THE
TRAVELER'S
READING GUIDE

THE TRAVELER'S READING GUIDE

*Ready-Made Reading Lists
for the Armchair Traveler*

Completely Revised and Updated

Maggy Simony, Editor

Facts On File
New York

The Traveler's Reading Guide
Completely Revised and Updated

Facts On File, Inc.
460 Park Avenue South
New York NY 10016
USA

Library of Congress Cataloging-in-Publication Data
The Traveler's reading guide : ready-made reading lists for the
armchair traveler / Maggy Simony, editor.
p. cm.
"Completely revised and updated."
Includes bibliographical references and index.
ISBN 0-8160-2648-3 (Hardcover)
ISBN 0-8160-2657-2 (Paperbound)
1. Travel—Bibliography.   I. Simony, Maggy
Z6004.T6T73   1992
[G151]
016.91—dc20   92-8175

A British CIP catalogue record for this book is available from the British Library.

Facts On File books are available at special discounts when purchased in bulk
quantities for businesses, associations, institutions or sales promotions. Please
call our Special Sales Department in New York at 212/683-2244 (dial 800/322-8755
except in NY).

Text design by Donna Sinisgalli
Composition and manufacturing by The Maple-Vail Book Manufacturing Group
Printed in the United States of America

10 9 8 7 6 5 4 3 2 1

This book is printed on acid-free paper.

The Georg Schneider quotation in the Preface was reprinted by permission from
Theory and History of Bibliography, by Georg Schneider, translated by Ralph Shaw
(Metuchen, N.J.: Scarecrow Press, 1962), copyright © 1962 by Ralph Shaw.

CONTENTS

PREFACE

"Bibliography is for books what Ariadne's thread was for Theseus in the labyrinths, and what the compass is to sea travel."
—Georg Schneider, *Theory and History of Bibliography.*

My interest in armchair travel, as a theme for library-browsing and reading, goes back so many years I can't remember when it started. I do know it was largely due to my father's influence.

After one adventurous spurt, when he emigrated from Stockholm to Brooklyn at age 17, my father could never afford to travel more than a few hundred miles from home. But he was an ardent armchair traveler. A trip to Maine led to Kenneth Roberts' novels. His characteristic parting comment to me (when I was leaving by car to move temporarily to California in 1948) was "Be sure now to stop at a library before you leave Reno to read about the Donner party." And he was right. Crossing the mountains into northern California for the first time, having just read the Donner story, was a far more memorable experience with the heartbreak of those earlier travelers vividly in mind.

For me, therefore, using the local library to enhance the anticipation for a trip and, again, to re-enjoy the experience of a completed trip, is an integral part of travel planning.

Moving from that avocational interest to compiling and publishing the first edition of this book was a long journey. It began when it struck me that, while I enjoyed the process of compiling reading lists for myself from standard library reference materials, most travelers would probably prefer "ready-made" lists to get them started.

The kind of book I had in mind (combining guides, fiction and non-fiction) did not exist, and I decided to tackle the job myself to fill the unfilled niche. That first edition, 1981–1984, was an independently published three-volume set of paperbacks. The first single-volume edition was published by Facts On File in 1987, with a paperback version following a year later.

To keep me on track through the long process of producing *Traveler's Reading Guide* I try to keep in mind a composite traveler that begins with me, but also includes other reader/travelers I've known and the many occupational travelers who move to foreign countries in connection with their jobs.

x   ○   P R E F A C E

For America, at the beginning, I had difficulty picturing a composite traveler to keep me on target—America didn't seem exotic enough. Two readers helped. One, a man involved with Meridian House International in Washington, D.C., wrote to say that the lists for America were useful as part of cultural orientation for travelers, business people and members of government delegations (who often take up residence for a period of time in the U.S., and read English well). With this audience in mind, I could think of America as a slightly exotic place.

Then I heard from a retiree who "full-times" it in a motor home—one of the RV crowd—who sent me a clipping from *Trailer Life* magazine with a review of *Traveler's Reading Guide.* That review revealed an audience I had never considered, the 20th-century populist American version of the 19th-century leisure-class traveler to Europe who took the traditional Grand Tour.

> "One of the best things about full-timing is that you can loll down the yellow brick road timelessly, taking all the days needed to savor the sights . . . immerse yourself in the moods and ambiences of each new area. Now I've discovered *Traveler's Reading Guides,* which are a boon to full-timers who love to read . . ."

Thereafter *all* retirees—in or out of RV's—who love to read, use libraries and travel, and have the time to do all three well, became part of my imaginary composite armchair traveler for America, and for the rest of the world as well.

I always appreciate letters with suggestions from armchair travelers, authors, travel writers and librarians—and I receive quite a few. Comments are welcome whether negative or positive; in fact, many reader suggestions have been incorporated into this new edition of *Traveler's Reading Guide.*

Maggy Simony
P.O. Box 1385
Meredith, NH 03253

ACKNOWLEDGMENTS

My appreciation to libraries in general, as well as to these local libraries in particular: Meredith Public Library, Plymouth State College, Laconia Public Library, New Hampton Public Library and Concord Public Library.

Also, my thanks to libraries used occasionally, while visiting friends and family: on Long Island, New York, public libraries in Patchogue, Sayville, West Islip and Farmingdale; in Florida, the Melbourne Public Library; in California, the public libraries in Coronado and San Diego.

ARMCHAIR TRAVEL

Armchair travel—described by Longfellow as "travels by the fireside . . . while journeying with another's feet"—is that delicious mix of reading and daydreaming about far-off places.

Armchair travel can be an exercise in pure fantasy—like reading the memoirs of travelers of an earlier day, or reading articles and books about places we will probably never see ourselves. Or it can be practical, helping us to decide where to go and what itinerary we'll follow.

In *Abroad*, Paul Fussell, commenting on the different approaches of explorers, travelers and tourists, says that while all three journey forth, the explorer is a discoverer, the traveler seeks "that which has been discovered by the mind working in history" and the tourist seeks what "entrepreneurship . . . mass publicity" offer. Reading beforehand is a way to acquire a "mind working in history" and thereby transform tourists into perceptive travelers.

For me, reading a novel or a mystery set in a place I've been, whether near or far away, is the best armchair traveling of all.

There's a new word—iterology—not yet in my *Webster's New World Dictionary*, which I understand means the relationship between authors, travels, books and readers. And that's as good a definition as any for the purpose of this book: encouraging iterology.

Traveler's Reading Guide is intended to get travelers started on locating background reading, travel literature, place-set novels, and travel guides. Background books introduce travelers to the culture, history, politics, foibles and characteristics of a place and its people. Travel literature can be read for the ambience and pure pleasure of reading first-rate writing. Novels and mysteries offer a sense of place, a glimpse of people leading ordinary or extraordinary lives. Family sagas are often a painless way of absorbing the history of an era through the lives of some prototypical people. Travel guidebooks offer much more than just practical tourist information, and can include a capsule history, background information, sometimes a suggested reading list—ideas for special travel interests you can pursue. Many travel guides provide a theme for planning an itinerary.

Traveler's Reading Guide is a "popular" bibliography, somewhat idiosyncratic, intended for the reasonably literate traveler, with some lowbrow reading thrown in here and there. Its tone and format are deliberately less formal than a traditional bibliography. The book is intended to be a starting point for readers, and to encourage them to explore the world of armchair travel beyond the contents of its pages. It is intended for browsing, much as one browses in a library or a bookstore. And, of course, it is intended to encourage readers to use their libraries to the fullest.

Getting Started

If you haven't already done so, read the Preface to get an idea of the basic philosophy of *Traveler's Reading Guide.* Then look over the Contents to understand how the book is organized geographically, and the Appendices.

The book is organized into seven parts divided by continent. These are further broken down by country and, in some cases, by state or province. The reading lists for each area are subdivided into Series Guidebooks, Background Reading, Guidebooks, History and Novels.

Classic travel guides of the 1920s, '30s, '40s, '50s—as well as the 19th-century travel classics—are increasingly reissued in new editions or exact reprints of the earlier versions. I have sprinkled a few of these reprints and new editions throughout and also added Appendix 2, which lists anthologies and books about travel writing and travelers. These can help you dip into and familiarize yourself with travel genre writing—both contemporary and classic.

In the case of some lengthy reading lists, Background Reading and Novels have additional subdivisions—categories such as travelogues, geographical subdivisions such as London, and counties under England's Novels section, or particular subjects such as Ghandi under India.

It should be obvious, but is worth emphasizing, that readers remember to look to the larger geographical entity first for series guidebooks and background reading that may have relevance to or information for the particular destination, i.e., continents before the countries to which they belong, the United States of America and its regions (east, south, midwest, west) before individual states.

Under England and Denmark check asterisked items for books relevant to all of Great Britain or all of the Scandinavian countries. Under the U.S.A., check asterisked items for books relevant to Canada and North America as a whole.

As you scan the "Background Readings" make a special note of anthologies, guides to literature, and books focused on authors and books; these can lead you beyond the material listed herein and provide in-depth critiques as well.

In this new edition of the *Reading Guide,* there are more Series Guides listed, fewer annotated guidebooks and no travel articles. Appendix I gives additional sources for guidebook information; Appendix II offers reading lists of books on travel literature; and Appendix III contains a list of authors who have written novels with English settings.

Find out more about what your library has to offer. Can you use your card to borrow books from nearby libraries, or must you go through a formal inter-library loan procedure? If you're lucky enough to have Infotrac or Magazine Index computer terminals, learn how to use them to find travel articles. Get in the habit of spending a few hours each month looking through travel and other magazines at the library and copying articles of particular interest. Newspapers and magazines such as *The New York Times* travel section, *Gourmet, Connoisseur, House & Garden* and many other consumer magazines, often carry travel articles of special interest to their readership.

Many of the books listed herein may be shelved with reference materials at your library.

In the instance of the United States and Canada, if you're vacationing in an area, stop by a local library. Most of them will have a regional or local collection of books about the area, fiction written by local authors that would not reach a more general bibliography like *Traveler's Reading Guide.*

A recent headline in the *New York Times* read, "Just Call It Russia Then? No, It's Not That Simple." In trying to decide what to do about the Soviet Union in this edition we came to the same conclusion as that *Times* article, which was a discussion of the semantic debate by the People's Deputies. The situation, and final affiliation and name of whatever countries emerge from the world-shaking events in the Soviet Union, are still too uncertain to simply rename the Soviet Union section "Russia." We considered adding sections for Estonia, Latvia and Lithuania, because they seem to have reverted to their original status and name for good, but there was an insufficient number of books and articles to list that meet the criteria of *Traveler's Reading Guide.*

What's NOT Included

For reasons of space—and the basic philosophy of this book—the following are generally not included herein (with always a few exceptions).

- outdoor travel books and guides—books on walking and trekking and camping and hiking—shopping guides, hotel and restaurant guides, B&B guides.
- biographies and autobiographies.
- mysteries—some are sprinkled throughout under novels, but this book has barely touched the surface of mystery and detective genre fiction.
- serious and/or classic novels—some are listed herein, but this book is not intended to be an introduction to the literature of a country. Again, most libraries have indexes or compendiums of world literature that can lead you to an in-depth exploration of a particular country's fiction.
- privately published materials, local histories, materials published by tourism organizations.

A Final Note

Traveler's Reading Guide generally reflects the volume of books for a particular country or state that are reviewed and the trends in books for that destination. Some places, such as England, California and New York, have an endless stream of new guidebooks, background books and novels from which to choose. Other places—for whatever reason—are sometimes rather neglected. But almost every place you want to go to has at least a good guidebook or two, and some guidebooks offer a good deal of background information.

Some places become suddenly "in" places to write about, while others are temporarily less favored depending on the political climate and current events. Some delightful countries and states never seem to inspire a piece of good travel writing or a bunch of place-set novels that reach the standard review sources for fiction used to compile the *Reading Guide.*

From my point of view, every state/country ought to have at least one block-buster novel or family saga, published in the United States, that makes that area's history and ambience come alive for armchair travelers. (The *Thornbirds* is a good example, which I suspect has more to do with a rise in Australian tourism than can be measured.)

If there are any authors looking through *Traveler's Reading Guide,* perhaps it can point out countries and states that will inspire the setting of their next novel or mystery, and by the next edition, there will be a few new novels or mysteries set in, say Scandinavia—or even Delaware.

THE TRAVELER'S READING GUIDE

I.
AFRICA

Series Guidebooks
(See Appendix 1)

Lonely Planet: Africa

Background Reading

See also books on Islam under Middle East, for Islam in Africa.

Braganti, Nancy and Devine, Elizabeth
THE TRAVELER'S GUIDE TO MIDDLE EASTERN AND NORTH AFRICAN CUSTOMS AND MANNERS
See entry under Middle East.

Daniels, Anthony
ZANZIBAR TO TIMBUKTU
An English doctor who has chosen to practice in Third World countries crosses 11 of Africa's—"alternately skeptical, anguished, and outraged" by the poverty. (PW) David & Charles, 1989. ○

Davidson, Basil
LET FREEDOM COME
A readable overview of the development of nationalism in Africa—1890–1970—that combines personalities and anecdotes, as well as European and African perspectives, and African responses. Atl Monthly Pr, 1978. ○

Dinesen, Isak
ISAK DINESEN'S AFRICA: IMAGES OF THE WILD CONTINENT FROM THE WRITER'S LIFE AND WORDS
A splendid work combining excerpts from the author's writings with photographs by various nature photographers. Sierra Club, 1985. ○

Duncan, David E.
FROM CAPE TO CAIRO: ONE MAN'S TREK ACROSS AFRICA
Travelogue of a bicycle trek in 1986–87—"his serendipitous cross-section of modern Africa combines solid first-hand reporting with tactile, lyrical sketches of myriad sites and people . . . without preconceptions, political axes to grind or romantic expectations." (PW) Weidenfeld, 1989. ○

Harden, Blaine
AFRICA: DISPATCHES FROM A FRAGILE CONTINENT
"Travel, history, politics, economics and generalities of African society" by a *Washington Post* correspondent—"for those who

1

don't know Africa this is a good place to start." (PW) Norton, 1990. ○

Heminway, John
NO MAN'S LAND

One reviewer felt this was an unfortunate title for the richly populated landscape captured in this classic travel book, first published in 1983. Its subject is the white expatriates who, Heminway says, "would like to belong, they are unable to belong, and the land that possesses them will never be theirs to possess." Many candid portraits of diverse people, from a flying woman doctor to the sultan of M'Simbati. Warner Bks, 1989. ○

Hone, Joseph
AFRICA OF THE HEART: A PERSONAL JOURNEY

By a BBC journalist looking for the romantic Africa of boyhood reading, finding colorful characters, a romance, urban poverty, depleted wildlife—"a provocative look . . . at what Africa is becoming." (LJ) Morrow, 1986. ○

Hudson, Peter
A LEAF IN THE WIND: TRAVELS IN AFRICA

"Lovely, startling, humorous book" by an English returnee to Africa seeking encounters in Mali, Zaire, Somalia and the Sahara. (PW) Walker, 1989. ○

Kodjo, Edem
AFRICA TOMORROW

A controversial and optimistic view of Africa's future—"no such statement of faith in the African continent has appeared in several decades." Continuum, 1987. ○

Lamb, David
THE AFRICANS

Written with humor and sympathy, by the *Los Angeles Times* correspondent for Africa—a combination of travelogue and news analysis, personal anecdotes, portraits of individual nations. Random, 1987. ○

Moorehead, Alan
THE BLUE NILE; THE WHITE NILE

The Nile River is a vehicle for recounting history and expeditions. *The Blue Nile* covers the early period from 1798, *The White Nile* 1856–1900, but each can be read separately. Har-Row, 1972, 1980. ○

Shoumatoff, Alex
AFRICAN MADNESS

Four essays that first appeared in *The New Yorker*—"reveals an Africa of incomprehensible savagery and awesome beauty." (BL) Knopf, 1988. ○

Stevens, Stuart
MALARIA DREAMS: AN AFRICAN ADVENTURE

Story of an overland journey through formerly French Africa. The reviewer says, "his off-beat African odyssey is a rollicking successor" to Stevens' *Night Train to Turkestan* (see under China). (PW) Atl Monthly Pr, 1989. ○

Ungar, Sanford J.
AFRICA: THE PEOPLE AND POLITICS OF AN EMERGING CONTINENT

Introduces the general reader to the "complexity, fascination and tragedy of Africa." Liberia, Nigeria, Kenya and South Africa are examined in depth with a summary of the situation today in many other countries. (PW) S&S, 1985. ○

AFRICAN CULTURE

Bebey, Francis
AFRICAN MUSIC: A PEOPLE'S ART

An overview of the place of music in African life. L. Hill Bks, 1975. ○

Davidson, Basil
THE AFRICAN GENIUS

In a unique synthesis, a general religious and social history makes African society intelligible to the lay reader. Little, 1970. ○

Gillen, Werner
A SHORT HISTORY OF AFRICAN ART
"Succinct but comprehensive history of the visual arts." (BL) Facts On File, 1985. ◯

Harris, Joseph E., ed.
AFRICA AND AFRICANS AS SEEN BY CLASSICAL WRITERS
Howard U Pr, 1977. ◯

Klein, Leonard S., ed.
AFRICAN LITERATURES IN THE 20TH CENTURY: A GUIDE
Essays, brief articles, bibliographies—a handy introduction based on the African section of *Encyclopedia of World Literature in the 20th Century*. Ungar, 1986. ◯

Mazrui, Ali
THE AFRICANS: A TRIPLE HERITAGE
Companion volume to a controversial TV series stressing Africa as a product, and transmitter, of Islamic, Western and indigenous cultures. Little, 1986. Also *The Africans: A Reader* (Praeger, 1986), a companion collection of essays. ◯

Murray, Jocelyn, ed.
CULTURAL ATLAS OF AFRICA
A panoramic view of Africa—text, photos, maps and articles by specialists explore the continent's cultural and ethnic diversity; includes information that brings each country up-to-date as to politics and economics. Facts On File, 1981. ◯

Schwartz, Brian M.
A WORLD OF VILLAGES
The author visited villages and obscure areas in Africa and Asia, traveling on less than a shoestring—"a love affair with poverty-stricken, primitive people and places" along with many adventures and memorable incidents. (BRD) Crown, 1986. ◯

Shostak, Marjorie
NISA: THE LIFE AND WORDS OF A KUNG WOMAN
A remarkable, outrageous story, told in her own words, of birth, marriage, life's events, from hundreds of taped conversations. Harvard U Pr, 1981. ◯

Turnbull, Colin
THE LONELY AFRICAN
Sketches of Africa, from powerful chiefs to the dispossessed city dwellers, centering on the importance and meaning of the tribe. S&S, 1968. ◯

Willett, Frank
AFRICAN ART: AN INTRODUCTION
A thematic approach, considered one of the best general introductions to, and surveys of, African art. Thames & Hudson, 1985. ◯

EXPLORERS AND EXPLORATIONS

Bass, Thomas A.
CAMPING WITH THE PRINCE AND OTHER TALES OF SCIENCE IN AFRICA
What happens when the paths of science and African tradition meet; seven scientific expeditions from Timbuktu to the Zambesi. HM, 1990. ◯

Boyles, Denis
AFRICAN LIVES
"White lies, tropical truth, darkest gossip, and rumblings of rumor . . . Beryl Markham, and beyond . . . wisecracks his way through the Dark Continent, singling out exploits of adventurers he has met or heard about." (PW) Weidenfeld, 1988. ◯

Hammond, Dorothy and Jablow, Alta
THE AFRICA THAT NEVER WAS: FOUR CENTURIES OF BRITISH WRITING ABOUT AFRICA
A critique of fiction and nonfiction "unveiling the myths that masquerade . . . as African reality." (BRD) Irvington, 1978. ◯

Hibbert, Christopher
AFRICA EXPLORED: EUROPEANS IN THE DARK CONTINENT, 1769–1889
Enthralling exploits of well-known (Mungo Park, Speke, Livingston and Stanley) and

not so well-known (Nachtigall, Rebmann) early travelers to Africa; based on diaries, letters and books of and by them. Norton, 1982.   ○

Severin, Timothy
THE AFRICAN ADVENTURE: FOUR HUNDRED YEARS OF EXPLORATION IN THE DANGEROUS CONTINENT
A fascinating account of the history of African explorers of all kinds—missionaries, sportsmen, the military and so on. Dutton, 1973.   ○

ANIMALS IN AFRICA

Bull, Bartle
SAFARI: A CHRONICLE OF ADVENTURE
An illustrated history. Viking Penguin, 1988.   ○

Camperapix
AFRICAN WILDLIFE SAFARIS
A Spectrum Guide; photographs and text. Facts On File, 1989.   ○

Fetner, P. Jay
THE AFRICAN SAFARI
The ultimate guide to photography, wildlife and adventure along with writings of naturalists and novelists. St. Martin, 1987.   ○

GUIDEBOOKS

See also guidebooks under separate areas of Africa.   ○

Capstick, Peter H.
SAFARI—THE LAST ADVENTURE: HOW YOU CAN SHARE IN IT
How to self-plan a safari: when to go, what you need to take along, how to select the right one and book it, chapters on hunting big game, etc. St. Martin, 1984.   ○

Estes, Richard D.
THE SAFARI COMPANION
A field guide to watching African wildlife. Chelsea Green, 1992.   ○

Nolting, Mark
AFRICA'S TOP WILDLIFE COUNTRIES
Complete guide to 10 top game-viewing countries, what's best seen where, with numerous maps and photos, walking safaris, birdwatching, gorilla safaris—a wealth of handy information. Global Travel, 1990.   ○

Taylor, Jane and Leah
LITERARY AFRICA
Specific itineraries that focus on the literary works of Isak Dinesen, Alan Moorehead, Elspeth Huxley and others, with historical and cultural background. Another guidebook by the Taylors is *African Safaris* (1986), 50 do-it-yourself safaris for various budgets and interests, from wildlife and spelunking to motorcycling and art collecting. Morrow, 1988.   ○

HISTORY

Fage, J.D.
A HISTORY OF AFRICA
An "outstanding one-volume narrative history." (BRD) Unwin, 1989.   ○

July, Robert W.
A HISTORY OF THE AFRICAN PEOPLE
Third edition of this history organized by regions. Scribner, 1985.   ○

McEvedy, Colin
THE PENGUIN ATLAS OF AFRICAN HISTORY
From pre-history to 1978, with many maps. Penguin, 1980.   ○

Oliver, Roland and Fage, J.D.
A SHORT HISTORY OF AFRICA
History dealt with chronologically and regionally. Facts On File, 1989.   ○

Wiseman, John A.
DEMOCRACY IN BLACK AFRICA: SURVIVAL AND REVIVAL
An overview of the emergence of democracy as a challenge to colonial authoritarianism,

its durability, and a prediction of even more democracy in Africa. Paragon Hse, 1991. ○

Novels

Bellow, Saul
HENDERSON THE RAIN KING
An American millionaire's "quest for revelation and spiritual power." (FC) Viking, 1959. ○

Cartwright, Justin
INTERIOR
Merging of past and present, a father's expedition 30 years earlier and his son's trip to Africa to make a documentary film. The book tells of the two treks "against the backdrop of the mysteries of African people, terrain, and wildlife." (FC) Random, 1989. ○

Gellhorn, Martha
THE WEATHER IN AFRICA
Three novellas that give a sense of the difference between what Europeans think about Africa and the reality. Hippocrene, 1989. ○

Gordimer, Nadine
LIVINGSTONE'S COMPANIONS
Short stories about Africa and the complex lives of people, black and white, who inhabit it. Ms. Gordimer is a leading novelist of African life; most of her titles are listed under South Africa/Novels. Viking, 1970. ○

Gordimer, Nadine
A GUEST OF HONOR
The "machinations of African politics" when the former administrator of a British colony returns to a mythical, composite African colony to help build it into a new nation. (FC) Viking, 1970. ○

Harrison, William
BURTON AND SPEKE
Based on the lives of the nineteenth-century explorer Richard Burton and his contemporary, John Speke, and their explorations in Africa, "this novel takes us on a tour of nineteenth-century manners and morals." (FC) St. Martin, 1982. ○

Ingalls, Rachel
BINSTEAD'S SAFARI
Binstead's wife goes along on his safari, and falls in love with their guide, believed to have "super-human, leonine powers." (BRD) S&S, 1988. ○

Montserrat, Nicholas
THE TRIBE THAT LOST ITS HEAD
This novel and its sequel concern neo-colonialism on a fictional African island—new tyrannies, intertribal hatreds. Sloane, 1956. *Richer Than All His Tribe* is the sequel. ○

Scholefield, Alan
THE LAST SAFARI
The story of a big-game hunter, turned author, who is arrested for murder; told through tapes reviewed by his son in attempting to help his father. St. Martin, 1987. ○

Updike, John
THE COUP
An imaginary state (a former French colony in upper Africa) is the setting for the narration of its dictator's present and former life. Knopf, 1978. ○

Waugh, Evelyn
BLACK MISCHIEF
A satirical tale of an Oxford-educated black, with a grandiose plan to found a new civilization on an island off the coast of Africa. FS&G, 1932. ○

CENTRAL AFRICA

Series Guidebooks (See Appendix 1)

Lonely Planet: Central Africa ○

Background Reading

Fossey, Dian
GORILLAS IN THE MIST
A remarkable woman's 13-year adventure in remote Africa rain forests with the greatest of the great apes—her observations and anecdotes, and her life. The book was made into a successful film. HM, 1983. ○

Gide, André
TRAVELS IN THE CONGO
Travel notebook by a distinguished French man of letters. Knopf, 1929. ○

Hoagland, Edward
AFRICAN CALLIOPE: A JOURNEY TO THE SUDAN
Travels in the Sudan in 1977, from the equator to the Sahara—people, small towns, the capital of Khartoum told with astonishing vividness. Random, 1981. ○

Hyland, Paul
THE BLACK HEART: A VOYAGE INTO CENTRAL AFRICA
The poet-author and his wife retrace the Zaire River routes of Joseph Conrad, missionary Dan Crawford and Roger Casement (an Irish nationalist) when it was the Congo River—"memorable account of Africa past and present." See also the Winternitz book listed below. (BL) HR&W, 1989. ○

Matthiessen, Peter
AFRICAN SILENCES
A description of two journeys to West and Central Africa, in 1978 and 1986, to find out about the animals in national parks, and specifically in search of the pygmy elephant—"dazzling, if dismaying report . . . offers his readers a superb vicarious experience." (PW) Random, 1991. ○

Mowat, Farley
WOMAN IN THE MISTS
This is a book about the remarkable Dian Fossey (see above) and her commitment to research in gorilla country in Africa. Warner Bks, 1988. ○

Murphy, Dervla
CAMEROON WITH EGBERT
Ms. Murphy "once again captivates armchair travelers." This time it's a three-month journey with her daughter and a packhorse through the mountains and jungle of Cameroon—"brilliantly captures the charm of the congenial Cameroonian people and their culture." (LJ) Overlook Pr, 1991. ○

Shoumatoff, Alex
IN SOUTHERN LIGHT: TREKKING THROUGH ZAIRE AND THE AMAZON
A journey to the land of the pygmies and to a nature preserve on Zaire's border with Uganda; and a trek to Rio Nhamunda in northwest Brazil. Extraordinarily colorful. (PW) S&S, 1986. ○

Tidwell, Mike
THE PONDS OF KALAMBAYI: AN AFRICAN SOJOURN
By a Peace Corps member sent to Africa to teach villagers how to build ponds and raise fish; tells of the lighter and serious aspects—"a riveting story." (PW) Lyons, 1990. ○

Verne, Jules
FIVE WEEKS IN A BALLOON
Reprint of a book originally published in 1863—"journeys and discoveries in Africa by three Englishmen" written from original notes. Amereon Ltd. ○

Winternitz, Helen
EAST ALONG THE EQUATOR
A 2,000-mile journey into Zaire, from Kinshasa to Kisangani, via the Congo and overland follows the path of *Heart to Darkness*. An adventure story and an introduction to

the politics of the region—"a vivid account . . . an eye-opening tour of Zaire." (PW) Atl Monthly Pr, 1987. ○

GUIDEBOOKS

Traveller's Guide Series, eds.
CENTRAL AND SOUTH AFRICA
Hunter Pub, 1990. ○

HISTORY

Needham, D.E.
**FROM IRON AGE TO
    INDEPENDENCE: A HISTORY**
Longman, 1984. ○

Wilson, Derek
**HISTORY OF SOUTH AND
    CENTRAL AFRICA**
Cambridge U Pr, 1975. ○

Novels

Ballard, J.G.
THE DAY OF CREATION
The narrator, a World Health Organization physician who works in a mythical country in Central Africa, searches for water and comes to believe that he has created a new river—"a blend of animated reveries, myth and adventure story." (FC) FS&G, 1988. ○

Conrad, Joseph
HEART OF DARKNESS
The classic novel of the Congo. Penguin, 1976 (first published 1902). ○

Forester, C.S.
THE AFRICAN QUEEN
Basis for the marvelous Hepburn/Bogart movie—a missionary's sister joins up with the owner of a dilapidated boat and devises a plan to blow up a German warship in World War I. Little, 1935. ○

Forester, C.S.
THE SKY AND THE FOREST
A Central African tribe builds an empire that falls to European exploitation by the Belgians. Little, 1948. ○

Griffin, W.E.B.
THE NEW BREED
The Congo in 1964, where Americans are trying to rescue American and Belgian hostages from the Congolese rebels. Book seven of a series with the overall title "Brotherhood of War." Putnam, 1988. ○

Haggard, H. Rider
FIVE ADVENTURE NOVELS
Nineteenth-century period pieces, including *King Solomon's Mines*. Dover, 1951 (first published 1885–1889). ○

Mudimbe, V.Y.
**BEFORE THE BIRTH OF THE
    MOON** (Zaire)
Set in the 1960s; story of a cynical state official's love for a prostitute, and their involvement in the political intrigue and tribal loyalties that destroy them. S&S, 1989. ○

Theroux, Paul
THE JUNGLE LOVERS (Malawi)
A Massachusetts insurance salesman comes to a small central African country during a revolution; dark comedy mixed with serious themes of race prejudice and colonialism. HM, 1971. ○

EASTERN AFRICA

Series Guidebooks
(See Appendix 1)

Berlitz: Travel Guide—Kenya
Fodor: Kenya, Tanzania and Seychelles

Frommer: Kenya
Hildebrand: Kenya
Insider's Guide: Kenya
Insight Guide: East African Wildlife; Kenya
Lonely Planet: East Africa; Kenya

Nelles Guide: Kenya
Real Guide: Kenya

Background Reading

Adamson, Joy
BORN FREE (Kenya)
This, along with *Living Free* (1961) and *Elsa* (1960), is a widely popular book about lions reared by the author and returned to the wilds. Also *The Peoples of Kenya* (1966), an account of her travels in Kenya to paint and photograph tribal people. Pantheon, 1960.   ○

Beckwith, Carol and Fisher, Angela
AFRICAN ARK
The sub-title is: "Ancient Cultures of Ethiopia and the Horn of Africa." A collection of "unexpected and stirring portraits" of the human societies of the region—"vivid photographs are stupendous." Abrams, 1990.   ○

Bentsen, Cheryl
MAASAI DAYS
A culture at odds with the Africa of today. Summit Bks, 1991.   ○

Boyles, Denis
MAN EATER'S MOTEL, AND OTHER STOPS ON THE RAILWAY TO NOWHERE: AN EAST AFRICAN TRAVELLER'S NOTEBOOK
Train travels on the Mombasa-Nairobi Express—"historical fact, personal anecdote, and droll humor." The reviewer goes on to say that the bleak impressions may be rough for armchair travelers. (LJ) Ticknor & Fields, 1991.   ○

Dinesen, Isak
OUT OF AFRICA/SHADOW ON THE GRASS
Two works that record the memoirs of Baroness Karen Blixen on a Kenyan coffee plantation during the early part of the century. Random, 1989. Also, *Letters from Africa, 1914–1931* (1984), her letters home to Denmark. Her writings were the basis for the movie *Out of Africa*.   ○

Goodall, Jane
THROUGH A WINDOW: MY THIRTY YEARS WITH THE CHIMPANZEES OF GOMBE
The author's first 10 years of researching the chimpanzee at Gombe resulted in the book *Shadow of Man* (1971); this book continues the saga of chimpanzee families observed. HM, 1990.   ○

Hemingway, Ernest
GREEN HILLS OF AFRICA
Account of a hunting expedition in the 1930s. Hudson River Ed (first published 1935).   ○

Heminway, John
AFRICAN JOURNEYS: A PERSONAL GUIDEBOOK
The author shares his passion for Africa in this armchair safari, away from usual tourist places and into the Serengeti. Among the places he takes you to is the area of Jane Goodall's chimps of Gombe. Warner Bks, 1990.   ○

Henriksen, A.
ISAK DINESEN/KAREN BLIXEN— ESSAYS ON THE WORK AND LIFE
A vibrant childhood memoir about growing up on a coffee plantation, by a leading writer about Africa. Penguin, 1982.   ○

Huxley, Elspeth
FLAME TREES OF THIKA (Kenya)
A vibrant childhood memoir about growing up on a coffee plantation. (BRD) Penguin, 1982. Also *Out In the Midday Sun: My Kenya* (1988), *The Mottled Lizard* (1982), *On the Edge of the Rift: Memories of Kenya* (1962), *The Sorcerer's Apprentice: A Journey Through East Africa* (1948).   ○

Huxley, Elspeth, ed.
NINE FACES OF KENYA
An anthology of writings about Kenya through firsthand accounts by writers ranging from Vasco da Gama and Churchill to Karen Blixen and Hemingway—"a colorful mosaic depicting Kenya's swirling diversity." (BL) Viking, 1991.   ○

Jackman, Brian
THE MARSH LIONS: THE STORY OF AN AFRICAN PRIDE
Well-written and entertaining account of the wildlife in Kenya's vast Masai Mara, from 1978 through 1981. Godine, 1983. ○

Latham, Aaron
THE FROZEN LEOPARD
One of the "Destinations" series of new travel writing, with an introduction by Jan Morris. The author of *Urban Cowboy* takes his family on safari to Kenya and Rwanda— "A revelation and a revitalization for the author . . . fine travel writing . . . a spellbinding story of self-discovery." (PW) S&S, 1991. ○

Leslie-Melville, Betty
A FALLING STAR
A true story of romance in the wilds of Africa, by an American who met a Scottish earl in 1963; about their life in Kenya managing a game preserve and hosting celebrities, and with a strong plea for conservation. Macmillan, 1986. Also by Leslie-Melville and her husband, *Elephants Have the Right of Way* (1973) and *There's a Rhino in the Rose Bed, Mother* (1973). ○

Markham, Beryl
WEST WITH THE NIGHT
This book, first published in 1942 and reprinted in 1983, became a bestseller second time around both for the author's writing style and the unique life she led—an eloquent memoir of an adventurous life in the early 1900s, in what was then British East Africa. N Point Pr, 1983. See also Markham's *African Stories* under Novels, below, and a biography of Markham, *Straight On Till Morning* (1987). ○

Matthiessen, Peter
THE TREE WHERE MAN WAS BORN, THE AFRICAN EXPERIENCE
A contemporary classic; impressions of African experiences (1960–70) in Sudan, Tanzania, to Lake Rudolf—Masai herdsmen, Serengeti. Dutton, 1983 (first published 1972). Also *Sand Rivers* (1981). ○

Murphy, Dervla
IN ETHIOPIA WITH A MULE
By the leading Irish travel writer; three months in the highlands—"enthusiastically recommended" for armchair travelers. (BRD) Transatlantic, 1970. ○

Nyabongo, Elizabeth
ELIZABETH OF TORO: THE ODYSSEY OF AN AFRICAN PRINCESS
The author is a princess who's also been a *Vogue* cover girl, foreign minister of Uganda— "eloquently written, spine-tingling . . . remarkable story" of Africa and events she observed. (PW) S&S, 1989. ○

Pavitt, Nigel
KENYA: THE FIRST EXPLORERS
Stories of those curious and courageous early explorers—"a book armchair explorers will love." (BL) St. Martin, 1989. ○

Waugh, Evelyn
REMOTE PEOPLE
Travel memoir of an ocean cruise and travel in Ethiopia and Kenya. One of a series of reprints of travel writing that also includes *They Were Still Dancing* and *A Tourist in Africa*. Ecco Pr, 1990. ○

GUIDEBOOKS

Bechky, Allen
ADVENTURING IN EAST AFRICA
The Sierra Club travel guide to the great safaris of Kenya, Tanzania, Rwanda, Eastern Zaire and Uganda. Sierra Club, 1990. ○

Brigden, John
VISITING KENYA
"Competent and attractive introduction for the first time visitor." (LJ) Hippocrene Bks, 1987. ○

Casimati, Nina
GUIDE TO EAST AFRICA: KENYA, TANZANIA, THE SEYCHELLES & MAURITIUS
Background history, geography, culture; treks and safaris; practical tourist information, cuisine and more. Hippocrene, 1989. ○

Cox, Thornton
KENYA AND NORTHERN TANZANIA: A TRAVELLER'S GUIDE

A guide to help plan a safari, along with practical information on hotels, transportation, wildlife parks and preserves; updated to reflect attention generated by the film of Dinesen's book *Out of Africa.* Hippocrene, 1988. ○

HISTORY

Oldhiambo, E.S. and others
A HISTORY OF EAST AFRICA

Longman, 1978.

Novels

Cody, Liza
RIFT

A freelance wardrobe assistant working on a movie in Kenya in 1974 is asked to deliver a letter to a woman in Ethiopia and gets involved in danger and intrigue. Scribner, 1988. ○

Dinesen, Isak
SHADOWS ON THE GRASS

Autobiographical short stories "recreate . . . the quality and texture of a past era in Kenya." (FC) Random, 1961. ○

Forbath, Peter
THE LAST HERO

A novelized account of Stanley's rescue of Emin Pasha; "paints a magnificent Stanley . . . equally glorious is Africa itself . . . an epic adventure." (FC) S&S, 1988. ○

Gellhorn, Martha
THE WEATHER IN AFRICA (Kenya)

Two novellas and a short story explore relationships between whites and blacks in post-colonial Kenya; set in a luxury hotel and brimming with the attitudes, atmosphere and landscape of Africa. Dodd, 1980. ○

Hagerfors, Lennart
THE WALES IN LAKE TANGANYIKA

Stanley's 1871 expedition to Lake Tanganyika to find Livingstone, told in diary form by an ex-sailor—"a visionary reverie, partly a satire, partly realistic." (BRD) Grove Pr, 1989. ○

Halkin, John
KENYA

Adventure and romance in an authentic novel of turn-of-the-century Kenya and building of a railroad from Mombasa to Uganda by a Scottish engineer. Beaufort, 1986. ○

Hanley, Gerald
CONSUL AT SUNSET

Story of English officialdom in an African outpost when the British are taking over the region from the Italians. Macmillan, 1951. Also *Gilligan's Last Elephant* (1962) and *Drinkers of Darkness* (1955). ○

Hemingway, Ernest
SNOWS OF KILIMANJARO, AND OTHER STORIES

Scribner, 1982 (*Snows* first published 1938). ○

Huxley, Elspeth
MURDER ON SAFARI

One of a series of old murder mysteries by this leading writer on Africa of the 1930s (see entries above, under Background Reading), now reprinted—"vivid descriptions of terrain . . . prescient protest against the slaughter of wildlife for fun and profit." Viking, 1989. Other titles reprinted are *Murder at Government House* and *The African Prison Murders*, about a fictitious country in East Africa. Also *Death in Zanzibar,* a revised version of a mystery first published in 1959 (1983). ○

Kaye, M.M.
DEATH IN KENYA

Revised version of a novel published in 1958. Eerie happenings culminate in the murder of Alice (wife of the heir to a cattle farm in the Rift Valley) and others. St. Martin, 1983. ○

Keneally, Thomas
TO ASMARA
A novel "of advocacy and engagement . . . unhesitatingly takes sides"—an Australian journalist goes to Eritrea to investigate charges that UN food shipments are being attacked by rebels. (FC) Warner Bks, 1989.　　○

Markham, Beryl
THE SPLENDID OUTCAST
African stories by the author whose repub-lished reminiscences about her life in British East Africa (see above) have become best-sellers. This is a collection of short fiction including adventures, romances, real events. N Point Pr, 1987.　　○

Ngugi Wa Thiong'o
DEVIL ON THE CROSS
Ngugi is a major Kenyan novelist and play-wright, and this is one of his recent books, published in 1981. Heinemann, 1981. Also *Petals of Blood*, set in rural Kenya and in-volving a triple murder and intertwined lives of the suspects (1978).　　○

Proffitt, Nicholas
EDGE OF EDEN
"Revelatory novel" by a former *Newsweek* correspondent—"makes the reader care about this gorgeous, tormented nation . . . superb word pictures of the . . . great central veld teeming with zebras, giraffes and elephants . . . and a glimpse of how a multitribal Africa, committed to a common task, might work." (NYT) Bantam, 1990.　　○

Smith, Wilbur
CRY WOLF (Ethiopia)
Adventures of a Briton and a Texan who sell arms at high profit to Ethiopia in 1935, as the Italians invade. Doubleday, 1977.　　○

Theroux, Paul
GIRLS AT PLAY
"The stresses of life in the tropics on a group of schoolteachers that concludes with an orgy of gore." (FC) HM, 1969.　　○

Thomas, Maria
ANTONIA SAW THE ORYX FIRST
　(Tanzania)
Friendship between a doctor in Dar-es-Sa-laam and a young black woman with spiri-tual healing powers. Each is intrigued by the other's world of medicine, reflecting the complexities of the relationship between Af-rica and the West. Soho Pr, 1987.　　○

Wood, Barbara
GREEN CITY IN THE SUN (Kenya)
Family saga, set in turn-of-the century Nai-robi—"cultures, lifestyles and differing ide-ologies are portrayed with stark reality." (FC) Random, 1988.　　○

INDIAN OCEAN ISLANDS

See also Eastern Africa, for overlap-ping background reading, guidebooks, history.　　○

Series Guidebooks
(See Appendix 1)

Hildebrand: Mauritius; Seychelles
Lonely Planet: Mauritius, Reunion & the
　Seychelles; Madagascar & the Comoros

Background Reading

Murphy, Dervla
**MUDDLING THROUGH IN
　MADAGASCAR**
Another of the intrepid woman travel writ-er's books, this time accompanied by her 14-year-old daughter. She encounters a country without reliable communications or trans-portation and a Christian people who retain some aspects of taboos and ancestor wor-ship. Adventures interwoven with island

history in an exotic setting. Overlook Pr, 1989.   ○

Severin, Tim
SINDBAD VOYAGE
See under "Middle East."   ○

GUIDEBOOKS

Casimati, Nina
GUIDE TO EAST AFRICA: KENYA, TANZANIA, THE SEYCHELLES & MAURITIUS
Hippocrene, 1989.   ○

Traveller's Guidebooks Series, eds.
EAST AFRICA AND THE INDIAN OCEAN
Hunter Pub, 1989.   ○

Novels

Durrell, Gerald
THE MOCKERY BIRD
Satirical story of British plans to establish a military airstrip and the potential effect on the ecology and on the mocking bird. S&S, 1982.   ○

Kaye, M.M.
TRADE WIND
Rewritten and expanded version of a book first published in 1963. The plot concerns a young Bostonian's journey to Zanzibar in 1859 with a mission to stop the slave trade— intrigue, romance, a pirate raid, evoke the beauty and barbarity of Zanzibar in the pe- riod. St. Martin, 1981. Also *Death in Zanzibar* (1983) that continues the story of gold buried a hundred years earlier.   ○

Waugh, Evelyn
BLACK MISCHIEF
Satirical story of an Oxford-educated black man determined to found a new civilization in his native state off the coast of Africa. Little, 1975 (first published 1932).   ○

NORTHERN AFRICA

*Series Guidebooks
(See Appendix 1)*

Fodor: North Africa

Background Reading

Asher, Michael
TWO AGAINST THE SAHARA: ON CAMELBACK FROM NOUAKCHOTT TO THE NILE
This feat had never been accomplished until 1987 when achieved by the author and his wife—all 4,500 miles! The story is of both a remarkable trip and its effects on a marriage. Morrow, 1989.   ○

Eberhardt, Isabelle
THE PASSIONATE NOMAD: THE DIARY OF ISABELLE EBERHARDT
This is the real-life inspiration for a 19th- century woman evoked by Lesley Blanch in *The Wilder Shores of Love*. A Swiss-born, middle-class woman, Eberhardt became a convert to Islam, traveled about in male disguise in North Africa—"absorbing piece of exotica" of a 1960s spirit in the 19th cen- tury. (PW) Virago, 1988.   ○

Edwards, Ted
BEYOND THE LAST OASIS: A SOLO WALK IN THE WESTERN SAHARA
Salem Hse, 1985.   ○

Gide, André
AMYNTAS
Journals of five years in the exotic cultures of Tunis and Algiers. Ecco Pr, 1988.   ○

MacKendrick, Paul L.
THE NORTH AFRICAN STONES SPEAK

A fascinating review of ancient history through the scrutiny of archaeological sites— for travelers who enjoy an archaeological theme. U of North Carolina Pr, 1980.   ○

Moorhouse, Geoffrey
THE FEARFUL VOID: ACROSS THE IMPLACABLE SAHARA, A MAN GOES IN SEARCH OF HIMSELF

This trip took place during 1972–73; like a 19th-century explorer, Moorhouse set forth without motorized transportation. The trip ended 1,600 miles short of his 3,600-mile objective, after losing guides and camels several times. What remains, however, is a unique and riveting story of that adventure and what it's like to spend time in this vast space. Originally published in 1974, the book has now been reissued, with maps and supply lists for anyone wishing to repeat the trip. CN Potter, 1989.   ○

Porch, Douglas
THE CONQUEST OF THE SAHARA

The French conquest of the Berbers in Central Sahara, which the author lays to France's intense pre-World War I nationalism and a desire to wield influence over the region. Knopf, 1984.   ○

GUIDEBOOKS

Canby, Courtlandt
GUIDE TO THE ARCHAEOLOGICAL SITES OF ISRAEL, EGYPT AND NORTH AFRICA

See entry under Egypt/Guidebooks.   ○

Traveler's Guide Series, ed.
NORTH AFRICA

Hunter Pub, 1988.

Novels

Bryher
THE COIN OF CARTHAGE

Carthage and ancient Rome during the Second Punic War and how the common people were cruelly dislocated by the endless warfare. HarBraceJ, 1963.   ○

Camus, Albert
EXILE AND THE KINGDOM

Short stories, four of which are set in North Africa. Knopf, 1958.   ○

Wren, Percival C.
BEAU GESTE

Adventure, mystery, and thrills in the highly romantic novel of life in the French Foreign Legion. Lippincott, 1927.   ○

ALGERIA

Series Guidebooks (See Appendix 1)

Berlitz: Country Guide—Algeria
Lonely Planet: Morocco, Algeria and Tunisia

Background Reading

Eberhardt, Isabelle
THE OBLIVION SEEKERS

And other writings, translated by novelist Paul Bowles. Story of Isabelle Eberhardt, a nineteenth-century woman who left Europe for Africa, dressed as a man. City Lights, 1975.   ○

Talbott, John E.
THE WAR WITHOUT A NAME

A concise account of France's war with Algeria. Knopf, 1981.   ○

Novels

Camus, Albert
THE PLAGUE

Impact of an epidemic of bubonic plague on an Algerian city. Knopf, 1977 (first published 1947).   ○

Daudet, Alphonse
TARTARIN OF TARASCON
Adventures of a Frenchman in Algeria. Dutton, 1954 (first published 1872).   ○

Driscoll, Peter
HERITAGE
The Algerian War of Independence (1954–1962) and its consequences for Algeria's first

family, which owns a huge wine-producing plantation. Doubleday, 1982.   ○

Irwin, Robert
MYSTERIES OF ALGIERS
A French intelligence agent is exposed as a double agent during the French-Algerian war—"investigation of the moral ambiguity of ideological belief." Viking, 1988.   ○

MOROCCO

Series Guidebooks
(See Appendix 1)

Berlitz: Morocco
Blue Guide: Morocco
Cadogan Guide: Morocco
Fodor: Morocco
Frommer: Morocco
Insight: Morocco
Lonely Planet: Morocco, Algeria, Tunisia
Real Guide: Morocco

Background Reading

Bowles, Paul
POINTS IN TIME
Takes the reader on a journey through the Moroccan centuries to create resonant images of the country, its landscape, the beliefs and characteristics of its inhabitants. First published 1982. Ecco Pr, 1991. Also *Days—Tangier Journal: 1987–1989* (1991).   ○

Canetti, Elias
THE VOICES OF MARRAKESH
An evocation of the magic of Marrakesh and of the author's response to the city. FS&G, 1984.   ○

Choukri, Mohamed
JEAN GENET IN TANGIER
Meetings in Tangier between Genet and a young Moroccan—"unexpected view [of the

writer] . . . a fascinating picture of cafe life in this city." (BL) Ecco Pr, 1990.   ○

Green, Michelle
THE DREAM AT THE END OF THE WORLD
Paul Bowles and the literary renegades in Tangier. HarperCollins, 1991.   ○

Harris, Walter
MOROCCO THAT WAS
Reprint of a 1921 travel book. Negro U Pr, 1970.   ○

Maxwell, Gavin
LORDS OF THE ATLAS
Morocco through the eyes of an adventurer, scholar and journalist. Hippocrene, 1983. ○

Mayne, Peter
A YEAR IN MARRAKESH
A memoir "filled with passion, awe and wonderful adventure." (TB) Hippocrene, 1984.   ○

Wharton, Edith
IN MOROCCO
A recent reprint of a book by the famous author—an account of her travels in 1918, courtesy of the French military mission. David & Charles, 1988 (first published 1920).   ○

GUIDEBOOKS

Bythines, Peter and Leocha, Charles A.
THE WHOLE EUROPE ESCAPE MANUAL: SPAIN, PORTUGAL, MOROCCO
Part of a series of guidebooks designed to put the fantasy and excitement back into travel. World Leis Corp, 1985.   ○

Kay, Shirley
MOROCCO
Short history and cultural overview. Charles River Bks, 1981.

HISTORY   ○

Porch, Douglas
THE CONQUEST OF MOROCCO
France's absorption of Morocco into its empire. Frommer Intl. Pub, 1986.

Novels

Bayer, William
TANGIER
A panoramic novel of Europeans, Moroccans, former Nazis, decadence. Dutton, 1978.   ○

Bowles, Paul
MIDNIGHT MASS
Short story collection. Black Sparrow, 1983. Also *The Delicate Prey, and Other Stories* (1980).   ○

Bowles, Paul
THE SHELTERING SKY
Existential novel of a man, wife and a male hanger-on, a "bizarre interior journey made in the Sahara by an American couple." (BRD) New Directions, 1949.   ○

Gilman, Dorothy
MRS. POLLIFAX AND THE WHIRLING DERVISH
The grandmotherly CIA spy meets up with a network of agents working to achieve independence for Western Sahara—"eye for background matches her marvelous sense of adventure." (BL) Doubleday, 1990.   ○

Luard, Nicholas
THE SHADOW SPY
A tale of espionage in Tangier. Macmillan, 1990.   ○

Maalouf, Amin
LEO AFRICANUS
Recreation of the era when the Moors were expelled from Spain, weaving protagonist Hassam's journeys (Morocco, Egypt, Italy, Spain) with accounts of famous contemporaries—Columbus, the Medicis, Suleiman, Luther. Norton, 1989.   ○

Serhane, Abdelhak
MESSAOUDA
"Poetic, disturbing, enlightening picture of a young Muslim boy's life in a small Arab town in Morocco in the 1950s" under French rule. (BRD) New Pr, 1986.   ○

TUNISIA

Series Guidebooks (See Appendix 1)

Berlitz: Tunisia
Cadogan Guide: Tunisia
Insight Guide: Tunisia
Lonely Planet: Morocco, Algeria and Tunisia
Real Guide: Tunisia

Background Reading

Douglas, Norman
FOUNTAINS IN THE SAND
A travel book of the period that praises what should be praised and is "coldly critical" of qualities the author disliked—he attributes "half the evils of this country to Mohammed." (BRD) Potts, 1912.   ○

Soren, David, and others
CARTHAGE: UNCOVERING THE MYSTERIES AND SPLENDORS OF ANCIENT TUNISIA

"Lively, interesting . . . Carthage as a civilized, cosmopolitan, physically attractive city." (PW) S&S, 1990.   ○

GUIDEBOOKS

Butler, Reg
WHERE TO GO IN TUNISIA
Hippocrene, 1989.   ○

Novels

Flaubert, Gustave
SALAMMBO
Classic of archaeology and ancient Carthage. Penguin, 1977 (first published 1863).   ○

SOUTHERN AFRICA

Series Guidebooks (See Appendix 1)

Berlitz: South Africa
Hildebrand: South Africa
Lonely Planet: South Africa

Background Reading

Alverson, Marianne
UNDER AFRICAN SUN (Botswana)
"Valuable . . . entertaining account of disappearing African society" based on the author's experience of living there with her husband and children in the early '70s. (PW) U of Chicago Pr, 1987.   ○

Becker, Peter
THE PATHFINDERS: THE SAGA OF EXPLORATION IN SOUTHERN AFRICA
Two centuries of exploration, from the Dutch landings at Capetown in the mid-seventeenth century to David Livingstone's travels on the Zambezi River. Viking, 1985.   ○

Caute, David
UNDER THE SKIN: THE DEATH OF WHITE RHODESIA
"Brilliant, atmospheric account of the last five years of Rhodesia before it became . . . Zimbabwe in 1980." (PW) Northwestern U, 1983.   ○

Gordimer, Nadine
THE ESSENTIAL GESTURE: WRITING, POLITICS, PLACES
Reflections on South Africa and her own life by the novelist/journalist whose writings span years of opposition to apartheid as a minority within a minority—a white woman in a black country and one who protests white rule of blacks. Knopf, 1988.   ○

Hochschild, Adam
THE MIRROR AT MIDNIGHT: A SOUTH AFRICAN JOURNEY
"Stunning blend of reportage, travelogue, history and meditation" that reenacts the Great Trek of the Boers (1836–39), their massacre of the Zulus and the role this plays in the present-day myth of Afrikaners as victims. Based on a visit to South Africa in 1988—"one of the most illuminating books ever written on contemporary South Africa." (PW) Viking, 1990.   ○

Kivnick, Helen Q.
WHERE IS THE WAY: SONG AND STRUGGLE IN SOUTH AFRICA
By an ethnomusicologist at the University of Chicago. It reflects time spent in South Africa at churches, homes and meetings and demonstrates how integral music is to the daily life of black South Africans, whether rooted in rural traditions, Christianity, the freedom movement or urban life—"provides real insight into the vital culture of those who struggle under apartheid." Anecdotes,

lyric excerpts, musicians, information on recordings and a bibliography. (BL) Penguin, 1990.   ○

Malan, Rian
MY TRAITOR'S HEART
Written by a great-nephew of Daniel Malan, who was an architect of South Africa's apartheid system. Rian Malan became a leftist, a crime reporter and a Los Angeles rock and roll critic before returning to South Africa in 1985. "A blistering book" of autobiography and reportage—"odyssey offers a first hand glimpse of South African apartheid." (PW) Atl Monthly Pr, 1989.   ○

North, James
FREEDOM RISING
The author hitchhiked across South Africa and this account of his venture is in the words of people he met—"attitudes toward their compatriots, other races, the underground organizations, the importance of sports . . . developments in Namibia . . . changes in neighboring Zimbabwe." (PW) Macmillan, 1985.   ○

Owens, Mark and Delia
CRY OF THE KALAHARI
Memoir of a couple's seven-year stint in the central Kalahari on a wildlife research project—"a thoroughly captivating account that should attract animal lovers and armchair adventurers." (BL) Houghton, 1984.   ○

Ransford, Oliver
LIVINGSTONE'S LAKE: THE DRAMA OF AFRICA'S INLAND SEA
The fabulous waters of Lake Nyasa and history of the surrounding Nyasaland (now Malawi). Transatlantic, 1977 (first published 1966). Also, Ransford's biography *Livingstone in Africa* (1973) and his *David Livingstone, The Dark Interior* (1978).   ○

Stengel, Richard
JANUARY SUN: ONE DAY, THREE LIVES, A SOUTH AFRICAN TOWN
Apartheid and life in a Transvaal town. The existence of an Indian merchant, an Afrika-

ner vet and a black political activist is portrayed by tracing the activities of a single day of the three prototypes. S&S, 1990.   ○

Taylor, Jane and Van Der Post, Laurens
TESTAMENT TO THE BUSHMEN
Story of the "tiny Stone Age people . . . once the sole occupants of the whole of Southern Africa and whose situation is now desperate." Van Der Post provides an essay on Bushman myth and folklore. (BL) Viking, 1985.   ○

Van Der Post, Laurens
THE HEART OF THE HUNTER
Story of the African Bushmen, and the aristocracy of spirit of this aboriginal race. HarBraceJ, 1980 (first published 1961). Also, *Lost World of the Kalahari* (1959) which continues the story of the African Bushmen. ○

GUIDEBOOKS

Shales, Melissa
ZIMBABWE
Hippocrene, 1989.   ○

Traveller's Guide Series, eds.
CENTRAL & SOUTHERN AFRICA
Hunter Pub, 1990.   ○

HISTORY

Morris, Donald R.
WASHING OF THE SPEARS
History of the rise and fall of the Zulu nation—"readable and lively narrative." (BRD) S&S, 1986.   ○

Sparks, Allister
THE MIND OF SOUTH AFRICA
"Sensitive . . . balanced" history of relationships among the people of South Africa—Dutch, English, Indian, black—and the inevitable blackening of the country. (PW) Knopf, 1990.   ○

Thompson, Leonard
A HISTORY OF SOUTH AFRICA
A succinct history for the general reader, emphasizing political history—"throws a

floodlight on South Africa's current crisis by examining the past." (PW) Yale U Pr, 1990.　○

Novels

All are for South Africa unless otherwise noted.

Abrahams, Peter
MINE BOY
"What happened to one country boy who sought the City of Gold" in Johannesburg. (BRD) Knopf, 1955. Also, *Wild Conquest* (1950), a historical novel of both sides of the Boer trek to the north in the 1830s and why the Africans tried to stop them; and *A Wreath for Udomo*, a political novel (published in 1956) of a "possible near-future in a hypothetical African country."　○

Bloom, Harry
TRANSVAAL EPISODE
Reprint of a classic. Life in apartheid South Africa—"violence and tragedy and destruction" result when a washerwoman is falsely accused of stealing. (FC) Second Chance Pr, 1981.　○

Bond, Larry
VORTEX
A thriller in which conservative Afrikaners have taken over the Pretoria government and invade Namibia, which brings in a Cuban counterforce, and the British and U.S. forces to restore order. Warner, 1991.　○

Breytenbach, Breyten
MEMORY OF SNOW AND DUST
An Ethiopian journalist and a film actor meet at a film festival in Burkina Faso. FS&G, 1989.　○

Cloete, Stuart
THE TURNING WHEELS
The founding of the Orange Free State and the Transvaal by the Dutch pioneers in South Africa, based on personal diaries of the author's grandfather. Houghton, 1937. Also, *The Fiercest Heart* (1960), about the Great Trek, and *Rags of Glory* (1963), about the Boer War.　○

Coetzee, J.M.
LIFE AND TIMES OF MICHAEL K.
A young black man's odyssey from municipal gardener to eking out "a numbing existence on an abandoned farm . . . war . . . labor camps . . . back into Cape Town . . . about what human beings do to fellow human beings in South Africa." (FC) Viking, 1984. Also, *From the Heart of the Country* (1977), a tale of madness set in the South African veldt, and *Age of Iron* (1990).　○

Courtenay, Bryce
THE POWER OF ONE
South Africa during World War II and an English boy in an Afrikaans boarding school—"appealing . . . masculine psychodrama of success through self-discipline and male bonding." (FC) Random, 1989.　○

Crane, J.K.
THE LEGACY OF LADYSMITH
Sophisticated mystery that shows a biographer in action as he researches a Scottish patriarch and discovers some truths about the man and the South African town of Ladysmith, which his family would like suppressed. S&S, 1989.　○

Driscoll, Peter
SPEARHEAD
A charismatic imprisoned black leader is taken to a clinic for cancer surgery; the authorities see a chance to engineer accidental death, the People's Congress an opportunity for escape. Little, 1987.　○

Ebersohn, Wessel
DIVIDE THE NIGHT
"Compelling story of hatred and misplaced priorities" as a South African psychologist treats a patient who has killed eight blacks. (FC) Pantheon, 1981. Also, *Store Up the Anger* (1981), about the cruelty of the South African racial system.　○

Francis, Dick
SMOKESCREEN
An English film star goes to South Africa to find out why a friend's racehorses are mysteriously collapsing—"tumultuous with thrills." (FC) Har-Row, 1973.　○

Gordimer, Nadine
A SPORT OF NATURE
A leading white voice through her novels and stories of contemporary Africa, and South Africa in particular. Knopf, 1987. Other titles include *My Son's Story* (1990), *July's People* (1982), *Burger's Daughter* (1979), *Conservationist* (1975), *Not For Publication* (1965), *Occasion for Loving* (1963), *The Lying Days* (1953). Collections of novellas and stories include *Something Out There* (1984), *A Soldier's Embrace* (1980), *Selected Short Stories* (1976). ○

Graham, Mark
THE HARBINGER
"Vividly detailed, convincing portrait of South Africa" with a plot involving the murder of a white union official and the return of an exiled black leader. (FC) Holt, 1988. ○

Havemann, Ernst
BLOODSONG, AND OTHER STORIES OF SOUTH AFRICA
The white author of Afrikaans descent grew up on a farm in Zulu country; the stories capture "the ironies of whites trapped in the collusion of sustaining black culture." (BRD) HM, 1987. ○

Head, Bessie
A QUESTION OF POWER
(Botswana/South Africa)
The emotional breakdown and recovery of a daughter of mixed African/English heritage. Pantheon, 1974. Also, *When Rain Clouds Gather* (1969) about a black South African who teaches farming techniques to village women in Botswana. ○

Hope, Christopher
KRUGER'S ALP
"A kind of Pilgrim's Progress dream sequence" as a priest begins to understand the mystery of Kruger's Alp—where the Boer leader supposedly hid a cache of gold—and repression in South Africa. (BRD) Viking, 1985. Also *A Separate Development* (1981), "wildly funny . . . the decline and fall into the . . . alleys of racial classification" when black genes surface in the son of white parents; and *The Hottentot Room* (1987), about South African exiles in London. ○

Lessing, Doris
THE GRASS IS SINGING
The life and disintegration of the wife of a South African farmer; ends in murder. Crowell, 1950. ○

McClure, James
THE BLOOD OF AN ENGLISHMAN
One of a series of police detective stories in which a white police lieutenant and his Zulu sergeant, Zondi, solve the mysteries. "First-rate mysteries . . . the psychology of life today in South Africa, and the racial and sexual tensions." (FC) Harper, 1981. Series includes: *The Steam Pig* (1972), *Snake* (1976), *The Sunday Hangman* (1977), *The Artful Egg* (1985). ○

Malan, Rian
MY TRAITOR'S HEART
"Brutally honest and riveting inquiry into apartheid's heart of darkness." (CNT) Atl Monthly Pr, 1990. ○

Michener, James A.
THE COVENANT
One of Michener's all-encompassing historic novels. This one traces South Africa's past from 500 years ago to contemporary events and is told from the perspective of three families—African, Afrikaans and English. Random, 1980. ○

Mphahlele, Ezekiel
RENEWAL TIME
A collection of some of the author's best stories—all but two set in South Africa. Readers Int, 1988. ○

Ndebele, Njabulo S.
FOOLS, AND OTHER STORIES
Five stories—vignettes of life in a South African black township—"evoke township life with remarkable immediacy for the non-South African reader." (BRD) Readers Int, 1986.
○

Nicol, Mike
THE POWERS THAT BE
By an award-winning poet and journalist, this book captures the history of South Af-

rica and the evils of apartheid, without ever using that word. Atl Monthly Pr, 1989.   ○

Paton, Alan
AH, BUT YOUR LAND IS BEAUTIFUL
Most recent novel of another leading South African writer whose novels of social protest against apartheid "make South Africa's old wounds bleed fresh again." (BRD) Scribner, 1982. Other titles include: *Cry the Beloved Country* (1948), *Too Late the Phalarope* (1953), and *Tales from a Troubled Land* (1961) (short stories).   ○

Rush, Norman
MATING (Botswana)
A comedy of manners. An American anthropologist falls for a man who runs a utopian community in the Kalahari Desert for unfortunate women—"extraordinarily stylish and intelligent, deeply resonant of place and character." (BL) Knopf, 1991.   ○

Rush, Norman
WHITES (Botswana)
Six stories by a Peace Corps worker who spent five years in Botswana; chiefly about American expatriates and foreign service workers passing through, and how good intentions can lead to both tragedy and farce. Knopf, 1986.   ○

Scholefield, Alan
THE SEA CAVE
A young woman and her family move from an Edinburgh slum to Africa and she is drawn into a "mysterious world involving family secrets, puzzling business dealings, and murder." (FC) Congdon & Weed, 1984.   ○

Scholefield, Alan
THE STONE FLOWER
A two-family saga—"the brawling boom days of Kimberley . . . the Boer War . . . the fluctuating fortunes of both greedy diamond hunters and struggling farmers." (FC) Morrow, 1982. Also, *Wild Dog Running* (1978) about emigrants from England to the Cape Colony in 1820.   ○

Serote, Mongane W.
TO EVERY BIRTH ITS BLOOD
Vignettes with a multitude of characters, set in Alexandria Township near Johannesburg in 1976. Thunder's Mouth, 1989.   ○

Seymour, Gerald
A SONG IN THE MORNING
A thriller with South African locales, involving a British agent sentenced to hang and his son's determination to free him. Norton, 1987.   ○

Sheldon, Sidney
MASTER OF THE GAME
The South African diamond mines are the focus of an adventure story involving a ruthless American woman's desire to control a conglomerate. Morrow, 1982.   ○

Sher, Antony
MIDDLEPOST
A Lithuanian Jew travels to Capetown in 1901, just after the Boer War, in search of a new life. Knopf, 1989.   ○

Silverberg, Robert
LORD OF DARKNESS
Based on a true incident, about a 16th-century seaman who is captured in Brazil and taken to Africa. Arbor Hse, 1983.   ○

Slaughter, Carolyn
DREAMS OF THE KALAHARI
The heroine's troubled life takes her, as the daughter of an English administrator, from convent school to England and back again as the lover of an exiled South African journalist. Scribner, 1987.   ○

Smith, Wilbur
THE ANGELS WEEP (Rhodesia)
The third volume of a family saga, set in Rhodesia (now Zimbabwe), in 1977, as the family is plagued by terrorist activity. (FC) Doubleday, 1983. Previous volumes in the saga are *Flight of the Falcon* (1982) and *Men of Men* (1983), which begin in nineteenth-century Africa—"a gripping tale of high adventure . . . historical authenticity and a

profound knowledge of the land and peoples of southern Africa." ○

Smith, Wilbur
THE COURTNEYS (Botswana)
Part of the saga that includes *The Sunbird, A Sparrow Falls, When the Lion Feeds, Sound of Thunder*. Begins when an archaeologist sets out from Johannesburg to find a lost city in Botswana; traces South Africa through the life of a powerful man and his family. Little, 1988. ○

Smith, Wilbur
RAGE
Third of a trilogy and family saga. It begins with *The Burning Shore*, as a young widowed Frenchwoman travels in World War I to her husband's family in South Africa. *Power of the Sword* continues the story with politics, adventure and romance, from the 1930s to post-World War II, and *Rage* continues from World War II on. Little, 1987. ○

Stengel, Richard
JANUARY SUN: ONE DAY, THREE LIVES, A SOUTH AFRICAN TOWN
The title tells the plot. The three lives are those of an Afrikaner, an Indian and a black living in a Transvaal town and the activities in a single day of these three prototypes. S&S, 1990. ○

WESTERN AFRICA

Series Guidebooks
(See Appendix 1)

Insight: Gambia & Senegal; West Africa
Lonely Planet: West Africa
Real Guide: West Africa

Background Reading

Alexander, Caroline
ONE DRY SEASON: IN THE FOOTSTEPS OF MARY KINGSLEY
The author uses Kingsley's *Travels in West Africa* (see below) to retrace that 1893 journey almost 100 years later, "juxtaposing the colorful details of her days with the writings of a vast cast of explorers from a century before . . . will fascinate." (PW) Knopf, 1990. ○

Belcher, Wendy
HONEY FROM THE LION: AN AFRICAN JOURNEY
Account of a young American woman's experiences in Ghana working for a Christian organization—"both artful and artless in her descriptions and insights." (LJ) Dutton, 1988. ○

Dodwell, Christina
TRAVELS WITH PEGASUS: A MICROLIGHT JOURNEY ACROSS WEST AFRICA
The author traveled by ultra-light plane and by solitary land explorations on foot, horseback, canoe and motorcycle—"a treat for vicarious adventurers." Walker, 1990. ○

Greene, Graham
JOURNEY WITHOUT MAPS
A journey into Sierra Leone, Liberia, French Guinea, ending on the Liberian coast, in an attempt to discover the author's spiritual home. Doubleday, 1936. ○

Haley, Alex
ROOTS
The book out of which the enormously popular TV series was developed. It traces the author's ancestors back seven generations to Gambia, where one of them was abducted and shipped as a slave to America. Doubleday, 1976. ○

Hudson, Mark
OUR GRANDMOTHERS' DRUMS
The author spent 14 months in an isolated village to study the lives of its women, be-

coming drawn into those lives. Grove Weidenfeld, 1990.   ○

Huxley, Elspeth
FOUR GUINEAS
A journey through West Africa. Greenwood, 1974 (first published 1954).   ○

Kingsley, Mary
TRAVELS IN WEST AFRICA
Reprint edition of this travel classic. Beacon Pr, 1988.   ○

Klitgaard, Robert
TROPICAL GANGSTERS
"Brilliant analysis of a financially devastated country [Equatorial Guinea] . . . a warm and affectionate memoir about the country and its people." (PW) Basic, 1990.   ○

Matthiessen, Peter
AFRICAN SILENCES
See entry under Central Africa.   ○

Packer, George
THE VILLAGE OF WAITING
Peace Corps experiences in 1982–83 as an English teacher in Togo; "comic . . . poignant . . . tragic experiences in sharp, descriptive prose. The author presents a full view of Togolese customs and society." (PW) Vintage, 1988.   ○

Spindel, Carol
IN THE SHADOW OF THE SACRED GROVE
By the wife of an agricultural geographer who accompanied him to spend a year in an Ivory Coast village; "intriguing memoir wittily and astutely records both her own adjustment to the village and her perceptions of its way of life." (PW) Vintage, 1989.   ○

Wilson, Ellen
THE LOYAL BLACKS
Definitive account of the first American blacks emancipated by the American Revolution who returned to Africa to establish their own country. Putnam Pub Group, 1976.   ○

Wright, Richard
BLACK POWER: A RECORD OF REACTIONS IN A LAND OF PATHOS
The black American novelist's report of a trip to Africa's Gold Coast—"passionate and subjective . . . important, informative and infuriating first-hand account." (BRD) Greenwood, 1974 (first published 1954).   ○

GUIDEBOOKS

Haag, Michael
GUIDE TO WEST AFRICA
Traces the Niger and Gambia, and caravan routes.   ○

Naylor, Kim
DISCOVERY GUIDE TO WEST AFRICA: NIGER AND GAMBIA
Includes Niger, Mali, Gambia, the village where *Roots* began. Hippocrene, 1989.   ○

Traveller's Guide Series, eds.
WEST AFRICA
Hunter Pub, 1988   ○

HISTORY

Fage, J.D.
HISTORY OF WEST AFRICA
History from the eleventh century to the twentieth, and the influences of North Africa, Western Europe, and the Americans. Cambridge U Pr, 1969.   ○

Novels

Achebe, Chinua
THINGS FALL APART (Nigeria)
A remote Nigerian village before the white man had made an impact—life and mores of an Ibo tribe. Astor-Honor, 1959. Also *Arrow of God* (1967), set in the 1920s (the conflict of Christianity and Westernization with tribal customs), *Girls at War* (1973), *A Man of the People* (1966) and *Anthills of the Savannah* (1987).   ○

Bagley, Desmond
JUGGERNAUT
Adventure story in which a huge transformer is moved up-country despite obstacles and a civil war. St. Martin, 1987.   ○

Boyd, William
A GOOD MAN IN AFRICA (West Africa)
Comic novel of a civil servant's plan for success that turns into disaster—recreates West Africa "in full and interesting detail." (FC) Morrow, 1982. ○

Boyle, T. Coraghessan
WATER MUSIC
A picaresque novel based on the adventures and misadventures of Mungo Park, the Scottish explorer who attempted to chart the Niger River in the eighteenth century—"reminiscent of *Tom Jones*." (FC) Little, 1981. ○

Cary, Joyce
COCK JARVIS (Nigeria)
A satire of the British bureaucracy, and a nonconformist, in colonial Nigeria in the 1920s and '30s. St. Martin, 1975. Also *Mister Johnson* (1951). ○

Dickinson, Peter
TEFUGA (Nigeria)
"Amusing and elegantly structured tour de force . . . interweaves a modern story with diary entries that recount events . . . in Northern Nigeria in the 1920s." (NYT) Pantheon, 1986. ○

Emecheta, Buchi
DOUBLE YOKE (Nigeria)
Two Nigerian young people face the choice of a traditional marriage or one that the woman seeks: "both worlds—wife, mother, and academician." (FC) Braziller, 1983. Other novels by Emecheta on the clash of modern and traditional, urban and rural, ways are *The Bride Price* (1976), *The Slave Girl* (1977), *The Joys of Motherhood* (1979), *Destination Biafra* (1982). ○

Greene, Graham
A BURNT-OUT CASE (West Africa)
An architect "flees the glory of the wide world" to retire to a leprosarium run by priests. (FC) Viking, 1961. Also *The Heart of the Matter* (1948), set in a coastal town—a parable of doom in which a British civil servant falls in love with a young widow, is blackmailed, and the result is tragedy. ○

Laing, B.K.
SEARCH SWEET COUNTRY (Ghana-Accra)
"Scintillating first novel" by a Ghanaian poet—"captures Accra, Ghana's capital, at a moment of recent history." Morrow, 1987. ○

Okri, B.
STARS OF THE NEW CURFEW (Nigeria)
A collection of short stories by a former poetry editor of a West African magazine—"a book on Nigerian life which perfectly captures the emotional temperature of that turbulent country." (BRD) Viking, 1989. ○

Schwarz-Bart, Andre
A WOMAN NAMED SOLITUDE
Recreates West African culture through the eyes of a little girl. Based on a historical incident; a child is conceived en route to Guadeloupe, grows up there and, when a brief era of freedom ends after the French Revolution, she refuses to go back to slavery. "She becomes both a moving legend and a symbol of human dignity." (FC) Atheneum, 1973. ○

Soyinka, Wole
ISAGA: A VOYAGE AROUND "ESSAY"
"Semi-fictionalized, multi-generational family saga" by a Nobel laureate author, about his schoolteacher father, grandparents and others—"musical quicksilver prose." Random, 1991. Also *Ake: The Years of Childhood* (1983). ○

Tutuola, Amos
THE PALM-WINE DRINKARD (Nigeria)
"An allegory . . . combining myth and legend and modern symbols" and written in

"young" (pidgin) English. (BRD) Grove, 1954.   o

Webb, Forrest
BRANNINGTON'S LEOPARD
"Splendid evocation of the West African landscape"—an Englishman's quest to kill a leopard and avenge the death of his two dogs. (BRD) Doubleday, 1974.   o

Wyllie, John
SKULL STILL BONE (West Africa)
Sleuth series set in "Arkhana" in West Africa, which does for West Africa what "Keating has done for India . . . full of delightful detail on a lively background." (LJ) Doubleday, 1975. Other titles in the series include: *The Butterfly Flood* (1975), *A Pocket Full of Dead* (1978), *The Killer Breath* (1979).   o

II.
THE MIDDLE EAST

Series Guidebooks
(See Appendix 1)

Traveller's Guide: The Middle East

Background Reading

Braganti, Nancy and Devine, Elizabeth
**THE TRAVELER'S GUIDE TO
    MIDDLE EASTERN AND NORTH
    AFRICAN CUSTOMS AND
    MANNERS**
Useful series to enlighten travelers to the
fact that American social customs are not
universal. St. Martin, 1991.   ○

Butor, Michel
**THE SPIRIT OF MEDITERRANEAN
    PLACES**
See entry under Europe—Cairo, Luxor and
Turkey are included.   ○

Carter, Jimmy
**THE BLOOD OF ABRAHAM:
    INSIGHTS INTO THE MIDDLE
    EAST**
Ex-President Carter's analysis of Middle East
politics. HM, 1985.   ○

Ceram, C.W.
GODS, GRAVES AND SCHOLARS
The modern classic that provides a popular
story of archaeology for travelers, the story
of the nineteenth-century discoveries in Troy
and other archaeological sites. Bantam, 1976
(first published 1967).   ○

Cornell, Tim and Matthews, John
ATLAS OF THE ROMAN WORLD
"A concise, extremely well illustrated intro-
duction to ancient Rome," which at its ze-
nith reached through the Middle East. (CSM)
Facts On File, 1984.   ○

Dalrymple, William
IN XANADU
Following in the footsteps of Marco Polo,
from Jerusalem to Xanadu. A correspondent
of the *London Sunday Times* recounts a journey during his student days—"brave and
fantastic . . . a delightful guide with the
bright-eyed perceptions of an explorer." (PW)
Vintage, 1990.   ○

Fargues, Philippe and Boustani, Rafic
ATLAS OF THE ARAB WORLD
A new, highly readable and comprehensive
reference for the general reader that de-
scribes culture, society and economy of the
Arab world in the Middle East, North Africa,
Mauritania and the Horn of Africa. Facts On
File, 1991.   ○

Friedman, Thomas L.
FROM BEIRUT TO JERUSALEM

By a Pulitzer Prize-winning *N.Y. Times* correspondent—a "provocative, absorbing memoir . . . condensed, incisive history of the Middle East." An elucidation of the complexity and agendas of various religious factions, daily life in Beirut, the Intifada, relationships between American and Israeli Jews. (PW) FS&G, 1989.   ○

Glass, Charles
TRIBES WITH FLAGS: A DANGEROUS PASSAGE THROUGH THE CHAOS OF THE MIDDLE EAST

"A literary and spiritual ramble through the countries of the Levant . . . comparing his impressions with those of earlier travelers such as Richard Burton, Benjamin Disraeli, Mark Twain." The book is by the TV correspondent who was picked up during his journey by the Hizbollah and held hostage. (PW) Atl Monthly Pr, 1990.   ○

Horwitz, Tony
BAGHDAD WITHOUT A MAP AND OTHER MISADVENTURES IN ARABIA

A *Wall Street Journal* reporter's memoir of travels in 1988–89 to 14 countries of the Arab world, plus Israel—"entertaining, often funny." (PW) Dutton, 1991.   ○

Hutchison, Robert
DANGER—HEAVY GOODS

Truckers race the devil and the clock on the toughest, most dangerous road in the world. See entry under Europe/Background Reading.   ○

Severin, Tim
TRACKING MARCO POLO

First published in 1964. A travelogue that integrates a dual story: one is a running narrative of Marco Polo's journey, the other tells of a motorcycle expedition by two college students and a photographer—"an illuminating contrast between present and past . . . intriguing glimpses [of] Turkey, Persia, and Afghanistan." (BL) Harper, 1986. Also by Severin, *Sinbad Voyage*, a trip via the ancient Arab sea routes in a replica of an Arabian wooden ship of the period (8th to 11th centuries), from the Arabian Gulf to China by way of Ceylon and Southeast Asia (1983).   ○

Stark, Freya
THE JOURNEY'S ECHO

"A chronological collection of purple passages and aphorisms" out of the author's travel writings, 1927–58—"the ideal bedside book" by one of the outstanding travel writers of the century. (BRD) Transatlantic, 1975 (first published 1964).   ○

Trench, Richard
ARABIAN TRAVELLERS—THE EUROPEAN DISCOVERY OF ARABIA

Explorers who succumbed to Arabia's fascination, from the first Danes to Burton, Doughty, T.E. Lawrence, oil companies, along with stories of minor travelers in the 19th century. Salem Hse, 1986.   ○

ISLAM

See also books listed under Israel/The Holy Land, Bible and Koran; Saudi Arabia.   ○

Lamb, David
THE ARABS: JOURNEYS BEYOND THE MIRAGE

Arab culture and history and a tour of the Arab world. The book focuses on people rather than events; "vividly portrays the humanity of a people too often misrepresented by Western media." (BRD) Random, 1988.   ○

Minai, Naila
WOMEN IN ISLAM

Childhood, adolescence, marriage, polygamy, the single, the widowed, working women. Seaview, 1981. Also *The Hidden Face of Eve* (1980) and *Women in the Arab World* (1982) by Hawal El Saadawi.   ○

Naipaul, V.S.
AMONG THE BELIEVERS

By a leading contemporary novelist, this is an exploration of the life and culture of four

Islamic countries. The author repeatedly finds in the very devotion to Islam the reason for the backwardness of these countries, and an expectation that the education and technology they need will come from alien lands. Knopf, 1981.   ○

Nydell, Margaret
UNDERSTANDING ARABS: A GUIDE FOR WESTERNERS

For people who plan to live or visit in an Arab country, or are just interested in learning about Arab culture. Intercultural Pr, 1988.   ○

Robinson, Francis
ATLAS OF THE ISLAMIC WORLD SINCE 1500

"More encyclopedia than atlas . . . lavishly illustrated . . . depicting everything from fourteenth-century tombs to contemporary Afghan nomads at prayer"—provides a framework for understanding the last 500 years of Muslim history. (BL) Facts On File, 1982.   ○

Wright, Robin
SACRED RAGE: THE WRATH OF MILITANT ISLAM

A survey of Middle Eastern terrorism and an argument for greater American understanding of the Islamic world. S&S, 1986. Also *In the Name of God: The Khomeini Decade, 1979–89* (1989).   ○

GUIDEBOOKS

Traveller's Guide Series, eds.
THE MIDDLE EAST
Hunter Pub, 1989.   ○

HISTORY

Goldschmidt, Arthur J.
A CONCISE HISTORY OF THE MIDDLE EAST

"Excellent . . . approach is conversational, direct and trenchant . . . a model of clarity." Designed to be an introduction to Middle East history from the seventh century to the present. (MEJ) Westview Pr, 1987.   ○

Hourani, Albert
A HISTORY OF THE ARAB PEOPLES

"Intended for beginning students and general readers . . . by one of the most distinguished scholars of the Arab world and the Middle East . . . written with grace and wisdom." (NYT) Belknap Pr/Harvard U Pr, 1991.   ○

Novels

Kanafani, Ghasse
MEN IN THE SUN, AND OTHER PALESTINIAN STORIES

Peter Theroux, in his book *Sandstorms: Days and Nights in Arabia* (see entry under Saudi Arabia/Background Reading), calls this "a thinking man's *Haj*." Three Continents, 1983.   ○

Poyer, David
THE GULF

A frigate in the Persian Gulf, convoying oil tankers through dangerous water, battles enemies and the ocean itself, while Navy divers undertake another dangerous mission of their own. St. Martin, 1990.   ○

Puzo, Mario
THE FOURTH K

A pope is assassinated, the daughter of a U.S. president is kidnapped and murdered and there's a nuclear explosion in Manhattan! "Astute characterizations, vivid drama . . . the paradoxes of evil detonate a top-notch thriller." (FC) Random, 1991.   ○

Renault, Mary
THE PERSIAN BOY

Historical novel of Alexander the Great's expeditions into Asia—"brings to life a great historical period." (FC) Pantheon, 1972.   ○

Saudray, Nicolas
THE HOUSE OF THE PROPHETS

The imaginary country of Marsana is a synthesis of middle eastern countries; the protagonist of the story is a young Christian architect whose design for a harbor mosque causes religious and political problems. Saudray is a pen name for an official in the French government who is also a novelist. This is the first of his novels published in the United States. Doubleday, 1985.   ○

Shagan, Steve
THE DISCOVERY

An archaeologist and companion find Syrian artifacts that seemingly lead to the actual words of Moses, discoveries that are "anathema in the current political climate." (FC) Morrow, 1984.   ○

Uris, Leon
THE HAJ

Sequel to *Exodus;* the story of a Muslim, head man of a Palestinian village, from 1922 through 1956 when he dies in a refugee camp. Doubleday, 1984.   ○

Whittemore, Edward
SINAI TAPESTRY

"The strange fortunes of a number of characters . . . over 100 years and several cultural genealogies." (BRD) HR&W, 1977.   ○

E G Y P T

Series Guidebooks
(See Appendix 1)

Baedeker: Egypt
Berlitz: Egypt
Blue Guide: Egypt
Fodor: Egypt
Frommer: Egypt (Country & Touring)
Insight Guide: Egypt
Langenscheidt: Self-Guided Egypt
Let's Go: Israel, Egypt and Jordan
Lonely Planet: Egypt and the Sudan
Moon Handbook: Egypt
Nagel's Encyclopedia Guide: Egypt
Nelles Guide: Egypt
Real Guide: Egypt
Visitor's Guide: Egypt

Background Reading

Drury, Allen
EGYPT: THE ETERNAL SMILE

The author has written novels set in early Egypt, and this book is a travelogue and personal impressions interwoven with information on Egyptian history, culture, religion. Doubleday, 1980. See also "Novels," below.   ○

Edwards, Amelia B.
A THOUSAND MILES UP THE NILE

This is a reprint of a travel classic. In 1873, the author departed Shepheard's Hotel in Cairo for a 1,000-mile trip up the Nile by boat, complete with servants and daily high

tea. "Wonderfully vivid tale of Egypt in the long, languid days when Britain's empire was at its height and Englishwomen . . . set forth on remarkable adventures." (Publisher) J.P. Tarcher, 1983.   ○

Forster, E.M.
ALEXANDRIA: A HISTORY AND A GUIDE

A love song to Alexandria divided into history and guide, carefully connected by cross-references to link present and past—considered by many to be the best thing written on the city. Oxford U Pr, 1986.   ○

Golding, William
AN EGYPTIAN JOURNAL

The author and his wife took a trip down the Nile "expecting mysteries and revelations . . . granted instead Pharaoic graffiti and interviews with displaced Nubians . . . sardonic, whimsical." (TL) Faber and Faber, 1985. Also *A Moving Target,* a collection of writings that includes two essays on Egypt, one written before he'd seen the country, the other afterwards (1982).   ○

Manley, Deborah
THE NILE: A TRAVELLER'S ANTHOLOGY

Excerpts of writings from more than 80 sources, ranging from Flaubert to Jan Morris, that takes its readers on a Nile journey—

"an impressive and stimulating historical overview." (BL) Sterling, 1991. ○

Moorehead, Alan
THE BLUE NILE; THE WHITE NILE
See entry under Africa/Background Readings. ○

Pye-Smith, Charlie
THE OTHER NILE
An account of two contrasting journeys in the Nile Valley, one earlier as a poor student, the other in 1982 as a journalist; the approach is one of frank comment—buying marijuana, brothels, not just the usual pyramids. "A tantalizing glimpse into a foreign land full of beauty and sadness." (BL) Viking, 1986. ○

Steegmuller, Francis, ed.
FLAUBERT IN EGYPT
Flaubert's travel notes and letters during a trip in 1849, with accompanying narrative by Steegmuller "providing perspective and background." (BRD) Academy Chi Pubs, 1979. ○

ANCIENT EGYPT & ARCHAEOLOGY

Baines, John and Malek, Jaromir
ATLAS OF ANCIENT EGYPT
"The most useful one-volume atlas and illustrated guide to ancient Egypt. . . . a journey down the Nile describing sites of archaeological or historical importance." (BL) Facts On File, 1980. ○

Clayton, Peter A.
THE REDISCOVERY OF ANCIENT EGYPT
"Egypt, from Alexandria to Abu Simbel, seen through the eyes of travelers. . . . makes it possible for the reader to experience something of the awe and excitement that nineteenth-century European travelers felt." (LJ) Thames & Hudson, 1983. ○

Johnson, Paul
THE CIVILIZATION OF ANCIENT EGYPT
Art, religion, social and political history for the general public library audience. Atheneum, 1978. ○

GUIDEBOOKS

Canby, Courtlandt
A GUIDE TO THE ARCHAEOLOGICAL SITES OF ISRAEL, EGYPT AND NORTH AFRICA
A guide for the general traveler or armchair traveler. Organized regionally with historical summaries to put sites in perspective— "clear and personable language . . . masterful command of archaeological and historical detail." (LJ) Facts On File, 1990. ○

Engstrom, Barbie
ENGSTROM'S GUIDE TO EGYPT AND A NILE CRUISE
A "travelogue and a travel guide [that] generates considerable enthusiasm for its subject." Personal experiences, practical information on planning and getting around, with appendices on Egyptian history, religion, hieroglyphics and basic conversation in Arabic. (BL) Kurios Pr, 1984. ○

Haag, Michael
GUIDE TO EGYPT
Practical information sections on accommodations, restaurants, entertainment, shopping and travel, an Arabic vocabulary, an Islamic calendar, a 5,000-year chronology, etc.—a guide that also explains the significance of what is seen. Hippocrene, 1989. Also *Guide to Cairo With the Pyramids and Saqqara* (1985). ○

Murnane, William J.
THE GUIDE TO ANCIENT EGYPT
A guide to the major and the less well-known historical sites of Egypt arranged by location to facilitate itinerary planning, history, architectural detail, maps. (BL) Facts On File, 1983. ○

Naylor, Kim
AFRICA: THE NILE ROUTE
Traveling between Cairo and Kenya (or the Sudan) for the budget traveler—low-cost hotels, buses or boats, "musts" to see, clean places to eat. Hippocrene, 1990. ○

West, John A.
TRAVELER'S KEY TO ANCIENT EGYPT
One of a series of guides to religious shrines; explores the country through the art and architecture of Ancient Egypt, various theories about the pyramids, Sphinx and other sacred sites. Knopf, 1985.   o

HISTORY

Aldred, Cyril
THE EGYPTIANS
Revised and enlarged edition of a survey history originally published in 1961. Thames Hudson, 1984.   o

Diop, Cheikh Anta
THE AFRICAN ORIGIN OF CIVILIZATION
Presents the theory that upper Egypt is a Negro civilization and birthplace of most Western ideas. Lawrence Hill, 1974.   o

Marsot, Afaf L.
A SHORT HISTORY OF MODERN EGYPT
Cambridge U Pr, 1985.   o

Novels

Bradshaw, Gillian
THE BEACON AT ALEXANDRIA
"By the time you finish . . . you will have learned about early Christian theology, Roman frontier politics and state-of-the-art fourth century medicine . . . and you will also have had a rousing good time." (FC) HM, 1986.   o

Christie, Agatha
DEATH ON THE NILE
A newly married woman is murdered aboard a Nile steamship—a Detective Poirot mystery. Dodd, 1970 (first published 1937). Also *Death Comes As the End* (from *Five Classic Murder Mysteries*), a murder mystery set in Thebes in 2000 B.C. (first published 1944).   o

Critchfield, Richard
SHAHHAT, AN EGYPTIAN
Evocative and impressionistic account (in novel form) of the daily life of an Egyptian peasant, living within walking distance of the Valley of the Kings. Syracuse U, 1978.   o

Cruz, M.M.
OCTOBER IN CAIRO
"Part political novel and part romance . . . reveals the author's familiarity with Egyptian culture." Plot concerns a journalist who becomes a pawn in a plot to kill Anwar Sadat. (FC) Permanent Press, 1988.   o

Drury, Allen
A GOD AGAINST THE GODS
Egypt in the fourteenth century B.C., during the reign of Nefertiti—recreates the period as the old gods are displaced. (FC) Doubleday, 1976. *Return to Thebes* (1977) is a sequel and continues with the story of Pharaoh Akhenaten—"warmly human but logical version" of the period.   o

Durrell, Lawrence
THE ALEXANDRIA QUARTET
Modern fiction classic, set in Alexandria. The sequence is *Balthazar, Clea, Justine, Mountolive.* Dutton, 1957–60.   o

Durrell, Lawrence
CONSTANCE
Part of the "Avignon" series of novels (see "France"). Novelist Blandford, and Constance's husband, Sam, are in Egypt in World War II. Blandford is crippled and Sam killed in an artillery accident. Viking, 1982.   o

Follett, Ken
THE KEY TO REBECCA
Suspense story of German espionage in World War II Egypt—"the evocation of wartime Cairo is a marvel of concise atmospherics." (FC) Morrow, 1980. Also *Triple* (1979), in which one hundred tons of uranium are hijacked—international espionage involving Egyptians, Palestinians, a KGB colonel and a Mafia don.   o

Gedge, Pauline
THE TWELFTH TRANSFORMING
Set in Egypt during the reign of Pharaoh Akhenaten—"a lustrous tale . . . told in the quiet tone of an intimate chronicle." (FC) Har-Row, 1984. Also, *Child of the Morning* (1979), about the only woman pharaoh, Hatshepsut.   ◯

Hawkes, Jacquetta
KING OF THE TWO LANDS: THE PHARAOH AKHENATEN
Historical novel that recreates the setting and mood of the period of Nefertiti and Akhenaten. Random, 1966.   ◯

Maalouf, Amin
LEO AFRICANUS
See entry under Morocco/Novels.   ◯

Mahfouz, Naguib
PALACE WALK
First of "The Cairo Trilogy" by the first Arab writer to receive the Nobel Prize for literature and considered an Egyptian Balzac. Originally published in Egypt in 1956–57, the novel centers on a family in Cairo during the period after World War I, including the 1919 revolution against the British. Doubleday, 1990. *Palace of Desire* is the second volume of the trilogy (1991), and *Sugar Street* (1992) the third. Other books now available by Mahfouz, in English, are *Wedding Song, The Beginning and the End, The Thief and the Dogs,* and it is anticipated that all of his works will be published in English given the Nobel Prize award.   ◯

Mailer, Norman
ANCIENT EVENINGS
Historical novel of Egypt, 1290–1100 B.C.— "magical, sensuous, and highly politicized atmosphere [portrayed with] stunning effect." (FC) Little, 1983.   ◯

Mann, Jessica
DEATH BEYOND THE NILE
An archaeologist, who is an avocational espionage agent, is assigned to guard a scientist on a Nile cruise. St. Martin, 1989.   ◯

Manning, Olivia
THE DANGER TREE
Continuation of *The Balkan Trilogy* (see Rumania/Novels), as Rommel's army advances. Atheneum, 1977. Following is *The Battle Lost and Won* (1979), set in World War II Cairo and the Egyptian desert, after El Alamein.   ◯

Newby, P.H.
KITH
Egypt in 1941 is recalled 30 years later, and an affair between a young English soldier and his uncle's Egyptian wife. Little, 1977. Other novels about the British colony in Egypt in the 1950s and '60s are: *The Picnic at Sakkara* (1955), *Revolution & Roses* (1957), *Something to Answer For* (1969).   ◯

Peters, Elizabeth
THE MUMMY CASE
"A disappearing mummy case and missing Coptic papyri are the clues in this slapstick comedy-mystery." (FC) Congdon & Weed, 1985. Also *Lion In the Valley* (1986) and *The Curse of the Pharaohs* (1981), which are set in 19th-century Egypt.   ◯

Salisbury, Carola
AN AUTUMN IN ARABY
"A Victorian fairy tale . . . glitters with romance, excitement, color and evocations of historic events played out in 1869"—the opening of the Suez Canal. (FC) Doubleday, 1983.   ◯

Waltari, Mika
THE EGYPTIAN
A fictional recreation of Egypt, before Christ, told by a physician—"we see, feel, smell and taste . . . Egypt." (FC) Putnam Pub Group, 1949.   ◯

ISRAEL

Series Guidebooks
(See Appendix 1)

Baedeker: Jerusalem; Israel
Berlitz: Jerusalem
Blue Guide: Jerusalem
Fodor: Israel
Frommer: Israel ($-A-Day)
Insight: Israel; Jerusalem
Langenscheidt: Self-Guided Israel
Let's Go: Israel
Lonely Planet: Israel
Michael's Guide: Jerusalem

Background Reading

Aronson, Geoffrey
CREATING FACTS: ISRAEL, PALESTINIANS AND THE WEST BANK

The demographic and political realities by an author who feels that the democratic and Jewish foundations of the state will erode unless some way of resolving the Palestinian situation is found. Institute for Palestine Studies, 1987. ○

Bar-Zohar, Michael
FACING A CRUEL MIRROR: ISRAEL'S MOMENT OF TRUTH

"Remarkably vivid portrayal of Israeli politics and society from the 1967 Six-Day War to the Intifada." Bar-Zohar is a Knesset member, journalist, soldier and author of espionage novels under pseudonyms of Michael Hastings and Michael Barak. He comes from a point of view that favors a Jordanian-Palestinian confederation rather than a separate Palestinian state. (PW) Scribner, 1990. ○

Binur, Yoram
MY ENEMY, MY SELF

An Israeli journalist assumes the identity of a Palestinian Arab for six months, living in a refugee camp in Gaza, working, sharing a Tel Aviv flophouse—even having a romance with a Jewish woman. He comes to the view that Israel's occupation of the West Bank and Gaza is disastrous. (PW) Doubleday, 1988. ○

Brook, Stephen
WINNER TAKES ALL: A SEASON IN ISRAEL

The author is a British Jew, and a travel writer; a travelogue with comments on the various factions, from frustrated Arabs to residents of a Kibbutz to Druzes, and an Ethiopian nun. Viking, 1991. ○

Chertok, Haim
STEALING HOME: ISRAEL BOUND AND REBOUND

Twenty-eight essays "offer a penetrating account of life in Israel during the last decade." (BL) Fordham U Pr, 1988. ○

Diqs, Isaak
A BEDOUIN BOYHOOD

An "idealized pastoral idyll" evoking the author's boyhood among Bedouins near the Negev Desert—a way of life that has ended. (PW) Universe, 1983 (first published 1967). ○

Gilead, Zerubavel and Krook, Dorothy
GIDEON SPRING: A MAN AND HIS KIBBUTZ

The author is a poet and active in the kibbutz movement and "maintains that its ideal of an egalitarian non-acquisitive society has survived." This is his life story with poems, photos and reminiscences—"a beautifully written, moving memoir." (PW) Ticknor & Fields, 1985. ○

Gorkin, Michael
DAYS OF HONEY, DAYS OF ONION

An American Jew, a clinical psychologist, has produced this book of oral testimony by a Palestinian Arab family—"intimate, revealing . . . a valuable and engaging report." (PW) Beacon, 1991. ○

Grossman, David
THE YELLOW WIND

By an Israeli novelist—"records the devastation that two decades of Israeli occupation . . . has wreaked on Palestinian and Israelis alike . . . one of the most stirring, refreshing voices of moral conscience to emerge." (PW) FS&G, 1988. ○

Harkabi, Y.
THE PALESTINIAN COVENANT AND ITS MEANING
The *"raison d'être* of the PLO"—written in the 1960s, it is the roots of the Palestinian movement and (the author believes) a straitjacket that will never allow recognition of Israel's claims. (BRD) Valentine, 1980. ○

Hasan, Sana
ENEMY IN THE PROMISED LAND
Account of the author's trip to Israel at a time when it was considered traitorous for this Harvard-educated Egyptian woman to do so. Pantheon, 1987. ○

Hazleton, Lesley
JERUSALEM, JERUSALEM
"Intimate memoir" of the author's years in Israel, encompassing both the Six Day and Yom Kippur Wars—"her evocation of the scents and stones of the Old City . . . heroic character of the Israelis . . . is moving and on target." (BRD) Atl Monthly Pr, 1986. ○

Kollek, Teddy
MY JERUSALEM
S&S, 1990. ○

Kreiger, Barbara
LIVING WATERS: MYTH, HISTORY, AND POLITICS OF THE DEAD SEA
"A rare natural, political, and human history of the 12,000-year-old Dead Sea, the lowest . . . and saltiest body of water in the world" that is unique also in the passion and curiosity it has engendered in travelers and scientists. (BL) Crossroad, 1988. ○

Kunstel, Marcia and Albright, Joseph
THEIR PROMISED LAND: ARAB AND JEW IN HISTORY'S CAULDRON
One valley in the Jerusalem Hills—the valley is the Sorek, "a microcosm of the Israeli-Palestinian conflict. Vivid, observant, ach-

ingly poignant" chronicle by two American correspondents. (PW) Crown, 1990. ○

Oz, Amos
IN THE LAND OF ISRAEL
"Candid, diverse, often passionate views of Israelis on divisions now wracking that land" based on conversations with people in all walks of life, by the Israeli novelist. (PW) HarBraceJ, 1983. ○

Peters, Joan
FROM TIME IMMEMORIAL
The author argues that a de facto exchange of Jews and Palestinians had already happened before the Israeli occupation and that many Palestinians are immigrants to Palestine, or children of immigrants, matched in number by Jews forced to leave Arab countries. Harper, 1983. ○

Said, Edward
BLAMING THE VICTIMS
Essays that attack the acceptance of Joan Peters' *From Time Immemorial* (see above) as part of the inability of Western media to accept the realities of Palestinian claims. Verso, 1988. Also *The Question of Palestine* (1979). ○

Shipler, David K.
ARAB AND JEW, WOUNDED SPIRITS IN A PROMISED LAND
The author was *New York Times* bureau chief in Jerusalem and this is his examination of the images and impressions Arab and Jew have of one another—"seems to leave no aspect of the complex Arab-Jewish relationship untouched . . . abundance of narratives, anecdotes, conversations." (BRD) Times Bks, 1987. ○

Sichrovsky, Peter
ABRAHAM'S CHILDREN: ISRAEL'S YOUNG GENERATION
Interviews with 26 young Israeli Jews from various backgrounds, by a Viennese journalist. "The narratives, earnest, impassioned . . . comprise a many-faceted portrait of Israel's 'young generation.' " (NYT) Pantheon, 1991. ○

Winternitz, Helen
A SEASON OF STONES: LIFE IN A PALESTINIAN VILLAGE
A year spent in a West Bank Village in 1988 by an American; the beginnings of the intifada. Atl Monthly Pr, 1991. ○

THE HOLY LAND, BIBLE & KORAN

Elon, Amos
JERUSALEM: CITY OF MIRRORS
"Rich, beautifully written, impartial meditation" on modern Jerusalem with its Jewish, Christian, Moslem, Armenian quadrants—"measures the clarity of Jerusalem's biblical landscape against a past and present choked with religious and political strife." (PW) Little, 1989. ○

Heilman, Samuel
A WALKER IN JERUSALEM
"An emotional and psychological pilgrimage through Jerusalem from the perspective of its diverse residents." (LJ) Summit Bks, 1986. ○

Indinopulos, Thomas A.
JERUSALEM BLESSED, JERUSALEM CURSED
"Jews, Christians, and Muslims in the Holy City from David's time to our own" is the lengthy subtitle. "Prodigous and imposing work, as timely as it is provocative," with maps and photographs. (BL) Ivan R. Dee, 1991. ○

Magnússon, Magnus
THE ARCHAEOLOGY OF THE BIBLE
A book on archaeology for the lay reader—"fun to read and educational." (The author did a TV documentary on the subject.) (LJ) S&S, 1978. ○

Millgram, Abraham E.
JERUSALEM CURIOSITIES
"Enchanting vignettes—facts and legends . . . a delightful look for the armchair traveler." (BL) Jewish Publication Society, 1990. ○

Morton, Henry C.
IN THE STEPS OF THE MASTER
This, and *In Search of the Holyland* (1984) are travel classics first published in 1934–35, based on Morton's journey in the 1930s. *In Search of the Holyland* is a book of photographs accompanied by text from *In the Steps of the Master*—"a you-are-there ambience." (PW) Dodd, 1984. ○

Pearlman, Moshe and Yanni, Yaacov
HISTORICAL SITES IN THE HOLY LAND
Historical and archaeological background to Israeli antiquities and restorations for travelers and armchair travelers. Judson, 1985. ○

Peters, F.E.
JERUSALEM
The long subtitle explains the book's contents: "The Holy City in the eyes of chroniclers, visitors, pilgrims and prophets from the days of Abraham to the beginnings of modern times"—first-hand impressions by people of all religions, over the centuries. Princeton U Pr, 1985. ○

Rabinovitch, Abraham
JERUSALEM ON EARTH: PEOPLE, PASSIONS AND POLITICS IN THE HOLY CITY
Co-existing Jews and Arabs, from its mayor to a Muslim specialist on Nietzsche to a matchmaker—"an absorbing portrait of an ancient city and its inhabitants." (BL) Free Press, 1988. ○

Rogerson, John
THE ATLAS OF THE BIBLE
History and transmission of biblical literature, biblical history, the Bible in art, geography of the Bible. Facts On File, 1985. ○

Thubron, Colin
JERUSALEM
Part of the Century Traveller Series. Random Cntry, 1988. ○

Uris, Leon and Jill
JERUSALEM SONG OF SONGS
History of this unique city, passionately told by two novelists. Doubleday, 1984. ○

Wilson, Edmund
**ISRAEL AND THE DEAD SEA
   SCROLLS**

By the distinguished literary critic—an account of the discovery of the scrolls with his interpretations of their significance for the Judeo-Christian tradition, along with views on Israel and modern Jewish literature, and a foreword by Leon Edel "to put it all in focus." (NYT) FS&G, 1978.   ○

GUIDEBOOKS

Canby, Courtlandt
**A GUIDE TO THE
   ARCHAEOLOGICAL SITES OF
   ISRAEL, EGYPT AND NORTH
   AFRICA**

See entry under Egypt/Guidebooks.   ○

Devir, Ari
**OFF THE BEATEN TRACK IN
   ISRAEL: A GUIDE TO
   BEAUTIFUL PLACES**

An Israel many tourists miss, including beauty spots, archaeological sites and natural wonders—a book also for armchair travelers. Adama Bks, 1986.   ○

Freeman-Grenville, G.S.P.
THE BEAUTY OF JERUSALEM

Ten itineraries outlining the Gospel story. Continuum, 1989.   ○

Kilgallen, John J.
**A NEW TESTAMENT GUIDE TO
   THE HOLY LAND**

"Adroit amalgam of practical travel information and scriptural reflection"—maps, photos, archaeological and geographic information, along with commentary on the significance to Christians of events that took place. (BL) Loyola U Pr, 1987.   ○

Lev, Martin
**TRAVELER'S KEY TO THE SACRED
   PLACES OF JERUSALEM**

One of a series of guides to places with religious or spiritual significance, the philosophical ideas that led to them, history, art. Knopf, 1989.   ○

Mehling, Marianne
**JERUSALEM & THE HOLY LAND:
   A PHAIDON CULTURAL GUIDE**

Succinct appreciation of the best the country has to offer in terms of national treasures and culture—churches, palaces, theaters, museums, monuments, maps and plans, all arranged alphabetically and cross-indexed. Phaidon Pr.   ○

Rosovsky, Nitza and Ungerleider-
   Mayerson, Joy
THE MUSEUMS OF ISRAEL

Jewish-, Christian- and Muslim-sponsored—both large and well-known, small and obscure museums are included. Arranged geographically with maps and subject/alphabetical/location indexes. Abrams, 1989.   ○

HISTORY

Johnson, Paul
**CIVILIZATIONS OF THE HOLY
   LAND**

Biblical civilizations, Byzantine and Islamic—"makes an exceedingly complex history intelligible without oversimplifying." (BRD) Atheneum, 1979.   ○

Sachar, Howard M.
A HISTORY OF ISRAEL

A history from the rise of Zionism to our time. Knopf, 1979.   ○

Novels

See also novels under "Egypt" and the "Middle East" by Caldwell, Fast, Slaughter and others.

Appelfeld, Aron
THE IMMORTAL BARTFUSS

A holocaust survivor who has "lost his great dream . . . distanced from everyone." Weidenfeld, 1988.   ○

Bayer, William
PATTERN CRIMES

Middle Eastern politics are involved in a series of pattern murders in this intricately plotted police procedural—"incisive prose

. . . carefully orchestrated sense of place . . . excellent and provocative fiction." (FC) Villard, 1987. ○

Courter, Gay
CODE EZRA
Suspense novel of an Israeli spymaster and the three coworkers he recruits. HM, 1986. ○

D'Alpuget, Blanche
WINTER IN JERUSALEM
A screenwriter returns to Israel to find her father—"stunningly evokes the passion and color of contemporary Israel."(PW) S&S, 1986. ○

Grossman, David
THE SMILE OF THE LAMB
The author also wrote *The Yellow Wind* (see above, under Background Reading) and a first novel, *See Under: Love* (1989). FS&G, 1990. ○

Kaniuk, Yaram
CONFESSIONS OF A GOOD ARAB
The Hebrew edition was originally published in 1984. The Arab-Israeli conflict told from the viewpoint of the son of an Israeli and a Palestinian scholar. Halban, 1987. Also *Rocking Horse* (1977), a "serious" comedy about a painter who deserts his family in New York for his native Israel in search of a new identity; and *His Daughter* (1989), a moral allegory of the disappearance of a daughter and the condition of contemporary Israel. ○

Kellerman, Jonathan
THE BUTCHER'S THEATER
An Israeli police inspector is assigned to solve a case in which young Arab women are being murdered, and must put together a team "who battle ancient prejudices . . . and their own rivalries" to find the killer. (FC) Bantam Bks, 1988. ○

Kemelman, Harry
ONE FINE DAY THE RABBI BOUGHT A CROSS
One of a series in which Rabbi David Small is the sleuth. The timely plot concerns a

cache of arms and the setting is historic Jerusalem. Morrow, 1987. Morrow has reprinted six or seven more in this series— *Monday the Rabbi Took Off, Saturday the Rabbi Went Hungry, Sunday the Rabbi Stayed Home* . . . and so on. ○

Le Carré, John
THE LITTLE DRUMMER GIRL
Spy novel by the master—this time involving the Israeli-Palestinian conflict. Knopf, 1983. ○

Levin, Meyer
THE SETTLERS
A family saga, interwoven with Israeli history, beginning in 1904. S&S, 1972. *The Harvest* (1978) continues the saga to 1948 and Israeli independence. ○

Oz, Amos
BLACK BOX
Contemporary Israel is the setting. Raises political, social, moral issues when Ilana, seeking help for their son, contacts her former husband. HB, 1988. Also *A Perfect Peace* (1985). ○

Quinnell, A.J.
THE SNAP
Based on the bombing of Iraq's nuclear reactor by Israel—a photojournalist is hired by Israel to photograph a delivery of uranium to prove its premise that the bombing was justified. Morrow, 1983. ○

Read, Piers Paul
ON THE THIRD DAY
An Israeli archaeologist finds a skeleton believed to be that of Jesus—"thought-provoking political and theological questions . . . a compelling tale." (FC) Random, 1991. ○

Roth, Philip
THE COUNTERLIFE
Israel is the setting for a sequel to the *Zuckerman Bound* trilogy. FS&G, 1986. ○

Roiphe, Anne
LOVINGKINDNESS
A young woman finds a new life in a fundamentalist Yeshiva in Israel; her New York

mother is horrified when an arranged marriage is proposed. Summit Bks, 1987. ○

Rosenberg, Robert
CRIMES OF THE CITY
The head of Jerusalem's CID, politicians, the prime minister, become involved in the death of mother/daughter nuns at the Russian Orthodox mission. "Neighborhoods that comprise the holy city are woven skilfully into the narrative." S&S, 1991. ○

Shabtal, Yaakov
PAST CONTINUOUS
"Thick but compelling literary labyrinth of connected families . . . a portrait of contemporary Israeli society." Jewish Publ Svc, 1985. ○

Shammas, Anton
ARABESQUES
The author, a Catholic Palestinian, writes of the traditional Arab village life in a Galilean village, the history of his family there and in Lebanon and Haifa, and his own life later on in Paris and Iowa—"renders beautifully" the village life and local customs, "excels with the vignette and the anecdote." (BRD) Har-Row, 1988. ○

Shaw, Robert
THE MAN IN THE GLASS BOOTH
A Jewish real estate tycoon confesses that he is actually a former Nazi, is arrested, and tried in Israel. HarBraceJ, 1967. ○

Singer, Isaac Bashevis
THE PENITENT
A wealthy businessman, disgusted with his life-style, goes to Israel, assumes the role of a penitent, marries a rabbi's daughter and devotes himself to prayer and study. FS&G, 1983. ○

Spark, Muriel
THE MANDELBAUM GATE
A novel involving a half-Jewish Catholic, her fiancé, a foreign officer, and the "piece of street between Jerusalem and Jerusalem."(FC) Knopf, 1965. ○

Uris, Leon
EXODUS
The history of Palestine and Zionism, from the 1940s on, with flashbacks and digressions that tell of Nazi persecutions—told from the point of view of a Christian nurse. Doubleday, 1958. Also *Mitla Pass* (1988). See also *The Haj*, listed under "Middle East" Novels. ○

Weisman, John
BLOOD CRIES
"The thorny problems of Israel's future . . . exquisite descriptions of Jerusalem" in a novel about an American journalist's personal/professional principles, and relationships between Israelis and American Jews. Viking, 1987. ○

Whittemore, Edward
JERUSALEM POKER
Sequel to *Sinai Tapestry*, see under "Middle East" Novels—begins in December 1921, as three men begin a twelve-year poker game in which the stakes are control of Jerusalem. HR&W, 1978. ○

Yehoshua, Abraham B.
FIVE SEASONS
"Subtly replaces the stereotypical view of Israel's war-torn, politically minded citizenry with an indelible portrait of an ordinary man's struggle to heal himself" when his wife dies after a long bout with cancer. (FC) Doubleday, 1989. Also *A Late Divorce*, set in a nine-day period around Passover as each character in a family relates the story that reveals their relationships. (1984). ○

BIBLICAL ISRAEL

NOTE: Also scan entries under Italy/Ancient Rome for appropriate titles.

Asch, Sholem
THE NAZARENE
"High level fiction of biblical background . . . extraordinary recreation of time and place." (BRD) Putnam, 1939. Also *The Apostle* (1943), *Mary* (1949), *Moses* (1951), *The Prophet* (1955). ○

Burgess, Anthony
THE KINGDOM OF THE WICKED
The early days of Christianity, when it was solidifying, and Rome in the beginning stages of decline. Arbor Hse, 1985. Also *Man of Nazareth,* based on the screenplay for the TV production "Jesus of Nazareth"; "masses of intriguing and funny historical detail" with Jesus portrayed as an ordinary man among his fellowmen, married and widowed, a carpenter, a teacher, a miracle worker (1979). o

Caldwell, Taylor
DEAR AND GLORIOUS PHYSICIAN
About St. Luke, author of the gospel, and his life as a physician, with scenes in Antioch, Rome, Alexandria and Judaea. Doubleday, 1959. Also *Great Lion of God* (1970), based on Paul of Tarsus, and *I, Judas,* which offers an explanation for his betrayal of Jesus (1977). o

Costain, T.B.
THE SILVER CHALICE
Based on the legend that grew after Christ's crucifixion about the frame intended to hold the sacred cup from which he drank at the Last Supper; with scenes in Antioch, Rome, Jerusalem. Doubleday, 1952. o

Douglas, Lloyd C.
THE BIG FISHERMAN
Fictional biography of Apostle Simon Peter. Houghton, 1948. Also *The Robe* (1942), about Roman soldier Marcellus, in charge of Christ's crucifixion. o

Heym, Stefan
THE KING DAVID REPORT
Novelization of events in Kings 1 and in Book 1 and 2 of Samuel. Putnam, 1973. o

Holmes, Marjorie
THE MESSIAH
Third in a series of novels recreating the life of Jesus—"the biblical framework is embellished in a respectful, non-doctrinaire narrative, with lively human dimensions." Har-Row, 1987. Preceding this novel are *Two from Galilee* (1972), about Jesus' youth, and *Three from Galilee,* portraying Jesus as a child with younger siblings (1985). o

Mann, Thomas
JOSEPH AND HIS BROTHERS
The biblical story recreated by a leading writer. Knopf, 1948. o

Martin, Malachi
KING OF KINGS
Biblical story of King David "in the cinematic style of Cecil B. De Mille." (FC) S&S, 1981. o

Michener, James A
THE SOURCE
An archaeological dig in Israel, and the varied team involved in the work, provide the focal point for a recreation of the history of Israel and the Jewish religion. Random, 1965. o

Schmitt, Gladys
DAVID THE KING
Biblical story of David, King of Israel—"serious, profound." (FC) Dial, 1973 (first published 1946). o

Segal, Brenda L.
THE TENTH MEASURE
Judaea in the first century, and the Jewish rebellion against the Romans, with a plot based solidly on historical fact. St. Martin, 1980. o

SAUDI ARABIA & THE ARABIAN, PENINSULA

Series Guidebooks
(See Appendix 1)

Berlitz: Saudi Arabia
Insight Guide: Yemen
Lonely Planet: Yemen (North and South)
Nagel's Encyclopedia Guide: Gulf Emirates

Background Reading

NOTE: See entries under Middle East/Background Reading/Islam for additional material.

Bullock, John
THE PERSIAN GULF UNVEILED
"Part travelogue, part history,part prophecy"—discovery of oil, rise of the great trading families, the sheikhs desire to hold onto traditional ways. The author prophesies a "cataclysmic twenty-first century scenario" when the Soviet Union and the United States compete for the region's oil. (PW) Congdon & Weed, 1985.   o

Dickey, Christopher
EXPATS: TRAVELS IN ARABIA, FROM TRIPOLI TO TEHERAN
The expatriate experience and the cultural collision between the West and Islam portrayed through meetings with Americans and Europeans who have lived and worked in Arab countries. Atl Monthly Pr, 1990. o

Dickson, H.R.P.
THE ARAB OF THE DESERT
The subtitle is: "A Glimpse into Badawin Life in Kuwait and Sau'di Arabia." A reader who has lived in Persian Gulf countries for over six years suggested inclusion of this book in *Traveler's Reading Guide*. It's an old book, written and published in 1949 and republished in new editions three more times. I couldn't locate a review of it, but unexpectedly found a copy at the local college library; judging from its worn appearance, the book has been heavily used over the years. If the Gulf War with Iraq increased your curiosity about Kuwait, try to locate a copy of this book. Allen & Unwin, 1967. o

Lacey, Robert
THE KINGDOM: ARABIA & THE HOUSE OF SAUD
"Thoroughly readable pop history . . . aims to provide a feel for the place, rather than orthodox analysis . . . titillating trivia on every aspect of life." (BRD) HarBraceJ, 1982.   o

Lawrence, T.E.
REVOLT IN THE DESERT
Shortened version of *Seven Pillars of Wisdom*—"tapestry of memoirs, philosophy, travel writing, anthropology and fiction." (BRD) Penguin, 1976 (first published 1926).   o

McGregor, Joy and Nydell, Margaret
UPDATE—SAUDI ARABIA
Intercultural Pr, 1990.   o

Musallam, Basim
THE ARABS
Aspects of the lives of Arabs—intellectual development, women, family, etc.—based on a TV documentary series, with the aim "to rectify incorrect Western impressions of the Arabs. . . . a delightful glance at a fascinating subject." (LJ) Salem Hse, 1985.   o

Seabrook, William B.
ADVENTURES IN ARABIA
An early 1920s memoir of travel by the author and his wife "among the Bedouins, Druses, Whirling Dervishes and Yezidee Devil Worshipers"—a last glimpse before oil changed everything. A reprint in the Athena Armchair Traveler Series, originally published 1927. Paragon Hse, 1991.   o

Stark, Freya
THE SOUTHERN GATES OF ARABIA
A recently reprinted travel adventure classic by an author who wanted to be the first woman to venture into Arabia along the old incense roads, and one with "rare ability to interpret and appreciate the oftentimes menacing natives and medieval Islamic traditions." She traveled with native guides, via donkey, car and foot. (Publisher) J.P. Tarcher, 1983 (first published 1936). ○

Tawfik, Heidi
SAUDI ARABIA: A PERSONAL EXPERIENCE
Views and impressions by an American woman who lived there in the 1980s. Windmill, 1991. ○

Theroux, Peter
SANDSTORMS: DAYS AND NIGHTS IN ARABIA
"Breezy, impressionistic travelogue . . . peppered with frank, telling glimpses of the Middle East." Also scenes in Egypt, Syria, Jerusalem. (PW) Norton, 1990. ○

Thesiger, Wilfred
ARABIAN SANDS
Five years among the nomadic Arab Bedouins in 1945—"vivid insight into nomad psychology." (BRD) Penguin, 1984 (first published 1959). ○

Tidrick, Kathryn
HEART-BEGUILING ARABY
A "captivating analysis of the Englishmen whose writings . . . enhanced a 'powerful imperial myth' "—Burton, Palgrave, Blunt and Doughty, the great Victorian travelers. (BRD) Cambridge U Pr, 1981. ○

Walker, Dale
FOOL'S PARADISE
A former employee of a multinational corporation returns to Saudi Arabia. His book is critical and acerbic; about cultural practices, corruption, anomalies. Vintage Departures Series. Random, 1988. ○

Wolfe, Michael
THE HADJ: AN AMERICAN'S JOURNEY TO MECCA
An American who converted to Islam recounts his journey as part of the Hadj, the pilgrimage to Mecca, starting in Morocco. He tells of his travels, meeting people in Muslim Africa, local mosques—"not since Sir Richard Burton's account of his pilgrimage to Mecca . . . has a Western writer described the Hadj in such fascinating detail." (Publisher) Atl Monthly Pr, 1992. ○

HISTORY

Encyclopaedia Britannica, eds.
THE ARABS
"Popularly written and . . . one of the best introductions to Arab history and Islam." (BRD) Bantam/Britannica, 1978. ○

Mansfield, Peter
THE ARABS
Social and political history from nomadic beginnings to individual portraits of modern Arab nations. Penguin, 1985. ○

Novels

Al-Rashid, Mohammad T.
THE VEILED SUN
"Horrifying, Kafkaesque tale about life in modern Saudi Arabia." (PW) Ashley, 1991. ○

Bulliet, Richard
THE GULF SCENARIO
An employee of the Harvard-MIT Strategic Research Group disappears with secret documents—Cambridge, Washington and "exotic locales in the Persian Gulf region" are settings for this spy novel. (FC) St. Martin, 1984. ○

TURKEY

Series Guidebooks
(See Appendix 1)

Baedeker: Istanbul; Turkey; Turkish Coast
Berlitz: Turkey; Istanbul
Blue Guide: Istanbul; Turkey
Cadogan: Turkey
Fodor: Turkey
Frommer: Turkey ($-A-Day & Touring)
Independent Traveler: Turkey
Insider's Guide: Turkey
Insight Guide: Istanbul; Turkey; Turkish Coast
Let's Go: Turkish Coast & Istanbul
Lonely Planet: Turkey
Nagel's Encyclopedia Guide: Turkey
Nelles Guide: Turkey
Real Guide: Turkey
Visitor's Guide: Turkey

Background Reading

Andersen, Hans Christian
A POET'S BAZAAR: A JOURNEY TO GREECE, TURKEY, AND UP THE DANUBE
The writer of all those fairytales was also a traveler, and this reprint is a memoir of his travels. First published in 1842. Kesend Pub, 1988.   ○

Dodwell, Christina
A TRAVELLER ON HORSEBACK: IN EASTERN TURKEY AND IRAN
"People, history, architecture and artifacts . . . first-rate travel adventure . . . in the tradition of fearless globe-trotters like Dame Freya Stark and Dervla Murphy." (PW) Walker, 1989.   ○

Fraser, Russell
THE THREE ROMES
The three Romes, in this author's concept, are Constantinople (now Istanbul), Moscow, and Rome—cities that felt they had "received divine missions to amass and rule empires." The book is historical commentary and anecdotes, an "entertaining overview . . . encounters with modern inhabitants . . . the shadowy past [implanted in] the mind of citizens today." (BL) HarBraceJ, 1985.   ○

Glazebrook, Philip
JOURNEY TO KARS
See under Europe.   ○

Hetherington, Paul
BYZANTIUM: CITY OF GOLD, CITY OF FAITH
"Splendidly recreates the spirit of Byzantium"—history, religious life, Byzantine art, and accompanied by photos that reflect the opulent art and architecture. (PW) Salem Hse, 1984.   ○

Orga, Irfan
PORTRAIT OF A TURKISH FAMILY
Extraordinary story of a prosperous family's survival after the 1914 war brought ruin and poverty to them in the old Turkey. The *London Observer* calls it "a wholly delightful book." Hippocrene Bks, 1989.   ○

Stark, Freya
ALEXANDER'S PATH: FROM CARIA TO CILICIA
Retracing by this leading travel writer in the early 1950s of the route of Alexander the Great along the coast of Turkey. Overlook Pr, 1990.   ○

Stark, Freya
GATEWAYS AND CARAVANS: A PORTRAIT OF TURKEY
A travel classic—"a text that mingles five thousand years of history with description of Turkey today [1970] . . . an irresistible book." (BRD) Macmillan, 1971.   ○

Tumpane, John D.
SCOTCH AND HOLY WATER
Vignettes of the author's 10 years back in the 1960s, working for an American company contracted by the U.S. Air Force to maintain their air bases. St. Giles, 1981.   ○

GUIDEBOOKS

Bean, George E.
AEGEAN TURKEY
And *Lycian Turkey* (1990), *Turkey's Southern Shore* (1989), *Turkey Behind the Meander* (1990), all by the same author; background information, maps, introduction to Turkey's ancient past. David & Charles, 1989.   o

Freely, John
CLASSICAL TURKEY
"Tourist guide to regional building styles and historical sites . . . for the traveler with an architectural bent." Includes visits to the lesser-known places often skipped on the usual tourist agenda. (BL) Chronicle, 1990.
o

Mehling, Marianne
TURKEY: A PHAEDON CULTURAL GUIDE
Succinct appreciation of the best the country has to offer in terms of national treasures and culture—churches, palaces, theaters, museums, monuments, maps and plans— all arranged alphabetically and cross-indexed. Phaidon Pr., n.d.   o

HISTORY

Browning, Robert
THE BYZANTINE EMPIRE
A balanced history centered in Istanbul (Constantinople), of the 1,000-year civilization. Scribner, 1980.   o

Lloyd, Seton
ANCIENT TURKEY: A TRAVELLER'S HISTORY OF ANATOLIA
History specifically intended for travelers who seek insight and background information, from prehistoric times to Christianity, and written by an archaeologist—"informal, almost chatty tone that only the best and most spellbinding college lecturers dare to adopt." (BL) U of California Pr, 1989.   o

Novels

Bradshaw, Gillian
THE BEARKEEPER'S DAUGHTER
The author adds an illegitimate son to this story of Empress Theodora and Justinian I—

"will entertain romantics as well as history buffs." (FC) Houghton, 1987.   o

Buchan, John
GREENMANTLE
Adventure story of the English secret service in Constantinople in World War I, and a classic. Doran, 1915.   o

Ennis, Michael
BYZANTIUM
Intrigue, romance and adventure played out against the Byzantium world of the 11th century and based on extensive research into primary resource materials. Atl Monthly Pr, 1989.   o

Gilliatt, Penelope
A WOMAN OF SINGULAR OCCUPATION
Dark intrigue of Istanbul during World War II and a love affair between two who meet on the Orient Express. Scribner, 1989.   o

Holland, Cecelia
THE BELT OF GOLD
Engrossing tale of a returning pilgrim from the Holy Land and a chance meeting with a Byzantine emperor in 9th-century Constantinople that embroils him in political intrigue. Knopf, 1984.   o

Kazan, Elia
AMERICA, AMERICA
Experiences of a Greek boy in Constantinople as he attempts to establish a rug business and secure money to go to America. Stein & Day, 1962.   o

Kemal, Yashar
THE UNDYING GRASS
"A tale of murder, revenge, love, hate, and compassion in modern Turkey." Kemal is a leading Turkish writer. Morrow, 1978. Other of his titles include: *Iron Earth, Copper Sky* (1979), *They Burn the Thistles* (1977), *Memed My Hawk* (1961), and *Seagull* (1981).   o

Settle, Mary Lee
BLOOD TIE
Set in the port city of Ceramos, with a plot involving Americans and the CIA in murder and corruption. Houghton, 1977.

Tarr, Judith
THE GOLDEN HORN
Constantinople at the time of the fourth crusade—plays out the personal story of Alfred of St. Ruan's "against . . . cataclysmic events." (FC) Bluejay Bks, 1985. Also *Alamut* (1989) and *A Fall of Princes* (1988).

Whitney, Phyllis A.
BLACK AMBER
Romantic, suspenseful novel, set in Istanbul. Appleton, 1964.

Yasar, Kemal
THE SEA-CROSSED FISHERMAN
A series of crimes near Istanbul are exaggerated by rumor—interweaving of the murderer's fate with that of a fisherman's dreams. Translated from the Turkish. Braziller, 1985.

III.
ASIA

○

Series Guidebooks
(See Appendix 1)

Fodor: Southeast Asia
Frommer: Southeast Asia
Insight Guide: East Asia; South Asia
Lonely Planet: Northeast Asia; Southeast Asia; West Asia; Karakoram Highway
Moon Handbook: Southeast Asia
2–22 Days Itinerary Planning Guide: Asia

Background Reading

See also Islam, under Middle East.

Braganti, Nancy and Devine, Elizabeth
THE TRAVELER'S GUIDE TO ASIAN CUSTOMS AND MANNERS

Useful series to enlighten travelers to the fact that American social customs are not universal. St. Martin, 1986.   ○

Buruma, Ian
GOD'S DUST: A MODERN ASIAN JOURNEY

"Essays search past and present for causes and effects of cultural emergence"—Burma, Thailand, Philippines, Malaysia, Singapore, Taiwan, South Korea, Japan. (PW) FS&G, 1989.   ○

Cameron, Ian
MOUNTAINS OF THE GODS

British 18th-century explorers in Central Asian mountains and climbers from the 19th century to the present, with quotes and excerpts from their writings; history, inhabitants, geology. Facts On File, 1985.   ○

Cordell, Michael
RED EXPRESS: THE GREATEST RAIL JOURNEY

From Eastern Europe to the Great Wall of China—"captivating rail odyssey" from Poland through Czechoslovakia and the Baltic republics, Moscow to Beijing, by a traveler "who generally interacts with the natives," and tied in with a TV documentary. (PW) P-H, 1991.   ○

DeGaury, Gerald and Winstone, H.V.F.
AN ANTHOLOGY OF WRITINGS ON ASIA

From Rudyard Kipling to Fitzroy MacLean— "strong on the romantic aspects of travel especially as seen through British eyes." (TB) Macmillan, 1982.   ○

Elegant, Robert
PACIFIC DESTINY: THE RISE OF THE EAST

By the novelist/journalist—"insightful, comprehensive, vivid, engaging survey of the

Orient." His view, while sympathetic to Asian culture cautions the West to understand that for the Japanese and Chinese, trade and commerce are "zero-sum games . . . trade is war." (PW) Crown, 1990.   ○

Fenton, James
ALL THE WRONG PLACES
"Adrift in the politics of the Pacific Rim" is the book's subtitle. A collection of essays—witnessing with humor, hope, tragedy and desperation—on political changes since the 1970s, the revolutions in Vietnam and the Philippines, and the revolution that didn't happen in Korea. Atl Monthly Pr, 1988.   ○

Fleming, Peter
NEWS FROM TARTARY
Report of a seven-month, 3,500-mile trip, in the early 1930s, despite a civil war, from Peking to Kashmir—"honest reporting, brilliantly written." J.P. Tarcher, 1982 (first published 1936). Also by this leading travel writer, *One's Company* (1934).   ○

Iyer, Pico
VIDEO NIGHT IN KATHMANDU
The author crisscrossed eastern Asia in 1985 to report on the spread of American pop-culture in Burma, China, Hong Kong, Japan, Philippines, Singapore, Thailand—"a book of warmth, charm and sensibility and anyone intending to visit the Orient will greatly benefit from his arresting descriptions and shrewd assessments." (PW) Knopf, 1988.   ○

Maillaret, Ella
FORBIDDEN JOURNEY
A new edition, with an introduction by Dervla Murphy, the Irish travel writer, of the journey made with Peter Fleming (see *News from Tartary*, above) from Peking to Northern India. Interesting, I would think, to compare to Fleming's account. Hippocrene, 1983.   ○

Morris, Mary
WALL TO WALL: FROM BEIJING TO BERLIN BY RAIL
In search of her Russian ancestors, the author finds herself in Chernobyl's nuclear disaster area and observing the end of the Cold War. She describes the history of Moscow, Leningrad, China's Forbidden city and people she meets as she describes her train journey—"has the rare touch of the true travel writer" in conveying to readers the feeling that they've been along for the journey. (PW) Doubleday, 1991.   ○

Naipaul, V.S.
AMONG THE BELIEVERS: AN ISLAMIC JOURNEY
Exploration of the life and culture of four Islamic countries. The author repeatedly finds in the very devotion to Islam the reason for the backwardness of these countries, and an expectation that the education and technology they need will come from alien lands. Knopf, 1981.   ○

Nelson, Theodora and Gross, Andrea
GOOD BOOKS FOR THE CURIOUS TRAVELER: ASIA AND THE SOUTH PACIFIC
Lengthy reviews of books on topics ranging from archaeology and food to literature and nature. Johnson Bks, 1989.   ○

Schwartz, Brian M.
A WORLD OF VILLAGES
See entry under Africa/African culture.   ○

Severin, Tim
THE ORIENTAL ADVENTURE: EXPLORERS OF THE EAST
Reading it "is an adventure in itself . . . and enjoyable account of a by-gone era" told through the explorations of diverse people from Marco Polo, scholars and merchants, to eccentrics and spies. (BRD) Little, 1976. See also *Tracking Marco Polo* under Middle East.   ○

Theroux, Paul
THE GREAT RAILWAY BAZAAR
A four-month lecture tour in 1973, via the Orient Express, Khyber Mail and Trans-Siberian Express, is the basis for these conversations and impressions of people encountered. Ballantine, 1981.   ○

Thubron, Colin
THE SILK ROAD: BEYOND THE CELESTIAL KINGDOM

"Shows readers the high points along the Silk Road . . . rich prose . . . stunning photographs . . . practical information and encouragement to travellers who want to experience it for themselves." (BL) S&S, 1990. ○

Welty, Thomas
THE ASIANS: THEIR HERITAGE AND THEIR DESTINY

A good overview of Asia, and introduction to the three major religions and variations thereof in the various countries. Har-Row, 1984. ○

MARCO POLO

Bellonci, Maria
THE TRAVELS OF MARCO POLO

A new Italian version of the classic translated into English to offer a readable, modern English version. Facts On File, 1984. Other versions of Marco Polo's travels retold in popular style include: *Marco Polo* by Richard Humble (1990), *Travels of Marco Polo* edited by Manuel Komroff (1982), *Marco Polo's Travels in Xanadu with Kublai Khan* by R.P. Lister (1977). ○

GUIDEBOOKS

Chambers, Kevin
THE TRAVELER'S GUIDE TO ASIAN CULTURE

Highlights and survey of history and culture from India to Japan. Muir, 1989. ○

Davis, Alison, ed.
THE ON-YOUR-OWN GUIDE TO ASIA

Based on experiences of volunteers; essentials for planning low-cost travel in Asia—10 countries in eastern and southeastern Asia. C.E. Tuttle, 1983. ○

Jacobs, Charles and Babette
FAR EAST TRAVEL DIGEST

Arranged alphabetically by country, from Burma to Thailand. Each segment includes a historical survey, description of people and customs, places to see, specific, useful how-to information. Travel Digest, 1988. ○

Steves, Rick and Gottberg, John
ASIA THROUGH THE BACK DOOR

This companion guide has the philosophy that spending less can enhance your travel; spending too much can build a wall between you and how you experience a country. John Muir, 1990. ○

HISTORY

Hall, Daniel G.
A HISTORY OF SOUTH-EAST ASIA

Updated edition of a "marvelous . . . prescriptive read" that covers Indonesia, Burma, Malaysia, Vietnam, Thailand. (BRD) St. Martin, 1981. ○

Welty, Thomas
THE ASIANS

Har-Row, 1984. ○

BURMA

Series Guidebooks (See Appendix 1)

Cadogan Guide: Thailand & Burma
Insight: Burma
Lonely Planet Guide: Burma
Passport: Burma

Background Reading

Bixler, Norma
BURMESE JOURNEY

The author accompanied her husband to Rangoon in 1958–60 where he set up a new university library. She recounts the details of setting up house, acquiring friends, understanding a new way of life—a Burma that is no more, with the influx later of many visitors and foreigners. Antioch Pr, 1970. Also *Burma, A Profile* (1971).   ○

Collis, Maurice
LORDS OF THE SUNSET: A TOUR IN THE SHAN STATES
"A particularly delightful book about [then] little-known and lovely land . . ." (BRD) AMS, 1977 (first published 1939).   ○

Courtauld, Caroline
IN SEARCH OF BURMA
"Takes the reader to remote corners of the 'authentic Orient'—a land of tranquillity and timelessness"—down the Irrawaddy River, to Mandalay, the Shwedagon Pagoda in Rangoon, Inle Lake and more. (Publisher) Salem Hse, 1985.   ○

Edmonds, Paul
PEACOCKS AND PAGODAS
Reprint of an English travel writer's impressions of Burma in the early twenties, and its people, which the author then found to be "perhaps the happiest and most contented in the world." (BRD) AMS, 1977 (first published 1924).   ○

Lewis, Norman
GOLDEN EARTH: TRAVELS IN BURMA
Travel to Burma in 1951 at a time of civil war—"brilliant descriptive passages that give the feel and flavor of Burma . . . brushes with bandits and Communist rebels." (BRD) Hippocrene, 1984 (first published 1952).   ○

Maugham, Somerset
GENTLEMAN IN THE PARLOUR
"A record of a journey from Rangoon to Haiphong . . . by canoe and riverboat, rickshaw, and on pony" taken in the late 1920s by the author, and his observations of Europeans and English colonists he met. "Vivid travel impressions," some of which became the plots for stories written later on. (BRD) Paragon Hse, 1989.   ○

Nicholl, Charles
BORDERLINES: A JOURNEY IN THAILAND AND BURMA
Three months of travel encounters in 1986 as the author goes on the road with a French gem trader and his girlfriend; with an unfailing sense of adventure. Viking, 1989.   ○

Strachan, Paul
PAGAN: ART AND ARCHAEOLOGY OF OLD BURMA
Seven Hills, 1990.   ○

GUIDEBOOKS

Stier, Wayne and Cavers, M.
WIDE EYES IN BURMA AND THAILAND—FINDING YOUR WAY
A travel guide "especially suited to the young, intrepid traveler." (BP) Meru Pub, 1983.   ○

HISTORY

Aung-Thwin, Michael
PAGAN: THE ORIGINS OF MODERN BURMA
U of Hawaii Pr, 1985.   ○

Novels

Bates, H.E.
THE JACARANDA TREE
The effects on British civilians, an Anglo-Burmese nurse, and other refugees fleeing before the advancing Japanese—the author "writes about Burma in a beautiful shimmering prose alive with . . . Gauguinesque color sense." (BRD) Atl Monthly Pr, 1949.   ○

Becker, Stephen
THE BLUE-EYED SHAN
Part of a trilogy that also includes *The Chinese Bandit* and *The Last Mandarin*—adventures of an American anthropologist in the Shan states on the Chinese border, before, during and after World War II and "the clash of cultures." (FC) Random, 1982.   ○

Gilman, Dorothy
INCIDENT AT BADAMYA
An orphaned 16-year-old girl in Burma, 1950, joins forces with a U.S. undercover agent, is imprisoned by General Wang and escapes—"authentic background . . . pleasant element of last-minute surprise." (FC) Doubleday, 1989.   ○

Law-Yone, Wendy
THE COFFIN TREE
"An odyssey . . . from the childhood of a girl born of well-to-do family in a modern Burma immersed in political turmoil, to the grown young woman forced . . . to immigrate . . . to America." (FC) Knopf, 1983.   ○

Orwell, George
BURMESE DAYS
A bitter, satirical picture of the white man's rule in Upper Burma. HarBraceJ, 1974 (first published 1934).   ○

CHINA

*Series Guidebooks
(See Appendix 1)*

Baedeker: China
Berlitz: China
Fodor: China; China's Great Cities
Hildebrand: China
Insider's Guide: China
Insight Guide: Beijing; China
Lonely Planet: China; Hong Kong, Macau & Canton
Nagel's Encyclopedia Guide: China
Passport China Guides: All China; Beijing; Fiijian; Guilin; Canton and Guangdong Province; Hangzhou and Zhejiang; Nanjing and Jiangsu Province; Shanghai; Xian; Yangzi River; Yunnan
Real Guide: China
2-22 Days Itinerary Planning Guide: China

Background Reading

Blunden, Caroline and Elvin, Mark
CULTURAL ATLAS OF CHINA
History, society, politics, religion, philosophy, literature and the visual arts—"demonstrates that it is possible to capture the vast span of history ranging from the magnificence of ancient China to the mystery of the present China within one volume." Facts On File, 1983.   ○

Bonavia, David
THE CHINESE
"Systematically illuminates . . . major aspects of the People's Republic. . . . A China seen sympathetically, but without rose-colored glasses"—by the chief correspondent for the *London Times* who has reported on the country since the 1960s. (NYTBR) Penguin, 1989. Also, *China Unknown* (1985), and *Peking* (1978).   ○

Bordewich, Fergus
**CATHAY: A JOURNEY IN SEARCH
    OF OLD CHINA**
"Delightful, surprising, compulsively readable"—the book is about the China that the communists have tried to destroy, with an introduction by Jan Morris. (PW) P-H Press, 1991.   ○

Buckley, Michael
CYCLING TO XIAN
An extraordinary travel adventure, by the coauthor of Lonely Planet's China and Tibet Traveler Survivor Kits. An account of a 4,000-

mile overland trip to Kathmandu (half of it by bike), from rural China to bleak central Tibet, and the characters he meets. Gordon Soules Bk, 1988. ○

Chang, Jung
WILD SWANS: THREE DAUGHTERS OF CHINA

Chinese history is experienced through the "riveting" history of three generations of the author's family—the end of old China and its repressions, Mao's regime, the Japanese occupation of Manchuria. "An intense, reflective, and probing testimony that combines the magnetism of fiction with the undeniable power of truth." (BL) S&S, 1991. ○

Ching, Julia
PROBING CHINA'S SOUL: RELIGION AND THE BODY POLITIC IN THE PEOPLE'S REPUBLIC

"Superb account . . . the author punctures the stereotype, still current among some China-watchers, that the Chinese people are somehow different from Westerners and not ready for democracy." (PW) Harper, 1990. ○

Clayre, Alasdair
THE HEART OF THE DRAGON

Companion book to the PBS series on China—"History/portrait of China and its people . . . depictions of Chinese life range from religious beliefs, marriage and concubinage, food and work to changing traditions of Chinese justice, art, crime and punishment." (PW) Houghton, 1985. ○

Dodwell, Christina
A TRAVELLER IN CHINA

The author followed the ancient Silk Route by local transportation, canoe and camel; "her adventurousness is reminiscent of the intrepid women travelers of Victorian England"—a treat for the armchair adventurer. (PW) Beaufort, 1986. ○

Endicott, Stephen
RED EARTH: REVOLUTION IN A SICHUAN VILLAGE

The son of a long line of missionaries who grew up in China, left before the communist revolution and returned several times during the '80s to record the impact of communism on the rural village—"detailed research and empathy . . . oral histories . . . a unique perspective." (PW) New Amsterdam, 1991. ○

Hanbury-Tenison, Robin
A RIDE ALONG THE GREAT WALL

A 1,000-mile expedition by horseback, by the author and his wife. "Blissful moments of oases of great natural beauty . . . industrial centers of unchecked pollution" are seen as few foreigners get the opportunity to see them. (PW) Salem Hse, 1988. ○

Hopkirk, Peter
FOREIGN DEVILS ON THE SILK ROAD

The story of the sacking by Europeans of art treasures on the historic Silk Road—"adventure and intrigue. . . . fascinating story." (BP) U of Massachusetts Pr, 1984. ○

Human Rights in China Staff
CHILDREN OF THE DRAGON: THE STORY OF TIANANMEN SQUARE

Interviews, newspaper articles from China; speeches, eyewitness accounts, chronicles, photographs of the student movement that ended in massacre. Macmillan, 1990. ○

Isherwood, Christopher and Auden, W.H.
JOURNEY TO A WAR

Classic travel book; a travel diary with sketches of celebrities interviewed, sonnets by Auden. The book was the result of a trip to China in 1938, and the outbreak of the Sino-Japanese war. Paragon Hse, 1990 (first published 1939). ○

Lord, Bette Bao
LEGACIES: A CHINESE MOSAIC

Updates her novel *Spring Moon* (see below, under Novels) with a study of China today, beginning April 1989 as the Tiananmen Square demonstrations begin. "Stunning collection of oral histories . . . franker, more penetrating and infinitely sadder than most journalistic accounts." (BL) Knopf, 1990. ○

Mosher, Steven W.
CHINA MISPERCEIVED: AMERICAN ILLUSIONS AND CHINESE REALITY

"An eye-opening polemic" that lambastes those who the author contends have idealized and misrepresented China, from Henry Kissinger and Edgar Snow to Pearl Buck and Tom Hayden. (PW) Basic, 1990. Also, *Broken Earth* (1983) and *Journey to the Forbidden China* (1985), based on earlier experiences as a graduate student.   o

Namioka, Lensey
CHINA: A TRAVELER'S COMPANION

"Fourteen concise, casually—sometimes amusingly—written chapters" on many aspects of China today from food and housing to sports and urban/rural livelihoods, with appendices on Chinese history, by a native Chinese (now a U.S. citizen) based on her childhood and recent return visits. (PW) Vanguard, 1985.   o

Peck, Stacey
HALLS OF JADE, WALLS OF STONE: WOMEN IN CHINA TODAY

Oral history of contemporary Chinese women "of all ages, in occupations ranging from athlete to doctor . . . to university president. . . . a unique look at the lives of women whose position in society has been radically altered in the past 35 years." (PW) Watts, 1985.   o

Salzman, Mark
IRON AND SILK

Perceptions of Chinese life "with the writerly eye of a young Hemingway . . . a bouquet of sketches . . . a quiet classic." (BRD) Random, 1987.   o

Schell, Orville
TO GET RICH IS GLORIOUS; CHINA IN THE 80s

The Westernization of China and the astonishing changes it is bringing, the about-face from Maoist ideology—"a riveting firsthand report" which appeared originally in the *New Yorker*. Another book by Schell, *In the*

People's Republic (1977) was a firsthand view of living and working in China, as visitor, worker and resident of a Chinese commune. As a follow-up in 1981 came *Watch Out for Foreign Guests*, about the social encounter between Chinese and Americans and the different country the author found on this second trip. *To Get Rich Is Glorious* is the last of this "trilogy." Pantheon, 1985.   o

Seth, Vikram
FROM HEAVEN LAKE: TRAVEL THROUGH SINKIANG AND TIBET

By an Indian, educated in the West, who speaks Chinese. The reader joins him on his "hitchhiking, walking, slogging" trip across China to India in 1981, spending nights in Chinese inns and truck parks—"the perfect travel book . . . a wonderful companion." The book won the Thomas Cook Award for travel writing in 1984. (BRD) Chatto & Windus, 1984.   o

Stevens, Stuart
NIGHT TRAIN TO TURKESTAN

Modern adventures along China's ancient Silk Road. The author retraces Peter Fleming's journey of 1935 and portrays both China and the Chinese in a rather negative, controversial perspective with occasional glimpses of kindness and individualism. Atl Monthly Pr, 1988.   o

Theroux, Paul
RIDING THE IRON ROOSTER: BY TRAIN THROUGH CHINA

"Conducts the reader through this enormous country with wisdom, humor and a crusty warmth." There is a final chapter on the subjugation of Tibet. Putnam, 1988. Also, for an account of Theroux's earlier trip by riverboat down the Yangtze River, *Sailing Through China* (1984).   o

Thubron, Colin
BEHIND THE WALL: A JOURNEY THROUGH CHINA

Rambles through small towns, cities, farm areas by an author who speaks fluent Mandarin. "With impressionistic color, vitality and immediacy, he creates images that linger in the memory." (PW) Atl Monthly Pr, 1988.   ○

Van Slyke, Lyman
YANGTZE: NATURE, HISTORY, AND THE RIVER
Using the Yangtze as focus, the author discusses aspects of China from ecology and boat-building to social structure and poetry; "by the end of it, the fellow-traveling reader has picked up nearly the equivalent of a course in Chinese history." (LJ) Addison-Wesley, 1988.   ○

Wang, Anyi
BAOTOWN
Translation from the Chinese. Life in an isolated Chinese village in the 1970s, with politics kept at a distance—"lucid . . . succinct." (BRD) Norton, 1989.   ○

Xinxin, Zhang and Ye, Sang
CHINESE PROFILES
Interviews with 100 ordinary Chinese—a cyclist, a bookstore salesman, a lady volleyball player—give an inkling of the diversity and provide insights into everyday life. Panda Pr, 1987.   ○

Zee, A.
SWALLOWING CLOUDS
"A stockpot of cuisine, history, poetry, etymology, linguistics, and personal experience" based on Chinese pictographs and assuming you love Chinese food. "Along the way you also learn the background of Chinese folkways and manners, history of foods . . . and even basic Confucian philosophy." (BL) S&S, 1990.   ○

MEMOIRS

Brown, J.D.
DIGGING TO CHINA: DOWN AND OUT IN THE MIDDLE KINGDOM
Account of teaching English in northern China in the '80s and two subsequent trips to China, one of which was after Tiananmen Square—"focus on the personal rather than the political . . . anecdotal images of daily life." (PW) Soho Pr, 1991.   ○

Noyes, Henry
CHINA BORN: MEMOIRS OF A WESTERNER
The author was born into a missionary family, and these memoirs are of three eras: pre-communism, post-cultural revolution and just prior to Tiananmen Square—"richly detailed view of China's variable moods" that foreshadowed the Tiananmen events. (PW) China Books, 1989.   ○

Pruitt, Ida
OLD MADAM YIN; A MEMOIR OF PEKING LIFE
Memoir of the friendship between a medical social worker and Madame Yin, along with her upper-class Chinese family. It explores family and values, and Peking life in the 1920s. "A new classic . . . a book to delight Old China Hands and to fascinate those who never set foot in China. A good book to take along . . . to visit the new China." (BRD) Stanford U, 1979.   ○

GUIDEBOOKS

Kaplan, Frederic M. and others
THE CHINA GUIDEBOOK 1991
New edition of a guidebook that has received highest praise—"a mass of facts systematically presented with accuracy, charm, and excellent readability . . . would serve tourist, businessperson, and academic visitor equally well." Contributions by experts on various aspects of Chinese life. HM, 1991.   ○

Lethbridge, H.J.
ALL ABOUT SHANGHAI: A STANDARD GUIDEBOOK
This is the reprint of a 1934 guide, including original photographs and ads that capture the feel of what travel was like in the 1930s. Oxford U Pr, 1986.   ○

Letson, Barbara
CHINA, SOLO: A GUIDE FOR INDEPENDENT TRAVEL IN THE PEOPLE'S REPUBLIC OF CHINA
For the traveler who wants to tackle China on his/her own; intended to supplement (not

replace) standard guidebooks. Jadetree Pr, 1984. ○

McCawley, James D.
THE EATER'S GUIDE TO CHINESE CHARACTERS
Food and menus made intelligible, by a linguistics professor—"as useful in San Francisco as in Beijing." (BP) U of Chicago Pr, 1984. ○

Reader's Digest Editors
TREASURES OF CHINA
An armchair journey to 352 legendary landmarks. RD Assn, 1989. ○

Wood, Frances
A COMPANION TO CHINA
"All-inclusive, covering food, language, religion, art, architecture, literature, science" and more. By the head of the Chinese Section of the British Library. (BL) St. Martin's, 1990. ○

HISTORY

Eberhard, Wolfram
A HISTORY OF CHINA
Considered one of the best one-volume histories. Revised 4th edition. U of California, 1977. ○

Huntington, Madge
TRAVELER'S GUIDE TO CHINESE HISTORY
Designed for travelers wishing to better understand China. H. Holt, 1987. ○

Morton, W. Scott
CHINA: ITS HISTORY AND CULTURE
"Cultural history . . . set in the fabric of its political development . . . will make China take on more meaning for the traveler . . . a leg up on the Great Wall of Understanding that separates the traveler from the Chinese." (LJ) McGraw, 1982. ○

Spence, Jonathan D.
THE SEARCH FOR MODERN CHINA
Chronicles the many wars and rebellions over the past 400 years, and ending with Tiananmen Square, that have transformed China. Norton, 1990. Note also Mr. Spence's novels, listed below under Novels. ○

Novels

Ballard, J.G.
EMPIRE OF THE SUN
"Gritty story of a child's miraculous survival" in a prison camp following the capture of Shanghai by the Japanese. (FC) S&S, 1984. ○

Barrett, William E.
THE LEFT HAND OF GOD
An American pilot assumes the role of a Catholic priest to escape from the local warlord and his duties as a priest present a moral struggle. Queens Hse, 1976 (first published 1951). ○

Bosse, Malcolm
FIRE IN HEAVEN
Sequel to *The Warlord*, whose former mistress and her German husband become antiques importers. Their daughter becomes involved with a Communist Party member. Depicts the changes in Asia, in China and Thailand, through the lives of this cast of characters. S&S, 1985. ○

Bosse, Malcolm
THE WARLORD
China in 1927—a "saga that involves the reader totally in a scene, a time and place and a group of characters." (Publisher) S&S, 1984. ○

Brent, Madeleine
MOONRAKER'S BRIDE
China at the time of the Boxer Rebellion is the setting; the plot involves an inheritance and a cache of emeralds. Doubleday, 1973. ○

Buck, Pearl S.
THE GOOD EARTH
Part of a trilogy that won the author a Pulitzer Prize, about a Chinese peasant family's rise to wealth and power, ending with a China in revolution and a now educated, Americanized generation. It is followed by

Sons (1932) and *A House Divided* (1935). Other titles by Buck set in China, in order of publication date, are *The Mother* (1934), *Dragon Seed* (1942), *Pavilion of Women* (1946), *Peony* (1948), *Kinfolk* (1949), *Imperial Woman* (1956). Crowell-Day, 1931. ○

Byrne, Donn
MESSER MARCO POLO
The fictionalized story of Marco Polo "as it should have been" and his love for Kublai Khan's daughter. (FC) Bentley, 1979 (first published 1921). ○

Cooney, Eleanor
THE COURT OF THE LION: A NOVEL OF THE T'ANG DYNASTY
"Intricate tapestry of 8th-century China unfolds . . . spellbinding novel with believable characters." (FC) Arbor Hse, 1988. ○

Cordell, Alexander
THE DREAM AND THE DESTINY
Historical novel of Mao Tse-tung's 6,000-mile march to begin the new Communist China, told through the experiences of a young medical student. Doubleday, 1975. ○

Courter, Gay
FLOWERS IN THE BLOOD
About a Victorian Jewish family's involvement in the flower trade (opium)—"compelling scenes of India and China in the late 1800s . . . history of the Jews in Calcutta, the tea and opium trades . . . Anglo-Indian society." (FC) Dutton, 1990. ○

Cronin, A.J.
THE KEYS OF THE KINGDOM
Story of a Scottish priest sent on a mission to China in the early 1900s. Little, 1941. ○

Duncan, Robert L.
CHINA DAWN
Recollections of a Japanese woman's life and loves, and involvement with fashion design, an American, a Japanese; history of the years from pre-World War II in Shanghai. Delacorte, 1988. ○

Ehrlichman, John
THE CHINA CARD
"Integrates compelling vignettes involving real-life personalities into this tense spy story." A fictional graduate of Harvard Law School, working for President Nixon in 1968, secretly negotiates with the Chinese People's Republic before Henry Kissinger ever did, paving the way for recognition of China by the U.S. in 1972. S&S, 1986. ○

Elegant, Robert S.
FROM A FAR LAND
Recreates the history of China, 1920–50, as Mao rises to power; focused around the life of a beautiful and enigmatic heroine. Random, 1987. Also *Dynasty*, saga of the Eurasian Sekloong family, told against the background of 20th-century events in China and Hong Kong, *Manchu* (1980) and *Mandarin* (1983). ○

Gilman, Dorothy
MRS. POLLIFAX ON THE CHINA STATION
Another in the series in which the intelligence agent is a grandmotherly American. This time the plot involves her assignment to free a strategically important prisoner from the Chinese interior. Doubleday, 1983. ○

Gulik, Robert van
JUDGE DEE MYSTERIES
A unique series of suspense stories by a Dutch Orientalist and diplomat, set in China. Judge Dee is a master detective based on an extraordinary, but real, seventh-century magistrate—"addictive . . . well-realized settings . . . detective stories with a surprisingly modern air." Titles in the series include: *The Chinese Gold Murders* (1959), *The Chinese Bell Murders* (1959), *The Haunted Monastery* (1969), *The Lacquer Screen* (1970), *Poets and Murder* (1972), *The Red Pavillion* (1968), *The Willow Pattern* (1965). Harper, Scribner. ○

Hardy, Ronald
THE WINGS OF THE WIND
"Powerful, elegant book" with a plot centering around an anti-communist missionary who has been corrupted by prison and be-

comes a spy for Chiang Kai-shek. (FC) Putnam, 1987.   ○

Hersey, John
THE CALL
The story of a dedicated, naive American missionary who becomes disillusioned and embittered by his lifetime cause. Knopf, 1985. Also *A Single Pebble* (1956), about an American engineer's trip by junk, taken in the 1940s and seen in retrospect.   ○

Lee, C.Y.
CHINA SAGA
One family's saga through the Boxer Rebellion, Sun Yat Sen, Mao Tse-Tung, World War II, invasion of Korea, the cultural revolution—"abounds with illuminating historical details." (FC) Weidenfeld, 1987.   ○

Lee, C.Y.
GATE OF RAGE
"Novel of one family trapped by the events of Tiananmen Square . . . examines China's so-called thaw and the attempt to woo foreign investors in the early 80s." (FC) Morrow, 1991.   ○

Lin, Yutang
LADY WU
Biographical novel based on the history of the rise of Lady Wu from chambermaid to Empress Dowager of China. Also: *The Vermillion Gate* (1953), *Moment in Peking* (1939). Putnam Pub Group, 1965.   ○

Lord, Bette Bao
SPRING MOON
Saga of a Mandarin Chinese family, from 1892–1972, through the eyes of daughter Spring Moon; recreates the cloistered upper-class life of the early years on to modern China—history interlaced with romance and culture. Har-Row, 1981.   ○

Mo, Timothy
AN INSULAR POSSESSION
See entry under Hong Kong and Macau/ Novels.   ○

Nathan, Robert S.
THE WHITE TIGER
Recreates contemporary Beijing—a Chinese policeman investigates the death of a friend and comes up against the Communist Party. S&S, 1987.   ○

Spence, Jonathan
THE DEATH OF THE WOMAN WANG
The ordinary life of a 17th-century woman comes alive—"the continual dilemma of women caught between ideal Confucian . . . behavior and the harsh demands of rural life." (BRD) Penguin, 1979.   ○

Tan, Amy
THE KITCHEN GOD'S WIFE
A Chinese woman recounts her "violent, war-wrenched youth . . . her arranged marriage" to her American-born daughter. (FC) Putnam, 1991.   ○

Zhang, Jie
LOVE MUST NOT BE FORGOTTEN
A collection of short stories, and one novella, by a woman considered a foremost Chinese feminist writer—"an after-the-Cultural-Revolution perspective of women's uncertain lives in a changing civilization." (BRD) China Bks, 1986.   ○

H O N G   K O N G   A N D   M A C A U

See also books listed under China.

*Series Guidebooks
(See Appendix 1)*

American Express Pocket Guide: Hong Kong

Baedeker: Hong Kong
Berlitz: Hong Kong
Frommer: Japan and Hong Kong; Hong Kong, Macau & Singapore
Gault/Milau: Best of Hong Kong
Hildebrand: Hong Kong
Insider's Guide: Hong Kong
Insight: Hong Kong

Lonely Planet: Hong Kong, Macau & Canton

Passport Asia Guides: Hong Kong

Post Guide: Hong Kong

Real Guide: Hong Kong

Background Reading

Coates, Austin
QUICK TIDINGS OF HONG KONG
Oxford U Pr, 1990.   ○

Crisswell, Colin N.
THE TAIPANS, HONG KONG'S MERCHANT PRINCES
Taipans were resident managers of China/India trade, with Hong Kong as their base. Oxford U Pr, 1981.   ○

Hinton, A.
FRAGRANT HARBOUR
Aimed at giving the general reader and visitor a better understanding of Hong Kong; includes a short history of Macau. Greenwood, 1977 (first published 1962).   ○

Morris, Jan
HONG KONG
A "total immersion" into history of the British era, the two races, architecture, crime, everyday life. "A lovely and balanced study of a unique society on the verge of drastic reformation." (BL) Random, 1989.   ○

HISTORY

Cameron, Nigel
HONG KONG, THE CULTURED PEARL
A history and contemporary account of Hong Kong—"articulate, richly illustrated account for the lay reader. . . . like a cultured pearl, its luster hides its flaws." (LJ) Oxford U, 1978.   ○

Novels

Black, Gavin
THE GOLDEN COCKATRICE
A Scottish shipping executive is the hero of this novel of international intrigue set in

Macau (Portuguese colony near Hong Kong). Har-Row, 1975.   ○

Booth, Martin
HIROSHIMA JOE
An Englishman, captured in Hong Kong during World War II, remains after the war as "Hiroshima Joe," living off the city's underworld—"remarkable piece of writing . . . scenes of war and imprisonment . . . intensely visual descriptions of post-war Hong Kong." (BRD) Atl Monthly Pr, 1985.   ○

Booth, Martin
THE JADE PAVILION
Set in Macau between 1937 and 1948. Follows the rise of Sean Mulrenan, an Ango-Irish nightclub pianist and gambler, and his spectacular fall, in this tiny enclave sealed off from World War II. Atl Monthly Pr, 1990.   ○

Clavell, James
NOBLE HOUSE
Takes place in 1963—an action-filled plot that evokes "sights, sounds, smells and history of Hong Kong . . . multi-national companies . . . narcotics and gold-smuggling." (FC) Delacorte Pr, 1981.   ○

Clavell, James
TAIPAN
"A novel of Hong Kong . . . and the most powerful trading company in the Orient" based there. "The backgrounds . . . surge with life and the plot is neatly dovetailed with history." (BRD) Atheneum, 1966.   ○

Davis, Gwen
JADE
Police Superintendent Clement Leslie "encounters every level of Chinese/British society" when he investigates the murder of two teenagers—"inspired repartee . . . settings and plots that are as diverting as they are realistic." (FC) Warner, 1991.   ○

Davis, John G.
YEARS OF THE HUNGRY TIGER
"The major presence is Hong Kong itself . . . a vivid feel of where modern China

came from." The plot is about a superintendent of police, his romantic involvement
with a Chinese girl, and their role in the
cultural revolution. (BRD) Doubleday,
1975.   o

Elegant, Robert
DYNASTY
Family saga of a Eurasian commercial house
in Hong Kong, from the mid-nineteenth
century through revolutions in the twentieth
century. McGraw, 1977.   o

Gash, Jonathan
JADE WOMAN
Taking over an international antiques company is the focus of this Lovejoy mystery
set in Hong Kong. St. Martin's, 1988.   o

Gilman, Dorothy
**MRS. POLLIFAX AND THE HONG
   KONG BUDDHA**
Terrorists plot to take over Hong Kong.
Doubleday, 1985.   o

Hoyt, Richard
THE DRAGON PORTFOLIO
A farce about what happens when Hong
Kong is transformed into a Chinese prov-
ince. Doherty, 1986.   o

Kenrick, Tony
NEON TOUGH
Thriller involving drugs and a DEA opera-
tive tracking a drug dealer to Hong Kong.
Putnam, 1988.   o

Leib, Franklin A.
SEA LION
An American lion in the world of international banking, and equally successful with
women, involved in a fast-paced plot from
Singapore to Hong Kong and back—the Orient, politics, tradition and cuisine depicted
in the process. NAL, 1990.   o

Ludlum, Robert
THE BOURNE SUPREMACY
A sequel to *The Bourne Identity*; David Webb
is still having flashbacks to his Jason Bourne
identity. In this, he is seeking a man in Hong
Kong posing as Bourne—"cliffhanger . . .
brims with assassination, torture . . . surprise and intrigue." (FC) Random, 1986. o

Marshall, William L.
OUT OF NOWHERE
One of the Yellowthread series—"successfully utilizes exotic, off-the-wall characters
. . . and an unusual locale, to great effect."
Other books in the Yellowthread mystery
series, and set in Hong Kong, are *Head First*
(1986), *The Far Away Man* (1985), *Roadshow*
(1985), *Perfect End* (1983), *Sci-Fi* (1981), *Skul-
duggery* (1980), *Thin Air* (1978).   o

Mo, Timothy
AN INSULAR POSSESSION
"Acute and brutal" study of the 19th-cen-
tury opium war. Two young Americans in
Canton and Macau start a newsletter to help
eradicate the drug trade. (BRD) Random,
1987.   o

Scott, Justin
THE NINE DRAGONS
The head of a trading company is murdered
and his daughter takes over. "Fresh writing,
memorable characters, an exotic locale, and
a surprise ending." (FC) Bantam, 1991.   o

Trenhaile, John
THE MAH-JOHNGG SPIES
The financial atmosphere in Hong Kong,
which is scheduled to become part of China—
"balances violent action with complex financial ploys and counterploys." (FC) Dutton,
1986. Also *The Gates of Exquisite View*, its
sequel (1988).   o

INDIA AND THE HIMALAYAN MOUNTAIN KINGDOMS

Series Guidebooks
(See Appendix 1)

Baedeker: India
Berlitz: India; Nepal
Cadogan Guide: India
Fodor: India; Himalayan Countries
Frommer: India ($-A-Day); Nepal
Hildebrand: India and Nepal; Kathmandu and the Kingdom of Nepal
Insider's Guide: India; Nepal
Insight Guide: Delhi/Agra/Jaipur; India; Indian Wildlife; Kashmir; Kathmandu Valley; Nepal; Rajasthan; South India
Lonely Planet: India; Kashmir, Ladakh and Zanskar; Kathmandu & Nepal
Nagel's Encyclopedic Guide: India & Nepal
Nelles Guide: Nepal; Northern India; Southern India
Passport Asia Guides: Bhutan; Bombay & Goa; Kathmandu; Delhi, Agra & Jaipur
Real Guide: Nepal
Times Travel Library: Delhi & Agra; India; Kathmandu
2-22 Days Itinerary Planning Guide: India

Background Reading

Ackerley, J.R.
HINDOO HOLIDAY

The journal of a young Englishman who accepts a position with the maharajah of a small Indian state in British India—"like reading Kipling with more than a dash of Lewis Carroll . . .exotic and charming." (BRD) S&S, 1990. ○

Alexander, Michael
DELHI AND AGRA: A TRAVELLER'S COMPANION

One of a series that is a compilation of excerpts from literature of the country—fiction, letters, memoirs, journals—to present a cultural overview. Extensive introductions by experts provide background history; will "captivate armchair travelers of a slightly bookish bent." Atheneum, 1987. Also *Lives of the India Princes*, Crown, 1984. ○

Allen, Charles, ed.
PLAIN TALES FROM THE RAJ

Anthology of reminiscences of India under British rule from Edwardian days to 1947; childhood memories, social life, "the daily round, the rains, hill holidays" and so on. (BRD) St. Martin, 1976. ○

Basham, A.L., ed.
THE WONDER THAT WAS INDIA

A cultural history of India; sourcebook of Indian culture, politics, history, village life, and so on. Oxford U, 1984. ○

Brata, Sasthi
INDIA: LABYRINTH IN THE LOTUS LAND

For "India-watchers" on India's economic system, caste system, film industry, temples, Westernization—"engrossing tour of an 'Oriental Sphinx' whose secret he unriddles." (PW) Morrow, 1985. ○

Brown, Barbara
TRAVELS THROUGH THE MIND OF INDIA

A guide to the spiritual aspect of India—gurus, yoga, some flimflammery, swamis, and so on. Saybrook Pub, 1989. ○

Bumiller, Elisabeth
MAY YOU BE THE MOTHER OF A HUNDRED SONS: A JOURNEY AMONG THE WOMEN OF INDIA

"Perceptive, alert travelogue" based on a four-year residence in India and focused on women and the customs that keep them powerless—from feminists and Indira Ghandi, to impoverished village women, painters and poets, Bombay actresses. (PW) Random, 1990. ○

Collins, Larry and Lapierre, Dominique
FREEDOM AT MIDNIGHT

An "insightful" account of the immediate events surrounding the independence of India in 1947–48, including interviews with Lord Mountbatten, Indian leaders, and those who murdered Gandhi. (LJ) S&S, 1975. ○

Corbett, Jim
JIM CORBETT'S INDIA
By a lifelong resident of Mokameh Ghat on the Ganges; sketches of village life, people and customs. Oxford U Pr, 1987. Also *My India* (1990). ○

Forster, E.M.
HILL OF DEVI
A series of letters to the novelist's friends while on the trip to India in 1912–13, which provided background for *A Passage to India*. HarBraceJ, 1971. ○

Garland, Nicholas
AN INDIAN JOURNAL
Travel journal of a British political cartoonist on a leisurely two-week journey—"in the style of a Victorian letter home . . . a refreshing view of a diverse and exotic land." (BL) Academy Chi, 1986. ○

Godden, Jon and Rumer
SHIVA'S PIGEONS: AN EXPERIENCE IN INDIA
The two writers who have written many novels set in India (see under Novels, below) in collaboration with a photographer, portray India "at its best, with artistry, sensitivity and intelligence." (BRD) Viking, 1972. Also *Two Under the Indian Sun* (1966), which are joint recollections by the sisters, of five childhood years in a small Indian river village—"the sights and smells of India, 1914–20, and leisurely domestic life of Englishmen in India." ○

Greenwald, Jeff
SHOPPING FOR BUDDHAS
See entry under the Mountain Kingdoms subhead below. ○

Griffith, Kenneth
THE DISCOVERY OF NEHRU: AN EXPERIENCE OF INDIA
The author filmed the life of Nehru as a one-man docudrama and recounts that experi-

ence, which required an immersion in Indian society, politics and culture. Viking, 1990. ○

Kaul, H.K.
TRAVELLERS' INDIA: AN ANTHOLOGY
Selections about India from ancient times to contemporary. Oxford U Pr, 1979. ○

Kaye, M.M.
THE SUN IN THE MORNING: MY EARLY YEARS IN INDIA AND ENGLAND
By the author of many novels set in Africa, Europe and Asia (see index). St. Martin, 1990. Also *the Golden Calm* (1980). ○

Kidman, Brenda
ONCE UPON A FAR HILLSIDE: THE LIFE AND TIMES OF AN INDIAN VILLAGE
"Pleasant, rambling account . . . of three generations of a Muslim family" in a village near Bombay. (LJ) Century, 1986. ○

Moorhouse, Geoffrey
INDIA BRITANNICA
British rule in India—"fresh, astute reconstruction of events, crisply written" with many illustrations. (BL) Har-Row, 1983. ○

Morris, Jan and Winchester, Simon
STONES OF EMPIRE
The buildings of the Raj. Oxford U, 1984. ○

Murphy, Dervla
ON A SHOESTRING TO COORG: AN EXPERIENCE OF SOUTHERN INDIA
The author travels by train and bus with her five-year-old daughter, discovering an atypical India that is neither crowded nor impoverished. Overlook, 1989. Also *Full Tilt: Ireland to India With Bicycle*, which is a reprint of a book first published in 1965 of the Irish author's diary of a bicycle trek from Dunkirk to India via the Himalayas and Pakistan (1986). ○

Naipaul, V.S.
INDIA: A MILLION MUTINIES NOW
Interviews with all sorts of men and women from Brahmins and gangsters to untouchables, screenwriters, politicians. In the process he sorts out for the reader the various castes and sects and political parties—kaleidoscopic travelogue of the profound changes in India since his 1962 trip, which was the basis for *India: A Wounded Civilization*. Viking, 1991. Also *An Area of Darkness*. ◦

Newby, Eric
SLOWLY DOWN THE GANGES
A trip by the travel writer with his wife in 1963–64, by boat, rail, bus and bullock cart, following the Ganges from Hardwar to the Bay of Bengal—"description of the river . . . cities and villages . . . temples . . . people. . . . holy men of all varieties." (BRD) Penguin, 1986. ◦

Raine, Kathleen
INDIA SEEN AFAR
The author's autobiography, but also a portrait of India that resulted from an invitation to lecture on Yeats at the University of Delhi—"interweaves a travel chronicle and a metaphysical journey . . . fusing her recollections and observations with her spiritual rebirth." (BL) Braziller, 1991. ◦

Theroux, Paul and McCurry, Steve
THE IMPERIAL WAY
A journey along the railroad lines of the old Raj, a route taken because "nothing has changed . . . for over one hundred and fifty years." Photographs with evocative description. (BL) HM, 1985. ◦

Wolpert, Stanley
INDIA
"If one were to read a single book about India in a lifetime, this should be it" is how *Library Journal* begins its review—"grand, sweeping synthesis of Indian civilization." The Ganges River serves as a thematic symbol of a book that represents the author's lifetime of learning—"vision, knowledge, and

superb prose." (LJ) U of California Pr, 1991. ◦

Wood, Heather
THIRD CLASS TICKET
The author had the opportunity to go along with a group of poor villagers who were able to see their country by train due to a special bequest, and this is the result of that experience. Penguin, 1990. ◦

GANDHI

Attenborough, Richard, ed.
THE WORDS OF GANDHI
"Conveys the simple eloquence of the man" through thematically arranged selections from his writings, compiled by the director of the movie *Gandhi*. Newmarket, 1982. ◦

Fischer, Louis
GANDHI
"Long, full, affectionate" biography by an American who knew Gandhi intimately. (BRD) Har-Row, 1983. Also *The Life of Mahatma Gandhi* (1983) and *The Essential Gandhi: An Anthology* (1983). ◦

Jack, Homer A., ed.
THE GANDHI READER
Grove, 1989. ◦

Nanda, B.R.
MAHATMA GANDHI: A BIOGRAPHY
Oxford U Pr, 1989. ◦

Richards, Glyn
THE PHILOSOPHY OF GANDHI
A cohesive summary of beliefs and ideas. B & N Imports, 1982. ◦

Shirer, William
GANDHI, A MEMOIR
Shirer's recollections and impressions of Gandhi and India in the early 1930s when Shirer was a foreign correspondent—"compellingly insightful." (BRD) WSP, 1982. ◦

THE MOUNTAIN KINGDOMS (NEPAL, BHUTAN, SIKKIM, ZANSKAR)

Bernstein, Jeremy
IN THE HIMALAYAS: JOURNEYS THROUGH NEPAL, TIBET AND BHUTAN

Journal of a 1983 trek, and three chapters on Tibet and Bhutan, by a *New Yorker* science writer—"welcome companion for both armchair and more active adventurers." (LJ) S&S, 1989.   ○

Greenwald, Jeff
SHOPPING FOR BUDDHAS

The author has been traveling to Nepal and India for 10 years looking for the perfect religious statue. One reviewer says that while the material is new, exciting, fascinating, the author's cavalier attitude toward Nepal's drug culture is 20-years-too-late anachronistic. "Cogent and funny . . . Woody Allenesque amusement about himself while witnessing revolutionary changes" in the Hindu kingdom. (BL) Har-Row, 1990. Also *Mister Raja's Neighborhood: Letters From Nepal* (1986).   ○

Harding, Mike
FOOTLOOSE IN THE HIMALAYA

The author is a British entertainer. "Splendid travel adventure . . . a memorable portrait of the awesome beauty of countries visited" (Zanskar, northwest India, Nepal, and Ladakh in Tibet). (PW) Viking, 1990. ○

Matthiessen, Peter
THE SNOW LEOPARD

"Radiant and deeply moving account of an expedition to Nepal"—a combination of "anthropological and natural history writing with old-fashioned adventure, plenty of introspection." (BRD) Penguin, 1987.   ○

Murphy, Dervla
WHERE THE INDUS IS YOUNG: A WINTER IN BALTISAN

By a middle-aged, Irish, intrepid woman-traveler and writer—"beautifully responsive to environment . . . sometimes exceedingly funny." (BRD) J. Murray, 1978. Also *Waiting*

Land: A Spell in Nepal (1979), about her seven months in Pokhara.   ○

Pye-Smith, Charlie
TRAVELS IN NEPAL: THE SEQUESTERED KINGDOM

"Knowledgeable and humane observer"— the author was eager to visit sites where foreign aid had been applied in conservation and training projects, and comes to the conclusion that despite good intentions they often do not benefit a country's poor. (NYT) Penguin, 1990.   ○

Sunquist, Fiona and Mel
TIGER MOON

The authors went to Nepal's Royal Chitwan National Park in 1974 to study its tiger population and returned 10 years later. This account of their travels is "delightful . . . a topnotch tale for readers interested in wildlife." (PW) U of Chicago, 1988.   ○

Unsworth, Walt
EVEREST

Historical study of climbing expeditions to Everest from 1921 to 1978, and based on published and unpublished materials made available to the author by the British Alpine Club and Royal Geographic Society (which organizations sponsored the expeditions). "The writing style is superb . . . hard to put down." (BRD) Cloudcap, 1989.   ○

GUIDEBOOKS

Engstrom, Barbie
ENGSTROM'S GUIDE TO INDIA, NEPAL & SRI LANKA

Kurios Pr, 1985.   ○

Gibbons, Bob and Ashford, Bob
THE HIMALAYAN KINGDOMS: NEPAL, BHUTAN AND SIKKIM

"Generous amount of background material on history, culture, climate and geography," along with suggestions for treks and climbing, visiting national parks and wildlife areas. (BL) Hippocrene, 1988.   ○

Nicholson, Louise
INDIA: A GUIDE FOR THE QUALITY CONSCIOUS TRAVELER
Atl Monthly Pr, 1986.   ○

Shearer, Alistair
TRAVELER'S KEY TO NORTHERN INDIA: A GUIDE TO SACRED PLACES
Introduction and guide to the three major religions, Hinduism, Buddhism, Islam—"unusual and intriguing . . . specific temples, palaces, shrines, traveling tips." (BL) Knopf, 1983.   ○

Stacy, Allan
VISITING INDIA
For pre-trip planning and the armchair traveler. In-depth introduction to customs, transportation, flora, fauna, religions, history—"astute suggestions for planning side trips." (BL) Hippocrene, 1988.   ○

HISTORY

Lannoy, Richard
THE SPEAKING TREE
Covers the whole range of Indian cultural history from prehistoric times to the death of Gandhi, relating India's history to its contemporary problems. Oxford U Pr, 1974. ○

Wolpert, Stanley
A NEW HISTORY OF INDIA
A survey from earliest times to the present—intended for the general reader. Oxford U Pr, 1989.   ○

Novels

Banerji, Bibhutibhushan
PATHER PANCHALI: SONG OF THE ROAD
An autobiographical novel of life in a Bengali village. Indiana U, 1969 (first published 1928).   ○

Bromfield, Louis
THE RAINS CAME
An "oldie" from which a movie was made in the 1940s—"diverse and interesting personalities . . . exotic detail" as a flood destroys years of work by an enlightened native prince. (FC) Aeonian, 1976 (first published 1937).   ○

Courter, Gay
FLOWERS IN THE BLOOD
About a Victorian Jewish family's involvement in the flower trade (opium)—"compelling scenes of India and China in the late 1800s . . . history of the Jews in Calcutta, the tea and opium trades . . . Anglo-Indian society." (FC) Dutton, 1990.   ○

Desai, Anita
CLEAR LIGHT OF DAY
The plot is concerned equally between the triennial visit of a younger sister and her diplomat husband to the family home near Old Delhi, and memories of the past the visit engenders. (FC) Har-Row, 1980. Also, *In Custody* (1984), "shattering and comic" novel about a college teacher who is asked to interview a famous visiting poet, and *Games At Twilight* (1980). Also the recent *Baumgartner's Bombay* (1989).   ○

Desai, Anita
FIRE ON THE MOUNTAIN
The story of a girl's summer with her great-grandmother in the hill country, ending tragically with rape and murder—set in post-British India. Har-Row, 1977.   ○

Forster, E.M.
A PASSAGE TO INDIA
A modern classic reveals "gross misunderstandings, and the subtler misunderstandings" that arise among various races in India, and the reactions of two visiting Englishwomen to Chandrapore. (BRD) HarBraceJ, 1924.   ○

Ghosh, Anutav
THE SHADOW LINES
"Brilliant" novel of two families, one in London the other in Calcutta, from World War II to contemporary times—"engaging characters abound." (FC) Viking, 1989. Also *The Circle of Reason* (1986), story of a suspected terrorist on the run from Bengal to Bombay, the Persian Gulf and North Africa.   ○

Godden, Rumer
COROMANDEL SEA CHANGE
Novel of "romance, love, tragedy, and . . . politics" set on the coast of the Coromandel Sea. (FC) Morrow, 1991.   ⊃

Godden, Rumer
THE DARK HORSE
Tale of an exiled thoroughbred horse, its trainer, a millionaire horseowner, a shrewd nun, and an ex-jockey—set in Calcutta in the early 1930s, in which Darkie wins the Viceroy Cup. Viking, 1982.   ⊃

Godden, Rumer
THE PEACOCK SPRING
The plot involves two girls sent to India to be with their diplomat father, where each becomes involved with an Indian—"vivid depiction" of the country. Viking, 1976. Other novels by Rumer Godden, noted for their evocative and sensitive rendering of Indian settings are *Black Narcissus* (1939), *Breakfast with Nikolides* (1942), *Kingfishers Catch Fire* (1953), *The River* (1946).   ⊃

Hoover, Thomas
THE MOGHUL
Based on the true story of Brian Hawksworth in the seventeenth century—"a fascinating and skillful mixture of romance, history, and adventure." (FC) Doubleday, 1983.   ⊃

Jhabvala, Ruth P.
HEAT AND DUST
A woman and her granddaughter lead parallel lives—abandoning their English husbands for marriage to Indians and life in a remote mountain village. Har-Row, 1976.   ⊃

Jhabvala, Ruth P.
OUT OF INDIA
Selected stories—"sensitively explores the tense juncture between Western and Indian cultures." (FC) Morrow, 1986. Also short stories collected in *A Stronger Climate* (1969) and *How I Became a Holy Mother* (1976).   ⊃

Jhabvala, Ruth P.
TRAVELERS
The effect of India on some young Anglo-Saxons looking for something in India or themselves. Har-Row, 1973. Also, *The Householder* (1960) set in New Delhi.   ⊃

Kaye, M.M.
DEATH IN KASHMIR
Revised version of a novel published in 1953. The intrepid heroine gets entangled in a treacherous plot that endangers the whole free world when she looks into a series of murders. The Kashmir setting comes exotically, enticingly alive. (FC) St. Martin, 1984. Also *The Far Pavilions* (1979) and *Shadow of the Moon* (1979).   ⊃

Keating, H.R.F.
INSPECTOR GHOTE MYSTERIES
Inspector Ghote of the Bombay police is the Sherlock Holmes of a series noted for authentic background and local color, in addition to being first-rate mysteries. Doubleday. Titles include: *The Iciest Sin* (1990); *The Body in the Billiard Room* (1987); *The Sheriff of Bombay* (1984); *The Murder of the Maharajah* (1981); *Bats Fly Up for Inspector Ghote* (1974); *Dead on Time* (1989), set in a country village; *Inspector Ghote Goes By Train* (1972); *Filmi, Filmi* (1977). Academy Chicago Ltd has also issued reprints of the following Inspector Ghote mysteries: *Inspector Ghote Breaks an Egg*, *Inspector Ghote Caught in Meshes*, *Inspector Ghote Draws a Line*, *Inspector Ghote Hunts the Peacock*, *Inspector Ghote Plays a Joker*, *Inspector Ghote Trusts the Heart*.   ⊃

Kipling, Rudyard
PLAIN TALES FROM THE HILLS
Short stories, first published in 1898. Doubleday, 1898.   ⊃

Markandaya, Kamala
TWO VIRGINS
Contemporary Indian family life—"love of land, custom and humanity pitted against India's agonizing evolution into the contemporary world." (FC) Day, 1973. Also, *Nectar in a Sieve* (1955), *A Handful of Rice* (1966), *The Golden Honeycomb* (1977), and *Shalimar* (1983).   ⊃

Masters, John
BHOWANI JUNCTION
An Anglo-Indian's dilemma in trying to identify with her mixed heritage; the setting is just prior to Indian independence. Viking, 1954. Two additional novels of the Savage family, preceding this one, are *Nightrunners of Bengal* (1951) and *Far, Far the Mountain Peak* (1957). Also *the Himalayan Concerto* (1976).   ◦

Mehta, Gita
RAJ
A saga that traces an Indian princess's life from 1897 to the mid-1920s—"counterpoints a vanished way of life . . . and the birth of the modern nations of India and Pakistan." (FC) S&S, 1989.   ◦

Narayan, R.K.
THE RAMAYANA
A short and readable modern version of the Indian epic passed on by word of mouth through the generations. Viking, 1972.   ◦

Narayan, R.K.
A TIGER FOR MALGUDI
One of a series of novels set in the small Indian town of Malgudi, written in English by a leading Indian writer, with all kinds of intriguing and delightful characters and diverse plots. Titles include: *Printer of Malgudi* (1957), *The Guide* (1958), *The Man Eater* (1961), *The Vendor* (1967), *A Horse and Two Goats* (1970), *Painter of Signs* (1976), *Malgudi Days* (1982), *Talkative Man* (1987) and *the World of Nagaraj* (1990). Viking, 1983.   ◦

Peters, Ellis
DEATH TO THE LANDLORDS!
Story of wealthy landholders, set in southern India, who are victims of a terrorist group. Morrow, 1972.   ◦

Rushdie, Salman
MIDNIGHT'S CHILDREN
Story of 1,001 children born on August 15, 1947, in the first hour of Indian independence and, in particular, about the fortunes of Shiva and Saleem, switched at birth by a nursemaid and destined to be enemies. Knopf, 1981.   ◦

Ryman, Rebecca
OLIVIA AND JAI
Historical romance between an American and the half-caste Jai—"suspense, exotic locales . . . a treat for romance readers." (FC) St. Martin, 1990.   ◦

Scott, Paul
THE RAJ QUARTET
The story of British India from 1942–45—"racist, heroic, exploitative, doomed"—brought to life through a variety of compelling characters. The four individual titles are *The Jewel in the Crown* (1966), *The Towers of Silence* (1972), *The Day of the Scorpion* (1968), *A Division of Spoils* (1975). A postscript to the *Quartet* is *Staying On* (1977) in which "a few Raj derelicts" linger in India, with their servants, in a hill town. Morrow.   ◦

Thomas, Craig
WILDCAT
A British intelligence agent confronts foes involved in a takeover of Nepal. Putnam, 1989.   ◦

Wolpert, Stanley
NINE HOURS TO RAMA
The story of Gandhi told from the viewpoint of a militant Hindu, and a member of the group that assassinated Gandhi. Random, 1962.   ◦

INDONESIA

*Series Guidebooks
(See Appendix 1)*

Cadogan Guide: Bali
Hildebrand: Indonesia

Insider's Guide: Indonesia; Bali
Insight: Indonesia; Bali
Lonely Planet: Indonesia; Bali and Lombok
Moon Handbook: Indonesia; Bali
Nelles Guide: West Indonesia

Passport: Bali
Post Guide: Indonesia
Times Travel Library: Bali; Borneo; Jakarta

Background Reading

Burbridge, F.W.
THE GARDENS OF THE SUN
"A naturalist's journal of Borneo and the Sulu Archipelago" is the subtitle. Oxford U Pr, 1989. ○

Corn, Charles
DISTANT ISLANDS: TRAVELS ACROSS INDONESIA
"Diverse and exotic Indonesia" by plane, train, boat and bus in the late 1980s and 1990s—"engrossing anecdotes." (LJ) Viking, 1991. ○

Gorer, Geoffrey
BALI AND ANGKOR
Reprint of a 1930s travel classic—"hilarious, unaffected personal memoir." Oxford U Pr, 1987. ○

Hansen, Eric
STRANGER IN THE FOREST: ON FOOT ACROSS BORNEO
First-rate adventure of a 1,500-mile solo walk in the rain forest of Borneo, first published in 1982. Viking, 1989. ○

Kayam, Umar
THE SOUL OF INDONESIA: A CULTURAL JOURNEY
A "sharply detailed travelogue" and photographs show how the country's traditional arts are faring as Indonesia is industrialized. (PW) Louisiana State U Pr, 1985. ○

Linklater, Andro
WILD PEOPLE: TRAVELS WITH BORNEO'S HEAD-HUNTERS
The author was sent by Time-Life to produce a coffee-table book of the Iban people; he found the people eager to embrace Western things, and therefore was unable to fulfill editorial expectations. Atl Monthly Pr, 1991. ○

Muller, Kal and Zach, Paul
INDONESIA: PARADISE ON THE EQUATOR
"Fascinating volume" by a pair of travelers who have fallen in love with the country— "readers will wish that the authors' adventure was their own." (LJ) St. Martin, 1988. Also *Borneo: Journey into the Tropical Rain Forest, East of Bali: from Lombok to Timor, Spice Islands: Exotic Eastern Indonesia* and *Bali: The Emerald Isle.* ○

Naipaul, V.S.
AMONG THE BELIEVERS
See entry under Middle East/Islam. Indonesia is one of the four Islamic countries the author explored. ○

O'Hanlon, Redmond
INTO THE HEART OF BORNEO
"A vastly entertaining report of . . . encounters with natives . . . discomforts of jungle life . . . as much escapade as adventure." (PW) Random, 1985. ○

Powell, Hickman
THE LAST PARADISE
Discovery of Bali in the 1920s—even then Westerners realized that Bali was an Eden that would be spoiled by tourism. Oxford U Pr, 1986. ○

Volkman, Toby A.
SULAWESI: ISLAND CROSSROADS OF INDONESIA
About the central Indonesian island that is crossroad of the spice trade. Passport Pr, 1990. ○

HISTORY

See also histories of Southeast Asia under Asia/History.

Neill, Wilfred T.
TWENTIETH-CENTURY INDONESIA
"Historical play of . . . influences—Malayan, Indian, Muslim, Portuguese, British and Dutch" on the Indonesian archipelago. (LJ) Columbia U Pr, 1977. ○

Rickfels, M.C.
A HISTORY OF MODERN INDONESIA
Indiana U Pr, 1981.   ○

Novels

Bosse, Malcolm J.
STRANGER AT THE GATE
An American builder in Indonesia of 1965 and his anthropologist wife who begins losing her Westernness, including falling in love with an Indonesian puppetmaster. S&S, 1989.   ○

Hartog, Jan de
THE SPIRAL ROAD
Effects of life in the then Dutch East Indies, on a young and smug doctor. Har-Row, 1957.   ○

Lofts, Norah
SCENT OF CLOVES
Story of an orphan who is raised by a sea captain and later sent to the Dutch East Indies as part of a complicated plot to marry her off to the idiot son of a wealthy planter—romance, suspense, local color. Doubleday, 1957. Also, a much earlier novel, *Silver Nutmeg* (1947), a romance with a complicated plot set on one of the Dutch islands.   ○

JAPAN

Series Guidebooks
(See Appendix 1)

American Express Pocket Guide: Tokyo
Baedeker: Tokyo; Japan
Berlitz: Japan
Crown Insider's Guide: Japan
Fisher's World: Japan
Fodor: Japan; Tokyo
Frommer: Tokyo; Japan & Hong Kong
Hildebrand: Japan
Insider's Guide: Japan
Insight Guide: Japan
Lonely Planet: Japan
Moon Handbook: Japan
Passport: Japan
Post Guide: Japan
2–22 Days Itinerary Planning Guide: Japan

Background Reading

Bohnaker, William
THE HOLLOW DOLL: A LITTLE BOX OF JAPANESE SHOCKS
"An acerbic portrait of Japan" by an author who resided there with his wife, and who sees it as a country beset by deception, competition, suspicion of foreigners, spiritual emptiness. (BL) Ballantine, 1990.   ○

Booth, Alan
THE ROADS TO SATA: A 2000-MILE WALK THROUGH JAPAN
A Japanese-speaking Englishman walks from northernmost tip of Hokkaido to the southernmost tip of Kyushu—"a delightful series of encounters with and impressions of local people" along the mostly rural route that he walked. (LJ) Viking, 1986.   ○

Cott, Jonathan
WANDERING GHOST: THE ODYSSEY OF LAFCADIO HEARN
A hybrid of selected excerpts from Hearn's writings and an informal biography of the 19th-century writer who led an unconventional life, from journalist in Ohio, to Martinique and New Orleans and ending his life in Japan and adopting Buddhism. See entry under Hearn, below. Knopf, 1991.   ○

Courdy, Jean C.
THE JAPANESE: EVERYDAY LIFE IN THE EMPIRE OF THE RISING SUN
By a French journalist and political scholar using "his personal experiences to illuminate . . . how the Japanese have come to terms both with the technological and social

changes of the post-World War II era and with the ancient traditions of their civilization. . . . intriguing look at today's Japan." (BL) Har-Row, 1984.　　o

Dalby, Liza
GEISHA
The author was awarded the privilege of being the first outsider to participate in Geisha training. Random, 1985.　　o

Downer, Lesley
ON THE NARROW ROAD: JOURNEY INTO A LOST JAPAN
This Londoner spends three months every year in rural Japan, and the book is her account of traditional Japan, retracing the footsteps of a 17th-century Japanese poet. Summit, 1989.　　o

Earhart, H. Byron
RELIGIONS OF JAPAN
Rituals, festivals, icons, social relationships of the various religions, history of religion in Japan. Includes Shintoism, Taoism, Buddhism, Christianity and various subsidiary sects. Har-Row, 1984.　　o

Fraser, Mary and Cortazzi, Hugh
A DIPLOMAT'S WIFE IN JAPAN
An abridged version of the original published in 1899. Letters describing turn-of-the-century Japan—"very readable. . . . with anecdotes that provide fascinating contrasts and continuities with the Japan of today." (BRD) Weatherhill, 1982.　　o

Hearn, Lafcadio
JAPAN: AN INTERPRETATION
Recognized as the first major American writer to interpret Japan to the West. Other books by Hearn include: *Writings from Japan, Glimpses of Unfamiliar Japan, Exotics and Retrospectives.* See entry under Jonathan Cott, above.　　o

Iyer, Pico
THE LADY AND THE MONK: FOUR SEASONS IN KYOTO
The author travels to a monastery to study Zen Buddhism, leading to a friendship with a Japanese housewife, and sets out to understand Japanese culture through this friendship. "A lyrical fable about the Japan of both yesterday and today." (LJ) Knopf, 1991.　　o

Katzenstein, Gary J.
FUNNY BUSINESS: AN OUTSIDER'S YEAR IN JAPAN
Account of the author's time in Japan as a Luce scholar at Sony and another smaller company, and the frustrations of foreigners who live in Japan—"overall, an entertaining if sometimes embittered discussion." (LJ) Prentice Hall, 1990.　　o

Keene, Donald
TRAVELERS OF A HUNDRED AGES
A collection of short pieces from Japanese diarists, ranging from literary greats to mothers and monks; published as a newspaper article series. Holt, 1989.　　o

MacIntyre, Michael
THE SHOGUN INHERITANCE
A coffee-table book "written to build on the BBC television series." See also the Clavell novel, under Novels, below. (BRD) A&W, 1982.　　o

Morley, John D.
PICTURES FROM THE WATER TRADE, ADVENTURES OF A WESTERNER IN JAPAN
The term "water trade" refers to Japanese bars, cafes, bordellos and the people the author encounters as a student in Japan, including his love affair with a Japanese woman. A *Travel & Leisure* reviewer said that this book reads like a collaboration by Henry James and Holden Caulfield! "So wise, erotic and complete" are the author's adventures and comments "that the Japanese people are now in imminent danger of being scrutable." (TL) Atl Monthly Pr, 1985.　　o

Morris, Ivan
THE WORLD OF THE SHINING PRINCE
Intended to tell of the realities underlying Murasaki's *Tale of the Genji* (see Novels, below). Penguin, 1979. Also *The Pillow Book*

of Sei Shonagon (1971), diary of a lady-in-waiting at court in pre-1000 A.D., edited by Morris. ○

Mura, David
TURNING JAPANESE: MEMOIRS OF A SANSEI

A third-generation Japanese-American in an account of his first visit to the land of his ancestors, and sampling Japan. Atl Monthly Pr, 1990. ○

Philip, Leila
THE ROAD THROUGH MIYAMA

Account of the author's apprenticeship to a potter in Miyama, "an eddy of tradition and ritual out of the mainstream of Japanese society." (PW) Random, 1989. ○

Reischauer, Edwin O.
THE JAPANESE TODAY: CONTINUITY AND CHANGE

Rewritten and updated version of *The Japanese* (1977). Harvard U, 1988. ○

Schoolland, Ken
SHOGUN'S GHOST: THE DARK SIDE OF JAPANESE EDUCATION

The author questions the accepted image of Japan's educational system as being near-perfect and one Americans should try to learn from. Bergin & Garvey, 1990. ○

Shapiro, Michael
JAPAN: IN THE LAND OF THE BROKENHEARTED

Observations on the journalist-author's five years in Japan, along with quotes from Lafcadio Hearn and reports on experiences of other American residents. Japan emerges as a xenophobic society—"a foreigner's love of Japan is rarely reciprocated" asserts the author. (PW) Holt, 1989. ○

Spry-Leverton, Peter and Kornicki, Peter
JAPAN

Companion book to a four-part PBS TV series presented in 1988, covering the history of Japan down to its contemporary role. Facts On File, 1988. ○

Stanley-Smith, Joan
JAPANESE ART

Authoritative survey from prehistoric times to contemporary and heavily illustrated. Thanes & Hudson, 1984. ○

Statler, Oliver
JAPANESE PILGRIMAGE

The author retraces an eight-century pilgrimage by a Buddhist monk in a two-month circular trek to shrines and temples associated with Buddhism—a "recreation of the priest's life. . . . history of medieval Japan. . . . the devotions of today's pilgrims." (BRD) Morrow, 1981. Also *Japanese Inn* (1962), a classic on Japanese life and customs. ○

Watson, Burton
THE RAINBOW WORLD: JAPAN IN ESSAYS AND TRANSLATIONS

Personal essays covering various aspects of the author's life in Japan as a U.S. sailor, a graduate student, and permanent resident since 1973. "Well-informed and sensitive . . . a strong sense of poetry . . . to be read slowly and savored both for cultural insights and the beauty of its writing." (LJ) Broken Moon Pr, 1990. ○

GUIDEBOOKS

Connor, Judith and Yoshida, Mayumi
TOKYO CITY GUIDE

Basic advice for tourists but also an exploration of the contemporary city and "what may be inscrutable to Occidental eyes." (BL) Kodansha, 1985. ○

DeMente, Boye
THE WHOLE JAPAN BOOK

An encyclopedia on things Japanese. The author lives in Japan and has written many other books on the country, including: *Everything Japanese, Japan Made Easy, Etiquette Guide, Discovering Cultural Japan, Japan at Night* and *The Tourist and the Real Japan,* which purports to be an unglamorized and frank report on the pitfalls and pleasures of the Japan experience. Phoenix, Books, 1983. ○

Demery, Leroy W., Jr. and others
JAPAN BY RAIL
Dedicated to encouraging tourists to travel by rail in a country with a remarkable dedication to rail travel. The Map Factory, 1985. ○

Kanno, Eiji
JAPAN SOLO: A PRACTICAL GUIDE FOR INDEPENDENT TRAVELERS
Practical trivia that can assume major importance for the independent traveler in Japan—how to use trains, key bus stop numbers, maps, Japanese/English printed conversation cards. A how-to-see book more than a what-to-see book. Warner Bks, 1988. ○

Kinoshita, June and Palevsky, Nicholas
GATEWAY TO JAPAN
"The best generalist guidebook for the curious and probing visitor . . . a huge amount of information at a very reasonable price." (LJ) Kodansha, 1990. ○

Sutherland, Mary and Britton, Dorothy
NATIONAL PARKS OF JAPAN
A guided tour of 27 parks, ranging from subarctic to subtropic—marine parks, mountains, waterfalls, crater lakes. Kodansha, 1981. ○

Ward, Philip
JAPANESE CAPITALS
A cultural, historical and artistic guide to Nara, Kyoto and Tokyo—successive capitals of Japan. Hippocrene, 1987. ○

Weatherly, James K.
JAPAN UNESCORTED
Kodansha, 1990. ○

HISTORY

Beasley, W.G.
THE RISE OF MODERN JAPAN
"Highly recommended for readers looking for a concise, well-written history of modern Japan." (LJ) St. Martin's, 1990. ○

Colcutt, Martin, and others
CULTURAL ATLAS OF JAPAN
Excellent general history. Facts On File, 1988. ○

Emmerson, John K. and Holland, Harrison M.
THE EAGLE AND THE RISING SUN
Japan and America in the 20th century, by former U.S. foreign service colleagues; a review of relations since World War II between Japan and the U.S., and other countries. Addison-Wesley, 1988. ○

Seidensticker, Edward G.
TOKYO RISING: THE CITY SINCE THE GREAT EARTHQUAKE
"Serendipitous social history" of the metamorphosis of Japan from 1923, after the earthquake, to its rebuilding following World War II, on through to the present. Knopf, 1990. ○

Tasher, Peter
THE JAPANESE: A MAJOR EXPLORATION OF MODERN JAPAN
Emphasis on political, economic and social developments by an author who lived in Japan for seven years. Dutton, 1988. ○

Varley, H. Paul
JAPANESE CULTURE
The evolution of the culture from antiquity to contemporary Japan, third edition. U of Hawaii Pr, 1984. ○

Novels

Abe, Kobo
THE ARK SAKURA
Sakura prepares a former quarry as a nuclear shelter and then looks for people to invite in—"dreamlike . . . a convincing sense of place . . . sickening and memorable" in its exploration of themes like ecology, old age, nuclear war, the role of outcasts in Japan. (BRD) Knopf, 1988. ○

Abe, Kobo
THE WOMAN IN THE DUNES
Probably the most well-known title by a leading Japanese author—story of a man,

vacationing on the seacoast, who is captured by villagers and must live in a house being engulfed by the dunes. Other titles include: *Secret Rendezvous* (1979), *The Box Man* (1974), *The Ruined Map* (1969). Knopf, 1964. ○

Akutagawa, Ryunosuke
RASHOMON

A collection of short stories. Liveright, 1970. ○

Albery, Nibuko
THE HOUSE OF KANZE

Historical novel of a 14th-century theatrical family. S&S, 1985. Also *Balloon Top,* about a young Japanese woman growing up in the early 1960s (1978). ○

Clavell, James
SHOGUN

Meeting of the East and West in seventeenth-century Japan, through a British sea pilot and his crew and a Japanese feudal lord—"creates a world, people, customs, settings, needs and desires . . . history infused with fantasy." (BRD) Atheneum, 1975. ○

Endo, Shusaku
THE SAMURAI

The plight of a seventeenth-century Spanish missionary who wants to preach Catholicism—by Japan's distinguished Roman Catholic novelist. Har-Row, 1982. Other novels by this writer include: *The Sea and Poison* (1980), *Silence* (1979), *Volcano* (1980), *When I Whistle* (1979). ○

Endo, Shusaku
SCANDAL

A celebrated artist and Catholic convert is forced to deal with the charge that he is a frequenter of Tokyo's brothels. Dodd, 1988. Also *Wonderful Fool,* picaresque tale about a naive, pacifist French penpal who shows up in Japan (1959). ○

Gardner, Mona
MIDDLE HEAVEN

Japan before and shortly after World War II—"absorbing . . . fascinating . . . percep-tive portrait of the Japanese way of life." (BRD) Doubleday, 1950. ○

Ishiguro, Kazuo
AN ARTIST OF THE FLOATING WORLD

"In postwar Japan, a retired painter . . . reflects on his career, the limits to loyalties . . . the life of art." Putnam, 1986. ○

Kawabata, Yasunari
THE OLD CAPITAL

Set in Kyoto—a young woman faces an identity crisis when she finds out that her real parents abandoned her. North Point Pr, 1987. ○

Kawabata, Yasunari
SNOW COUNTRY and THOUSAND CRANES

Kawabata won the Nobel Prize in literature for these novels. Knopf, 1969. Other titles by the same author include: *The Lake* (1974), *The Master of Go* (1972), *The Sound of the Mountains* (1970), *Beauty and Sadness* (1975). ○

Kita, Mario
THE HOUSE OF NIRE

Along with *The Fall of the House of Nire,* both published originally in one book in 1964. Saga of three generations of a Japanese family between World Wars I and II, ending when Pearl Harbor is bombed. Kodansha, 1985. ○

Lustbader, E.V.
WHITE NINJA

Trilogy of the Ninja whose mother was Japanese and father, a British officer—"a distinctly good time for the unabashed thriller-reader." The first two books in the trilogy are *The Ninja* (1985) and *The Miko* (1984). (FC) Columbine, 1990. ○

Maruya, Salichi
RAIN IN THE WIND

Four atmospheric stories of postwar Japan. Kodansha, 1990. ○

Matsubara, Hisako
SAMURAI
Novel of a marriage, set in turn-of-the-century provincial Japan, and the lives of the wife in Japan, and her husband in America as an immigrant—"lovely . . . as a Japanese flower arrangement . . . brilliant evocation of Japanese culture." (BRD) Times Bks, 1980.   ⊃

McInerney, Jay
RANSOM
An American in Kyoto trying to find himself and rid himself of his past—"vivid, acerbic . . . the scenes in the karate dojo . . . are stunning." (FC) Random, 1985.   ⊃

Melville, James
THE NINTH NETSUKE
Detective Superintendent Otani, using his wife as a cover, registers in a notorious Kobe hotel where there's been a murder, and she provides a critical clue by finding an ivory figurine (netsuke). "The details of Japanese culture, history and daily life . . . create a very satisfying and intriguing mystery." (FC) St. Martin, 1982. Other mysteries set in Japan by Melville are: *Sayonara, Sweet Amaryllis* (1984), *The Chrysanthemum Chain* (1982), *A Sort of Samurai* (1981), *The Death Ceremony* (1985), *Go Gently Gaijin* (1986), *Kimono for a Corpse* (1987), *The Reluctant Ronin* (1988), *A Haiku for Henae* (1989), and *The Bogus Buddha* (1991).   ⊃

Michener, James A.
SAYONARA
An American Air Force major falls in love with a Japanese girl. Random, 1954.   ⊃

Mishima, Yukio
THE SEA OF FERTILITY
A cycle of four novels: *Spring Snow* (1972), *Runaway Horses* (1973), *The Temple of Dawn* (1973), and *The Decay of the Angel* (1974). This series begins in turn-of-the-century Tokyo and ends with modern industrial Japan—"an absolute evocation of a Japanese way of life that is completely intelligible." (FC) Knopf, 1972. Also by Mishima, *After the Banquet* (1963), *Forbidden Colors* (1968),

The Sound of the Waves (1956), *The Temple of the Golden Pavilion* (1959).   ⊃

Murasaki, Shikibu
THE TALE OF GENJI
Considered the greatest single work in Japanese literature, and possibly the world's first novel—a "vast chronicle of court life" of the Heian period that "centers on the career of Prince Genji and the women with whom he was associated." (FC) Knopf, 1976 (dating from tenth-eleventh centuries).   ⊃

Schwartz, John B.
BICYCLE DAYS
A coming-of-age novel, but the twist is that this young man's version is set in Japan where he's working for a Tokyo branch of an American computer company. Summit Bks, 1989.   ⊃

Sheard, Sarah
ALMOST JAPANESE
A Canadian teenager becomes infatuated with a Japanese conductor and Japanese culture; she later visits Japan—"the pain of adolescence and the seductiveness of a new culture." (BRD) Scribner, 1987.   ⊃

Skimin, Robert
CHIKARA!
The subtitle reads: "A sweeping novel of Japan and America from 1907 to 1983." Three generations of a Japanese family, those in Japan and those who emigrate to America— "personal dramas are played out against a canvas that includes the rise of . . . militarism in Japan and anti-Japanese sentiments . . . the Tokyo earthquake . . . the Depression, and two world wars. . . . plenty of well-researched history and exotic details." (FC) St. Martin, 1984.   ⊃

Stroup, Dorothy
IN THE AUTUMN WIND
Story of one family in Hiroshima when the bomb falls. Scribner, 1987.   ⊃

Tanizaki, Junichiro
NAOMI
Written in the 1920s, this is the first English translation—"it is Tanizaki's *Daisy Miller;* like

Henry James, Tanizaki created . . . the type of the modern young woman." The narrator is obsessed with a girl half his age who becomes a torment as he indulges her, eventually marries her—"a clever, oblique evocation of a neurotic period in Tokyo." (BRD) Knopf, 1985. ○

Toland, John
OCCUPATION
This and *Gods of War* (1985) chronicle two families—the American McGlynns and the Japanese Todas—linked by marriage and their experiences in World War II and the ensuing occupation of Japan. Doubleday, 1987. ○

Wynd, Oswald
THE GINGER TREE
In 1903 a girl sailed from Scotland to the Far East to marry the Peking military attaché. She has an affair with a Japanese soldier, and this is the story of her survival in an alien culture. Eland, 1989. ○

MALAYSIA AND SINGAPORE

Series Guidebooks
(See Appendix 1)

American Express Pocket Guide: Hong Kong, Singapore & Bangkok
Baedeker: Singapore
Berlitz: Singapore
Fodor: Singapore
Frommer: Hong Kong, Macau & Singapore
Hildebrand: Malaysia/Singapore
Insight: Malaysia; Singapore
Lonely Planet: Malaysia, Singapore and Brunei; Singapore
Moon Handbook: South Pacific (includes Malaysia)
Passport: Malaysia; Singapore
Post Guides: Malaysia; Singapore
Times Travel Library: Singapore

Background Reading

Bird, Isabella
THE GOLDEN CHERSONESE
Letters to the author's sister while on a visit to the Malay Peninsula in 1879; new reprint. Hippocrene, 1983. ○

Naipaul, V.S.
AMONG THE BELIEVERS
See entry under Middle East/Islam. Malaysia is one of the four countries explored by the author on which the book is based. ○

O'Hanlon, Redmond
INTO THE HEART OF BORNEO
An account of a hazardous journey into central Borneo—"a vastly entertaining report of . . . encounters with natives . . . discomforts of jungle life . . . as much escapade as adventure." (PW) Random, 1985. ○

White, Walter G.
THE SEA GYPSIES OF MALAYSIA
A "very readable" anthropological study of the nomadic sea peoples of the Malaysian archipelago and their way of life. AMS, 1981 (first published 1922). ○

GUIDEBOOKS

Stier, Wayne and Cavers, Mark
TIME TRAVEL IN THE MALAY CRESCENT
For the adventurous traveler—travel tips, maps, how to get around, history, culture, people. Meru Pub, 1984. ○

HISTORY

See also books on history of Southeast Asia under "Asia/History." ○

Turnbull, C.M.
A HISTORY OF SINGAPORE
"From Raffles's emporium to Lee Kuan Yew's barracks state." (BRD) Oxford U Pr, 1977. Also, *A Short History of Malay, Singapore & Brunei* (1981). ○

Winstedt, Richard O.
THE MALAYS: A CULTURAL HISTORY
Three Continents, 1981 (first published 1961). ○

Novels

Boulle, Pierre
THE BRIDGE OVER THE RIVER KWAI
(Singapore)

The story on which the memorable movie was based—"a stirring and imaginative book . . . soaked in Kipling atmosphere . . . unforgettable character sketches." The plot concerns a Japanese prison camp during World War II and a stiff-upper-lip British officer who builds a bridge using prison labor. (FC) Vanguard Bks, 1954.   o

Burgess, Anthony
THE LONG DAY WANES: A MALAYAN TRILOGY

Three short novels set in Malay in the period of waning British rule just before Malay's independence—"one of the most revealing narratives about the East and the West" relationship. (BRD) Norton, 1965.   o

Clavell, James
KING RAT

Corruption, fear, despair in a World War II prison camp in Singapore. Little, 1962.   o

Conrad, Joseph
LORD JIM

A classic story of a man who becomes a demigod. Knopf, 1979 (first published 1899). Also, *Almayer's Folly* (1895).   o

D'Alpuget, Blanche
TURTLE BEACH

"Meld of movements, cultures, and beliefs ranging from feminism to mysticism" set in an exotic Malaysia. (FC) S&S, 1984.   o

Drummond, Emma
SOME FAR ELUSIVE DAWN
(Singapore)

The time is just after World War I, as two newcomers into the world of the English-in-exile and their rigid protocols of behavior set off sparks—"Singapore's steamy atmosphere is evoked well." (PW) St. Martin's, 1991.   o

Leib, Franklin A.
SEA LION

See entry under Hong Kong.   o

Maugham, W. Somerset
THE CASUARINA TREE

Short stories fashioned in typical Maugham style "out of dramatic and melodramatic situations in the lives of European exiles." (BRD) Doran, 1926.   o

Overgard, William
THE MAN FROM RAFFLES
(Singapore)

Adventures "not for the faint hearted," a merchant seaman returns to Singapore to investigate his estranged father's death—"splendid reading." (PW) S&S, 1991.   o

Reeman, Douglas
THE PRIDE AND THE ANGUISH

The fall of Singapore in 1941. Putnam, 1969. Also, *The Deep Silence* (1968) and *The Greatest Enemy* (1971).   o

Shute, Nevil
THE LEGACY

See entry under Australia/Novels.   o

Theroux, Paul
THE CONSUL'S FILE

Tales of "how uprooted individuals connect or fail to connect with each other" and places they've ended up, set in post-colonial Malaysia. (BRD) Houghton, 1977. Also *Saint Jack* (1973).   o

PAKISTAN

Series Guidebooks (See Appendix 1)

Insight Guide: Pakistan

Lonely Planet: Pakistan
Moon Handbook: Pakistan
Passport: Pakistan

Background Reading

Duncan, Emma
**BREAKING THE CURFEW: A
  POLITICAL JOURNEY
  THROUGH PAKISTAN**
"An exciting journey of political discovery
into the murkier side of Pakistani society
. . . good basic overview." (LJ) Viking,
1989.   ○

Khan, Imram
**INDUS JOURNEY: A PERSONAL
  VIEW OF PAKISTAN**
"Moving and evocative introduction to Pak-
istan and its people" with numerous color
photographs. The author traveled along the
Indus River from the Arabian Sea to the
Himalayas, recounting the history of Paki-
stan and recalling his childhood. (BL) Chatto
& Windus, 1991.   ○

Moorhouse, Geoffrey
TO THE FRONTIER
Account of a journey to Baluchistan, Lahore,
the Khyber Pass and the Afghan border by
a leading travel writer. "Wherever he went
he observed both visiting foreigners and the
local people . . . keenly, respectfully and
humorously." (PW) HR&W, 1985. *On the
Other Side* (1991) continues journey where
To the Frontier left off near the Pakistan
border.   ○

Naipaul, V.S.
AMONG THE BELIEVERS
See entry under Middle East/Islam. Pakistan
is one of the four Islamic countries the author explored.   ○

Reeves, Richard
A PASSAGE TO PESHAWAR
"Absorbingly describes [his] experiences
during a 1983 visit to Pakistan . . . the conflicts arising from the drive toward modern-
ization . . . and the Muslim fundamentalism
. . . their recent yen for TV and video
games." (PW) S&S, 1984.   ○

Suleri, Sara
MEATLESS DAYS
Autobiographical memoir of a professor of
English at Yale, weaving her personal and
family history with that of Pakistan. U of
Chicago Pr, 1989.   ○

Theroux, Paul and McCurry, Steve
THE IMPERIAL WAY
See under "India."   ○

GUIDEBOOKS

See also under India/Guidebooks.

Camerapix
SPECTRUM GUIDE TO PAKISTAN
Facts On File, 1989.   ○

HISTORY

Singhal, Damodar P.
PAKISTAN
History of the nation state, created in 1947.
P-H, 1972.   ○

Novels

Mojtabai, A.G.
A STOPPING PLACE
Novel of the "explosive . . . Moslem religious zealotry and ethnic power politics,"
with a plot that involves the disappearance
of a holy relic of the Prophet Muham-
mad. (FC) S&S, 1979. Also *Ordinary Time*
(1989).   ○

Rushdie, Salman
SHAME
By a Pakistani who is a Westerner by adop-
tion and choice; and "blessed with the gift
of authenticity . . . able to portray unfamiliar places and people with such clarity and
conviction, the reader knows he is in the
presence of truth." The novel is a "sort of
modern fairy tale . . . the link between certain bizarre happenings . . . and events in
a nation that is 'not quite Pakistan' is ines-
capable." (Publisher) Knopf, 1983. Also,
Midnight's Children, listed under India. ○

Sidhwa, Bapsi
THE BRIDE
Set at the time of India's partition. A widower adopts a girl who cannot accept the
harsh life of his ancestral tribe—"marriage,
loyalty, honor, and the conflict with old
ways in this well-told tale." (FC) St. Martin,
1983.   o

Zameenzad, Adam
THE 13TH HOUSE
A middle-aged clerk is beset by poverty and
problems when he meets a holy man who
seemingly offers hope and help. "Partly a
realistic description of the small and large
indignities of poverty . . . [also] ghost story,
nightmare, vision." (BRD) Random, 1989. o

THE PHILIPPINES

Series Guidebooks
(See Appendix 1)

Insight: Philippines
Lonely Planet: Philippines
Moon Handbook: Philippines
Nagel's Encyclopedia Guide: Philippines
Post Guide: Philippines

Background Reading

Bain, David H.
**SITTING IN DARKNESS:
    AMERICANS IN THE
    PHILIPPINES**
"Unique blend of history and adventure"
told through the exploits of U.S. General
Funston and Philippine rebel Aguinaldo, and
the volatile situation in the Philippines today. (BL) Houghton, 1984.   o

Gersi, Douchan
EXPLORER
By a documentary filmmaker—"incredible
adventures among primitive tribes of the
Philippines and Borneo." (LJ) St. Martin's,
1987.   o

Hamilton-Paterson, James
**PLAYING WITH WATER: PASSION
    AND SOLITUDE ON A
    PHILIPPINE ISLAND**
"Lyrical meditation on sea, sunlight . . .
analysis of consciousness." (NYT) New Amsterdam, 1989.   o

Johnson, Bryan
THE FOUR DAYS OF COURAGE
A correspondent for the *Toronto Globe* evokes
the celebration and optimism as the Philip-

pine people overthrow Marcos in 1986. Free
Pr, 1987.   o

Nance, John
THE GENTLE TASADAY
A journalist's story of the Stone Age people
in the rain forests of the Philippines. Nonpareil, 1988.   o

Romulo, Beth D.
**INSIDE THE PALACE: THE RISE
    AND FALL OF FERDINAND AND
    IMELDA MARCOS**
"Gossipy, meaty expose . . . contrasts the
glamorous life of the privileged few . . .
with the dire poverty of the Philippine people." (PW) Putnam, 1987.   o

HISTORY

Steinberg, David
**THE PHILIPPINES, A SINGULAR
    AND PLURAL PLACE**
Westview, 1982.   o

Novels

Hagedorn, Jessica
DOGEATERS
"A political fable of life in Marcos' Manila."
(BL) Pantheon, 1990.   o

Kluge, P.F.
MACARTHUR'S GHOST
A travel journalist on a press junket to Manila to cover the 40th anniversary of the
beginning of World War II is focus of a plot

that presents a portrait of life in Manila before the Marcoses fled. Arbor Hse, 1987.   ○

Nolledo, Wilfrido D.
BUT FOR THE LOVERS
The Philippines in World War II during the Japanese and American occupations—"personalities and events [merge] into one stunning nightmare." (BRD) Dutton, 1971.   ○

Thomas, Ross
ON THE RIM
A suddenly-fired expert on terrorism is offered a job as liaison between Philippine

guerillas and a shadowy group from Hong Kong—"spinetinglers don't come much better." (PW) Mysterious Pr, 1987.   ○

Ty-Casper, Linda
AWAITING TRESPASS
Manila 1981 is the setting at a time of terrorism and martial law. "Complex drama of a gathered family shares equal time with the political and religious mood of the Philippines in 1981." (BRD) Readers Int, 1985.   ○

SOUTH KOREA

*Series Guidebooks
(See Appendix 1)*

Fodor: Korea
Hildebrand: Korea
Insider's Guide: Korea
Insight Guide: Korea
Lonely Planet: Korea
Moon Handbook: South Korea
Passport: Korea
Times Travel Library: Seoul

Background Reading

Bird, Isabella
KOREA AND HER NEIGHBORS
Bird was one of those intrepid women who travelled in the 19th century, and this is her account of customs, daily life, politics and the Sino-Japanese War. C E Tuttle, 1986. ○

Hoare, James and Pares, Susan
KOREA: AN INTRODUCTION
Intended to whet the appetite of the general reader—geography, history, family relationships, culture, religion and contemporary issues. Routledge, 1988.   ○

Howe, Russel W.
**THE KOREANS: PASSION AND
   GRACE**
Primer—art, education, family, cuisine, religious beliefs, sports, etc.—on a country

that has changed from an agricultural economy to industrialized prosperity, yet manages to preserve many traditions. HarBraceJ, 1988.   ○

Kearney, Robert P.
**THE WARRIOR WORKER: THE
   CHALLENGE OF THE KOREAN
   WAY OF WORKING**
Story of Korea's economic success "both grand and troubling"—the author's view is that Korea's economic model is militaristic and that "Korea is, above all, a glimmering advertisement for the benefits of fascism." (NYT) H Holt, 1991.   ○

Shapiro, Michael
**THE SHADOW IN THE SUN: A
   KOREAN YEAR OF LOVE AND
   SORROW**
Political, social, and economic events that have made Korea the crucible it is today and a 1987 journal of events when the dictatorship was transformed into a budding democracy. Atl Monthly Pr, 1991.   ○

Stephens, Michael
**LOST IN SEOUL AND OTHER
   DISCOVERIES ON THE KOREAN
   PENINSULA**
Creative non-fiction—"beautiful, hilarious" chapters that touch on aspects of Korea and

Koreans based on the author's visit to his wife's family in the 1970s. (BL) Random, 1990. ○

Winchester, Simon
KOREA: A WALK THROUGH THE LAND OF MIRACLES
"Engaging, informed, often humorous distillation of . . . observations on the culture, people, language, economy, and politics." P-H, 1988. ○

GUIDEBOOKS

Kaplan, Frederic M. and others
THE KOREA GUIDEBOOK
HM, 1991. ○

HISTORY

Knox, Donald
THE KOREAN WAR: PUSAN TO CHOISIN
Oral history told by U.S. soldiers who fought in Korea. "This book is the war . . . no one who reads this book is likely to forget it." (NYT) HarBracJ, 1985. Also *The Korean War: Uncertain Victory* (1988). ○

Rees, Davis
A SHORT HISTORY OF MODERN KOREA
"Traces the restless march of events . . . highlights the cultural continuity . . . the endurance of the Korean nation." (Publisher) Hippocrene, 1988. ○

Yi, Ki-baek
A NEW HISTORY OF KOREA
"Spans Korean political, social, military, and cultural history to 1960." (LJ) Harvard U Pr, 1985. ○

Novels

Bond, Larry
RED PHOENIX
"Wonderfully entertaining," but probably an unlikely scenario since glasnost; of a chain reaction that results in the U.S. once again joining South Korea in a war against North Korea and the Soviet Union. (FC) Warner, 1989. ○

Brown, Diana
THE BLUE DRAGON
A missionary in Korea in the 1890s becomes involved in court intrigues and political events, and a relationship with an American adventurer. (FC) St. Martin's, 1988. ○

Buck, Pearl S.
THE LIVING REED
A family saga, the history of Korea through four generations from 1881 to the Korean War in 1952. Day, 1963. ○

Hooker, Richard
MASH
The beginning of the TV series on the Mobile Army Surgical Hospital unit in Korea that established Hawkeye, Trapper John, etc., in TV history. Morrow, 1968. ○

Shagan, Steve
THE CIRCLE
A Korean general's plan for oriental world supremacy by China, Japan and Korea —"non-stop . . . intrigue, betrayal" set in a half dozen countries. (FC) Morrow, 1982. ○

Wiley, Richard
FESTIVAL FOR THREE THOUSAND MAIDENS
"A Peace Corps volunteer coming of age and confronting an alien society in South Korea in 1967. The commentary is provided in the journal musings of an aging Korean whose observations of and reflections on this young foreigner reveal why it is that America both repels and enchants." (NYT) Dutton, 1992. ○

SRI LANKA
(Including the Maldives)

Series Guidebooks
(See Appendix 1)

Berlitz Travel Guide: Sri Lanka
Fodor: India, Nepal & Sri Lanka
Hildebrand: Sri Lanka
Insight Guide: Sri Lanka
Lonely Planet: The Maldives and the Isles of East Indian Ocean; Sri Lanka
Nagel's Encyclopedia Guide: Ceylon (Sri Lanka)
Post Guide: Sri Lanka

Background Reading

Gooneratne, Yasmine
RELATIVE MERITS
Personal memoir of an aristocratic Sri Lankan family over three generations, through the mix of ancient and modern social and cultural conditions. St. Martin, 1986.   ○

Heyerdahl, Thor
THE MALDIVE MYSTERY
By a noted writer on primitive sea travel, this is an account of his investigation into the artifacts of a lost early civilization of the Maldives, in the Indian Ocean, and the possible connection to pre-Viking tombs in Sweden. Harper, 1986.   ○

Palmer, Nigel and Page, Tim
SRI LANKA
Photographs and "enchanting essays . . . splendidly [capture] the spirit of this Garden of Eden"—history, daily life, sacred places, wildlife reserves of exotic birds and animals, folk tales and ancient customs. (PW) Thames & Hudson, 1984.   ○

HISTORY

De Silva, K.M.
A HISTORY OF SRI LANKA
U of California, 1981. Also, *Sri Lanka, a Survey* (1977).   ○

Novels

DeSilva, Colin
THE WINDS OF SINHALA
Portrays Ceylon's (Sri Lanka's) heroic age in the second century B.C. when Gamini was its warrior king. Doubleday, 1982.   ○

Hudson, Christopher
WHERE THE RAINBOW ENDS
Ceylon, and the world of rubber plantations, on the eve of Pearl Harbor as the Japanese, having overrun Hong Kong and Singapore, head toward the Island. Atheneum, 1987.   ○

Ondaatje, Michael
RUNNING IN THE FAMILY
The author departed for the West, and recently revisited Sri Lanka and the result is a "poet's nimble, impressionistic portrait of a social milieu." (BL) Norton, 1982.   ○

TAIWAN

Series Guidebooks
(See Appendix 1)

Hildebrand: Taiwan
Insight: Taiwan
Lonely Planet: Taiwan
Times Travel Library: Taipei

Background Reading

See also Background Reading under China.

Long, Simon
TAIWAN: CHINA'S LAST FRONTIER
How events in China affect demands for economic and political democracy. St. Martin, 1991.   ○

Wood, Christopher
TAIWAN
Viking, 1982.   ○

GUIDEBOOKS

Nerbonne, J.J.
**TAIWAN: GUIDE TO TAIPEI AND
ALL TAIWAN**
Heinemann, 1985.   ◦

HISTORY

Davidson, James W.
**THE ISLAND OF FORMOSA PAST
& PRESENT.**
Oxford U Pr, 1989.   ◦

Novels

Arnold, William
CHINA GATE
The Asian underworld and how a hard-working youth can, Horatio Alger style, rise in its hierarchy; set in Taiwan in the late 1950s—fascinating . . . gripping . . . disquieting.'' (Publisher) Villard, 1983.   ◦

THAILAND

*Series Guidebooks
(See Appendix 1)*

American Express Pocket Guide: Hong Kong, Singapore & Bangkok
Baedeker: Bangkok
Berlitz: Thailand
Cadogan: Thailand and Burma
Fodor: Thailand
Frommer: Thailand; Bangkok
Gault/Milau: Best of Thailand
Hildebrand: Thailand
Insider's Guide: Thailand
Insight Guide: Bangkok; Thailand
Lonely Planet: Thailand
Nagel's Encyclopedia Guide: Thailand
Nelles Guide: Thailand
Passport: Thailand
Post Guide: Thailand
2-22 Days Itinerary Planning Guide: Thailand

Background Reading

Blackwood, Sir Robert
THAILAND
A ''definitive work'' by one who worked and traveled in the country for over twenty years—''beautiful color photographs and splendid descriptions.'' (Publisher) Hippocreme, 1983.   ◦

Bristowe, W.S.
LOUIS AND THE KING OF SIAM
Louis was Anna's son (see Landon entry below), who visited the country between 1860 and 1910. This is an attempt to seek the truth about Louis' ''fabulous life.'' (BRD) Thai-Am, 1976.   ◦

Landon, Margaret D.
ANNA AND THE KING OF SIAM
Story on which the musical was based, of the Welsh widow, hired by the King of Siam in 1862 to teach his many children. Harper, 1944.   ◦

Lewis, Paul and Elaine
**PEOPLES OF THE GOLDEN
TRIANGLE**
Six culturally distinct people in Thailand, each struggling to maintain its own identity. Photos and text document their skills, houses, villages, arts and crafts. Thames Hudson, 1984.   ◦

Nicholl, Charles
**BORDERLINES: A JOURNEY IN
THAILAND AND BURMA**
See entry under Burma.   ◦

Smithies, Michael
OLD BANGKOK
Cultural traditions, canals and buildings that are still relatively unchanged in old Bangkok. Oxford U Pr, 1986.   ◦

Toth, Marian Davies
TALES FROM THAILAND: FOLKLORE, CULTURE AND HISTORY
C.E. Tuttle, 1983.   ○

GUIDEBOOKS

Hoskins, John
A GUIDE TO BANGKOK
Pacific Rim, 1987.   ○

Kaplan, Frederic, and others
THE THAILAND GUIDEBOOK
HM, 1992. Also, *The Four Dragons Guidebook* includes Thailand.   ○

Rutledge, Len
THAILAND
Maverick Guide to Thailand, typically comprehensive as are all of the Maverick Guides. Pelican, 1991.   ○

Stier, Wayne and Cavers, M.
WIDE EYES IN BURMA AND THAILAND—FINDING YOUR WAY
A travel guide "especially suited to the young, intrepid traveler." (BP) Meru Pub, 1983.   ○

HISTORY

See also Southeast Asia histories under "Asia/ Background Reading."

Sharp, Lauriston
BANG CHAN
"Jargon-free social history" of the change from an agrarian life to Westernized social customs—a rare look at a culture in transition. (BRD) Cornell U, 1978.   ○

Wyatt, David K.
THAILAND: A SHORT HISTORY
A new, one-volume history by a Cornell professor. Yale U Pr, 1984.   ○

Novels

Boulle, Pierre
THE BRIDGE OVER THE RIVER KWAI
The story on which the memorable movie was based. "A stirring and imaginative book . . . soaked in [Kipling] atmosphere . . . unforgettable character sketches." The plot concerns a Japanese prison camp during World War II and a "stiff-upper-lip" British officer who builds a bridge using prison labor. (FC) Vanguard Bks, 1954.   ○

Gilman, Dorothy
MRS. POLLIFAX AND THE GOLDEN TRIANGLE
While on a simple vacation with her husband, Emily's boss back at the C.I.A. receives a cryptic message from a Thai village, and she is contacted to pick up a significant package in that village. Doubleday, 1988. ○

TIBET
(Including Ladakh)

Series Guidebooks

Lonely Planet: Tibet
Passport: Tibet

Background Reading

Avedon, John F.
IN EXILE FROM THE LAND OF SNOWS
"The first full account of the Dalai Lama and Tibet since the Chinese conquest" is the subtitle. "Fascinating" account of the history of Tibet, its loss of freedom to China, and how Tibetan culture continues in exile. (BL) Knopf, 1984.   ○

Bernstein, Jeremy
IN THE HIMALAYAS: JOURNEYS THROUGH NEPAL, TIBET AND BHUTAN
See entry under India/The Mountain Kingdoms.   ○

Brignoli, Frank J. and Christine J.
TIBET'S FORBIDDEN CITY
Text and photos go behind Lhasa's walls—
"a reminder of how little Lhasa has changed
. . . how its timeless culture continues to
exist." (BL) Creative Focus, 1989.   ○

The Dalai Lama and Rowell, Galen
MY TIBET
Collaboration between a renowned photographer and the 14th Dalai Lama, winner of
the 1989 Nobel Prize for Peace—personal
views on peace, environment and his country. U of California Pr, 1990.   ○

David-Neel, Alexandra
MY JOURNEY TO LHASA
One of a series of books by a remarkable
Frenchwoman, the first white woman who
succeeded in entering the forbidden city,
and also a practicing Buddhist and lama.
Great Eastern, 1983 (first published 1927).
Also *Magic and Mystery in Tibet* (1932), *Ti-
betan Journey* (1936). There's also a recent
biography of David-Neel by Barbara M. and
Michael Foster, *Forbidden Journey* (1987).   ○

Fleming, Peter
BAYONETS TO LHASA
Story of a British expedition to Tibet's forbidden city in 1904, with a summary of later
developments that led to the Communist
invasion. Oxford U Pr, 1986 (first published
1961).   ○

Harrer, Heinrich
RETURN TO TIBET
The author wanted to spend the rest of his
life in Tibet but was forced to leave when
the Communists took over. This is about a
brief return to the country in 1982, reintro-
ducing some of the friends from *Seven Years
in Tibet* (1982). Schocken, 1985.   ○

Harvey, Andrew
A JOURNEY IN LADAKH
A travel odyssey to this remote area between
Kashmir and Tibet, as well as a spiritual
quest—written by an English poet and Shak-
espearian scholar. Houghton, 1983.   ○

Hopkirk, Peter
**TRESPASSERS ON THE ROOF OF
   THE WORLD**
An account of "an extraordinary contest that
spanned a century, as travellers from nine
different countries attempted to enter . . .
and be the first to penetrate Lhasa, its sacred
capital." A "poignant" story of a variety of
people with various motives—some never
returned. It ends with the invasion by the
Chinese Communists of "the world's last
stronghold of mystery and romance." (BRD)
J.P. Tarcher, 1983.   ○

Johnson, Russell and Moran, Kerry
**THE SACRED MOUNTAIN OF
   TIBET: ON PILGRIMAGE TO
   KAILAS**
"Part adventure story and part religious pil-
grimage" about the authors' expedition to
Mount Kailus, which has significance for
both Hindus and Buddhists. (BL) Traditions,
1989.   ○

Miller, Luree
**ON TOP OF THE WORLD: FIVE
   WOMEN EXPLORERS IN TIBET**
A travel narrative about five women of the
1800s who tackled Tibet, a closed country
with the highest mountains in the world.
Even by today's standards these women
could be called "intrepid"—as Victorian
women, truly remarkable. Included in the
book are Alexandra David-Neel, Fanny
Workman, Isabella Bird, Annie Taylor and
Nina Mazuchelli. Mountaineers, 1984.   ○

Norbu, T.J.
TIBET IS MY COUNTRY
The country's story, told by the elder brother
of the Dalai Lama, "as only a native-born
Tibetan could. . . . fact and fancy, truth and
myth, reality and imagination subtly intertwined." (BRD) Wisdom Pubs, 1986.   ○

Normanton, Simon
TIBET: A LOST CIVILIZATION
"Story of the unveiling and subsequent destruction of the old Tibet" following Chinese
occupation in the 1960s—"by turn delightful
and horrific" with remarkable and rare photos and a highly readable introduction to the
country. (PW) Viking, 1989.   ○

Trungpa, Chogyam
BORN IN TIBET
Autobiographical account of Tibetan Buddhism, monastery life, escape to India. Random, 1985.   ○

GUIDEBOOKS

Batchelor, Stephen
THE TIBET GUIDE
With a forward by the Dalai Lama—history, culture, food, how to get there, what to see. Wisdom Pubs, 1987.   ○

Booz, Elizabeth B.
TIBET
There's an introduction by David Bonavia on the takeover of Tibet by China—capsule of Tibetan history, culture, religion, along with touristic information on what to see, tips on customs and how to get the most out of a trip to Tibet, avoiding altitude sickness, sketches of religious art explaining symbols, restaurants, hotels. Passport Bks, 1987.   ○

HISTORY

Richardson, Hugh E.
TIBET AND ITS HISTORY
Revised edition of a history first published in 1962. Shambhala, 1986.   ○

Novels

Easterman, Daniel
THE NINTH BUDDHA
"A solid thriller . . . a man willing to risk all to regain his family"—set mainly in India, Tibet and Mongolia in 1921 when an intelligence officer's son is kidnapped and the search leads to a Tibetan monastery. (FC) Doubleday, 1989.   ○

Harvey, Andrew
ONE LAST MIRROR
By an Anglo-Indian don; a 70-year-old Sri Lankan woman takes in a bi-sexual Anglo-Indian student. HM, 1985. See entry above for *A Journey in Ladakh,* by this author.   ○

Hilton, James
LOST HORIZON
That classic story of adventure and fantasy—an airplane is forced down in Tibet, and its passengers become guests at a Tibetan lamasery—Shangri-La. Morrow, 1933.   ○

Hyde-Chambers, Frederick R.
LAMA: A NOVEL OF TIBET
Politics, the Tibetan and Buddhist philosophies, and the invasion of Tibet by China in the late 1950s. McGraw, 1985.   ○

IV.
THE PACIFIC
AND OCEANIA

Series Guidebooks
(See Appendix 1)

Fisher's World: Australia, New Zealand and South Pacific

Fodor: South Pacific

Frommer: South Pacific

Lonely Planet: Fiji; Micronesia; New Caledonia; Papua New Guinea; Rarotonga Cook Islands; Samoa; Solomon Islands; Tahiti & French Polynesia; Tonga

Moon Handbook: Fiji; Micronesia; South Pacific; Tahiti/Polynesia

Times Travel Library: Tahiti

Background Reading

Brower, Kenneth
MICRONESIA: THE LAND, THE PEOPLE, AND THE SEA

Reports on scenery, customs, languages, history, marine life, ruins of the islands of Micronesia, with maps and photos to help keep your bearings. Louisiana State U Pr, 1982.   ○

Brower, Kenneth
A SONG FOR SATAWAL

A magical passage to a faraway Eden—life and culture on the islands of Yap, Satawal and Palau, concentrating on three individuals who represent past and future. Har-Row, 1983.   ○

Ellison, Joseph W.
TUSITALA OF THE SOUTH SEAS

The story of Robert Louis Stevenson's life in the South Pacific ("Tusitala" means "teller of tales"). Hastings House, 1953.   ○

Freeman, Derek
MARGARET MEAD AND SAMOA

The subtitle, "the making and unmaking of an anthropological myth," indicates that this is a debunking of the anthropologist's landmark book, *Coming of Age in Samoa*. It disputes her scientific methods and presents the author's description of Samoan culture at the time Mead's work was published. Harvard U Pr, 1983.   ○

Kluge, P.F.
THE EDGE OF PARADISE:
AMERICA IN MICRONESIA

"A thoughtful journey through time and circumstances, and an evocative portrayal of a paradise lost." The author spent time in Micronesia as a member of the Peace Corps in the mid-60s; he returned some 20 years later to find that his "enchanted islands" had been turned into "a polluted 'U.S. territory in disguise.' " (BL) Random, 1991. ○

Malcomson, Scott L.
TUTURANI

Story of a six-month odyssey by the editor of *Village Voice*—"travel, adventure and politics blend in this involving, serendipitous journey." (PW) Poseidon Pr, 1990. ○

Martini, Frederic
EXPLORING TROPICAL ISLES AND SEAS

An introduction for the traveler and amateur naturalist. This is a combination of natural history text on the South Pacific, Hawaiian Islands and the Caribbean, for the nonspecialist, and a travel guide. P-H, 1984. ○

Michener, James A.
A RETURN TO PARADISE

Informal essays and stories telling readers what he thought about a given island, and then a fictional story reflecting what the island thought about itself. Fawcett, 1988 (first published 1951). Also *Rascals in Paradise* (1957). ○

Moorehead, Alan
THE FATAL IMPACT

The effects of Captain Cook's first three voyages on the native culture and wildlife— "scrupulously honest, yet colorful and very much alive." (BRD) HarRow, 1987. ○

Nelson, Theodora and Gross, Andrea
GOOD BOOKS FOR THE CURIOUS TRAVELER

See entry under Asia/Background Reading. Johnson Bks, 1989. ○

Stevenson, Robert Louis
IN THE SOUTH SEAS: THE MARQUESAS, PAUMOTU AND THE GILBERT ISLANDS

Reprint of a classic. Routledge, 1971. ○

Varawa, Joanna M.
CHANGES IN LATITUDE: AN UNCOMMON ANTHROPOLOGY

A California-born woman who is an environmentalist and anthropologist marries a Fiji fisherman half her age. Empathetic account of "this oddly archaic society and her relation to it . . . utterly disarming. It would make a remarkable movie." (PW) Atl Monthly Pr, 1989. ○

Wright, Ronald
ON FIJI ISLANDS

Vivid descriptions of the author's experiences traveling throughout the islands—"not just a travel book but a weaving of contemporary impressions with underlying history." (LJ) Viking, 1986. ○

PACIFIC VOYAGES

Buck, Peter H.
VIKINGS OF THE SUNRISE

By a scholar of Polynesian history, and descendant of a Maori mother—an account of a Stone Age people who crossed the Pacific and colonized its lands long before Columbus. Greenwood, 1985 (first published 1938). ○

Christian, Glynn
FRAGILE PARADISE: THE DISCOVERY OF FLETCHER CHRISTIAN, BOUNTY MUTINEER

By a descendant of Fletcher Christian, of the *Bounty* voyage—"the definitive biography" using family records—"an exciting bit of history interestingly researched." (BL) Little, 1982. ○

Daws, Gavin
A DREAM OF ISLANDS

"Voyages of self-discovery in the South Seas" is the subtitle of these biographical sketches of "five restless Victorians" in search of the "frontier between civilization and savagery—only to discover themselves." The five are authors Melville and Stevenson, missionary John Williams, political adventurer Walter M. Givson, and artist Paul Gauguin. (Publisher) Norton, 1980. ○

Heyerdahl, Thor
EASTER ISLAND: THE MYSTERY SOLVED
Account of author's return to Easter Island, and resumption of diggings and oral history research. Random, 1989. Also *Aku Aku*, published in 1958, which resulted from that earlier trip in 1950. ○

Heyerdahl, Thor
THE KON-TIKI EXPEDITION
A "log turned into literature" of the author's raft journey from Peru to Polynesia, following (by his theory) the journey taken by the Polynesians who first discovered and settled the islands. Rand, 1950. Also *Fatu Hiva* (1976). ○

Thomas, Stephen D.
THE LAST NAVIGATOR
"A story of travel and adventure . . . a splendid glimpse into an exotic society." The author set out to learn an ancient system of navigation from natives of the Carolines. (PW) Holt, 1987. ○

TAHITI

Gauguin, Paul
NOA NOA
The French artist's account of his desertion of Europe, and civilization, in 1891, and subsequent life in Tahiti. Archer, 1976 (first published 1920). See also *Moon and Sixpence* by Somerset Maugham under "Novels," below. ○

Howarth, David
TAHITI: A PARADISE LOST
Charts the decline of this island paradise through journals of 18th and 19th century visitors—Captains Cook and Bligh, Darwin, Melville, Robert Louis Stevenson, etc. Viking, 1983. ○

THE STONE AGE ISLAND—NEW GUINEA

Connolly, Bob and Anderson, Robin
FIRST CONTACT
Fifty-year-old photos and stills of film coverage on the first confrontation in the 1930s, when a team of Australians went into unexplored New Guinea; the authors tracked down survivors for a series of extraordinary interviews. Viking, 1987. ○

Cousteau, Jean-Michel and Richards, Mose
COUSTEAU'S PAPUA NEW GUINEA JOURNEY
Day-by-day account and magnificent photographs of a major expedition to Papua New Guinea and offshore islands— "an exciting, instructive re-creation of the journey-adventure." Abrams, 1989. ○

Schneebaum, Tobias
WHERE THE SPIRITS DWELL
An odyssey in the jungle of New Guinea. Grove, 1989. ○

GUIDEBOOKS

Jacobs, Charles and Babette
SOUTH PACIFIC TRAVEL DIGEST
Includes Oceania, Papua New Guinea, Australia and New Zealand. Historical and general background as well as much practical information on each area, including how to route a trip of your own; used by travel agents as a planning guide to this complex area of the world. Travel Digests, 1984. ○

HISTORY

Bellwood, Peter S.
THE POLYNESIANS: PREHISTORY OF AN ISLAND PEOPLE
Prehistory (to 1800 A.D.) of peoples, culture, geography of each island group, for the general reader and for those with an interest in archaeology, with a chapter on Easter Island. Thames Hudson, 1987. ○

Dodd, Edward
THE ISLAND WORLD OF POLYNESIA
The last of the Ring of Fire series, a multivolume cultural history of Polynesia: art, seafaring, the rape of Tahiti, pre-history to 1850, when a deluge of explorers, adventurers and missionaries descended upon Tahiti. Windmill, 1990. ○

Sahlins, Marshall
ISLANDS OF HISTORY
U. of Chicago Pr, 1987.   ○

Spate, O.H.K.
THE SPANISH LAKE
"Superb history of early European discovery and rivalry in Oceania and Australasia." (BRD) U of Minnesota, 1979.   ○

Novels

Astley, Thea
BEACHMASTERS
A revolution is launched against an island's French and British officials—"Third World setting and politics evoke comparisons to the work of V.S. Naipaul and Graham Greene." (BRD) Viking, 1986.   ○

Bagley, Desmond
NIGHT OF ERROR
"Tense, fast-paced romp" as two shiploads of men go after underwater treasure. (FC) St. Martin, 1987.   ○

Barber, Noel
THE OTHER SIDE OF PARADISE
Adventure and romance set in the 1930s. A British doctor falls in love with a grand-daughter of Paul Gauguin. Macmillan, 1987.   ○

Conrad, Joseph
VICTORY
A Swedish nobleman rescues a traveling girl musician resulting in "exciting and tragic happenings." (BRD) State Mutual, 1982 (first published 1915).   ○

Conran, Shirley
SAVAGES
The wives of five mining executives have to survive in the jungle when their husbands are murdered—"horror-struck fascination that makes this tall tale an entertaining page turner." (FC) S&S, 1987.   ○

Day, A. Grove and Stroven, Carl
BEST SOUTH SEA STORIES
Anthology of 15 varied and fresh selections from writers such as Michener, Maugham,

Jack London, with biographical sketches of the authors. Mutual Pub 1985.   ○

Jay, G. Charlotte
BEAT NOT THE BONES (Papua New Guinea)
A mystery classic with "authentic horror and atmosphere—beautifully deft plot [and] subtle picture of the interaction of an 'advanced' and a primitive race." (BRD) Har-Row, 1952.   ○

Jay, G. Charlotte
VOICE OF THE CRAB (Papua New Guinea)
A thriller set on Kipi Island, involving "a disparate bunch of white settlers [and] natives . . . spoiled by well-meaning meddlers." (BRD) Har-Row, 1974.   ○

London, Jack
SOUTH SEA TALES (Solomon Islands)
Eight stories about pearl divers, missionaries, cannibals—the inevitable white man in a land whose law, says the author, is "eat or be eaten." (BRD) Macmillan, 1911.   ○

McCullough, Colleen
AN INDECENT OBSESSION
By the author of the hugely successful *Thorn Birds* (see "Australia/Novels"), this novel takes place at the close of World War II and its plot revolves about a mental ward and its nurse, Sister Honor Langtry. Har-Row, 1981.   ○

Maugham, W. Somerset
THE MOON AND SIXPENCE (Tahiti)
Story of a European artist who deserts his family to live in Tahiti dedicated to his art—based on the life of Gauguin. Ayer, 1977 (first published 1919).   ○

Maugham, W. Somerset
TREMBLING OF A LEAF
Six short stories of the South Sea islands, about the effects of "the indolent enervation of life of the islands" on men from colder

climes. First published in 1921. Mutual Pub, 1985.   o

Melville, Herman
TYPEE and OMOO
Classic novels "recording the adventures of a whaling voyage in the Pacific. . . . give a vivid picture of a civilized man in contact with the exotic dreamlike life of the tropics." (FC) Northwestern U, 1968 (first published 1846–47).   o

Michener, James A.
TALES OF THE SOUTH PACIFIC
Stories of World War II in the South Pacific, some of which were the basis for the musical *South Pacific*. Fawcett, 1978 (first published 1947). See also *A Return to Paradise* under Background Reading, above.   o

Nordhoff, Charles and Hall, James N.
THE BOUNTY TRILOGY
Based on the true story of mutiny of English sailors against Captain Bligh of the ship *Bounty* and the settlement by the mutineers of Pitcairn Island. The three individual books are *Mutiny on the Bounty* (1932), *Men Against the Sea* (1934), and *Pitcairn's Island* (1934). (*Men Against the Sea* tells of Captain Bligh and those loyal to him who sailed 3,600 miles in an open boat, following the mutiny, to reach the East Indies.) Little, 1946 (first published 1932–34).   o

Nordhoff, Charles and Hall, James N.
THE HURRICANE (Polynesia)
Polynesian life from the point of view of a French medical officer. The climax is a hur-

ricane—"description of the hurricane is a masterpiece." (BRD) Little, 1936.   o

Saxton, Mark
THE ISLAR; TWO KINGDOMS; HAVOC IN ISLANDIA
A trilogy of novels set on a wholly created, mythical island continent in the South Pacific, taking place prior to the year 1200. Houghton, 1982. Readers should first try to read *Islandia* by Austin Wright (see below), which began it all.   o

Warner, Sylvia Townsend
MR. FORTUNE'S MAGGOT
One of the novels in *Four in Hand*. A Pacific Island missionary decides that a white man's efforts there will hurt its natives rather than help. First published in 1927. Norton, 1986.   o

Wendt, Albert
THE BIRTH AND DEATH OF THE MIRACLE MAN
Short stories about the impact of the West on the islands of Samoa—"gentle but powerful tales . . . have the tone of timeless, and very savvy fables." (BRD) Viking, 1986.   o

Wright, Austin
ISLANDIA
Long novel of life on an imaginary South Pacific continent called Islandia, created by a law professor—"gentle philosophical novel . . . with [people] who come to life." (BRD) Ayer, 1971 (first published 1942). The Saxton trilogy, listed above, continues the story. o

AUSTRALIA

Series Guidebooks (See Appendix 1)

American Express Pocket Guide: Australia
Berlitz: Australia
Cadogan Guide: Australia
Fielding: Australia
Fisher's World: Australia, New Zealand & South Pacific

Fodor: Australia
Frommer: Australia ($-A-Day, Country & Touring); Sydney
Hildebrand: Australia
Insider's Guide: Australia
Insight Guide: Australia; Islands of Australia's Great Barrier Reef; Melbourne; Sydney

Lonely Planet: Australia
Post Guide: Australia
2-22 Days Itinerary Planning Guide:
   Australia

Background Reading

Abbey, Edward
SLUMGULLION STEW: AN
EDWARD ABBEY READER

Anthology of essays and novel excerpts covering "thirty years and thousands of miles of desert, canyon and river rapids [by] one of America's most articulate and engaging environmentalists . . . will delight his fans (while bedeviling his foes)." The book contains material on the Australian outback. Dutton, 1984.   ○

Alexander, Lamar
SIX MONTHS OFF

Humorous and pleasant memoir by the former governor of Tennessee (now secretary of education) who packed up his wife and four children and took off for six months in Australia with side trips elsewhere "to reconnect with his family." Morrow, 1988.   ○

Brewster, Barbara
DOWN UNDER ALL OVER: A LOVE
AFFAIR WITH AUSTRALIA

The author spent three years in Australia as a young woman and returned 20 years later with her husband. This is an account of their travels, "reveling in the joy and warmth of renewed friendships and revisited memories." (BL) Four Winds, 1991.   ○

Burt, Jocelyn
THE UNIQUE CONTINENT

Vegetation, wildlife, geography unique to Australia in text and photos, of 60 natural wonders—"sure to inspire even the most sedentary armchair traveler." (BL) Houghton, 1989.   ○

Chatwin, Bruce
THE SONGLINES

Two companions, traveling and talking together, "explore the hopes and dreams that animate both them and the people they encounter." "Songlines" (or Dreaming Tracks)

to the aborigines are the labyrinth of pathways travelled and marked by occasions of song, dance, marriage. "A narrative of mild adventure . . . novelistic dialogue . . . musings and observations." (BRD) Viking, 1987.   ○

Christmas, Linda
THE RIBBON AND THE RAGGED
SQUARE: AN AUSTRALIAN
JOURNEY

"Personal and impressionistic account" of a counter-clockwise journey around Australia ("the ribbon"), visiting cities, mining camps, ranches and talking with a variety of people about all sorts of topics. (LJ) Viking, 1986.   ○

Colebrook, Joan
A HOUSE OF TREES: MEMOIRS OF
AN AUSTRALIAN GIRLHOOD

Memoir of a Victorian family of pioneers at the turn of the century and their clinging to English proprieties. FS&G, 1987.   ○

Conrad, Peter
BEHIND THE MOUNTAIN:
RETURN TO TASMANIA

The author left for Oxford 20 years ago and this is an account of his rediscovery of his homeland—"powerful images of a remote, desolate, exotic land . . . wholly memorable." (PW) Poseidon, 1989.   ○

Finkelstein, Dave and London, Jack
GREATER NOWHERES: A
JOURNEY THROUGH THE
AUSTRALIAN BUSH

The authors alternate in writing the chapters of an eight-month jeep trip and encounters with aborigines, escapists, pioneers, hunters and more—"entertaining and well-written." (LJ) Harper, 1988.   ○

Flood, Josephine
ARCHAEOLOGY OF THE
DREAMTIME

"Dreamtime" symbolizes creation in the aborigine tradition. "Eye-opening portrait of past (and present) aboriginal life . . . how this culture adapted and flourished in the harsh Australian environment." (BL) U of Hawaii, 1983.   o

Horwitz, Tony
ONE FOR THE ROAD: HITCHHIKING THROUGH THE AUSTRALIAN OUTBACK
"As much a chronicle of the pubs along the way as of the scenery . . . delightfully wry style and an eye for absurdity." The author set out to hitchhike alone across the interior of Australia. (PW) Vintage Departures, 1988.   o

Hughes, Robert
THE FATAL SHORE
"Dense yet swiftly moving . . . aggressively engaging account" of the early settlement of Australia (1788–1868) by boatloads of prisoners from Great Britain and Ireland. (BL) Knopf, 1987.   o

Irvine, Lucy
CASTAWAY
An account of the author's "treacherous one-year adventure on a desert island in the Torres Strait off the northernmost coast of Australia"—spent there as a result of answering a newspaper ad. (BL) Random, 1984.   o

Keneally, Thomas
OUTBACK
The celebrated Australian novelist writes of Australia's Northern Territory—the wide-open, magnificent part of the continent—history of its European settlement, geology, aborigine culture, life of the white population. Rand-McNally, 1984.   o

Keneally, Thomas, and others
AUSTRALIA: BEYOND THE DREAMTIME
"A spectacular threefold vision of Australia, the one book to read for a true appreciation of life on the Island Continent." (Publisher) Facts On File, 1989.   o

Marshall, Catherine and Daniell, Jo
THORNBIRD COUNTRY
A diary with snippets of history and legend, recording impressions of a three-month trip through Australia. Warner, 1983.   o

Moorhouse, Frank
AUSTRALIA
"Brilliant pieces, exchanging barbs, witticisms and stinging insights on the ways of people." (PW) Penguin, 1987.   o

Morgan, Sally
MY PLACE
Autobiography by a good storyteller with a great deal to say about Australia—"one very interesting society" as the author relates stories of her aboriginal roots. (BL) Holt, 1988.   o

Newby, Eric
THE LAST GRAIN RACE
By the prolific travel writer (see index for some of his works); this is an humorous "gritty" account of his apprentice seamanship, at age 18, in the Australian grain trade. Penguin, 1986.   o

Pierce, Peter
THE OXFORD LITERARY GUIDE TO AUSTRALIA
"Illustrated panorama of Australian literature . . . identifying every place that has some kind of literary significance . . . eminently readable." Oxford U Pr, 1988.   o

Pilger, John
A SECRET COUNTRY: THE HIDDEN AUSTRALIA
The author's premise is that Australia's popular image—koalas, "Crocodile Dundee," etc.—has a dark past of inhumanity to the aboriginal peoples, and a present that is a trans-national country dominated by Britain and America, thus facing a dismal future. Knopf, 1992.   o

Terrill, Ross
THE AUSTRALIANS
Geographical and psychological tour—"fascinating portrait . . . history and sociology . . . skillfully woven together." (PW) S&S, 1987.   o

Vandenbeld, John
NATURE OF AUSTRALIA: A PORTRAIT OF THE ISLAND CONTINENT

Based on the PBS television series and emphasizing land, climate, flora and fauna. Facts On File, 1989.   ○

GUIDEBOOKS

Bone, Robert W.
THE MAVERICK GUIDE TO AUSTRALIA

"Practical, extremely interesting, very specific, colorful, and spritely. . . . easy to use, easy to read." (ARBA) Pelican, 1989.   ○

Goodyear, Lauren and Skinner, Thalassa
AUSTRALIA: WHERE THE FUN IS

Divided into eight geographic areas, and providing comprehensive coverage of all aspects of travel. "Emphasis is on budget traveling, safety, and fun," and the author encourages exploration beyond the popular attractions. (LJ) Mustang, 1991.   ○

Odgers, Sally F.
TASMANIA, A GUIDE
Kangaroo Pr, 1989.   ○

Salem House, Editors of
EXPLORE AUSTRALIA: THE COMPLETE TOURING COMPANION

A complete guide for Americans for touring Australia by car, everything from maps and pre-planning to itinerary planning and how to handle actual driving and possible breakdowns. Salem Hse, 1989.   ○

Werchik, Ruth and Arne
THE GREAT BARRIER REEF—A GUIDE TO THE ISLANDS AND THE REEFS
Wide World, 1988.   ○

Wilson, Robert
THE BOOK OF AUSTRALIA

An encyclopedic guide, with maps and photographs, in gazetteer format. Lansdowne, 1983.   ○

HISTORY

Cameron, Roderick
AUSTRALIA: HISTORY AND HORIZONS

"Easy-to-read, skillful evocation" of Australian history by a traveler/writer, with emphasis on the "style and quality of life" in Australia from the late eighteenth through the nineteenth centuries. (LJ) Columbia U Pr, 1971.   ○

Carter, Paul
THE ROAD TO BOTANY BAY: AN EXPLORATION OF LANDSCAPE AND HISTORY

A bicentennial book on Australia's origins, discovery and settlement, from early journals, letters, and other writings and maps by emigrants, explorers, the military and convicts. Knopf, 1988.   ○

Novels

Anderson, Jessica
THE ONLY DAUGHTER

A family comedy—"of class and manners . . . descriptions of contemporary life in Sydney glitter and bustle . . . sun-drenched, vibrant harbor." (BRD) Viking, 1985. Also *Tirra Lirra by the River* (1984).   ○

Astley, Thea
TWO BY ASTLEY: THE ACOLYTE AND AKC

First published 1972 and 1974, respectively. "Quirky, strong-willed characters . . . lyrical sense of place." (FC) Putnam, 1988.   ○

Astley, Thea
REACHING TIN RIVER

Growing up in Australia—"eerie, hypnotic." (NYT) Putnam, 1990.   ○

Battle, Lois
THE PAST IS ANOTHER COUNTRY

Characters introduced in 1958 at age 12, as fellow students in a West Australia convent school, return to their roots in the 1980s. Viking, 1990.   ○

Carey, Peter
OSCAR AND LUCINDA
A Church of England minister defrocked for gambling meets an Australian who shares his vice. Harper, 1988. Also *Illywhacker*, which means a professional liar and scam artist—"a huge, funny, imaginative account of the life and loves of Herbert Badgery" (1985). ○

Cato, Nancy
THE HEART OF THE CONTINENT
Traces the lives of a mother and daughter who try to bring adequate medical care to the aborigines of Queensland. St. Martin's, 1989. Also *Forefathers* (1983). ○

Cleary, Jon
NOW AND THEN, AMEN
A nun is found murdered on the steps of a Sydney whorehouse—"urbane wit blunts the sting in this story." (FC) Morrow, 1989. Other police procedurals by this author include *Murder Song* (1990), *Babylon South* (1990), *Dragons At the Party* (1988) and *Helga's Web* (1970). *Sundowners* (n.d.), on which a popular movie was based about an Australian sheep drover's family, is also one of Mr. Cleary's books. ○

Drewe, Robert
THE BODYSURFERS
"Spare . . . sharp" character sketches in a dozen short stories of the beaches of Australia (and California). Harper., 1984. ○

Ekert-Rotholz, Alice
THE SIDNEY CIRCLE
Romance and intrigue as an English girl marries an Australian architect. Fromm, 1983. ○

Elliott, Sumner, L.
WAITING FOR CHILDHOOD
Seven children choose a variety of roles after the death of their parents—"enough romance and coincidence and wish fulfillment here to make an absorbing television series . . . difficult not to be captivated by the sheer literary virtuosity of it all." (FC) Har-per, 1987. Also *Careful, He Might Hear You* (1963). ○

Ferrars, E.X.
THE CRIME AND THE CRYSTAL
A retired botany professor from England vacationing with a former student in Australia becomes involved in a mystery when his host's new wife is accused of murder. Doubleday, 1985. ○

Franklin, Miles
MY BRILLIANT CAREER
A young Australian woman is rescued by her affluent grandmother from her dreary life in the Australian outback but, in the end, "chooses spiritual independence over physical comfort and emotional security." (FC) St. Martin, 1980 (first published 1901). *The End of My Career* is a sequel (published in 1946) in which the author relates how she came to write *My Brilliant Career*, and the reactions of those people depicted in it. ○

Franklin, Miles
UP THE COUNTRY: A SAGA OF PIONEERING DAYS
First published in 1928; tells the 19th-century story of three Australian families and individualism versus industrialism. Beaufort, 1987. ○

Green, Evan
ADAM'S EMPIRE
Saga of an orphan, an aboriginal and a German immigrant, set in opal mine country of the Australian outback. St. Martin's, 1987. ○

Grenville, Kate
JOAN MAKES HISTORY
A collection of heroines, all named Joan, and their vision of Australian history. British Am Pub, 1988. ○

Hall, Rodney
CAPTIVITY CAPTIVE
Three children were murdered on the Australian frontier in 1898, and this is a younger brother's fictional account of what happened

from a perspective of sixty years later. FS&G, 1988.   ○

Holt, Victoria
THE ROAD TO PARADISE ISLAND
The heroine discovers a diary, a map and a murdered namesake leading to an island off the coast of Australia. Doubleday, 1985. Also *The Pride of the Peacock,* a mystery set in the opal fields of Australia and England (1976), and *Shadow of the Lynx,* a gothic set in England and the Australian gold mines of the 1880s (1971).   ○

Jolley, Elizabeth
THE NEWSPAPER OF CLERMONT STREET
The "newspaper" is the weekly cleaning lady, the incidents she encounters amongst her employers and her ambitions to own a piece of land. Viking, 1987.   ○

Jolley, Elizabeth
THE SUGAR MOTHER
"Wonderfully engrossing" novel about a childless professor of English literature, and surrogate motherhood—"ends with entirely satisfying inconclusiveness on all fronts." (BRD) Har-Row, 1988.   ○

Keneally, Thomas
THE PLAYMAKER
Based on an incident in 1789 and a Restoration play using a cast of convicts. S&S, 1987. Also *Three Cheers for the Paraclete,* about conflict amongst the Catholic clergy (1969), and *The Chant of Jimmy Blacksmith* (1972).   ○

Koch, C.J.
THE DOUBLEMAN
Three young folk musicians of the 1960s from Tasmania and their rise to musical stardom in Sidney. McGraw, 1986. Also *The Year of Living Dangerously* (1979).   ○

Lansbury, Coral
THE GROTTO
Daughter of an English mother and Sicilian father grows to adulthood—begins in Sicily, ends in rural Australia and Sydney. Knopf, 1989.   ○

McCullough, Colleen
THE THORNBIRDS
The blockbuster novel of the Cleary clan in Australia, from 1915 to 1969—an old-fashioned family saga. Har-Row, 1977. Also *The Ladies of Missalonghi,* about the blossoming of a poor spinster in a small town in the Blue Mountains (1986).   ○

Malouf, David
HARLAND'S HALF ACRE
An "eccentric and solitary painter . . . obsessed with restoring to his kin acreage an ancestor gambled away." (FC) Knopf, 1984.   ○

Marshall, James V.
WALKABOUT
A brother and sister (nine and thirteen years old) are the sole survivors of a plane crash in an uninhabited area of northern Australia. They set out to walk the 1,400 miles to Adelaide and are saved by a young aborigine on a "walkabout ordeal" that is part of his tribe's rites. The children manage to "bridge across the gap of more than a hundred thousand years that lies between the cultures that have produced them." Also a 1971 film. (BRD) Doubleday, 1961.   ○

Marshall, James V.
A WALK TO THE HILLS OF THE DREAMTIME
The adventures of two Japanese-aborigine orphans, raised in a Christian mission, who are stranded in a desert and decide to make the trek to the "hills of dreamtime"—the perfect land of the aborigines—and are finally rescued by a wandering tribe. Morrow, 1970.   ○

Masters, Olga
A LONG TIME DYING
"Quality of life in a dusty depression-era village in the Australian outback." (FC) Norton, 1989.   ○

Nordhoff, Charles and Hall, James N.
BOTANY BAY
The story of the Australian penal colony at Botany Bay and some of the English prisoners sent there. Little, 1941.   ○

Park, Ruth
MISSUS
The Darcy saga of Irish immigrants in Australia. A prequel to the author's *The Harp in the South* (1948) and *Poor Man's Orange* (1949). St. Martin's, 1987.   ○

Richardson, Henry H.
FORTUNES OF RICHARD MAHONEY
The overall title of a trilogy and Australian saga of Richard Mahoney. *Australian Felix* tells of his early years in Australia as a storekeeper in Ballarat during the gold rush days. He becomes a doctor, and in *The Way Home* leaves Australia for England, but realizes he is an "Australian" and returns to build *Ultima Thule* (title of the third book) to begin his medical practice all over again. It's a series "packed with woe" but an "unforgettable picture of the development of Australia." (BRD) Norton, 1929, 1930 (first published 1917).   ○

Shute, Nevil
THE LEGACY
This was published as *A Town Like Alice* in England, and therefore is the basis for the TV series made about a woman's return, after the war, to repay debts of gratitude that take her to Malaya and Australia. Morrow, 1950.   ○

Talbot, Michael
A WILFUL WOMAN
Chronicle of Australia's settlement, and sequel to *The Ends of the Earth* (1985). Knopf, 1989.   ○

West, Morris L.
CASSIDY
An unscrupulous politician, his labyrinth of deals and secrets that must be dealt with after his death by his son-in-law. Doubleday, 1986.   ○

White, Patrick
THE EYE OF THE STORM
The author is a leading Australian writer who won the Nobel Prize in literature in 1973. Viking, 1973. Other titles include: *The Tree of Man* (1955), *Voss* (1957), *Riders in the Chariot* (1961), *The Solid Mandala* (1966), *The Vivisector* (1970), *A Fringe of Leaves* (1977). ○

Wongar, B.
BABARU; THE TRACK TO BRALGU
Two books of short stories by an Australian aborigine. The stories deal with the "white man's devastation of Australian aboriginal culture . . . lethal conflict between a race that sees the earth as no more than a quarry and another and more ancient one to whom it is an extension of body, soul, and family." (FC) U of Illinois, 1982 and 1977.   ○

Wongar, B.
GABO DJARA
Last book of a trilogy about aborigines, told from the viewpoint of an immortal, giant green ant, who returns when white intruders plan to mine for uranium. In the process he encounters Queen Elizabeth, Ghengis Khan, the Australian parliament. First two titles in the trilogy are *Walg* (1983) and *Karan* (1985).   ○

Wood, Barbara
THE DREAMING: A NOVEL OF AUSTRALIA
In claiming her inheritance, a 19th-century woman travels to Australia and must confront the family's aboriginal past. Random, 1991.   ○

NEW ZEALAND

*Series Guidebooks
(See Appendix 1)*
Berlitz: New Zealand

Fisher's World: Australia, New Zealand & South Pacific
Fodor: New Zealand

Frommer: New Zealand ($-A-Day)
Hildebrand: New Zealand
Insight: New Zealand
Lonely Planet: New Zealand
Moon Handbook: New Zealand
Times Travel Library: New Zealand North;
  New Zealand South
2–22 Days Itinerary Planning Guide: New
  Zealand

Background Reading

Barker, Lady Mary Anne
STATION LIFE IN NEW ZEALAND

Reprint of an 1870s account of ranching life in frontier New Zealand. Beacon Pr, 1987.   ○

Barrow, Terence
**AN ILLUSTRATED GUIDE TO
  MAORI ART**

Guide to a unique art in the context of Maori culture. U of Hawaii Pr, 1984.   ○

Hanbury-Tenison, Robin
**FRAGILE EDEN: A RIDE THROUGH
  NEW ZEALAND**

A farmer-author-environmentalist who travels by horseback, with insights on environmental effects of farming. Salem Hse, 1989.   ○

Leland, Louis S., Jr.
KIWI-YANKEE DICTIONARY

Humorous introduction, in dictionary format, to New Zealand's slang and terms for various things. Pelican, 1984.   ○

Marsh, Ngaio
NEW ZEALAND

Reprint of a personal interpretation of the country written for young people, by the prolific writer of mysteries who was a New Zealander. Amereon, 1976 (first published 1942). Also, her autobiography *Black Beech and Honeydew* (1965).   ○

O'Biso, Carol
**FIRST LIGHT: A MAGICAL
  JOURNEY**

The author went to New Zealand to prepare a collection of Maori treasures for exhibition in the U.S.—"hilarious account . . . the setbacks, cultural clashes, and final insights." (Publisher) Paragon Hse, 1991.   ○

Pownall, Glen
UNIQUE NEW ZEALAND

Flora, fauna, Maori culture. Viking Sevenseas, 1980. Also *Maori Arts and Crafts* (1980) from the same author and publisher.   ○

GUIDEBOOKS

Bone, Robert W.
**THE MAVERICK GUIDE TO NEW
  ZEALAND**

A combination of lecture, gossip session and practical guidebook—where to go, what to see, hotels, food and shopping—"the best guide to New Zealand ever seen by this New Zealander." (LJ) Pelican, 1989.   ○

Shadbolt, Maurice
**READER'S DIGEST GUIDE TO NEW
  ZEALAND**

Basic travel data, in-depth background information in gazetteer's format, over 500 hundred color photos. Random, 1988.   ○

HISTORY

Oliver, W.H. and Williams, B.R.
**THE OXFORD HISTORY OF NEW
  ZEALAND**
Oxford U, 1981.   ○

Sinclair, K.
HISTORY OF NEW ZEALAND
Penguin, 1986.   ○

Novels

Ashton-Warner, Sylvia
GREENSTONE

Maori legend, history and tradition woven into the story of an English writer's family that includes a grandchild who is daughter of a Maori princess. S&S, 1966.   ○

Ashton-Warner, Sylvia
INCENSE TO IDOLS

"Portrait of a lost lady . . . who invades New Zealand and the orbits of several men." (BRD) S&S, 1960.   ○

Ashton-Warner, Sylvia
SPINSTER
A spinster schoolteacher's struggles to teach a group of seventy mostly Maori children in an outpost school—"funny . . . delightful . . . deeply poetic and strikingly apropos." (FC) S&S, 1959. Also, *Bell Call* (1964), in which an unconventional mother defies school authorities. ○

Goudge, Elizabeth
GREEN DOLPHIN STREET
Historical novel of frontier life in New Zealand in the nineteenth century. Coward, 1944. ○

Hulme, Keri
THE BONE PEOPLE
Provocative novel about Maori myth and Christian symbols, set on South Island. Louisiana State U, 1985. Also *Te Kaihau* (1983), a collection of stories about Maori culture. ○

Marsh, Ngaio
PHOTO FINISH
By the popular mystery writer—lively and amusing murder mystery of a temperamental opera singer in New Zealand. Little, 1980. Also *Colour Scheme* (1943), reprints of *Vintage Murder* (1937) and *Died in the Wool* (1945). ○

Shadbolt, Maurice
SEASON OF THE JEW
Te Kooti was the leader of a Maori revolt in the 1860s and whose followers considered themselves like Israelites in bondage. Norton, 1987. ○

Shadbolt, Maurice
STRANGERS AND JOURNEYS
A two-family saga—one a pioneer farm family, the other a Communist working class family—covers forty years in the lives of the two male protagonists just after World War I, and the social and political forces of the period—"enhanced by the authentic New Zealand setting." (BRD) St. Martin, 1972. Also *Lovelock Version* (1981), *Among the Cinders* (1965) and *The New Zealanders* (1961). ○

Sherwood, John
A BOTANIST AT BAY
Celia Grant is a botanist who solves crimes through her knowledge of vegetation; in this novel, she returns to New Zealand for the birth of a grandchild and becomes involved in a conservationist battle and a murder investigation. Scribner, 1985. ○

Sligo, John
FINAL THINGS
Three novellas, a "first novel" that won an award for the author. "Creates a rich and vibrant world peopled by old Maoris, provincial boors and Russian mystics." (NYT) Penguin, 1988. ○

Worboys, Anne
AURORA ROSE
Pioneers set sail for life in New Zealand in 1826. Dutton, 1988. ○

V.
EUROPE

Series Guidebooks
(See Appendix 1)

Birnbaum: Europe
Berlitz: Europe
Fielding: Budget Europe; Europe
Fisher's World: Europe
Fodor: Budget Europe; Europe's Great Cities; Great Trips Through Europe; Eastern Europe; Europe
Frommer: Europe ($-A-Day); Eastern Europe ($-A-Day)
Insight Guide: Continental Europe; Inland Waterways of Europe
Langenscheidt: Self-Guided European Cities
Let's Go: Europe; Eastern Europe
Lonely Planet: Eastern Europe
2–22 Days Itinerary Planning Guide: Europe

Background Reading

Barzini, Luigi
THE EUROPEANS
"Examines with great shrewdness and a delightful dry wit" why political unification of Europe has not happened—a character analysis of Britain, Germany, France, Italy, Holland. (BRD) S&S, 1983.   ○

Braganti, Nancy and Devine, Elizabeth
THE TRAVELER'S GUIDE TO EUROPEAN CUSTOMS AND MANNERS
Useful series to enlighten travelers to the truth that American social customs are not universal. S&S, 1984.   ○

Bryson, Bill
NEITHER HERE NOR THERE
"Splendidly provocative example" of the armchair travel genre. The author duplicates a backpacking trip he took 20 years ago, balancing "former impressions with fresh new observations" by blending accounts of the two journeys. (BL) Morrow, 1992.   ○

Butor, Michel
THE SPIRIT OF MEDITERRANEAN PLACES
Translated from the French. Includes, in Europe: Salonika, Delphi, Crete in Greece, Ferrara, Mantua in Italy, Cordoba in Spain. Marlboro Pr, 1987.   ○

Cather, Willa
WILLA CATHER IN EUROPE
Memoir of a trip she took in the early 1900s, her own story of her first journey. U of Nebr Pr, 1988.   ○

Cordell, Michael
RED EXPRESS
See entry under Asia.   ○

Enzensberger, Hans M.
**EUROPE, EUROPE: FORAYS INTO
A CONTINENT**
A disillusioned view of six countries by a
German essayist and poet (Hungary, Italy,
Poland, Portugal, Spain, Sweden). 1989. ○

Fermor, Patrick
A TIME OF GIFTS
Travel memoir of a walk, in 1933, from the
Netherlands to Istanbul by an author (only
18) "with the head of a classicist and the
heart of romantic . . . frequently hilarious."
His impressions give a unique view of Germany just before the Nazis took over; the
pre-Communist Hungarian and Rumanian
countryside. (BRD) Penguin, 1988. Also, *Between Woods and the Water: the Middle Danube
to the Iron Gates,* its sequel covering the second stage of his journey decades ago and
"recalled with splendid freshness." (BL)
(1986).   ○

Gill, Anton
**BERLIN TO BUCHAREST: TRAVELS
IN EASTERN EUROPE**
"Experiences and conversations" with citizens of Albania, Bulgaria, Czechoslovakia,
East Germany, Hungary, Poland, Romania
and Yugoslavia—"offers intriguing introduction to the history, politics and culture
of each country." (LJ) David & Charles,
1990.   ○

Glazebrook, Philip
JOURNEY TO KARS
This is the account of a trip by a novelist
who wanted to find out why earlier middle-
class Victorians left comfortable England to
travel in discomfort and danger to distant
lands. Therefore he, his wife and children
set out from Dorset, traveling via Yugoslavia, Greece and Turkey to the border of the
Soviet Union, returning via Bulgaria, Rumania and Hungary. He "succeeds in involving the reader with lands and people
perhaps more satisfying to read about than
to visit.[and] in bringing life to the familiar

sites of cathedrals, palaces, ruins, and museums . . . the book's combination of history and humor makes it ideal for browsing."
(PW) Atheneum, 1984.   ○

Hardyment, Christina
HEIDI'S ALP
A mother and her four daughters set out
from England to find locales of favorite heroes, heroines and authors of children's stories, e.g., Hans Brinker, Pied Piper,
Pinocchio, ending with Heidi's Alp—"down-
to-earth quandaries . . . magical moments."
(BL) Atl Monthly Pr, 1987.   ○

Hogarth, Paul
**THE MEDITERRANEAN SHORE:
TRAVELS IN LAWRENCE
DURRELL COUNTRY**
Durrell's writings and settings illustrated by
Hogarth watercolors. Viking, 1989.   ○

Holmes, Richard
**FOOTSTEPS: ADVENTURES OF A
ROMANTIC BIOGRAPHER**
A visit to the houses in which they so-
journed, tracing the landscapes traveled, for
Robert Louis Stevenson's *Travels With a Don-
key,* Mary Wolstonecraft and Paris during
the French Revolution, Percy and Mary
Shelley in Italy, Gerard de Verval. Viking,
1985.   ○

Hutchison, Robert
DANGER—HEAVY GOODS
"Truckers race the devil and the clock on
the toughest, most dangerous road in the
world." This is about the ultimate truck route
between Europe and the Middle East. The
author describes his trip with truckers from
England to Saudi Arabia through Belgium,
Czechoslovakia, Germany, Greece and
Hungary in Europe, and Iraq and Turkey in
the Middle East—"does a superb job of re-
creating the milieu . . . difficult to put
down." (PW) Morrow, 1988.   ○

Huxley, Aldous
ALONG THE ROAD
A reissue of Huxley's travel essays on Europe. First published in 1925. Ecco Pr,
1989.   ○

Kramer, Jane
EUROPEANS
Thirty articles that originally appeared in *The New Yorker*—"superior reportage" of individuals and events and what they reveal about a particular country. (BL) FS&G, 1988.   ○

Laufer, Peter
IRON CURTAIN RISING
A journalist visits countries of Eastern Europe following the fall of the Berlin Wall—"a personal journey through the changing landscape of Eastern Europe . . . anecdotes humanize issues . . . readable, entertaining, enlightening." (BL) Mercury, 1991.   ○

Lewis, Flora
EUROPE: A TAPESTRY OF NATIONS
A *New York Times* columnist's highly readable survey of modern Europe, with portraits of each country, its priorities, attitudes, flavor, combined with historical perspective and the role of each today. S&S, 1987.   ○

Magris, Claudio
DANUBE
"A multifaceted picture of the Danube's role and personality" in the formation of Western civilization—"essay of enthralling character and stylistic distinction" by an Italian cultural critic. (BL) FS&G, 1989.   ○

Miller, Stuart
PAINTED IN BLOOD
An analysis of Europe as a spiritual entity "contrasting it and European materialism with the American psyche and consumerism." (PW) Atheneum, 1987.   ○

Morris, Mary
WALL TO WALL: FROM BEIJING TO BERLIN BY RAIL
See entry under Asia.   ○

Morris, Wright
AN AMERICAN DREAMER IN EUROPE
Reprint of a book of the '30s—"recaptures his first trip to Europe during the depths of the depression . . . episodes and adventures . . . minutely detailed yet dreamlike, bizarre, compellingly readable." (PW) Penguin, 1984.   ○

Selby, Bettina
RIDING TO JERUSALEM
An account of a bicycle trip from London to Jerusalem following a route taken during the Crusades by medieval knights; combines history, sights and personal encounters—"A unique tapestry of spiritual reflection, adventure, and humor." (BL) Har-Row, 1986.   ○

Tanner, Marcus
TICKET TO LATVIA: JOURNEY FROM BERLIN TO THE BALTIC
Travel from Germany and Berlin to Prague, Cracow, Riga, Vilnius and Leningrad. HR&W, 1990.   ○

GUIDEBOOKS

Apple, R.W., Jr.
APPLE'S EUROPE: AN UNCOMMON GUIDE
Tribute by a *New York Times* correspondent who has traveled and lived in Europe. This is his tribute to his favorite places in fifteen countries; almost fifty essays with a decidedly opinionated viewpoint. Macmillan, 1987.   ○

Barber, Richard
THE PENGUIN GUIDE TO MEDIEVAL EUROPE
Organized around themes and topics, rather than geographically—the Papacy, pilgrimages, and so on. Introduces the great medieval religious and historic treasures and buildings in the larger context in which they were created. Penguin, 1984.   ○

Bassett, Richard
A GUIDE TO CENTRAL EUROPE
Guide to those regions that were part of the Hapsburg Empire in 1911—Austria, Czech-

oslovakia, Hungary, Rumania,Yugoslavia—
by a British journalist. Viking, 1987.   ○

Brunhouse, Jay
**ADVENTURING ON THE EURAIL
EXPRESS**
Rail tours for 18 European countries dis-
cussed in detail; a wealth of practical information for both experienced and
inexperienced train travelers. Pelican,
1989.   ○

Bryson, William
THE PALACE UNDER THE ALPS
Subtitle: And over 200 other unusual, unspoiled, and infrequently visited spots in 16
countries. "Features an outstanding castle
here, an odd but intriguing museum there,
a celebration, a lake" etc. (BL) Congdon &
Weed, 1985.   ○

Chandler, David
**BATTLES & BATTLESCENES OF
WORLD WAR II**
Macmillan, 1990.   ○

Eastman, John
**WHO LIVED WHERE IN EUROPE: A
BIOGRAPHICAL GUIDE TO
HOMES AND MUSEUMS**
Arranged alphabetically—residences or work
places of 300 authors, composers, artists,
statesmen and others, including fees and
hours if open to the public. Includes the
British Isles and East Germany. Facts On
File, 1985.   ○

Hobhouse, Penelope and Taylor,
    Patrick, eds.
THE GARDENS OF EUROPE
Seven hundred gardens described by specialists in the area where they are located:
the country's gardening history, maps, symbols for outstanding gardens and plant collections. Random, 1990.   ○

Johnson, Margaret M.
FESTIVAL EUROPE!
Fairs and celebrations throughout Europe.
Mustang, 1991.   ○

McQuown, Judith H.
KEEP ONE SUITCASE EMPTY
Shopping guides are generally not included
in this book, but a guide to factory outlets
in Europe seemed too good an idea to ex-
clude. Arbor Hse, 1987. There is also a separate factory outlet guide for the British
Isles.   ○

Manston, Peter B.
**MANSTON'S TRAVEL KEY
EUROPE**
A take-along guide—how to make a phone
call, do laundry, find a toilet, get around
easily, etc. Travel Keys, annual update.   ○

Meras, Phyllis
**EASTERN EUROPE: A TRAVELER'S
COMPANION**
"Provides hours of fascinating reading . . .
historical and cultural background . . . zesty
legend and myth" along with tourist information on what to expect in terms of lodging
and eating, and some suggestions for off-
the-beaten track adventures. Includes Bulgaria, Czechoslovakia, Germany, Hungary,
Poland and Romania. (BL) HM, 1991. Also,
The Mermaids of Chenonceaux (1952), European anecdotes.   ○

Murphy, Michael and Laura
**TRAVELER'S GUIDE TO OCEAN-
GOING FERRY LINES OF
EUROPE**
Volume 1: Southern Seas; Volume 2: North-
ern Seas. Hippocrene, 1986.   ○

Spring, Michael
GREAT EUROPEAN ITINERARIES
Everything you need to know to plan your
own memorable vacation, one region in each
of eight countries described for those who
want self-directed travel by car or public
transportation. Eating, shopping, where to
stay, special attractions, sources for additional information—"European vacations in
the style that Europeans would experience."
(LJ) Doubleday, 1987.   ○

Steves, Rick
**EUROPE THROUGH THE BACK
DOOR**
"Vital how-to's" for travel in Europe . . .
"sure to make you a seasoned traveler—on

your first trip"—to the less-traveled corners of Europe. For the independent traveler and the budget-minded, told with "wit and readability." John Muir, 1984.   o

Wignall, Harrison J.
IN MOZART'S FOOTSTEPS
A travel guide for music lovers. See full entry under Austria/Guidebooks.   o

Willes, Burl
UNDISCOVERED ISLANDS OF THE MEDITERRANEAN
John Muir, 1990.   o

RELIGIOUS TRAVEL GUIDES

Note: See also *Guide to Medieval Europe,* listed above, and *Riding to Jerusalem,* under Background Reading.

Gruber, Ruth
JEWISH HERITAGE TRAVEL
A guide to the Jewish past in Bulgaria, Czechoslovakia, Hungary, Poland, Romania and Yugoslavia. Wiley, 1992.   o

Higgins, Paul L.
PILGRIMAGES: A GUIDE TO THE HOLY PLACES OF EUROPE FOR TODAY'S TRAVELER
"Spiritual sites of Europe north of the Alps: ancient cathedrals, abbey ruins, burial grounds. Tips on how to reach these places (many are off the beaten track) and lodging." (PW) P-H, 1984.   o

Krinsky, Carol H.
SYNAGOGUES OF EUROPE: ARCHITECTURE, HISTORY, MEANING
Country-by-country survey and social/architectural history. MIT Pr, 1985.   o

McNaspy, C.J.
A GUIDE TO CHRISTIAN EUROPE
Loyola, 1984.   o

Pepper, Elizabeth
MAGICAL AND MYSTICAL SITES: EUROPE AND THE BRITISH ISLES
Delphi, Malta, Stonehenge, Granada and other sites reputed to have magical qualities. Har-Row, 1977.   o

ART, MUSIC, LITERATURE GUIDES

Berntein, Ken
MUSIC LOVER'S EUROPE
"For the traveler who is serious but not solemn about music . . . general tourist information with facts and lore about major festivals . . . places of historical interest." (LJ) Scribner, 1983.   o

Couch, John Philip
THE OPERA LOVER'S GUIDE TO EUROPE
Covers opera in Western Europe with occasional excursions into Hungary, describing the theaters, performance schedules, repertory, how to get tickets ahead or at the last minute, music festivals. An appendix with useful addresses is also included. Limelight, 1991.   o

Morton, Davis L.
TRAVELER'S GUIDE TO THE GREAT ART TREASURES OF EUROPE
Art, but also in churches, palaces, monasteries. G K Hall, 1987.   o

Nelson, Theodora and Gross, Andrea
GOOD BOOKS FOR THE CURIOUS TRAVELER: EUROPE
Lengthy reviews of books on topics ranging from archaeology and food to literature and nature. Johnson Bks, 1989.   o

Rabin, Carol Price
MUSIC FESTIVALS IN EUROPE AND BRITAIN
Comprehensive guide to 91 music festivals in 21 countries from the British Isles to Austria. Berkshire Traveller, 1984.   o

Steves, Rick and Openshaw, Gene
EUROPE 101: HISTORY, ART AND CULTURE FOR THE TRAVELER
An overview of 5,000 years of European culture, history, art "written in hip jargon," with appendices covering palaces, museums, festivals, ruins. (BL) John Muir, 1985.　　○

Steves, Rick and Openshaw, Gene
MONA WINKS: SELF-GUIDED TOURS OF EUROPE'S TOP MUSEUMS
Very down to earth—"unabashedly low-brow"—approach to getting the most out of visiting museums. The author says, "This book speaks your language—you're no art

historian, but hey, you're no dummy either!" John Muir, 1988.　　○

Zietz, Karyl
OPERA! THE GUIDE TO WESTERN EUROPE'S GREAT HOUSES
John Muir, 1991.　　○

HISTORY

Laquer, Walter
EUROPE IN OUR TIME: A HISTORY, 1945–1992
"Excellent and timely study of postwar Europe . . . clear and engaging writing style." (LJ) Viking, 1992.　　○

AUSTRIA

Series Guidebooks

(See Appendix 1)

Baedeker:　Vienna; Austria
Berlitz:　Tyrol
Blue Guide:　Austria
Exploring Rural Europe:　Austria
Fodor:　Austria; Vienna
Frommer:　Austria & Hungary
Insight Guide:　Austria; Vienna
Michelin:　Austria
2-22 Days Itinerary Planning Guide:　Germany, Austria & Switzerland
Visitor's Guide:　Austria, Tyrol

Background Books

Brook, Stephen
VANISHED EMPIRE
The three capital cities of the Hapsburg Empire (Vienna, Budapest, Prague) as seen today—"wonderful eye for those details that reveal the quirks, fissures and strengths of each nation's psyche." (PW) Morrow, 1990.　　○

Davenport, Marcia
MOZART
Reprint of a standard biography of the Austrian composer. Hippocrene, 1987.　　○

Gainham, Sarah
HABSBURG TWILIGHT
Eight essays by a novelist who knows Vienna well, describing life in late nineteenth-century Vienna. (See also her novels listed below.) Atheneum, 1979.　　○

Gallup, Stephen
A HISTORY OF THE SALZBURG FESTIVAL
Salem Hse, 1988.　　○

Gardiner, Muriel
CODE NAME "MARY"
Memoirs of an American woman in the Austrian underground in the years leading up to World War II. "An authentic heroine [who] does everything to convince you she is . . . ordinary"—she hid people, helped them escape, smuggled forged documents, and got out in June 1938 one step ahead of the Gestapo. (BRD) Yale U Pr, 1983.　　○

Hofmann, Paul
THE VIENNESE: SPLENDOR, TWILIGHT, AND EXILE

By a *New York Times* journalist who served as correspondent for Vienna—"penetrating, engaging, vivid cultural history" that also captures aspects of its darker side that was won over by Nazism. Doubleday, 1988. ○

Kallir, Jane
ARNOLD SCHOENBERG'S VIENNA

Fin-de-siècle Vienna of the early twentieth century—"describes the political, intellectual and artistic climate of the day [and a] discussion of Schoenberg's own creations." (PW) Rizzoli, 1985. ○

Lehmann, John and Bassett, Richard
VIENNA: A TRAVELLER'S COMPANION

One of a series that compiles excerpts from literature of the country—fiction, letters, memoirs, journals—to present a cultural overview. Extensive introductions by experts provide background history; will "captivate armchair travelers of a slightly bookish bent." Atheneum, 1988. ○

Morton, Frederic
THUNDER AT TWILIGHT: VIENNA 1913/1914

"An astonishing work of literary energy and historical insight . . . captures the elegant decadence" of the period preceeding Franz Ferdinand's assassination, which led to World War I. Macmillan, 1989. Also *A Nervous Splendor,* which centers around the suicides at Mayerling of Prince Rudolf and his mistress and offers anecdotal portraits of individuals, gossip, daily life (1979); and *The Forever Street,* under Novels, below. ○

Olsen, Donald J.
THE CITY AS A WORK OF ART: LONDON, PARIS, VIENNA

"Delightful and gripping, richly illustrated social history." (PW) Yale U Pr, 1988. ○

Spiel, Hilde
VIENNA'S GOLDEN AUTUMN

From the watershed year 1866 to Hitler's Anschluss. Grove-Weidenfeld, 1987. ○

GUIDEBOOKS

Endler, Franz
VIENNA: A GUIDE TO ITS MUSIC & MUSICIANS

Amadeus Oregon, 1989. ○

Hurdle, Jonathan
WALKING AUSTRIA'S ALPS HUT TO HUT

Eleven tours in 10 areas of Austria, ranging from four to 11 days with stopping overnight at huts or hostels. The tours are said to be easy enough for a beginner (but fit) walker, with sufficient information to evaluate the difficulty of the tour for yourself. The Mountaineers, 1988. ○

Kitfield, James and Walker, William
WHOLE EUROPE ESCAPE MANUAL: GERMANY, AUSTRIA, SWITZERLAND

Part of a series of guidebooks "designed to . . . put the fantasy and excitement back into travel." (Publisher) World Leis Corp, 1984. ○

Mehling, Franz N.
AUSTRIA; A PHAIDON CULTURAL GUIDE

Succinct appreciation of the best the country has to offer in terms of national treasures and culture—churches, palaces, theaters, museums, monuments, maps and plans—all arranged alphabetically and cross-indexed. Phaidon Pr., n.d. ○

Wignall, Harrison J.
IN MOZART'S FOOTSTEPS: A TRAVEL GUIDE FOR MUSIC LOVERS

A guide for following in Mozart's footsteps in Europe—Austria, Czechoslovakia, France, Germany, Italy, England. In all he toured nine countries and over 70 cities. Arranged alphabetically by country and city, listing churches and public buildings he visited, places where he lived or lodged, and palaces, salons and concert halls where he performed. Atl Monthly Pr, 1991. ○

HISTORY

Crankshaw, Edward
THE FALL OF THE HOUSE OF HABSBURG

The monarchy from 1848 to 1918—"brings the past alive . . . with unusual force and clarity." (BRD) Penguin, 1983 (first published 1963). ○

Novels

Appelfeld, Aron
BADENHEIM 1939

A novel of self-delusion as Jewish guests at a pleasure resort near Vienna refuse to worry even though this is 1939, with Nazis in control of Austria—"the most shocking thing . . . is not its satirical humor but its charm . . . [an] appalling theme with grace." (FC) Godine, 1980. Also, *The Age of Wonders* (1981) and *The Retreat* (1984). ○

Bernhard, Thomas
WOODCUTTERS

A novel in the form of "an extended interior monologue" as the writer-narrator relives the past two decades and his relationships to the people present at a literary dinner party—"a penetrating and satirical glimpse into contemporary Austrian society." (BRD) Knopf, 1988. ○

Bernstein, Marcelle
THE RUSSIAN BRIDE

Story of Salka, sent out of Russia by her parents to save her from an anti-Semitic pogrom, who lives as a poor relation in Germany until she meets a wealthy Viennese banker, marries him, and is brought into the family business—"believable characters and . . . careful attention to atmosphere and historical detail." (FC) S&S, 1987. ○

Drucker, Peter F.
THE LAST OF ALL POSSIBLE WORLDS

The financial and romantic intrigues of three wealthy partners in a fictional banking firm; Austria and London in 1906. Har-Row, 1982. ○

Gainham, Sarah
NIGHT FALLS ON THE CITY

This is the first of a trilogy that tells of a prominent actress, and her world in Vienna, beginning with the war years 1938–45. HR&W, 1967. Following is *A Place in the Country* (1969), post World War II, and *Private Worlds* (1971), the final volume, which takes the plot to the 1950s. ○

Greene, Graham
THE THIRD MAN

The story *A Sense of Reality,* from this collection, was the basis for that marvelous movie *The Third Man,* about black marketeering, an amoral American (he's British in the book), and his longtime writer-friend in Vienna who tries to find out how he supposedly died. Viking, 1950. ○

Irving, John
SETTING FREE THE BEARS

In *3 by Irving,* a three-novel omnibus edition. The plot involves "a madcap scheme to liberate zoo animals, [a] balance between the humorous and the macabre." (FC) Random, 1969. ○

Jelinek, Elfriede
THE PIANO TEACHER

A "neurotic love triangle" involving a piano teacher at the Vienna Conservatory and her student—"some may find the ruthlessly unsentimental approach . . . image of Vienna as a bleak city . . . too much to take." (BRD) Weidenfeld, 1988. ○

MacInnes, Helen
THE SALZBURG CONNECTION

A chest, buried during World War II by the Nazis in an Austrian lake near Salzburg, is the focal point of the plot, with agents from Russia, Austria, Britain and America interested in its contents. HarBraceJ, 1968. Also *Prelude to Terror* (1978). ○

Meyer, Nicholas
THE SEVEN-PER-CENT SOLUTION

"Pastiche" is the term used to describe this detective story in which Sherlock Holmes and Sigmund Freud join forces to solve a criminal conspiracy—set in Vienna. Dutton, 1974. ○

Morton, Frederic
THE FOREVER STREET
Saga of a family dynasty, based on the author's memories of his family. It begins with the family's journey from Slovakia to Vienna in the nineteenth century and ends with their dispersal when the Nazis take over. The family (although "Jewish outsiders") prospers—"vividly realized, both in its . . . personal meanings and its social and cultural context." (FC) Doubleday, 1984. ○

Musil, Robert
THE MAN WITHOUT QUALITIES
Major Austrian fiction that was to be a four-volume novel but ended with the author's death in 1942 after only two. This first volume, complete in itself, is a panoramic study of upper class Viennese society on the eve of World War I. The second volume takes the plot to the point where the hero decides to leave Vienna. Coward, 1953–54. ○

Pryce-Jones, David
THE AFTERNOON SUN
Portrayal of three generations of a family beginning with Gustav, a German-Jewish orphan who achieves fame and money in Vienna in the early 1900s; his daughter who takes over the family company in 1919 and flees to England following the German takeover; and her son who returns to Vienna in 1940—"fine, disciplined, moving . . . unsentimental novel." (BRD) Weidenfeld, 1986. ○

Roth, Joseph
THE RADETSKY MARCH
A new translation of a novel written in 1932 traces the lives of three generations from 1859 to 1914. "Beautiful, elegiac novel [that] conveys the tenuousness with which the empire was held together: the many races, disparities . . . seemingly under the authority of a frail old man until World War I blows the illusion to shards." (PW) Overlook, 1984. ○

Schnitzler, Arthur
THE LITTLE COMEDY, AND OTHER STORIES
Stories set against the background of Vienna describing "with great charm the social and cultural atmosphere of Vienna before World War I." Several were made into a haunting series presented by PBS-TV, under the title "Tales of Love and Death." (FC) Ungar, 1977. ○

Stewart, Mary
AIRS ABOVE THE GROUND
An English lady veterinarian helps her husband solve a mystery involving "Lipizzan horses, a medieval Austrian castle, a circus, a murder, and a narcotics ring." (FC) Morrow, 1965. ○

Stone, Irving
THE PASSIONS OF THE WIND
Fictionalized story of Sigmund Freud's life from his twenty-sixth year and on through half a century. Doubleday, 1971. ○

BELGIUM AND LUXEMBOURG

*Series Guidebooks
(See Appendix 1)*

Baedeker: Brussels; Belgium & Luxembourg
Berlitz: Brussels
Blue Guide: Belgium & Luxembourg
Fielding: Benelux
Fodor: Belgium & Luxembourg

Frommer: Brussels; Belgium, Holland & Luxembourg
Michael's Guide: Brussels and Antwerp

Background Reading

Bailey, Anthony
REMBRANDT'S HOUSE
The artist's home (now a museum) is the takeoff point to tell the story of Rembrandt's

life as well as seventeenth-century life in general in and around Amsterdam. Houghton, 1978.   ○

Dolibois, John E.
PATTERN OF CIRCLES (Luxembourg)
An ambassador's story. Kent St U Pr, 1989.   ○

Fitzmaurice, John
THE POLITICS OF BELGIUM
Crisis and compromise in a plural society. St. Martin, 1983.   ○

Newcomer, James
THE GRAND DUCHY OF LUXEMBOURG
The evolution of its nationhood from 963 A.D. to 1983. U Pr of America, 1984.   ○

GUIDEBOOKS

Blyth, Derek
FLEMISH CITIES EXPLORED
Art, architecture and walks in each city—Antwerp, Bruges, Brussels, Ghent, Mechelen.   ○

Green, Kerry and Bythines, Peter
THE WHOLE EUROPE ESCAPE MANUAL: FRANCE, HOLLAND, BELGIUM WITH LUXEMBOURG
One of a series of guidebooks "designed to bring Europe to life and put the fantasy and excitement back into travel." (Publisher) World Leis Corp, 1984.   ○

MacDonald, Roger
OVER FROM DOVER: THE BBC BREAKAWAY CROSS CHANNEL GUIDE
Intl Spec Bk, 1987.   ○

Neuberg, Victor
A GUIDE TO THE WESTERN FRONT: A COMPANION FOR TRAVELERS
Penguin, 1989.   ○

Shilling, Marvina A.
UPDATE BELGIUM
Intercult Pr, 1989.   ○

HISTORY

Kossman, E.H.
THE LOW COUNTRIES, 1780–1940
Oxford U Pr, 1978.   ○

Novels

Brontë, Charlotte
THE PROFESSOR
This and *Villette* are set in Brussels and were written out of the author's own experiences as a teacher in Belgium. Penguin, 1980 (first published 1857, 1853 respectively).   ○

Claus, Hugo
THE SORROW OF BELGIUM
Coming-of-age novel, with 10-year-old Louis at the brink of World War II—"filters the gruesome historical record through his adolescent eyes . . . from rollicking realism to frightening symbolism and back again." (BL) Pantheon, 1990.   ○

Dunnett, Dorothy
NICCOLÒ RISING
"Strong characterization, subtle with . . . lively action and labyrinthine plot . . . evocation of a social and material scene that . . . compels belief"—the low countries in the 15th century is the setting for this first installment of a serial. (FC) Knopf, 1986.   ○

Johnson, Pamela H.
THE UNSPEAKABLE SKIPTON
A "swift-moving, witty, wicked comedy" of a self-exiled British novelist pursuing his writing in an attic in Bruges while also conniving to profit out of the British tourists. (FC) HarBraceJ, 1959. Also *The Holiday Friend* (1973).   ○

Plante, David
THE ACCIDENT
A novel "in the tradition of . . . the French existentialists"—a college student from New England spending his junior year abroad in Belgium and a fellow-American student, along with the daughter of an American businessman and her "slightly sinister" boyfriend, take a trip to Spain that results in tragedy. (FC) Ticknor & Fields, 1991.   ○

Sarton, May
THE BRIDGE OF YEARS
Chronicle of a Belgian family, 1919–40—"rich family life which remains serene even under the shadow of the impending . . . war." (FC) Norton, 1971.

Stone, Irving
LUST FOR LIFE
A novelization of artist Van Gogh's tortured life, ending with his suicide at age 37. Doubleday, 1954 (first published 1934).

BULGARIA

Series Guidebooks

Nagel's Encyclopedia Guide: Bulgaria

Background Reading

Gill, Anton
BERLIN TO BUCHAREST: TRAVELS IN EASTERN EUROPE
See entry under Europe/Background Reading.

Hall, Brian
STEALING FROM A DEEP PLACE: TRAVELS IN SOUTHEASTERN EUROPE (Bulgaria, Hungary, Romania)
Account of a sabbatical bike trip behind the then-Iron Curtain—"hints of ideological differences and social ramifications . . . the real joy of Hall's book is the infectious enthusiasm he has put into his adventures." (BL) Hill & Wang, 1988.

MacKendrick, Paul
THE DACIAN STONES SPEAK
Archaeology and history based on archaeological sites in the Roman province of Dacia, roughly Rumania/Bulgaria. U of NC Pr, 1975.

GUIDEBOOKS

Mihailov, Dimiter
BULGARIA
Past history, contemporary Bulgaria and eight itineraries to tour the country. Hippocrene Bks, 1990. Also *Sofia,* which has an overview and a half-dozen itineraries for seeing the city and its environs.

Ward, Philip
BULGARIA: A TRAVEL GUIDE
A quote from the Bulgarian newspaper *Sofia News* says: "The best book about Bulgaria in any language since the 1930s." Oleander, 1989.

HISTORY

Crampton, R.J.
A SHORT HISTORY OF MODERN BULGARIA
Cambridge U Pr, 1987.

Ristelhueber, Rene and Spector, S.P.
A HISTORY OF THE BALKAN PEOPLES
General historical information for the many nationalities of the Balkan peninsula—Greeks, Rumanians, Bulgarians, Albanians, Serbs, Turks, others. Irvington, 1978.

Novels

Littell, Robert
THE OCTOBER CIRCLE
A group of Bulgarian performers resist the invasion of Czechoslovakia. Houghton, 1976.

Talev, Dimitur
THE IRON CANDLESTICK
First of a trilogy and family saga beginning in the early nineteenth century and continuing to the early twentieth century. The second and third titles in the trilogy are *St. Elijah's Day* (1953) and *The Bells of Prespa* (1954). Twayne, 1952.

CZECHOSLOVAKIA

Series Guidebooks
(See Appendix 1)

Baedeker: Prague
Berlitz: Prague
Insight Guide: Prague
Nagel's Encyclopedia Guide:
Czechoslovakia
Real Guide: Czechoslovakia

Background Reading

Ash, Timothy G.
THE MAGIC LANTERN
The revolution of 1989 witnessed in
Prague, Berlin, Budapest, Warsaw. Random,
1990. ○

Bauer, Maria
BEYOND THE CHESTNUT TREES
The author returned to Prague after an absence of 40 years; she writes a nostalgic
memoir about the city between World War
I and II, and of contemporary Prague. Overlook Pr, 1984. ○

Brook, Stephen
VANISHED EMPIRE
The three capital cities of the Hapsburg Empire (Vienna, Budapest, Prague) as seen today—"wonderful eye for those details that
reveal the quirks, fissures and strengths of
each nation's psyche." (PW) Morrow,
1990. ○

Gill, Anton
BERLIN TO BUCHAREST: TRAVELS
IN EASTERN EUROPE
See entry under Europe/Background
Reading. ○

Havel, Vaclav
DISTURBING THE PEACE
"Mingling of autobiography . . . politics,
literature and theater" since the departure
of the communist-dominated government,
by then first president of a democratic
Czechoslovakia. (PW) Knopf, 1990. ○

Kavan, Rosemary
LOVE AND FREEDOM: MY
UNEXPECTED LIFE IN PRAGUE
The English-born wife of a Czech diplomat
tells the story of their life in Czechoslovakia
as she moves from faithful support of the
regime to disillusionment and involvement
in the 1960s underground. Hill & Wang,
1988. ○

Martin, Pat
CZECHOSLOVAK CULTURE:
RECIPES, HISTORY AND FOLK
ARTS
Penfield, n.d. ○

Zeman, Zbynek
THE MASARYKS: THE MAKING
OF CZECHOSLOVAKIA
A readable history and biography of the two
Masaryks, father and son. The father was
one of the Republic's founders; the son was
foreign minister after World War II until his
suicide (believed by many to have been his
murder, by the communists). Also *Prague
Spring* (1979). Har-Row, 1976. ○

GUIDEBOOKS

Haymon, Simon
GUIDE TO CZECHOSLOVAKIA
Hippocrene, 1991. Completely updated and
expanded, with comprehensive details for
the traveler including opportunities for hiking, canoeing, climbing and caving. ○

HISTORY

Korbel, Josef
TWENTIETH-CENTURY
CZECHOSLOVAKIA: THE
MEANING OF ITS HISTORY
Columbia U Pr, 1977. ○

Renner, Hans
HISTORY OF CZECHOSLOVAKIA
SINCE 1945
Routledge, 1989. ○

Novels

Aleichem, Sholem
MARIENBAD

A "mischievous comedy of gossip, jealousy and deceit" as some bored women amuse themselves at a spa while their husbands remain at work in Warsaw. (BRD) Putnam Pub Group, 1982.   o

Chatwin, Bruce
UTZ

Utz is a "nondescript little man" and a survivor. Part-Jewish, he's survived the Nazis and obsessively collects porcelain, which according to the political rules he must bequeath to the state. "What he does about that insult . . . becomes his own peculiar final solution." (BRD) Viking, 1989. Also *The Journey from Prague Street,* a sequel that takes the narrator, after World War II, to Germany, New York City, Cambridge (Massachusetts) and Bethlehem (Pennsylvania).   o

Gellhorn, Martha
A STRICKEN FIELD

Part of the Virago Modern Classics reprint series. The experiences of a woman war correspondent in Europe between the Munich Pact and the Czechoslovakian takeover by the Nazis, and the heartbreak of two German refugees caught up in it. Martha Gellhorn was a noted World War II correspondent, and this is a novelized version of some of what she saw. Penguin, 1986.   o

Gruša, Jiři
THE QUESTIONNAIRE, OR PRAYER FOR A TOWN AND A FRIEND

This novel was originally published in an underground edition (nineteen typed copies) resulting in the arrest of its author. It has been translated into "crisp and vivid English." The plot is about a man who applies for a job which, in Czechoslovakia, means filling out a questionnaire on himself, family, neighbors, and on and on—"a satirical view of the past and an oblique criticism of the present." (BRD) FS&G, 1982.   o

Herlin, Hans
SOLO RUN

When the Eastern bloc countries plan an emergency summit in Prague, the West German Intelligence recalls a retired agent because he once had an affair with a woman in the East German secretariat. "More contemplative than action-propelled." (LJ) Doubleday, 1983.   o

Hrabal, Bohumil
I SERVED THE KING OF ENGLAND

"Picaresque allegory" of 20th-century Czech history narrated by a waiter who rises to wealth during World War II under the Nazis, only to lose it all under communism. (BRD) HarBraceJ, 1989.   o

Klima, Ivan
MY FIRST LOVES

Four stories of adolescence, love, writing, politics—"haunting and disorienting." (BRD) Har-Row, 1988.   o

Kundera, Milan
THE JOKE

A college student, and prankster, is stigmatized for life for having written an irreverent postcard as a joke; many years later he seeks vengeance with another "joke" by seducing the wife of the Communist leader who turned him in to the Party. Har-Row, 1982 (first published 1969). Also *The Farewell Party* (1976), *Life Is Elsewhere* (1974) and *Laughable Loves* (1974).   o

Kundera, Milan
THE UNBEARABLE LIGHTNESS OF BEING

"Refreshingly readable and colloquial novel of ideas"—a successful surgeon, and "relentless womanizer" gets into conflict with the state, leaves for Switzerland and there sacrifices a promising career for his wife's sake. (FC) Har-Row, 1984.   o

McCrum, Robert
THE FABULOUS ENGLISHMAN

"Depicts the hopelessness of life . . . a novel of sad nostalgias." The Englishman has carried on a correspondence with a Czech bookseller since the Czech girl he loved was killed by the Soviets. He travels to meet his penpal and finds that the bookseller has died, and the correspondence maintained is part of an escape plan. (BRD) HM, 1985.   o

Roth, Philip
THE PRAGUE ORGY
Part of Roth's *Zuckerman Bound* trilogy—Zuckerman visits Czechoslovakia to rescue a manuscript. FS&G, 1985.   ○

Škvorecký, Josef
THE MIRACLE GAME
Twenty years of Czech political history culminating in the 1968 Prague Spring, and invasion by the Soviets. Knopf, 1991. Also *The Engineer of Human Souls* (1984) and *Miss Silver's Past* (1975).   ○

Škvorecký, Josef
THE END OF LIEUTENANT BORUVKA/RETURN OF LIEUTENANT BORUVKA
Detective stories by the noted Czech author set in Czechoslovakia. Norton, 1990/1991. Also in this genre, *Mournful Demeanor of Lieutenant Boruvka* (1987), *Sins for Father Knox* (1989).   ○

Škvorecký, Josef
THE SWELL SEASON
A trilogy published backwards, thus this novel is about Danny as a high school student in Czechoslovakia in 1967. He is 18 in *The Bass Saxophone* (1979); 20 in *The Cowards* (published in 1958)—"the fluctuating moods of adolescence" as they escape the political situation "in an underground cult of jazz." (BRD) L & O Dennys, 1982.   ○

Sovakova, Lidmilla
THE DROWNING OF A GOLDFISH
"Bittersweet look at the troubled post-World War II years" narrated by a young woman who moves from a bourgeois upbringing through the communist takeover and a marriage. (PW) Permanent Pr, 1990.   ○

Weil, Jiřl
LIFE WITH A STAR
A timid bank clerk records the humiliation of living as a Jew in Nazi-occupied Prague. FS&G, 1989.   ○

D E N M A R K
(Including Scandinavia)

Note: All asterisked entries (*) are for Scandinavia as a whole. Books listed under Denmark/Vikings, of course, are pertinent to the other Scandinavian countries, including Iceland.

Series Guidebooks
(See Appendix 1)

Baedeker: *Scandinavia; Copenhagen; Denmark
Berlitz: Copenhagen
Fielding: *Scandinavia
Fodor: *Scandinavia; *Scandinavian Cities
Frommer: *Scandinavia ($-A-Day); Copenhagen ($-A-Day)
Insight: Denmark
Nagel's Encyclopedia Guide: Denmark/Greenland
Real Guide: *Scandinavia

*2-22 Days Itinerary Planning Guide: Norway, Sweden & Denmark
Visitor's Guide: Denmark

Background Reading

Aistrup, I.
DENMARK—TOWN AND COUNTRY
Vanous, 1986.   ○

*Anderson, John C.
SCANDINAVIAN HUMOR & OTHER MYTHS
Har-Row, 1989.   ○

Eriksen, Peter and others
FUNEN—THE HEART OF DENMARK
Nordic Bks, 1980.   ○

*Fiske, Arland O.
THE SCANDINAVIAN HERITAGE
N Amer Heritage Pr, 1987. ◦

Gronlund, J.
THE DENMARK BOOK
Vanous, 1988. ◦

*Lunden, Rolf
DREISER LOOKS AT SCANDINAVIA
Coronet Bks, 1977. ◦

McCamant, Kathryn M. and Durrett, Charles R.
COHOUSING: A CONTEMPORARY APPROACH TO HOUSING OURSELVES
An account of Denmark's innovative approach to housing, which began a movement that has spread to California and New England. Habitat Pr, 1988. ◦

MacHaffie, Ingeborg and Nielsen, Margaret
OF DANISH WAYS
Part of a series, provides a panorama of the land and heritage of Denmark—history, customs, art, inventions, government, food, hospitality, more. B&N Bks, 1984. ◦

*Petrow, Richard
THE BITTER YEARS
The invasion and occupation of Denmark and Norway, from 1940 to 1945. Morrow, 1979. ◦

Thomas, John O.
THE GIANT KILLERS
The story of the Danish resistance movement, 1940–45—the Danes' communal and individual acts of resistance against their Nazi occupiers and the rescue of nearly all Danish Jews. Taplinger, 1976. ◦

*THE VIKINGS

*Jones, Gwyn
A HISTORY OF THE VIKINGS
History based on surviving documents and archaeological finds—"a vivid and living picture of the Viking adventure." (BRD) Oxford U Pr, 1984. ◦

*Wilson, David
THE VIKINGS AND THEIR ORIGINS
Thames Hudson, 1989. ◦

GUIDEBOOKS

*Cowie, Peter, ed.
SCANDINAVIAN GUIDE
NY Zoetrope, 1987. ◦

Ensig, Kirsten
YOUR COPENHAGEN GUIDE BOOK
Politiken, 1987. ◦

Melchior, Arne
THERE IS SOMETHING WONDERFUL IN THE STATE OF DENMARK
Lyle Stuart, 1987. ◦

HISTORY

*Derry, T.K.
A HISTORY OF SCANDINAVIA
U of Minnesota Pr, 1979. ◦

Jones, Glyn W.
DENMARK, A MODERN HISTORY
Routledge, 1986. ◦

Jacobsen, Helge S.
DENMARK, AN OUTLINE HISTORY
Nordic Bks, 1986. ◦

Lauring, Palle
A HISTORY OF THE KINGDOM OF DENMARK
Nordic Bks, 1986. ◦

Novels

Andersen Nexø, Martin
PELLE THE CONQUEROR
Pelle is introduced as he and his grandfather migrate to Denmark in this first book of a four-volume Danish classic. Fjord Pr, 1989. ◦

Bjarnhof, Karl
THE STARS GROW PALE

A young, near-blind boy must leave the security of home for a special institute for the blind in Copenhagen. In a sequel, *The Good Light* (1960), the story is continued, following the boy into adolescence, manhood, discovery of the arts, his first love affair, and acceptance of the total blindness he knows must eventually come. The setting is pre-World War I Denmark—an "autobiographical memoir within the framework of a novel. . . . A haunting and evocative reminiscence." (FC) Knopf, 1958.   ○

Brown, Cecil
THE LIFE AND LOVES OF MR. JIVEASS NIGGER

A first novel out of the black student movement of the '60s, first published in 1976. A black anti-hero in Copenhagen and his "affairs with Danish and American girls, raps and brawls . . . in Danish taverns." Reprinted as part of a new series of fiction and non-fiction by Afro-American writers. (Publisher) Ecco Pr, 1991.   ○

Canning, Victor
RAVEN'S WIND

Historical novel of the Danes' invasions of England; in this plot they capture an Englishman and take him back to Denmark as a slave. Morrow, 1983.   ○

Dinesen, Isak
WINTER'S TALES

Seven gothic short stories, most of which are set in the Danish landscape. Random, 1942.   ○

Kurtén, Björn
SINGLETUSK: A NOVEL OF THE ICE AGE

Sequel to *Dance of the Tiger* (1980). "Scandinavia of 35,000 years ago . . . an imaginative reconstruction of the meeting of Neanderthal and Cro-Magnon." (FC) Pantheon, 1986.   ○

Lofts, Norah
THE LOST QUEEN

Historical novel of the eighteenth century; the sister of George III is married off to the crown prince of Denmark. Doubleday, 1969.   ○

Peters, Elizabeth
THE COPENHAGEN CONNECTION

A romantic suspense novel in which the heroine takes the place of secretary to her favorite author, following an accident at Copenhagen's airport. Congdon & Lattes, 1982. Also *Street of the Five Moons* (1978).   ○

Stegner, Wallace
THE SPECTATOR BIRD

A man in 20th-century California recalls his "great adventure, a visit to Denmark . . . entangled with aristocrats of endless roots and alarming commitments" and contrasts it with his own life as an uncommitted spectator. U of Nebraska Pr, 1979.   ○

E N G L A N D
(Including Great Britain)

Note: All asterisked entries (*) indicate that "Britain" or "Great Britain" is stated or implied and therefore may contain material on Ireland, Scotland, and/or Wales in addition to England.

Series Guidebooks
(See Appendix 1)

American Express Pocket Guide: London
At Its Best Guide: *Britain; London

Baedeker: London; *Great Britain
Berlitz: *Britain; London; Oxford & Stratford
Birnbaum: *Great Britain
Blue Guide: England; London; Oxford & Cambridge; Channel Islands; Cathedrals & Abbeys of England/Wales; Churches & Chapels: Northern England; Churches & Chapels: Southern England
Crown Insider's Guide: *Britain
Exploring Rural Europe: England & Wales
Fielding: *United Kingdom
Fisher's World: *Britain; London
Fodor: *Great Britain; Pocket Guide to London; London; London Companion
Frommer: London (City, $-A-Day & Touring); England & Scotland; England ($-A-Day)
Gault/Milau: Best of London
Insight Guide: Channel Islands; *Great Britain; London; Oxford
Langenscheidt: Self-Guided England
Let's Go: *Britain & Ireland; London
Michael's Guide: London
Michelin: England, the West Country; *Great Britain; London
Nagel's Encyclopedia Guide: *Great Britain
2–22 Days Itinerary Planning Guide: *Great Britain
Visitor's Guide: Cornwall; Cotswolds; Devon; East Anglia; Guernsey, Alderney & Sark; Hampshire & the Isle of Wight; Jersey; Kent; Lake District; North York Moors; Northumbria; Peak District; Severn & Avon; Somerset & Dorset; Sussex; Yorkshire Dales

Background Reading

Bradford, Ernie
THE STORY OF THE MARY ROSE
History and salvage story of this ship destined to be a prime tourist attraction and a treasure of knowledge on Tudor life; the author "infuses his story with a wonderful sense of excitement." (BL) Norton, 1982.   ◦

Burke, John
LOOK BACK ON ENGLAND
"Fascinating and informative journey into England's past . . . that lives visibly in the architecture, countryside and villages . . . rather than by studying dates, battles, and cumbersome facts." (Publisher) Salem Hse, 1983.   ◦

Calder, Nigel
THE ENGLISH CHANNEL
The author uses ports and landmarks as a jump-off for a book about both coasts of the Channel. Touches on natural history, geography, sailing lore, shipwrecks, building the tunnel, English/French relations and much more, as his ketch traces a route from Ushant on the French coast along England's shoreline to the Scilly Isles. A unique travelogue by a learned writer. Viking, 1986. ◦

Chamberlin, Russell
THE ENGLISH CATHEDRAL
"Eminently approachable survey . . . gracefully presented . . . suitable for both travel-minded and art history-minded readers." Michael Joseph, 1987.   ◦

*Crookston, Peter, ed.
THE AGES OF BRITAIN
Nine authors guide us through British history—Stone Age through the Victorians, plus sections on daily life over the entire period by eight more experts. Illustrated gazetteer arranged by periods and types of objects, relevant museums and sights. St. Martin, 1983.   ◦

Daniell, Christopher
A TRAVELLER'S HISTORY OF ENGLAND
"A delightful source" for travelers who want a refresher course in English history, from hunter-gatherers to Margaret Thatcher's resignation; written by a British historian and archaeologist—"amazingly concise yet delivers a solid, comprehensive and entertaining overview." (LJ) Interlink Pub, 1991.   ◦

*Deighton, Len
BATTLE OF BRITAIN
Illustrated review of a pivotal battle of World War II; day-by-day account of the summer of 1940. Coward, 1980. Also *Fighter: The True Story of the Battle of Britain* (1978).   ◦

*Gelb, Norman
THE BRITISH: A PORTRAIT OF AN INDOMITABLE ISLAND PEOPLE
"Personal, informal definition of the British people . . . generally laudatory." Topics include the class society, sexuality and feminism, relations with America, royalty, how it is different from Scotland and Wales. (BL) Everett Hse, 1982.   ○

Hibbert, Christopher
THE ENGLISH: A SOCIAL HISTORY, 1066–1945
What they ate for dinner, worked at, amused themselves with—high to low social levels—history of daily life. (BL) Norton, 1987.   ○

Jones, Christopher
THE GREAT PALACE: THE STORY OF PARLIAMENT
Companion book to a BBC TV series—setting and history of the U.K.'s legislative body, traditions and operations. Parkwest, 1985.   ○

Kaplan, Philip and Smith, Rex
ONE LAST LOOK
An informal, anecdotal history of life at American air bases in East Anglia during World War II. Abbeville Pr, 1983.   ○

*Marwick, Arthur
BRITAIN IN OUR CENTURY: IMAGES AND CONTROVERSIES
"The flavor of each decade from 1900 to the present . . . succinct commentary"—how Britain has changed yet remains in many ways unchanged. (PW) Thames Hudson, 1985.   ○

*Morris, James
SPECTACLE OF EMPIRE
Overall title of a remarkable trilogy that is popular history, written by a renowned travel writer. Volume 1, *Heaven's Command: An Imperial Progress,* begins with Queen Victoria's accession to the throne in 1837 and ends with her Jubilee in 1897. Volume 2, *Pax Britannica, the Climax of an Empire,* is the British Empire in 1897, at its zenith. Volume 3, *Farewell the Trumpets: The Decline of an*

Empire, takes the reader on to Churchill's funeral in 1965. (BRD) Doubleday, 1982.   ○

*Norwich, John Julius, ed.
BRITAIN'S HERITAGE
Geology, geography, life-styles, cities, country houses, religion, arts, leisure and more—sumptuously illustrated. Continuum, 1983.   ○

*Sampson, Anthony
CHANGING ANATOMY OF BRITAIN
An update of Sampson's earlier work, *Anatomy of Britain*—a journalist's analysis of Britain. Random, 1984.   ○

Smith, Godfrey
THE ENGLISH COMPANION
Subtitle: An idiosyncratic guide to England and Englishness from A to Z. A "charming, witty, and lively companion to English life, letters, and history" arranged alphabetically. (LJ) Potter, 1985.   ○

TRAVELOGUES, SPECIAL PERSPECTIVES

Bailey, Anthony
ENGLAND, FIRST AND LAST
A sequel to *America, Lost and Found*—the author's homecoming in 1944 and on through his West African military service in 1952—"details and insights of adolescence and awakening in fading postwar Britain." (LJ) Viking, 1985.   ○

Chesshyre, Robert
THE RETURN OF THE NATIVE REPORTER
The author served in the United States as a reporter for *The Observer,* and these are his observations after returning to England. He blames 10 Downing Street for appalling conditions of crime, indifference of the rich to the poor, a continuing class system—"ruthlessly brutal, exceptionally well written." (BRD) Viking Penguin, 1988.   ○

Christmas, Linda
CHOPPING DOWN THE CHERRY TREES

Another portrait of Britain in the 1980s that is very anti-England. Viking Penguin, 1990. ◦

*Critchfield, Richard
AN AMERICAN LOOKS AT BRITAIN

Extended conversations between the author and 50 Britons, resulting from a trek through the country at the behest of *The Economist;* what makes contemporary Britain tick— "sympathetic . . . an absorbing read." (PW) Doubleday, 1990. ◦

*Fowles, John and others
BRITAIN: A WORLD BY ITSELF

For Anglophiles, a "banquet" of writing by eleven authors describing "country nooks and vistas special to each"—for example, Jan Morris on the Black Mountains in Wales, R. S. Thomas on Lleyn, John Fowles on Dorset. (PW) Little, 1984. Also, by Mr. Fowles, *A Short History of Lyme Regis* (1983), providing a portrait of this "home of notables and eccentrics." See also *The French Lieutenant's Woman* under "England/Novels" (Devon). ◦

*Frater, Alexander
STOPPING-TRAIN BRITAIN: A RAILWAY ODYSSEY

Originally a series of *Observer* articles—narrative of the author's "journeys on 10 small train lines [whose existence he says are in jeopardy] in rural England and Scotland . . . in crisp style they relate the landscapes and people the author encountered." (BL) Hodder & Stoughton, 1984. ◦

Hazleton, Lesley
ENGLAND, BLOODY ENGLAND: AN EXPATRIATE'S RETURN

Highly critical account of her country by an Englishwoman who admittedly never felt at home there—"perhaps unfairly harsh . . . will.be a dose of reality to those who worship at the *Brideshead Revisited* altar." (LJ) Atl Monthly Pr, 1990. ◦

*Morton, H.V.
MORTON'S BRITAIN

The "In Search of" series of travel guides, classics written in the 1920s and 1930s, have been culled for excerpts in this newer book, with updating editorial comments. Dodd, 1970. The originals from which the excerpts were taken—*In Search of England* (1927), *In Search of Ireland* (1931), *In Search of Scotland* (1930), *In Search of Wales* (1932)—have also been recently reissued (Dodd, 1984). ◦

*Theroux, Paul
THE KINGDOM BY THE SEA: A JOURNEY AROUND THE COAST OF BRITAIN

The author, who has lived part-time in Britain for years, writes of a three-month tour around its coast via foot, bus and train, "observing the British public on holiday. . . . merciless in his portrayal of the tawdry seaside resorts . . . apathy of people." His aim was to write a book on the British themselves like the ones Britons have been writing for years about every place else— Anglophiles be forewarned! (PW) Houghton, 1983. ◦

Waugh, Auberon
BRIDESHEAD BENIGHTED

Collection of articles from *Spectator* magazine on the "mores and morons" of modern Britain—"polished flights of waspish fancy" on subjects ranging from generation gaps and class war to the decline and fall of the country. (LJ) Little, 1986. ◦

THE ROYAL FAMILY

*Delderfield, Eric R.
KINGS AND QUEENS OF ENGLAND AND GREAT BRITAIN

Illustrated survey of the lines of succession since the ninth century—"packed with information . . . ideal one-stop reference . . . about the livees and careers of the monarchs of England and Great Britain." (Publisher) Facts On File, 1991. ◦

Edgar, Donald
PALACE

Subtitle: A fascinating behind-the-scenes look at how Buckingham Palace really works.

"Relates the history of the structure and its grounds . . . the queen's average working day . . . roles of functionaries. . . . uses the recent state visit of Queen Beatrix of the Netherlands as an example of how lavishly important guests are treated." Photographs and watercolors done especially for the book. (BL) Salem Hse, 1984.   o

Fraser, Antonia
WARRIOR QUEENS
Knopf, 1989.   o

Morton, Andrew
ROYALTY WATCHING
Officially part of the Fodor Guides series, the focus is to assist afficionados in encountering the family at business or play, and includes who lives where, where they shop, and so on. Fodor, 1987.   o

Packard, Jerrold M.
THE QUEEN AND HER COURT: A GUIDE TO THE BRITISH MONARCHY TODAY
"An excellent sorting out of the intricacies surrounding the functioning of the British crown." (BL) Scribner, 1981.   o

COUNTRY & VILLAGE ENGLAND

Bailey, Brian
THE ENGLISH VILLAGE GREEN
"A lovely look at the center of English village life . . . anecdotes . . . charming illustrations. . . . 600 of the most important and attractive village greens in all parts of England." (Publisher) Salem Hse, 1985. Also *Villages of England* (1984).   o

DuMaurier, Daphne
VANISHING CORNWALL
A new edition of a book first published in 1967, with new photos and an epilogue. "Celebrates the beauty and mourns lost elements of the Cornish countryside . . . stirring text that includes reminiscences, literary references, history and legends." (BL) Doubleday, 1981.   o

Girouard, Mark
LIFE IN THE ENGLISH COUNTRY HOUSE; A SOCIAL AND ARCHITECTURAL HISTORY
Houses as architectural digs. Yale U Pr, 1978. Also The *Victorian Country House* (1979).   o

Hill, Susan
THE MAGIC APPLE TREE: A COUNTRY YEAR
"Reflections on life in a country village" in Oxfordshire where the author, her husband and daughter moved into an eighteenth-century cottage—gardening, food, villagers, local church and festivals, and so on. (PW) HR&W, 1983.   o

Thompson, Flora
LARK RISE TO CANDLEFORD
An omnibus edition of the trilogy that includes *Lark Rise, Over to Candleford* and *Candleford Green*—life in a country hamlet and nearby market towns in the 1880s and 1890s. Penguin, 1983 (first published 1945).   o

Whiteman, Robin
THE ENGLISH LAKES
Text and photography that emphasizes literary places, history, customs and wonderful scenery. Grove Weidenfeld, 1989.   o

LITERARY & BOOK-RELATED GUIDES FOR TRAVELERS

*Adams, Robert M.
THE LAND AND THE LITERATURE OF ENGLAND: A HISTORICAL ACCOUNT
Retelling the "entire history of England (with side glances at Ireland, Scotland, and Wales) . . . to make clear . . . what was going on while all those plays, novels, essays and poems were being written." (BL) Norton, 1983.   o

Benningfield, Gordon
HARDY COUNTRY
Text and illustrations of the area indigenous to the Hardy classics—depicts England as it appeared to the novelist. (PW) Allen Lane, 1983.   o

Blythe, Ronald
DIVINE LANDSCAPES
"A series of meditations on sites associated with English mystical writers and visionary poets . . . The image of the parish priest carrying on his duties through centuries of English history binds the chapters together." (LJ) HarBraceJ, 1986. Also *Places: An Anthology of Britain* (1981), in which a number of authors (Bawden, Sillitoe, Pym, etc.) share their memories and views of favorite residences or scenic spots.   ○

Davis, Stephen M.
ROBIN HOOD'S ENGLAND
The historical Robin Hood and step-by-step tours of Nottingham and Sherwood Forest. Time Traveler Pr, 1991.   ○

*Drabble, Margaret
A WRITER'S BRITAIN: LANDSCAPES IN LITERATURE
A series of "quotation-studded essays about aspects of English landscape and writers who have responded to them." (LJ) Thames & Hudson, 1987.   ○

*Eagle, Dorothy and others
THE OXFORD ILLUSTRATED LITERARY GUIDE TO GREAT BRITAIN AND IRELAND
"Identifies the many towns, homes, lakes and other places associated with British and Irish writers." (BRD) Oxford U, 1992.   ○

Fisher, Lois H.
A LITERARY GAZETTEER OF ENGLAND
Reference work of literary associations (settings of novels, authors' birthplaces, etc.) for 1,200 English localities with associations to some 500 authors—"an almost overwhelming mass of detail [presented] in a clear, precise, and engaging fashion." (BL) McGraw, 1980.   ○

Graham, Winston
POLDARK'S CORNWALL
The author of the Poldark saga "describes how the novels came to be written and how the TV epic based on the saga came to be made . . . stunning array of photographs." (Publisher) Bodley Head, 1983.   ○

Hammer, David L.
FOR THE SAKE OF THE GAME: BEING A FURTHER TRAVEL GUIDE TO THE ENGLAND OF SHERLOCK HOLMES
Sequel to *The Game Is Afoot: A Travel Guide to the England of Sherlock Holmes* (1983). "New perambulations about the country, from London . . . to provincial cities and towns . . . in-depth coverage for the Holmes aficionado." (See also entries on Holmes under London, below.) (BL) Gasogene Pr, 1986.   ○

Herriot, James
THE BEST OF JAMES HERRIOT
Excerpts from the veterinarian author of books about Yorkshire, made into a widely popular PBS TV series; and *James Herriot's Yorkshire* (1979). St. Martin, 1983.   ○

Jackson-Stops, Gervase, ed.
WRITERS AT HOME: NATIONAL TRUST STUDIES
A dozen British authors' homes that are now literary properties of the National Trust—buildings, landscapes, anecdotes, lives of Kipling, Lawrence, Shaw, Hardy, etc. Facts On File, 1985.   ○

Keates, Jonathan
COMPANION GUIDE TO THE SHAKESPEARE COUNTRY
P-H, 1983.   ○

Lynch, Tony
DICKENS' ENGLAND
A gazetteer of real and imaginary places that figure in the life and novels of Charles Dickens. Facts On File, 1987.   ○

*Morley, Frank
LITERARY BRITAIN: A READER'S GUIDE TO ITS WRITERS AND LANDMARKS
"Journey through the literary highways and byways of England, Scotland and Wales in company with a remarkable and enthusiastic

bibliophile." The book has a unique format in that it is organized around six ancient roads out of London and back again (now main "A" highways). (Publisher) Har-Row, 1980. ○

Read, Miss (Doris Saint)
THE WORLD OF THRUSH GREEN
The author and artist John S. Goodall created 31 books together about a Cotswold Village. Here are photographs, paintings and text showing the real village (Wood Green) that was the inspiration for the series, along with character prototypes "dear to readers who have met them in Miss Read's sometimes funny, often poignant, always absorbing chronicles." (PW) HM, 1989. See under Novels/Gloucestershire. ○

Wechsler, Robert, ed.
**IN A FOG: THE HUMORIST'S
    GUIDE TO ENGLAND**
This is part of a new series of anthologies of humor about the foibles of travelers, and the countries they visit—anecdotes, poems, cartoons, by leading humorists. Catbird Pr, 1989. ○

STONEHENGE

Chippindale, Christopher
STONEHENGE COMPLETE
Cornell U Pr, 1987. ○

Fowles, John
THE ENIGMA OF STONEHENGE
With text by novelist John Fowles; covers the most credible of the myriad theories about Stonehenge. Summit Bks, 1980. ○

Hawkins, Gerald S.
STONEHENGE DECODED
A reprint, first published in 1965. Hippocrene, 1988. Also, *Beyond Stonehenge* (1973). ○

OXFORD

Conrad, Peter
**WHERE I FELL TO EARTH: A LIFE
    IN FOUR CITIES**
The four cities—Oxford, London, Lisbon and New York—provide a map for a memoir

evoking the settings "with particular distinction . . . a number of marvelous and disturbing images of the human condition." Poseidon, 1990. ○

Fothergill, John
AN INNKEEPER'S DIARY
Recollections—some hilarious—of guests at Spreadeagle Inn, in Oxford. Faber & Faber, 1988. ○

Morris, Jan
OXFORD
New revised edition of the book originally published in 1965—a comprehensive guide that is a "mixture of rhapsody and anecdote"—perfect preparatory reading for a visit. (BRD) Oxford U Pr, 1988. ○

Morris, Jan, ed.
THE OXFORD BOOK OF OXFORD
An anthology—traces the history of the university from its foundation in the Middle Ages through to 1945, combining extracts from contemporary observers with Jan Morris's own linking commentary." (BRD) Oxford U. Pr, 1978. ○

THE ISLANDS OF BRITAIN

Bailey, Anthony
SPRING JAUNTS
A series of jaunts, originally appearing as articles in *The New Yorker,* one of which is to the Isle of Wight—"a book to savour . . . wise, funny." (LJ) FS&G, 1986. ○

Gladwin, Mary Fane
**CHANNEL ISLAND HOPPING: A
    GUIDE FOR THE INDEPENDENT
    TRAVELLER**
Jersey, Guernsey, Alderney, Sark and Herm—history, accommodations, inter-island travel, etc. Hippocrene, 1984. ○

*ISLANDS OF THE WORLD SERIES
Individual books by various authors that emphasize history, culture, geography, climate, geology and wildlife of the various islands. Available in the series are Aran Islands (1973), Guernsey (1977), Bute (1973), Arran (1985), Isle of Wight (1979), Jersey

(1976), Kintyre (1974), Lundy (1984), Orkney (1985), Shetland (1984), the Uists and Barra (1974). David.   ○

GUIDEBOOKS TO INSPIRE AN ITINERARY OR EXPLORE A THEME

NOTE: See also guidebooks listed under London, below.   ○

*Adams, Richard
A BOOK OF BRITISH MUSIC FESTIVALS
Riverdale Co, 1986.   ○

Ashe, Geoffrey
THE LANDSCAPE OF KING ARTHUR
An itinerary-planning resource for Camelot-inspired touring. H Holt, 1988. Also *King Arthur, the Dream of a Golden Age* (1990).   ○

*Awdry, W. and Cook, Chris
A GUIDE TO THE STEAM RAILWAYS OF GREAT BRITAIN
Preserved and/or restored steam railway lines in Britain (a few in Ireland)—illustrated account for all train buffs—history, equipment in use, what the ride is like, etc. Michael Joseph, 1983.   ○

Bacon, David & Maslov, Norman
THE BEATLES' ENGLAND: THERE ARE PLACES I'LL REMEMBER
For Beatles fans—birthplaces, childhood homes, "landmarks identified in their works (Penny Lane, Albert Hall, the Abbey Road crosswalk)"—then and now. (BL) 910 Press, 1982.   ○

*Bence-Jones, Mark
THE NATIONAL TRUST GREAT ENGLISH HOMES OF ENGLAND AND WALES AND THE PEOPLE WHO LIVED IN THEM
"Anglophiles can explore the histories of 61 houses . . . all currently open to the public . . . profiled architecturally [and the] passage of lives under their roofs." (BL) Heritage, 1984.   ○

*Botting, Douglas
WILD BRITAIN: A TRAVELER'S AND NATURALIST'S GUIDE
Information to explore Britain's wild places, local phone numbers and addresses. Maps and photos, practical tourist information, where to get guides or detailed trail guides and Ordnance Survey maps, accommodations, making reservations, etc. Prentice Hall, 1989.   ○

Brereton, Peter
PETER BRERETON'S TOURING GUIDE TO ENGLISH VILLAGES
"A guide to the charming towns and villages of England . . . itineraries, historical details, information on where to eat and sleep." (BL) P-H, 1984.   ○

*Fedden, Robin & Joekes, Rosemary
THE NATIONAL TRUST GUIDE TO ENGLAND, WALES AND NORTHERN IRELAND
"National Trust properties that help to preserve Britain's heritage and history"—arranged by category (houses, gardens, archaeological sites, etc.). (BL) Norton, 1984.   ○

*Green, Kerry and Leocha, Charles
THE WHOLE EUROPE ESCAPE MANUAL: U.K./IRELAND
Part of a series of guidebooks "designed to . . . put the fantasy and excitement back into travel." World Leis Corp, 1985.   ○

*Hanson, Neil and Gilles, Andrea
THE BEST PUBS OF GREAT BRITAIN
The American version of the British *Good Beer Guide*. Traditional taverns that serve authentic English ale—over 5,000 pubs that meet CAMRA's (Campaign for Real Ale) standards for authenticity—are listed for England, Wales, Scotland, Northern Ireland, Channel Islands and the Isle of Man. Cartoons and comments add an entertaining touch. Globe Pequot, 1989.   ○

*Hudson, Kenneth and Nicholls, Ann

THE CAMBRIDGE GUIDE TO THE MUSEUMS OF BRITAIN AND IRELAND

Brief descriptions of 2,000 museums and galleries, from toys to theater, with practical tourist information. Cambridge U Pr, 1987. ⟳

*Jacobs, Michael

KNOPF TRAVELER'S GUIDE TO ART: GREAT BRITAIN & IRELAND

Suggested tours, routes, museums (including hours and fees and museum plans), guides to collections. The book is organized geographically by region, city and site, with an introduction to each. Knopf, 1984. ⟳

*Kinross, John

WALKING & EXPLORING THE BATTLEFIELDS OF BRITAIN

Guide to 65 battlefields that can be explored on foot, some famous, some little-known. The story of each, maps, photos and walking tours of various lengths described, how to get there, where to stay. Hunter Pub, 1989. ⟳

*Manston, Peter B.

MANSTON'S FLEA MARKETS OF BRITAIN, INCLUDING ANTIQUE FAIRS AND AUCTIONS

Travel Key, 1987. ⟳

*Mehling, Franz N.

GREAT BRITAIN & IRELAND: A PHAIDON CULTURAL GUIDE

Succinct appreciation of the best the country has to offer in terms of national treasures and culture—churches, palaces, theaters, museums, monuments, maps and plans, all arranged alphabetically and cross-indexed. Phaidon Pr. ⟳

*Rose, Graham and King, Peter

GOOD GARDENS GUIDE 1991

Over 1,000 of the best gardens open to the public in the British Isles. Trafalgar Sq, 1991. ⟳

Whitaker, Terence

HAUNTED ENGLAND: ROYAL SPIRITS, CASTLE GHOSTS, PHANTOM COACHES & WAILING GHOULS

The title tells it all. Contemporary Books, 1987. ⟳

*Wilkinson, Gerald

WOODLAND WALKS IN BRITAIN

Four hundred rambles, with maps and photographs for the walker (rather than the hiker.) HR&W, 1985. ⟳

*Winks, Robin W.

AN AMERICAN'S GUIDE TO BRITAIN

Second edition of one of the best books to read before you go, by a Yale history professor. A congenial and literate source for information, with the American traveler in mind. Scribner, 1987. ⟳

HISTORY

Briggs, Asa

A SOCIAL HISTORY OF ENGLAND

"Traces the evolution of English society . . . politics . . . literature and the arts . . . science and technology . . . balances a depth of detail and interpretation with an ability [to] isolate" major events and influences. (BL) Viking, 1984. ⟳

*Churchill, W.S.

A HISTORY OF THE ENGLISH-SPEAKING PEOPLES

Abridged edition. Bantam, 1976. ⟳

*Morgan, Kenneth O.

THE OXFORD ILLUSTRATED HISTORY OF BRITAIN

Oxford U, 1984. ⟳

Muir, Richard

TRAVELLER'S HISTORY OF BRITAIN AND IRELAND

Interlink Pub, 1990. ⟳

Trevelyan, G.M.

A SHORTENED HISTORY OF ENGLAND

Penguin, 1976. ⟳

Background Reading/ London

Hibbert, Christopher
LONDON: THE BIOGRAPHY OF A CITY
"A delight to read or merely to peruse" with photos and maps showing London's growth from a "walled city-port to the sprawl" of today—"a mine of information and . . . nostalgic reminiscence." (BRD) Penguin, 1983.   ○

Jones, Christopher
NO. 10 DOWNING STREET: THE STORY OF A HOUSE
"Glowing history of the house . . . a unique domestic slant to the political history of Britain." (BL) Salem Hse, 1986.   ○

Kiek, Jonathan
EVERYBODY'S HISTORIC LONDON
"Absorbing information . . . in very short space, it combines history of the British capital with advice on what sights to see . . . which pertain to each epoch covered." (BL) Salem Hse, 1985.   ○

Kramer, Jane
UNSETTLING EUROPE
Refugee families from Algeria, Uganda, Yugoslavia, living in France, London and Sweden, respectively, and an Italian Communist family in Italy—their isolation from traditions of those around them and the implications for Europe's future of these rootless people. Compelling reading. FS&G, 1989.   ○

Kureishi, Hanif
THE BUDDHA OF SUBURBIA
Asian immigrants living in London. Viking Penguin, 1990.   ○

Montgomery-Massingberd, Hugh
THE LONDON RITZ
A social and architectural history of the hotel, and the role it has played in London's history. Salem Hse, 1983.   ○

Morton, Brian N.
AMERICANS IN LONDON
Guide to residences and favorite haunts of illustrious Americans, from Abigail Adams and James Fenimore Cooper to Wallis Simpson and Joseph Kennedy. Morrow, 1986. ○

Olsen, Donald J.
THE CITY AS A WORK OF ART: LONDON, PARIS, VIENNA
"Delightful and gripping, richly illustrated social history." (PW) Yale U Pr, 1988.   ○

TRAVEL MEMOIRS & SPECIAL PERSPECTIVES/LONDON

Conrad, Peter
WHERE I FELL TO EARTH: A LIFE IN FOUR CITIES
See entry under England/Oxford, above. ○

Hanff, Helen
84 CHARING CROSS ROAD; THE DUCHESS OF BLOOMSBURY STREET
These are almost classics—delightful armchair travel reading. The first is correspondence between the author, a New Yorker, and a bookstore in London. As a result of publication of the letters, the author became something of a celebrity and was invited to visit the London she so yearned to see over the years, and the second book is an account of that visit. Avon, 1978.   ○

Pritchett, V.S.
LONDON PERCEIVED
A photo book, but one with superior text by a leading British critic and travel writer. HarBraceJ, 1966.   ○

Simon, Kate
LONDON PLACES AND PLEASURES
Out-of-date on practical information but a classic—highly descriptive, uncommon guidebook by a leading travel writer. Putnam, 1970.   ○

Woolf, Virginia
THE LONDON SCENE: FIVE ESSAYS

The subjects are Oxford Street, Westminster Abbey, the House of Commons, St. Paul's Cathedral and great men's houses—leading to views on less tangible subjects such as commerce, the perishability of human structures, the nature of democracy. Random, 1982. ○

LITERARY AND BOOK-RELATED BOOKS FOR TRAVELERS/LONDON

Ackroyd, Peter
DICKENS' LONDON: AN IMAGINATIVE VISION

The London Dickens knew—"an evocative guide." (BL) David & Charles Pubs, 1988. ○

Dale, Alzina S. and Hendershott, Barbara S.
MYSTERY READER'S WALKING GUIDE: LONDON

The actual mysteries, or private lives of their authors, are the focus of 11 walking tours. It is arranged by neighborhood, rather than by author, beginning and ending at a tube stop. Includes general tourist information and places to eat. Passport Bks, 1991. ○

Davies, Andrew
LITERARY LONDON

"Concise, chatty history" of London neighborhoods, fictional characters, in a series of essays. St. Martin, 1989. ○

Kobayashi, Tsukasa
SHERLOCK HOLMES'S LONDON

Follow in the footsteps of London's master detective. Chronicle Bks, 1989. ○

Miller, Luree
LITERARY VILLAGES OF LONDON

Describes the rich literary life of the city with portraits of writers associated with seven neighborhoods, evoking diverse worlds of Edith Wharton, I.B. Singer, Zora Neale Hurston, Auden, Millay, others. Starrhill, 1990. ○

Pease, Martha R.
THE BOOKSHOPS OF LONDON

A guide for bibliophiles. Salem Hse, 1985. ○

GUIDEBOOKS/LONDON

Banks, F.R.
THE NEW PENGUIN GUIDE TO LONDON

Won a prize as Guide Book of the Year—36 sightseeing routes via foot and bus, with maps and street plans. Penguin, 1984. ○

Danto, Eloise
THE UNDISCOVERED MUSEUMS OF LONDON

A travel guide to little-known and hard-to-find museums, galleries, churches, palaces. Eldan Pr, 1990. ○

Fido, Martin
MURDER GUIDE TO LONDON

Locations and backgrounds of noted murder trials from King James to the present, including a Jack the Ripper walking tour. Academy Chi Pubs, 1990. ○

Humleker, Ruth
LONDON FOR THE INDEPENDENT TRAVELER

A pocket-sized guide of over 100 walking tours arranged by themes such as art lovers, shoppers, royalty buffs. Planned, mapped, timed, with restaurants and pubs. Marlor Pr, 1987. ○

Jones, Edward and Woodward, Christopher
A GUIDE TO THE ARCHITECTURE OF LONDON

Van Nostrand, 1983. ○

Lawson, Andrew
DISCOVER UNEXPECTED LONDON

Recommended highly by London afficionados (such as John Bainbridge who writes the "London Journal" for *Gourmet* magazine). This is a reissue, with an introduction by Hugh Trevor-Roper to assist tourists in discovering London for themselves. Salem Hse, 1986.   o

Turner, Christopher
OUTER LONDON STEP BY STEP
Intended for absolute novices in London—take-along walking guide arranged logically to catch English life on the periphery of London, but reachable by public transportation. "Fully edifying but very easy to absorb on the run." (BL) Faber & Faber, 1986. Also in this series, *Windsor and Eton, Greenwich and East London, London Churches.*   o

Novels

NOTE: Appendix 3 has additional information for England/Novels.   o

LONDON

Ackroyd, Peter
HAWKSMOOR
A century-spanning mystery of contemporary murders at various 18th-century churches in London, involving the architect who built them. Har-Row, 1985.   o

Amis, Kingsley
DIFFICULTIES WITH GIRLS
The 1960s scene, chronicles the married life of the Standishes, whose courtship began in an earlier novel, *Take a Girl Like You* (1961). Summit, 1989. Also *The Riverside Villa Murders,* set in a prosperous London suburb in the 1930s (1973).   o

Amis, Martin
LONDON FIELDS
"Satirical portrait of present-day London life . . . packed with jokes too"—the plot concerns a woman (in 1999) who knows what will happen and knows she is to be murdered. (BRD) Harmony Bks, 1989. Also *Money,* about a British movie director obsessed with money whose personal and professional life is in turmoil—"exuberantly tuned to a contemporary beat" (1985); and *Success,* about competition between two brothers (1987).   o

Archer, Jeffrey
FIRST AMONG EQUALS
The careers of three people hoping to be prime minister, 1964–91—"manages the labyrinthine British Parliamentary system with an adroit hand and generates real suspense in the race." (FC) S&S, 1983.   o

Barnard, Robert
POLITICAL SUICIDE
"Funny . . . scathing look at politics as practiced today in England"— the plot is about the scramble of three candidates to fill the empty seat in Commons of a drowned M.P. (FC) Scribner, 1986. Also *Bodies* (1986) *A Scandal in Belgravia* (1991) and, set outside of London, *Death and the Chaste Apprentice* (1988).   o

Bermant, Chaim
THE HOUSE OF WOMEN
A family of rich, eccentric sisters, who must eventually confront their Jewish heritage— "entertaining saga of a unique British family." (FC) St. Martin, 1983. Also *The Diary of an Old Man* (1966) and *The Last Supper* (1975).   o

Bowen, Elizabeth
THE DEATH OF THE HEART
A "psychological study of a young girl . . . brought into conflict with the sophisticated futility of life in her half-brother's home in Regency Park." (FC) Knopf, 1939. Also *The Heat of the Day* (1949), set in wartime London.   o

Brookner, Anita
FAMILY AND FRIENDS
Saga of an Eastern European family in London between the wars. Pantheon, 1985. For Brookner enthusiasts, several novels have a London setting: *The Debut* (1981), *Look At Me* (1983), *Providence* (1984), *The Misalliance* (1986), *A Friend from England* (1987), *Latecomers* (1989), *Lewis Percy* (1990).   o

Butler, Gwendoline
ALBION WALK
"The sophisticated ambiance of chancy show business life is captured" in this novel—the

member of a theatrical family inherits a run-down theatre, restores it, and manages it for four decades. (FC) McCann, 1982. Also *Windsor Red* (1988).   ○

Cadell, Elizabeth
THE YELLOW BRICK ROAD
The heroine manages her sister's household and commutes to London as well, giving home beauty treatments, until one day she's found unconscious, which leads to adventure and romance—"essentially a mystery [but] . . . full of startling psychological insights." (FC) Morrow, 1960. Also *The Round Dozen*, suspense novel involving missing family treasure set in London and environs (1978).   ○

Campbell, Ramsey
ANCIENT IMAGES
"Guaranteed to furnish readers with the macabre joy of horrific dread" and a plot about a film editor who sets out to track down an unreleased Karloff/Lugosi film. (FC) Scribner, 1989.   ○

Cary, Joyce
THE HORSE'S MOUTH
Picaresque novel of painter Gully Jimson; last part of a trilogy beginning with *Herself Surprised* (1948) and *To Be a Pilgrim* (1949). Har-Row, 1950.   ○

Clark, Mary Higgins
THE ANASTASIA SYNDROME AND OTHER STORIES
The title story is of a woman historian's research into British history, which seems "mirrored in the present as a series of terrorist bombings . . . follow the historian's path around England." (FC) S&S, 1989. ○

Cooper, William
SCENES FROM PROVINCIAL LIFE AND SCENES FROM METROPOLITAN LIFE
One volume edition of two books first published separately in 1950 and 1982, respectively. (FC) Dutton, 1984. This is followed by *Scenes From Married Life and Scenes From Later Life* (1983), first published separately in 1961 and 1983, respectively. Collectively they

recount the life of Joe Lunn, science teacher in a small town, beginning in 1939, his move to London in 1946, becoming a novelist and civil servant, and on through thirty years of marriage and later life. "The atmosphere of the era is caught perfectly . . . the peculiar tensions and idiosyncrasies of London civil servantdom are remarkably rendered."   ○

Cronin, A.J.
THE CITADEL
"Moving and absorbing novel" that has been made into both a classic old movie and a British TV series presented on PBS. The plot is about a young doctor's career, from poverty in Wales to success in London. Little, 1937.   ○

Donleavy, J.P.
THE GINGER MAN
Picaresque novel that begins in Dublin, but is set partially in London. Delacorte Pr, 1965. Also *Schultz* (1979) and *Are You Listening, Rabbi Low?* (1988).   ○

Drabble, Margaret
THE MIDDLE GROUND
A journalist decides, in sorting out her life at 40, "to examine the paths taken by former schoolmates . . . London life in the 1970s, with traditional British values surviving amidst foreign immigration, terrorism and inflation." (FC) Knopf, 1980. Also, *The Needle's Eye* (1972), *Jerusalem the Golden* (1967) and *The Waterfall* (1969).   ○

Duffy, Maureen
CAPITAL: A FICTION
A history professor and an oddball student who audits his course give a composite picture of London from the earliest days to the present—"a celebration of London" told with irony and humor. (BRD) Braziller, 1976. ○

Fitzgerald, Penelope
OFFSHORE
"Perfectly absorbing little novel . . . casting an understanding but humorous light" on a group of eccentrics living on barges moored on the Thames. HR&W, 1987.   ○

Follett, Ken
PAPER MONEY
Plot takes place on a single day and involves sex, robbery and an oil scam. Morrow, 1987.   o

Frankau, Pamela
SING FOR YOUR SUPPER
First in a trilogy about an English theatrical family. This book is set in a seaside town in the summer of 1926. Random, 1964. *Slaves of the Lamp* (1965) and *Over the Mountains* (1967), which follow, are set in London and take the family on through World War II.   o

Fraser, Antonia
THE CAVALIER CASE
"An upscale tennis club and modern London society" is the milieu for this Jemima Shore mystery, and there's the ghost of a 17th-century poet involved. (FC) Bantam, 1991.   o

Gaskin, Catherine
FAMILY AFFAIRS
"A long, well-done family saga . . . of two endowed families whose destinies are intertwined by pride of place"; set in London and on a sheep ranch. (FC) Doubleday, 1980.   o

Godwin, Gail
MR. BEDFORD
One of five stories in *Mr. Bedford and the Muses*, of writers in various life stages. Viking, 1983.   o

Graham, Winston
A GREEN FLASH
An ambitious man's rise in the 1960s and '70s to a baronetcy. Random, 1987.   o

Greene, Graham
END OF THE AFFAIR
"A love affair in wartime England and . . . a woman's reluctant turning to religion is told with the air of suspense of a mystery story." First published in 1951. (FC) S&S, 1978. Also *Ministry of Fear*, a story of espionage in World War II (1943).   o

Hardwick, Mollie
THE DUCHESS OF DUKE STREET
Adaptation of the public TV series about the woman who owned an exclusive residential hotel in Edwardian London where prominent people stayed and dined. HR&W, 1977.   o

Hilton, James
RANDOM HARVEST
Romantic story of lost memory and enduring love, and made into that classic movie with Greer Garson as heroine. Little, 1941.   o

Huxley, Aldous
POINT COUNTER POINT
"Satiric picture of London intellectuals and . . . upper-class society during the 1920s." (FC) Har-Row, 1928.   o

James, P.D.
A TASTE FOR DEATH
"About murder . . . also about the human condition in London today . . . a wonderful writer." (FC) Knopf, 1986.   o

Le Carré, John
THE LOOKING GLASS WAR
"A bitter, cruel, dispassionate" story of a former military espionage unit in London. Coward, 1965. Also, *The Honorable Schoolboy* (1977); *Smiley's People* (1980); and *Tinker, Tailor, Soldier, Spy* (1974).   o

Lessing, Doris
THE GOOD TERRORIST
The "good" terrorist keeps house for a bunch of radicals, rebelling against her mother's middleclass values, but in doing so "winds up just like her mother . . . decorating . . . cooking for her comrades." (FC) Knopf, 1985.   o

Llewellyn, Richard
NONE BUT THE LONELY HEART
First published in 1943, revised later. A character study of a young Cockney in London's slums just before World War II—London's East End "made very real." This was the

subject of a movie classic with Cary Grant as the hero. Macmillan, 1969. ○

Lurie, Alison
FOREIGN AFFAIRS
Two American professors on leave in London to do research, and their romantic entanglements and reactions—"a wry, wonderful book." Random, 1984. ○

MacKenzie, Donald
RAVEN'S SHADOW
Death of a British Airways pilot leads to a "trail of corpses through the seamy London underworld of dope dealers and crime bosses." (FC) Doubleday, 1985. ○

Maugham, W. Somerset
OF HUMAN BONDAGE
The classic story of a young doctor's struggles in London and his obsessive love for the waitress Mildred (Bette Davis' great role in the film), and eventual happiness. First published 1915. Penguin, 1978. ○

Mortimer, John
LIKE MEN BETRAYED
A solicitor discovers that his son is involved in possible illegal manipulation of funds. Viking, 1989. Also *Paradise Postponed* (1986), a look at postwar England through a group of villagers from a London suburb, and *Titmus Regained* (1990). ○

Pearson, John
THE BELLAMY SAGA
The book version of that marvelous public TV series, "Upstairs, Downstairs." Praeger, 1976. ○

Pym, Barbara
AN UNSUITABLE ATTACHMENT
The "vanished world [of the] Anglican parish" and a cast of characters "no longer quite appropriate to the present day." (FC) Dutton, 1982. Also, about the "doings" of an Anglo-Catholic parish is *A Glass of Blessings* (1980). Other London novels include *No Fond Return of Love* (1982), *Excellent Women* (1978), *Less Than Angels* (1980), *The Sweet Dove Died*

(1979). All Pym novels were originally published in the '50s and '60s. ○

Read, Piers Paul
A SEASON IN THE WEST
A Czech defector and writer is taken under the wing of a shallow rich woman and lionized by her social set—"biting pictures of British publishing and banking circles . . . sedate lives moved by unruly passions." (FC) Random, 1989. ○

Rendell, Ruth
TALKING TO STRANGE MEN
A plant store owner becomes obsessed with deciphering the coded messages of a group of precocious schoolboys—"electrifying consequences . . . enhancing the story are the author's evocation of locales, especially the wonderful gardens found only in England." (FC) Pantheon, 1987. Also set in or near London are *The Bridesmaid* (1989), *A Tree of Hands* (1984), *A Demon in My View* (1977), *Murder Being Once Done* (1972), *Going Wrong* (1990). ○

Settle, Mary Lee
CELEBRATION
London in the 1960s—a widow, a geologist and a variety of friends looking for love and a sense of belonging. FS&G, 1986. ○

Sharp, Margery
BRITANNIA MEWS
Family chronicle from 1865 to 1940 as the Mews change from slum to fashionable residential area. Little, 1946. Also *The Faithful Servants* (1975), vignettes of beneficiaries of a family trust, the trustees, and the family descendants. ○

Sillitoe, Alan
HER VICTORY
A complicated love story spanning two generations. Watts, 1982. ○

Somers, Jane
THE DIARY OF A GOOD NEIGHBOR
Diary of Janna, a "modish Londoner" who befriends "an ancient bundle of smelly rags"

and the love-hate relationship of two needy people. (FC) Knopf, 1983. Following is *If the Old Could* . . . (1984), in which Janna "stumbles upon her destined love . . . when it is impossible to take advantage of their mutual attraction." ○

Spark, Muriel
THE BALLAD OF PECKHAM RYE
Set in an industrial town near London. Lippincott, 1960. Also *The Girls of Slender Means* (1963), set in a London residence for women at the close of World War II, and *Loitering With Intent* (1981) in which an aspiring novelist takes a job as secretary to a group who are composing their memoirs in advance. Also *A Far Cry From Kensington* (1988)—recollections of earlier years as a war widow, living in a Kensington rooming house, and beginnings of a publishing career. ○

Stevenson, Robert L.
THE STRANGE CASE OF DR. JEKYLL AND MR. HYDE
Reissue of the classic story. Dufours Eds, 1986. ○

Theroux, Paul
THE LONDON EMBASSY
An American diplomat's experiences at the London Embassy—"a sparkling portrait gallery of eccentric Brits and misplaced Americans." (Publisher) Houghton, 1984. Also *The Family Arsenal* (1976) in which an American ex-State Department employee becomes involved with the IRA. ○

Thomas, Rosie
BAD GIRLS, GOOD WOMEN
Three decades of relationships as two women run off to London in 1955—"engaging portrait of the 60s . . . provincial theaters . . . Soho clubs." (FC) Bantam, 1989. Also *Strangers* (1987), about a London housewife and an advertising executive who share several hours of self-revelation before being rescued from a bomb attack, and *A Woman of Our Time* (1990). ○

Van Slyke, Helen
NO LOVE LOST
Four generations of a family's women "embellished with a historical backdrop featur-

ing New York City and London of the past forty years." (FC) Lippincott, 1980. ○

Waller, Leslie
EMBASSY
An Army Intelligence officer is assigned to secure the embassy's holiday gala—intrigue, violence, pleasantly diverting glimpses of London embassy life. McGraw, 1987. ○

Woods, Sara
AWAY WITH THEM TO PRISON
A London barrister-sleuth is chief protagonist of a series of mysteries set in London that "combine the vagaries of English trial law with detective-story excitement." (FC) St. Martin, 1985. Also *Most Deadly Hate* (1986), *An Obscure Grave* (1986), *Put Out the Light* (1985), which involves an actors' group rehearsing a Restoration comedy. ○

AVON/SOMERSET

Gill, B.M.
SEMINAR FOR MURDER
A mystery writers' convention in a Victorian mansion near Bristol is the setting. Scribner, 1986. ○

Livingston, Nancy
FATALITY AT BATH AND WELLS
Murder in the control room of the local TV studio. St. Martin, 1987. ○

BEDFORDSHIRE

Veryan, Patricia
THE WAGERED WIDOW
The period is the Jacobite rebellions—an impecunious (wagered) widow is won by the right man. St. Martin, 1984. ○

BERKSHIRE

Ferrars, E.X.
THE OTHER DEVIL'S NAME
Several people have disappeared from a Berkshire village, and a botany professor visiting a former colleague gets involved. Doubleday, 1987. Also by Ferrars are *Blood Flies Upward, Death of a Minor Character, Something Wicked*. ○

BUCKINGHAMSHIRE

Lovesey, Peter
BERTIE AND THE SEVEN BODIES
Bertie is the Prince of Wales, and the mystery is narrated by him. During a hunt in Buckinghamshire, Bertie bags a murderer along with other game—"a wonderfully put together puzzle." (FC) Mysterious Pr, 1990.   ○

Milne, A.A.
MR. PIM
Novel version of an English comedy of manners in which Mr. Pim (having died) briefly returns to the household where his widow lives with her second husband. Dutton, 1930.   ○

CAMBRIDGESHIRE

Gloag, Julian
SLEEPING DOGS LIE
"Not an ordinary whodunit . . . an excellent psychological thriller." (FC) Dutton, 1980. Also *Our Mother's House* (1963), about a Cambridge psychiatrist and a student with an unusual phobia.   ○

James, P.D.
AN UNSUITABLE JOB FOR A
WOMAN
A woman detective's first case is to investigate the death of a microbiologist's son—"Cambridge in the summer is beautifully evoked." (FC) Scribner, 1973.   ○

Johnson, Pamela Hansford
THE GOOD LISTENER
Three men begin their lives at Cambridge in 1950. Scribner, 1975. *The Good Husband* (1979) continues the saga of one of them in the 1960s.   ○

CHANNEL ISLANDS & GUERNSEY

Edwards, G.B.
THE BOOK OF EBENEZER LEPAGE
A "fictionalized memoir of a simple but not simpleminded Guernsey-man . . . looking back from the 1960s on a life that began at

the turn of the century." (FC) Knopf, 1981.   ○

Marsh, Ngaio
LAST DITCH
A university don, vacationing on one of the Channel Islands, becomes involved in drug smuggling and a fatal accident. Little, 1977.   ○

Webster, Noah
WITCHLINE
Murder and a suspiciously sunken vessel bring an insurance investigator to the Channel Islands. Doubleday, 1988.   ○

CHESHIRE

Hill, Fiona
THE COUNTRY GENTLEMAN
Regency tale of a heroine forced from London into the country life of Cheshire when her fortune is lost. St. Martin, 1987.   ○

CORNWALL

Brent, Madeleine
TREGARON'S DAUGHTER
A Gothic romance set in a Cornish fishing village in the early twentieth century. Doubleday, 1971.   ○

Burley, W.J.
WYCLIFFE AND THE TANGLED
WEB
Wycliffe investigates the disappearance of an unwed mother. Doubleday, 1987. Also by Burley, *Wycliffe and the Quiet Virgin* (1986), *Wycliffe and the Winsor Blue* (1987), *Wycliffe and the Cycle of Death* (1991).   ○

Carr, Philippa
MIDSUMMER'S EVE
Romantic suspense centered around the evil witnessed by the local squire's daughter on a midsummer's eve. Putnam, 1986. Also, set in Victorian London and the Cornish countryside, *The Changeling* (1989), and *The Black Swan* (1990) sequels to *The Pool of St. Branok* (1988).   ○

DuMaurier, Daphne
JAMAICA INN
One of several novels by DuMaurier, historic and contemporary, set in Cornwall. Buccaneer, 1979 (first published 1936). Other titles include: *The King's General* (1946), *Frenchman's Creek* (1942), *The House on the Strand* (1969), *Rule Britannia* (1973), *Rebecca* (1938), *My Cousin Rachel* (1952).   ○

George, Elizabeth
A SUITABLE VENGEANCE
Detective Inspector Thomas Lynley of Scotland Yard brings his fiance to Cornwall to meet his mother, and they become embroiled in a series of local murders. Bantam, 1991.   ○

Godden, Rumer
CHINA COURT
Family chronicle of life in a house through five generations. Viking, 1961.   ○

Graham, Winston
THE GROVE OF EAGLES
Historical novel of Elizabethan times and the Second Armada, and the hero's service under Sir Walter Raleigh. Doubleday, 1964.   ○

Graham, Winston
THE POLDARK NOVELS
The series on which the public TV series was based. Doubleday titles include: *The Black Moon* (1974), *The Four Swans* (1977), *The Angry Tide* (1978), *The Stranger from the Sea* (1982), *The Miller's Dance* (1983), *The Loving Cup* (1985), *The Twisted Sword* (1991).   ○

Holt, Victoria
BRIDE OF PENDORRIC
Suspense novel by the prolific master storyteller. Doubleday, 1963. Other Cornwall novels by Holt include: *Curse of the Kings* (1973), *Legend of the Seventh Virgin* (1965), *Manfreya in the Morning* (1966), *Mistress of Mellyn* (1960), *Lord of the Far Island* (1975), *The Landower Legacy* (1984).   ○

Meek, M.R.D.
A MOUTHFUL OF SAND
"Superb village settings"—the plot involves murder and a beheaded corpse that turns up in a fisherman's net. (FC) Scribner, 1989. Also *Remembrance of Rose* (1989).   ○

Michaels, Barbara
WAIT FOR WHAT WILL COME
A young American schoolteacher inherits a mansion with a family curse—has a "nice spoofing tongue-in-cheek tone." (FC) Dodd, 1978.   ○

Pearce, Mary E.
POLSINNEY HARBOUR
Following a family tragedy, a young woman flees her native village for a Cornish fishing village, to start over with her unborn child—"has all the stark simplicity of an enchanting ballad . . . a melodic commentary on the enduring powers of love and the sea." (FC) St. Martin, 1984.   ○

Pilcher, Rosamunde
VOICES IN SUMMER
Feeling alienated from her husband's past and his family, Laura goes to visit with his aunt and uncle for a recuperative stay in their lovely home in Cornwall. St. Martin, 1984. See also *The Shell Seekers* under Gloucestershire/The Cotswolds, below.   ○

Quiller-Couch, Arthur and DuMaurier, Daphne
CASTLE D'OR
The story of a modern-day Tristan and Isuelt, started by Quiller-Couch and finished, at the request of his daughter, by Miss DuMaurier. Doubleday, 1962.   ○

Ross-Macdonald, Malcolm
AN INNOCENT WOMAN
A "robust" romance set in 19th-century Cornwall—"evokes the natural landscape of Cornwall and the dialect and class distinctions of its inhabitants." (FC) St. Martin, 1991.   ○

Shannon, Dell
THE MANSON CURSE
An American "visits his novelist friend in Cornwall and becomes curious about the writer's obsession with the occult." (FC) Morrow, 1990.   ○

CUMBRIA/LAKE DISTRICT

Forster, Margaret
THE BRIDE OF LOWTHER FELL
When her twin sister is killed, Alexandra is left responsible for their thirteen-year-old nephew and decides to move, with him, to an isolated cottage to "overcome her own restlessness and change the child . . . shrewd and peppery insight into the psychology of both young woman and boy who must work out their destinies together . . . even face possible death together." (FC) Atheneum, 1981.   o

Grimes, Martha
THE OLD CONTEMPTIBLE
A mystery that takes place in the Old Contemptible Pub in the Lake District, which is a favored meeting place for local denizens. Melrose Plant arrives, posing as a librarian, to help clear his friend being suspected of a murder—"eccentric, appealing characters." (FC) Little, 1991.   o

Hill, Reginald
THE LONG KILL
A political assassin misses his target, resigns and later meets the man he recognizes as his target. Countryman Pr, 1988.   o

DERBYSHIRE

Hilton, John B.
PASSION IN THE PEAK
A local Passion Play leads to murder—"great dollops of Derbyshire scenery." St. Martin, 1985. Also by Hilton: *Slickensides; Mind of Mr. Mosley; What, Me, Mr. Mosley?*   o

DEVONSHIRE

Canning, Victor
THE KINGSFORD MARK
Murder plans of a guest and his host with some of the trappings of a Gothic novel—(the author's) "way with the Devonshire landscape heightens the drama of this well-told, suspenseful tale of love, betrayal and tangled heritage." (FC) Morrow, 1976. Also *Queen's Pawn* (1975), in which a man is blackmailed into stealing gold bullion from the *QE 2*, and *The Mask of Memory* (1975),

an "absorbing study of adult civil servants who are in the messy business of intelligence."   o

Cary, Joyce
EXCEPT THE LORD
The Devonshire childhood and young manhood of Chester Nimmo, in the 1870s, revealing the "conditions and people that determined his life as preacher, labor leader and politician." (FC) Har-Row, 1953. This is the middle volume of a trilogy, preceded by *Prisoner of Grace* (1952) and followed by *Not Honour More* (1955).   o

Delderfield, R.F.
A HORSEMAN RIDING BY
This and *Green Gauntlet* (1968) comprise a family saga beginning in 1902, as a young man returns from the Boer War to a run-down estate in Devonshire, and ending in the 1960s after following the family through World War II. S&S, 1966.   o

Delderfield, R.F.
TO SERVE THEM ALL MY DAYS
A schoolmaster's cavalcade of life at a West Country public school between World Wars I and II. S&S, 1972.   o

Harris, Marilyn
THIS OTHER EDEN
Historical saga of eighteenth-century England peopled with the likes of Thomas Paine, Emma Hamilton and Lord Nelson. Putnam Pub Group, 1977. It is the first of four novels and is followed by *The Prince of Eden* (1978), *The Eden Passion* (1979) and *The Women of Eden* (1980).   o

Holt, Victoria
THE TIME OF THE HUNTER'S MOON
The heroine of this Gothic teaches at an exclusive academy in Devon and the story is set in the nineteenth century. Doubleday, 1984.   o

Sharp, Margery
CLUNY BROWN
An amusing novel of a young girl who simply will not remember her social place as a

plumber's niece and who ends up running off with a Polish emigré. Little, 1944.   o

DORSET

Cody, Liza
HEAD CASE
Private detective Anna Lee becomes involved with a 16-year-old genius in a Dorset hospital. Scribner, 1986.   o

Fowles, John
THE FRENCH LIEUTENANT'S WOMAN
Lyme Regis is the setting for a love story told Victorian style but with contemporary insights. Little, 1969.   o

Hart, Roy
A FOX IN THE NIGHT
Police procedural, solved by Superintendent Roper, involving a drowned widow. St. Martin, 1988.   o

James, P.D.
THE BLACK TOWER
Commander Dalgleish is invited to visit a family friend in Dorset, but the friend is dead by the time Dalgleish arrives. Scribner, 1975. Also *The Skull Beneath the Skin* (1982).   o

DURHAM

Cookson, Catherine
THE MOTH
A romantic entanglement between a carpenter and a lady sets up a controversy between the social classes. Summit Bks, 1986.   o

Cookson, Catherine
TILLY
A chronicle of a girl born into poverty and the hard life that meant in Victorian days, but who ends up as mistress of Sopwith Manor in Durham (with one part of her life spent in Texas). Morrow, 1980. First of a trilogy, followed by *Tilly Wed* (1981) and *Tilly Alone* (1982).   o

EAST ANGLIA

Gash, Jonathan
PEARLHANGER
East Anglia is home territory of mysteries in which antiques dealer Lovejoy is the chief protagonist—this series has also been filmed for TV. St. Martin, 1985. Also *Moonspender* (1986), and *The Very Last Gambado* (1990).   o

James, P.D.
DEVICES AND DESIRES
A serial killer is loose in coastal Norfolk, and Dalgleish is visiting the area to settle his aunt's estate; employees of the nuclear plant at Larksoken are key to the plot as well. Knopf, 1990. Also *Death of an Expert Witness* (1977).   o

Lofts, Norah
THE HOMECOMING
Chronicle of a house and its inhabitants, over 350 years. Doubleday, 1976.   o

Sharp, Margery
SUMMER VISITS
Events at a country estate from mid-nineteenth century to 1940. Little, 1978. Also *The Innocents* (1972), about a retarded child, her mother, and the foster mother who wishes to care for her.   o

Wilson, A.N.
INCLINE OUR HEARTS
First of a trilogy about an orphan raised in a Norfolk village, describing his life as a series of English Gulags from public school to National Service. Viking, 1989.   o

GLOUCESTERSHIRE/THE COTSWOLDS

Gosling, Paul
THE WYCHFORD MURDERS
A Cotswold butcher is murdering women—"discreetly delightful scenery . . . terror-laden plot twists." (FC) Doubleday, 1986. Also *The Wychford House* (1987).   o

Guthrie, A.B.
MURDER IN THE COTSWOLDS
Montana Sheriff Chick Charleston exercises his sleuthing talents in a Cotswold village

while traveling with his wife—"limpid prose, tidy plot . . . comfy atmosphere." (FC) HM, 1989. ○

Huxley, Elspeth
THE PRINCE BUYS THE MANOR
A "comic extravaganza" set in a market town in the Cotswolds, occasioned by the decision of an African royal prince to buy a nearby manor house. (FC) Chatto & Windus, 1983. ○

Lively, Penelope
PASSING ON
An unmarried brother and sister, living in the family home in the Cotswolds, and their reaction to their mother's death—". . . wonderful writing." (FC) Grove, 1990. ○

Pearce, Mary E.
THE TWO FARMS
Rural 19th-century England and daily farm life. St. Martin, 1986. ○

Pilcher, Rosamunde
THE SHELL SEEKERS
This is the extremely popular novel about an older woman coming to terms with her children and her life of gardening and living in a village. Cornwall is also featured in the plot. St. Martin, 1987. ○

Read, Miss
THRUSH GREEN NOVELS
Miss Read's long Doris Saint series of novels about the school and village of Thrush Green are set in the Cotswolds. The thing to do is check your local library, arrange the Read novels they have according to date of publication, and start from the beginning. If you don't care for the first one, you probably won't like any of the rest; if you do like the very low-key, nothing-much-happens, daily life of an idyllic Cotswold village, you may become addicted. The series began in 1955 with *Village School*. Note also *The World of Thrush Green* (1989), listed under Literary and Book-related Guides for England. ○

HAMPSHIRE

Aiken, Joan
MANSFIELD REVISITED
A return to Jane Austen's novel, *Mansfield Park*. Doubleday, 1985. ○

Goudge, Elizabeth
THE BIRD IN THE TREE
A family chronicle that begins on the Hampshire coast in 1938 and ends following World War II, with an Austrian refugee and concert pianist sharing in the family's life—"exquisite portrayal of children, grownups, animals and the English countryside." Coward, 1940. First of a trilogy, followed by *Pilgrim's Inn* (1948) and *Heart of the Family* (1953). ○

Grimes, Martha
THE DEER LEAP
One of a series of mysteries in which Superintendent Richard Jury is the detective protagonist, and "The Deer Leap" is the name of the local pub. Little, 1985. ○

HERTFORDSHIRE

Amis, Kingsley
THE GREEN MAN
The *Green Man* is a pub and also a "very nasty thing conjured up by the resident ghost." (FC) HarBraceJ, 1970. ○

ISLE OF MAN

Gash, Jonathan
GOLD BY GEMINI
A mystery involving buried Roman coins, and a search for lost treasure by an antique dealer. Har-Row, 1978. ○

KENT

Bruce, Leo
A BONE AND A HANK OF HAIR
Disappearance of a woman leads to possibility that there's been a whole series of murdered wives in Canterbury. Academy Chi Pubs, 1985. ○

Godden, Jon
IN HER GARDEN
A 75-year-old widow in Kent "falls in love with her newly-hired [30-year-old] gardener, and tragedy results. . . . a genteel modern sketch of manners and morals." (FC) Knopf, 1981.   o

Hardwick, Mollie
MALICE DOMESTIC
Doran Fairweather, an antiques dealer in Abbotsbourne, Kent, involved in chilling events and a series of deaths. St. Martin, 1986. Also featuring Ms. Fairweather are *Perish in July* (1990) and *The Dreaming Damozel* (1991).   o

Holt, Victoria
THE SHIVERING SANDS
A gothic involving a piano teacher's search for her archaeologist sister. Doubleday, 1969.   o

Pearson, Diane
THE SUMMER OF THE BARSHINSKEYS
A three-part novel of the Willoughby family: the first part concerns the arrival in 1902 of an exotic Russian family with "odd gypsy ways" that has a profound effect on the 11-year-old Willoughby daughter; part two involves the love between the now-grown Willoughby son and the Barshinskey daughter; part three finds the oldest Willoughby daughter in love with Ivan Barshinskey—"a most entertaining and poignant novel." (FC) Crown, 1984.   o

Simpson, Dorothy
SUSPICIOUS DEATH
A Luke Thanet mystery set in Telford Green—". . . intriguingly complex relationships with the villagers." Also *Element of Doubt* (1988), *Dead on Arrival* (1987), *Last Seen Alive* (1985). Scribner, 1988.   o

LANCASHIRE

Bainbridge, Beryl
QUIET LIFE
The setting is a village near Southport—story of acute family strife told in flashback. Braziller, 1977. Also *Harriet Said* (1973).   o

Bentley, Ursula
THE NATURAL ORDER
Three sisters working in a Catholic boys' school in Manchester and "trying to act out the genius of the Brontë myth" are each ensnared by the school's "most promising Sixth Former ever." (BRD) St. Martin, 1982.   o

Greenwood, John
MOSLEY BY MOONLIGHT
Police procedural involving bizarre commercials being filmed in bucolic Lancashire. Walker, 1985.   o

Hartog, Jan de
THE PEACEABLE KINGDOM
Story of Quaker life, this first volume beginning in England, 1652–53, and dealing with George Fox's work with prison and mental hospital inmates. Atheneum, 1972.   o

Stubbs, Jean
BY OUR BEGINNINGS
The saga of the Howarth family in Lancashire—"social ferment and family history are vigorously blended" in this chronicle that begins in 1760 and ends following the Industrial Revolution, with the first railroad brought to the valley. St. Martin, 1979. First in a trilogy, followed by *An Imperfect Joy* (1981), *The Vivian Inheritance* (1982) and *The Northern Correspondent* (1984).   o

NORTHUMBERLAND

Cookson, Catherine
THE BANNAMAN LEGACY
The plot grows out of the machinations of a local squire. Summit Bks, 1985.   o

Cookson, Catherine
THE BLACK VELVET GOWN
A penniless widow's daughter rises from her lowly laundress position to that of lady's maid and becomes the center of a family scandal. Summit Bks, 1984. Also *Pure as a Lily* (1973), chronicle of a working class family, 1933–1973, and *The Cinder Path* (1978). o

Cookson, Catherine
THE MALLEN STREAK
A family saga with unusual and complicated relationships, from mid-nineteenth century to World War I. Dutton, 1973. This book is followed by *The Mallen Girl* (1973) and *The Mallen Lot* (1974). ○

Cronin, A.J.
THE STARS LOOK DOWN
Life in a mining community during the first half of this century. Little, 1935. ○

Gilliatt, Penelope
MORTAL MATTERS
Lady Corfe recalls her life from suffragette days to the 1980s as she flees London for her Northumberland home—"gracefully combines past and present to . . . define [an] odd and interesting heroine." (FC) Coward, 1983. ○

Stewart, Mary
THE IVY TREE
A Canadian girl is mistaken for a dead heiress—vivid descriptions of the Northumberland countryside. Morrow, 1961. ○

NOTTINGHAMSHIRE

Sillitoe, Alan
OUT OF THE WHIRLPOOL
"An expert observer of lower-class British life"—a plot involving Peter Granby and a wealthy widow who hires him as caretaker. Har-Row, 1987. Also *Men, Women and Children* (1974), short stories of Nottingham. ○

Sillitoe, Alan
SATURDAY NIGHT AND SUNDAY MORNING
An angry young man and his working-class life in industrial Britain, from which a memorable movie was made. Knopf, 1959. Also *The Widower's Son* (1977). ○

OXFORDSHIRE

Beerbohm, Max
THE ILLUSTRATED ZULEIKA DOBSON
A facsimile edition of the author's own copy of this novel "of love and dandyism, set in Edwardian Oxford." (BRD) Yale U Pr, 1985. ○

Colegate, Isabel
THE SHOOTING PARTY
The year 1913 in Oxfordshire; leading sportsmen and their wives are invited to a pheasant shoot—"deftly evokes the vanished confident world of the British aristocracy just before World War I. . . . vivid observations of . . . social snobbery are suffused with a brooding Chekhovian melancholy." (FC) Viking, 1981. ○

Fowles, John
DANIEL MARTIN
Two friends at Oxford marry sisters and realize years later that each chose the wrong one. Little, 1977. ○

Fraser, Antonia
OXFORD BLOOD
A Jemima Shore mystery in the "exclusive reaches of Britain's titled aristocracy." (FC) Norton, 1985. ○

Goudge, Elizabeth
THE SCENT OF WATER
At fifty, a woman inherits a house and the journals of an earlier resident, and gains from them spiritual regeneration and happiness. Coward, 1963. ○

Murdoch, Iris
THE BOOK AND THE BROTHERHOOD
A group of 1980s students at Oxford form a coalition to fund one of their members in his major writing project, which involves life's serious questions. Viking, 1988. ○

Pym, Barbara
A FEW GREEN LEAVES
A woman anthropologist hopes to do an article on village life—"several people make a significant impact on her and eventually bring her to grips with reality." (FC) Dutton, 1980. Also for Barbara Pym addicts, a newly discovered novel written and set at Oxford, with a plot revolving around "a pair of em-

inently unsuitable attachments": the title is *Crampton Hodnet*. ○

Stewart, J.I.M.
ANDREW AND TOBIAS
The adopted heir to a large estate finds his double in the new gardener—"souffle of erudition and ingenuity, insubstantial but . . . delightful." (FC) Norton, 1980. ○

Stewart, J.I.M.
THE GAUDY
First of a series of novels on Oxford "attuned to the finer nuances of Oxford life," with the collective title *A Staircase in Surrey*. They were written by an Oxford don who writes mysteries under the name Michael Innes. A "gaudy" is an alumni gathering. (FC) Norton, 1975. Followed by *Young Patullo* (1976), *A Memorial Service* (1976), *Madonna of the Astrolabe* (1977). ○

Trapido, Barbara
NOAH'S ARK
After courtship, an American surgeon takes Alison and her daughter from squalid London to idyllic Oxford, but a former love enters the scene—"warm portrayal of middle-aged renewal."(BRD) Watts, 1985. ○

SHROPSHIRE

Peters, Ellis
FLIGHT OF A WITCH
A mystery revolving around "the sheer beauty of 18-year-old Annet Beck" and her identification as being near a murder scene in Birmingham. "Deeply satisfying murder novel . . . the central challenge lies in unraveling the mystery of a young woman's character." First published in 1964. (FC) Mysterious Pr, 1991. ○

Peters, Ellis
THE HERETIC'S APPRENTICE
Brother Cadfael is the main protagonist—"provides darker characters . . . somber view of Shrewsbury life . . . the true subject . . . is human misery." Also *The Potter's Field* (1990), another chronicle of Brother Cadfael, a Benedictine monk. (FC) Mysterious Pr, 1990. ○

Webb, Mary
PRECIOUS BANE
A novel about farming life and country people and a plot in which a disfigured woman finds a husband who appreciates her. Dutton, 1926. ○

SOMERSET

Canning, Victor
BIRDS OF A FEATHER
Suspense novel of an art-collecting aristocrat marked for assassination by his clients and government agents. Morrow, 1985. ○

Heyer, Georgette
BATH TANGLE
A "saucy Regency novel" of mismatched, entangled lovers with the tangles skillfully unraveled by the author. Also, *Lady of Quality* another Regency novel by a writer noted for her authenticity of historical detail. Putnam Pub Group, 1972. ○

STAFFORDSHIRE

Heaven, Constance
THE WILDCLIFFE BIRD
"The backdrop of England during the period of incipient unionism provides added interest" to a historical romance with a heroine who discovers a "web of mysterious accidents and murder" in the family that offers her a position. (FC) Coward, 1983. ○

SUFFOLK

Lofts, Norah
THE CLAW
"Character study of a contemporary small town . . . shaken out of apathy into terror" by a rape-murder. (FC) Doubleday, 1982. ○

Lofts, Norah
THE OLD PRIORY
Elizabethan England is evoked in this novel about three generations of a family living in a cursed priory. Doubleday, 1982. Two other novels by Ms. Lofts that chronicle the lives of occupants of a house over the years are *Bless This House* (1954) and *The House at Old Vine* (1961). ○

Lofts, Norah
A WAYSIDE TAVERN

"In an engaging conceit" the novel chronicles English history from the late Roman period to the present in "the evolution of a wayside inn and its proprietors through the generations." (FC) Doubleday, 1980.   ○

Radley, Sheila
FATE WORSE THAN DEATH

A young woman is murdered and all the "eccentric male inhabitants of . . . a quaint Suffolk hamlet, are suspect." (FC) Scribner, 1986. Also set in Suffolk by Radley: *The Quiet Road to Death* (1984), *A Talent for Destruction* (1982), *Who Saw Him Die?* (1988).   ○

Rendell, Ruth
MAKE DEATH LOVE ME

A thriller with psychological insight involving two teenaged bank robbers and a bank manager who is a romantic at heart. Doubleday, 1979.   ○

SURREY

Braddon, Russell
THE FINALISTS

Suspense story with a Wimbledon setting; a Russian defector must thwart a plan to assassinate the Queen during the singles finals. Atheneum, 1977.   ○

Gardner, John
THE WEREWOLF TRACE

A furniture importer living in Surrey is discovered to have been present in the bunker where Hitler died, and is his spiritual heir. Doubleday, 1977.   ○

SUSSEX

Benson, E.F.
MAKE WAY FOR LUCIA

Like Miss Read, E.F. Benson's "Lucia" novels have almost a cult following, and in the past few years were the source for a BBC series that was run here on PBS. This is the second edition of an omnibus printing of six of her novels, plus a short story. According to an article in the *New York Times*, February 18, 1990, in the Sunday travel section, the

town of Rye, in Sussex, is the "Tilling" of the Lucia novels. Har-Row, 1986.   ○

Birkhead, Margaret
TRUST AND TREASON

Historical novel about two generations of the Woodfall family of Sussex, beginning in the years prior to the reign of Elizabeth I. St. Martin, 1991.   ○

Heyer, Georgette
THE RELUCTANT WIDOW

A Regency-period mystery of a governess who is married off to a dying man. Putnam Pub Group, 1971.   ○

Laker, Rosalind
WARWYCK'S CHOICE

"Saga of the contentious, wealthy Warwycks . . . the England of 1884" set in the seaside community of Easthampton. (FC) Doubleday, 1980. It is a sequel to *Warwyck's Woman* (1978) and *Claudine's Daughter* (1979).   ○

Morice, Anne
DESIGN FOR DYING

The owner returns to Sussex after a 20-year absence, and later her husband is found murdered—"this solid mystery is social comedy as well." (FC) St. Martin, 1988.   ○

Rendell, Ruth
THE VEILED ONE

One of a series of Rendell mysteries set in the created Sussex town of Kingsmarkham, with Detective Wexford as chief protagonist. Pantheon, 1988. Also *An Unkindness of Ravens* (1985), *Speaker of the Mandarin* (1983), *Death Notes* (1981), *Means of Evil* (1979), *A Sleeping Life* (1978).   ○

Wright, Patricia
I AM ENGLAND

An historical novel, in five separate stories linked by a Sussex ridge, spanning from 70 A.D. to the mid-1500s—"superior historical detail and a deeply rooted sense of place makes the whole come alive as a portrait of the English people." Its sequel is *That Near and Distant Place* (1988). (FC) St. Martin, 1987.   ◦

WARWICKSHIRE

Hardwick, Mollie
PARSON'S PLEASURE

On a working holiday, antiques dealer Doran Fairweather finds a gypsy dealer murdered. St. Martin, 1987.   ◦

Lively, Penelope
NEXT TO NATURE, ART

The Framleigh Creative Study Centre in the Warwickshire countryside is an "artistic sanctuary," but really run by some con artists who entice "non-artists . . . fleeing their mundane lives [to] pay good money to spend a week there." (FC) Heinemann, 1983.   ◦

WILTSHIRE

Belle, Pamela
WINTERCOMBE

Set in Wiltshire at the time of the Roundhead revolt against King Charles. A young wife must try to protect her lands and its workers from the Cavaliers—"rich in . . . lore about gardens, furnishings, arms, and herb medicine." (FC) St. Martin, 1988.   ◦

Cutter, Leela
WHO STOLE STONEHENGE?

An aged mystery writer and a local newspaper reporter solve the mystery when Stonehenge is literally stolen from its site. St. Martin, 1983.   ◦

Golding, William
THE SPIRE

Building of the highest spire ever becomes an obsession of the dean of a medieval cathedral. HarBraceJ, 1964. Also *The Pyramid* (1967), about three separate incidents in a boy's life while growing up (1920–40).   ◦

Harrison, Harry and Stover, Leon
STONEHENGE

A fictionalized account of the origins of Stonehenge by a novelist and an anthropologist—"vivid, valid archaeological background and a psychology and ferocity of behavior

appropriate to the age and peoples depicted." (FC) Scribner, 1972.   ◦

Howatch, Susan
GLITTERING IMAGES

This is the first of a series of "ecclesiastical novels"—sort of a 20th-century Barchester Towers series, with modern problems and situations. Following are *Glamorous Powers* (1988), *Ultimate Prizes* (1989), *Scandalous Risks* (1990), and *Mystical Paths* (1992). The characters and plots are loosely connected and set in the 1930s and on through World War II. Starbridge Cathedral is center of the fictional diocese around which the series is written, and Starbridge is supposedly taken from Salisbury Cathedral in Wiltshire. Knopf, 1987.   ◦

Naipaul, V.S.
THE ENIGMA OF ARRIVAL

Autobiographical novel—the narrator departs Trinidad and begins a second life in England—"irritates, tires and confuses while also exciting, informing and satisfying." (FC) Knopf, 1987.   ◦

Rutherfurd, Edward
SARUM: THE NOVEL OF ENGLAND

The history of England through the Salisbury landscape and the generations of five fictional families that reflect history, social and political change—"fascinating . . . will appeal to Anglophiles, history buffs, and fans of epic novels . . . well-written . . . thoroughly researched." (BRD) Crown, 1987.   ◦

Trollope, Joanna
A VILLAGE AFFAIR

A married woman's lesbian relationship scandalizes a village near Salisbury. HarRow, 1989.   ◦

WORCESTERSHIRE

Pearce, Mary E.
CAST A LONG SHADOW

A blissful marriage in a "closed, watchful English village" is shattered by distortion of the husband's character through a horrifying experience—"people one cares about and low-key charm." (FC) St. Martin, 1983.   o

Pearce, Mary E.
THE LAND ENDURES
An old-fashioned family chronicle, with this volume commencing just after World War I. St. Martin, 1981. Sequel to *Apple Tree Lean Down* (1976).   o

YORKSHIRE

Barnard, Robert
FETE FATALE
The new vicar in a Yorkshire town is disapproved of by some, and then at a town fete the local veterinarian is murdered— "mixing satire and suspense in a rousing display of intelligence and wit." Scribner, 1985. Also *A City of Strangers* (1990).   o

Braine, John
ROOM AT THE TOP
Story of a man with an "insatiable lust for wealth, social prestige and power. . . . narrow but deadly accurate account of contemporary northern [England] small town life." (FC) Houghton, 1957. The sequel about what happens after the man has attained his ambition, is *Life at the Top* (1962). Also *The Queen of a Distant Country* (1973), about a successful novelist's reexamination of his life.   o

Carr, J.L.
A MONTH IN THE COUNTRY
Regeneration of a young veteran of World War I who arrives in a Yorkshire village to restore the wall painting in a local church— "the folk and landscape of Yorkshire play a crucial role . . . a small masterpiece." (FC) St. Martin, 1983.   o

Crowe, Cecily
BLOODROSE HOUSE
Contemporary gothic of strange happenings when an American writer settles in a house in Yorkshire. Saint Martin's, 1986.   o

George, Elizabeth
A GREAT DELIVERANCE
A bizarre murder in the wilds of Yorkshire. Bantam Bks, 1988.   o

Giroux, E.X.
A DEATH FOR A DARLING
A London barrister invited to a country home for a vacation finds ensconced a cast and crew working on a remake of *Wuthering Heights*. St. Martin, 1983.   o

Haines, Pamela
THE KISSING GATE
A three-generation family saga of two intertwined Yorkshire families. Doubleday, 1981.   o

Hylton, Sara
THE WHISPERING GLADE
Gothic about an orphan from southern Rhodesia sent to live with her uncle, and her involvement with Greythorn Hall and its family. St. Martin, 1985.   o

Storey, David
A PRODIGAL CHILD
Pre-World War II is the setting—"concerns itself with class differences that are bridged by the budding artistic abilities of [the] son of a farm-worker father." (FC) Dutton, 1983.   o

Wainwright, John W.
THE FORGOTTEN MURDERS
A riderless horse, crashing out of the dark at 2 A.M., begins this Constable Parker mystery. St. Martin, 1987.   o

FINLAND

Series Guidebooks
(See Appendix 1)

Berlitz: Helsinki
Nagel's Encyclopedia Guide: Finland

Visitor's Guide: Finland
See also Series Guides for Scandinavia (*) under Denmark.

Background Reading

NOTE: See also Denmark for books with an asterisk (*), which offer additional background reading on Scandinavia as a whole and may include material on Finland. Also, see Norway for background books on Lapland.

Engman, Max and Kirby, David, eds.
FINLAND: PEOPLE, NATION, STATE
Ind U Pr, 1989.   ○

Jones, David H.
NIGHT TIMES AND LIGHT TIMES: A JOURNEY FROM LAPLAND
See entry under Norway.   ○

Rajanen, Aini
OF FINNISH WAYS
A cultural guide and history of what makes a Finn a Finn—keeping their national identity through hundreds of years of rule by Sweden, 42 wars with Russia, and finally independence. An introduction to the day by day rituals, festivals, saunas. B&N Bks, 1984.   ○

Yinger, Don L.
FINLAND (Suomi)
Yinger, 1986.   ○

GUIDEBOOKS

Ward, Philip
FINNISH CITIES: TRAVELS IN HELSINKI, TURKU, TAMPERE AND LAPLAND
"Packed with information . . . on art, architecture, culture, and history"—inval-

uable guide for visitors. Hippocrene, 1988.   ○

HISTORY

Jutikkala, E.
A HISTORY OF FINLAND
Vanous, 1984.   ○

Singleton, Fred
A SHORT HISTORY OF FINLAND
Cambridge U Pr, 1989.   ○

Novels

Schoolfield, G.C., ed.
SWEDO-FINNISH SHORT STORIES
Regional and modern psychological stories by Finns whose native tongue is Swedish. Twayne, 1975.   ○

Sillanpaa, F.E.
THE MAID SILJA
A Finnish classic and a book that won a Nobel Prize for literature in 1939. The story is about a well-to-do family brought to ruin by the father's ineptitude. N S Berg, 1974 (first published 1939).   ○

Thayer, Nancy
STEPPING
A young stepmother in Finland while her husband is on a Fulbright grant, struggling to resolve problems with her stepdaughters and the neurotic ex-wife who is their mother. Doubleday, 1980.   ○

Thomas, Craig
SNOW FALCON
Members of the anti-peace faction of the Red Army plan to sabotage Soviet/Western arms limitation talks in Helsinki—for espionage addicts. HR&W, 1980.   ○

FRANCE
(Including Corsica)

Series Guidebooks
(See Appendix 1)

Access Guide: France

American Express Pocket Guide: Paris; South of France

At Its Best: France; Paris

Baedeker: Paris; France; Loire; Provence

Berlitz: France; French Riviera; Paris; Brittany; Loire Valley; Normandy

Birnbaum: France

Blue Guide: Corsica; France; Paris & Versailles

Cadogan: South of France

Exploring Rural Europe: France

Fisher's World: France; Paris

Fodor: France; Loire Valley; Paris; Pocket Guide to Paris

Frommer: Paris (City, $-A-Day & Touring); France

Gault/Milau: The Best of France; The Best of Paris

Hildebrand: France

Insider's Guide: France

Insight Guide: Alsace; Brittany; France; Loire Valley; Paris; Provence

Langenscheidt: Self-Guided France

Let's Go: France; Paris

Michael's Guide: Paris

Michelin: France; Paris

Nagel's Encyclopedia Guide: France

Off the Beaten Track: France

Real Guide: France; Paris

2–22 Days Itinerary Planning Guide: France

Visitor's Guide: Corsica; France—Alps & Jura; Brittany; Dordogne; French Coast; Loire; Normandy; Normandy Battlefields; Provence & Cote D'Azur; South of France

Background Reading

Adams, Henry
MONT SAINT MICHEL AND CHARTRES

A classic—"eloquent and profound . . . expression concerning the glory of medieval art and the elements that brought it into being." (BRD) Berg, 1978 (first published 1914).   ○

Ardagh, John
CULTURAL ATLAS OF FRANCE

"A spectacular re-creation of a unique culture through a brilliant integration of text, maps and illustrations . . . A must for Francophiles, invaluable for armchair travelers." (PW) Facts On File, 1991.   ○

Ardagh, John
WRITER'S FRANCE: A REGIONAL PANORAMA

"Will delight Francophiles"—writing inspired by the French countryside that provides an overview of French literature as well as regional customs and historical settings for novels, locales of memoirs, social history, philosophy. (BL) Viking, 1990. Also *Rural France* (1985), a celebration of the people and countryside of France.   ○

Ash, Russell and Higton, Bernard
PROVENCE: SPIRIT OF PLACE

Part of a series of similar books—words of writers that capture the spirit of a place accompanied by illustrations of the chosen excerpts. Arcade Pub Inc, 1989.   ○

Bernstein, Richard
FRAGILE GLORY: A PORTRAIT OF FRANCE AND THE FRENCH

"Spirited introduction to a prosperous, complacent, Americanized people 'leached out of their particularity.' " (PW) Knopf, 1990.   ○

Braudel, Fernand
THE IDENTITY OF FRANCE

Volume I: *People and Production;* Volume II: *History and Environment.* "The riches of this book . . . are inexhaustible for anyone who loves France . . . history as autobiography . . . immense erudition . . . Gallic charm and wit." This was to be a four-part study of France, but the author died after just two volumes were completed. Har-Row, 1988.   ○

Brown, Michael
SOUTH TO GASCONY
Gascony stretches from the Pyrenees to Bordeaux, and the author owns a home there. "This delightful volume . . . presents Gascony's outstanding cuisine, unrivaled brandy, colorful history" as well as breathtaking scenery. (LJ) Viking, 1990.   o

Calder, Nigel
THE ENGLISH CHANNEL
See entry under England.   o

Daley, Robert
PORTRAITS OF FRANCE
Nineteen vignettes "mixing travelogue, history and offhand cultural commentary . . . serendipitous journey appraises France's soul." (PW) Little, 1991.   o

Durrell, Lawrence
CAESAR'S VAST GHOST: ASPECTS OF PROVENCE
Explores the culture and history of Provence, where the author has lived for over 30 years—"brilliant descriptive passages, esoteric theories on love and culture, colorful local characters, bizarre sexual escapades." (LJ) Little, 1990.   o

Flower, John
PROVENCE
Text and photographs of an area the author claims is one of France's most varied, far more so than St. Tropez. Salem Hse, 1987.   o

Fried, Eunice
BURGUNDY: THE COUNTRY, THE WINES, THE PEOPLE
A profile by an American who has worked as a wine broker—history, cultivating and harvesting, and the daily routine of wine production, Burgundian restaurants and recipes. Har-Row, 1986.   o

Goldman, William
HYPE AND GLORY
The novelist/author was invited to be a judge at the 1989 Cannes film festival and then to help choose Miss America—"sharp-witted

and howlingly funny" commentary on the two events. Random, 1990.   o

Harte, Glynn B.
MR. HARTE'S HOLIDAY
"Graceful text and brilliant watercolors" of the north coast of France, a world somewhat apart, celebrated by generations of writers and painters. (Publisher) Atl Monthly Pr, 1991.   o

Jackson, Stanley
INSIDE MONTE CARLO
"A social history of Monaco's past one hundred years and of its resident and visiting celebrities and reigns of the Grimaldi princes." (BRD) Scarborough Hse, 1975. o

Kramer, Jane
UNSETTLING EUROPE
Refugee families from Algeria, Uganda, Yugoslavia, living in France, London and Sweden, respectively, and an Italian Communist family in Italy, their isolation from traditions of those around them and the implications for Europe's future of these rootless people. FS&G, 1989.   o

Marnham, Patrick
LOURDES: A MODERN PILGRIMAGE
The author participated in an organized tour with a British group and gives an account of that experience, his conversations with tour members and local people. Vignettes, local color, and commentary. (NYT) Coward, 1981.   o

Raison, Laura
THE SOUTH OF FRANCE: AN ANTHOLOGY
Writings about southern France—Belloc on Arles, Evelyn Waugh on Marseilles, Sitwell on Monte Carlo, and so on. Beaufort, 1986.   o

Rambali, Paul
FRENCH BLUES
"A not-so-sentimental journey through lives and memories in modern France" is the

subtitle—"an entertaining *tour d'horizon.*" (BL) Heinemann, 1991.   ○

Reperant, Dominique
THE MOST BEAUTIFUL VILLAGES OF FRANCE

Photographs of the best preserved, unspoiled villages, with brief histories and notes on architecture, along with information on nearby hotels and restaurants. Thames & Hudson, 1990.   ○

Root, Waverly
THE FOOD OF FRANCE

Considered the ultimate book on the subject for travelers—history, food and wine for every region, secret inns, recipes. Random, 1977.   ○

Sinclair-Stevenson, Christopher
WHEN IN FRANCE

"Stylish evocations of storied people and places, past and present . . . a witty and entertaining book that may greatly increase French tourism." (PW) S&S, 1987.   ○

Smith, Bonnie G.
CONFESSIONS OF A CONCIERGE

Biography and oral history—20th-century France through the eyes of the concierge of a Paris apartment building. Yale U Pr, 1985.   ○

Wechsler, Robert, ed.
SAVOIR RIRE: THE HUMORIST'S GUIDE TO FRANCE

This is part of a new series of anthologies of humor about the foibles of travelers, and the countries they visit—anecdotes, poems, cartoons by leading humorists. Catbird Pr, 1989.   ○

White, Freda
THREE RIVERS OF FRANCE

"Her intelligence, wit and curiosity bring the countryside to life"—lovely photos, a classic. Arcade, 1989.   ○

TRAVELOGUES, MEMOIRS

Bailey, Anthony
SPRING JAUNTS

A series of jaunts, originally appearing as articles in *The New Yorker*, one of which is to Nice—"a book to savour . . . wise, funny." (LJ) FS&G, 1986.   ○

DeLarrabeiti, Michael
THE PROVENCAL TALES

Recreation of a trekking experience decades earlier, with the shepherds of Provence and the medieval folk tales related by locals "a magical tour into the past." (BL) St. Martin's, 1989.   ○

Delbanco, Nicholas
RUNNING IN PLACE: SCENES FROM THE SOUTH OF FRANCE

By a novelist who "explores the lure of the Provencal landscape" as a magnet for artists and writers—"elegant depiction of the effect of time on character and place." (LJ) Atl Monthly Pr, 1989.   ○

Fisher, M.F.K.
LONG AGO IN FRANCE, THE YEARS IN DIJON

Part of the new Destinations Series, with an introduction by travel writer Jan Morris. The author's recollections of the tastes, sounds, sights and smells of Dijon where she first learned to appreciate good food and life as a young newlywed back in 1929. P-H, 1992.   ○

Fisher, M.F.K.
TWO TOWNS IN PROVENCE

Two books in one: *A Considerable Town*, about Marseilles—"its glory and wickedness, past and present; its life, its legends its mystery"; and *Map of Another Town, A Memoir of Provence*—two years lived in Aix-en-Provence. Vintage, 1983.   ○

Ford, Ford Madox
PROVENCE: FROM MINSTRELS TO THE MACHINE

"Delightful reminiscences . . . builds up a picture of the past and present of Provence.'' (BRD) Ecco Pr, 1979 (first published 1935).   ○

Helias, Pierre-Jakez
THE HORSE OF PRIDE: LIFE IN A BRETON VILLAGE
Memoirs of how the village was between World Wars I and II—''whimsical folk stories, adventures and initiations . . . affectionate and touching portraits'' of a people. (TL) Yale U Pr, 1980.   ○

Mayle, Peter
A YEAR IN PROVENCE
''Highly entertaining . . . teaches a lesson in social life and customs.'' It is a chronological story of how the author and his wife move to Provence and restore a farmhouse—won a ''Best Travel Book of the Year'' from British Book Awards. Also *Toujours Provence*, more stories (1991). (LJ) Knopf, 1990.   ○

Millar, George
ISABEL AND THE SEA
Sailing the canals of France in the *Truant*, by an inexperienced yachtsman and his wife. Random, 1988.   ○

Niles, Bo
A WINDOW ON PROVENCE
One summer's sojourn into the simple life. Viking, 1990.   ○

Pagnol, Marcel
MY FATHER'S GLORY AND MY MOTHER'S CASTLE
Memories of childhood in Provence at the turn of the century. N Point Pr, 1987.   ○

Stevenson, Robert Louis
TRAVELS WITH A DONKEY IN THE CEVENNES
Reprint of a travel classic (1879) of his trip with Modestine in southern France, with a new introduction about his life as a traveler and writer. Evman England, 1984.   ○

Zbigniew, Herbert
BARBARIANS IN THE GARDEN
Ten travel essays by a Polish poet, translated from the French. He writes lyrically of French and Italian towns—''impressions . . . historical data, musings on art history . . . delightful anecdotes.'' The towns in France are Arles, Lascaux, Valois. (PW) Carcanet, 1985.   ○

GUIDEBOOKS

Green, Kerry and Bythines, Peter
THE WHOLE EUROPE ESCAPE MANUAL: FRANCE, HOLLAND, BELGIUM, WITH LUXEMBOURG
One of a series of guidebooks ''designed to bring Europe to life and put the fantasy and excitement back into travel.'' (Publisher) World Leis Corp, 1984.   ○

Jacobs, Michael and Stirton, Paul
THE KNOPF TRAVELER'S GUIDE TO ART: FRANCE
Suggested tours and routes, guides to collections, hours and fees, museum plans. Organized geographically by region, city, site. Knopf, 1984.   ○

Jacobs, Michael
A GUIDE TO PROVENCE
Alphabetical list of sights with an introduction explaining the special qualities of Provence in southern France. Penguin, 1989.   ○

James, John
THE TRAVELER'S KEY TO MEDIEVAL FRANCE
One of a series of guides to places with religious or spiritual significance, the philosophical ideas that led to them, history, art. Knopf, 1986.   ○

Lichine, Alexis and Perkins, Samuel
ALEXIS LICHINE'S GUIDE TO WINES AND VINEYARDS OF FRANCE
Suggested itineraries, maps, hotels, all the information needed to plan a tour that combines wine and travel as an experience. Knopf, 1986.   ○

Manston, Peter B.
MANSTON'S FLEA MARKETS, ANTIQUE FAIRS, AND AUCTIONS OF FRANCE

Lists both serious antique sources and junk/flea markets as well as providing information on how to deal with shipping and customs. Travel Keys, 1987. ○

Mehling, Marianne
FRANCE: A PHAIDON CULTURAL GUIDE

Succinct appreciation of the best the country has to offer in terms of national treasures and culture—churches, palaces, theaters, museums, monuments, maps and plans, all arranged alphabetically and cross-indexed. Phaidon Pr., n.d. Also separate volumes— *The Loire Valley, Provence and the Cote D'Azur.* ○

O'Toole, Christopher and Losito, Linda
THE HOLIDAY NATURALIST IN FRANCE

For those who love the outdoors, this is a take-along guide, illustrated in color, to birds, flowers, butterflies, etc., as well as jellyfish and mollusks for beach visitors. It is aimed at both the average tourist without specific knowledge of natural history, and those who already know flora and fauna. Stephen Greene Pr, 1987. ○

Reuss, Henry and Margaret
THE UNKNOWN SOUTH OF FRANCE: A HISTORY BUFF'S GUIDE

Events from 400,000 B.C. to 1945. HCP, 1991. ○

Sanger, Andrew
EXPLORING RURAL FRANCE

Regional tours for a day to a week with an emphasis on the unexpected and including reasonably-priced places to stay and to eat. Passport, 1988. Also *Exploring Languedoc & Roussillon* (1989). ○

Wells, Patricia and others
THE FOOD LOVER'S GUIDE TO FRANCE

An itinerary that includes 3-star restaurants, rural cafes, B&B's, elegant chateaux, food markets of the country's varied regions. Workman, 1987. ○

HISTORY

Castries, René de la Croix
THE LIVES OF THE KINGS AND QUEENS OF FRANCE

A survey of royalty from the Merovingian dynasty through Louis-Philippe (1848). It makes obvious that the direction taken by the evolution of the French state was greatly the result of the personalities of its monarchs. Knopf, 1979. ○

Cole, Robert
TRAVELER'S HISTORY OF FRANCE

One of a series of introductory histories for travelers. Interlink Pub, 1989. ○

Law, Joy
FLEUR DE LYS: THE KINGS AND QUEENS OF FRANCE

Anecdotal, entertaining view of French monarchs from inside the palace, using contemporary accounts. McGraw, 1976. ○

Maurois, André
A HISTORY OF FRANCE

FS&G, 1957. ○

PARIS

Background Reading and Guides

Ash, Russell and Higton, Bernard
PARIS: SPIRIT OF PLACE

Part of a series of similar books—words of writers that capture the spirit of a place, accompanied by illustrations of the chosen excerpts. Arcade Pub Inc, 1989. ○

Cody, Morrill and Ford, Hugh
THE WOMEN OF MONTPARNASSE

A collective biography of English and American women on the Left Bank between World War I and II who, the authors claim, shaped and directed the life of the under-thirties of the Anglo-American art colony—profiles of Josephine Baker, Gertrude Stein, others. Cornwall Bks, 1984. ○

Culbertson, Judi and Randall, Tom
**PERMANENT PARISIANS: AN
ILLUSTRATED GUIDE TO THE
CEMETERIES OF PARIS**

Biographies of such people as Colette, Gertrude Stein, Alexander Dumas, others, suggested walks, photographs and maps. Chelsea Green, 1986.   o

Danto, Eloise
**THE UNDISCOVERED MUSEUMS
OF PARIS**

A travel guide to little-known and hard-to-find museums, galleries, churches and palaces. Surrey Bks, 1991.   o

Fitch, Noel R.
LITERARY CAFES OF PARIS

"A sparkling book" packed with anecdotes of literary life in Paris that evoke scenes from places like Deux-Magots and Harry's Bar. Includes practical information on metro stops to get there, hours and the cafe's food and drink. Starrhill Pr, 1990.   o

Fitch, Noel R.
WALKS IN HEMINGWAY'S PARIS

Seven walks, with maps and photos, of where Hemingway ate, slept, wrote as described in *A Moveable Feast* (see below). "A joy to read . . . conveys the irresistible patina of passion and sense of place." (BL) St. Martin's, 1990.   o

Gajdusek, Robert E.
HEMINGWAY'S PARIS

A "loving compilation of photographs of places mentioned by Hemingway and his friends, interspersed with passages from his writings." (TBL) Scribner, 1982.   o

Hansen, Arlen J.
**EXPATRIATE PARIS: A CULTURAL
AND LITERARY GUIDE TO
PARIS IN THE 1920s**

"For travelers, Francophiles and the curious . . . gossipy retrospective . . . hundreds of short entries organized geographically around 32 neighborhoods." (PW) Arcade, 1990.   o

Harriss, Joseph
**TALLEST TOWER, EIFFEL AND
BELLE EPOQUE**

Social history of the Tower. Houghton, 1975.   o

Hemingway, Ernest
A MOVEABLE FEAST

Personal reminiscences and sketches of the years in Paris, 1921–26, in a new edition. Collier, 1988.   o

Jordan Haight, Mary Ellen
**WALKS IN GERTRUDE STEIN'S
PARIS**

Five walking tours for the literary traveler through the Bohemian Paris where Stein and her literary and artist friends hung out at a period when Paris was home to expatriate literati and artists from many countries (1900 to the German occupation of Paris in World War II). Gibbs Smith, 1988.   o

Littlewood, Ian
PARIS: A LITERARY COMPANION

This book begins with writings by historian Gibbons and includes writings by Rabelais, Dickens, going on to contemporary writings that illuminate Paris past and present. Harper, 1989.   o

Lurie, Patty
**A GUIDE TO THE IMPRESSIONIST
LANDSCAPE: DAYTRIPS FROM
PARIS**

By an art historian who lives in Paris; itineraries out of Paris to the places where Impressionist landscape paintings were created, along with practical information for walking trips around Paris to sites where painters such as Monet and Cezanne worked. Little, 1990.   o

Mehling, Marianne
**PARIS: A PHAIDON CULTURAL
GUIDE**

Succinct appreciation of the best the country has to offer in terms of national treasures and culture—churches, palaces, theaters, museums, monuments, maps and plans, all arranged alphabetically and cross-indexed. Phaidon Pr., n.d. ○

Meral, Jean
PARIS IN AMERICAN LITERATURE
Translated from the French; an analysis of Paris in American literature (fiction, drama, poetry) of the last 150 years. U of North Carolina, 1989. ○

Olsen, Donald J.
THE CITY AS A WORK OF ART: LONDON, PARIS, VIENNA
"Delightful and gripping, richly illustrated social history." (PW) Yale U Pr, 1988. ○

Wells, Patricia
THE FOOD LOVER'S GUIDE TO PARIS
See entry under France/Guidebooks. ○

Whitman, William B.
LITERARY CAFES OF PARIS
Anecdotes, pen and ink sketches, maps and walks, with a glossary of terms used in restaurants and cafes. Starrhill Pr, 1990. ○

Novels

Barber, Noel
THE WEEPING AND THE LAUGHTER
Saga of an aristocratic Russian family in France, forced to flee Russia when the communists took over. McGraw, 1985. ○

Boissard, Janine
CECILE
Last of a three-part saga of the Moreau family that began with *Christmas Lessons* (1984) and *A Time to Choose* (1985)—"worldly wisdom and ebullience are captured in a lively translation that brings this attractive family saga to a satisfying conclusion." (FC) Little, 1988. ○

Bond, Michael
MONSIEUR PAMPLEMOUSSE TAKES THE CURE
The inspector for a culinary guide finds that all's not what it seems to be at a luxury spa whose "guests" are treated like inmates rather than paying customers. Random, 1988. Also *Monsieur Pamplemousse Investigates Columbine* (1990). ○

Chandernagor, Françoise
THE KING'S WAY
Biographical novel in the form of a memoir of Louis XIV's marriage to Françoise D'Aubigné, French court life and intrigue; "will appeal to the discerning reader." (FC) HarBraceJ, 1984. ○

Collins, Larry
FALL FROM GRACE
A novel of espionage, D-Day of World War II, and an American agent who seeks to find out the fate of a woman years after the war. S&S, 1985. ○

Deforges, Regine
THE BLUE BICYCLE
France during World War II and a glimpse of life of the period at a family estate and in Paris. Stuart L., 1986. ○

Durand, Loup
DADDY
"Superb plotting, mesmerizing characters" in a suspense novel of the Nazi era, about a young genius with financial secrets fleeing his pursuer. (FC) Villard, 1988. ○

Durrell, Lawrence
LIVIA (Avignon)
Chronologically the first of the projected five-part sequence of novels. Following are *Monsieur* (1975) and *Constance* (1982). Viking, 1979. ○

Freeling, Nicolas
WOLFNIGHT
Just one of the many marvelous mysteries by this author. In this one the plot "reeks of Chappaquiddick" in its parallel events and the "tug of war . . . between police efforts to solve the mystery [of a young woman's death] and political efforts to cover it up." (FC) Pantheon, 1982. Other books by Freeling, set in France, include: *Those in Peril* (1990), *Not As Far As Velma* (1989), *The Back*

of the North Wind (1983), *Arlette* (1981), *The Bugles Blowing* (1976) and *The Dressing of Diamond* (1974).   ○

Hebden, Mark
PEL AND THE PARTY SPIRIT
Murder on Route Nationale 6—"police procedural with a . . . fair amount of droll humor." (FC) St. Martin, 1991. Also *Death Set to Music* (1982).   ○

Hemingway, Ernest
THE GARDEN OF EDEN
Begun in 1946 and worked on intermittently for many years, this Hemingway novel was finally published in 1986. It's based on his honeymoon, back in 1927, with his first wife—an idyllic existence in a French fishing village in the Camargue becomes a love triangle. Scribner, 1986.   ○

Malraux, André
THE WALNUT TREES OF ALTENBURG
Translated from the French—"juxtaposing the beginnings of the two great European wars . . . depictions of France overrun by the Germans in 1940." (FC) Fertig, 1989. ○

Read, Piers Paul
THE FREE FRENCHMAN
The three elements of wartime France—a free Frenchman, a communist and a collaborator—in an "unusually engrossing" epic. (FC) Random, 1986.   ○

Sagan, Françoise A.
A RELUCTANT HERO
Vichy of 1942 is the setting—French Resistance operatives try to convince an industrialist to open his factory to political refugees. Dutton, 1987. Also *Salad Days* (1984), about a timid bookkeeper who discovers a cache of jewels that changes his life.   ○

Wallace, Irving
THE MIRACLE (Lourdes)
The Catholic Church reveals the date that Bernadette predicted the Virgin Mary would appear in Lourdes and as the time approaches "an explosive mix of petitioners, journalists, and opportunists" descend upon Lourdes. Who is to be the one to whom Mary reveals herself, or to be blessed with a miraculous cure, or to "sniff out" fraud—these are questions around which the plot develops. (FC) Dutton, 1984.   ○

Wharton, William
TIDINGS
Several days of the Christmas holidays as a philosophy professor and his wife, living in France, invite their four children to spend the holidays with them. Holt, 1987.   ○

BORDEAUX

Daley, Robert
STRONG WINE RED AS BLOOD
An American businessman sent to buy a wine chateau becomes enthralled with the life and the winemaking process—novel of the region and of winemaking. Harper's Magazine Pr, 1975.   ○

Mauriac, François
A MAURIAC READER
Five novels set in Bordeaux and environs for which the author won the Nobel Prize for literature in 1952; includes *Woman of the Pharisees* (1946). FS&G, 1968 (first published 1952).   ○

Mauriac, François
QUESTIONS OF PRECEDENCE
Explores the moral implications of using another person for an unworthy purpose—in this case to enter Bordeaux society. FS&G, 1959. Also *Maltaverne* (1970).   ○

BRITTANY

Francis, Clare
NIGHT SKY
The heroine, unwed and pregnant, ends up with relatives in Brittany where she becomes part of a dangerous operation to evacuate Allied servicemen during World War II. Morrow, 1984.   ○

Holland, Cecelia
LORDS OF VAUMARTIN
Brittany in the 14th century is the setting for a story of a young man's claim to knighthood. HM, 1988. ○

Loti, Pierre
AN ICELAND FISHERMAN
Breton fishermen and their lives of danger and hardship, by a nineteenth-century writer. Dutton, 1935 (first published 1896). ○

MacInnes, Helen
ASSIGNMENT IN BRITTANY
A British officer is sent on a mission to Brittany following the Dunkirk disaster in World War II. HarBraceJ, 1971. ○

Shute, Nevil
MOST SECRET
Exceptionally skillful adventure-and-espionage story of English and Free French officers sent to a Breton village to wreak havoc on German patrols. Morrow, 1945. ○

Stewart, Mary
MERLIN TRILOGY
Omnibus edition of a trilogy about Merlin and the Arthurian legend that includes *The Crystal Cave* (1970), *The Hollow Hills* (1973), *The Last Enchantment* (1979)—"high adventure, mystery and romantic intrigue. . . . produce an extremely entertaining tale." (FC) Morrow, 1980. ○

BURGUNDY

Colette
MY MOTHER'S HOUSE and **SIDO**
Autobiographical novels of the author's early years in the region. FS&G, 1975 (first published 1922 and 1929, respectively). ○

Hebden, Mark
PEL AND THE PICTURE OF INNOCENCE
One of a series of police procedurals featuring Chief Inspector Pel. St. Martin, 1989. Also *Pel and the Touch of Pitch* (1988), *Pel and the Faceless Corpse* (1982). ○

CORSICA

Swindells, Madge
THE CORSICAN WOMAN
An American archaeologist helps a beautiful Corsican woman to escape a lynch mob after she shoots her father-in-law. Warner, 1988. ○

MEDITERRANEAN COAST

Daley, Robert
THE DANGEROUS EDGE
Story about an egotistical expatriate American who plans a bank robbery—the author's "knowledge of [French] police procedure . . . insight into human nature . . . add up here to a gripping detective novel [and] romantic, moving love story." (FC) S&S, 1983. ○

Shaw, Irwin
EVENING IN BYZANTIUM
A has-been Hollywood producer at the Cannes film festival. Delacorte Pr, 1973. ○

Tournier, Michel
THE GOLDEN DROPLET
Originally published in France in 1985. Follows a Berber shepherd who leaves the Sahara for Marseilles—"at once a fairy tale, a philosophical parable . . . and a traditional naturalist novel." Doubleday, 1987. ○

Waller, Leslie
AMAZING FAITH
San Sebastian is a Monaco-like principality on the Mediterranean with a Grace Kelly-like princess, and the plot concerns a scheme for organized crime to take over the lush gambling casinos. McGraw, 1988. ○

NORMANDY

Holt, Victoria
DEMON LOVER
A typical Holt romance, set in Normandy during the Second Empire—"innocent heroine . . . roguishly incorrigible hero . . . happy ending." (FC) Doubleday, 1982. ○

Prescott, H.F.M.
SON OF DUST
A historical romance set in eleventh-century
Normandy—weaves "a rich tapestry, glow-
ing with color and quick life." (FC) Macmil-
lan, 1956 (first published 1932).   ○

Shipway, George
THE PALADIN
Historical novel, and a good suspense story,
of eleventh-century England and Normandy—the plot revolves around the Norman knight Tirel. HarBraceJ, 1973.   ○

PROVENCE

Conrad, Joseph
THE ROVER
An old sea captain throws his life away in a
scheme for outwitting Lord Nelson, and
blockading Toulon. Doubleday, 1923.   ○

Durrell, Lawrence
QUINX
Fifth title of the Avignon quintet; preceding
are *Monsieur* (1975), *Livia* (1979), *Constance*
(1982), *Sebastian* (1984). Viking, 1985.   ○

Fisher, M.F.K.
THE BOSS DOG
Adventures of a "proud if scruffy mongrel"
and a soujourn in France with two daughters in the early 1950s—"inimitable observations of place, taste and character." (FC)
N Point Pr, 1991.   ○

Pagnol, Marcel
**THE WATER OF THE HILLS: JEAN
   DE FLORETTE AND MANON OF
   THE SPRINGS**
"Greek tragedy in the hillsides north of Mar-
seilles" as the daughter of a hunchbacked
tax collector seeks retribution for his treat-
ment by local people. N Point Pr, 1988.   ○

Stewart, Mary
MADAM WILL YOU TALK?
A young widow befriends a thirteen-year-
old boy and discovers that his father is suspected of murder—a warm Provençal background. Morrow, 1956.   ○

PARIS

Aiken, Joan
THE GIRL FROM PARIS
Romantic suspense novel of a twenty-one-
year old English girl faced with earning her
own way as a governess in mid-nineteenth-
century Paris. Doubleday, 1982.   ○

Barber, Noel
A FAREWELL TO FRANCE
A love story and a war story of the French
occupation and resistance movement through
the eyes of an American journalist. Macmillan, 1983.   ○

Beauvoir, Simone de
THE MANDARINS
"A group portrait of the Existentialist clique
. . . the political role played . . . from the
liberation to the late 1940s." (BRD) World,
1956. Also *Les Belles Images* (1968), which
considers the heroine's involvements with
people in her life.   ○

Boissard, Janine
A NEW WOMAN
Portrait of "a woman starting at zero in mid-
life" when her husband leaves her for a
younger woman. (FC) Little, 1982. Also *A
Matter of Feeling* (1980).   ○

Briskin, Jacqueline
THE NAKED HEART
A daughter pledges to avenge the death
of her parents by the Nazis. Delacorte,
1989.   ○

Cadell, Elizabeth
THE MARRYING KIND
"A pleasant story with lots of local color"—
the plot involves a young Englishwoman
"not the marrying kind" who must deal
with a problem father in Paris, and finds
herself in love. (FC) Morrow, 1980.   ○

Colette
THE COMPLETE CLAUDINE
Omnibus edition of *Claudine at School, Clau-
dine in Paris, Claudine Married, Claudine and
Annie*—semi-autobiographical novels writ-

ten in 1900–1903. Also, set in Paris, are *Gigi, Julie De Carneilhan, Chance Acquaintances, The Innocent Libertine* (1909), and *The Vagabond* (1910). FS&G, 1976.   o

Deforges, Regine
THE BLUE BICYCLE
France during World War II and glimpses of the life of the period at a family estate and in Paris. Berkley Pub, 1987.   o

Eberstadt, Isabel
NATURAL VICTIMS
"A singularly elegant horror story . . . about madness and money and the interaction between them" set in Paris where the heroine has fled from her mother. (FC) Knopf, 1983.   o

Ferlinghetti, Lawrence
LOVE IN THE DAYS OF RAGE
A French banker and an American expatriate artist are caught up in a love affair and the student riots in Paris in 1968. Dutton, 1988.   o

Forsyth, Frederick
THE DAY OF THE JACKAL
Meticulous plans for the assassination of de Gaulle, and the search when authorities are alerted to the plan under way—almost seems like an actual event as real people move in and out of the plot. Viking, 1971.   o

Gallant, Mavis
OVERHEAD IN A BALLOON
Short stories inter-connected by their characters—"Paris milieu is well captured." (FC) Random, 1987.   o

Gary, Romain
KING SOLOMON
A taxi driver narrates the plot; he is general helper in SOS, an organization in Paris that is a "combination of Amnesty International and Meals on Wheels." (FC) Har-Row, 1983.   o

Grayson, Richard
CRIME WITHOUT PASSION
"Clever plotting and the ambience of the glittering city during the last century ensure

. . . a dandy entertainment"—Gautier of the Sureté investigates a crime-of-passion murder. (FC) St. Martin, 1984.   o

Hemingway, Ernest
THE SUN ALSO RISES
Novel of the post-World War I lost generation, with scenes shifting between Paris and Spain. Scribner, 1926.   o

Hill, Reginald
THE COLLABORATORS
Set mostly in Paris during World War II— "the conflict between social and personal responsibility . . . the collaborator in various guises from the self-serving black marketeer to the loving mother and wife." (BRD) Countryman Pr, 1989.   o

Hotchner, A.E.
THE MAN WHO LIVED AT THE RITZ
Set mostly at the Paris Ritz in the 1940s with "intimate glimpses of the famous and infamous" (Chanel, Goering, etc.) and "a lively, often vivid piece of chase-thriller narrative." (FC) Putnam Pub Group, 1981.   o

Miller, Henry
TROPIC OF CANCER
Autobiographical novel of an American in Paris in the early '30s. Modern Lib, 1983 (first published 1961).   o

Perec, Georges
LIFE; A USER'S MANUAL
A novel of unusual literary devices, first published in 1978. It is set in a Paris apartment house, in a single day, with 99 chapters and an epilogue. It describes the building's 100 rooms and the life stories of their occupants, while a single Englishman paints. Godine, 1987.   o

Remarque, Erich Maria
ARCH OF TRIUMPH
Refugees from the Nazis in Paris just before World War II. This is another novel you can still catch in a movie version on late-night TV occasionally. Appleton, 1945.   o

Rhys, Jean
QUARTET
An English girl in Paris is victim of a rather sick couple. Har-Row, 1971 (first published 1928). Also *Good Morning, Midnight* (1939), in which the heroine—"beauty and youth dribbled away"—returns to Paris.   ○

Rice, Luanne
THE SECRETS OF PARIS
"Paris settings and themes of betrayal and forgiveness" when the heroine spends a year in Paris with her husband. (FC) Viking, 1991.   ○

Romains, Jules
THE DEPTHS AND THE HEIGHTS
A political novel of Paris heading toward World War I. Knopf, 1937. Also *The Earth Trembles* (1936) and *Men of Good Will* (1932).   ○

Sagan, Françoise
A CERTAIN SMILE
Love affair of a young student and an older married man. Dutton, 1956. Also, set in Paris, *La Chamade* (1966).   ○

Sartre, Jean Paul
THE AGE OF REASON
Existentialism in Paris, 1938. Knopf, 1947.   ○

Signoret, Simone
ADIEU, VOLODYA
Traces the "trajectory of European history" in the years following the Russian Revolution through the lives of two Jewish families from the Ukraine and Poland who settle in Paris. (FC) Random, 1986.   ○

GERMANY

Series Guidebooks
(See Appendix 1)

At Its Best Guide: Germany (East and West)
Baedeker: Berlin, Cologne; Frankfort; Hamburg; Munich; Stuttgart; Rhine
Berlitz: Germany; Berlin; Munich; Rhine Valley
Blue Guide: Germany
Exploring Rural Europe: Germany
Fisher's World: Germany
Fodor: Germany
Frommer: Germany; Berlin ($-A-Day)
Insight Guide: Berlin; Dusseldorf; Germany East/West; Munich; The Rhine
Langenscheidt: Self-Guided Berlin
Let's Go: Berlin
Michael's Guide: Frankfort
Michelin: Germany
Nagel's Encyclopedia Guide: German Federal Republic (West)
Off the Beaten Track: West Germany
Real Guide: Germany; Berlin
2–22 Days Itinerary Planning Guide: Germany, Austria & Switzerland

Visitor's Guide: Bavaria; The Black Forest; The Rhine, Mosel and Eifel

Background Reading

Ardagh, John
GERMANY AND THE GERMANS
"An information-packed view of present-day Germany . . . admiring, chatty, frank look at daily life in West Germany"—guest-worker problems, pollution; includes a chapter on East Germany. (PW) Harper, 1987.   ○

Ash, Timothy G.
THE MAGIC LANTERN
See entry under Czechoslovakia.   ○

Craig, Gordon A.
THE GERMANS
"A literate, eminently readable book . . . fundamental facets of German life and culture. . . . chapters on religion, money, women, romantics, soldiers, students, Germany and Jews, literature and society [trace]

attitudes and experiences" over the last centuries. (NYTBR) NAL, 1989.   ○

Gill, Anton
BERLIN TO BUCHAREST: TRAVELS IN EASTERN EUROPE
See entry under Europe/Background Reading.   ○

Grzesinski, Albert C.
INSIDE GERMANY
Reprint of the 1939 edition. AMS Pr.   ○

Laqueur, Walter
GERMANY TODAY: A PERSONAL REPORT
"A blend of reportage and reminiscence, of impressions and erudition—served up lightly." (NYTBR) Little, 1985.   ○

Marsh, David
THE GERMANS: THE PIVOTAL NATION
By a London correspondent for *Financial Times*—"a clarifying view of German attitudes, trends and issues." (PW) St Martin, 1990.   ○

Rippley, Lavern J.
OF GERMAN WAYS
Legend and lore, folkways and fact of the German people, both in Germany and America. Crown, 1986.   ○

Shirer, William L.
THE RISE AND FALL OF THE THIRD REICH
A classic on the whole history of the Nazi movement through World War II. Random, 1984 (first published 1960). Also *Berlin Diary* (1988, first published 1941).   ○

Shlaes, Amity
GERMANY: THE EMPIRE WITHIN
The author is a European correspondent for *The Wall Street Journal*—"impressionistic travelogue . . . telling observations." The author deliberately sought out small and odd groups within the society. (PW) FS&G, 1991.   ○

Stern, Fritz
DREAMS AND DELUSIONS: THE DRAMA OF GERMAN HISTORY
Essays on the German experience, from a biography of Einstein to post-World War II relations with the United States. Knopf, 1987.   ○

BERLIN

Agee, Joel
TWELVE YEARS; AN AMERICAN BOYHOOD IN EAST GERMANY
A unique view of life inside East Germany where the author (son of James Agee) lived with his American mother and German Communist stepfather from age eight until 1960. FS&G, 1981.   ○

Bornstein, Jerry
THE WALL CAME TUMBLING DOWN
Chronology of European events leading to the fall of communism in East Germany and the wall—photos that capture the dramatic events, history of Berlin 1945–89, and an introduction by Willy Brandt. Arch Cape Pr, 1990.   ○

Darnton, Robert
BERLIN JOURNAL, 1989–90
An academic year in Berlin at the time of the uprising that brought down the Wall. Some chapters appeared in *New Republic* in shorter versions. (PW) Norton, 1991.   ○

Gelb, Norman
THE BERLIN WALL
A vivid recreation of the night that construction of the wall started and the escape attempts by East Berliners that followed. Times Bks, 1987.   ○

Reinfrank, Karin and Arno
BERLIN: TWO CITIES UNDER SEVEN FLAGS
A kaleidoscopic A-to-Z that captures the many faces of Berlin. This is an unconventional collection of 80 anecdotal selections in alphabetic format. St. Martin, 1987.   ○

Ryan, Cornelius
THE LAST BATTLE
Story of the last three weeks of World War II in Europe, culminating in the fall of Berlin to the Soviets in 1945. PB, 1985 (first published 1966).   o

Walker, Ian
ZOO STATION: ADVENTURES IN EAST AND WEST BERLIN
"Rambling exploration of life on both sides of the cold war's line of demarcation . . . Walker's private and decidedly pro-Communist political leanings are also given free rein." (PW) Atl Monthly Pr, 1988.   o

Wyden, Peter
WALL: THE BERLIN STORY
Written by a Berlin native, now an American journalist. This is a history with anecdotes, personal stories, spies—"a dramatic narrative that is as entertaining as it is revealing." (BL) S&S, 1989.   o

GUIDEBOOKS

Kitfield, James and Walker, William
WHOLE EUROPE ESCAPE MANUAL: GERMANY, AUSTRIA, SWITZERLAND
Part of a series of guidebooks "designed to . . . put the fantasy and excitement back into travel." (Publisher) World Leis Corp, 1984.   o

Manston, Peter B.
MANSTON'S FLEA MARKETS, ANTIQUE FAIRS AND AUCTIONS OF GERMANY
Lists both serious antique sources and junk/flea markets as well as providing information on how to deal with shipping and customs. Travel Keys, 1987.   o

Mehling, Franz N.
GERMANY: A PHAIDON CULTURAL GUIDE
Succinct appreciation of the best the country has to offer in terms of national treasures and culture—churches, palaces, theaters, museums, monuments, maps and plans, all arranged alphabetically and cross-indexed. Phaidon Pr, n.d.   o

HISTORY

Bendersky, Joseph W.
A HISTORY OF NAZI GERMANY
Nelson-Hall, 1984.   o

Detwiler, Donald S.
GERMANY: A SHORT HISTORY
A very concise, one-volume history. Southern Illinois U, 1989.   o

Fulbrook, Mary
A CONCISE HISTORY OF GERMANY
First of a new series for the general reader, and college students; illustrated histories with the "main emphasis on broader historical currents." Covers the period from medieval times to the recent reunification. (BL) Cambridge U Pr, 1991.   o

Novels

Abish, Walter
HOW GERMAN IS IT
"About the new Germany, but the ghost of the old one is lurking in the background." The plot focuses on two brothers—"an exploration of the psyche of modern Germany." (BRD) New Directions, 1980.   o

Boll, Heinrich
THE STORIES OF HEINRICH BOLL
Arranged chronologically, represents the entire span of Boll's career from early postwar stories to "masterfully satirical tales . . . of the new German sociopolitical order." (BRD) Knopf, 1986.   o

Boll, Heinrich
WOMEN IN A RIVER LANDSCAPE
Thirty years after starting a life of politics to make a new government, a couple "are ill with moral defeat" and around them members of various groups (lawyers, bankers, etc.) step forward to deliver his/her "load of fear, shame or arrogance." (BRD) Knopf, 1988. Also *The Safety Net* (1982), *And Never Said a Word* (1978), *The Bread of Those Early*

Years (1976), *Lost Honor of Katharina Blum* (1975), *The Clown* (1965).   o

Briskin, Jacqueline
THE OTHER SIDE OF LOVE
An American basketball player and a beautiful German sprinter meet at the 1936 Olympic Games in Berlin, and fall in love. The author has "impressively conveyed a sense of time and place . . . Hitler's Germany" (and wartime England as well). (FC) Delacorte, 1991.   o

Brückner, Christine
FLIGHT OF CRANES
Document of a woman's survival from the end of World War II, fleeing the Russian troops, to middle-age in postwar Germany. Fromm, 1982. The companion book, about the woman's life up to the point of *Flight of Cranes*, is *Gillyflower Kid* (1982).   o

Grass, Günter
HEADBIRTHS; OR, THE GERMANS ARE DYING OUT
"Collage of intellectual and ideological jabs at Germany . . . on the eve of the . . . 1980 elections." (FC) HarBraceJ, 1982.   o

Grass, Günter
THE MEETING AT TELGTE
Historical novel set in 1647 (at the end of the Thirty Years War) "brings together a fictional meeting of literati—theorists, poets, prose writers . . . for the purpose of strengthening the last bond within a divided nation: its language and literature." It "mirrors a real meeting [of] Group 47, at the end of another ravaging war 300 years later." (FC) HarBraceJ, 1981. Also *Dog Years* (1965), *The Tin Drum* (1963), *Local Anesthetic* (1970).   o

Harrington, William
THE ENGLISH LADY
Espionage novel about a British aristocrat "married to a German cousin, friend of Hitler [and other] upper echelon Nazis" who becomes an agent for the British. (FC) Seaview, 1982.   o

Herlin, Hans
SOLO RUN
See under "Czechoslovakia/Novels."   o

Hughes, Richard
THE FOX IN THE ATTIC
A young man leaves England to visit relatives in Germany at the time Hitler comes to power—"sketches of the young Hitler are brought off brilliantly [as are] scenes and characterizations that represent the festering Germany of that time." (FC) Har-Row, 1961.   o

Kirst, Hans H.
THE AFFAIRS OF THE GENERALS
Fictionalized reconstruction of how Goering and Heydrich, with Hitler, destroyed two high-ranking army officers, making their way clear for a complete takeover of the Wehrmacht—"a vivid portrait of the Nazi organization." (FC) Coward, 1979.   o

Kirst, Hans H.
REVOLT OF GUNNAR ASCH
Chronicle, in four novels, of the adventures of a German army sergeant beginning just before World War II—grim drama, suspense, high comedy, satire. Little, 1956. The titles that follow are *Forward Gunnar Asch* (1956), *Return of Gunnar Asch* (1957), *What Became of Gunnar Asch* (1964).   o

Leahy, Syrell R.
ONLY YESTERDAY
An American student allows her host family to raise her illegitimate daughter. Putnam, 1989.   o

Le Carré, John
A SMALL TOWN IN GERMANY
    (Bonn)
Britain must solve the mystery of a missing "green" file in Bonn. Coward, 1968.   o

Leffland, Ella
THE KNIGHT, DEATH AND THE DEVIL
Fictionalized depiction of Goering's life that presents a fascinating portrait of the era. Morrow, 1990.   o

Maron, Monika
FLIGHT OF ASHES

A woman journalist in East Germany decides to tell the truth about Bitterfield—the dirtiest city in Europe, environmentally speaking—and the consequences affect both her personal and professional life. Readers Int, 1986.   ○

Paretti, Sandra
THE WISHING TREE

Begins on New Year's Eve, 1900; the riches to rags and back again saga of Camilla Hofmann—"strong dose of historical vicissitudes of the early twentieth century." (FC) St. Martin, 1977.   ○

Peters, Elizabeth
TROJAN GOLD

Part of series in which Vicky Bliss, an art historian, is chief protagonist. This involves ancient gold jewelry missing since 1945—"scintillating, captivating tale." (FC) Atheneum, 1987.   ○

Uhlman, Fred
REUNION (Stuttgart)

Two young male friends, one Jewish, the other the son of a count whose family supports Hitler. Their friendship disintegrates, and one is forced to leave Germany. "The novella is simply, elegantly, and sweetly written . . . Arthur Koestler has said of the apparently autobiographical story, 'It is as though Mozart had re-written the Gotterdammerung.' " (FC) FS&G, 1977.   ○

Uris, Leon
ARMAGEDDON: A NOVEL OF BERLIN

See below under Berlin.   ○

Walser, Martin
THE INNER MAN

A chauffeur who is the seeming epitome of self-control copes with his job and family by turning inward—"the hero's musings are often glitteringly humorous, and the dialogue is splendid." (BRD) HR&W, 1985. ○

Walser, Martin
NO MAN'S LAND

Story of conflicted loyalties. A spy for the East Germans, living in Bonn, hopes Germany will be reunited. HR&W, 1989. Also *The Swan Villa* (1982) and *Runaway Horse* (1980).   ○

Wellershoff, D.
WINNER TAKES ALL

Story of a young man in Germany obsessed with making money; first published in 1983. "Dramatic and devastating picture of the glittering and cruel world of fast-buck financiers and takeover artists"—German style. (BRD) Carcanet Pr, 1986.   ○

Wolf, Christa
ACCIDENT; A DAY'S NEWS

One day in the life of a woman writer in a small East German village at the time of Chernobyl—"connections she finds . . . between the monstrous creations of technology and love or lack of love." (BRD) FS&G, 1989.   ○

BERLIN

Baum, Vicki
GRAND HOTEL

Two days in the lives of hotel guests and employees, in Berlin of the 1920s. Doubleday, 1931.   ○

Berger, Thomas
CRAZY IN BERLIN

An American G.I. of German background at the end of World War II, complicated relationships and guilt about the treatment of Jews by the Nazis. Scribner, 1958.   ○

Deighton, Len
BERLIN GAME

A British agent assists an undercover agent to escape from East Berlin but a security leak threatens the operation—"elaborately plotted [but] its best moments derive from the setting [in Berlin] and from the force of this particular setting upon behavior and psychology." Knopf, 1984. Also *Funeral in Berlin* (1965), about a Russian scientist smuggled out of East Berlin. *London Match* follows in this Berlin-based suspense series (1985). ○

Deighton, Len
WINTER: A NOVEL OF A BERLIN FAMILY
"Gives recognizably human form to the shape of German history from 1900 through 1945." Knopf, 1987. ○

Döblin, Alfred
A PEOPLE BETRAYED
This book and *Karl and Rosa* (1983), are the first two in a trilogy—"Interweaves the lives of historical personages . . . and fictional characters to portray the chaos of war and the failure of revolution." (FC) Fromm, 1983 (first published 1948–50). Also *Berlin Alexanderplatz*. ○

Isaacs, Susan
SHINING THROUGH
Most of the plot is preamble to the heroine's involvement in a dangerous mission to Berlin during World War II; made into a movie, 1992. Har-Row, 1988. ○

Isherwood, Christopher
THE BERLIN STORIES
Stories that reflect life in Berlin in the early 1930s and on which the play *I Am a Camera* and the musical *Cabaret* are based. New Directions, 1954. ○

Johnson, Uwe
THE THIRD BOOK ABOUT ACHIM
"A somewhat Joycean, somewhat Kafka-esque" story of the author's views on the split in Germany—"offers a dual perspective on life in East Germany." HarBraceJ, 1967. Also *Two Views* (1966), *Speculations About Jacob* (1962). ○

Kaufelt, David A.
SILVER ROSE
Suspenseful story of a young Jewish woman who assumes the identity of a gentile cabaret singer and succeeds in moving into Hitler's inner circle through marriage to a high-ranking Nazi—"period details and plenty of excitement" for melodrama fans. (FC) Delacorte Pr, 1982. ○

Kaye, M.M.
DEATH IN BERLIN
Reprint of a book first published in 1955 with a plot concerning a cache of Dutch diamonds stolen by the Nazis—set mostly in West Berlin. St Martin, 1985. ○

Kerr, Philip
MARCH VIOLETS
Berlin in 1936 is the setting. A hard-boiled detective must find the murderer of his daughter and son-in-law, and gets involved in political scandal. Viking, 1989. ○

Knebel, Fletcher
CROSSING IN BERLIN
"A tense, exciting, entertaining novel of suspense" at the Berlin wall as a woman tries to get out of East Germany. "One should have a taste for unstressed satire and covert irony"—there are "weak, venal, stupid [characters], or the reverse" on each side of the Wall. (FC) Doubleday, 1981. ○

Kotzwinkle, William
THE EXILE
"Two distinct adventures . . . suspense-fully intertwined"—a contemporary film star is telepathically transported to wartime Berlin where he is a black marketeer and must "grapple with the practical implications of this sinister alter ego." (FC) Dutton, 1987. ○

McEwan, Ian
THE INNOCENT
An "innocent" is assigned to work on a British-American espionage operation in Berlin of 1955—"a city of 5,000 or maybe 10,000 spies . . . of stimulating menace and unsettling temptation." (NYT) Doubleday, 1990. ○

Pickering, Paul
THE BLUE GATE OF BABYLON
A British Intelligence officer is banished to Berlin in 1961 to set up a cafe intended to trap Eastern Zone officers, and years later is called on to tie up a loose end—"highly literate, brooding and sad." (BRD) Random, 1989. ○

Schneider, Peter
THE WALL JUMPER
A novel about the Berlin wall. Marvelous stories of wall-jumpers "balanced between the mythic, and the plausible, boundary-walking tales that create . . . the unreal reality of Berlin." (NYTBR) Pantheon, 1984. ○

Uris, Leon
ARMAGEDDON: A NOVEL OF BERLIN
Saga of Berlin from the end of World War II to the Berlin airlift when the Allies and the Russians first came into conflict over Berlin and its access. There's a love story as well, between an American military government

officer and a German girl. Doubleday, 1964. ○

Wallace, Irving
THE SEVENTH SECRET
The daughter of an Oxford don picks up her father's cause of proving that Hitler did not really die in that bunker in Berlin; she acquires three protectors in her conflict with neo-Nazis who wish to perpetuate Hitler's image. Dutton, 1986. ○

Welt, Elly
BERLIN WILD
The holocaust, 1943–45, seen from a sideline perspective of one man who is protected and survives. Viking, 1986. ○

GREECE
(Including Cyprus)

Series Guidebooks
(See Appendix 1)

American Express Pocket Guide: Greece
Baedeker: Athens; Greek Islands
Berlitz: Greece; Athens; Corfu; Crete; Cyprus; Greek Islands; Peloponnese; Rhodes; Salonika
Blue Guide: Crete; Cyprus; Greece
Cadogan Guide: Greek Islands
Exploring Rural Europe: Greece
Fisher's World: Greece
Fodor: Greece
Frommer: Athens; Greece ($-A-Day)
Independent Traveller: The Greek Islands; Mainland Greece
Insight Guide: Athens, Crete, Greece; Greek Islands
Let's Go: Cyprus, Greece
Michelin: Greece
Nelles Guide: Crete
Real Guide: Greece

Background Reading

Amos, H.D. and Lang, A.G.
THESE WERE THE GREEKS
"A general introduction to Greek culture . . . they convey much historical fact without losing either the reader's attention or

the shape of the period treated." (BL) State Mutual Bk, 1988. ○

Bell, Robert E.
PLACE NAMES IN CLASSICAL MYTHOLOGY
Fascinating dictionary that brings to life those ancient places for the reader or traveler. ABC-Clio, 1989. ○

Biers, William R.
THE ARCHAEOLOGY OF GREECE
"An overview of Greek art and architecture from Minoan to Hellenistic times . . . functions well as an introduction for lay readers." (BL) Cornell, 1987. ○

Butor, Michel
THE SPIRIT OF MEDITERRANEAN PLACES
Translated from the French—includes Salonika, Delphi, Crete. Marlboro Pr, 1987. ○

Ceram, C.W.
GODS, GRAVES AND SCHOLARS
The story of archaeology for the general reader/traveler and accounts of discoveries

in Crete, Pompeii, Troy, the Middle East. Random, 1986.   ○

Gage, Nicholas
HELLAS: A PORTRAIT OF GREECE
An informal book about people, landscape, art, food and more, originally published 1971 as *Portrait of Greece*—"the wonder and appreciation . . . an invitation to join in an emotional and enjoyable" tour of the country. (BL) Random, 1987. Also *Eleni: A Savage War, a Mother's Love and Son's Revenge* (1983), about the author's dramatic and moving search for the people who killed his mother in 1948.   ○

Grant, Michael
FROM ALEXANDER TO CLEOPATRA: THE HELLENISTIC GREECE
"A deceptively uncomplicated history of a very complicated era. . . . in Mr. Grant's experienced hands, history becomes a revelation." One of several histories of ancient Greece by Grant. (NYTBR) Macmillan, 1990.   ○

Levi, Peter
ATLAS OF THE GREEK WORLD
The text "traces the history and culture of Greece from Minoan times to the Roman conquest . . . augmented by a profuse assortment of maps, photographs, and drawings . . . special inserts highlight different sites or aspects of Greek life." (BL) Facts On File, 1981.   ○

MacKendrick, Paul
THE GREEK STONES SPEAK
An introduction to archaeology and discoveries at Troy and Knossos, "cultural history based on a selection of archaeological evidence." (BL) Norton, 1982 (first published 1962).   ○

Simonsen, Thordis
DANCING GIRL
A high school anthropology teacher's record of her experiences in Greece over many years of visiting and restoring a house there, and her experiences with villagers, daily life, neighbors—"a delightful ode to a people

and their homeland." (BL) Fundamental Note, 1991.   ○

TRAVEL MEMOIRS

Andersen, Hans Christian
A POET'S BAZAAR: A JOURNEY TO GREECE, TURKEY, AND UP THE DANUBE
The writer of all those fairytales was also a traveler, and this reprint is a memoir of his travels. First published in 1842. Kesend Pub, 1988.   ○

Fermor, Patrick L.
ROUMELI: TRAVELS IN NORTHERN GREECE
"Long, probing examination" of the author's adopted homeland—"encyclopedic knowledge and grasp of the language, customs and history bring him into contact with . . . characters far out of reach of the ordinary traveler." Penguin, 1984 (first published 1933). Also *Mani: Travels in the Southern Peloponnese* (1984, first published 1960), "an extraordinary journey through the most remote and wildest region of Greece."   ○

Miller, Henry
THE COLOSSUS OF MAROUSSI
Travel memoir by the noted American writer. New Directions, 1973 (first published 1941).   ○

GUIDEBOOKS

See also Guidebooks listed below under Greek Islands.

Geldard, Richard G.
THE TRAVELER'S KEY TO ANCIENT GREECE: A GUIDE TO THE SACRED PLACES OF ANCIENT GREECE
A cultural and anthropological walking tour of 30 Greek sites plus background history—for travelers and armchair travelers. Knopf, 1989.   ○

Haag, Michael and Lewis, Neville
TRAVELAID GUIDE TO GREECE
Practical handbook for the independent traveler, for all budgets. Hippocrene, 1986. ○

Mehling, Marianne
ATHENS & ATTICA: A PHAIDON CULTURAL GUIDE ○

Mehling, Franz N.
GREECE: A PHAIDON CULTURAL GUIDE
Succinct appreciation of the best the country has to offer in terms of national treasures and culture—churches, palaces, theaters, museums, monuments, maps and plans, all arranged alphabetically and cross-indexed. Phaidon Pr, n.d. ○

Pausanias
GUIDE TO GREECE
Yes, a traveler's guide that was written in the second century A.D.—for history buffs. It includes history of the various statues, tombs, buildings of Ancient Greece. Volume 1, *Central Greece;* Volume 2, *Southern Greece.* Penguin, 1984. ○

GREEK ISLANDS

Durrell, Lawrence
THE GREEK ISLANDS
"Description, history and myth . . . personal reminiscence" by a leading writer in the travel genre. Also, *Reflections on a Marine Venus* (1978), chronicles the author's sojourn on the island of Rhodes with a British occupation unit at the end of World War II. *Prospero's Cell* (1978) is about Corfu, and *Spirit of Place* is a compilation of (Durrell's) fact and fiction (1969) that includes a piece on Corfu. (BRD) Penguin, 1980. ○

Eperon, Arthur
EPERON'S GUIDE TO THE GREEK ISLANDS
By a famous British travel writer. Hunter, 1988. ○

Freely, John
CRETE
"At once a guide, a short history, and a tribute . . . detailed maps and itineraries for extended excursions" in a format compact enough to take along. (BL) New Amsterdam Bks, 1989. ○

Hopkins, Adam
CRETE: ITS PAST, PRESENT AND PEOPLE
A complete guide, including anthropology, history, what you absolutely must see and things you can miss. Faber & Faber, 1979. ○

CYPRUS

Durrell, Lawrence
BITTER LEMONS
Experiences as a visitor, and as a resident teaching English; villages and ways of life in the 1950s. Dutton, 1959. ○

Parker, Derek and Julia
TRAVELER'S GUIDE TO CYPRUS
Trafalgar Sq, 1990. ○

Thubron, Colin
JOURNEY INTO CYPRUS
Just before the Turkish invasion of 1974, the author traveled extensively in Cyprus, meeting all the various factions. Now the Greek and Turkish Cypriots are separated and this gives a glimpse of the "halcyon time" when it was one island. Combines myth, personal adventure, history, anecdotes from all sorts of people. Now released in a new edition as a travel classic. Atl Monthly Pr, 1990. ○

HISTORY

Boatswain, Timothy and Nicolson, Colin
TRAVELLER'S HISTORY OF GREECE
Interlink Pub, 1990. ○

Clogg, R.
A SHORT HISTORY OF MODERN GREECE
Cambridge U Pr, 1987. ○

Woodhouse, Christopher M.
MODERN GREECE: A SHORT HISTORY
Faber & Faber, 1984.   ○

Novels

Ambler, Eric
A COFFIN FOR DIMITRIOS
"An English writer traces the life history of a nondescript Greek fig-picker" to explain his criminal record and death—"social comment, authentic current history . . . at the same time providing all the surprises . . . that every thriller needs." (FC) Knopf, 1939.   ○

Benford, Gregory
ARTIFACT
The artifact—a black cube—discovered by an American archaeologist becomes the object of a struggle between the American and Greek governments. Tor Bks, 1985.   ○

Brett, Simon
MRS. PARGETER'S PACKAGE
A tour of Greece with a recently widowed friend leads to an apparent suicide, and Melita Pargeter takes on the case. Scribner, 1991.   ○

Dunnett, Dorothy
RACE OF SCORPIONS
Historical novel of 15th-century Cyprus, part of the Niccolo Series. This one is about a dynastic power struggle over Cyprus—"precisely rendered scenes . . . fascinating images . . . admirable narrative web." (FC) Knopf, 1990.   ○

Durrell, Lawrence
TUNC
An inventor recounts his strange adventures in business, love, marriage. Set in Athens, Istanbul and London—"Athens . . . is vividly with us in this book." (FC) Dutton, 1968.   ○

Fowles, John
THE MAGUS
The "harrowing misadventures" of a British schoolteacher who takes a teaching job on the island of Phraxos—"engrossing entertainment [blending] sensuous realism, suspenseful romanticism, hypertheatrical mystification . . . a gallery of unusual or exotic characters . . . vivid setting . . . of an isolated Greek island." (FC) Little, 1978 (first published 1966).   ○

Hodge, Jane A.
STRANGERS IN COMPANY
Intrigue and romance as two women with a guided-tour bus group become unwilling participants in a plot to free a political prisoner because one of them is the prisoner's look-alike. Coward, 1973.   ○

Kazantzakis, Nikos
ZORBA THE GREEK (Crete)
The adventures and philosophy of Zorba ("hedonist raconteur and roué"), narrated by his employer ("a rich and cultivated dilettante"). "It is in every sense a minor classic . . . among the significant and permanent characters in modern fiction." (FC) S&S, 1952. Also *The Fratricides* (1964), a "modern parable" of a priest's attempts to mediate between Communists and Loyalists in the Greek civil wars of the 1940s, and *Freedom or Death* (1956), about the Cretan Revolt of 1889.   ○

MacInnes, Helen
DECISION AT DELPHI
Plot revolves about two friends sent to Greece on a magazine assignment; one, a Greek-American, disappears en route—"landscapes from Taormina to Sparta, all freshly observed" and the Acropolis, the streets of Athens are part of the plot's action, with a "panoramic finale on the noble heights of Delphi." (FC) HarBraceJ, 1960.   ○

MacInnes, Helen
THE DOUBLE IMAGE (Mykonos)
The plot is about a supposedly-dead Nazi war criminal—"an intelligent amateur [becomes] part of the mixed crew of agents, double agents and bystanders involved in Operation Pear Tree" on Mykonos. HarBraceJ, 1966.   ○

Olson, Toby
DORIT IN LESBOS
A painter travels to Lesbos "in search of peace, fulfillment, love, and the perfection of his art." (BL) S&S, 1990. ○

Sarton, May
JOANNA & ULYSSES
A young woman on an idyllic holiday on a Greek island rescues a little donkey from ill-treatment and in the process recovers herself from a decade of family troubles. Norton, 1963. ○

Stewart, Mary
THIS ROUGH MAGIC (Corfu)
An English actress, vacationing on the isle reputed to be the setting of Shakespeare's *Tempest,* becomes involved in a smuggling plot. Morrow, 1964. Also by Miss Stewart, are mystery-romances set in Crete and Delphi, respectively, *The Moon Spinners* (1963) and *My Brother Michael* (1960). ○

Vassilikos, Vassilis
Z (Salonika)
The assassination of a left-wing deputy in 1963, based on the actual, brutal assassination of Deputy Lambrakis. FS&G, 1968. ○

ANCIENT GREECE

Bradley, Marion Z.
THE FIREBRAND
The Trojan War as seen through the eyes of a princess with the gift of "sight." S&S, 1987. ○

Graves, Robert
HERCULES, MY SHIPMATE
Story of Jason and the Argonauts in quest of the golden fleece—"marked factual quality . . . painstakingness of the [voyage's]

details . . . a lively story . . . of violent death, double-dealing, grand larceny and seduction. . . . A remarkable book." (FC) Creative Age, 1945. ○

Kazantzakis, Nikos
AT THE PALACES OF KNOSSOS
Retelling of the story of Theseus and the Minotaur, written many years ago and only published recently. Ohio U Pr, 1988. Also, *Alexander the Great* (1982), a fictionalized biography. ○

Renault, Mary
FIRE FROM HEAVEN
This, *Persian Boy* (1972) and *Funeral Games* (1981), comprise a fictionalized version of the story of Alexander the Great—"an astounding grasp of the facts and the spirit of the ancient world . . . brings to life a great historical period." Pantheon, 1969. ○

Renault, Mary
THE KING MUST DIE
The story of Theseus, followed by its sequel *The Bull from the Sea* (1962). Others in the series of masterful novels by this author: *The Praise Singer* (1978), based on the story of Simonides; *The Mask of Apollo* (1966), about an actor's life in Syracuse and Athens in the fourth century B.C.; *The Last of the Wine* (1956), which recreates what it was like to be a well-to-do Athenian youth of that day as one of Socrates' pupils. Pantheon, 1958. ○

Wolfe, Gene
SOLDIER OF THE MIST
A Roman soldier, unable to remember who he is, wanders through 5th-century Greece in the company of a variety of people—"myth and history merge into a semireality." (FC) Doherty Assocs, 1986. ○

HUNGARY

Note: Books and novels on the Hapsburg monarchy and the Austro-Hungarian Empire, listed under "Austria," are also relevant.

Series Guidebooks
(See Appendix 1)

Baedeker: Budapest; Hungary
Berlitz: Hungary; Budapest
Blue Guide: Hungary
Fodor: Hungary
Frommer: Austria & Hungary
Insight Guide: Budapest; Hungary
Nagel's Encyclopedia Guide: Hungary
Nelles Guide: Hungary
Real Guide: Hungary

Background Reading

Ash, Timothy G.
THE MAGIC LANTERN
See entry under Czechoslovakia.   ○

Brook, Stephen
VANISHED EMPIRE: VIENNA, BUDAPEST, PRAGUE
See entry under Austria.   ○

Dobai, Peter
BUDAPEST
A photographic essay. Intl Spec Bk, 1986.   ○

Enzensberger, Hans M.
EUROPE, EUROPE: FORAYS INTO A CONTINENT
See entry under Europe/Background Reading. Hungary is one of six European countries analyzed by the German essayist.   ○

Gadney, Reg
CRY HUNGARY!: UPRISING 1956
Radio bulletins, eyewitness observations and remarkable photos give a sense of immediacy—"forces the reader to feel the emotional intensity of the uprising." (LJ) Atheneum, 1986.   ○

Gill, Anton
BERLIN TO BUCHAREST: TRAVELS IN EASTERN EUROPE
See entry under Europe/Background Reading.   ○

Hall, Brian
STEALING FROM A DEEP PLACE: TRAVELS IN SOUTHEASTERN EUROPE
See entry under Bulgaria.   ○

Lukacs, John
BUDAPEST 1900
"Account of a beautiful city at the zenith of its prosperity, with a brief final chapter describing the subsequent 80 years." (Harpers) Weidenfeld & Nicolson, 1988.   ○

Porter, Monica
THE PAPER BRIDGE: A RETURN TO BUDAPEST
Affecting story of a woman's return to Budapest in search of her roots, twenty-five years after fleeing the 1956 revolution. Quartet, 1982.   ○

Sisa, Stephen
THE SPIRIT OF HUNGARY
"A panorama of Hungarian history and culture [that] 'seeks to illuminate the spirit of Hungary' . . . a rich, popular amalgam of national legends, myth and history." Delves into art, music, science and literature. (LJ) Vista, 1991.   ○

Völgyes, Ivan
HUNGARY: A NATION OF CONTRADICTIONS
"An excellent brief introduction to Hungary for students as well as tourists," by an expatriate professor. (BRD) Westview Pr, 1982.   ○

GUIDEBOOKS

Nemeth, Gyula
A COMPLETE GUIDE TO HUNGARY
History, culture, art and museums, along with everything a traveler needs to know about hotels, food, transportation, weather, currency, sightseeing. Hippocrene, 1989.   ○

Torok, Andras
BUDAPEST: A CRITICAL GUIDE
Officina Nova and Park Bks, 1989.   ○

Zentai, P.
**SEVENTY-TWO HOURS IN
    BUDAPEST: A GUIDEBOOK**
State Mutual Bk, 1989.   ∘

HISTORY

Sinor, Denis
HISTORY OF HUNGARY
Greenwood, 1976 (first published 1959). ∘

Sugar, Peter F. and others
A HISTORY OF HUNGARY
Twenty historians provided the essays—
"aimed at collegiate undergraduates and
better-informed or interested general readers." (LJ) Indiana U Pr, 1990.   ∘

Novels

Elman, Richard M.
THE 28TH DAY OF ELUL
This, *Lilo's Diary* (1968) and *The Reckoning*
(1969), form a trilogy about the town of Clig,
Hungary—a portrait of the town and its
inhabitants. Scribner, 1967.   ∘

Holland, Cecelia
ROKÓSSY
Historical novel of sixteenth-century Hun-
gary during a period of Turkish incursions.
Atheneum, 1967.   ∘

Korda, Michael
WORLDLY GOODS
Saga of a Hungarian family "at once a Holocaust novel . . . and a look at love, hate,
power and sex in the stratosphere of
the modern corporation." (FC) Random,
1982.   ∘

Pearson, Diane
CSARDAS
Saga of the Ferenc family "who are as en-
slaved to their [aristocratic] social class as
are the peasants." Their fortunes crumble
before two wars and communism and, sym-
bolically, a peasant boy "rises well above
his class and eventually marries into the
Ferenc family." (FC) Lippincott, 1975.   ∘

Petrovics-Ofner, Laszlo
BROKEN PLACES
An autobiographical novel of a Hungarian
Jew at the crossroads of the wars of Europe,
and exile. It begins in 1938 and ends in 1956,
when Soviet tanks came into Budapest to
put down the Hungarian revolt. Atl Monthly
Pr, 1990.   ∘

Zilahy, Lajos
CENTURY IN SCARLET
Saga of the Dukay family from 1815 to World
War I. McGraw, 1965.   ∘

ICELAND

*Series Guidebooks
(See Appendix 1)*

Nagel's Encyclopedia Guide: Iceland
Visitor's Guide: Iceland
See also Series Guides for Scandinavia (*)
    under Denmark.

Background Reading

Note: See also Denmark for books with an
asterisk (*), which offer additional background reading on Scandinavia as a whole
and may include material on Iceland and
Denmark/Vikings.   ∘

Auden, W. H. and MacNeice, Louis
LETTERS FROM ICELAND
"Amusing collection of letters and impressions of two English poets from their 1937
trip to Iceland . . . genuinely funny." First
published in 1937, this new edition is part
of a series of reprinted travel literature. Paragon Hse, 1990.   ∘

Coles, John
SUMMER TRAVELING IN ICELAND
Reprint of 1882 edition. AMS Pr, 1978.   ∘

Edwards, Ted
FIGHT THE WILD ISLAND: A SOLO WALK ACROSS ICELAND
Salem Hse Pubs, 1987.　ο

Jones, Gwyn
NORSE ATLANTIC SAGA
A dramatic narrative history of the Norse voyages of discovery and settlement in Iceland (and Greenland). Oxford U Pr, 1984.　ο

Magnussen, S.
ICELAND: COUNTRY AND PEOPLE
Vanous, 1987.　ο

Magnússon, Sigurdur
NORTHERN SPHINX
A general introduction to Iceland—settlement and history from A.D. 900 to present, the Icelandic people, state of commerce, industry, literature, arts, music. McGill-Queens U, 1977. Also *Stallion of the North* (1979).　ο

Metcalfe, Frederick
THE OXONIAN IN ICELAND
Notes of travel in Iceland during the summer of 1860. Reprint of 1861 edition. AMS Pr.　ο

Millman, Lawrence
LAST PLACES
See entry under Norway.　ο

Roberts, David
ICELAND: LAND OF THE SAGAS
Iceland's history and culture examined through the 13th-century Icelandic sagas, with many photographs. Abrams, 1990.　ο

Saminel
GOLDEN ISLAND
M Evans, 1988.　ο

Saunders, Pamela
ICELAND
Based on a series of trips with photographer Roloff Beny; tells of visits to persons and places, "a striking informal introduction to

Ultima Thule, and end of the world." (BL) Salem Hse, 1985.　ο

Vander-Molen, Paul
ICELAND BREAKTHROUGH
Haynes Pubns, 1985.　ο

GUIDEBOOKS

Hamar, H.J.
ICELAND: THE SURPRISING ISLAND OF THE ATLANTIC
Vanous, n.d.　ο

HISTORY

Guthmundson, Barthe
THE ORIGIN OF ICELANDERS
U of Nebr Pr, 1967.　ο

Stefansson, Vilhjalmur
ICELAND: THE FIRST AMERICAN REPUBLIC
A history and study of an island that was a republic by A.D. 900 and once had peasants who spoke Latin—from settlement to contemporary times. Greenwood, 1971 (first published 1939).　ο

Tomasson, Richard F.
ICELAND: THE FIRST NEW SOCIETY
U of Minnesota Pr, 1980.　ο

Novels

Cooper, Dominic
MEN AT AXLIR
Story of a violent family feud in eighteenth-century Iceland—harsh passions in a harsh land. St. Martin, 1980.　ο

Gunnarsson, Gunnar
THE GOOD SHEPHERD
The life of a shepherd and his dog in the isolated and rugged mountains of Iceland. Bobbs, 1940 (first published 1910). Also the *Black Cliffs* (1929).　ο

Holland, Cecelia
TWO RAVENS
Historic novel set in twelfth-century Iceland involving family feuds and conflicts between

those converted to Christianity and those who remained loyal to Icelandic pagan beliefs. Knopf, 1977.　　　　　　　　　○

Jones, Gwyn
EGIL'S SAGA
Am Scandinavian, 1960.　　　　　　○

Laxness, Halldór
FISH CAN SING
Contrasts the simple life-style and unworldly values of fishermen in Iceland with those who have come in contact with a more

sophisticated world. Laxness is a major Icelandic writer who has won a Nobel Prize for his literature. Also *Independent People* (1946), a story of sheep-raising and rural life in Iceland, and *World Light* (1969), based on the life of Icelandic poet Magnusson. Crowell, 1967.　　　　　　　　　　　○

Seton, Anya
AVALON
A recreation, from early Anglo-Saxon and French manuscripts, of eleventh-century England and the lands colonized by Norsemen (Iceland). Houghton, 1965.　　　○

IRELAND

Note: See also all asterisked entries (*) under "England" for additional Series Guides and background books that may include Ireland.

Series Guidebooks

Baedeker: Ireland
Berlitz: Ireland
Birnbaum: Ireland
Blue Guide: Ireland
Cadogan Guide: Ireland
Fisher's World: Ireland
Fodor: Ireland
Frommer: Ireland ($-A-Day); Dublin
Insight Guide: Dublin; Ireland
Let's Go: Britain & Ireland
Nagel's Encyclopedia Guide: Ireland
Real Guide: Ireland

Background Reading

Bailey, Anthony
SPRING JAUNTS
A series of jaunts, originally appearing as articles in *The New Yorker*, one of which is to Tara—"a book to savour . . . wise, funny." (LJ) FS&G, 1986.　　　　　　　○

Buckley, Vincent
MEMORY IRELAND: INSIGHTS INTO THE CONTEMPORARY IRISH CONDITION
"A controversial, disturbing, beautifully written" recollection by a current visitor to

the country who finds the reality of Ireland in "fatalism and aimless despondency."(BL) Penguin, 1986.　　　　　　　　　○

DeBreffny, Brian
IRELAND: A CULTURAL ENCYCLOPEDIA
The most recent of three books that taken together, provide great background for a trip to Ireland. The *Encyclopedia* "provides 600 entries on a wide range of cultural subjects extending from the Abbey Theatre to William Butler Yeats." (LJ) Facts On File, 1984.　　　　　　　　　　　○

Delaney, Mary M.
OF IRISH WAYS
History, landscape, traditions—for travelers to Ireland or for Irish-Americans who want a look at their heritage. B&N Bks, 1979.　○

Donleavy, J.P.
J.P. DONLEAVY'S IRELAND
"In all her sins and in some of her graces . . . wonderfully told anecdotes about people and places" by the author of *The Ginger Man* (see under Novels), remembering attending Trinity College and living in Ireland in the 1940s and '50s. (BL) Viking, 1986.　○

Morton, H.V.
IN SEARCH OF IRELAND
"To encourage the English to become acquainted" with the country and first

published just eight years after Irish independence—"the book's observations are [still] completely up-to-date." Dodd, 1984 (first published 1930). See also *Morton's Britain* under "England."   ○

Murphy, Dervla
IRELAND
"Ireland in terms of four modern revolutions: economic, journalistic, historigraphical and theological . . . freewheeling, whimsical, thoroughly engaging . . . probes the Irish psyche, culture, politics, English and Irish violence, the arts, economics and the sexual revolution." (BL) Salem Hse, 1985. Also *A Place Apart,* Ms. Murphy's attempt to understand the divisions in Northern Ireland, and *Wheels Within Wheels* (1980).   ○

Newby, Eric
ROUND IRELAND IN LOW GEAR
The author and his wife, biking around Ireland in middle age, is the basis for this book by a major travel writer. Blends history, people, culture with their travel for a memorable experience. Penguin, 1988.   ○

O'Brien, George
THE VILLAGE OF LONGING AND DANCEHALL DAYS
"Exquisite evocation of an Irish childhood set in County Waterford . . . a microcosm of Ireland in the 1950s that is both delightful and disturbing." (PW) Viking, 1990.   ○

O'Faolain, Sean
THE IRISH: A CHARACTER STUDY
The development of Ireland from its Celtic beginnings—"urban, shrewd, witty" and considered one of the best books on the Irish. (BRD) Devin, 1979 (first published 1949).   ○

Robinson, Tim
STONES OF ARAN: PILGRIMAGE
"An exquisitely detailed portrait of a special landscape . . . an exploration of geology, topography, history, language and folklore." (PW) Viking, 1989.   ○

Ryan, Kathleen Jo and Share, Bernard, eds.
IRISH TRADITIONS
"17 short, bright essays by Irish specialists in fiction, poetry, archaeology, architecture, sports, art and other fields . . . from prehistoric people to neighborliness in rural areas." (BL) Abrams, 1985.   ○

Sharkey, Olive
OLD DAYS, OLD WAYS
A folk history of Ireland's daily life, with illustrations—house and farm activities in the thatched houses, cooking over an open hearth, farming chores done by hand or with horses. Syracuse U Pr, 1987.   ○

Taylor, Alice
TO SCHOOL THROUGH THE FIELDS: AN IRISH COUNTRY CHILDHOOD
The author takes care of the market and post office of Inishcannon—"delightful evocation of Irishness . . . with its rituals of religion and the antics of local characters has universal appeal." St. Martin, 1990.   ○

Webster, Bryce
IN SEARCH OF MODERN IRELAND: AN AMERICAN TRAVELER'S ODYSSEY
Retraces the journey of H.V. Morton's classic of the 1930s (see above)—"usually interesting and often delightful . . . excels in presenting oddments of information." (BL) Dodd, 1986.   ○

Williams, Niall and Breen, Christine
O COME YE BACK TO IRELAND: OUR FIRST YEAR IN COUNTY CLARE
The alternating journal of two New York City graduate students who met in Dublin and decided to return to the land of their forebears by settling in a village on the west coast. There's a sequel, *When Summer's in the Meadow,* which continues their story and personal disappointment in trying to have a child and finally adopting one. "Entertaining and instructive . . . captures a way of life foreign to most readers." (PW) FS&G, 1987.   ○

Williams, Niall and Breen, Christine
THE PIPES ARE CALLING: OUR JAUNTS THROUGH IRELAND
Continues this couple's journals (see above), but this time the authors take off to popular attractions as well as more remote islands and seacoasts and beaches and share "their joy in Ireland's largely unspoiled natural beauty." (PW) Soho Pr, 1990.   ○

DUBLIN

See also books listed under Literary Guides and Theater in Ireland, below.   ○

Armstrong, Alison
THE JOYCE OF COOKING: FOOD AND DRINK FROM JAMES JOYCE'S DUBLIN
Dublin Station Hill, 1986.   ○

Delaney, Frank
JAMES JOYCE'S ODYSSEY: A GUIDE TO THE DUBLIN OF ULYSSES
An "ingratiating guide to Joyce's *Ulysses*, to the actual city of Dublin . . . on June 16, 1904, and to the city as it exists today"—18 chapters correspond to 18 in the novel, with maps tracing movements of the characters. (PW) HR&W, 1982.   ○

Lalôr, Brian
ULTIMATE DUBLIN GUIDE: AN A-Z OF EVERYTHING
Dufour, 1991.   ○

McCarthy, Jack
JOYCE'S DUBLIN: A WALKING GUIDE TO ULYSSES
Revised and updated version of a book first published in 1986; a list of buildings intact as Joyce wrote about them, and bus and train information have been added. St. Martin, 1991.   ○

Pakenham, Thomas and Valerie, eds.
DUBLIN: A TRAVELLERS' COMPANION
One of a series that is a compilation of excerpts from literature of the country—fiction, letters, memoirs, journals—to present a cultural overview. Extensive introductions by experts provide background history—will "captivate armchair travelers of a slightly bookish bent." (BL) Atheneum, 1988.   ○

LITERARY GUIDES AND THEATER IN IRELAND

Hunt, Hugh
THE ABBEY: IRELAND'S NATIONAL THEATRE, 1904–1979
A history commissioned to celebrate the Theatre's seventy-fifth birthday. Columbia U Pr, 1979.   ○

O'Farrell, Padraic
SHANNON THROUGH HER LITERATURE
Mercier Pr, 1983.   ○

Trevor, William
A WRITER'S IRELAND: LANDSCAPE IN LITERATURE
"A walk through [Ireland's] history with native writers (from Yeats to Seamus Heaney), who have been inspired by the events and landscape of their homeland." (BL) Penguin, 1986.   ○

SOME IRISH LIVES, ECCENTRIC AND OTHERWISE

Court, Artelia
PUCK OF THE DROMS: THE LIVES AND LITERATURE OF THE IRISH TINKERS
Scholarly overview of a unique sub-culture—the life-style of "travelers" in biographies of three of them in their own words and collected songs, folklore, poems. U of California, 1985.   ○

O'Donnell, E.E., ed.
FATHER BROWNE'S IRELAND
Remarkable images of people and places. Wolfhound Pr, 1990.   ○

Scherman, Katherine
**THE FLOWERING OF IRELAND:
  SAINTS, SCHOLARS AND
  KINGS**
"Colorful figures" from the Ice Age through
the Norman Period, written with "great flair."
(PW) Little, 1981.   ○

Wallace, Martin
100 IRISH LIVES
Biographies, historic sites. David, 1983.   ○

GUIDEBOOKS

Day, Catharina
AROUND IRELAND
Part of the "Island Hopping" series of guides
for independent travelers—island descriptions, how to get there, background information on local customs and history,
where to stay and what to do. Hippocrene,
1982.   ○

Fullington, Don
**THE CONNOISSEUR'S GUIDE TO
  IRELAND: A SELECT
  COMPENDIUM FOR THE
  DISCRIMINATING TRAVELER**
For the traveler with lots of time and money—
practical information and itineraries. Owl
Bk, 1989.   ○

Green, Kerry and Leocha, Charles
**THE WHOLE EUROPE ESCAPE
  MANUAL: U.K./IRELAND**
Part of a series of guidebooks "designed to
. . . put the fantasy and excitement back
into travel." (Publisher) World Leis Corp,
1985.   ○

Hudson, Kenneth and Nicholls, Ann
**THE CAMBRIDGE GUIDE TO THE
  MUSEUMS OF BRITAIN AND
  IRELAND**
Brief descriptions of 2,000 museums and
galleries, from toys to theater, with practical
tourist information. Cambridge U Pr,
1987.   ○

Jacobs, Michael and Stirton, Paul
**THE KNOPF TRAVEL GUIDE TO
  ART: GREAT BRITAIN &
  IRELAND**
Knopf, 1984.   ○

Mehling, Franz N.
**GREAT BRITAIN & IRELAND: A
  PHAIDON CULTURAL GUIDE**
Succinct appreciation of the best the country
has to offer in terms of national treasures
and culture—churches, palaces, theaters,
museums, monuments, maps and plans, all
arranged alphabetically and cross-indexed.
Phaidon, Pr, n.d.   ○

Mulligan, Fergus
SEE IRELAND BY TRAIN
Irish Bks Media, 1986.   ○

Watney, John
**SECRET WATERS: A GUIDE TO THE
  QUIET & UNSPOILT RIVERS,
  LAKES & CANALS OF BRITAIN
  & IRELAND**
Penguin, 1988.   ○

HISTORY

Bottigheimer, Karl S.
**IRELAND AND THE IRISH: A
  SHORT HISTORY**
Columbia U Pr, 1982.   ○

Foster, R.F.
**THE OXFORD ILLUSTRATED
  HISTORY OF IRELAND**
Lavish illustrations, essays by scholars. Ox-
ford U Pr, 1989. Also *Modern Ireland*, 1600–
1972. Allen Lane, 1989.   ○

MacManus, Seumas
THE STORY OF THE IRISH RACE
Devin, 1990.   ○

Ranelagh, John O'B.
A SHORT HISTORY OF IRELAND
Cambridge U Pr, 1983. Also *Ireland: An Il-
lustrated History* (1981).   ○

Novels

Anthony, Evelyn
A PLACE TO HIDE
The Anglo-Irish Arbuthnot family and the Irish situation—"slickly-paced adventure . . . a carefully balanced perspective." (FC) Putnam, 1987. ○

Binchy, Maeve
FIREFLY SUMMER
Set in an Irish town of the 1960s as an American's attempt to bring prosperity to the village disrupts the whole lifestyle. Delacorte, 1988. Also *Echoes* (1986), set in a seaside community, about a shopkeeper's daughter who challenges the community's social strictures, and *Light a Penny Candle* (1983), about a long friendship between two men, from World War II to mutual widowhood. ○

Carroll, James
SUPPLY OF HEROES
"The complexity and irony" of Ireland's relationship with England and World War I, told through the lives of one family. Dutton, 1986. ○

Donleavy, J.P.
THE DESTINIES OF DARCY DANCER, GENTLEMAN
Tale of an Irish Tom Jones and squire of Andromeda Park. Delacorte Pr, 1977. There's a sequel, *Leila; Further in the Destinies of Darcy Dancer, Gentleman* (1983)—"riotous exuberance and invention. If Smollett were reborn today, it's tempting to think that he might write like this." (FC) ○

DuMaurier, Daphne
HUNGRY HILL
Saga of a family of mine owners through four generations, each with its own "tragedy of weak characters." (FC) Bentley, 1971 (first published 1943). ○

Flanagan, Thomas
THE TENANTS OF TIME
Three decades of Irish history through four men who participated in the Rising of 1867—"simply, a remarkable book; convincing as history . . . and compelling as fiction." (FC) Dutton, 1988. ○

Flanagan, Thomas
THE YEAR OF THE FRENCH (Mayo)
Historical novel of 1798, when people of County Mayo revolted, aided by French revolutionists. HR&W, 1979. ○

Haien, Jeanette
THE ALL OF IT
"Captures both the essence of life in the rural west of Ireland and . . . conflict between official morality and the private compromise" people make to live their lives—a couple's secret that they are, in fact, brother and sister is confessed to a priest upon the death of the man. Godine, 1986. ○

Holland, Cecelia
THE KINGS IN WINTER
Historical novel of eleventh-century Ireland and attempts to unify the country. Atheneum, 1968. ○

Keane, Molly
GOOD BEHAVIOR
Decline and fall of a genteel, Anglo-Irish family from Edwardian times through the twenties. Knopf, 1981. Also *Time After Time* (1984)—"decaying siblings in a decaying Irish country house." ○

Keane, Molly
QUEEN LEAR
The Forester family of Deer Forest—an idyllic world is shattered when Lady Forester runs off with a steward and, later, her daughter repeats the pattern. "Acutely perceptive . . . plumbs deeper than the delicious mockery of its surface." (FC) Dutton, 1989. ○

Kiely, Benedict
A LETTER TO PEACHTREE AND NINE OTHER STORIES
"The beauty and bitterness of Irish life." (FC) Godine, 1988. Also *The State of Ireland*, a novella and 17 stories (1980). ○

Lavin, Mary
COLLECTED STORIES
"Cover almost every aspect of Irish life—the farmers, the fishermen, the well-off, the servant girls, lovers, husbands, wives, spinsters, bachelors and children. The dialogue is superb." (BRD) Houghton, 1971. Also, *The Shrine and Other Stories* (1977).   o

Leonard, Hugh
PARNELL AND THE ENGLISHWOMAN
Based on the true story of Charles Parnell, member of Parliament involved in the struggle for Irish Home Rule and his love affair with Kitty O'Shea. Atheneum, 1991.   o

O'Brien, Edna
NIGHT
Introspective monologue of a modern Molly Bloom as she recalls her early life in a small town, Dublin and beyond. FS&G, 1987.   o

O'Connor, Frank
COLLECTED STORIES
One of several volumes of short stories by a leading Irish writer—"The Ireland he evokes . . . is the provincial life of his Cork boyhood. Loving but acute . . . reveals a humanity peculiarly Irish in its stubborn divisive ways." (FC) Knopf, 1981. Also, *The Stories of Frank O'Connor* (1952) and *More Stories* (1954).   o

O'Faolain, Julia
NO COUNTRY FOR YOUNG MEN
A nun is returned to her family in America when her convent is closed, and a traumatic experience involving the IRA comes to light. Carroll & Graf, 1986.   o

O'Faolain, Sean
A NEST OF SIMPLE FOLK
(Southwest Ireland)
Three generations of a family, through poverty and revolution, 1854–1916. Viking, 1934. Also, *The Finest Stories of Sean O'Faolain* (1957) and *Selected Stories of Sean O'Faolain* (1978), the *Collected Stories of Sean O'Faolain*.   o

Shannon, Dell
THE SCALPEL AND THE SWORD
A historical novel of an Irish doctor and his experiences as a military surgeon in the Napoleonic wars of the early 19th century. Morrow, 1987.   o

Spellman, Cathy C.
AN EXCESS OF LOVE
Story of the varied fortunes of two sisters drawn into the Irish Republican Brotherhood through the men they love. Delacorte, 1985.   o

Uris, Leon
TRINITY
The years 1840–1916 from the viewpoints of the trinity—British, Irish Catholics, and Ulster-Protestant families. Doubleday, 1976.   o

DUBLIN

Binchy, Maeve
CIRCLE OF FRIENDS
"Wonderfully absorbing story" of three women who travel from a village to Dublin and university life. (FC) Delacorte, 1991.   o

Bringle, Mary
THE MAN IN THE MOSS-COLORED TROUSERS
A body found on a racecourse near Dublin is the heart of this mystery—"absolutely splendid unforeseen conclusion." (FC) Doubleday, 1986.   o

Brown, Christy
DOWN ALL THE DAYS
Semi-autobiographical story of a large Dublin working-class family, through the eyes of one member severely crippled with cerebral palsy—"brutally, bawdily, joyfully (and sadly) real." (FC) Stein & Day, 1970.   o

Donleavy, J.P.
THE GINGER MAN
Picaresque novel of an ex-G.I., begins in Dublin and moves on to London. Delacorte Pr, 1965. Also *The Beastly Beatitudes of Balthazar B.* (1968), about the lives and loves of

the protagonist from youth in Paris, through adventures in an English prep school, to Trinity College, Dublin.   ○

Gill, Bartholomew
McGARR AND THE P.M. OF BELGRAVE SQUARE
Peter McGarr, head of the Irish murder squad, must solve the death of an antiques dealer—"the Irish background is splendidly handled to give . . . the feel of the sights and smells of Dublin." (FC) Viking, 1983. Also *The Death of a Joyce Scholar* (1989), *McGarr and the Legacy of a Woman Scorned* (1987), *McGarr and the Method of Descartes* (1986).   ○

Hynes, James
THE WILD COLONIAL BOY
Chilling thriller of internal strife in the I.R.A.—"descriptions of Belfast and Dublin are outstanding." (FC) Atheneum, 1990.   ○

Joyce, James
ULYSSES
The classic, first published in 1922, of thoughts and actions of a group of people in Dublin through a single day. Random, 1967. Also *The Dubliners* (1914) (short stories), *Portrait of the Artist as a Young Man* (1914) and its earlier version *Stephen Hero* (1944), *Finnegan's Wake* (1939) and *A Shorter Finnegan's Wake* (1958). See also books listed under "Literary Guides and Theatre in Ireland."   ○

Murdoch, Iris
THE RED AND THE GREEN
Stories of an Anglo-Irish family in Dublin during Easter Week, 1916. Viking, 1965.   ○

O'Flaherty, Liam
THE INFORMER
The classic story of a former Irish revolutionary who betrays his comrades. Knopf, 1925.   ○

I T A L Y
(Including Malta)

Series Guidebooks
(See Appendix 1)

Access Guide: Florence; Milan; Rome; Venice
American Express Pocket Guide: Florence & Tuscany; Rome; Venice
At Its Best Guide: Italy
Baedeker: Florence; Rome; Venice; Italy; Tuscany
Berlitz: Italy; Rome, Venice; Florence; Italian Adriatic; Italian Riviera; Malta; Rome & the Vatican; Sicily
Birnbaum: Italy
Blue Guide: Florence; Malta & Gozo; Northern Italy/Alps to Rome; Rome & Environs; Sicily; Southern Italy; Venice
Cadogan Guide: Italy Northeast; Italy Northwest; Italy South; Italian Islands; Rome; Tuscany & Umbria; Venice
Crown Insider's Guide: Italy
Exploring Rural Europe: Italy
Fielding: Italy

Fisher's World: Italy
Fodor: Italy
Frommer: Rome; Italy; Florence; Venice
Gault/Milau: Best of Italy
Independent Traveler: Southern Italy
Insight Guide: Florence; Italy; Malta; Rome; Sardinia; Tuscany; Umbria; Venice
Langenscheidt: Self-Guided Italy
Let's Go: Italy; Rome
Michelin: Italy; Rome
Nagel's Encyclopedia Guide: Italy; Malta
Off the Beaten Track: Italy
Real Guide: Italy; Venice
Visitor's Guide: Florence & Ruscany; Italian Lakes

Background Reading

Barzini, Luigi
THE ITALIANS
A full-length portrait that touches on many aspects of Italian life, its virtues and vices, achievements and failures—"enjoyable, in-

dispensable introduction" to Italy. Penguin, 1984 (first published 1964). Also, *From Caesar to the Mafia, Sketches of Italian Life* (1971). ○

Ceram, C.W.
GODS, GRAVES AND SCHOLARS
The story of archaeology for the general reader/traveler; discoveries in Crete, Pompeii, Troy, the Middle East and Central America. Random, 1986. ○

Cornell, Tim and Matthews, John
ATLAS OF THE ROMAN WORLD
"A superbly compact yet thorough, heavily illustrated and well-written history of the rise, zenith and decline of the Roman Empire." (Publisher) Facts On File, 1982. ○

Enzensberger, Hans M.
EUROPE, EUROPE: FORAYS INTO A CONTINENT
See entry under Europe—Italy is one of six European countries analyzed by the German essayist. ○

Gray, Patience
HONEY FROM A WEED—FASTING AND FEASTING IN TUSCANY, CATALONIA, THE CYCLADES AND APULIA
Food and traditions in rural Italy. Har-Row, 1987. ○

Harrison, Barbara G.
THE ISLANDS OF ITALY
"Affectionate tribute" in memory of the author's grandparents, of a visit to Sicily, Sardinia and the Aeolian Islands in 1990, with photographs. Ticknor & Fields, 1991. ○

Harrison, Barbara G.
ITALIAN DAYS
"A rare pleasure: a book of almost Victorian amplitude . . . eloquent, witty, colorful and lyrical"—the journalist author goes to Italy in search of her past and the national ethos of Italy. (PW) Weidenfeld, 1989. ○

Haycraft, John
ITALIAN LABYRINTH: ITALY IN THE 1980S
"Thorough, readable study of postwar Italy's economic growth and cultural change

. . . updates Luigi Barzini's *The Italians*." (LJ) Penguin, 1987. ○

Hofmann, Paul
CENTO CITTA
A hundred cities and towns, the author's favorite locales (see entry below). Capsule histories, sketches, notes on special festivals and events, residents, economic conditions, etc. HR&W, 1988. ○

Hofmann, Paul
THAT FINE ITALIAN HAND
"Entertaining and shrewd appraisal" by a former *New York Times* Rome bureau chief, and obviously an author with a continuing love affair with Italy. "He nevertheless recognizes the blemishes . . . especially the cultural differences and tensions between the progressive North and the still semifeudal, Mafia-plagued South." (PW) HR&W, 1990. ○

Kramer, Jane
UNSETTLING EUROPE
See entry under Sweden. ○

MacKendrick, Paul
THE MUTE STONES SPEAK
The story of archaeology in Italy by two archaeologists who, as R.A.F. officers stationed in Italy at the end of World War II, asked permission to use aerial photography on behalf of archaeological research, and the profound change it had in Italy's knowledge of its own ancient settlements. Norton, 1983. ○

Murray, William
THE LAST ITALIAN
The essence of the Italian character in a portrait of Italian life, with an introduction by Jan Morris. P-H, 1990. Also *Italy—The Fatal Gift* (1981), in which the author puts us in touch with the fatal gift of beauty that is characteristic of that land—a collection of essays about the author's sojourns in Rome and his love affair with the country. ○

Newby, Eric
LOVE AND WAR IN THE APENNINES
This memoir by travel writer Newby reflects a time in Italy that was not a pleasure trip. He had escaped from a POW camp in World War II, and the book gives delightful accounts of the Italians who captured him but then helped with his escape. Penguin, 1990.   ○

Norwich, John J., ed.
THE ITALIANS: HISTORY, ART AND THE GENIUS OF A PEOPLE
A cultural history of Italy from mythological origins to the twentieth century. Various experts contribute "highly individual and readable essays" of chronological periods—history, art, politics, music, literature, philosophy. Beautifully illustrated. (LJ) Abrams, 1983.   ○

Root, Waverly
THE FOOD OF ITALY
See entry for *Food of France,* its companion volume.   ○

Simon, Kate
ITALY, THE PLACES IN BETWEEN
Revised and expanded edition of the original published in 1970—"preserved are the author's superb qualifications as a travel companion, guide, and stylist [directing] the tourist . . . to a pleasant and fulfilling adventure. . . . travel outside the country's major cities." (BL) Har-Row, 1984.   ○

Simon, Kate
A RENAISSANCE TAPESTRY: THE GONZAGA OF MANTUA
Recreates the days of the Renaissance through exploring the city of Mantua and its ruling family; enhanced by Simon's superior writing. Har-Row, 1989.   ○

Wechsler, Robert
WHEN IN ROME: A HUMORISTS' GUIDE
This is part of a new series of anthologies of humor about the foibles of travelers, and the countries they visit—anecdotes, poems, cartoons, by leading humorists. Catbird Pr, 1989.   ○

Whitman, William B.
LITERARY CITIES OF ITALY
Guides the reader, by foot and by water taxi, to places that inspired writers such as Forster, Henry James, the Brownings—with maps. Starrhill Pr, 1991.   ○

Willinger, Faith H.
EATING IN ITALY
"A food lover's guide to the gastronomic pleasures of wining and dining in Northern Italy." For each of 11 regions north of Rome, there's an introduction to the best regional foods and wines, and the author's top-secret address list of restaurants, markets, shops (from humble to deluxe) culled from years as a leader of gastronomic tours. (LJ) Morrow, 1989.   ○

TRAVELOGUES, MEMOIRS

Dickens, Charles
PICTURES FROM ITALY
One of a series of reprinted travel memoirs from the past; Dickens took the social conscience of his novels along with him on his travels. Ecco Pr, 1988.   ○

Howells, William Dean
ITALIAN JOURNEYS
The author was American consul to Venice for Abraham Lincoln, and these impressions of Italy were published in 1867, now reprinted in response to the increased interest in early travel writings. Marlboro, 1988.   ○

Huxley, Aldous
ALONG THE ROAD
"A score of entertaining essays written during the interludes of tourist travel in Flanders and Italy"—mostly Italy. Ecco Pr, 1989.   ○

James, Henry
ITALIAN HOURS
Travel essays by the 19th-century novelist, in a new edition. Ecco Pr, 1987.   ○

Lawrence, D.H.
TWILIGHT IN ITALY
A new omnibus edition that includes three of Lawrence's travel books under one cover, originally published between 1916 and 1932— *Twilight in Italy, Sea and Sardinia, Etruscan Places.* Penguin, 1985.   o

Morton, H.V.
A TRAVELLER IN ITALY
Also *A Traveller in Southern Italy* and *A Traveller in Rome,* all originally published in the 1950s and 1960s—collections of essays on the author's sojourns in Italy and his love affair with the country. Dodd, 1981.   o

O'Faolain, Sean
A SUMMER IN ITALY
Also *An Autumn in Italy*—travel memoirs by the Irish writer of trips in 1948 to Italy—"amusing, wholly unpredictable, humorous, description of persons and places." (BRD) Devin, 1950 and 1953, respectively.   o

Wharton, Edith
ITALIAN BACKGROUNDS
Quoting the author from this account of her travels in Italy at the turn of the century: "The onset of impressions and memories is at times so overwhelming that observation is lost in mere sensation." Ecco Pr, 1989. o

Zbigniew, Herbert
BARBARIANS IN THE GARDEN
See entry under France/Travelogues and Memoirs—the towns in Italy are Siena and Orvieto.   o

ROME & THE VATICAN

Bowen, Elizabeth
A TIME IN ROME
Impressions of Rome, past and present by the novelist—"describing, reminiscing about, and explicating a city." (BRD) Penguin, 1990.   o

Bull, George
INSIDE THE VATICAN
The day-to-day life and work of the Pope and those who run the whole Vatican com-plex of museums, archives, radio station, etc. St. Martin, 1983.   o

Clark, Eleanor
ROME AND A VILLA
"Evocative portrait of a city . . . teeming with life, memory, history, smells, and sights." (NYTBR) Atheneum, 1982 (first published in 1950; revised in 1974). Also *A Time in Rome* (1960), a reminiscence, descrip-tion, explication, by a novelist.   o

Fraser, Russell
THE THREE ROMES
The three Romes, in this author's concept, are Constantinople (now Istanbul), Moscow and Rome—cities that felt they had "re-ceived divine missions to amass and rule empires." The book is historical commen-tary and anecdotes, an "entertaining over-view . . . encounters with modern inhabitants . . . the shadowy past [im-planted in] the mind of citizens today." (BL) HarBraceJ, 1985.   o

Hofmann, Paul
O VATICAN! A SLIGHTLY WICKED VIEW OF THE HOLY SEE
"A lively discourse on personalities, mo-tives, and morals" of the powers behind St. Peter's throne. (BL) Congdon & Weed, 1984. Also *Rome: the Sweet Tempestuous Life* (1982).   o

Mehling, Marianne
ROME & LATINUM: A PHAIDON CULTURAL GUIDE
Succinct appreciation of the best the country has to offer in terms of national treasures and culture—churches, palaces, theaters, museums, monuments, maps and plans, all arranged alphabetically and cross-indexed. Phaidon Pr., n.d.   o

Mewshaw, Michael
PLAYING AWAY: ROMAN HOLIDAYS AND OTHER MEDITERRANEAN EXCURISONS
By an American novelist who's lived in Rome for 10 years—"explores the contradictory pleasures of living in an ancient city . . . in

the light-hearted mood of a hip travelogue."
(BL) Atheneum, 1988. ○

Packard, Jerrold M.
**PETER'S KINGDOM: INSIDE THE
PAPAL CITY**
A guide to the history, operations and build-
ings, museums and art collections. Scribner,
1985. ○

Simon, Kate
ROME: PLACES AND PLEASURES
Ideal companion to *The Places in Between*,
above. Knopf, 1972. ○

Vance, William L.
AMERICA'S ROME
"The image and idea of ancient Rome in the
American imagination . . . traces the influence of Rome on American painting, sculpture and literature" produced by travelers
in the 19th and 20th centuries. There are
two volumes: Volume 1, *Classical Rome*; Volume 2, *Catholic and Contemporary Rome*. (LJ)
Yale U Pr, 1989. ○

FLORENCE & TUSCANY

Acton, Harold
**FLORENCE: A TRAVELLER'S
COMPANION**
Excerpts from fiction, letters, memoirs, journals for "an impressive historical and cultural overview . . . to lead tourists to
significant sights . . . will captivate armchair travelers of a slightly bookish bent."
(BL) Atheneum, 1986. ○

Ash, Russell and Higton, Bernard
TUSCANY: SPIRIT OF PLACE
Part of a series of similar books—words of
writers that capture the spirit of a place
accompanied by illustrations of the chosen
excerpts. Arcade Pub Inc, 1989. ○

Bentley, James
A GUIDE TO TUSCANY
"Enlightening, incisive, personalized guide
to the joys of Tuscany . . . perfect joining

of information and excitement." (BL) Penguin, 1988. ○

Hibbert, Christopher
**THE HOUSE OF MEDICI: ITS RISE
AND FALL**
Their personal lives, political squabbles and
a picture of Renaissance city-state politics.
Morrow, 1980. ○

McCarthy, Mary
STONES OF FLORENCE
A profile of Florence—history, architecture,
art and people—"perceptive . . . interpre-
tation of this heart of the Renaissance." (BRD)
HarBraceJ, 1987 (first published 1959). ○

Mehling, Marianne
**FLORENCE & TUSCANY: A
PHAIDON CULTURAL GUIDE**
Succinct appreciation of the best the country
has to offer in terms of national treasures
and culture—churches, palaces, theaters,
museums, monuments, maps and plans, all
arranged alphabetically and cross-indexed.
Phaidon Pr., n.d. ○

More, Julian and Carey
**VIEWS FROM A TUSCAN
VINEYARD**
"Sights, impressions and thoughts evoked
from their journeys through the region"—
history, literature, arts, landscapes, architecture, people. (PW) Holt, 1987. ○

Origo, Iris
**WAR IN VAL D'ORCIA: AN
ITALIAN WAR DIARY**
The author's diary from 1943 to 1944 when
her family estate in southern Tuscany was
opened up to aid anyone trying to escape
the war, as the Allied forces invaded and
the Germans retreated—"a monument to
the kindness and courage of the Origos
and the peasants who lived with them . . .
enhanced by the excellent introduction."
(NYT) Godine, 1984. ○

Raison, Laura
TUSCANY: AN ANTHOLOGY
An illustrated anthology of prose excerpts,
letters, poetry, stories, recipes—"a treasure

trove of great writers sharing their delight in discovering some new and delightful facet of Tuscany." (NYT) Facts On File, 1984.   ○

Romer, Elizabeth
THE TUSCAN YEAR
Details the cycle of her neighbors' year as farmers in a remote valley of Tuscany "in what is fundamentally a cookbook but one of particular interest to the traveler . . . in the Italian countryside." (NYT) Atheneum, 1985.   ○

SOUTHERN ITALY & CAPRI, MALTA, SICILY

Bonville, William J.
SICILIAN WALKS
Exploring the history and culture of the two Sicilys. Mills Sanderson, 1988.   ○

Cornelisen, Ann
WOMEN OF THE SHADOWS
An American Protestant ran a day nursery for ten years in Lucania (south of Naples). She introduces the town, her neighbors and acquaintances, and their children in the "bare sepia world of Southern Italy." (BRD) Random, 1977. Also *Torregreca: Life, Death, Miracles* (1969) and *Where It All Began: Italy 1954* (Dutton, 1990).   ○

Douglas, Norman
SIREN LAND
" 'Sirenland' is Capri and the Peninsula of Sorrento . . . observations and reflections upon men, nature, and history of a gladly-tempted sojourner." Reprint of a classic. (BRD) David, 1983 (first published 1911).   ○

Durrell, Lawrence
SICILIAN CAROUSEL
Lighthearted and humorous tour of Sicily on a carousel bus. Viking, 1977.   ○

Kanzler, Peter
PRACTICAL TRAVELER A TO Z: MALTA
Hayit, 1992.   ○

Seward, Desmond
NAPLES: A TRAVELLER'S COMPANION
One of a series that is a compilation of excerpts from literature of the country—fiction, letters, memoirs, journals—to present a cultural overview. Extensive introductions by experts provide background history—will "captivate armchair travelers of a slightly bookish bent." Atheneum, 1986.   ○

Simeti, Mary Taylor
ON PERSEPHONE'S ISLAND: A SICILIAN JOURNAL
Journal of a year in Sicily, in Palermo and the countryside, by the American wife of a Sicilian professor—"beautifully written," perceptive insights into the people and social customs. (PW) Knopf, 1986.   ○

VENICE

Ash, Russell
VENICE: SPIRIT OF PLACE
Part of a series of similar books—words of writers that capture the spirit of a place accompanied by illustrations of the chosen excerpts. Arcade Pub Inc, 1990.   ○

Hibbert, Christopher
VENICE: THE BIOGRAPHY OF A CITY
Chronological narrative laced with anecdotes—"capturing the mood and beauty of Venice at its peak and in decline." (PW) Norton, 1989.   ○

Links, J.G.
VENICE FOR PLEASURE
For dawdling and walking about Venice. FS&G, 1985.   ○

McCarthy, Mary
VENICE OBSERVED
A book of photographs with superior text reflecting the author's "astonishing comprehension of the Venetian taste and character." (BRD) HarBraceJ, 1963.   ○

Mehling, Marianne
VENICE & THE VENETO
Succinct appreciation of the best the country has to offer in terms of national treasures

and culture—churches, palaces, theaters, museums, monuments, maps and plans, all arranged alphabetically and cross-indexed. Phaidon Pr., n.d.   ○

Morris, James
THE WORLD OF VENICE
A new edition of a classic book first published 1961. Not a guidebook, "recommended for all who really want to capture the essence of the fair city . . . will give joy to all those who have visited Venice." (BRD) HarBraceJ, 1985.   ○

Morris, Jan
A VENETIAN BESTIARY
"She uses the factual and fantastic animals of Venice to tell again that magic city's story." (TBS) Thames Hudson, 1982.   ○

Morris, Jan
THE VENETIAN EMPIRE: A SEA VOYAGE
A travel guide to the Venetian empire of the twelfth to eighteenth centuries—a reconstruction of the period. HarBraceJ, 1980.   ○

Norwich, John J.
A HISTORY OF VENICE
The author "has managed to compress 1,000 years of . . . events [in] one book . . . a living book . . . full of blood, naval battles, sieges, adventures, conquests, strokes of luck, stupendous defeats, glorious victories, secret plots . . . sharp profiles of the protagonists [yet] found space to describe the incredible beauty of Venice and its Circean charm." (BRD) Knopf, 1982.   ○

Ruskin, John
THE STONES OF VENICE (abridged)
A new "festive" edition of a "classic of art history and social criticism . . . enriched by splendid old and new photos, reproductions of Ruskin's diagrams, sketches, and watercolors, and a sensitive prefatory evaluation by editor Jan Morris—[a] selective abridgement [for] modern readers." (BL) Little, 1981.   ○

SARDINIA

Crawshaw, Gerry
CORSICA AND SARDINIA: A VISITOR'S GUIDE
W.H. Allen, 1987.   ○

Lawrence, D.H.
SEA AND SARDINIA
Travelogue describing a trip from Sicily to Sardinia, first published 1921. Penguin, 1981. Also *D.H. Lawrence and Italy* (1985).   ○

GUIDEBOOKS/Italy

(See also guidebooks listed under various cities/regions.)

Atlee, Helena and Ramsay, Alex
ITALIAN GARDENS: A GUIDE FOR VISITORS
McCarta, 1990.   ○

Goldsmith, James and Anne
THE DOLOMITES OF ITALY
"Chosen by the Italian government as the best guide to the Dolomites" (LJ) Hunter, 1989.   ○

Green, Kerry and Leocha, Charles
ESCAPE MANUAL: ITALY
One of a series of guidebooks designed to bring Europe to life and put the fantasy and excitement back into travel. World Leis Corp, 1984.   ○

Langdon, Helen
THE KNOPF TRAVELER'S GUIDES TO ART: ITALY
One of a series that covers major museums, art treasures, churches, important buildings that appear on most travel itineraries, along with essays on artists and periods, and a star system to identify museums or works of particular interest. Knopf, 1984.   ○

Mehling, Franz N.
ITALY: A PHAIDON CULTURAL GUIDE
Succinct appreciation of the best the country has to offer in terms of national treasures

and culture—churches, palaces, theaters, museums, monuments, maps and plans, all arranged alphabetically and cross-indexed. Phaidon Pr., n.d.   ○

O'Toole, Christopher and Losito, Linda
THE HOLIDAY NATURALIST IN ITALY
See entry under France/Guidebooks.   ○

Whitman, William B.
LITERARY CITIES OF ITALY
Literary life of Rome, Florence and Venice with maps and tours by foot (and by water taxi) to places that inspired such authors as Forster, Proust, and so on. Starrhill, 1990.   ○

HISTORY

Grant, Michael
FROM ALEXANDER TO CLEOPATRA
"Outstanding popular history of a fascinating era" in Roman history. It is followed by *The Rise of the Greeks* (1988) and *The Classical Greeks* (1989). (Choice) Scribner, 1983.   ○

Guicciardini, Francesco
THE HISTORY OF ITALY
Princeton U Pr, 1984.   ○

Hadas, Moses
GIBBON'S THE DECLINE AND FALL OF THE ROMAN EMPIRE
A modern abridgement. Fawcett, 1987.   ○

Hearder, H.
SHORT HISTORY OF ITALY
Cambridge U Pr, 1966.   ○

Lintner, Valerie
TRAVELER'S HISTORY OF ITALY
One of a series of introductory histories for travelers. Interlink Pub, 1989.   ○

Novels

Bassani, Giorgio
THE GARDEN OF THE FINZI-CONTINIS (Ferrara)
Set in Ferrara of the 1920s and '30s, and an aristocratic Italian-Jewish family at the out-

break of World War II. Atheneum, 1965. Also *The Smell of Hay* (1975) and *The Heron* (1970).   ○

Crichton, Robert
THE SECRET OF SANTA VITTORIA
A wonderful movie was made of this novel about a town in Italy that uses a variety of stratagems to outwit the German occupiers' search for their cache of wine. S&S, 1966.   ○

DeWohl, Louie
LAY SIEGE TO HEAVEN (Siena)
Story of St. Catherine of Siena. Lippincott, 1961.   ○

Duranti, Francesca
THE HOUSE ON MOON LAKE
Translated from the Italian; the plot concerns a translator who tracks down an obscure novel and creates a biography for its author. Random, 1986.   ○

Eco, Umberto
THE NAME OF THE ROSE
"An antidetective-story detective story . . . extraordinary work of novelistic art." The story is set in a 14th-century Benedictine monastery and involves a series of bizarre deaths taking place in seven days in November 1327. (BRD) HarBraceJ, 1983. Also *Foucault's Pendulum* (1990), "not a novel in the strict sense . . . a long erudite joke"—a student in the 1970s is doing his thesis on the monastic Templars, disbanded in the 1300s for their practices, and explores the theory that the Templars have carried out a secret revenge for seven centuries.   ○

Elliott, Janice
THE ITALIAN LESSON
Two British couples on vacation in Italy—"a delight for the senses, a feast of tears and laughter." (FC) Beaufort Bks, 1986.   ○

Godden, Rumer
THE BATTLE OF THE VILLA FIORITA
Two English children, victims of divorce, battle to force their mother to return home from the villa. Viking, 1963.   ○

Guareschi, Giovanni
THE LITTLE WORLD OF DON CAMILLO
The first in a series of humorous books about the ongoing war between Don Camillo, local village priest, and the communist mayor. This and the titles that follow recount various contretemps involving local villagers, social activist younger priests, and flower children, and give a highly readable and insightful account of a country that can have a large Communist party and yet remain very Catholic. Pelligrini, FS&G, 1951. Also *Don Camillo and His Flock* (1952), *Don Camillo's Dilemma* (1954), *Don Camillo Takes the Devil By the Tail* (1957), *Comrade Don Camillo* (1964). ○

Heller, Joseph
CATCH-22
The contemporary classic about an American bombing squadron in World War II, stationed in Italy. S&S, 1961. ○

Hemingway, Ernest
A FAREWELL TO ARMS
A doomed love affair between an American and an English nurse during World War I. Scribner, 1983 (first published 1929). ○

Holme, Timothy
THE ASSISI MURDERS
An Italian police inspector accompanies his sister on a package tour to Assisi and becomes involved in solving a murder. Walker, 1988. ○

Hoving, Thomas
DISCOVERY
"Arch, nicely crafted" story of murder and suspense when a New York art director and his wife are invited to help with an archaeological dig. (FC) S&S, 1989. ○

Kennedy, William P.
TOY SOLDIERS
Suspenseful international thriller in which terrorists capture a school for well-off American boys in Italy. St. Martins, 1988. ○

Maalouf, Amin
LEO AFRICANUS
See entry under Morocco/Novels. ○

Morante, Elsa
HISTORY
A novel with the theme that history obscures individual lives and "our perception of past wars blurs the degradation and destruction" inflicted. The plot centers on a man conceived as the result of wartime rape; his life and that of his family unfold and are intertwined with headlines about events of the period. Knopf, 1977. ○

Sherwood, John
MENACING GROVES
A tour of Italian gardens is the setting—"events . . . a bit farfetched, but the botanical lore is fascinating." (FC) Scribner, 1989. ○

Spark, Muriel
THE TAKEOVER
"A duel between the effete Hubert and the earthy Maggie" over possession of a home in Nemi, Italy. (FC) Viking, 1976. ○

Stewart, Fred M.
CENTURY
Saga of two branches of an Italian family encompassing two world wars, Hollywood, the worlds of mansion and ghetto in New York, decadent aristocracy and beleaguered peasant in Italy. (FC) Morrow, 1981. ○

FLORENCE & TUSCANY

Cornelisen, Ann
ANY FOUR WOMEN COULD ROB THE BANK OF ITALY
Funny novel based on the premise that in chauvinist Italy women are invisible, hence the title. Set in a "deliciously detailed" Tuscan hilltop community. (FC) HR&W, 1984. ○

DeWohl, Louis
LAY SIEGE TO HEAVEN
The story of St. Catherine of Siena. Lippincott, 1961. ○

Forster, E.M.
A ROOM WITH A VIEW
The heroine is an upper-middle-class Englishwoman who exchanges rooms with

lower-middle-class Mr. Emerson at her Florence hotel so that she can have a room with a view. The exchange leads to a profound change in her life and prejudices. Knopf, 1923 (first published 1908).   o

Howells, William D.
INDIAN SUMMER
Story of the American colony in nineteenth-century Florence, by one of America's leading writers of that period. Indiana U, 1972 (first published 1886).   o

Johnston, Velda
THE ETRUSCAN SMILE
The plot centers on a young woman seeking her missing older sister in Tuscany, which leads to "Mafioso connections . . . the smuggling of ancient art objects out of Italy." (FC) Dodd, 1977.   o

Langton, Jane
THE DANTE GAME
Homer Kelly, as part of the faculty of the American School of Florentine Studies, and his students read through Dante's *Divine Comedy* and draw parallels to contemporary Florence. After three murders Homer and a friend become involved in the investigation. "Descriptions of the city's visual delights are as voluptuously detailed as any armchair traveler might desire." (FC) Viking, 1991.   o

Lawrence, D.H.
AARON'S ROD
A novel of "the chaos of impulses and incoherent aspirations in the break-up" of established moral standards . . . life in Florence is charmingly pictured. Seltzer, 1922.   o

Maugham, W. Somerset
THEN AND NOW
Novel about Machiavelli in 1502. Doubleday, 1948.   o

Michaels, Barbara
THE GREY BEGINNING
Mystery in which a young widow visits the ancestral home, outside Florence, of her dead husband. Congdon & Weed, 1984.   o

Mortimer, J.C.
SUMMER'S LEASE
Responding to an ad for a Tuscan villa takes the Pargenter family to Italy—"elements of social satire and mystery . . . an entertaining story whose atmosphere of mounting tension culminates in a disturbing climax." Viking Penguin, 1988.   o

Nabb, Magdalen
THE MARSHAL AND THE MADWOMAN
One of a series of Marshal Guarnaccia mysteries set in Florence and environs. Clementina, a madwoman in middle-class Florence, is found murdered, seemingly without motive—"superb . . . rises far above the staples of the genre." Scribner, 1988. Also *The Marshall's Own Case* (1990), *Marshall and the Murderer* (1987), *Death in Springtime* (1985), *Death in Autumn* (1985), *Death of a Dutchman* (1983) and *Death of an Englishman* (1982).   o

Stone, Irving
THE AGONY AND THE ECSTASY
A fictionalized life of Michelangelo, the renaissance artist, sculptor and poet. Doubleday, 1961.   o

SOUTHERN ITALY & CAPRI, MALTA, SICILY

Douglas, Norman
SOUTH WIND
Capri is the fictional isle of Nepenthe in this classic. The novel is about the effect of the Capri life-style on visitors. Scholarly Pr, 1971 (first published 1917).   o

Dunnett, Dorothy
DISORDERLY KNIGHTS
Part of a series of historical novels set in the sixteenth century. This one is about the Knights of Malta, the Turkish invasion and shifts from Malta to Tripoli to Scotland. Buccaneer Bks, 1981.   o

Hazzard, Shirley
THE BAY OF NOON
An English girl grows up when she spends a year in Naples as a spectator to, and is influenced by, the life of a novelist to whom

she's been given a letter of introduction. Little, 1970. ○

Hersey, John
A BELL FOR ADANO
A Pulitzer Prize novel about American soldiers in World War II Italy. Knopf, 1944. ○

Lampedusa, Giuseppe di
THE LEOPARD
The fortunes of Don Fabrizio, a cultivated Sicilian prince and the noble house he heads. The time is 1860–1910—Don Fabrizio is considered a major fictional character creation and the period evoked "congeals a moment of time past and makes it timeless." (FC) Pantheon, 1960. ○

Llewellyn, Caroline
THE LADY OF THE LABYRINTH
Blends modern with ancient—"action-packed tale of international intrigue" set in Libya and Sicily. (BL) Scribner, 1990. ○

Puzo, Mario
THE SICILIAN
"Fine, fast-paced novel about Sicily in the mid-1940s" following the career of a renegade who incurs the enmity of the Mafia. (FC) S&S, 1984. ○

Seton, Cynthia Propper
A FINE ROMANCE
The lives of two American families area changed when they meet on a tour bus over Christmas in Italy. Norton, 1976. ○

Warner, Marina
THE LOST FATHER
Family saga narrated by a woman working in a London museum who recalls her family's violent history. S&S, 1989. ○

ROME & THE VATICAN

Gash, Jonathan
THE VATICAN RIP
A suspenseful caper in which an antiques dealer is forced to steal a piece of Chippendale from the Vatican. Ticknor & Fields, 1982. ○

Ginzburg, Natalia
THE CITY AND THE HOUSE
"dissolution of family and love in the contemporary world" told through a series of letters. (FC) Seaver, 1987. ○

Martin, Malachi
VATICAN
Inner workings and history of the Vatican state—"will stun readers with its revelations and intrigue them with its multi-textured plot." (FC) Har-Row, 1986. ○

Moravia, Alberto
THE WOMAN OF ROME
Story of a prostitute in Fascist Rome, FS&G, 1949. Also *Two Women* (1958)—the ordeal of a widow and her daughter in the closing days of World War II; *Roman Tales* (1957), *More Roman Tales* (1964), *Mistaken Ambitions* (1955). ○

Peters, Elizabeth
THE SEVENTH SINNER
An art history student becomes involved in a murder, which also involves a beautiful art historian. Dodd, 1972. ○

Tucci, Niccoló
THE SUN AND THE MOON
A family saga. (BRI) Knopf, 1977. This is a sequel to *Before My Time* (1962), conveying the social levels and the spirit of Rome at the turn of the century. ○

West, Morris L.
THE SHOES OF THE FISHERMAN
A fictional new pope is from the Ukraine, and has spent many years as prisoner of the Russians in Siberia—"fantastic novel . . . a whopper, a spellbinder, a cliffhanger, an annoyance and a delight." (FC) Morrow, 1963. Also *The Devil's Advocate* (1959). ○

Williams, Tennessee
THE ROMAN SPRING, OF MRS. STONE
A fading beauty of fifty meets a gigolo in Rome. New Directions, 1950. ○

Yourcenar, Marguerite
A COIN IN NINE HANDS
"A fictional cross section of Italian society" in 1933, in the 1980s remains "an elegant but sharp slap at . . . political degeneracy." (FC) FS&G, 1982.   ○

ANCIENT ROME

Note also novels listed under Biblical Israel.

Asch, Sholem
THE NAZARENE
"A historical background against which the figure of Jesus [moves] authentically." The story is narrated by a scholar who, as a Roman official in an earlier incarnation, was involved in the persecution of Jesus. (FC) Putnam Pub Group, 1939.   ○

Bradshaw, Gillian
THE BEACON AT ALEXANDER
See entry under Egypt/Novels.   ○

Bryher
THE COIN OF CARTHAGE
See under North Africa/Novels.   ○

Bulwer-Lytton, Sir Edward G.
THE LAST DAYS OF POMPEII
Pompeii just before and during the Vesuvius eruption in A.D. 79—"full of learning and spirit . . . a charming novel." (FC) Dodd, 1946 (first published 1834).   ○

Burgess, Anthony
THE KINGDOM OF THE WICKED
The early days of Christianity in Rome— "masses of intriguing and funny historical detail." (FC) Arbor Hse, 1985.   ○

Caldwell, Taylor
DEAR AND GLORIOUS PHYSICIAN
See under Middle East/Novels. Also *The Pillar of Iron* (1965), a "massive fictional biography of Cicero . . . against a panoramic background of Imperial Rome."   ○

Costain, Thomas B.
THE SILVER CHALICE
Based on legends of the years following Christ's crucifixion. The silver chalice was meant to hold the cup from which Christ drank at the Last Supper. Doubleday, 1964.   ○

Davis, Lindsay
THE SILVER PIGS
Marcus Didius Falco is hired in ancient Rome to solve a murder and locate a ring of silver smugglers—"humor, suspense, romance." (FC) Crown, 1989.   ○

Douglas, Lloyd C.
THE ROBE
The story of Christ's robe and the influence it had on the soldier who won it in dice— Christianity during those first years after the crucifixion. Houghton, 1942.   ○

Duggan, Alfred
CHILDREN OF THE WOLF
Fictionalized version of the founding of Rome. Coward, 1959.   ○

Graves, Robert
I, CLAUDIUS
The fascinating story of Imperial Rome, and the basis for the public TV series. A "work of the imagination that has the effect of history." Random, 1977 (first published 1934). The sequel is *Claudius the God* (1977, first published 1934).   ○

McCullough, Colleen
FIRST MAN IN ROME
Rome between 110 and 100 B.C.—"astonishing work, the first of five planned volumes about life . . . in ancient Rome." (FC) Morrow, 1990.   ○

Murphy, Walter F.
UPON THIS ROCK
St. Peter and the first century of the Christian Church. Macmillan, 1987.   ○

Sienkiewicz, Henryk
QUO VADIS
Historical novel of Nero's Rome and the Christian martyrs—won a Nobel Prize for literature in 1905. Airmont, 1968 (first published 1896).   ○

Wallace, Lew
BEN HUR
Ben Hur is sentenced to be a Roman gal-
leyslave as the result of a false accusation,
and his family are also sentenced to dreadful
punishments. He escapes, seeks revenge,
and finds his family who are miraculously
cured by Jesus. Buccaneer Bks, 1981 (first
published 1880). ○

Waltari, Mika
THE ROMAN
Setting is first century A.D., and the reigns
of Claudius and Nero—the decadence of
Rome, the rise of Christianity and the existence of other religions. Putnam Pub Group,
1966. ○

Wilder, Thornton
THE IDES OF MARCH
"Historical novel or fantasy . . . the life of
Julius Caesar and some other Romans dur-
ing the months preceding Caesar's assassi-
nation." (FC) Har-Row, 1948. ○

Wood, Bari
SOUL FLAME
The heroine is a "healer woman" in 1st-
century Rome—"dramatic, unpredictable
narrative with intriguing material about history, spirituality and the medical practices
of antiquity." (FC) Random, 1987. ○

VENICE

Byrne, Donn
MESSER MARCO POLO
See entry under China/Novels. ○

Gash, Jonathan
THE GONDOLA SCAM
The narrator is an antiques dealer/detective;
the story "takes him from an illegal auction
in England to the canals of Venice . . . can
almost serve as a travel guide. . . . conveys
the feeling of all who first visit Venice." (FC)
St. Martin, 1984. ○

Habe, Hans
PALAZZO
A woman struggles to save her palazzo from
collapse and deals in fraudulent art to raise

the needed money—"portrayal of Venetian
life at every level, from that of the communist gondolier to the cheap chic . . . the
bored, idle rich kids, the elderly eccentrics."
(FC) Putnam Pub Group, 1977. ○

Hemingway, Ernest
**ACROSS THE RIVER AND INTO
THE TREES**
An American colonel and his love affair
in post-World War II Venice. Scribner,
1950. ○

Holme, Timothy
A FUNERAL OF GONDOLAS
"Re-creates the busy vibrance of Venice in
a plot as delightfully tortuous as the streets
and canals of this strange city." An "off-
beat police procedural" involving a gondo-
liers' betting syndicate. (FC) Coward,
1982. ○

James, Henry
THE ASPERN PAPERS
Novelette set in Venice by the nineteenth-
century writer, in *The Complete Tales of Henry
James*. Lippincott, 1975. ○

Jong, Erica
SERENISSIMA
Literary fantasy in which an American
actress at a film festival for a role in the
Merchant of Venice is transported back to
the Shakespearean Venice of 1592. HM,
1987. ○

Mann, Thomas
DEATH IN VENICE
A successful writer on a visit to Venice becomes aware of decadent potentialities in
himself. Knopf, 1965 (first published
1925). ○

Pasinetti, P.M.
VENETIAN RED
Fortunes and passions of two Italian families in the period 1938 to 1941. Random,
1960. ○

Shellabarger, Samuel
PRINCE OF FOXES
Historical novel of Renaissance Venice and
the house of the Borgias. Little, 1947. Also,

Lord Vanity (1953), historical novel of eighteenth-century Venice. ○

Spark, Muriel
TERRITORIAL NIGHTS
An international comedy of manners. Coward, 1979. ○

Unsworth, Barry
STONE VIRGIN
The plot centers around the restoration of a Renaissance madonna—"provides knowledgeable discourses on art, breathtaking scenes of Venice and a ripe plot." (FC) HM, 1986. ○

THE NETHERLANDS

Series Guidebook
(See Appendix 1)

American Express Pocket Guide: Amsterdam
At Its Best: Holland
Baedeker: Amsterdam; Netherlands
Berlitz: Amsterdam
Blue Guide: Holland
Fodor: Amsterdam, Holland
Frommer: Amsterdam & Holland
Insight Guide: Amsterdam; Netherlands
Let's Go: Amsterdam
Michelin: Netherlands
Real Guide: Amsterdam
Visitor's Guide: Holland

Background Reading

Bailey, Anthony
REMBRANDT'S HOUSE
Rembrandt's house, now a museum, is the point of departure for an account of both his life and life in the seventeenth century. Houghton, 1978. ○

Colijn, Helen
OF DUTCH WAYS
By an author who was born and educated in the Netherlands and returns annually—culture from Rembrandt to mud-flat hiking, personal experiences in everyday living. The director of the Dutch National Bureau for Tourism says: "With a few deft strokes [Helen Colijn] has described our complex political system, our unique educational system and the problems of living in a country that, except for Bangladesh, is the most densely populated in the world." B&N Bks, 1984. ○

Frank, Anne
DIARY OF A YOUNG GIRL
The experiences of a Jewish family, living in hiding in Amsterdam during the Nazi occupation. PB, 1985. ○

Golding, William
A MOVING TARGET
A collection of the noted author's writings, including an article on the Dutch waterways. FS&G, 1982. ○

Hoffman, William
QUEEN JULIANA: THE STORY OF THE RICHEST WOMAN IN THE WORLD
HarBraceJ, 1979. ○

Hopkins, Adam
HOLLAND, ITS HISTORY, PAINTINGS AND PEOPLE
Historical overview that features the lives of Holland's many prominent artists. Faber & Faber, 1988. ○

Schama, Simon
EMBARRASSMENT OF RICHES: AN INTERPRETATION OF DUTCH CULTURE IN THE GOLDEN AGE
"Traces the development of simple farming, fishing and shipping communities . . . into a formidable world empire . . . Explores the land and collective personality of the Dutch people" using documents, literature, paintings, even recipes. (Choice) U of California Pr, 1988. ○

GUIDEBOOKS

Green, Kerry and Bythines, Peter
THE WHOLE EUROPE ESCAPE MANUAL: FRANCE, HOLLAND, BELGIUM WITH LUXEMBOURG
One of a series of guidebooks "designed to bring Europe to life and put the fantasy and excitement back into travel." World Leis Corp, 1984. ○

Leitch, Michael
SLOW WALKS IN AMSTERDAM
Leisurely walks to see the city, shops, museums, cafes, and excursions to Haarlem, Leiden and Utrecht. Har-Row, 1990. ○

Mehling, Franz N.
HOLLAND: A PHAIDON CULTURAL GUIDE
Succinct appreciation of the best the country has to offer in terms of national treasures and culture—churches, palaces, theaters, museums, monuments, maps and plans, all arranged alphabetically and cross-indexed. Phaidon Pr., n.d. ○

Penguin, eds.
THE TIME-OUT AMSTERDAM GUIDE
"Amsterdam by Amsterdammers"—all the major attractions and hundreds of the lesser-known, from specialty shops and contemporary art to how to book a session with a personal philosopher. (Publisher) Penguin, 1991. ○

Pilkington, Roger
SMALL BOAT THROUGH HOLLAND
State Mutual Bk, 1985. ○

Stoutenbeck, Jan, and others
A GUIDE TO JEWISH AMSTERDAM
Hermon, 1985. ○

HISTORY

Burnchurch, R.
AN OUTLINE OF DUTCH HISTORY
E J Brill, 1982. ○

Novels

Camus, Albert
THE FALL
A successful lawyer in Amsterdam bares his soul to a stranger. Knopf, 1957. ○

Freeling, Nicolas
THE LOVELY LADIES
A seemingly senseless murder in Amsterdam leads to Dublin for an answer. Harper, 1971. Other mysteries in the Inspector Van der Valk series set in the Netherlands are *Criminal Conversation* (1966), *Auprés de ma Blonde* (1972), *Love in Amsterdam* (1990), *Sand Castles* (1990). ○

Hartog, Jan de
THE INSPECTOR
Story of a "heroic, middle-aged Dutch policeman" who undertakes to get a young Dutch-Jewish girl to Israel in 1946. Atheneum, 1960. Also *The Captain* (1966), story of a Hollander who escapes from the Nazis and does convoy duty on the Iceland-Murmansk run, *The Little Ark* (1953) and *The Lost Sea* (1966). ○

Holland, Cecelia
THE SEA BEGGARS
Historical novel set in the sixteenth century; a brother and sister fight for freedom with William of Orange. Knopf, 1982. ○

Koning, Hans
DEWITT'S WAR
An "intelligent thriller" set in a small town in Holland during World War II—one of Europe's richest men is murdered and the Germans have removed critical documents. (FC) Pantheon, 1983. ○

MacLean, Alistair
FLOODGATE
A group of terrorists threaten to blow up the dikes and flood the Netherlands to force England to withdraw her troops from Northern Ireland—set in and around Amsterdam. Doubleday, 1984. ○

Moyes, Patricia
DEATH AND THE DUTCH UNCLE
Inspector Henry Tibbetts pursues a killer through Holland's canals. H. Holt, 1983. ◌

Mulisch, Harry
LAST CALL
An aging actor, and former Nazi collaborator, is asked to star in a play that seems to him like an opportunity for redemption. Viking, 1989. Also *The Assault* (1985), a political thriller. ◌

Schmitt, Gladys
REMBRANDT
Fictionalization of the life of Rembrandt. Random, 1961. ◌

Van de Wetering, Janwillem
THE STREETBIRD
A murder mystery set in the red light district of Amsterdam with a pimp as the murder victim—"night-watch tale of this bizarre, seamy city within a city is full of life, death, intrigue and a shadowy magic." Putnam, 1983. Others in the series of murder mysteries by this author, solved by the team of Grijpstra and deGier and set in Amsterdam, include: *The Mind-Murders* (1981), *The Corpse on the Dike* (1976), *Tumbleweed* (1976), *Outsider in Amsterdam* (1975), *The Japanese Corpse* (1977) (Japan and Amsterdam), *Death of a Hawker* (1977), *Blond Baboon* (1978). ◌

N O R W A Y
(Including Lapland)

Series Guidebooks
(See Appendix 1)

Berlitz: Oslo & Bergen
Insight Guide: Norway
Visitor's Guide: Norway
See also Series Guides for Scandinavia (*) under Denmark.

Background Reading

NOTE: See also Denmark for books with an asterisk (*), which offer additional background reading on Scandinavia as a whole and may include material on Norway, and Denmark/Vikings. ◌

Bjercke, Alf and Tomkinson, Michael
NORWAY, A PICTORIAL
TRAVELOGUE
Seven Hills, 1991. ◌

Bruemmer, Fred
THE ARCTIC WORLD
A comprehensive survey of the northern circumpolar world—essays on history, people, animals and plant life of the Arctic countries, including the Lapps. Crown, 1989. ◌

Carlson, Signe H.
FROM FOG TO FLARK
Adventures of Norwegian homesteaders in Swedish Lapland. Midgard Pr. ◌

Jones, David H.
NIGHT TIMES AND LIGHT TIMES:
A JOURNEY THROUGH
LAPLAND
Chronicles the author's love affair with Lapland (really Samiland) and a personal memoir as well—"superbly describes and photographs the natural wonders." (BL) Viking, 1990. ◌

Millman, Lawrence
LAST PLACES: A JOURNEY IN THE
NORTH
Follows the Viking route from Bergen, Norway, to Newfoundland (via Shetlands, Faeroes, Iceland, Greenland, Labrador). "Describes the beauty . . . relates the history . . . tells tales of local mythology . . . encounters with the native residents . . .

acerbic wit makes the book extremely entertaining." (LJ) HM, 1990. ○

Valkeapaa, Nils-Aslak
GREETINGS FROM LAPPLAND: THE SAMI, EUROPE'S FORGOTTEN PEOPLE.
Humanities, 1983. ○

Vanberg, Bent
OF NORWEGIAN WAYS
"A humorous, quite irreverent, and highly interesting history and description of Norway, of the Norwegian people, and also of their cousins overseas." (Publisher) Har-Row, 1984. ○

GUIDEBOOKS

Lundevall, E.
NORWAY TOURIST
Vanous, 1983. ○

Welle-Strand, Erland
TWO THOUSAND FIVE HUNDRED MILES OF THE NORWEGIAN COASTAL STEAMER
One of a series of guides to Norway by this author. Vanous, 1984. Also *Tourist in Norway, Motoring in Norway, Angling, Mountain Touring Holidays*. ○

HISTORY

Derry, T.K.
HISTORY OF SCANDINAVIA
U of Minnesota Pr, 1979. Also *Short History of Norway*, Greenwood, 1979, and *Oslo*, published by Vanous. ○

Midgaard, J.
NORWAY: A BRIEF HISTORY
Vanous, 1982. ○

Semmingsen, Ingrid
NORWAY TO AMERICA: A HISTORY OF THE MIGRATION
U of Minnesota Pr, 1978. ○

Novels

Barnard, Robert
THE CHERRY BLOSSOM CORPSE
A conference of romance writers in Norway is the setting for this mystery. Dell, 1988. Also *Death In a Cold Climate* (1980). ○

Francis, Clare
WOLF WINTER (Lapland)
When a mountain climber is killed, his widow is drawn into espionage, the cold war, and events rooted in World War II—"a violent struggle for truth and survival in Lapland's frozen wastes." (FC) Morrow, 1988. ○

Francis, Dick
SLAYRIDE
One of Francis's many mysteries involving horseracing. An investigator for the British Jockey Club is brought to Oslo to solve the disappearance of racing receipts—"more than a suspense story . . . [a] novel with humor and authenticity of setting and characters." (FC) Har-Row, 1974. ○

Hamsun, Knut
GROWTH OF THE SOIL
A novel of "rude peasant life in an out-of-the-way corner of Norway"—it won the Nobel Prize for literature in 1920. Knopf, 1968 (first published 1917). Other novels by Hamsun include: *Hunger* (1890), about a struggling writer; *Pan* (1894), a "game of love" ends in a ruined life for the man; also *Mysteries* (1892), *The Wanderer* (1909), *Victoria* (1898). ○

Holt, Tom
WHO'S AFRAID OF BEOWULF
A fantasy in which an archaeologist (Hildy) discovers the tomb of an ancient Norse king (Hrolf). Hildy helps Hrolf (who was only sleeping) to do battle with his 20th-century enemy, a computer buff—"pokes gentle fun at ancient stories of the gods, and at modern technology." (FC) St. Martin, 1989. ○

Laker, Rosalind
THE SHINING LAND
A love story, and a story of the Resistance in occupied Norway during World War II—

"packed with fascinating details of the wartime dangers faced." Doubleday, 1985. ○

Undset, Sigrid
KRISTIN LAVRANSDATTER: A TRILOGY

Originally published singly as *The Bridal Wreath* (1923), *The Mistress of Husaby* (1925), and *The Cross* (1927)—it takes its heroine from "happy childhood and later romance as wife and mother on a great estate, to her old age and loneliness . . . one of the most realistic stories of a woman's life ever written." The setting is medieval Norway and the book is considered a masterpiece; its author won the Nobel Prize for literature in 1928. (FC) Knopf, 1959. Also *The Master of Hestviken* (1952), a portrait of thirteenth- and fourteenth-century Norwegian life in four volumes: *The Axe* (1928), *The Snake Pit* (1929), *In the Wilderness* (1929), and *The Son Avenger* (1930), which ends in 1814. ○

POLAND

*Series Guidebooks
(See Appendix 1)*

Nagel's Encyclopedia Guide: Poland
Real Guide: Poland

Background Reading

Ash, Timothy G.
THE MAGIC LANTERN

See entry under Czechoslovakia. This book is about the revolution of 1989; Ash's *The Polish Revolution: Solidarity* describes events in 1980–81 (1984). ○

Bloch, Alfred, ed.
THE REAL POLAND: AN ANTHOLOGY OF NATIONAL SELF-PERCEPTION

Selections of Polish writing-fiction and non-fiction—with the intent to acquaint non-Poles "with the unique way in which Poles view the world." (LJ) Continuum, 1982. ○

Brandys, Kazimierz
A WARSAW DIARY: 1978–1981

By a Polish novelist, diary excerpts that convey the atmosphere and reality of life in Poland just prior to imposition of martial law in 1982. "An extraordinary book." (BRD) Random, 1984. ○

Döblin, Alfred
JOURNEY TO POLAND

The author, an important writer of the twentieth century, traveled to Poland from Germany in 1924, in search of his Jewish roots. "*Journey to Poland* is the chronicle of Döblin's travels, capturing both the rich Yiddish culture of Eastern Europe and the proudly independent Poland of the years between two world wars." Reprint of the 1968 edition. (Publisher) Paragon Hse, 1991. ○

Enzensberger, Hans M.
EUROPE, EUROPE: FORAYS INTO A CONTINENT

See entry under Europe. Poland is one of six European countries analyzed by the German essayist. ○

Gill, Anton
BERLIN TO BUCHAREST: TRAVELS IN EASTERN EUROPE

See entry under Europe/Background Reading. ○

Kaufman, Michael T.
MAD DREAMS, SAVING GRACES: POLAND AND ITS PEOPLE—A NATION IN CONSPIRACY

"Trenchant observations" of a Polish-American who was also based in Warsaw for several years as *New York Times* correspondent. It includes reactions from his father who comes to visit Poland after a 50-year absence in America. (PW) Random 1989. ○

Konwicki, Tadeŭsz
NEW WORLD AVENUE: AND VICINITY

Reminiscences of the Polish-Lithuanian novelist who moved to New World Avenue in

Warsaw after Vilnius was annexed by the Soviet Union in 1947—"essays, sketches and reminiscence . . . by turns cranky, urbane . . . sad, and funny . . . a self-portrait that reflects its social context." (PW) FS&G, 1991.   ○

Michener, James A.
PILGRIMAGE
"Fans of *Poland* [see under Novels, below] will certainly want to read about the fall-out from that best-seller" and Michener's side trip to Rome to visit John Paul II, another Pole. (BL) Rodale, 1990.   ○

Sebastian, Tim
NICE PROMISES
"Presenting a side of Poland rarely seen on the network news . . . an intimate, colorful and personal account of events in Poland from 1979 and the Pope's first visit through to the imposition of martial law." (Publisher) Chatto & Windus, 1985.   ○

Stewart, Steven
THE POLES
A book "rich in history and analysis" that describes the Polish people, their heritage, country and city life, politics, religion. By a British journalist with a Polish-born wife and access to people Westerners would not ordinarily meet. (BL) Macmillan, 1983.   ○

Swick, Thomas R.
UNQUIET DAYS
Married to a Polish woman, the author lived in Warsaw for two years (1980–82), at the time of Solidarity's rise and during its suppression. This is a diary of his experiences, with observations on Poland's history, politics, local folklore and traditions. "His book is framed as a literary appreciation of 'the special character of people who live under harsher climes and regimes.' " (NYT) Ticknor & Fields, 1992.   ○

Wedel, Janine
THE PRIVATE POLAND
The author visited Poland for two long stays as a social anthropologist doing research. This book, for the general reader, is is guide to everyday life with many anecdotes and

experiences on how Poles cope. Facts On File, 1985.   ○

Weschler, Lawrence
THE PASSION OF POLAND: FROM SOLIDARITY TO THE STATE OF WAR
Previously published in *Rolling Stone* and the *New Yorker*, and based on three trips to Poland during 1981–82. "The first outbreak of optimism . . . the crushing opposition by the government . . . martial law . . . voices and opinions [of Solidarity representatives, workers, government officials] in vividly related conversations . . . the role of the Catholic church . . . in the Polish national character and in [now] muted resistance." (BL) Pantheon, 1984.   ○

GUIDEBOOKS

Jordan, Alexander
INSIDER'S GUIDE: POLAND
In addition to typical guidebook material there are lists of insider activities from friendship societies to bridge and chess clubs. "Following Jordan's tips, the tourist has the means for creating a unique travel experience." (BL) Hippocrene, 1989.   ○

Stephenson, Jill & Bloch, Alfred
COMPANION GUIDE TO POLAND
People, culture, history, along with practical information. Hippocrene, 1991.   ○

Ward, Philip
POLISH CITIES
Travels in Cracow and the south, Gdansk, Malbork and Warsaw. Pelican, 1989.   ○

HISTORY

Davies, Norman
HEART OF EUROPE: A SHORT HISTORY OF POLAND
The Solidarity movement serves as a frame for the nation's history. Oxford U, 1986. Also *God's Playground*, a two-volume history (NYTBR) (Columbia U Pr, 1982)—"superbly readable, rich in detail . . . recounts both fact and legends that [have] contributed to the Poles' perception of their own history

. . . a biography of Poland and a work of art." ○

Novels

Agnon, S.Y.
THE BRIDAL CANOPY
The setting is early nineteenth-century Galicia, and the story is about a Jew who must find dowries for three daughters. Schocken, 1967 (first published 1922). Also *A Guest for the Night* (1937), *A Simple Story* (1985). ○

Begley, Louis
WARTIME LIES
"Recounts the wounded moral development" of its narrator, who grew up in Poland, as a Jew, during the Nazi occupation. (FC) Knopf, 1991. ○

Bienek, Horst
EARTH AND FIRE
Latest of a series of novels, set in a Silesian town beginning in the 1940s. Atheneum, 1988. Earlier titles in the tetralogy are *The First Polka* (1984), *September Light* (1986), *Time Without Bells* (1988). ○

Grass, Gunter
THE DANZIG TRILOGY
Omnibus edition of three serious novels with bizarre characters—*Cat and Mouse* (1963), *Dog Years* (1965), *The Tin Drum* (1963)—of Danzig and villages along the Vistula River. HBJ, 1987. ○

Hodge, Jane A.
POLONAISE
Historical novel of Poland in 1802, caught between the forces of Napoleon and Russia. Putnam, 1987. ○

Kosinski, Jerzy
THE PAINTED BIRD
Wanderings of a dark-haired child in Poland in World War II and the cruelties visited upon him because he is different-looking than the typical Polish child—an indictment of man's inhumanity to man. Houghton, 1976. ○

Kuniczak, W.S.
THE THOUSAND-HOUR DAY
The first thousand hours of World War II as Poland surrenders to the Germans. Dial, 1967. ○

Lem, Stanislaw
HOSPITAL OF THE
TRANSFIGURATION
A doctor is employed in a provincial insane asylum in 1939 as Poland falls to the Nazis— "gripping, introspective novel challenges popularly held conceptions of sanity and provokes the reader with its cynicism." HarBraceJ, 1988. ○

Michener, James A.
POLAND
The author uses a fictional village on the Vistula River and vignettes from the 1200s to the 1980s to tell the saga of three families, and thereby the story of Poland—"historically accurate . . . highly vivid . . . an engrossing and fast moving novel by a superb storyteller." (FC) Random, 1983. ○

Milosz, Czeslaw
THE SEIZURE OF POWER
Begins in the summer of 1944; the author "catalogues the reactions of a broad swath of Poles to . . . first the splintered resistance to the Nazis and then the . . . compromises and killing that arrives with the Russians. . . . based on actual characters of the period." (FC) FS&G, 1982. ○

Read, Piers Paul
POLONAISE
Saga of an aristocratic family from 1925 to 1958, set in Poland and later in Paris—whirls through "sexual escapades, the Spanish Civil War, flight from the Russians, and a jewel theft." (FC) Lippincott, 1976. ○

Sienkiewicz, Henryk
WITH FIRE AND SWORD
The first volume of a trilogy that is Poland's *War and Peace* and *Gone With the Wind*— appeared in 1890 and now republished in a new translation. Volume 2 (*The Deluge*) and volume 3 (*Fire in the Steppe*, previously known

as *Pan Michael)* will follow. Hippocrene, 1991. ○

Singer, Isaac Bashevis
THE MANOR

Portrays the period between the Polish insurrection of 1863 and the end of the nineteenth century. FS&G, 1967. Its sequel, *The Estate* (1969) covers the same period. Other novels by this Nobel Prize-winning author, set in Poland, include: *Yoshe Kalb* (1933), *The Brothers Ashkenazi* (1936), *The Magician of Lublin* (1960), *The Slave* (1962), *Satan in Goray* (1955), *The Seance and other Stories* (1968), and a recent novel, *Reaches of Heaven: A Story of the Baal Shem Tov* (1980). See also under ''Warsaw,'' below. ○

WARSAW

Hersey, John
THE WALL

The resistance of Polish Jews as they are systematically exterminated by the Nazis. Knopf, 1962. ○

Konwicki, Tadeǔsz
A MINOR APOCALYPSE

Chronicle of the Warsaw vagaries of a writer who has been asked to set himself afire as a protest in front of Communist party headquarters—''combines the surrealist detail of a dream with the repartee and reflection of a novel of ideas.'' (FC) FS&G, 1983. ○

Singer, Isaac Bashevis
SHOSHA

A young writer in Warsaw of the 1930s escapes political confrontations by involving himself with women, including his early love, Shosha. FS&G, 1978. Also *The Family Moskat* (1950), story of a Jewish family from the nineteenth century to the beginning of World War II. ○

Uris, Leon
MILA 18

Story of ''the handful of men and women who, knowing they had to die, defied the whole German Army with their homemade weapons''—Mila 18 was their command post. (FC) Doubleday, 1961. ○

PORTUGAL

Series Guidebooks (See Appendix 1)

Baedeker: Portugal
Berlitz: Algarve; Lisbon; Madeira
Birnbaum: Spain & Portugal
Blue Guide: Portugal
Cadogan Guide: Portugal
Fielding: Spain & Portugal
Fisher's World: Portugal
Fodor: Lisbon; Portugal
Frommer: Lisbon, Madrid & Costa del Sol; Portugal, Madeira & the Azores
Independent Traveler: Portugal
Insight Guide: Portugal; Madeira; Lisbon
Let's Go: Spain & Portugal
Michelin: Portugal
Real Guide: Portugal
Times Travel Library: Lisbon
2–22 Days Itinerary Planning Guide: Portugal

Background Reading

Conrad, Peter
WHERE I FELL TO EARTH: A LIFE IN FOUR CITIES

Lisbon is one of the cities. See entry under England/Oxford. ○

Dos Passos, John
THE PORTUGAL STORY

''Three centuries of exploration and discovery'' is the subtitle for this book by the American novelist, which tells of the extraordinary explorations of the Portuguese and establishment of the first extensive overseas empire of the period. Doubleday, 1969. ○

Kaplan, Marion
**THE PORTUGUESE: THE LAND
    AND ITS PEOPLE**
By a British photojournalist—"sprawling . . .
view of modern Portugal mingles straight
history with travel information . . . digressions into art and architecture, capturing the
beauty of sun-drenched cathedrals, castles
and cities." (PW) Viking, 1992.   o

Macaulay, Rose
**FABLED SHORE: FROM THE
    PYRENEES TO PORTUGAL**
Reprint of a travel classic. Oxford U Pr,
1986.   o

MacKendrick, Paul L.
THE IBERIAN STONES SPEAK
Introduction to archaeology and cultural history through archaeological findings in Spain
and Portugal. Funk & Wagnall, 1969.   o

GUIDEBOOKS

Cox, Thornton
**THORNTON COX'S TRAVELLERS'
    GUIDE TO PORTUGAL**
"Highly readable introduction to the area
under consideration. . . . necessary data for
getting there and getting about . . . suggested itineraries [designed for] economy of
time and movement." (Publisher) Hippocrene, 1987.   o

Kubiak, T.
COMPLETE GUIDE TO PORTUGAL
Hippocrene, 1989.   o

Leocha, Charles
**WHOLE EUROPE ESCAPE
    MANUAL: SPAIN & PORTUGAL**
Part of a series of guidebooks designed to
put the fantasy and excitement back into
travel. World Leis Corp, 1985.   o

Rogers, Barbara R. and Stillman
**THE PORTUGAL TRAVELER:
    GREAT SIGHTS AND HIDDEN
    TREASURES**
A guidebook with the tone of a first-person
narrative. Includes the Azores and Madeira.
Mills & Sanderson, 1989.   o

Thackery, Susan
**LIVING IN PORTUGAL: A
    COMPLETE GUIDE**
Trans-Atl Phila, 1985.   o

HISTORY

Livermore, H.V.
A NEW HISTORY OF PORTUGAL
Cambridge U Pr, 1976.   o

O'Callaghan, J.F.
HISTORY OF MEDIEVAL SPAIN
The author's Spain "is the entire peninsula
[and] Islamic, Jewish, Christian, Portuguese, and Catalonian as well as Castilian"
Spain and Portugal. (BRD) Cornell U, 1983
(first published 1975).   o

Novels

Boyle, Thomas
THE COLD STOVE LEAGUE
Set in an Algarve resort, a suspense novel
about an international currency scam. Academy Chi Pubs, 1987.   o

Cornwell, Barnard
SHARPE'S COMPANY
One of a series of historical novels about the
adventures of an English soldier of fortune.
Penguin, 1987. Also *Sharpe's Gold*.   o

Hodge, Jane A.
THE WINDING STAIR
A suspenseful Gothic romance set in early
nineteenth-century Portugal with a plot con-
cerning a secret society determined to con-
trol Portugal. Doubleday, 1969. Also, set in
Regency England and Portugal, *Marry in
Haste* (1970).   o

Lambert, Derek
THE JUDAS CODE
A complicated plot in which a Russian in
Lisbon (an illegitimate son of Stalin) is re-
cruited by British Intelligence to help Chur-
chill's "plan to embroil Germany and Russia
in a mutually destructive war"; for "World
War II buffs and espionage devotees alike."
(FC) Stein & Day, 1984.   o

L'Engle, Madeleine
THE LOVE LETTERS
A contemporary woman learns to deal with her own marriage after reading a packet of old love letters. FS&G, 1966.   o

Saramago, José
BALTASAR AND BLIMUNDA
Panorama of the 18th-century, organized as a series of contrasts in the lives of the rulers and the ruled. The plot focuses on a promise by the king to build a huge convent for the Franciscans if he is granted an heir, with a love story between an ex-soldier and a visionary. HarBraceJ, 1987.   o

Saramago, José
THE YEAR OF THE DEATH OF RICARDO REIS
Translation of an acclaimed Portuguese novel published in 1984. The setting is 1936, as a doctor returns to Lisbon from Brazil—"evokes an unforgettable image of Lisbon . . . full of poetry and surreal and ludicrous philosophical musings." (PW) HarBraceJ, 1991.   o

Sherwood, Valerie
LISBON
Historical romance, a saga of Lisbon in her 18th-century golden era. NAL, 1989.   o

Slavitt, David
SALAZAR BLINKS
A burlesque on 20th-century politics—a journalist is hired to convince Salazar with bogus news broadcasts that although incapacitated by a stroke, he is still in power. Atheneum, 1988.   o

RUMANIA

*Series Guidebooks
(See Appendix 1)*

Nagel's Encyclopedia Guide: Rumania

Background Reading

Codrescu, Andrei
A HOLE IN THE FLAG: A ROMANIAN EXILE'S STORY OF RETURN AND REVOLUTION
By a poet and commentator for National Public Radio who left Rumania as a teenager and returned to observe the shocking events and joys of the revolution from 1989 to January 1991. Morrow, 1991.   o

Daniels, Anthony
UTOPIAS ELSEWHERE
By a psychiatrist/travel writer, and based on his travels in 1989—"may astound even those . . . well versed in the perversities of the one party state." (BL) Crown, 1991.   o

Fermor, Patrick
BETWEEN WOODS AND WATER
See entry under Europe/Background Reading.   o

Florescu, Radu R. and McNally, Raymond T.
DRACULA, PRINCE OF MANY FACES
The real-life sources for Stoker's fictional vampire. Little, 1989.   o

Gill, Anton
BERLIN TO BUCHAREST: TRAVELS IN EASTERN EUROPE
See entry under Europe/Background Reading.   o

Hall, Brian
STEALING FROM A DEEP PLACE: TRAVELS IN SOUTHEASTERN EUROPE
See entry under Bulgaria.   o

MacKendrick, Paul
THE DACIAN STONES SPEAK
Archaeology and history based on archaeological sites in the Roman province of Dacia, now roughly the country of Rumania. U of North Carolina Pr, 1975. ◦

Pakula, Hannah
THE LAST ROMANTIC
Biography of the the flamboyant Queen Marie of Rumania who reigned from 1914 to 1927. S&S, 1985. ◦

Sitwell, Sacheverell
ROUMANIAN JOURNEY
An account of a journey made in the 1930s, with a new introduction by Patrick Fermor, and the best of the illustrations from the original edition published in 1938. The author comes into contact with gypsies at country fairs, the aristocracy, the landscape of Transylvania, Carpathia, the Danube delta. Oxford U Pr, 1991. ◦

GUIDEBOOKS

Brinkle, Lydle
COMPANION GUIDE TO ROMANIA
History, background and information for travelers. Hippocrene Bks, 1990. ◦

HISTORY

Georgescu, Vlad
THE ROMANIANS: A HISTORY
By the director of Radio Free Europe's Romanian Service, first published in 1984 and updated with an epilogue on the overthrow of Ceausescu's regime. Ohio State U Pr, 1991. ◦

Novels

Bellow, Saul
THE DEAN'S DECEMBER
A Chicago newspaperman travels to Bucharest to help his wife care for her mother who is dying, while back in Chicago his articles have embroiled him in controversy. A "political, social and philosophical [novel] rather than personal. The rapid switching back and forth between Bucharest and Chicago endows the book with a nervous, flickering energy." (FC) Har-Row, 1982. ◦

Eliade, Mircea
YOUTH WITHOUT YOUTH
Three novellas that portray the increasingly paranoic bureaucracy. Ohio State U Pr, 1988. Also *The Old Man and the Bureaucrats* (1980) and *The Forbidden Forest* (1978). ◦

Manning, Olivia
THE BALKAN TRILOGY
Three novels: *The Great Fortune* (1960), *The Spoilt City* (1962), *Friends and Heroes* (1965). The first takes place in Rumania at the outbreak of World War II and the plot revolves about an English lecturer at the local university in Bucharest and his wife, as Poland falls to the Nazis and refugees begin flooding in. The second is set in the 1940s and the last days of King Carol's reign. In the third, the couple have fled from German-occupied Rumania to Greece. The trilogy is "full of intriguing minor characters . . . evocative of both place and mood . . . an amazingly full and colorful canvas [that] hardly seems like fiction." Penguin, 1982 (first published 1960–65). ◦

SCOTLAND

NOTE: See also all asterisked entries (*) under England for additional series guides and background books, that may include Scotland. ◦

Series Guidebooks
(See Appendix 1)

Berlitz: Scotland
Blue Guide: Scotland

Cadogan Guide: Scotland
Exploring Rural Europe: Scotland
Fodor: Scotland
Frommer: England & Scotland; Scotland & Wales ($-A-Day); Scotland
Insight Guide: Edinburgh; Glasgow; Scotland
Michael's Guide: Scotland
Michelin: Scotland
Visitor's Guide: Lowlands & Edinburgh

Background Reading

Begley, Eve
OF SCOTTISH WAYS
"A wealth of information on Scotland and the Scottish conveyed in a bright, spritely . . . style." (Publisher) B&N Bks, 1978. ○

Campbell, James
INVISIBLE COUNTRY: A JOURNEY THROUGH SCOTLAND
"Witty and insightful look at a fascinating, romantic land by a native son . . . meeting the locals." (LJ) New Amsterdam, 1990. ○

Daiches, David, ed.
EDINBURGH: A TRAVELLER'S COMPANION
For the traveler and armchair traveler, a collection of historical readings arranged by locale, excerpted from writings of John Knox, Sir Walter Scott and so on. Atheneum, 1986. ○

Gordon, Sheila
A MODEST HARMONY: SEVERN SUMMERS IN A SCOTTISH GLEN
"A graceful, entertaining" account of the novelist's summers spent with her family in Perthshire—"characterizations of the people . . . regional lore and history." (BL) Seaview, 1982. ○

Harris, Paul, ed.
SCOTLAND: AN ANTHOLOGY
"Snatches of poetry, history, humor, fiction and anecdotal prose reveal the nature and soul of Scotland." Arranged geographically, culturally and historically. (BRD) Little, 1986. ○

Hawken, Paul
THE MAGIC OF FINDHORN
An account of this unique international community in northeastern Scotland, from its beginnings to "spiritual greenhouse" for thousands of people who visit each year. Harper, 1975. Also *Findhorn Garden* (1976). ○

MacGregor, Geddes
SCOTLAND FOREVER HOME
An introduction to the homeland for American and other Scots—great introductory reading by a Scottish-American. Dodd, 1980. Also *Scotland: An Intimate Portrait* (1990). ○

Maxwell, Gavin
RING OF BRIGHT WATER
For anyone who loves nature and animals— description of a remote and lovely area of coastal (Highland) Scotland, and the author's unique relationship with two sea otters. Penguin, 1987. ○

Miller, Christian
A CHILDHOOD IN SCOTLAND
Amusing, nostalgic memories of life in the 1920s in a castle with friendly ghosts. David & Charles, 1989. ○

Morris, Jan
SCOTLAND: THE PLACE OF VISIONS
Scotland's people, cities, countryside, history—"lovely collaboration between Jan Morris and photographer Paul Wakefield . . . A colorful excursion from the borderlands in the south to the Highlands in the north, and all around the rocky, irregular coast." (LJ) Potter, 1986. ○

Morton, H.V.
IN SEARCH OF SCOTLAND
Reprint of a travel classic. Dodd, 1984 (first published 1930). See also *Morton's Britain* under "England." ○

Prebble, John
JOHN PREBBLE'S SCOTLAND
Survey of the land by a novelist and clan historian—"cordial prose intertwines historical, literary, geographical, and autobiographical anecdotes delightfully." (BL) Secker & Warburg, 1985.   ○

Shenker, Israel
IN THE FOOTSTEPS OF JOHNSON & BOSWELL
The author follows the itinerary of Johnson and Boswell (taken and written about some 200 years earlier) to tell what they saw and to talk to descendants of those Johnson and Boswell talked to; visits to castles, churches, great homes, inns, ruins—"often witty, always deft and engaging." (PW) Houghton, 1982.   ○

Slavin, Ken and Julie
AROUND SCOTLAND: A TOURING GUIDE
A "pre-trip planning guide especially for travelers intending to tour by car, but useful for anyone considering a visit to Scotland"—arranged by region. (PW) Hippocrene, 1983.   ○

Steel, Tom
SCOTLAND'S STORY
Scotland's love-hate relationship with England, its influence on Britain, the fate of Scots who moved away—"brings history alive using the words of contemporary people wherever possible." Salem Hse, 1986.   ○

ISLANDS

MacLean, Charles
ISLAND ON THE EDGE OF THE WORLD
The story of St. Kilda, which, until 1930, was home for an isolated community with commonly held property and an economy based on agriculture, sheep, birds, feathers and oil. Nineteenth-century travelers brought disease and a decline in the economy until remaining residents were evacuated in 1930. David & Charles, 1990.   ○

Millman, Lawrence
LAST PLACES: A JOURNEY IN THE NORTH
See entry under Norway. The Viking route followed by the author includes the Faeroes and Shetlands.   ○

Schei, Liv and Moberg, Gunnie
THE ORKNEY STORY
Comprehensive guide to the Orkneys off Scotland's northeast coast—history, folklore, language, culture, government, lives, occupations, photographs. Hippocrene, 1985.   ○

Tomkies, Mike
BETWEEN EARTH AND PARADISE
"A naturalist's outlook . . . on his lonely wilderness life on a beautiful coastal island in the Scottish highlands . . . natural history laced with drama and humor." (BL) Doubleday, 1982.   ○

GUIDEBOOKS

Crowl, Philip A.
THE INTELLIGENT TRAVELLER'S GUIDE TO HISTORIC SCOTLAND
Companion to the author's guide to historic Britain—narrative history and gazetteer. Congdon & Weed, 1985.   ○

Hamilton, David
GOOD GOLF GUIDE TO SCOTLAND
A guided tour to championship courses, one-hole layouts, remote clubs, town clubs; maps, directions, nearby attractions. Pelican, 1984.   ○

Newton, Norman
ROADS TO THE ISLES
An island hopper's guide to the Hebrides—Clyde, Aran, Bute, Cumbrae. Seven Hills, 1992.   ○

Perrott, David
THE EDINBURGH GUIDE
Walking tours, easy and hard, and day trips out of the city. Also, material on the Edin-

burgh festival and practical advice for the traveler. Robert Nicholson Pubns, 1989. ○

Tindall, Jemima
SCOTTISH ISLAND HOPPING
A handbook for the independent traveler—an uncommon travel ground, the remote (Hebrides, Orkneys, Shetlands) islands off the Scottish coast. Practical travel information, history and an introduction to the islands. Hippocrene, 1983. ○

Tranter, Nigel
TRAVEL GUIDE TO THE SCOTLAND OF ROBERT THE BRUCE
Natl Hist Soc, 1985. ○

Wainwright, A. and Brabbs, Derry
WAINWRIGHT IN SCOTLAND
Tour by foot and car of the Pennine Way—"an inspiration and guide for prospective Scottish excursions and an amiable armchair ramble for stay-at-homes." (BL) Michael Joseph, 1988. ○

HISTORY

Jenner, Michael
SCOTLAND THROUGH THE AGES
"Stunningly illustrated . . . cogent and exciting—the perfect introduction to Scottish history." (BL) Viking, 1987. ○

Judd, Denis
TRAVELLER'S HISTORY OF SCOTLAND
One of a series of introductory histories for travelers. Interlink Pub, 1990. ○

Maclean, Fitzroy
A CONCISE HISTORY OF SCOTLAND
Scotland's complex history enlivened with wit and scholarship. Thames Hudson, 1983. ○

Novels

Barrie, J.M.
LITTLE MINISTER
The classic romance—"skilful portrayal of the complexities of Scotch character." (FC) AMS, 1975 (first published 1891). ○

Crane, John K.
THE LEGACY OF LADY SMITH
An American writer is hired to write a biography of a family's noted grandfather—"a sophisticated mystery story which presents a writer in action." (FC) S&S, 1986. ○

Gray, Alasdair
THE FALL OF KELVIN WALKER, A FABLE OF THE SIXTIES
About a successful London TV host brought down when the Calvinist ideals of his provincial youth conflict with the TV world of money—"ferociously funny satirist of a society bent on . . . stripping its citizens of . . . humanity." (BRD) Braziller, 1986. Also *Lanark* (1980) and *Janine* (1984). ○

Hill, Pamela
MY LADY GLAMIS
Historical novel about the reign of James IV and power struggles between clans and the king—"a very human portrait of a troubled, momentous period of Scottish history." (FC) St. Martin, 1987. ○

Knox, Bill
THE CROSSFIRE KILLINGS
Intricate plot, interesting characters and intriguing local color—a young policewoman is murdered near Loch Ness while vacationing at a peace camp, and an attack on the detective investigating the murder while at a Glasgow museum arcade leads to a solution. Doubleday, 1986. ○

Plaidy, Jean
THE CAPTIVE QUEEN OF SCOTS
Historical novel of the last eighteen years of Queen Mary of Scots. Putnam Pub Group, 1970 (first published 1963). Also *Royal Road to Fotheringay* (1955) (story of Mary's childhood and early reign in France and Scotland). ○

Stevenson, D.E.
VITTORIA COTTAGE
First in a family trilogy. Holt, 1971 (first published 1949). *Music in the Hills (1950)* and *Shoulder in the Sky* (1951), complete the series. Two other Scottish family sagas by Stevenson are *Mrs. Tim Christie* (1940), *Mrs. Tim Carries On* (1941), *Mrs. Tim Gets a Job* (1952), *Mrs. Tim Flies Home* (1952); and *Celia's House*, (1977) forty years of a family's life in the Scottish border country.　　○

PROVINCIAL & RURAL SETTINGS

Beaton, M.C.
DEATH OF AN OUTSIDER
A Hamish Macbeth mystery set in a Highland village with "a wildly ghoulish twist" supplied by ravenous lobsters! Also, *Death of a Hussy* (1990) and *Death of a Cad* (1987). (FC) St. Martin, 1988.　　○

Caird, Janet
THE UMBRELLA-MAKER'S DAUGHTER
Into a "tight, Scottish village" moves the umbrella-maker and his daughter with a penchant for writing "trenchant verses"—amorous attentions and a clash with townspeople result from her sharp wit. (FC) St. Martin, 1980. Two other mysteries with rural settings are *Murder Remote* (1973) (a West Scotland fishing village) and *In a Glass Darkly* (1966) (a modern gothic that begins with murder in a museum).　　○

Cronin, A.J.
THE GREEN YEARS
Story of a boy growing up in a small Scottish village. Little, 1944. The sequel is *Shannon's Way* (1948). Also *Hatter's Castle* (1931).　　○

Gash, Jonathan
THE TARTAN SELL
One of a series of mysteries featuring antique dealer Lovejoy—this one set in the Scottish Highlands. St. Martins, 1985.　　○

George, Elizabeth
PAYMENT IN BLOOD
"Red herrings abound" in an intricate suspense story set at a country estate where a troupe of actors are gathered to read a new play. Bantam Bks, 1989.　　○

Gibbon, Lewis G.
A SCOTS QUAIR
Three novels—*Sunset Song, Cloud Howe,* and *Grey Granite*—tell of Christine Guthrie's life in a small Scottish village; subsequently made into a public TV series. Schocken, 1977 (first published 1932–34).　　○

Grayson, Richard
THE WHISKY MURDERS
A fired management consultant goes to the countryside to consider this unfortunate event and gets involved in solving a murder. Walker, 1987.　　○

Johnston, Velda
I CAME TO THE HIGHLANDS
Romantic novel involving Scottish politics and intrigue at the time of Prince Charlie; a Scot, banished from a pre-Revolution colony in America, returns to Scotland. Dodd, 1974.　　○

Llewellyn, Sam
DEADEYE
Nautical thriller—a divorce lawyer must deal with environmental danger to a Scottish village, violence and murder. Summit, 1991.　　○

Ogilvie, Elisabeth
THE SILENT ONES
A specialist in folklore "falls in love with an enigmatic Highlander and finds herself enmeshed in a web of greed . . . murder." (FC) McGraw, 1981. Also *Jennie About to Be* (1984), set at the turn of the nineteenth century in the Highlands, and with a heroine who has a social conscience—"captivating start of a promised trilogy . . . a natural heroine."　　○

Pilcher, Rosamunde
SEPTEMBER
An intergenerational saga—a coming-out party in the Highlands "brings together characters whose lives change . . . during

the novel's four-month span." (FC) St. Martin, 1990. ○

Stirling, Jessica
TREASURES ON EARTH
First of a trilogy about 19th-century Scotland—"has style . . . its characters really do breathe and come to vibrant life." Following is *Creature Comforts* (1986). (FC) St. Martin, 1985. ○

EDINBURGH

Brett, Simon
SO MUCH BLOOD
An actor/director becomes involved with a group of young drama students when he arrives in Edinburgh to put on a one-man play, and in the investigation of the murder of one of them. "Conveys the behind-the-scenes atmosphere . . . evokes the sights and malty smell of Edinburgh." (FC) Scribner, 1977. ○

Douglas, Colin
THE HOUSEMAN'S TALE
Serio-comic novel of backstairs and inside of the Royal Charitable Institute—a new intern (houseman, in Scottish parlance) is put in charge of a ward and has to deal with patients for the first time—infighting with peers and superiors, escapes into sex and alcohol. "Fresh and entertaining hospital drama with universal appeal." (FC) Taplinger, 1978. Continues with *The Greatest Breakthrough Since Lunchtime* (1979). ○

Meek, M.R.D.
THE SPLIT SECOND (Edinburgh and Glasgow)
A London private investigator is hired to find his boss's niece—"crackerjack plot, startling image of . . . contrasts of weather and soul to be found in Scotland." (FC) Scribner, 1987. ○

Spark, Muriel
THE PRIME OF MISS JEAN BRODIE
Set in Edinburgh of the 1930s—a character sketch of a schoolteacher at a girls' school. "A story that is funny, true, unpleasant . . .

gloriously human—or ingloriously human—both, actually." (FC) Lippincott, 1962. ○

GLASGOW

Bermant, Chaim
THE PATRIARCH
Saga of a Jewish boy, sent at sixteen to Glasgow from Russia, who eventually brings over other members of his family—a family epic with the backdrop of the World Wars. St. Martin, 1981. Also *The Second Mrs. Whitberg* (1976), about the Pakistani influence on a Jewish neighborhood. ○

Kelman, James
A DISAFFECTION
A week in the life of a disaffected schoolteacher whose job adds to his despair. FS&G, 1989. ○

Knox, Bill
THE HANGING TREE
A videotape piracy racket is the focus of this mystery—"interesting characters, a lively race and vivid descriptions of Glasgow's urban ills." (FC) Doubleday, 1984. ○

McIlvanney, William
THE PAPERS OF TONY VEITCH
"Glasgow, 'city of the stare,' is richly depicted" in a novel for mystery fans of the Police Detective Jack Laidlaw series. "Sure to be compared with Higgins's Boston and Wambaugh's Los Angeles." (FC) Pantheon, 1983. Also *Laidlaw* (1977). ○

Stirling, Jessica
THE GOOD PROVIDER
First of a trilogy about a 19th-century Glasgow couple. Its sequel is *The Asking Price* (1990). St. Martin, 1989. ○

Turnbull, Peter
CONDITION PURPLE
A prostitute is murdered—"heart-wrenching action . . . unforgiving streets of Glasgow." (FC) St. Martin, 1989. Also in the "brutal crime" genre and set in Glasgow, by Turnbull, are *Two Way Cut* (1988) and *Dead Knock* (1983). ○

THE HEBRIDES AND OTHER ISLANDS

Beaton, M.C.
DEATH OF A SNOB
Hamish Macbeth (see under Provincial & Rural, above) visits an island in the Hebrides to investigate a woman's suspicions that she is in danger—"efficient little caper, full of gentle humor." (FC) St. Martin, 1991.   ○

Beckwith, Lillian
A PROPER WOMAN (Hebrides)
Novel about a woman in a violent marriage of convenience. St. Martin, 1987. Also *A Shine of Rainbows* (1984) and *The Hills Is Lonely* (1959).   ○

Brown, George M.
THE MASKED FISHERMAN AND OTHER STORIES (Orkney)
An author seeks his ancestral roots and a new life in 21 tales—"capturing the isles' austere beauty, daily rhythms of the fisherfolk and villagers." (PW) John Murray, 1990. Also *Greenvoe* (1970) and *A Time to Keep* (1969).   ○

Carothers, Annabel
KILCARAIG
Family saga set on the island of Mull in the Hebrides with "local color . . . lovingly supplied in the detailed description of the landscape and people." (FC) St. Martin, 1982.   ○

Grindal, Richard
DEATH STALK
"Lots of wild scenery and misty atmosphere [and] information about the making of Scotch whiskey" plus a plot in which an American is suspected of rape and murder on a remote isle in the Hebrides. (FC) St. Martin, 1982.   ○

Mackenzie, Compton
TIGHT LITTLE ISLAND
What happens on two little islands in the Outer Hebrides when whiskey runs short during World War II—"packed with chuckles"—made into a great and funny movie many years ago. Houghton, 1950.   ○

Stewart, Mary
THE STORMY PETREL
Two young men intrude on a young professor's holiday on Moila Island and seem "jumpy, evasive, and mutually antagonistic . . . vivid rendering of Moila's lochs, glens and wild birds." (FC) Morrow, 1991. Also *Wildfire at Midnight* (1961).   ○

SOVIET UNION

Series Guidebooks
(See Appendix 1)

Berlitz: Moscow & Leningrad
Baedeker: Moscow; Leningrad
Blue Guide: Moscow & Leningrad
Fodor: Soviet Union
Independent Traveller: The Soviet Union
Insight Guide: Leningrad; Moscow; USSR
Let's Go: USSR
Moon Handbook: Moscow-Leningrad
Nagel's Encyclopedia Guide: U.S.S.R.

Background Reading

Binyon, Michael
LIFE IN RUSSIA
A thematic approach and filled with quotations and anecdotes as it comments on Soviet women, youth, workers, culture, health care system, life for the average citizen and social problems that parallel those in the West, from alcoholism and high divorce rates to "crazes" and status symbols. The author is a former Moscow correspondent for the *London Times* and sees the Soviet Union as

being in "the midst of its [turbulent] adolescence as a nation." (BL) Pantheon, 1984. ○

Bookbinder, Alan, and others
COMRADES: PORTRAITS OF SOVIET LIFE

A look at the daily lives of some Soviet citizens, by a group of BBC correspondents—weaves in impressions and information about Soviet society in general. Plume, 1986. ○

Cullen, Robert
TWILIGHT OF EMPIRE

The former Moscow bureau chief for *Newsweek* reports on his firsthand observations of the unrest at the edges of the Soviet Empire—deterioration of the Warsaw Pact, independence movements in the Baltic nations and Caucasus, ethnic and religious violence. (Publisher) Atl Monthly Pr, 1991. ○

Deriabin, Peter and Bagley, T.H.
KGB: MASTERS OF THE SOVIET UNION

"The fate of the Soviet system hangs upon the KGB" is the premise, with the conclusion that there will not be true and lasting change for the better until the KGB has been dismantled. (BL) Hippocrene, 1990. ○

De Villiers, Marq
A JOURNEY THROUGH MOTHER RUSSIA IN A TIME OF TROUBLES

Account of a journey in 1990, traveling alone and with others—"Probing, knowledgeable report on heartland Russia . . . relates tales going back to the Huns and Tartars . . . the Cossacks, the Revolution, World War II . . . nostalgia for a noble dream corrupted." (PW) Viking, 1992. ○

Forest, Jim
A PILGRIM TO THE RUSSIAN CHURCH

An American journalist encounters a vibrant religious faith in the Soviet Union. Crossroad, 1988. ○

Fraser, Russell
THE THREE ROMES

The three Romes, in this author's concept, are Moscow, Constantinople (now Istanbul) and Rome—cities that felt they had "received divine missions to amass and rule empires." The book is historical commentary and anecdotes, an "entertaining overview . . . encounters with modern inhabitants . . . the shadowy past [implanted in] the mind of citizens today." (BL) HarBraceJ, 1985. ○

Gray, Francine du Plessix
SOVIET WOMEN: WALKING THE TIGHTROPE

The effect of glasnost on women's lives—"will confound, amaze, and inspire . . . cuts through the more stilted images of that country's society and culture." (BL) Doubleday, 1990. ○

Kort, Michael
THE SOVIET COLOSSUS

A new "popular" history of Russia that presents a balanced view of their achievements and failures. The theme is "continuity of tradition and social structures from Tsarist Russia [and the] author's style is lively and holds the reader's attention." (LJ) Scribner, 1984. ○

Lourie, Richard
RUSSIA SPEAKS

Oral history that reads like a novel and gives a capsule history of Russia. "Dramatic oral history . . . engrossing recollections capture the havoc of civil war . . . perpetual paranoia . . . World War II . . . stirrings of glasnost." The characters range from ordinary people to Elena Bonner, wife of the late Sakharov. (PW) HarperCollins, 1991. ○

Massie, Suzanne
LAND OF THE FIREBIRD, THE BEAUTY OF OLD RUSSIA

Dazzling cultural history of pre-revolutionary Russia, profusely illustrated. S&S, 1982. ○

Milner-Gulland, Robin and Dejevsky, Nikolai
CULTURAL ATLAS OF RUSSIA AND THE SOVIET UNION
"Compelling, concise history . . . enlivened and enhanced by more than forty detailed maps and 250 color illustrations." (BL) Facts On File, 1989. ○

Polonsky, Marc
USSR: FROM AN ORIGINAL IDEA BY KARL MARX
The title is clue to the tone of this book— funny and irreverent. Faber & Faber, 1986. ○

Salisbury, Harrison E.
THE 900 DAYS
The siege of Leningrad. Da Capo, 1985 (first published 1969). ○

Sinyavsky, Andrei
SOVIET CIVILIZATION: A CULTURAL HISTORY
By an emigre writer who survived Soviet labor camps—"a devastating, mordantly witty appraisal." (PW) Arcade, 1990. ○

Smith, Hedrick
THE NEW RUSSIANS
Follow-up to Smith's earlier book *The Russians,* published in 1976 and updated and republished in 1983. Thematic chapters, including three on the non-Russian republics, and character sketches. "Riveting, in-depth report" of 10 trips from Lithuania to Central Asia over a period of two years. (PW) Random, 1990. ○

Voslensky, Michael
NOMENKLATURA
The Soviet ruling class described by one who was a member of "this happy band." Gives "a vivid picture of a state where a few have very much and the mass has very little, with no prospect of reversing that equation." (LJ) Doubleday, 1984. ○

Wachtel, Andrew and Zykov, Eugene
AT THE DAWN OF GLASNOST: SOVIET PORTRAITS
Forty-two people, ranging from the mayor of Samarkand to a Moscow jazz pianist, speak about their lives, work, attitudes, along with 200 photos recording the authors' 8,000-mile trip. Proctor Jones, 1988. ○

Willis, David K.
KLASS: HOW RUSSIANS REALLY LIVE
How the rising class in Russia uses connections and money for everything from theater tickets to food, with the thesis that this cultivation of status and privilege will, in the end, undermine the Communist Party's power. Written by a Moscow bureau chief for the *Christian Science Monitor.* St. Martin, 1985. ○

TRAVELOGUES AND SOME UNIQUE PERSPECTIVES

See also "Moscow & Leningrad," and "Siberia & the Trans-Siberian Railroad," below. ○

Cheuse, Alan
FALL OUT OF HEAVEN: AN AUTOBIOGRAPHICAL JOURNEY
Three books in one—a journey back to places where the author's father had spent his youth as a pilot in the Red Army's air force in the 1930s, their life together in New Jersey, and this journey as a quest to resolve father and son relationship. The author is a novelist who traveled, with his photographer son, to the Soviet Union in the summer of 1986. Atl Monthly Pr, 1989. ○

Custine, Marquis de
EMPIRE OF THE CZAR: A JOURNEY THROUGH ETERNAL RUSSIA
A memoir and travelogue written in 1839 and republished as part of the increased interest in early travel writing. Anchor Pr, 1990. ○

Dull, Christine and Ralph
SOVIET LAUGHTER, SOVIET TEARS

Memoir of the authors' half-year exchange with Ukrainian counterparts as each couple worked the other's farms—one a collective in Ukraine, the other a farm in Ohio. Stillmore, 1992.   ○

Leighton, Ralph
TUVA OR BUST!

A Nobel Laureate physicist (Richard Flynman) and the author make a pact to visit Tannu Tiva, an area of Mongolia controlled by the Soviet Union, and live up to it despite the illness of Flynman—"poignant account of Flynman's last escapade." (LJ) Norton, 1991.   ○

Moorhouse, Geoffrey
ON THE OTHER SIDE: A JOURNEY THROUGH SOVIET CENTRAL ASIA

"Superb travel narrative" of a seven-week journey sponsored by the National Geographic Society through Central Asia, where eastern and western culture mingle—"command of history . . . elegant, evocative prose . . . engrossing." (PW) Holt, 1991.   ○

Schecter, Jerrold and others
BACK IN THE U.S.S.R.: AN AMERICAN FAMILY RETURNS TO MOSCOW

Sequel to *An American Family in Moscow,* which was an account of the Schecter family's time in the U.S.S.R. in the late 1960s. Glasnost tempted them back. "Full of insights—small and weighty . . . This rich book will profit anyone interested in contemporary Soviet history." (BL) Scribner, 1989.   ○

Soloukin, Vladimir
LAUGHTER OVER THE LEFT SHOULDER

Remembrance of childhood, with adult hindsight, in a Russian village in the '20s and '30s as it becomes part of a collective farm. Peter Owen, 1991.   ○

Taubman, William and Jane
MOSCOW SPRING

Two academics provide first-hand experience of their visit to Moscow in spring of 1988 as part of an educational exchange— captures the ambivalence as momentous change and promises of reform also bring fear for loss of security. Summit, 1989.   ○

Thubron, Colin
WHERE NIGHTS ARE LONGEST: TRAVELS BY CAR THROUGH WESTERN RUSSIA

Account of a unique travel experience as the author manages to get permission to drive over hundreds of miles of the Soviet Union, camping and "chatting with whomever crossed his path." (BL) Random, 1984.   ○

Van der Post, Laurens
JOURNEY INTO RUSSIA

Reprint of a travelogue of a three-month trip, twenty years ago, alone and by plane, train and ship, from north to south and from west to east—the longest solitary journey made through Russia by a non-Communist. Island Pr, 1984 (first published 1964).   ○

Vishnevskaya, Galina
GALINA: A RUSSIAN STORY

Autobiography of a Russian singer that provides an unusual perspective—"candid, often devastating, depiction of cultural life in postwar Russia . . . the care and feeding of a Muscovite" prima donna. (NYTBR) HarBraceJ, 1984.   ○

THE REVOLUTION AND DISSIDENTS

Aksyonov, Vasily and others, eds.
METROPOL: LITERARY ALMANAC

A collection of poems, essays and stories by some of Russia's most respected literary figures in a failed experiment to challenge Soviet censorship. Norton, 1983.   ○

Crankshaw, Edward
THE SHADOW OF THE WINTER PALACE

Russia's drift to Revolution, 1825–1917—a portrait of Russia through its last four czars. Penguin, 1978.   ○

Massie, Robert K.
NICHOLAS AND ALEXANDRA

"Intimate history at its magnificent best"—motivations and personal emotions of the royal family whose son's illness with hemophilia led to Alexandra's dependence on Rasputin for help, which in turn led to disastrous decisions that helped Kerensky and Lenin gain power. (BRD) Dell, 1978 (first published 1968).   ○

Pearlstein, E.W., ed.
REVOLUTION IN RUSSIA!

The revolution as reported in contemporary accounts by the *New York Tribune* and the *New York Herald*, 1894–1921. Viking, 1967.   ○

Pearson, Michael
SEALED TRAIN

Lenin's return to Russia from exile in Switzerland, in 1917, via a sealed train through Germany as events led to power seizure by the Bolsheviks—"generates excitement as though it were a contemporary account." (BRD) Putnam Pub Group, 1975.   ○

Sakharov, Andrei
MOSCOW & BEYOND

Sequel to his *Memoirs* (1990). The book picks up with Sakharov's return from exile to Moscow in 1986 and shares his views of Gorbachev, the myriad difficulties inherent in perestroika, etc. Knopf, 1991.   ○

Sakharov, Andrei
MY COUNTRY AND THE WORLD

A book by a Russian emigré and dissident who believes that detente has only strengthened the Soviet Union and will eventually undermine American democracy. Random, 1975.   ○

Salisbury, Harrison E.
BLACK NIGHT, WHITE SNOW

Russia's revolutions, 1905–1917. Da Capo Pr, 1981.   ○

Solzhenitsyn, Aleksandr
THE GULAG ARCHIPELAGO

His own personal experiences and those of 227 other survivors. Har-Row, 1974.   ○

Solzhenitsyn, Alexsandr
REBUILDING RUSSIA

A "prescient essay, written in 1990" by the exiled writer, and his plan for a post-communist U.S.S.R. that includes divestiture of the non-Slav republics, a decentralized economy, local self-government and built from the bottom up with rejection of Western pop culture. FS&G, 1991.   ○

MOSCOW & LENINGRAD

Butler, Reg
MOSCOW-LENINGRAD: ESSENTIAL GUIDE FOR SOPHISTICATED VISITORS

Hippocrene, 1989.   ○

Kelly, Laurence, ed.
MOSCOW/A TRAVELLERS' COMPANION; ST. PETERSBURG/A TRAVELLERS' COMPANION

A "You-are-there experience [for each city] . . . excerpts from old novels, biographies, letters, poems, diaries, that describe or give impressions" of St. Petersburg (now Leningrad) and Moscow, with contemporary prints and photographs. They make ideal traveling companions. (BL) Atheneum, 1983.   ○

Lee, Andrea
RUSSIAN JOURNAL

Account of an eight-month residence in Moscow, and two in Leningrad, by a young woman from Harvard who "knows how to write . . . informative, ingratiating . . . moving." (TBS) Random, 1984.   ○

Semler, Helen B.
DISCOVERING MOSCOW: THE COMPLETE COMPANION GUIDE

A guide and cultural journal; divides the city into walking tours of a day or less to historical sites, churches, palaces, galleries, and so on, with descriptions of sites and historical detail provided. Art and history are emphasized. St. Martin, 1990.   ○

SIBERIA & THE TRANS-SIBERIAN RAILROAD

Grossfeld, Stan
THE WHISPER OF STARS: A SIBERIAN JOURNEY
A five-week journey, beginning in Leningrad, with photos by a Pulitzer Prize-winning photographer, and "atmospheric text . . . supplements his affecting portrait of a warm people in a cold place." (BL) Globe Pequot, 1988. ○

Magowan, Robin
FABLED CITIES OF CENTRAL ASIA: SAMARKAND, BUKHARA, KHIVA
A British traveler and a Russian photographer capture the paradoxical world of Siberia with text and spectacular photographs. Abbeville, 1990. ○

Mowat, Farley
THE SIBERIANS
An account of two lengthy visits in 1966 and 1969 by a Canadian novelist. The author challenges "the myth of Siberia as . . . a desolate wilderness" and makes Siberia and the Siberians come alive for the reader as a "teeming and productive country." (BRD) Bantam, 1984. ○

Newby, Eric
THE BIG RED TRAIN RIDE
Newby's trip from Moscow to Vladivostok with his wife, a photographer, and their companion from the Soviet tourist agency. Observations of people and scenes along the way, with some background history thrown in. Penguin, 1985. ○

Niven, Alexander C.
COMPANION GUIDE FOR TRAVELERS ON THE TRANS-SIBERIAN RAILROAD
Intl Inst Adv Stud, 1985. ○

Theroux, Paul
THE GREAT RAILWAY BAZAAR
A four-month lecture tour in 1973, via the Trans-Siberian Express (and the Orient Express and Khyber Mail), is the basis for these "conversations and impressions of people encountered." Ballantine, 1981. ○

Yevtushenko, Yevgeny
DIVIDED TWINS: ALASKA & SIBERIA
Penguin, 1988. ○

GUIDEBOOKS

Brinkle, Lydle
AN AMERICAN'S GUIDE TO THE SOVIET UNION
By a professor who is also a frequent visitor to the country; major cities and smaller cities are covered, as well as religious centers, resorts, ethnic diversity. Hippocrene, 1990. ○

Louis, Victor E. and Jennifer M.
LOUIS MOTORISTS' GUIDE TO THE SOVIET UNION
Pergamon, 1987. Also *The Complete Guide to the Soviet Union* (1991). ○

Ovsianikov, Yuri and Bouchet, Guy
INVITATION TO RUSSIA
A tour of imperial Russian architecture in text and photos—"puts the Soviet Union's most charming face forward for travelers and browsers." (BL) Rizzoli, 1990. ○

Scott, Gini G.
THE OPEN DOOR: TRAVELING IN THE USSR
Based on the author's 1988 trip under sponsorship of the Center for U.S.-U.S.S.R. Initiatives. "Engaging and refreshingly offbeat travel book" with an appendix of useful resources and organizations that sponsor citizen diplomacy trips. (BL) New World Library, 1990. ○

Ward, Charles A.
NEXT TIME YOU GO TO RUSSIA
A guide to historical landmarks and art museums; the information was originally compiled for the University of Wisconsin's Soviet Seminar, and then expanded for use by Smithsonian Associates tours. It fills the gap between a straight tour guide and a cultural

history and includes maps and floorplans for places visited. Scribner, 1980.   ○

HISTORY

Carmichael, Joel
A HISTORY OF RUSSIA
The author "discerns a continuous theme . . . an irresoluble conflict between arbitrary force and intellectual idealism" binding over 1,000 years of Russia's social and political development.   (Publisher)   Hippocrene, 1990.   ○

Dmytryshyn, Basil
USSR: A CONCISE HISTORY
"Brief, accurate, balanced survey." Scribner, 1984 (first published 1977).   ○

Neville, Peter
TRAVELLER'S HISTORY OF RUSSIA & THE USSR
One of a series of introductory histories for travelers. Interlink Pub, 1990.   ○

Pipes, Richard
HISTORY OF THE RUSSIAN REVOLUTION
A gripping history and one that will be explosive in the Soviet Union. Its premise is that the Russian Revolution of November 1917 was more accurately a coup d'état, and terror was used from the outset by the Bolsheviks. "No single volume . . . begins to cater so adequately to those who want to discover what really happened in Russia . . . [or] better designed to help Soviet citizens to struggle out of the darkness." (NYT) Random, 1990. Also *Russia Under the Old Regime* (1976).   ○

Riasanovsky, Nicholas V.
A HISTORY OF RUSSIA
Oxford U, 1984 (first published 1977).   ○

Novels

Aksyonov, Vassily
THE BURN
A novel in three volumes, written in the 1960s and '70s (the author was forced to emigrate to the U.S. in 1980). "Five gifted, sophisticated, cynical yet hopeful young denizens of Moscow" each represent an aspect of Tolya Von Steinbock who spent his childhood in Siberian work camps. Random, 1984. Also *The Island of Crimea* (1983).   ○

Aleichem, Sholom
THE NIGHTINGALE
Or *The Saga of Yoselle Solovey the Cantor*—set in a Russian village in the 1880s, about a cantor's son with a voice like a nightingale. Putnam, 1985.   ○

Anatoli, A.
BABI YAR
The period 1941–43 when the Nazis systematically murdered two million people at Babi Yar, outside of Kiev, including 50,000 Jews. FS&G, 1970.   ○

Berberova, Nina
THE ACCOMPANIST
Originally published in Russian in 1936— story of a girl lifted out of her depressing origins to become traveling companion to a singer. Atheneum, 1988.   ○

Bolger, Daniel P.
FEAST OF BONES
"Outstanding fiction debut" by a U.S. Army officer who has written on military topics. The plot revolves about Captain Dimitri Donskov and his Reconnaissance Company in Afghanistan, charged with the mission of ensuring Gorbachev's rise to premier. Presidio, 1990.   ○

Brien, Alan
LENIN
Biographical novel—"meticulous research . . . completely convincing narrative voice." (FC) Morrow, 1988.   ○

Buckley, William F.
MARCO POLO, IF YOU CAN
One of Buckley's Blackford Oakes spy novels—involves a covert operation to locate a leak to the Russians from within the National Security Council; "top notch spy thriller." (FC) Doubleday, 1982.   ○

Clancy, Tom
RED STORM RISING

Credible suspense story of a Soviet attack on Germany when terrorists destroy a key Soviet oil installation and fuel shortages threaten the country. Putnam, 1986.   ○

DeMille, Nelson
THE CHARM SCHOOL

An American tourist stumbles into a secret charm school where Soviets are taught to imitate Americans, but their instructors are not there by their own choosing—"action and adventure . . . a fascinating psychological study." (FC) Warner Bks, 1988.   ○

Der Nister
THE FAMILY MASHBER (Ukraine)
Saga of a Jewish Hasidic family set in Ukraine of the 1870s—"massive social chronicle . . . superb portrait of a now vanished culture." Summit Bks, 1987.   ○

Gray, Francine du Plessix
WORLD WITHOUT END

Three women, linked by a long friendship, "are pilgriming in Russia, seeking inspiration to give meaning to the last third of their lives." (FC) S&S, 1981.   ○

Grekova, I.
RUSSIAN WOMEN

Consists of two stories, *The Hotel Manager* and *Ladies' Hairdresser*—"both stories depict contemporary Russian life as unending struggles with a rigid government, echoed in the male-female relationships." (FC) HarBraceJ, 1983.   ○

Grossman, Vasily
LIFE AND FATE

Translated from the Russian; the battle of Stalingrad, 1942–43, and ranging throughout Eastern Europe and occupations by the Nazis and communists—"as remarkable a document of the conflicts of daily working lives under political and moral stress as we are likely to be given." (FC) Har-Row, 1985.   ○

High, Monique R.
THE FOUR WINDS OF HEAVEN

Based on diaries of the author's grandmother, living in St. Petersburg, the Crimea, Switzerland, Paris; "this superior saga recreates the lives of a family that in its heyday considered itself 'the First Jewish Family of Russia' . . . destroyed at one blow by the Bolshevik Revolution . . . brims with social history, tragedy, romance." (FC) Delacorte Pr, 1980.   ○

Hyman, Vernon T.
SEVEN DAYS TO PETROGRAD

"Lenin's legendary journey to the Finland Station becomes . . . the center-piece in an Anglo-American plot to assassinate the famous Bolshevik" in this fictional history. (FC) Viking, 1988.   ○

Iskander, Fazil
SANDRO OF CHEGEM

A comic epic of the adventures of Sandro, 1880 to 1960, which "touch on just about every conceivable subject: erotica, Joseph Stalin (known as 'Beloved Leader' and the 'Big Mustache'), ethnic antagonisms . . . Islam . . .collective agriculture." This irreverent book by an author who lives in Moscow was published in the Soviet Union ten years ago but "only about 10 percent of the present manuscript appeared in print. The real surprise is that the censors managed to leave one-tenth [of this] comedy of the blackest hue." (NYTBR) Vintage, 1985.   ○

Jones, Donald
RUSSIAN SPRING

The chief protagonist is a guerrilla combat specialist in Afghanistan who is nephew to the new Russian leader. There's a coup and civil war with nuclear weapons—"superb plotting." (FC) Beaufort, 1984. Also *Rubicon One* (1983), another novel of "nail-biting tension" about the delicate balance created by nuclear missiles.   ○

Joseph, Mark
TO KILL THE POTEMKIN

The novel takes the disappearance of the American submarine *Scorpion* in 1968 and posits a theory that a secret underwater war existed between the United States and the Soviet Union. Fine, 1986.   ○

Koestler, Arthur
DARKNESS AT NOON
First published in 1940, Koestler's disillusionment with the Communist party and the revolution—"a grimly fascinating interpretation of the logic of the Russian Revolution, indeed of all revolutionary dictatorships." MacMillan, 1987.   ○

Krotkov, Y.
THE NOBEL PRIZE
Based on Pasternak's winning of the Nobel Prize for *Dr. Zhivago*. S&S, 1980.   ○

Littell, Robert
THE REVOLUTIONIST
Two young men leave poverty in New York City for Russia, in 1917, while a third goes to Palestine. They meet 35 years later at Stalin's death. "A mix of history and fiction, carefully researched and vigorously written." (FC) Bantam, 1988.   ○

Lourie, Richard
FIRST LOYALTY
A New York translator has a Russian double who is a poet and works for the KGB-"labyrinthine plot that twists from Siberia to the Bronx . . . works as polemic and page turner." HarBraceJ, 1985. Also *An Oral History of the U.S.S.R.* under Background Reading, above.   ○

Pasternak, Boris
DOCTOR ZHIVAGO
"Brilliant kaleidoscopic chronicle [that] illuminates the period of the Russian Revolution, the violent, proletarian upheaval and the Communist succession." (BRD) Pantheon, 1958.   ○

Peters, Ralph
RED ARMY
Told from the point of view of the Russians as their army gathers on the East-West German border to attack. Pocket Bks, 1989.   ○

Pohl, Frederik
CHERNOBYL
Recreation of the 1986 disaster—"the tale is gripping, and the locale well established." (FC) Bantam, 1987.   ○

Rand, Ayn
WE, THE LIVING
By the philosophical heroine of political libertarians and originally published in 1936. The novel takes place in post-Revolution Russia, and plot concerns a woman torn between a communist and an aristocrat. Random, 1959.   ○

Rubens, Bernice
BROTHERS
Saga of six generations of a Jewish family from the nineteenth century to Russia of today—"a window into the family life of each Blindel generation" and how they apply the lessons of survival taught by the family patriarch, through pogroms, the Nazis, the Soviet psychiatric hospitals. (FC) Delacorte Pr, 1983.   ○

Rutherfurd, Edward
RUSSKA
"Immense yet intimate dramatization of Russia's conflictful past" that begins in 180 A.D. and works through the centuries as it focuses on various families. "Tales of survival, adventure, and romance are infused with insight into ethnic distinctions, sexual mores, and political intrigue . . . blending knowledge with imagination." The author follows a format used earlier in his novel *Sarum* (see under England/Novels). (BL) Crown, 1991.   ○

Rybakov, Anatoli N.
CHILDREN OF THE ARBAT
Autobiographical novel of a student in the Soviet Union in the 1930s; first published in the Soviet Union in 1987. "Personal, sensitive, and subtle in its detail . . . overwhelming in its impact." (FC) Little, 1988.   ○

Scott, Justin
THE WIDOW OF DESIRE
"A female James Bond . . . is utterly unbelievable and just as entertaining" in a plot

that involves the death of her husband, Gorbachev, glasnost, perestroika. (FC) Bantam,
1989.   ○

Sholokhov, Mikhail
AND QUIET FLOWS THE DON
First of a series of novels about the Cossacks
and their region of Russia, the effects of the
revolution and collectivization. Knopf, 1934.
See also *Tales of the Don* (1962), *The Don Flows
Home to the Sea* (1941), *Harvest on the Don*
(1961), *Seeds of Tomorrow* (1959), *The Silent
Don* (1961).   ○

Sinyavsky, Andrey
GOODNIGHT!
Novelized autobiography—"bawdy, mystical, satiric, philosophical . . . stream of consciousness interspersed with fragments of
surrealist fiction, drama . . . verse." (BRD)
Viking, 1989.   ○

Smith, Martin Cruz
POLAR STAR
Former Moscow investigator Renko (from
Gorky Park) now toils as a seaman on a joint
U.S./Soviet fishing venture in the Bering Sea
and gets involved in investigating a Russian
girl's death—"endlessly entertaining and
deeply serious." (FC) Random, 1989.   ○

Solzhenitsyn, Aleksandr
AUGUST 1914
A new translation of this novel, originally
published in 1971, about Russia at the out-
break of World War I. FS&G, 1989. Also *The
Cancer Ward* (1969) and *For the Good of the
Cause* (1970).   ○

Ulam, Adam B.
THE KIROV AFFAIR
Begins with the death of Kirov in 1934 and
the ensuing mass purges, and Khrushchev
era and finally the more open 1982. "Chronicles the rise of a politburo member who
loosely combines . . . Andropov and Gorbachev . . . a compelling political thriller."
(BRD) HarBraceJ, 1988.   ○

Voinovich, Vladimir
THE FUR HAT
"Gogolian poetry and Jewish humor"—a
member of the Writers' Union is disturbed

when he hears that fur hats are to be a
symbol of W.U. membership and he is offered one of a fluffy tomcat. (BRD) Har-
BraceJ, 1989.   ○

Wiesel, Elie
THE TESTAMENT
As he awaits his mother's arrival in Israel,
with a planeload of Russian immigrants,
Grisha rereads the memoirs of his father—
"an idealist . . . an innocent victim of the
machinations of the Soviet regime." European political history "revealed in brand-
new dimensions when recalled from the
perspective . . . of a Jew-turned-Commu-
nist." (FC) Summit, 1981.   ○

LENINGRAD

Butler, Gwendoline
THE RED STAIRCASE
Set in St. Petersburg in 1912—a Scottish girl
hired as companion to a young member of
an aristocratic family finds that she's really
been hired for her healing powers to help
break Rasputin's hold on the czarina by
helping the young crown prince who is ill
with hemophilia. Coward, 1979.   ○

Hanlon, Emily
PETERSBURG
Recreation of the "dress rehearsal" in 1905
for the 1917 Bolshevik revolution. Putnam,
1988.   ○

Voznesenskaya, Julia
THE WOMEN'S DECAMERON
Ten women of varied backgrounds who are
quarantined in a Leningrad hospital for 10
days tell their stories—some of hardship and
disaster, some funny, absurd, touching.
"Reveals more about Soviet life than anything to be read in a newspaper." (BRD) Atl
Monthly Pr, 1986.   ○

Williams, David
TREASURE IN ROUBLES
"Traditional British mystery"—high-brow
festivities of a group of British patrons of
culture are interrupted by murder and an
art theft from the Leningrad Art Museum.
(FC) St. Martin, 1987.   ○

MOSCOW

Ageyev, M.
NOVEL WITH COCAINE

First published in an emigre magazine in Paris over 50 years ago; confessional novel of a promising young man from school days to death, during the years that span the Russian revolution—"a compulsive read, much more than a period piece." Har-Row, 1984.   ○

Aksyonov, Vasily P.
SAY CHEESE!

Forced to emigrate in 1980, this is the author's first major novel written in the West and a novelized version of the incident that lead to his emigration—"an evocative insider's view of the Moscow intellectual scene in the last years of the Brezhnev era." (BRD) Random, 1989.   ○

Cullen, Robert
SOVIET SOURCES

An American correspondent in Moscow becomes the pawn between East and West and must pit his integrity against that of both the U.S. and the U.S.S.R. "From exclusive journalists's eating clubs to the blackmarket porno trade . . . a charming writers' colony . . . a state-of-the-art political thriller . . . authentic post-glasnost Russia." Atl Monthly Pr, 1991.   ○

Finder, Joseph
THE MOSCOW CLUB

A CIA Kremlinologist in a complicated plot involving communist history, an Armand Hammer-like figure, an attempted coup to end glasnost, and the vindication of his father. Viking, 1991.   ○

Fitzgerald, Penelope
THE BEGINNING OF SPRING

"Slightly exotic atmosphere—daily life in pre-Revolutionary (1913) Moscow"—a British expatriate is deserted by his wife and must hire a peasant girl to care for his three children. Holt, 1988.   ○

Kaletski, Alexander
METRO

"One young Muscovite's transformation from lukewarm citizen to rebel determined to escape abroad . . . Metro is a joy, funny and profound." Viking, 1985.   ○

Kaminsky, Stuart M.
A FINE RED RAIN

Inspector Rostnikov tries to save a circus aerialist from the fate met by two of her colleagues—the finale is in the center ring of the Moscow Circus big top. Also The Man Who Walked Like a Bear (1990). Scribner, 1988.   ○

Le Carre, John
THE RUSSIA HOUSE

An English publisher is sent to Moscow to establish contact with the author of a leaked manuscript—"a thriller that demands a second reading as a treatise on our time." (FC) Knopf, 1989.   ○

Moody, John
MOSCOW MAGICIAN

Post-glasnost Russia is the setting for this thriller, as a charming fixer and his Jewish friend plan their escape—"ingenious efforts, the places they go and the colorful people they meet form the core of this intriguing thriller." (PW) St. Martin, 1991.   ○

Smith, Martin Cruz
GORKY PARK

"Believable, realistic and gripping portrayals of certain segments of Soviet society, and of one man's search for meaning." The plot involves three mutilated bodies found in Gorky Park and two police investigators—one Soviet, one American—determined to solve the mystery of their deaths. (FC) Random, 1981.   ○

Sorokin, Vladimir
THE QUEUE

Dialogue and conversation while waiting in line to purchase some desirable item, never really identified; "a major charm . . . is its depiction of the queue as a not necessarily miserable place to be," as in between the conversations people read the paper, do a crossword puzzle, flirt, argue. Readers Int, 1988.   ○

Topol, Edward and Neznansky, Fridrikh
RED SQUARE
Both authors are Russian emigrés and have been part of the bureaucracy "a veritable rogues' gallery of fictitious black marketeers, procurers, middlemen, officials on the take, and ladies of pleasure who are at times the strange bedfellows of the Kremlin elite." Fascinating characters and plot. (NYTBR) Quartet, 1985.   ○

Yevtushenko, Y.A.
ARDABIOLA
A plant psychologist believes he's developed a cure for cancer but becomes disillusioned, gives up on his research, only to find that the plant—ardabiola—has a life of its own, a metaphor for the Russian spirit. "Excellent local color . . . science-fiction flavor . . . entertaining." (BRD) St. Martin, 1985. Also, *Wild Berries* (1984).   ○

SIBERIA

Huffaker, Clair
THE COWBOY AND THE COSSACK
Epic novel of an 1880s Siberian cattle drive in which Cossacks and Montana cowboys join forces. Trident Pr, 1973.   ○

Kaminsky, Stuart M.
A COLD RED SUNRISE
Inspector Rostnikov is sent to Siberia to solve the mysterious deaths of a dissident's daughter and the commissar sent to investigate that death. Scribner, 1988.   ○

L'Amour, Louis
LAST OF THE BREED
An Air Force pilot is forced down over the Soviet Union, imprisoned and escapes with some Russians. Bantam, 1986.   ○

Olcott, Anthony
MAY DAY IN MAGADAN
The hotel security officer of *Murder at the Red October* (see under Moscow, above), now exiled to Magadan in Siberia, stumbles on fur pelts connected to an airline disaster. "The dense atmosphere of squalor, coarseness, drunkenness, corruption, despair . . . is depressingly persuasive." (FC) Bantam, 1983.   ○

Solzhenitsyn, Aleksandr
ONE DAY IN THE LIFE OF IVAN DENISOVICH
A modern classic by the Soviet dissident writer about prison life in a Siberian labor camp. Dutton, 1963.   ○

Topol, Edward
RED SNOW
Mystery and suspense story of ritual murders in Moscow in 1983, just as the city is planning to welcome foreigners in celebration of the new pipeline to Europe—"may be most fascinating for its depiction of . . . the complex, fragile state of race relations in the Soviet Union." (FC) Dutton, 1987.   ○

S P A I N
(Including Gibraltar)

Series Guidebooks

American Express Pocket Guide: Spain
At Its Best: Spain
Baedeker: Madrid; Costa Brava; Mediterranean Islands; Spain
Berlitz: Barcelona; Madrid; Canary Islands; Costa Blanca; Costa Brava; Costa del Sol and Andalusia; Costa Dorada & Barcelona; Ibiza & Formentera; Mallorca & Minorca; Seville
Cadogan Guide: Spain
Exploring Rural Europe: Spain
Fielding: Spain & Portugal
Fisher's World: Spain/Portugal
Fodor: Madrid & Barcelona; Spain
Frommer: Spain & Morocco; Madrid

Independent Traveler's Guide: Spain
Insider's Guide: Spain
Insight Guide: Barcelona; Costa Brava; Costa del Sol; Gran Canaria; Madrid; Mallorca, Ibiza, Menorca; Spain; Tenerife
Let's Go: Spain & Portugal
Michael's Guide: Madrid
Michelin: Spain
Nagel's Encyclopedia Guide: Spain
Nelles Guide: Spain—Vol. 1 (North); Vol. 2 (South)
Off the Beaten Track: Spain
Real Guide: Spain
2–22 Days Itinerary Planning Guide: Spain & Portugal

Background Reading

Brenan, Gerald
SOUTH FROM GRANADA
"A book of discovery and exploration . . . anatomy of village life [and] inquiry into character"—considered one of the most perceptive writers on Spain in the English language. Cambridge U Pr, 1980 (first published 1957). Also *The Face of Spain* (the author's return to his Andalusian house and village after many years of absence and travels in Madrid, Cordova, Toledo, Granada), reproduction of 1950 edition (1976).   ○

Cela, Camilo José
JOURNEY TO ALCARRIA
Awarded the 1989 Nobel Prize for literature; a book of travels—sketchbook of a region. Alcarria is northeast of Madrid, and Cela the urban intellectual wandering through villages, farms, country roads, encounters with local people—"vignettes are narrated in a fresh, clear prose that is wonderfully evocative." Atl Monthly Pr, 1991.   ○

Crow, John A.
SPAIN: THE ROOT AND THE FLOWER
"The substance of Spanish culture—art, literature, architecture and music is emphasized [over] straight politics . . . taps the very marrow of Spanish consciousness." This is the third edition and expands coverage of the post-Franco period. (BL) U of California, 1985.   ○

Enzensberger, Hans M.
EUROPE, EUROPE: FORAYS INTO A CONTINENT
See entry under Europe/Background Reading. Spain is one of six European countries analyzed by the German essayist.

Goodwin, Godfrey
ISLAMIC SPAIN
One of a series of books for travelers with an interest in architecture (see entry under Turkey, by Freely). Chronicle, 1990.   ○

Graham, Robert
SPAIN: A NATION COMES OF AGE
A report by a non-Spanish correspondent on Spain's transition from Franco's authoritarianism to a democracy with king and parliament. St. Martin, 1985.   ○

Hemingway, Ernest
DEATH IN THE AFTERNOON
His classic on bullfighting in Spain. Macmillan, 1978.   ○

Hooper, John
THE SPANIARDS: A PORTRAIT OF THE NEW SPAIN
Penguin, 1987.   ○

Hughes, Robert
BARCELONA
The author, it is alleged, set out to write a simple guide to Barcelona's architecture for travelers, and ended up with a *Mont-Saint-Michel*-length book on architecture, art, religion, literature—a cultural history of Barcelona and Catalonia. "It is destined to become, like Forster's *Alexandria* and Mary McCarthy's *Venice Observed*, a classic of urban history." (NYT) Knopf, 1992.   ○

Irving, Washington
ALHAMBRA
A travel classic of 1829. Washington Irving (who was the ambassador to Spain) rode from Seville to Granada on horseback and wrote this memoir about the experience and about the Alhambra where he lived for sev-

eral months. Reproduction of 1851 edition. Sleepy Hollow, 1982. ○

Jackson, William G.
THE ROCK OF THE GIBRALTARIANS
Fairleigh Dickinson, 1988. ○

Jones, Tristran
SEAGULLS IN MY SOUP
An unlikely pair–the sister of an Anglican bishop and an itinerant sailor—tell of adventures and people met over several months on the Mediterranean, mostly around Ibiza—"interesting, readable tale." (BL) Sheridan Hse, 1991. ○

Laxalt, Robert
A TIME WE KNEW
Images of yesterday in the Basque homeland. U of Nevada Pr, 1990. ○

Lewis, Norman
VOICES OF THE OLD SEA
Intimate portrait of a remote Spanish fishing village where the author lived for several years and what happens when it becomes part of the tourism industry. "Not so much a travelogue as a rich biography of a town." (TL) Viking, 1985. ○

Macaulay, Rose
FABLED SHORE: FROM THE PYRENEES TO PORTUGAL
Reprint of a travel classic. Oxford U Pr, 1986. ○

MacKendrick, Paul
THE IBERIAN STONES SPEAK
See under Portugal. ○

Maugham, W. Somerset
DON FERNANDO
The author intended to write a novel on sixteenth-century life in Spain; instead he incorporated his notes with results of reading and observations into a series of informal chapters on a variety of topics from Spanish food and wines to El Greco and Cervantes, in his "intelligent and crafted style." First

published 1935. (BRD) Paragon Hse, 1990. ○

Michener, James A.
IBERIA
A travelogue and interpretation of Spanish art, history, customs, politics, chapters on bullfighting, Las Marismas (wildlife preserve). Essential reading for Spain. Fawcett, 1988. ○

Morris, Jan
SPAIN
One reviewer says: "One of the best descriptive essays on that country ever written." Originally written in 1965, the author revisited and retraced some of her travels. (BRD) Prentice Hall Pr, 1988. ○

Pritchett, V.S.
THE SPANISH TEMPER
A pocket analysis of the Spanish character—and an important addition to the literature on Spain by British writers (Brenan, Maugham, Morris, Morton). Ecco Pr, 1989. ○

Thomas, Hugh
MADRID: A TRAVELLER'S COMPANION
One of a series that is a compilation of excerpts from literature of the country—fiction, letters, memoirs, journals—to present a cultural overview. Extensive introductions by experts provide background history—will "captivate armchair travelers of a slightly bookish bent." Atheneum, 1990. ○

THE SPANISH CIVIL WAR

Brenan, Gerald
THE SPANISH LABYRINTH
Cambridge U Pr, 1950. ○

Orwell, George
HOMAGE TO CATALONIA
A soldier-author's account of the Spanish Civil War. HarBraceJ, 1969 (first published 1952). ○

Sender Barayon, Ramon
A DEATH IN ZAMORA
The author's mother was murdered by a fascist firing squad during the Civil War and this book (like *Elena,* under Greece) is about his mission to find out who those murderers were. U of New Mexico Pr, 1989. ○

Thomas, Hugh
THE SPANISH CIVIL WAR
A history, from the origins of the war to Barcelona's fall in 1939. Har-Row, 1977 (first published 1961). ○

GUIDEBOOKS

Burns, Tom
EVERYTHING UNDER THE SUN
A series of guides for cities in Spain in time for their Olympics and world's fair. Titles include: Barcelona, Cordoba, Granada, Madrid, Marbella, Palma de Majorca, Salamanca, Seville, Toledo. Passport Bks, 1988. ○

Casas, Penelope
DISCOVERING SPAIN: AN UNCOMMON GUIDE
Covers all regions of the country. By the author of *The Foods and Wines of Spain,* and she evaluates restaurants, hotels, shops, etc. Knopf, 1991. ○

Grunfeld, Frederic V.
WILD SPAIN
A guide for those interested in the outdoors, flora, fauna, national parks, scenic attractions. P-H, 1989. ○

Hewson, David
TRAVELS IN SPAIN: SEVILLE AND WESTERN ANDALUSIA
A new series of comprehensive guides for traveling Spain by car and by foot, with 12-day itineraries that can be shortened or lengthened. David & Charles, 1990. Also *Granada and Eastern Andalusia* and *Mallorca.* ○

Howells, John and Magee, Bettie
CHOOSE SPAIN
Intended for those planning an extended stay or relocation, detailed comparisons between Spain and America as to amenities, health care, automobiles, real estate, etc. Gateway, 1990. ○

Jacobs, Michael
THE ROAD TO SANTIAGO DE CAMPOSTELA
One of a series of architectural guides for travelers; this one follows the ancient pilgrimage route. Chronicle, 1991. Also, *A Guide to Andalusia* (1990), an historical, archaeological, cultural examination of the region. ○

Mehling, Franz N.
SPAIN: A PHAIDON CULTURAL GUIDE
Succinct appreciation of the best the country has to offer in terms of national treasures and culture—churches, palaces, theaters, museums, monuments, maps and plans, all arranged alphabetically and cross-indexed. Phaidon Pr., n.d. ○

HISTORY

Kamen, Henry A.
A CONCISE HISTORY OF SPAIN
From first settlements to Franco. Scribner, 1974. ○

Lalaguna, Juan
A TRAVELLER'S HISTORY OF SPAIN
One of a series of introductory histories for travelers. Interlink Pub, 1990. ○

O'Callaghan, J.F.
HISTORY OF MEDIEVAL SPAIN
The author's Spain "is the entire peninsula [and] Islamic, Jewish, Christian, Portuguese, and Catalonian as well as Castilian" Spain and Portugal. Cornell U, 1983 (first published 1975). ○

NOVELS

Alarcón, Pedro A. de
THE THREE-CORNERED HAT
A classic based on a Spanish folktale of a miller and his perfect wife, first published 1874. Penguin, 1975. ○

Blasco-Ibañez, Vincente
BLOOD AND SAND
The novel of Spanish bullfighters—"no detail . . . is spared." (FC) Ungar, 1958 (first published 1908).   ◦

Cervantes, Miguel de
THE PORTABLE CERVANTES
An anthology that includes an abridged version of *Don Quixote de la Mancha,* and some of his novellas. Viking, 1951 (first published 1605).   ◦

Conrad, Barnaby
MATADOR (Seville)
Story of a bullfighter about to retire who is challenged by a newcomer into making a comeback—"aims at a tragic denouement of classical proportions." (FC) Houghton, 1952.   ◦

Conrad, Joseph
THE ARROW OF GOLD
"Beautiful but transitory love idyll" of a gunrunning English sea captain and the Spanish woman who finances his operations. (FC) Doubleday, 1919.   ◦

Coppel, A.
THE MARBURG CHRONICLES
"A 40-year story line . . . historical background and local color" centering around Aaron Marburg and his father's second wife. (FC) Dutton, 1985.   ◦

Cornwell, Bernard
SHARPE'S SWORD
The adventures of a nineteenth-century British infantryman in the Salamanca campaign—realistic historic novel. Viking, 1983. Also *Sharpe's Honour* (1985), about the battle of Vitoria.   ◦

Feibleman, Peter S.
THE COLUMBUS TREE
American tourists in Spain in the 1950s, and the outcome of an encounter between an American girl and a Spanish count. Atheneum, 1973.   ◦

Fuentes, Carlos
TERRA NOSTRA
"An amalgam of the historical and religious consciousness and heritage of Spain; a biblical allegory; a sensuous, erotic, and fantastic journey through time." (FC) FS&G, 1976.   ◦

Gironella, José Mariá
THE CYPRESSES BELIEVE IN GOD
    (Catalonia)
First of a trilogy, by one of Spain's leading writers. The novel takes place in the years prior to the Spanish Civil War, and is told through the experiences of a middle-class family. Knopf, 1955. Following is *One Million Dead* (1963) (during the War) and *Peace After War* (1969) (following the War).   ◦

Hemingway, Ernest
FOR WHOM THE BELL TOLLS
Four days of an American working for the Loyalists in the Spanish Civil War—thought by many to be Hemingway's best novel. Scribner, 1940.   ◦

Hemingway, Ernest
THE SUN ALSO RISES (Pamplona)
A group of English and American expatriates in the 1920s drift between Paris and Spain. Scribner, 1983 (first published 1926). See also *Death in the Afternoon* (1932) for a nonfiction book on bullfighting.   ◦

Maalouf, Amin
LEO AFRICANUS
See entry under Morocco/Novels.   ◦

Plante, David
THE FOREIGNER (Barcelona)
A naive American's travels in 1959—"he finds himself embroiled in a world of violence, conspiracy and sexuality for which he is ill-prepared." (FC) Atheneum, 1984.   ◦

Schoonover, Lawrence
THE PRISONER OF TORDESILLAS
Historical novel of the reigns of Ferdinand and Isabella. Little, 1959. Also *The Queen's Cross* (1955), a fictionalized biography of Queen Isabella, and *The Key of Gold* (1968),

in which the first novella is set in fifteenth-century Spain. ❍

Sheldon, Sidney
THE SANDS OF TIME
Novel in which the Basque national guerrilla organization (ETA) and its adversary, Opus Mundo, are the protagonists. Morrow, 1988. ❍

Viertel, Peter
AMERICAN SKIN (Costa del Sol)
An American "in Costa del Sol to find love and money among the rich expatriate exploiters of Spanish coastal real estate." (NYTBR) Houghton, 1984. ❍

MADRID

Pérez Galdós, Benito
OUR FRIEND MAUSO
First published in Spain in 1882, written by one of Spain's great novelists. "Rich in terms of observation of nineteenth-century Spanish society . . . a delight for serious fiction readers." (FC) Columbia U Pr, 1987. ❍

Pérez Galdós, Benito
TORQUEMADA
Omnibus edition of the Torquemada tetralogy of middle-class life in Madrid—originally published in the late 19th century. Columbia U Pr, 1986. ❍

Serafin, David
MADRID UNDERGROUND
A Superintendent Bernal police procedural, set in Madrid, where bloody corpses (first dummies, then the real thing) show up on the subway—"writes knowingly about life in contemporary Spain." (FC) St. Martin, 1984. ❍

BALEARIC ISLANDS (Minorca, Majorca)

Innes, Hammond
MEDUSA
A deal to swap a half-finished villa and fishing boat for a catamaran leads into arms smuggling and a military coup—"absorbing narrative rich in character and exotic atmosphere" (of Minorca). (FC) Atheneum, 1988. ❍

Jeffries, Roderic
DEAD CLEVER
One of a series of Inspector Alvarez mysteries—"thoroughly entertaining, intricate plotting . . . exotic settings." (FC) St. Martin, 1989. Also in the series, *Too Clever by Half* (1990), *Relatively Dangerous* (1987), *Death Trick* (1988), *Three and One Make Five* (1984), *Unseemly End* (1982). ❍

GIBRALTAR

Masters, John
THE ROCK
A two-track book that dramatizes Gibraltar's past. There are thirteen chapters arranged chronologically, each with its own historical essay and followed by a fictional section that traces one family in each of the eras, beginning with Gibraltar's earliest days and ending in contemporary times with questions about the future of the "rock." The author "crams a painless course in Western civilization into this novel [with] real live characters to keep history moving briskly along." (FC) Putnam Pub Group, 1970. ❍

S W E D E N

Series Guidebooks
(See Appendix 1)
Berlitz: Stockholm
Fodor: Sweden
Frommer: Stockholm ($-A-Day)
Insight: Sweden
Nagel's Encyclopedia Guide: Sweden

Visitor's Guide: Sweden
See also Series Guides for Scandinavia (*) under Denmark.

Background Reading

NOTE: See also Denmark for books with an asterisk (*), which offer additional background reading on Scandinavia as a whole and may include material on Sweden. Also, see Norway for background books on Lapland.

Barton, H. Arnold
THE SEARCH FOR ANCESTORS
A Swedish-American family saga. Swedish-Am, 1979. ○

Conforti, Michael and Walton, Guy, eds.
SWEDEN: A ROYAL TREASURY
National Gallery Art, 1988. ○

Enzensberger, Hans M.
EUROPE, EUROPE: FORAYS INTO A CONTINENT
See entry under Europe; Sweden is one of the six European countries analyzed by the German essayist. ○

Jones, David H.
NIGHT TIMES AND LIGHT TIMES
(Lapland)
See entry under Norway. ○

Kramer, Jane
UNSETTLING EUROPE
Refugee families from Algeria, Uganda, Yugoslavia, living in France, London and Sweden respectively, and an Italian Communist family in Italy, their isolation from traditions of those around them and the implications for Europe's future of these rootless people. FS&G, 1989. ○

Lorénzen, Lilly
OF SWEDISH WAYS
"A lively account of the customs and traditions of that Northern Nation." (Publisher) B&N Bks, 1978. ○

Moberg, Vilhelm
A HISTORY OF THE SWEDISH PEOPLE FROM RENAISSANCE TO REVOLUTION
Popular history by a novelist (see below under "Novels")—an introduction to Sweden's history and its people. Pantheon, 1973. ○

HISTORY

Scott, Franklin D.
SWEDEN: THE NATION'S HISTORY
U of Minnesota, 1979. ○

Novels

Barroll, Clare
SEASON OF THE HEART
Historical novel of fifteenth-century Sweden. Scribner, 1976. ○

Jonsson, Reidar
MY LIFE AS A DOG
Focuses on two years in the life of a young Swedish boy whose mother is dying of tuberculosis. FS&G, 1990. ○

Krotkov, Y.
THE NOBEL PRIZE
Novel based on Pasternak's winning of the prize. S&S, 1980. ○

Lagerlöf, Selma
THE GENERAL'S RING
A ring belonging to Charles XII brings disaster and death to three generations who come to possess it. Doubleday, 1928. Also *The Eternal Smile* (1954), short stories. ○

Lagerlöf, Selma
GÖSTA BERLING'S SAGA
The adventures of a young man with a gift for drawing people to him—particularly women—but who eventually marries and leads a life "that more nearly approximates his own ideals." (FC) American-Scandinavian Foundation, 1918 (first published 1891). ○

Moberg, Vilhelm
THE EMIGRANTS
Classic story of the Swedish migration to the American Midwest in the nineteenth century. S&S, 1951. ○

Moberg, Vilhelm
A TIME ON EARTH
A transplanted Swede in California reflects on his life and early days in Sweden. S&S, 1965. ○

Ozick, Cynthia
THE MESSIAH OF STOCKHOLM
A book reviewer for a Stockholm newspaper believes he is the son of a Polish Jew murdered by the Nazis—"complex and fascinating meditation on the nature of writing . . . manages to capture the atmosphere of Stockholm." (FC) Knopf, 1987.   ○

Peters, Elizabeth
SILHOUETTE IN SCARLET
One of a series of romantic adventures involving art historian Vicky Bliss—in this one she is invited to Stockholm and finds herself, along with a former lover, held captive by a criminal organization. Congdon & Weed, 1983.   ○

Sjöwall, Maj and Wahlöö, Per
THE TERRORISTS
The last of the Swedish husband-and-wife team's crime novels in which Martin Beck, head of the National Homicide Squad, is the sleuth. The series has been reviewed as being much more than simply stories of murders and police investigations—they present a picture of contemporary Sweden, "among the best—perhaps, they are the best—writers of detective fiction today." Pantheon, 1976.

Additional titles by this couple, set in Sweden, are *Roseanna* (1967), *The Man on the Balcony* (1968), *The Fire Engine That Disappeared* (1970), *The Laughing Policeman* (1970), *Murder at the Savoy* (1971), *The Abominable Man* (1972), *The Locked Room* (1973), *The Cop Killer* (1975).   ○

Wallace, Irving
THE PRIZE
Behind-the-scenes machinations and intrigues of the Nobel Prize ceremonies. S&S, 1962.   ○

SWITZERLAND
(Including Liechtenstein)

Series Guidebooks
(See Appendix 1)

At Its Best Guide: Switzerland
Baedeker: Switzerland
Berlitz: Switzerland
Blue Guide: Switzerland
Fodor: Switzerland
Frommer: Switzerland
Michelin Touring Guide: Switzerland
Off the Beaten Track: Switzerland
2–22 Days Itinerary Planning Guide: Germany, Austria & Switzerland
Visitor's Guide: Switzerland

Background Reading

Hardyment, Christina
HEIDI'S ALP
See entry under Europe.   ○

Kubly, Herbert
NATIVE'S RETURN
By an American academic of Swiss descent—"an observant, though quite subjective, set of vignettes, travel notes, and ruminations. . . . His characterizations of city and village life are entertaining, his analysis of the *malaise suisse* is provocative." (BL) Scarborough Hse, 1981.   ○

McPhee, John
LA PLACE DE LA CONCORDE SUISSE
The paradox of a country that has not fought a war in nearly 500 years, yet has one of the world's biggest militia armies in proportion to its population—"puts his reader inside Switzerland with elegance and insight." (Publisher) FS&G, 1984.   ○

Steinberg, Jonathan
WHY SWITZERLAND
"The Swiss success story through the ages" based on the author's premise that Switzerland is a unique country from which the world can learn much—"democracy rests ultimately on the community level." The author is a lecturer in history at Cambridge

and is married to a Swiss-German woman. (BRD) Cambridge U Pr, 1981.

LIECHTENSTEIN

Greene, Barbara
LIECHTENSTEIN—VALLEY OF PEACE
Liech-Verlag, 1967.

Schlapp, Manfred
THIS IS LIECHTENSTEIN.
Seewald, 1980.

GUIDEBOOKS

Kitfield, James and Walker, William
WHOLE EUROPE ESCAPE MANUAL: GERMANY, AUSTRIA, SWITZERLAND
Part of a series of guidebooks "designed to . . . put the fantasy and excitement back into travel." (Publisher) World Leis Corp, 1984.

Lieberman, Marcia & Philip
WALKING SWITZERLAND THE SWISS WAY
Walking and stopping at mountain huts for the night. Mountaineers, 1987.

Mehling, Franz N.
SWITZERLAND: A PHAIDON CULTURAL GUIDE
Succinct appreciation of the best the country has to offer in terms of national treasures and culture—churches, palaces, theaters, museums, monuments, maps and plans, all arranged alphabetically and cross-indexed. Phaidon Pr, n.d.

Spencer, Brian
WALKING IN SWITZERLAND
Hunter Pub, 1986.

HISTORY

Hughes, Christopher S.
SWITZERLAND
Praeger, 1975.

Novels

Brookner, Anita
HOTEL DU LAC
A sedate Swiss hotel is the setting for an "oddly detached, very small-scale, faintly humorous" novel. Pantheon, 1985.

Duerrenmatt, Friedrich
THE PLEDGE
A genius detective seeks a killer of little girls to fulfill his pledge to a victim's mother— "an unusual and arresting level of crime and detection . . . some tantalizing moral questions." (FC) Knopf, 1959. Also *The Quarry* (1962), about the search for and execution of a former Nazi criminal—a doctor.

Durrell, Lawrence
SEBASTIAN (Geneva)
Part of the Avignon quartet series of novels, set in post-World War II Geneva. Viking, 1984.

Freemantle, Brian
THE RUN AROUND
The KGB is planning to assassinate a Western politician in Geneva and British agent Muffin is called in to handle the situation. Bantam, 1988.

Frisch, Max
MAN IN THE HOLOCENE (Ticino)
Profound novel of a man living alone in a mountain valley under threat from rockslides and avalanches. HarBraceJ, 1980.

James, Henry
DAISY MILLER (Vevey)
An international episode—will an English nobleman marry a "beautiful, dainty, innocent and very foolish" American girl? (FC) Har-Row, 1975 (first published 1878).

Solzhenitsyn, Aleksandr
LENIN IN ZURICH
Fictional account of Lenin's time in exile in Switzerland during World War I, until his departure in 1917 for Russia. FS&G, 1976.

Spark, Muriel
NOT TO DISTURB (Geneva)

A witty comedy about the aristocracy as seen through the eyes of servants. Viking, 1972. ○

Ullman, James R.
THE WHITE TOWER

"Development and revelation of several characters" who attempt to climb "the White Tower," never before scaled from a particular side, and an adventure story as well. (FC) Lippincott, 1945. ○

Waller, Leslie
THE SWISS ACCOUNT (Basel)

Novel of high-level banking as an American is sent to Basel to take over the assets of the Staeli family—"crisply told with a splendid denouement." (FC) Doubleday, 1976. ○

Whiteman, John
GENEVA ACCORD

A thriller that also provides an armchair way to learn about arms control; it was written by a former CIA employee who was a member of the U.S. Salt II negotiating team. Crown, 1985. ○

WALES

Note: See also all asterisked entries (*) under "England" for additional series guidebooks and background reading that may include Wales.

Series Guidebooks
(See Appendix 1)

Note also guides for Great Britain/Britain listed under England, above.

Blue Guide: Wales; Cathedrals & Abbeys of England & Wales
Exploring Rural Europe: England & Wales
Frommer: Scotland & Wales ($-A-Day)
Insight Guide: Wales
Visitor's Guide: South & West Wales; North Wales & Snowdonia

Background Reading

Barber, Chris
MYSTERIOUS WALES

"Folklore for armchair adventurers and real travelers. . . . thoroughly entertaining." (BL) David, 1982. ○

Barber, W.T.
EXPLORING WALES

A lively guide to Welsh history, literature, architecture, archaeology, legend, fable and countryside, arranged in fourteen regions and organized into favorite tours by foot, car, train and boat. David, 1982. ○

Ellis, Alice T.
WALES

An anthology. David & Charles, 1990. ○

Fishlock, Trevor
TALKING OF WALES

By the *London Times* correspondent for Welsh affairs, a companion book to *Wales and the Welsh People.* Academy Chi Pubs, 1978. ○

McMullen, Jeanine
MY SMALL COUNTRY LIVING

Life on a thirteen-acre farm, on a Welsh mountainside, owned by a BBC broadcaster who is star of a successful radio program on rural life—"a gem of the genre." (PW) Norton, 1984. The sequel, *Wind in the Ashtree: More Tales of My Small Country Living* (1988), converts bad weather and a hard Welsh family life into an enchanting saga with various endearing animals and people. ○

Morgan, John
JOHN MORGAN'S WALES: A PERSONAL VIEW

Longwood Pub Group, 1987. ○

Morris, Jan
THE MATTER OF WALES: EPIC VIEWS OF A SMALL COUNTRY

This noted travel writer's celebration of her native country: "what is special about it—

from rocks and soil to history and religion to the prevailing national character." (BL) Oxford U, 1985. ○

Morris, Jan
WALES: THE FIRST PLACE
"Sensitively written, history-haunted and marvelously ambient celebration of Wales . . . unique, impassioned interweaving of Welsh character, geography, history and legend." (BL) Crown, 1982. ○

Morton, H.V.
IN SEARCH OF WALES
Reprint of a travel classic. Dodd, 1984 (first published 1932). See also *Morton's Britain*, under "England." ○

White, Jon M.
THE JOURNEYING BOY, SCENES FROM A WELSH CHILDHOOD
Travelogue by a distinguished Anglo-Welsh writer who returns to Wales after an absence of 20 years, mixing history and personal reminiscences, odd Welsh characters, the singular nature of the Welsh people. Atl Monthly Pr., 1991. ○

GUIDEBOOKS

Automobile Association of Britain
WALES: GOING PLACES
One of a series of books by the Automobile Association of Britain. Also *Mid Wales, South Wales, North Wales* guides for visitors. Salem Hse, 1985. ○

HISTORY

Dodd, A.H.
SHORT HISTORY OF WALES
Welsh life and customs from prehistoric times to the present day. David & Charles, 1988. ○

Jones, Gareth Elwyn
MODERN WALES: A CONCISE HISTORY
History since the Tudors—"always striving to isolate what it is about the Welsh and their history that makes them special." (BL) Cambridge U Pr, 1985. ○

Novels

Amis, Kingsley
THE OLD DEVILS
The lives of three couples in South Wales are turned upside down by the return of a TV poet and his wife. Summit, 1987. ○

Cordell, Alexander
THE RAPE OF THE FAIR COUNTRY
A family chronicle, and story of the iron-workers' attempts to unionize. Doubleday, 1975 (first published 1959). Its sequel is *Robe of Honour* (1960). Another novel of union struggles is *This Sweet and Bitter Earth* (1978). ○

Cronin, A.J.
THE CITADEL
"Moving and absorbing novel" of pre-socialized medicine. A kind of classic about a young doctor's start from poverty in Wales, to prominence as a London doctor, and the estrangement from principles, and his wife, that come about. Both a classic oldie movie and a British TV series have been made from the book. Little, 1937. ○

Ellis, Alice T.
UNEXPLAINED LAUGHTER
A London journalist on holiday in a Welsh village and trying to recover from a painful love affair—"wickedly funny . . . the beautiful, haunted Welsh landscape . . . comes to dominate this atmospheric story." Har-Row, 1987. ○

Fuller, John
FLYING TO NOWHERE
A "monastic horror tale" that is set on a Welsh island during the Middle Ages. (FC) Braziller, 1984. ○

Gill, B.M.
NURSERY CRIMES
A psychological suspense novel set in the '40s about a young woman surrounded by violent death since childhood. Scribner, 1987. ○

Gower, Iris
FIDDLER'S FERRY
Swansea after World War I through the lives of a ferryman and his seven sons. St. Martin, 1988.   ○

Gregory, Stephen
THE CORMORANT
"Sensual tale of inexorable dread"—an English couple and their child move to a cottage inherited from an uncle, with the stipulation that they care for his pet cormorant. (FC) St. Martin, 1988.   ○

Grumbach, Doris
THE LADIES
Based on the real and infamous "ladies of Llangollen" of the eighteenth century—two women who spurned convention and left Ireland to live together in a Welsh village. (FC) Dutton, 1984.   ○

Llewellyn, Richard
HOW GREEN WAS MY VALLEY
The story of Welsh mining country related by the youngest son of the family, and the gradual laying waste of the once-lovely countryside—"a remarkably beautiful novel

of Wales." Macmillan, 1940. Its sequels are: *Up Into the Singing Mountain* (1960) and *Green, Green, My Valley Now* (1975), which takes the main character to Patagonia and back, to retire in Wales.   ○

Meredith, Christopher
SHIFTS
"Bitter, angry . . . sad, loving" novel of a steel mill town in 1977. Seren, 1988.   ○

Penman, Sharon
HERE BE DRAGONS
Thirteenth-century Wales—"the stuff of high adventure and romance . . . carefully researched history lesson . . . engrossing to the last page." (FC) HR&W, 1986.   ○

Roberts, Dorothy J.
KINSMEN OF THE GRAIL
Historical novel of the twelfth-century quest for the Holy Grail. Little, 1963.   ○

Stewart, Mary
THE MERLIN TRILOGY
An omnibus edition of the Arthurian legend trilogy—*The Crystal Cave, The Hollow Hills, The Last Enchantment*. Morrow, 1980.   ○

YUGOSLAVIA

*Series Guidebooks
(See Appendix 1)*

Baedeker: Yugoslavia
Berlitz: Yugoslavia; Dubrovnik & Southern Dalmatia; Istria & the Croatian Coast; Split & Central Dalmatia
Blue Guide: Yugoslavia
Fodor: Yugoslavia
Insight Guide: Yugoslavia
Real Guide: Yugoslavia
Visitor's Guide: Adriatic

Background Reading

Adamic, Louis
NATIVE'S RETURN
Adamic was an American journalist of Yugoslavian background. This is an account of

the underground struggle, and the Partisans, in 1943, with portraits of the Serbs, Croats, Slovenes, the various ethnic groups in this country. Reprint of a 1934 edition. Greenwood, 1975.   ○

Doder, Dusko
THE YUGOSLAVS
An emigrant from Yugoslavia returns twenty years later as Bureau Chief for the *Washington Post*—a panoramic, personal survey by a sympathetic and skilled observer. Description of the history, culture, ideology, profiles of Tito and Djilas. Random, 1978.   ○

Gill, Anton
BERLIN TO BUCHAREST: TRAVELS IN EASTERN EUROPE
See entry under Europe/Background Reading. ○

Jones, E. Michael
MEDJUGORJE: THE UNTOLD STORY
This is about Yugoslavia's version of Lourdes or Fatima, where young girls supposedly have seen visions of the Virgin Mary. Their story has not been accepted as yet by the Vatican—nevertheless, the village attracts an enormous number of travelers, both believers and unbelievers. Fidelity Pr, 1988. ○

Lees, Michael
THE RAPE OF SERBIA: THE BRITISH ROLE IN TITO'S GRAB FOR POWER
A Secret Service cache of files unearthed 40 years later is catalyst and source for this book that says Churchill was fooled by a disinformation campaign to transfer British support from pro-West Mihailovic to Tito, and that Churchill later considered this decision one of his great blunders. HarBraceJ, 1990. ○

West, Rebecca
BLACK LAMB AND GREY FALCON
A classic and important book. History, brilliant analysis of European culture and ideas, and a travel diary of a trip through Yugoslavia at Easter in 1937. Penguin, 1982. ○

Westerlind, Eva S.
CARRYING THE FARM ON HER BACK: A PORTRAIT OF WOMEN IN A YUGOSLAV VILLAGE
"A fine work that gives a glimpse of rural, isolated Croatian farm villages" with the women maintaining farms alone while men migrate to towns for work. Rainier Bks, 1989. ○

GUIDEBOOKS

Gavranic, N. Kola
YUGOSLAV WINE COUNTRY
Ragusan Pr, 1983. ○

Letcher, Piers
YUGOSLAVIA: MOUNTAIN WALKS AND HISTORICAL SITES
Emphasizes some of the lesser-known areas away from the crowded beaches, including historical sights, where to eat and stay. Hunter Pub, 1989. ○

Tomaševic, Nebojša, ed.
TREASURES OF YUGOSLAVIA: AN ENCYCLOPEDIC TOURING GUIDE
Reference guide to Yugoslavia's cultural treasures, historical landmarks, art, architecture, etc.—illustrated. Yugoslavia Pubns, 1983. ○

Trifunovic, Lazar
YUGOSLAVIA: MONUMENTS OF ART
Yugoslavia has been a crossroads of routes linking Asia Minor, central Europe and the Aegean Sea since prehistoric times, and the various cultures have left their mark. This is an alphabetical, comprehensive guide to the sites, with location, diagrams, illustrations. State Mutual Bk, 1988. ○

HISTORY

Singleton, Fred
A SHORT HISTORY OF THE YUGOSLAV PEOPLES
Cambridge U Pr, 1985. ○

Wilson, Duncan
TITO'S YUGOSLAVIA
"Good account of the events of World War II, of the Yugoslav Revolution," and 1948 on as an independent state. (BRD) Cambridge U Pr, 1980. ○

Novels

Andrić, Ivo
THE BRIDGE ON THE DRINA
First novel in the Bosnian trilogy. Chronicle of a bridge near Visograd over three and a half centuries. Allen Unwin, 1959 (first published 1945). The sequels are *Bosnian Chronicle* (1945), set in the capital of Bosnia in the years just before the fall of Napoleon; *The*

Woman from Sarajevo (1945), set in the Balkans during the early twentieth century and including Sarajevo at the time of the assassination that started World War I (the "woman" is a girl, turned into an embittered miser by the bankruptcy and death of her father).   ○

Ćosić, Dobrica
A TIME OF DEATH

First in a trilogy. This is a story of Serbia during World War I and its fight for survival. HarBraceJ, 1978. It is followed by *Reach to Eternity* (1980), which tells of the aftermath of a decisive battle in 1914 when the Serbs defeated the Austrian forces. The third novel is *South to Destiny* (1981), which takes the story through 1916 when Serbia is defeated and abandoned by its allies.   ○

Djilas, Milovan
UNDER THE COLORS

The "roots of nationalism" and the story of a peasant family in the 1870s engaged in the "seemingly hopeless task of rebelling against their Turkish overlords." (FC) HarBraceJ, 1971.   ○

Handke, Peter
REPETITION

"An odyssey of self-discovery" as a writer retraces his brother's steps of 20 years earlier. (FC) FS&G, 1988.   ○

Jovanovski, Meto
COUSINS

The first novel to be translated from Macedonian to English—two Macedonian cousins try to return to their village during World War I; an indictment of war and a novel that has significance as a predictor of Yugoslavian political problems. Mercury Hse, 1987.   ○

MacLean, Alistair
PARTISANS

A MacLean suspense story of World War II and the Nazi/partisan struggle—the vastness of the Balkan mountains is the setting. Doubleday, 1983. Also *Force 10 From Navarone* (1968).   ○

VI.
LATIN AMERICA

Background Reading

Arciniegas, Germán
THE GREEN CONTINENT
An anthology of writings on Latin America by historians, essayists and novelists. 1944. ○

Braganti, Nancy and Devine, Elizabeth
THE TRAVELERS' GUIDE TO LATIN AMERICAN CUSTOMS AND MANNERS
One of a useful series to enlighten travelers that American social customs are not universal. St. Martin, 1989. ○

Fagan, Brian
KINGDOMS OF GOLD, KINGDOMS OF JADE
A scholarly and readable treatment of the civilizations present before the arrival of Columbus. Thames & Hudson. ○

Harvey, Robert
FIRE DOWN BELOW: A JOURNEY OF EXPLORATION FROM MEXICO TO CHILE
"More probing than most travel books, the author's acute sense of observation . . . and evocative prose convey not only the flavor and variety . . . but the suffering, horror and poverty." (PW) S&S, 1988. ○

Hinds, Harold E., Jr. and Tatum, Charles
HANDBOOK OF LATIN AMERICAN POPULAR CULTURE
Ten chapters examine comics, sports, festivals, music, religion and more—"the average traveler who marvels at the sights and sounds of urban Latin America will welcome its cultural insights." (Americas) Greenwood, 1985. ○

Hopkins, Jack W., ed.
LATIN AMERICA: PERSPECTIVES ON A REGION
"Consistently approachable" collection of essays on the region about subjects ranging from soil and climate, and history, to contemporary aspects of religion, education, etc.—"use for dipping . . . in search of specific information . . . a compelling narrative when read cover to cover." (BL) Holmes & Meier, 1987. ○

Krich, John
EL BEISBOL: TRAVELS THROUGH THE PAN-AMERICAN PASTIME
Baseball is the unifying theme; it is more a travel book providing insights into Latin America, with comments on politics and social structure. Atl Monthly Pr, 1989. ○

Naipaul, V.S.
THE MIDDLE PASSAGE

Impressions of Trinidad, British Guiana, Surinam, Martinique and Jamaica in the West Indies and South America, by an author who is a Trinidadian of East Indian descent. "A descriptive travel book . . . combines a novelist's sketches of character with an amateur historian-sociologist's speculation . . . an armchair traveler's joy." First published in 1962. (BRD) Vintage, 1981. Also *The Loss of El Dorado* (1970).   ○

Parry, J.H.
THE DISCOVERY OF SOUTH AMERICA

Spanish explorations in Central America, Mexico, South America and the Antilles, based on contemporary chronicles and diaries. "Superbly written . . . the reader experiences with the conquistadores the wonder of the New World . . . conjures time, places [and] bedazzled Europeans' curiosity about exotic races, spectacular plans, unknown beasts." (BRD) Taplinger, 1979.   ○

Prescott, W.H.
PRESCOTT'S HISTORIES—THE RISE AND DECLINE OF THE SPANISH EMPIRE

Selections from four of the author's historical classics: *Ferdinand and Isabella, The Conquest of Mexico, The Conquest of Peru, Philip II*. Viking, 1963 (first published 1837 through 1858).   ○

Theroux, Paul
THE OLD PATAGONIAN EXPRESS: BY TRAIN THROUGH THE AMERICAS

Theroux's insights and characterizations as he travels (mostly by train) through North and South America. HM, 1989.   ○

Tschiffely, A.F.
SOUTHERN CROSS TO POLE STAR—TSCHIFFELY'S RIDE

Reprint of a travel classic. A Swiss schoolmaster and his two aging Criollo-bred ponies travelled 10,000 miles in a two-and-a-half-year journey from Buenos Aires to Washington, D.C.—"remarkable often terrifying exploits." Tarcher, 1982 (first published 1925).   ○

Von Hagen, Victor
THE ANCIENT SUN KINGDOMS OF THE AMERICAS

"Exciting *magnum opus* on the life and times of the highly cultured peoples of the Sun Kingdoms"—Aztec, Maya and Inca. (BRD) Beekman, 1977 (first published 1960). Also *Maya Explorer* (1990).   ○

HISTORY

Burns, E. Bradford
LATIN AMERICA: A CONCISE INTERPRETIVE HISTORY
P-H, 1990.   ○

Hennessy, Alistair
THE FRONTIER IN LATIN AMERICAN HISTORY

Comparative history of the frontier experience—missionaries, mining, cattle and cowboys, etc.—with that of the United States, Canada and Australia. U of New Mexico, 1978.   ○

Picon-Salas, Mariano
A CULTURAL HISTORY OF SPANISH AMERICA: FROM CONQUEST TO INDEPENDENCE
U of Cal Pr, 1962.   ○

T H E   C A R I B B E A N

*Series Guidebooks
(See Appendix 1)*

Alive Guide: Virgin Islands Alive

Baedeker: Caribbean
Berlitz: French West Indies; Southern Caribbean; Virgin Islands

Birnbaum: The Caribbean, Bermuda & Bahama

Cadogan Guide: Caribbean

Caribbean Guide: Antigua & Barbuda; Adventure Guide to Barbados; Curacao Close-up; Dominica; Grenada; Nevis; Saint Lucia; St. Kitts; Trinidad & Tobago; Turks & Caicos; Adventure Guide to the Virgin Islands; British Virgin Islands; Islands to the Windward

Crown Insider's Guide: The Caribbean

Fielding: Caribbean

Fisher's World: Caribbean; Puerto Rico & the Virgin Islands

Fodor: The Caribbean; Barbados; Saint Martin and Saint Maarten; Virgin Islands

Frommer: Caribbean; Virgin Islands

Hildebrand: Hispaniola (Dominican Republic & Haiti)

Insight Guide: Caribbean; Barbados; Trinidad & Tobago

Moon Handbook: Puerto Rico & the Virgin Islands (includes Dominican Republic)

Nelles Guide: Caribbean (North); Caribbean (South)

2–22 Days Itinerary Planning Guide: West Indies

Background Reading

Barry, Tom, and others
THE OTHER SIDE OF PARADISE: FOREIGN COUNTRIES IN THE CARIBBEAN
A study of the negative effect of foreign investment. Grove, 1985.   ○

Carr, Archie
THE WINDWARD ROAD
Adventures of a naturalist on remote Caribbean shores. U Presses Fl, 1979.   ○

Curran, Carolyn J.
THE CARIBBEAN, A CULTURAL JOURNEY
Gumbs & Thomas, 1988.   ○

Fermor, Patrick Leigh
TRAVELLER'S TREE: A JOURNEY THROUGH THE CARIBBEAN ISLANDS
First published in 1950, an account of travels in the Caribbean; a plant species is metaphor

for the diverse inhabitants of the Antilles. "Each island is recorded in rich, evocative imagery with an eye to unique cultural histories and landscapes." (BL) Penguin, 1991.   ○

Fleming, Carrol
ADVENTURING IN THE CARIBBEAN
"A general feel and appreciation for the entire region"—general information on the Caribbean with descriptive, specific information on 40 of the islands. (BL) Sierra Club, 1989.   ○

Garreau, Joel
THE NINE NATIONS OF NORTH AMERICA
A *Washington Post* reporter's view of North America argues that arbitrary state and national boundaries mean nothing. His "nine nations" are based on economics, emotional allegiance, and attitudes, and each has its own capital and distinctive web of power and influence. Under this concept, the Caribbean is part of Miami. A highly readable and perceptive analysis. Houghton, 1981.   ○

Gosner, Pamela
CARIBBEAN GEORGIAN
The great houses, and the small, of the Caribbean. Three Continents, 1982.   ○

Howes, Barbara, ed.
FROM THE GREEN ANTILLES
Excerpts of writings from forty Caribbean authors representative of the four language groups—English, French, Spanish and Dutch. Macmillan, 1966.   ○

Jinkins, Dana and Bobrow, Jill
ST. VINCENT AND THE GRENADINES: A PLURAL COUNTRY
A travelogue with "celebratory comments" by Margaret Atwood and Raquel Welch. (PW) Norton, 1985.   ○

Kaplan, Eugene H.
A FIELD GUIDE TO SOUTHEASTERN & CARIBBEAN SEASHORES
From Cape Hatteras to the Gulf Coast, Florida and the Caribbean. HM, 1988.   ○

Kincaid, Jamaica
A SMALL PLACE (Antigua)
The author of *Annie John* (see Novels, below) reveals what tourists rarely see and travels back in history and in her past to describe conditions in Antigua—"a bleak travelogue, fueled by fire, passion and love." (BL) FS&G, 1988.   ○

Kurlansky, Mark
A CONTINENT OF ISLANDS— SEARCHING FOR THE CARIBBEAN DESTINY
"Alternately social history, political history and travel essay . . . brims with enthusiasm and thoroughness." (PW) Addison-Wesley, 1992.   ○

LaBrucherie, Roger A.
IMAGES OF BARBADOS
The reviewer said of its companion volume *Images of Puerto Rico*, "a compact overview of the true spirit of this Caribbean island." Tuttle, 1985.   ○

Murray, John A., ed.
THE ISLANDS AND THE SEA
Five centuries of nature writing from the Caribbean of Columbus to present. Oxford U Pr, 1991.   ○

Nunley, John W. and Bettelheim, Judith
CARIBBEAN FESTIVAL ARTS: EACH AND EVERY BIT OF DIFFERENCE
Festival incarnations where dance, sculpture, painting, music and poetry are intertwined—the differences among the islands and political, social, historical backgrounds. St. Louis Art Museum/U of Washington Pr, 1989.   ○

Sale, Kirkpatrick
THE CONQUEST OF PARADISE
A "demythologizing biographical adventure . . . Columbus as seed-bearer of a European civilization of conquest, violence, ecological plunder and intolerance." (PW) Knopf, 1990.   ○

Seabury, Paul and McDougall, Walter A., eds.
THE GRENADA PAPERS
Edited, annotated documents seized during the Grenada invasion that illustrate the Communist threat. ICS Pr, 1984.   ○

Waugh, Alec
A FAMILY OF ISLANDS
Unique popular history—"a kind of novel with islands instead of individual characters as the protagonists." Covers the period from 1492 to 1898, with an epilogue sketching in events from the Spanish-American War up to the 1960s. "Packed with vivid portraits" of historical figures. (BRD) Doubleday, 1964.   ○

Waugh, Alec
LOVE AND THE CARIBBEAN
Tales, characters and scenes of the West Indies, a collection of the author's best writing about the Caribbean, bringing to life the past and present of the area. "Should be a delight to the armchair traveller as well as the sophisticated tourist," said *Kirkus Review* of this collection. Paragon Hse, 1991.   ○

GUIDEBOOKS

Adkins, Leonard
A WALKING GUIDE TO THE CARIBBEAN
From the Virgin Islands to Martinique—on beaches and in the hills. Johnson Bks, 1988.   ○

Curran, Patrick L.
THE CARIBBEAN
A cultural journey. Gumbs & Thomas, 1991.   ○

Dean, John
DIVERS TRAVEL GUIDE TO THE CARIBBEAN & THE BAHAMAS
Travel & Sports, 1987.   ○

Gravette, A. Gerald
THE FRENCH ANTILLES: A GUIDE TO GUADELOUPE, MARTINIQUE, ST. BARTHOLOMEW AND ST. MARTIN
All the usual information plus a writing style that evokes the flavor of the islands "making the reader eager to be on the next plane or cruise ship." (LJ) Hippocrene, 1989. Also *The Netherlands Antilles,* 1989.   ○

Keown, Ian
CARIBBEAN HIDEAWAYS
How to avoid neon, plastic, piped-in music, conventions, children, cruise-ship passengers. (BL) P-H, 1989.   ○

Showker, Kay
CARIBBEAN PORTS OF CALL: A GUIDE FOR TODAY'S CRUISE PASSENGERS
Globe Pequot, 1990. Also *Eastern Caribbean Ports of Call,* 1991.   ○

Showker, Kay
OUTDOOR TRAVELER'S GUIDE TO THE CARIBBEAN
Comprehensive guide to flora, fauna, birds, forests and outdoor activities of all kinds. Stewart, Tabori & Chang, 1989.   ○

Willes, Burl
UNDISCOVERED ISLANDS OF THE CARIBBEAN
The author has tracked down islands off the coasts of Central America, Puerto Rico, Venezuela, the Bahamas and Antilles, where there are few tourists and no big hotels. John Muir, 1990.   ○

HISTORY

Ajlouny, Joe
THE ISLANDS OF THE CARIBBEAN SEA
A concise and colorful history; part of the Tourist Companion Histories Series. J.S.A. Pubs, 1988.   ○

Knight, Franklin W. and Palmer, Colin A., eds.
THE MODERN CARIBBEAN
U of NC Pr, 1989.   ○

Rogoziński, Jan
A BRIEF HISTORY OF THE CARIBBEAN
Overview of the geography and environment, discussion of the early settlers, chronicle of the complete history beginning with Columbus and on to the present day, including tourism and the invasion of Grenada. Facts On File, 1992.   ○

Williams, Eric
FROM COLUMBUS TO CASTRO: THE HISTORY OF THE CARIBBEAN
By a prime minister of Trinidad and Tobago—"interesting and well written essay on slavery and sugar cane . . . the effects of their interaction on the peoples of the Caribbean." First published 1971. (BRD) Random, 1984.   ○

Novels

Anthony, Evelyn
THE TAMARIND SEED (Barbados)
Espionage and romance; a British widow meets a Russian agent. Coward, 1971.   ○

Anthony, Michael
GREEN DAYS BY THE RIVER (Trinidad)
"Novel of adolescence of a Trinidad island boy . . . outstanding writing and characterization." First published in 1967. Heinemann, 1985.   ○

Atwood, Margaret
BODILY HARM
An introspective, successful journalist takes a working holiday on a Caribbean island to restore normalcy to her life after a bout with cancer and loss of her lover. S&S, 1982.   ○

Benchley, Peter
THE ISLAND

A variation on *Jaws* but with "bloodthirsty buccaneers replacing the sharks" as the enemy. A writer for a newsmagazine and his son are kidnapped in the British West Indies and taken to a remote island in the Turks and Caicos. (BRD) Doubleday, 1979.　ↄ

Bissoondath, Neil
A CASUAL BRUTALITY

An Indian, raised on a fictional island, studies medicine in Toronto, marries and returns to the island—"a powerful story of exploitation and violence set on a West Indian colonial island." Ivy Books, 1990.　ↄ

Christie, Agatha
A CARIBBEAN MYSTERY

In *Five Complete Miss Marple Novels*. Avenal, 1980 ("Caribbean" first published 1965).　ↄ

Coulter, Catherine
IMPULSE

A reporter goes under cover at a gangster-owned Caribbean resort—"dashing men, beautiful women, sex, intrigue and international high stakes." (FC) NAL, 1990.　ↄ

DeBoissiere, Ralph
CROWN JEWEL (Trinidad)

Story of a charismatic black activist and his attempts to unify blacks in Trinidad for social progress. Allison & Busby, 1981.　ↄ

Edwards-Yearwood, Grace
IN THE SHADOW OF THE PEACOCK

Set in New York City and the Caribbean. A "token black" in publishing falls in love in the Caribbean and begins to question her ambitions. McGraw-Hill, 1988.　ↄ

Fermor, Patrick L.
THE VIOLINS OF ST. JACQUES, A TALE OF THE ANTILLES
(Martinique)

Nostalgic novel of a Creole island—"a lush, heady mixture." (BRD) Oxford U Pr, 1985.　ↄ

Forester, C.S.
ADMIRAL HORNBLOWER IN THE WEST INDIES

Classic Hornblower adventure set in the West Indies involving a Bonapartist uprising, piracy and the slave trade. Little, 1958. Also *The Captain from Connecticut* (1941).　ↄ

Galvan, Manuel de Jesus
THE CROSS AND THE SWORD

Historical novel of the Columbus and post-Columbus period of Caribbean history, translated from the Spanish by Robert Graves. AMS, 1975 (first published 1954).　ↄ

Gaskin, Catherine
FIONA

Mystery romance set on a small Caribbean island in 1833. Doubleday, 1970.　ↄ

Guy, Rosa
MY LOVE, MY LOVE

A modern fable set on a Caribbean island—"allegory abounds in vivid, sensual images . . . many of which parallel Hans Christian Andersen's *Little Mermaid* but with a last scene that is 'devastating in its ugliness.' " (FC) HR&W, 1985.　ↄ

Holland, Isabelle
KILGAREN

A gothic—a girl returns to her ancestral home in the West Indies and finds mystery and romance. Weybright & Talley, 1974.　ↄ

Kincaid, Jamaica
ANNIE JOHN (Antigua)

"A magical coming-of-age tale" of Annie John from 10 to 17, with "special ambiance of its tropical setting . . . a poetic and intensely moving work." (FC) FS&G, 1985.　ↄ

Lamming, George
IN THE CASTLE OF MY SKIN
(Barbados)

An autobiographical novel of a boyhood in Barbados—"rarely has any island of the West Indies been presented to feelingly." (BRD) Schocken, 1983 (first published 1953).　ↄ

Lauder, Peter
NOBLE LORD
A black police sergeant from Antigua is assigned to solve the mystery of his brother-in-law's death, and finds it is connected to a terrorist plot to kill Queen Elizabeth on Derby Day. Stein & Day, 1986.   o

Lehmann, Rosamond
A SEA-GRAPE TREE
"A short idyll on a lush, romantic Caribbean island [with a] supernatural aura." (BRD) HarBraceJ, 1980.   o

Lovelace, Earl
A BRIEF CONVERSION AND OTHER STORIES (Trinidad)
Part of a Caribbean Writers Series. Heinemann, 1988.   o

Lovelace, Earl
THE WINE OF ASTONISHMENT (Trinidad)
Eva, wife of a "Spiritual Baptist" minister in Trinidad during World War II narrates the story in Trinidadian speech patterns. The plot concerns the demoralization of the community when the government bars the exercise of her husband's religion as uncivilized. Vintage, 1984. Also *The Dragon Can't Dance*.   o

Marshall, Paule
THE CHOSEN PLACE, THE TIMELESS PEOPLE
Complex racial relationships as a group of Americans working on a research development project arrive on a West Indian island, and their interraction with an islander— "impressive, important—a parable of Western civilization and its relations with the undeveloped world." (BRD) Vintage, 1985 (first published 1969). Also *Praisesong for the Widow* (1983).   o

Matthiessen, Peter
FAR TORTUGA
A remote islet, south of Cuba, is the setting—men search for the last turtles of the season on Grand Cayman and the cays and reefs of Nicaragua. Random, 1975.   o

Michener, James A.
CARIBBEAN
One of Michener's historical sagas, starting from the days of the Arawak Indians and moving to a contemporary tour of today's still lush, but troubled paradise, with historical figures from pirate Henry Morgan and Sir Francis Drake, to Fidel Castro, in the cast of characters. Random, 1989.   o

Morris, Mervyn
THE FABER BOOK OF CONTEMPORARY CARIBBEAN SHORT STORIES
Stories from Antigua, Barbados, Jamaica, other islands and including writers both well known and new. Faber & Faber, 1990.   o

Morrison, Toni
TAR BABY
A novel of relationships between blacks and whites as a fugitive American is discovered in the retirement house of a wealthy Philadelphia couple. Knopf, 1981.   o

Moyes, Patricia
ANGEL DEATH
One of several Inspector Henry Tibbett mysteries set in the British Caribbean. HR&W, 1980. Also *The Coconut Killings* (1985) and *Black Girl, White Girl* (1991).   o

Naipaul, V.S.
GUERILLAS
The novel creates an island in the Caribbean complete with a history, geography, and population; it's a troubled island with a mixed population of British colonials, Africans, Americans and Asians. Knopf, 1975.   o

Naipaul, V.S.
A HOUSE FOR MR. BISWAS (Trinidad)
Story of a poverty-stricken Indian journalist and a major novel of West Indian life in Trinidad. McGraw, 1961. Also *The Chip Chip Gatherers* (1971)   o

Naipaul, V.S.
THREE NOVELS: THE MYSTIC MASSEUR, THE SUFFRAGE OF ELVIRA, MIGUEL STREET
(Trinidad)
The characters are mostly East Indians and the setting is Trinidad of the 1940s—"each . . . is a charming and delightful celebration of innocence, and readers will find the Calypso lilt of the dialogue quite wonderful." (FC) Knopf, 1982.   ○

Phillips, Caryl
THE FINAL PASSAGE
"Creates a strong impression of the two worlds it spans" with a plot that is about the events leading up to emigration from an unnamed Caribbean island to London. Faber & Faber, 1985.   ○

Phillips, Caryl
A STATE OF INDEPENDENCE (St. Kitts)
A man returns after a 20-year absence to St. Kitts, and this coincides with the island's independence. FS&G, 1986.   ○

Plain, Belva
EDEN BURNING
"Eden" is an island in the Caribbean; half-brothers become enemies when the island explodes in a revolution—"interesting descriptions of the native habitat, culture, cuisine and history." (FC) Delacorte Pr, 1982.   ○

Rhys, Jean
WIDE SARGASSO SEA (Dominica)
A Creole heiress (based on the mad Mrs. Rochester in *Jane Eyre*) is the main character—"this detailed and frightening study of the disintegration of a woman is played out in the lush and captivatingly sensuous environment of the tropics." Norton, 1967. ○

Schwarz-Bart, Simone
A WOMAN NAMED SOLITUDE
(Guadeloupe)
The recreation of the life of a West African child, conceived on a slave ship en route to Guadeloupe, who refuses to return to slavery after the brief period of freedom that followed the French Revolution—based on an actual historical figure. Atheneum, 1973. Also *The Bridge of Beyond* (1974) and *Between Two Worlds* (1981).   ○

Shacochis, Bob
EASY IN THE ISLANDS
A short-story collection of "the flip side of paradise, a world the tourist never sees." (TL) Crown, 1984.   ○

Steinbeck, John
CUP OF GOLD
The subtitle is: a life of Sir Henry Morgan, buccaneer, with occasional reference to history. The novel begins in Wales, and tells of Morgan's life, first as a slave in Barbados, then as a buccaneer and on to his respectable death. R.M. McBride, 1980 (first published 1929).   ○

HAITI

Series Guidebooks (See Appendix 1)

Hildebrand: Hispaniola (Dominican Republic & Haiti)
Moon Handbook: Jamaica (includes Haiti)

Background Reading

Gold, Herbert
BEST NIGHTMARE ON EARTH: A LIFE IN HAITI
An "impassioned memoir" of Haiti over four decades as a scholar, novelist and journalist.

Reflections on history and folklore, arrival of AIDS, encounters with people, voodoo, cockfights, politics of Duvalier—"captures the essence of this land." (Publisher) Prentice Hall Pr, 1991. ○

Laguerre, Michel S.
VOODOO AND POLITICS IN HAITI
"Unabashed defense of Haitian voodoo." The author argues that voodoo temples in colonial Haiti were like liberation theology churches in Latin America today—"the loci for revolutionary nationalistic political movements." (BRD) St. Martin, 1989. ○

Lemoine, Maurice
BITTER SUGAR
The author alleges near-slave conditions as the fate of sugar workers employed by both Haitian and American companies. Banner Pr, 1985. ○

Parkinson, Wanda
THIS GILDED AFRICAN: TOUSSAINT L'OUVERTURE
Biography of the black general and diplomat who rose from slavery to lead his people against European colonialism. Quartet, 1982. ○

Price-Mars, Jean
SO SPOKE THE UNCLE
"Series of essays tracing voodoo to its African roots . . . its similarities with the dominant Western religions . . . its central role in Haitian folk culture." The author, a Haitian physician and diplomat, wrote these essays in 1928 at a time when most educated Haitians were repudiating their heritage, so he was stating an early version of ethnic pride. (NYT) Three Continents, 1983. ○

Rodman, Selden
HAITI: THE BLACK REPUBLIC
A new edition (the seventh) of a book first published in 1954. It is both a background book and a guide to Haiti and includes history, customs, a basic Creole-French vocabulary, art, the wilderness, religion and voodoo, along with a great deal of practical information for travelers on hotels, shop-

ping and touring. Devin, 1985. Also, *Where Art Is Joy: Haitian Art—The First Forty Years* (1988). ○

Seabrook, William B.
THE MAGIC ISLAND
Reprint of a travel classic first published in 1929, of the first-hand adventures and experiences of the author in Haiti, with drawings by Alex King, plus photos. He lived with the family of a voodoo princess and was initiated into the cult. The book treats four aspects: Haiti as a final stronghold of voodoo worship, Haiti as a black republic, the attitude of the U.S. Marines during their period of control and Haiti as a place of beauty. Paragon Hse, 1989. ○

Wilentz, Amy
THE RAINY SEASON: HAITI SINCE DUVALIER
The author left her job at *Time* magazine to live in Haiti for a few years. She describes developments since Duvalier left, 1986–89. "The flavor of Haiti is superbly conveyed . . . as are some unsavory aspects." (PW) S&S, 1989. ○

HISTORY

Abbott, Elizabeth
HAITI UPDATED
"The most intimate and revealing examination to date of the Duvalier years . . . of corruption, greed and relentless slaughter." (PW) S&S, 1991. ○

Bellegarde-Smith, Patrick
HAITI: THE BREACHED CITADEL
Summary of history from colonization in the 18th century through the fall of General Namphy in 1988. Westview, 1988. ○

Novels

Carpentier, Alejo
THE KINGDOM OF THIS WORLD
"Recreates the 18th-century era of foreign misrule in Haiti, the subsequent native uprising and . . . new conquerors" who turned out to be just as tyrannical. Historic figures are mixed with fictitious characters in a pic-

aresque story. (FC) Knopf, 1957 (first published 1948).   ○

Greene, Graham
THE COMEDIANS
Life in a run-down tourist hotel in Haiti with a group of diverse characters, "most of them in varying degrees comedians on the stage of life." (FC) Viking, 1966.   ○

Roberts, Kenneth
LYDIA BAILEY
By the author of many historical novels about Maine; in this, a man from Maine finds love in Haiti and the period is 1791–1804. Doubleday, 1947.   ○

Roumain, Jacques
MASTERS OF THE DEW
A novel of Haitian peasant life—"of the African heritage . . . impulsive, gravely formal folk, poetry of their speech [and] the love of a land and its people." (BRD) Heinemann, 1978 (first published 1947).   ○

Thoby-Marcelin, Philippe
ALL MEN ARE MAD
A comic novel of Catholicism in Haiti as a young French priest tries to eradicate ancestral religious influences in its practice there. FS&G, 1970.   ○

JAMAICA

Series Guidebooks
(See Appendix 1)

Berlitz: Jamaica
Caribbean Guide: Jamaica
Fodor: Jamaica
Hildebrand: Jamaica
Insight Guide: Jamaica
Moon Handbook: Jamaica

Background Reading

Barrett, Leonard E.
**THE RASTAFARIANS: SOUNDS OF
    CULTURAL DISSONANCE**
The "belief system . . . rituals, art and music" of the Jamaican cult—"an enlightening book on that strange sect." (BRD) Beacon Pr, 1988.   ○

Cargill, Morris, ed.
**IAN FLEMING INTRODUCES
    JAMAICA**
Ian Fleming, Morris Cargill, and other writers—Jamaicans or long-term residents of Jamaica—contribute to a book that covers people, history, politics, religions, dialects, birds, food, natural history, etc. Hawthorn, 1965.   ○

Dance, Daryl C.
**FOLKLORE FROM
    CONTEMPORARY JAMAICANS**
An anthology of stories, songs, poetry that offers a fascinating introduction to Jamaican culture and life. U of Tennessee Pr, 1985.   ○

Marrish, Ivor
OBEAH, CHRIST & RASTAMAN
Jamaica and its religion. Attic Pr, 1982.   ○

White, Timothy
**CATCH A FIRE: THE LIFE OF BOB
    MARLEY**
About the recently deceased "King of Reggae" who made that music a social and political statement. HR&W, 1983.   ○

Novels

Banks, Russell
THE BOOK OF JAMAICA
An American novelist in Jamaica on a grant. "Provides armchair tourists with a rare . . . fictional view [of] history, landscape, language, religion and politics" of Jamaica. (BRD) Houghton, 1980.   ○

Battle, Lois
A HABIT OF THE BLOOD
"Larger-than-life novel . . . a glimpse into the tawdry politics and the drug subculture of Jamaica." (FC) St. Martin, 1989.   ○

Cliff, Michelle
ABENG
A young girl's rite of passage that explores Jamaican society's sensitive racial issues, and her "growing awareness of the gulf created by color and caste." (FC) Crossing Pr, 1984.   ○

Fleming, Ian
DOCTOR NO
One of several James Bond thrillers set partly in Jamaica. Macmillan, 1958. Also *Live and*

Let Die (1955), *For Your Eyes Only* (1960), and *The Man With the Golden Gun* (1965).   ○

Reid, V.S.
NEW DAY
Jamaica from the rebellion in 1865 to 1944 when it became self-governing to a degree— "true to historical fact . . . a liquid, lyrical thing" by a Jamaican black. (BRD) Knopf, 1949.   ○

Waugh, Alec
ISLAND IN THE SUN
The regime of a British governor confronts questions of colonialism, racial equality and self-government. FS&G, 1955.   ○

PUERTO RICO

*Series Guidebooks
(See Appendix 1)*

American Guide Series: WPA Guide Reprint—Puerto Rico: A Guide to the Island of Boriquen
Berlitz: Puerto Rico
Caribbean Guide: The Adventure Guide to Puerto Rico; The Other Puerto Rico
Fisher's World: Puerto Rico and the Virgin Islands
Fodor: Puerto Rico Pocket Guide
Insight Guide: Puerto Rico
Moon Handbook: Puerto Rico & the Virgin Islands (includes Dominican Republic)

Background Reading

LaBrucherie, Roger A.
IMAGES OF PUERTO RICO
"A compact overview of the true spirit of this Caribbean island." (LJ) C.E. Tuttle, 1985.   ○

Levine, Barry
BENJY LOPEZ: A PICARESQUE TALE OF EMIGRATION AND RETURN
Basic Bks, 1980.   ○

Lewis, Oscar
LA VIDA
Chronicle of Puerto Rican life, a study of one thousand families from San Juan and their New York relatives. Irvington, 1982 (first published 1966).   ○

Morales, Arturo, ed.
PUERTO RICO: A POLITICAL AND CULTURAL ODYSSEY
By Puerto Rican scholars "but addressed to the general reader on the U.S. mainland"— essays that function as a social, cultural and political history. (BL) Norton, 1983.   ○

Novels

Babin, Maria Teresa
BORINQUEN: AN ANTHOLOGY OF PUERTO RICAN LITERATURE
Vintage, 1974.   ○

Baldwin, James
IF BEALE STREET COULD TALK
New York City and Puerto Rico are the settings for a novel of a love between two young people that helps them to deal with racial oppression. Dial, 1974.   ○

Sánchez, Luis R.
MACHO CAMACHO'S BEAT
"Macho Camacho's Beat" is a popular song
that plays on the radio as a persistent background to a series of interrelated incidents. Pantheon, 1981.   ○

THE BAHAMAS

Series Guidebooks
(See Appendix 1)

Berlitz: Bahamas
Birnbaum: The Caribbean, Bermuda & Bahamas
Caribbean Guide: The Bahamas
Fielding: Bermuda & Bahamas
Fisher's World: Bahamas
Fodor: Bahamas; Pocket Guide to the Bahamas
Frommer: Bermuda & Bahamas
Insight Guide: Bahamas

Background Reading

Pye, Michael
THE KING OVER WATER
The Duke of Windsor's years as governor of the Bahamas—in the process it gives an admirable history of the country, its colorful characters, the money-laundering business, and "charts the Windsors' decline in the exotic, politically corrupt Bahamian society." (BRD) HR&W, 1981.   ○

Zink, David
THE STONES OF ATLANTIS
The author's theories of the legendary Atlantis being near Bimini. P-H, 1990.   ○

GUIDEBOOKS

Braun, Jerome R.
THE BEST OF GRAND BAHAMA ISLAND: A SURVIVAL GUIDE
Intercon Pub, 1988.   ○

Dean, John
DIVERS TRAVEL GUIDE TO THE CARIBBEAN & BAHAMAS
Travel & Sports SF, 1987.   ○

Moore, James F.
THE PELICAN GUIDE TO THE BAHAMAS
"By far the most comprehensive guide to the more than 700 diverse islands . . . people, customs, and colorful history" and including practical tourist information. (LJ) Pelican, 1988.   ○

HISTORY

Ajlouny, Joe
THE BAHAMAS
A concise and colorful history and part of the Tourist Companion Histories Series. J.S.A. Pubs, 1988.   ○

Novels

Hemingway, Ernest
ISLANDS IN THE STREAM
Posthumous novel of a man's reflections on his two marriages and his children. Bimini and Cuba. Scribner, 1970.   ○

Mason, F. Van Wyck
STARS ON THE SEA
Part of a saga on the American Revolution; this part is about the involvement of privateers in the Bahamas. Lippincott, 1940.   ○

Wilder, Robert
AN AFFAIR OF HONOR
The Bahamas as reflected in the parallel lives of a white Bahamian "with an insatiable greed for wealth and power" and a black Bahamian's ambition to establish a black government. Putnam Pub Group, 1969.   ○

Wilder, Robert
WIND FROM THE CAROLINAS
A family chronicle beginning with an American family's migration to the Bahamas fol-

lowing the American Revolution, and continuing to the Civil War when they become involved in the blockade and rumrunning. Putnam Pub Group, 1964. ○

B E R M U D A

Series Guidebooks (See Appendix 1)

Berlitz: Bermuda
Birnbaum: The Caribbean, Bermuda & Bahamas
Fielding: Bermuda & Bahamas
Fisher's World: Bermuda
Fodor: Bermuda
Frommer: Bermuda & the Bahamas

Background Reading

Kusche, Larry
THE BERMUDA TRIANGLE MYSTERY—SOLVED
"Debunking is such a delight . . . if it is done with the quiet precision of this book"—written by a reference librarian who has collected information on all the legends and myths about the triangle, and then points out discrepancies and "comprehensible causes" for the vast majority of incidents. (BRD) Prometheus Bks, 1986. ○

LaBrucherie, Roger A.
IMAGES OF BERMUDA
C.E. Tuttle, 1981. ○

Tucker, Terry
BERMUDA: TODAY AND YESTERDAY
St. Martin, 1975. ○

GUIDEBOOKS

Hay, Nelson E.
GUIDE TO THE ALTERNATIVE BERMUDA: HOW TO HAVE A WONDERFUL TIME IN BERMUDA AT A PRICE YOU CAN AFFORD
Sea Pr, 1984. ○

Irwin–Wiener, Susan
BERMUDA
World of Travel, 1989. ○

HISTORY

Wilkinson, Henry C.
BERMUDA FROM SAIL TO STEAM
The history of the Island from 1784 to 1901. Oxford U, 1973. Also the *Adventures of Bermuda* (1976). ○

Novels

Benchley, Peter
BEAST
By the author of *Jaws*. This time a giant squid is the enemy, and he's eating swimmers and anything else he can—"suspense is consistent and compelling." (FC) Random, 1991. ○

Benchley, Peter
THE DEEP
Underwater diving explorations of a sunken World War II cargo ship lead to a heroin cache—"constant flow of information on history, sociology, climate of Bermuda . . . as well as the alarms and beauty" of underwater exploration. (BRD) Doubleday, 1976. ○

Kinsolving, William
BORN WITH THE CENTURY
Story of Magnus MacPherson's rise from Scottish poverty to corporate power. Putnam Pub Group, 1979. ○

Mason, F. Van Wyck
THE SEA VENTURE
Historical novel of Jamestown-bound pioneers who end up in Bermuda. Doubleday, 1961. ○

Mason, F. Van Wyck
THREE HARBOURS
Part of a series on the American Revolution. This part tells of Bermuda's assistance, 1774–78. Lippincott, 1938.   ○

Spikol, Art
THE PHYSALIA INCIDENT
"The Drowning of a Millionaire Is the Focus for This Mystery Set in Bermuda." Viking Penguin, 1988.   ○

CENTRAL AMERICA

Series Guidebooks
(See Appendix 1)

Alive Guide: Guatemala Alive
Fodor: Central America
Frommer: Costa Rica ($-A-Day)
Lonely Planet: La Ruta Maya: Yucatan, Guatemala & Belize; South America (includes Central America & Mexico)
Moon Handbook: Mexico & Central America
Nagel's Encyclopedia Guide: Central America
Real Guide: Guatemala & Belize

Background Reading

NOTE: Books on the Mayas and Aztecs are listed under Mexico.

Barns, Bob
NICA NOTES: A COLLECTION OF NEWSLETTERS FROM A PEACE ACTIVIST'S STAY IN NICARAGUA
The author spent eight months in the country. Friendsview Pr, 1988.   ○

Berryman, Philip
INSIDE CENTRAL AMERICA
The essential facts, past and present, on El Salvador, Nicaragua, Honduras, Guatemala and Costa Rica. Pantheon, 1985.   ○

Davis, Peter
WHERE IS NICARAGUA?
"Thoroughly integrated portrait of Nicaragua's history, culture, politics, personalities and contemporary ambience . . . interpretations favor the Sandinistas nevertheless he paints a clear picture." Things have changed

since the election but this still provides good background reading. (LJ) S&S, 1987.   ○

Evans, G. Russell
SWINDLE: THE PANAMA CANAL TREATIES
The treaties treated from a highly negative viewpoint. Signal Bks, 1984. See also La-Feber, below.   ○

Ford, Peter
AROUND THE EDGE
"Unusual travelogue . . . full of odd bits of chaotic history, languages and local customs." An exploration of Central America's east coast, Belize to Panama by a former *Christian Science Monitor* correspondent for the area—by foot, a barge, a yacht, canoes, all manner of transport. (PW) Viking, 1991.   ○

Huxley, Aldous
BEYOND THE MEXIQUE BAY
A travel diary by the noted writer with "digressions upon many matters suggested by the places visited" in Central America and Mexico. (BRD) Greenwood, 1975 (first published 1934).   ○

Kinzer, Stephen
BLOOD OF BROTHERS: LIFE AND WAR IN NICARAGUA
"Information-rich survey" of Nicaragua by the former *New York Times* bureau chief. (PW) Putnam, 1991.   ○

Knapp, Herbert and Mary
RED, WHITE AND BLUE PARADISE: THE AMERICAN CANAL ZONE IN PANAMA
The authors spent sixteen years in the Zone as teachers, leaving when the treaty went

into effect giving the Canal to Panama. "Notable for its elegantly ironic style . . . a lively examination of the political, sociological and cultural dynamics." (PW) HarBraceJ, 1984. ○

Krauss, Clifford
INSIDE CENTRAL AMERICA
Its people, politics, history and an updating of the issues that dominate each country. Summit Bks, 1991. ○

LaFeber, Walter
THE PANAMA CANAL: THE CRISIS IN HISTORICAL PERSPECTIVE
Updated edition; "disabuses concepts on both sides of the debate and comes up with an extremely readable, cogent argument for the new treaties." (BRD) Oxford U Pr, 1990. ○

McCullough, David
THE PATH BETWEEN THE SEAS
Story of the creation of the Panama Canal, 1870–1914—"readable, informative, exciting. . . . steers readers through political, financial and engineering intricacies without fatigue or muddle." (BRD) S&S, 1978. ○

McGuire, Stryker
STREETS WITH NO NAMES: A JOURNEY INTO CENTRAL & SOUTH AMERICA
The author covered the Nicaraguan revolution for *Newsweek,* and years later this led to his driving 20,000 miles through the two areas and writing this travelogue. "A look at Latin America from the ground up, from the inside out . . . the human reality of everyday life . . . travel writing of the first order." (Publisher) Atl Monthly Pr, 1990. ○

Marnham, Patrick
SO FAR FROM GOD: A JOURNEY TO CENTRAL AMERICA
"A book of travels—though not a travel book"—impressions and images of people encountered, incidents along the way in California, Mexico and Central America by a British reporter. (NYTBR) Viking, 1985. ○

Morris, Mary
NOTHING TO DECLARE
Memoirs of a woman traveling alone through Mexico and Central America. Penguin, 1989. ○

Rolbein, Seth
NOBEL COSTA RICA
A portrait of the country, travelogue and political analysis, including depictions of Arias, its Nobel Prize-winning president (hence the title), his leadership, and history of the country. St. Martin, 1988. ○

Rushdie, Salman
THE JAGUAR'S SMILE: A NICARAGUAN JOURNEY
Generally sympathetic impressions by the novelist who was invited to visit as a guest of the Sandinistas. Viking, 1987. ○

Schwantes, V. David
GUATEMALA: A CRY FROM THE HEART
A Minnesota businessman joins an ecumenical study group visiting Guatemala and the experience has a profound effect as he observes the people and feels he must confront American policy. Health Initiatives Pr, 1990. ○

Setzekorn, William D.
FORMERLY BRITISH HONDURAS: A PROFILE OF THE NEW NATION OF BELIZE
By an architect and travel writer—"provides a mini-encyclopedia on the subject of Belize . . . geographical, cultural and social features [and] tracing its history from its founding in 1638." (TA) Ohio U, 1981. ○

West, Richard
HURRICANE IN NICARAGUA: JOURNAL IN SEARCH OF REVOLUTION
Travelogue, history and personal anecdotes. Viking, 1990. ○

Wright, Ronald
TIME AMONG THE MAYA: TRAVELS IN BELIZE, GUATEMALA & MEXICO

Writes of this area as one contiguous with the United States yet removed by centuries of culture and history, based on his visits to sites of Mayan Indians, ancient and Modern, in Guatemala, Belize, Mexico—"Fuses adventure, politics, archaeology and history in a riveting read." (PW) Weidenfeld, 1989. ○

GUIDEBOOKS

Barry, Tom
BELIZE, COSTA RICA, EL SALVADOR, GUATEMALA, PANAMA

Five individual "country guides." Inter-Hemispheric Education Resource Ctr, 1990. ○

Blake, Beatrice and Becher, Anne
THE NEW KEY TO COSTA RICA

The English-language newspaper *The Tico Times* calls this a gem that's bursting with information for visitors and residents. Wingbow Pr, 1990. ○

Glassman, Paul
BELIZE, COSTA RICA AND GUATEMALA GUIDES

Each guide includes historical background along with usual practical information for tourists and for adventurers and those who want to explore opportunities for fishing, diving. Passport Pr, 1991. ○

Norsworthy, Kent
NICARAGUA: A COUNTRY GUIDE

Inter-Hemispheric Education Resource Center, 1990. ○

Searby, Ellen
THE COSTA RICA TRAVELER

Updated edition of a favorite guide, with critical evaluations of all aspects of travel, shopping, sightseeing, sports, fishing, hunting, parks, museums and theater, as well as how to plan an itinerary and get around in Costa Rica. Windham Bay, 1990. ○

Seavey, William
EDEN-SEEKER'S GUIDE (Costa Rica)
Loompanics, 1989. ○

Sheck, Ree S.
COSTA RICA: A NATURAL DESTINATION

Focuses on the natural splendor of Costa Rica—its park system, rivers, wildlife and wildlife reserves, biological reserves, private nature reserves. Muir, 1990. ○

HISTORY

Brignoli, Hector
A BRIEF HISTORY OF CENTRAL AMERICA

U of California Pr, 1989. ○

Helms, Mary W.
MIDDLE AMERICA: A CULTURE HISTORY OF HEARTLAND AND FRONTIERS

"Crisp, clear introduction" to Mexico and Central America, for the general reader—covers the cultural development from earliest aboriginal people to the twentieth century. (BRD) U. Pr of America, 1982. ○

Jorden, William J.
PANAMA ODYSSEY: FROM COLONIALISM TO PARTNERSHIP

U of Texas, 1984. ○

Parker, Franklin D.
THE CENTRAL AMERICAN REPUBLICS

Survey history of Guatemala, Nicaragua, Honduras, El Salvador and Costa Rica. Greenwood, 1981 (first published 1964). ○

Woodward, Ralph Lee
CENTRAL AMERICA: A NATION DIVIDED

Recommended by *Library Journal* as the best history in English. Oxford U Pr, 1985. ○

Novels

Asturias, Miguel A.
STRONG WIND
First of a trilogy on plantation life in a banana republic in Central America. In this, an enlightened American entrepreneur tries to influence the relationship of American companies and native growers. Delacorte Pr, 1968 (first published 1962). Following is *The Green Pope* (1954) in which a tramp steamer captain becomes representative ("green pope") for a banana company; he meets his downfall in *The Eyes of the Interred* (1960). Also *Mulata* (1967) and *El Señor Presidente* (1964).   ○

Didion, Joan
A BOOK OF COMMON PRAYER
"The quintessential American innocent" involved in a political coup. (FC) S&S, 1977.   ○

Fast, Howard
THE CONFESSION OF JOE CULLEN
A thriller involving a priest, a hooker, the CIA, the Contras and cocaine. Houghton, 1989.   ○

Goldman, Francisco
THE LONG NIGHT OF WHITE CHICKENS (Guatemala)
"Combining the magic realism of Gabriel Garcia Marquez with the distinctly American voice of a young Salinger"—a bicultural novel set in the 1980s, and about a young man, raised in Boston, and his relationship with a Guatemalan orphan who is later murdered in Guatemala. (Publisher) Atl Monthly Pr, 1992.   ○

Macaulay, Rose
STAYING WITH RELATIONS (Guatemala)
Reprint of a novel first published in 1930. A young novelist visits relatives in Guatemala and finds "a motley assortment of relations . . . in a rococo dwelling . . . on the edge of a steaming Central American jungle" where all sorts of things happen, given the effect of members of the group upon one another. (BRD) Ecco Pr, 1987.   ○

Mason, Robert
WEAPON
An anti-Contra, anti-CIA science fiction thriller in which the main character is a robot—"straightforward thriller . . . fascinating exploration into . . . artificial intelligence." (FC) Putnam, 1989.   ○

Overgard, William
A FEW GOOD MEN
Historical novel of Sandino and Nicaragua with a plot involving the kidnapping of the American consul's daughter. St. Martin, 1988.   ○

Peters, Daniel
TIKAL; A NOVEL ABOUT THE MAYA (Guatemala)
Tikal was a Mayan city in southern Central America (Guatemala) more than 1,000 years ago, which was mysteriously evacuated. The novel creates a hypothesis of reasons for the exodus—"rich in texture [and] thorough knowledge of Mayan customs." (FC) Random, 1983.   ○

Stone, Robert
A FLAG FOR SUNRISE
A political novel of ideas, and a thriller, set in a fictional Central American country. Knopf, 1981.   ○

Theroux, Paul
THE MOSQUITO COAST
An American inventor, accompanied by his family, pursues his obsession to be totally self-sufficient on the wild coast of Honduras. Houghton, 1982.   ○

Thomas, Ross
MISSIONARY STEW
"Intricately plotted, entertaining literary romp . . . witty dialogue . . . unconventional situations" in a novel set in twentieth-century Central America—an "examination of the abuse of power." (FC) S&S, 1983.   ○

Westbrook, Robert
NOSTALGIA KILLS
Lieutenant Rachmaninoff of Beverly Hills Police Department, while vacationing in Nicaragua, gets involved in a scheme to restore the Sandinistas to power—a thriller

and social satire of Hollywood's leftist community. Crown, 1988.   o

Westlake, Donald E.
HIGH ADVENTURE (Belize)
Art theft among the Mayan ruins of Belize. Mysterious Pr, 1985.   o

MEXICO

*Series Guidebooks
(See Appendix 1)*

American Express Pocket Guide: Mexico
Baedeker: Mexico
Berlitz: Mexico City
Birnbaum: Mexico
Crown Insider's Guide: Mexico
Fielding: Mexico
Fisher's World: Mexico
Fodor: Acapulco; Cancun, Cozumel & Yucatan Peninsula; Mexico; Mexico City
Frommer: Mexico City & Acapulco; Cancun, Cozumel & the Yucatan; Mexico ($-A-Day)
Hildebrand: Mexico
Insider's Guide: Mexico
Insight Guide: Mexico; Mexico City
Langenscheidt: Self-Guided Mexico
Let's Go: Mexico; California & Hawaii (includes Baja Peninsula)
Lonely Planet: South America (includes Central America & Mexico); Baja California; Mexico
Michelin: Mexico
Moon Handbook: Cancun; Yucatan
Nagel's Encyclopedia Guide: Mexico
Real Guide: Mexico
2–22 Days Itinerary Planning Guide: Mexico

Background Reading

Horgan, Paul
GREAT RIVER: THE RIO GRANDE IN NORTH AMERICAN HISTORY
"A joy to read"—history of the river and the entire border region of New Mexico and Texas from ancient days to modern times. Part 1 is about the Indians and Spain, Part

2 about Mexico and the United States. (BRD) Texas Monthly Pr, 1984 (first published 1954).   o

Kandell, Jonathan
LA CAPITAL: THE BIOGRAPHY OF MEXICO CITY
By a Latin American correspondent for *The New York Times*. Recreates Mexico City from prehistoric time to present day through its political and cultural evolution—"narrative skill is superb . . . scholarship impeccable . . . deliciously detailed, animated book that gives the reader a definite sense of what it was like to live in Mexico City during each of its tumultuous epochs." (BL) Random, 1988.   o

Lewis, Oscar
THE CHILDREN OF SANCHEZ
An in-depth study of one family in Mexico City. Random, 1966 (first published 1961). Also *Death in the Sanchez Family* (1969).   o

Lockwood, C.C.
THE YUCATAN PENINSULA
Informal narration of the author's adventures, with photographs, of an exploration over eight months into this "naturalist's paradise." (PW) Louisiana State U Pr, 1989.   o

Oster, Patrick
THE MEXICANS: A PERSONAL PORTRAIT OF A PEOPLE
"A realistic and captivating view of Mexico" through a series of biographies of a cross-section of Mexicans—men, women, gays, intellectuals, farm workers and more, who

reflect Mexican society and its problems. (LJ) Morrow, 1989.   ○

Parmenter, Ross
LAWRENCE IN OAXACA: A QUEST FOR THE NOVELIST IN MEXICO

Scenes and sketches of Lawrence's life in Oaxaca that led to *Mornings in Mexico* (1927) and *The Plumed Serpent* (1926), and other writings during the period 1922–25—"fresh glimpses of [Lawrence's] extraordinarily changeable personality." (NYTBR) Peregrine Smith, 1985.   ○

Paz, Octavio
THE LABYRINTH OF SOLITUDE

An analysis of Mexican life and thought by a major poet. Grove, 1983 (first published 1962).   ○

Riding, Alan
DISTANT NEIGHBORS: PORTRAIT OF THE MEXICANS

By a foreign correspondent for the *New York Times*—"short historical background . . . the diverse heritage [and] economic situation and monumental problems" with profiles of major figures on the Mexican scene. "Assessments are pungent and provocative." (BL) Knopf, 1984.   ○

Rodman, Selden
A SHORT HISTORY OF MEXICO

This is a newly revised edition of *The Mexico Traveler; a Concise History and Guide*, published in 1969, and is a summary of history, painting, architecture and literature by an art critic and travel writer. Stein & Day, 1982.   ○

Walker, Ronald G.
INFERNAL PARADISE: MEXICO AND THE MODERN ENGLISH NOVEL

The book is an analysis of the fascination Mexico has held for writers Lawrence, Huxley, Graham Greene and Malcolm Lowry, the journeys they made and an analysis of the fiction that emerged. U of California, 1978.   ○

TRAVELOGUES, MEMOIRS

Adams, Alice
MEXICO: SOME TRAVELS AND SOME TRAVELERS THERE

Part of the "Destinations" series of travel books—a novelist explains her love for Mexico. "Shows a different side of Mexico from the guidebooks . . . bleaker [yet] more colorful and exotic." (LJ) S&S, 1991.   ○

Conrad, Jim
ON THE ROAD TO TETLAMA: MEXICAN ADVENTURES OF A WANDERING NATURALIST

A biologist from Kentucky takes off for "a summer of anarchy" in this travelogue of his adventures and misadventures in the central Mexican back country as an "observer and intimate participant." (LJ) Walker, 1991.   ○

Diaz Del Castillo, Bernal
CONQUEST OF NEW SPAIN

Eyewitness account, by a man of letters and a soldier, under Cortes, which has come to be a favorite "travel" book. Late in life the author wrote this retrospective account. Penguin, 1963.   ○

Flandrau, Charles M.
VIVA MEXICO! A TRAVELLER'S ACCOUNT OF LIFE IN MEXICO

Mexico of 1908, that is—reprint of Flandrau's travelogue that touches on religious and political issues and a range of topics. Hippocrene, 1985.   ○

Greene, Graham
ANOTHER MEXICO

"Impressionistic, personal account . . . with a jaundiced eye" of the author's visit in the spring of 1938. (BRD) Viking, 1981 (first published 1939). Also *The Lawless Roads* (1971), another memoir of Mexico which led to his novel *The Power and the Glory* (1940).   ○

Lawrence, D.H.
MORNINGS IN MEXICO

"Pleasant, sun-baked essays . . . studies of the Mexican Indian in his life and at his rites." (BRD) Peregrine Smith, 1982 (first published 1927). ο

Lincoln, John
ONE MAN'S MEXICO
Based on this English writer's travel experiences (1958–64), about the "intrepid" school of travel. One reviewer comments: "best exposition of Mexico's past and present predicament" to have come to his attention—people watching, travels along the coast and in the mountains, experiences with LSD. (BRD) Hippocrene, 1983 (first published 1968). ο

Simon, Kate
MEXICO: PLACES AND PLEASURES
Essays, vignettes, sketches and a travel guide, by a noted travel writer. Har-Row, 1988. ο

Steinbeck, John
SEA OF CORTEZ
A leisurely journey of travel and research on marine animals by the novelist. Appel, 1971 (first published 1941). ο

THE MAYAS AND THE AZTECS

Bernal, Ignacio
A HISTORY OF MEXICAN ARCHAEOLOGY: THE VANISHED CIVILIZATIONS OF MIDDLE AMERICA
Traces prehistoric Mexican society through accounts by early travelers and conquerors, and modern archaeologists—read for pleasure or information. Thames Hudson, 1980. ο

Coe, Michael D.
THE MAYA
Distills "the essence of Maya civilization for the average reader." (BRD) Thames Hudson, 1987. ο

Fagan, Brian M.
THE AZTECS
Introduction to the Aztec world—"a complete and accurate portrait of the people and their culture." (BL) Freeman, 1984. ο

Morley, Sylvanus G. and George W.
THE ANCIENT MAYA
Originally written twenty-five years ago, new discoveries and interpretations have been added while retaining features that originally made this book the most popular introduction to the Mayan world at the time it was first published. Stanford U, 1981 (first published 1956). ο

Pearce, Kenneth
THE VIEW FROM THE TOP OF THE TEMPLE
Guides the reader "through ruins and resorts . . . rituals and customs the modern Maya have steadfastly preserved . . . mingles tales of archaeological shenanigans with tips on what roads to take and where and what to expect when you arrive." (TL) U of New Mexico, 1984. ο

Perry, Richard and Rosalind W.
MAYA MISSIONS: EXPLORING THE SPANISH COLONIAL CHURCHES OF YUCATAN
One of a projected series of regional guides to Mexican missions, 16th-century monasteries set atop ancient pyramids, quaint village chapels, religious folk art, vernacular architecture. Includes itineraries, maps and plans, original drawings—for travelers, art and architecture aficionados. Espadana Pr, 1988. ο

BAJA CALIFORNIA

Krutch, Joseph
THE FORGOTTEN PENINSULA
By a leading naturalist and writer about nature—flora, fauna, whales, desert and sea. U of Arizona Pr, 1986. ο

Miller, Tom
BAJA BOOK III
Also *Angler's Guide* and *Baja California Diver's Guide*. Baja Trail, 1989. ο

Nelson, Mike and Zamba, Michael, Jr.
BAJA FOR BEGINNERS: ACCESSIBLE, IRRESISTIBLE AND SENSATIONAL
One of a series—Mexico By Land. Travelog, 1991. ο

Williams, Jack, ed.
THE MAGNIFICENT PENINSULA
A comprehensive guide to Baja California.
HJ Williams, 1989.   ○

GUIDEBOOKS

Note also guidebooks listed above under
"Archaeology" and "Baja California."   ○

Babcock, Judy and Kennedy, Judy
THE SPA BOOK
See under "Caribbean/Guidebooks."   ○

Barker, Joanne H. and Stone, Jack
**MOTORING MEXICO: COMPLETE
GUIDE TO TOURING MEXICO
BY CAR**
"Touts the joys . . . ends it with a lot of
cautions." (LJ) Doubleday, 1987.   ○

Barroso, Memo
**THE PACIFIC COAST OF MEXICO:
FROM MAZATLAN TO IXTAPA-
ZIHUATANEJO**
"An upbeat guide with good coverage of
practical matters"—does not include Aca-
pulco. Crown, 1986.   ○

Burleson, Bob & Riskind, David H.
**BACKCOUNTRY MEXICO: A
TRAVELER'S GUIDE & PHRASE
BOOK**
U of Texas Pr, 1986.   ○

Farley, Michael & Lauren
**DIVER'S GUIDE TO UNDERWATER
MEXICO**
Marcor Pub, 1986.   ○

Franz, Carl
THE PEOPLE'S GUIDE TO MEXICO
A classic by an author who, it is said, knows
Mexico better than anyone. The *Los Angeles
Times* says, "The text is whimsically refresh-
ing . . . expertly detailed . . . after reading
it . . . a resident could mistake you for a
native." John Muir, 1990.   ○

Nelson, Mike
**FOREIGN AFFAIRS FOR
WEEKENDERS**
One of a series called Mexico by Land. Trav-
elog, 1991.   ○

HISTORY

Miller, Robert Ryal
MEXICO: A HISTORY
"A superb synthesis of Mexico's complex
history." (LJ) U of Oklahoma Pr, 1985.   ○

Prescott, William H.
**THE HISTORY OF THE CONQUEST
OF MEXICO**
Abridged edition of a classic history, origi-
nally published in 1843. U of Chicago Pr,
1985.   ○

Rodman, Selden
SHORT HISTORY OF MEXICO
Scarborough Hse, 1982.   ○

Novels

Adams, Harold
WHEN RICH MEN DIE
A former TV anchorman is hired to find
a corpse—"glittering scenes of Mexico
make this a real thriller." (FC) Doubleday,
1987.   ○

Azuela, Mariano
**TWO NOVELS OF THE MEXICAN
REVOLUTION**
The Flies and *The Bosses*. First published 1915,
1918. U of Cal Pr, 1956. Also *Underdogs*. ○

Bagley, Desmond
THE VIVERO LETTER (Yucatan)
An archaeological thriller—a London ac-
countant solves his brother's murder. Doubleday, 1968.   ○

Brawley, Ernest
THE ALAMO TREE
A saga of two contrasting families set in
Manzanillo and Acapulco and how the po-
litical, economic and social conditions shape
their lives. S&S, 1984.   ○

Doerr, Harriet
STONES FOR IBARRA
An American couple move to a small town in Mexico where they hope to revitalize a copper mine. Episodes of village life alternate with those of the couple's experiences. Viking, 1984.   ○

Elkins, Aaron J.
CURSES!
The setting is an archaeological dig on the Yucatan Peninsula; the plot concerns a scandal five years earlier and an ancient curse. Mysterious Pr, 1989.   ○

Fuentes, Carlos
THE OLD GRINGO
"Clever fictional use of an actual literary mystery"—journalist/writer Ambrose Bierce's last days with Pancho Villa. (BRD) FS&G, 1985.   ○

Fuentes, Carlos
TERRA NOSTRA
"Fusion of history, myth and fiction on a grand scale. . . . the major work of the most important Mexican writer." (BRD) FS&G, 1976. Also, by Fuentes, *Where the Air Is Clear* (1960), *A Change of Skin* (1968), *The Death of Artemio Cruz* (1964), *The Hydra Head* (1978), *Burnt Water* (1980).   ○

Greene, Graham
THE POWER AND THE GLORY
A Catholic priest on the run is the central character—"the atmosphere and detail [of Mexico] are convincing." (FC) Viking, 1968 (first published 1940). See also *Another Mexico* under Background Reading, above.   ○

Hall, Oakley
THE CHILDREN OF THE SUN
"A strange, bloody, haunting historical novel" of a failed Spanish expedition to Florida and an historic 1,600-mile journey to Mexico to search for Cibola. (FC) Atheneum, 1983.   ○

Hebden, Mark
PEL AMONG THE PUEBLOS
Pel is a detective normally working out of the Burgundy section of France; in this he has to locate a killer in Mexico. Walker, 1988.   ○

Highwater, Jamake
THE SUN HE DIES: A NOVEL ABOUT THE END OF THE AZTEC WORLD
Narrated by Montezuma's chamberlain, it tells how the 2000-year old Aztec civilization was destroyed by Cortez in six years. Lippincott, 1980.   ○

Jennings, Gary
AZTEC
Reminiscences of an Aztec Indian before and after Cortez—accurate history blended with fictional drama. Atheneum, 1980.   ○

Lawrence, D.H.
THE PLUMED SERPENT
"A powerful, vivid evocation of Mexico and its ancient Aztec religion." (FC) Random, 1955 (first published 1926).   ○

Lea, Tom
THE BRAVE BULLS
A famous bullfighter recalls his past life. Little, 1949. Also, *The Wonderful Country* (1952).   ○

Lowry, Malcolm
UNDER THE VOLCANO
Remembrances of things past of a British ex-consul drinking himself to death. Har-Row, 1984 (first published 1947).   ○

MacDonald John D.
DRESS HER IN INDIGO
Travis McGee murder mystery set in Oaxaca "among the gay, the depraved . . . drug addicted and the violent." (FC) Lippincott, 1971. Also, set in Mexico, *Cinnamon Skin* (1982), *A Deadly Shade of Gold* (1965).   ○

Michener, James A.
THE EAGLE AND THE RAVEN
Fictional account of Sam Houston and Santa Anna, and their encounter that led to the annexation of Texas by the United States— "engaging slice of Americana and Texas lore." (FC) State House Pr, 1990.   ○

Moss, Robert
MEXICO WAY
"An incredible scenario" of an attempt by a cabal in the U.S. government to create a new state in northern Mexico. (FC) S&S, 1991.   ○

Murphy, Pat
THE FALLING WOMAN
An archaeologist, deeply involved with her work in Yucatan, conjures up the ghost of a Mayan priestess. Tor Bks, 1986.   ○

Murray, William
THE KING OF THE NIGHTCAP
Tiajuana's Caliente racetrack is the setting and focus for this story of a scam to smuggle Mayan artifacts across the border. Bantam Bks, 1989.   ○

Portis, Charles
GRINGOS
"Murder, adventure . . . animate a Mexico aswarm" with a motley group of expatriates. (FC) S&S, 1991.   ○

Shellabarger, Samuel
CAPTAIN FROM CASTILE
A young Spaniard joins Cortez in the capture of Mexico City in the sixteenth century. Little, 1945.   ○

Shiner, Lewis
DESERTED CITIES OF THE HEART
Fast-moving adventure story about modern-day Mexico. Doubleday, 1988.   ○

Steinbeck, John
THE PEARL
A parable based on a Mexican folk tale of a fishing family and the finding of a great pearl. Viking, 1947.   ○

Stone, Robert
CHILDREN OF LIGHT
The claustrophobic world of a movie set on the coast of Mexico is the setting—"crackles with conflict, intrigue, and malice." (FC) Knopf, 1986.   ○

Traven, B.
THE TREASURE OF THE SIERRA MADRE
Basis for the classic movie of the search by three American "have-nots" for gold in the mountains of Mexico. Hill & Wang, 1967 (first published 1927). Also *The Carreta* (1931), about the poverty and naivete of the Mexican peasantry.   ○

SOUTH AMERICA

Series Guidebooks (See Appendix 1)

Birnbaum: South America
Fodor: South America
Frommer: South America ($-A-Day)
Insight: South America
Lonely Planet: South America (includes Central America & Mexico)
Michael's Guide: South America
Moon Handbook: South America

Note: Books on the Incas are entered under "Peru"; on Patagonia see under "Argentina."

Background Reading

Bemelmans, Ludwig
THE DONKEY INSIDE
South American travels by the famous illustrator/author of *Madeline* books for children. Paragon Hse, 1990.   ○

Daniels, Anthony
COUPS AND COCAINE: TWO JOURNEYS IN SOUTH AMERICA
"Lively, unexpected" commentary of a British physician traveling in Brazil, Bolivia, Chile, Ecuador, Paraguay and Peru—talking to peasants, tourists, clerics, physicians, descriptions of landscapes and people

"often with merciless malice." (BL) Viking, 1987.   o

Kandell, Jonathan
PASSAGE THROUGH EL DORADO: THE CONQUEST OF THE WORLD'S LAST GREAT WILDERNESS
Account of a journey through the Amazon basin, an area that involves six nations, and the land rush going on in that part of the world today, with comparisons to our own westward migration in the nineteenth century. A "serious, probing and revealing book"—the author traveled the area and talked to many, from squatters and Indians to drug dealers and ranchers. (LJ) Morrow, 1984.   o

Leitch, William C.
SOUTH AMERICA'S NATIONAL PARKS
A guide for visitors to national parks that offers spectacular scenery, and unusual and rare flora and fauna for the nature enthusiast. Both a background book for pre-travel planning and a source of practical tourist information. Mountaineers, 1990.   o

McGuire, Stryker
STREETS WITH NO NAMES
See entry under Central America/Background Reading.   o

McIntyre, Loren
EXPLORING SOUTH AMERICA
A photographic journey with essays that makes the case for the diversity of South America as a continent—for people who think of it as a homogeneous place. Clarkson N Potter, 1990.   o

Matthiessen, Peter
THE CLOUD FOREST: A CHRONICLE OF THE SOUTH AMERICAN WILDERNESS
Chronicle of an eight-month journey by air, land and water to the Amazon, Macchu Picchu and other parts of the continent. Penguin, 1987 (first published 1961).   o

Morris, Arthur S.
SOUTH AMERICA
A handbook that emphasizes the variety of geography, history, cultures and economies in South America. B&N Imports, 1987.   o

Rodman, Selden
SOUTH AMERICA OF THE POETS
Describes a journey through most of South America, meetings with the outstanding writers—a travel book with insights into the culture of each country. Southern Illinois U, 1972.   o

Topolski, Daniel and Feliks
TRAVELS WITH MY FATHER: A SOUTH AMERICAN JOURNEY
An itinerary covering most of the continent with emphasis on "pursuit of the erotic and dangerous." (BL) Hamish Hamilton, 1984.   o

Tschiffely, A.F.
SOUTHERN CROSS TO POLE STAR—TSCHIFFELY'S RIDE
Reprint of a travel classic which recounts the "remarkable, often terrifying exploits" of a Swiss schoolmaster and his two aging Criollo-bred ponies in a 10,000-mile, two-and-one-half year journey from Buenos Aires to Washington, D.C. (BRD) Tarcher, 1982 (first published 1933).   o

THE AMAZON AND THE ANDES

Cameron, Ian
THE KINGDOM OF THE SUN GOD: A HISTORY OF THE ANDES AND THEIR PEOPLE
"A richly detailed account of the mountain range's geology, natural history, and cultural heritage from prehistoric times to the modern era . . . a lively text and beautiful illustrations." (Publisher) Facts On File, 1991.   o

Cousteau, Jacques-Yves
JACQUES COUSTEAU'S AMAZON JOURNEY
Combination of Cousteau's journals, coauthor Mose Richards' account of the logistics,

and wonderful photographs. Abrams, 1984.   ○

Dwyer, Augusta
INTO THE AMAZON: THE STRUGGLE FOR THE RAIN FOREST
Chronicles of a freelance journalist based in Brazil—"pithy details and a poetic touch . . . an air of the unexpected." (PW) Sierra Club, 1991.   ○

Fawcett, P.H.
LOST TRAILS, LOST CITIES
A classic in its field written by an explorer following his seventh trip into the Amazon area (he vanished on his eighth trip). Book Club, 1974. Also *Exploration Fawcett*, 1988.   ○

Kane, Joe
RUNNING THE AMAZON
Account of a group of 10 that set out to travel from the source of the Andes to the Atlantic Ocean—only four survived the weather, bandits, mutiny and illness. Knopf, 1990.   ○

Kelly, Brian and London, Mark
AMAZON
Colorful, evocative account of the frontier being developed and exploited by entrepreneurs. The book is based on a trip sponsored by the *Chicago Sun-Times* and calls to mind parallels in the expansion of our own Wild West. HarBraceJ, 1983.   ○

Morrison, Tony and others
LIZZIE: A VICTORIAN LADY'S AMAZON ADVENTURE
Morrison discovered her great-aunt Lizzie's letters in the 1970s; Lizzie had been the wife of a rubber company manager 1896–99. This book is the result. "A gripping book . . . Lizzie's lively, uninhibited, uncomplaining reports are more vivid" than the period and modern photos of the area that are part of the book. Parkwest, 1987.   ○

Murphy, Dervla
EIGHT FEET IN THE ANDES
The "eight feet" are those of Dervla, her young daughter and the mule—account by an adventurous woman traveler following Pizarro's route through the Andes. Overlook Pr, 1986.   ○

O'Hanlon, Redmond
IN TROUBLE AGAIN: A JOURNEY BETWEEN THE ORINOCO AND THE AMAZON
By the author of *Into the Heart of Borneo*, one of the best contemporary travel writers. An account of a four-month trip up the Orinoco and across the Amazon Basin, encounters with diseases and exotic wildlife. "This is Monty Python meets Dr. Livingstone . . . [without] palaver about noble motivations or thwarted expectations. He travels in order to see how bad things can get, reveling in the perversity of the human spirit." Atl Monthly Pr, 1989.   ○

Peters, Daniel
THE INCAS: FROM ANDEAN PEAKS TO AMAZONIAN JUNGLE
The last years of the Incas before the arrival of Pizarro. Random, 1991.   ○

Shoumatoff, Alex
THE RIVERS AMAZON
A multi-faceted travelogue of jungle life, flora and fauna for the lay naturalist, a stay in a village, a cross-country trek, and a search for the source of the Amazon. Sierra Club, 1986. See also *In Southern Light* (1986) under Central Africa.   ○

Shukman, Henry
SONS OF THE MOON
A solo trip from Argentina to Peru via Bolivia by walking, hitchhiking and lorry— "vivid descriptions . . . dance across the pages . . . one of the most enjoyable travel books in years"—along with some history and myth. The purpose of the trip was to seek the Aymara culture that pre-dates that of the Incas, in the Altiplano area of the Andes. (LJ) Scribner, 1990.   ○

Smith, Anthony
EXPLORERS OF THE AMAZON
History of explorations and explorers of the river. Viking, 1990.   ○

Stone, Roger D.
DREAMS OF AMAZONIA
History, personal experiences and interviews to support the author's thesis that human nature has an "inevitable need to pursue the dream of a conquered land." (BL) Viking, 1985.   ◦

Tomlinson, H.M.
THE SEA AND THE JUNGLE
Firsthand account of a trip made in the early 1900s from Swansea, Wales, across the ocean, and up the Amazon for 2,000 miles—observations and yarns about shipmates. Marlboro Pr, 1989 (first published 1912).   ◦

Wakefield, Celia
HIGH CITIES OF THE ANDES
Memoir of a septuagenarian's adventures in the Andes. The reviewer found her emphasis on Latin American stereotypes off-putting, but when describing "sights, sounds, and smells . . . Inca lore she is top-notch." Includes an excellent supplementary reading list. Wide World Pub, 1988.   ◦

Werner, Dennis
AMAZON JOURNEY: AN ANTHROPOLOGIST'S YEAR AMONG BRAZIL'S MEKRANOTI INDIANS
Research among one of the few tribes that still preserves its traditional way of life—"a fascinating and charming work." (BL) S&S, 1984.   ◦

Zalis, Paul
WHO IS THE RIVER: GETTING LOST AND FOUND IN THE AMAZON AND OTHER PLACES
Two counterculture survivors from California, with a guide, wander the river looking

for ancient pyramids—"offbeat travel writing . . . raucous and thoroughly involving adventure." (BL) Atheneum, 1986.   ◦

THE FALKLANDS

Charlton, Michael
THE LONG STRUGGLE FOR THE FALKLANDS
Basil Blackwell, 1989.   ◦

Strange, Ian J.
FALKLAND ISLANDS
All aspects of the islands—history, geography, wildlife, the people and their daily lives in the countryside—and updated to include the recent conflict. David, 1983.   ◦

GUIDEBOOKS

Brooks, John, ed.
SOUTH AMERICAN HANDBOOK
Includes all of Latin America, with comprehensive information on history and culture along with information for travelers on accommodations, what to see, recommended excursions, many maps. S&S, 1990.   ◦

Frazier, Charles and Secreast, Donald
ADVENTURING IN THE ANDES
The Sierra Club traveler's guide to Ecuador, Peru, Bolivia, the Amazon Basin and Galapagos Islands. Sierra, 1985.   ◦

Jacobs, Charles & Babette
SOUTH AMERICAN TRAVEL DIGEST
Designed for travel agents—the "bible" on South America. Travel Digests, 1986.   ◦

ANTARCTICA

Background Reading

Adams, Richard and Lockley, Ronald
VOYAGE THROUGH THE ANTARCTIC
An account of a tour to Antarctica (and

Argentina and New Zealand) by a naturalist (author of *Watership Down*), as part of a Lindblad *Explorer* tour—"a delightful book . . . a birdwatcher's dream." (PW) Knopf, 1982.   ◦

Fogg, G.E.
THE EXPLORATIONS OF ANTARCTICA: THE LAST UNSPOILT CONTINENT

"Lucid text recreates explorations . . . geography, landscape and wildlife . . . the only place on earth that all major nations have agreed not to exploit"—with photographs, reproductions of oil and watercolor paintings. Cassell, 1990.   ○

Gould, Laurence M.
ANTARCTIC COLD

Richard Byrd called this account of the Byrd expedition in 1929–30 "a story without parallel in Antarctic literature." (BRD) Carleton Coll, 1984.   ○

Huntford, Roland
THE LAST PLACE ON EARTH

The race of Amundsen and Scott to reach the South Pole. Atheneum, 1985.   ○

May, John
THE GREENPEACE BOOK OF ANTARCTICA: A NEAR VIEW OF THE SEVENTH CONTINENT

Armchair travelers can be transported to this remote place. "Insights into Antarctica's geography, geology, flora and fauna . . . human impact . . . plea for a world park to preserve the last, vast, relatively pristine area of the globe." (LJ) Doubleday, 1989. ○

Mickleburgh, Edwin
BEYOND THE FROZEN SEA

A colorful history of explorations from 1773, when Captain Cook first sighted the continent, and on to contemporary scientific expeditions and a warning against exploitation. St. Martin, 1988.   ○

Parfit, Michael
SOUTH LIGHT: A JOURNEY TO THE LAST CONTINENT

An account of the author's adventurous visit to Antarctica—"exceptionally well told story . . . filled with humor and awe." (BL) Macmillan, 1986.   ○

Novels

Batchelor, John C.
THE BIRTH OF THE PEOPLE'S REPUBLIC OF ANTARCTICA

A band of Swedish exiles, at the end of the twentieth century, after epic voyages from the Baltic to the South Atlantic, flee to Antarctica where the group leader becomes a "berserker warlord." (FC) Dial, 1983.   ○

Charbonneau, Louis
THE ICE: A NOVEL OF ANTARCTICA

"Timely, credible and suspenseful eco-thriller"—a marine biologist and her associates foil a U.S. conglomerate's plans for the Antarctic. Fine, 1991.   ○

Herbert, Marie
WINTER OF THE WHITE SEAL

Diary epic of a hero marooned on an island and the seal pup he befriends who, in turn, gives him the heart to persevere. Morrow, 1982.   ○

Holt, Karé
THE FACE: A NOVEL OF POLAR EXPLORATION

Documentary novel about the race between Scott and Amundsen to reach the South Pole. Delacorte Pr, 1976.   ○

Sillitoe, Alan
THE LOST FLYING BOAT

An RAF bomber crew at the close of World War II unknowingly becomes part of a treasure hunt for gold buried beneath Antarctic ice. Little, 1984.   ○

ARGENTINA

Series Guidebooks
(See Appendix 1)

Alive Series: Buenos Aires Alive
Insight Guide: Argentina; Buenos Aires

Lonely Planet: Argentina
Michael's Guide: Argentina, Chile, Paraguay & Uruguay

Background Reading

Chatwin, Bruce
IN PATAGONIA
A collection of "good stories" of the region's past—"a work of travel, observation . . . learning, reflection and art." The author is a descendant of a British sea captain who lost his ship in the Strait of Magellan when that was the only way to go from the Atlantic to the Pacific. (BRD) Summit Bks, 1977. Also *Patagonia Revisited* (1985), with Paul Theroux.   ○

Fraser, Nicholas and Navarro, Marysa
EVA PERON
"Thoroughly researched and historically accurate . . . fascinating story of her life, achievements and shrewdness." (LJ) Norton, 1985.   ○

Graham-Yooll, Andrew
A STATE OF FEAR: MEMORIES OF ARGENTINA'S NIGHTMARE
The author was news editor for the *Buenos Aires Herald* for 10 years, as friends and acquaintances disappeared; a frightening, chilling picture of life under a dictatorship that allowed no deviation of opinion whatsoever. After being forced to flee, he nevertheless made return journeys. Hippocrene, 1986.   ○

Hudson, W.H.
FAR AWAY AND LONG AGO
An autobiography of the author's early days on the pampas, of which he later wrote in essays and stories—"like a mixture of a Conrad novel and Robinson Crusoe." Reprint of 1923 edition. AMS Pr, n.d. Also *Idle Days in Patagonia*, his classic book of a journey on the Rio Negro to Patagonia; from a 1923 edition, reprint by AMS Pr, n.d.   ○

Partnoy, Alicia
THE LITTLE SCHOOL
Tales of disappearance and survival in Argentina. Gleis Pr, 1987.   ○

Taber, Sara Mansfield
DUSK ON THE CAMPO: A JOURNEY IN PATAGONIA
"Revealing, candid, look at a remote corner of the world." Oral histories of descendents of Basque and Spanish pioneers—"the rites and rhythms of the sheepherder's year, the exotic flora and fauna." (PW) Holt, 1991. ○

HISTORY

Crawley, Eduardo
A HOUSE DIVIDED: ARGENTINA, 1880–1980
St. Martin, 1984.   ○

Mainwaring, Michael
FROM THE FALKLANDS TO PATAGONIA
Schocken, 1984.   ○

Novels

Borges, Jorge L.
BORGES: A READER
Selections from his writings that offer a good survey of early and late writing, prose and poetry. Dutton, 1981. Also, *A Personal Anthology* (1967), those writings on which Borges would like his reputation to rest.   ○

Costantini, Humberto
THE GODS, THE LITTLE GUYS, AND THE POLICE
Involves a police plot to massacre a "sadly deluded poetry circle." On one level the novel is "whimsical fantasy [but] beneath the quirky humor lies a frightening picture of political terror." (FC) Har-Row, 1984. ○

Greene, Graham
THE HONORARY CONSUL
Story of political kidnapping that combines violent action with religious speculation. S&S, 1973.   ○

Guiraldes, Ricardo
DON SEGUNDO SOMBRA
"A series of swift and brilliant impressions" of a legendary gaucho of the Argentine pampas told by a boy who works on a ranch

and rides with Don Segundo. (BRD) Farrar, 1935.   ○

Higgins, Jack
EXOCET

A novel about the war in the Falklands and the struggle by the Argentinians to obtain Exocet missiles. Stein & Day, 1983.   ○

Langley, Bob
FALKLANDS GAMBIT

The politics and people of the Falklands and Argentina's attempt to annex it—"portraits of Falklanders as 'more British than the British,' piercing glimpses of Antarctica's beauty and valid political points about Antarctic oil." (PW) Walker, 1985.   ○

Martínez, Tomás E.
THE PERON NOVEL

Originally printed in Argentina in 1985. The rise and fall of Peron, political intrigue and the psyche—"masterfully written, absorbing." (FC) Pantheon, 1988.   ○

Puig, Manuel
BETRAYED BY RITA HAYWORTH

Toto—"born in 1932 in the bleakest flatland pampas of the Argentine"—and his friends are compulsive moviegoers who talk about their own lives through films. (FC) Dutton, 1971. Also *Buenos Aires Affair* (1976), *Heartbreak Tango* (1973) and *Kiss of the Spider Woman* (1979).   ○

Soriano, Osvaldo
WINTER QUARTERS

Two "losers"—a boxer and an ex-tango singer—are invited to a small town to participate in a celebration of the local military. "Manages to convey the decadence of a military regime, the pathos of friendship . . . the callousness of politics." (BRD) Readers Int, 1989.   ○

Thornton, Lawrence
IMAGINING ARGENTINA

When a journalist disappears in 1976, her playwright husband discovers a psychic gift— when someone tells him the last details known of a missing person, he has a vision of that person's present situation. Doubleday, 1987.   ○

BOLIVIA

Series Guidebooks (See Appendix 1)

Lonely Planet: Bolivia
Michael's Guide: Bolivia & Peru
Nagel's Encyclopedia Guide: Bolivia

Background Reading

NOTE: Books on the Andes are listed under South America/The Amazon & the Andes. See also Peru, for books on the Incas.

Lawlor, Eric
IN BOLIVIA

Illuminating vignettes of a country seemingly "in chronic economic and emotional depression." (BL) Random, 1989.   ○

Nash, June
WE EAT THE MINES AND THE MINES EAT US

An anthropological study of a tin-mining town from its "mythological past to the . . . 1952 revolution"—family life, values, and religious and ritual beliefs. (BRD) Columbia U, 1979.   ○

Nouwen, Henri J.M.
GRACIAS! A LATIN AMERICAN JOURNAL

Account of a six-month stay in Bolivia and Peru by a Dutch theologian who lived among the people. Har-Row, 1983.   ○

GUIDEBOOKS

Meisch, Lynn
A TRAVELER'S GUIDE TO EL DORADO AND THE INCA EMPIRE
See under "Peru/Guidebooks." ◯

HISTORY

Morales, Waltrand Q.
BOLIVIA: LAND OF STRUGGLE
Westview Pr, 1991. ◯

Morner, Magnus
THE ANDEAN PAST (Peru, Bolivia, Ecuador)
Columbia U Pr, 1984. ◯

Novels

Pausewang, Gudrun
BOLIVIAN WEDDING
The events of a single All Soul's Day in a Bolivian mountain town. Knopf, 1972. ◯

BRAZIL

Series Guidebooks
(See Appendix 1)

Alive Guide: Rio Alive
Berlitz: Brazil Highlights; Rio de Janeiro
Fisher's World: Brazil
Fodor: Brazil; Rio de Janeiro
Frommer: Rio de Janeiro; Brazil
Insight Guide: Brazil; Rio de Janeiro
Lonely Planet: Brazil
Michael's Guide: Brazil
Nagel's Encyclopedia Guide: Brazil
Real Guide: Brazil

Background Reading

NOTE: See also books entered above under South America/The Amazon & the Andes.

Allen, Benedict
WHO GOES OUT IN THE MIDDAY SUN?
Since the author's adventure ends with him alone, with only a dog, no maps, no canoe, and a 30-day cross-jungle walk, the title is apt—"one of the most harrowing tales of survival in the literature of travel." (PW) Viking Penguin, 1986. ◯

Dos Passos, John
BRAZIL ON THE MOVE
The American novelist spoke Portuguese and visited Brazil in 1948, 1956 and 1962. This is his report on Brasilia at each stage—"gives

the feel of Brazil's wondrously contrasting landscapes." (BRD) Paragon Hse, 1991 (first published 1963). ◯

Fleming, Peter
BRAZILIAN ADVENTURE
Class British travel book of the 1930s of an expedition to Brazil—"it became an adventure for which Rider Haggard might have written the plot, P.G. Wodehouse supplied the characters, and Joseph Conrad designed the scenery." (BRD) Tarcher, 1983 (first published 1933). ◯

Guillermoprieto, Alma
SAMBA
Follows the carnival preparations from the beginning until the Samba school parade in which the author participated—"must reading for anyone who wants to understand the social and spiritual forces that make cariocas move at carnaval time." (CNT) Knopf, 1990. ◯

Morley, Helena
THE DIARY OF HELENA MORLEY
First published privately in Brazil in 1942, it became something of a success among literary circles and is now considered a classic and compared to *Diary of Anne Frank* for the freshness of its insights. Written by a teenage girl, it "vividly captures the landscape of a small provincial Brazilian town." Edited

by Elizabeth Bishop. (Publisher) Ecco Pr, 1991.   ○

O'Hanlon, Redmond
IN TROUBLE AGAIN
See entry under the Amazon and the Andes, above.   ○

Rodman, Selden
THE BRAZIL TRAVELER
Background history for travelers, people and culture, with emphasis on the arts. Devin, 1975.   ○

Shoumatoff, Alex
THE CAPITAL OF HOPE
The story of Brasilia, its people, politics, economic rigors, flora, fauna, climate and architecture. The author, who married into a Brazilian family in the course of doing this book, "wears his knowledge lightly [and] conveys his own sense of wonder" at the creation of the city. (BRD) U of NM Pr, 1987.   ○

Thomsen, Moritz
THE SADDEST PLEASURE
"Imagine that Joseph Conrad, Henry Miller, and Gabriel Garcia Marquez had collaborated on a book about living in Ecuador and traveling through Brazil . . . brooding and evocative, witty and profane, mystical, morbid, full of delight." Tells of an epic journey he made in 1978 up the coast of Brazil, and then by river steamer to Manaus, "seduced by Bahia" en route. (TL) Graywolf Pr, 1990.   ○

Waugh, Evelyn
NINETY-TWO DAYS
See under "Guianas."   ○

GUIDEBOOKS

Bradbury, Alex
BACKCOUNTRY BRAZIL
Hunter Pub, 1990.   ○

Greenberg, Arnold
BRAZIL ON YOUR OWN
Passport Bks, 1988.   ○

Pickard, Christopher
INSIDER'S GUIDE TO RIO DE JANEIRO
Luso-Brazilian Bks, 1986.   ○

Potter, Everett
THE BEST OF BRAZIL
"Fills the bill perfectly by focusing on the *best* things to do . . . not necessarily the most expensive . . . complete and well organized." (BL) Crown, 1988.   ○

HISTORY

Barman, Roderick J.
BRAZIL
Stanford U Pr, 1988.   ○

Burns, E. Bradford
A HISTORY OF BRAZIL
Updated version of a standard history. Columbia U, 1980.   ○

Novels

Alegria, Ciro
THE GOLDEN SERPENT
Story of primitive Indian life on the Marañon River, and a white engineer who comes to make his fortune. FS&G, 1935.   ○

Amado, Jorge
PEN, SWORD, CAMISOLE: A FABLE TO KINDLE A HOPE
Intrigue and political maneuvering to fill a seat in the Brazilian Academy of Letters. Godine, 1985. Also *Showdown* (1988).   ○

Amado, Jorge
TEREZA BATISTA: HOME FROM THE WARS
One of many novels by this author that provide insights for the traveler into Latin American culture—"the warmth, gaiety and romance of an Amado novel are always a special treat." Knopf, 1975. Other titles set in Brazil are: *Tieta the Goat Girl* (1979), *Tent of Miracles* (1971), *Dona Flor and Her Two Husbands* (1969), *Gabriela Clove and Cinnamon* (1962), *Shepherds of the Night* (1967), *Home is the Sailor* (1964), *The Violent Land* (1965).   ○

Courter, Gay
RIVER OF DREAMS

A young American from New Orleans sets off to join her parents—a saga that captures the atmosphere and spirit of post-civil war Brazil and "large chunks of Brazilian history." (FC) Houghton, 1984.   ○

Fonseca, Rubem
HIGH ART

"Elegant and subtle" detective novel with bizarre, violent characters, about a criminal attorney who becomes a quarry when his investigation into the deaths of prostitutes connects to a criminal organization. (BRD) Carroll & Graf, 1987.   ○

Levin, Ira
THE BOYS FROM BRAZIL

An organization of ex-Nazis tries to establish a Fourth Reich—"good, clean horror." (FC) Random, 1976.   ○

Lins Do Rego, Jose
PLANTATION BOY

Part of the sugar cane cycle of novels by this author, begun in the 1930s. Knopf, 1966. ○

McDonald, Gregory
CARIOCA FLETCH

Romance and murder at carnival time in Rio. Warner Bks, 1984.   ○

Machado de Assis, Joachim Maria
ESAU AND JACOB

By a leading nineteenth-century Brazilian writer—a novel of social criticism about the rivalry of twin brothers at the end of the Brazilian empire. Also *Epitaph of a Small Winner* (1881) and *Helena* (1876). U of California, 1965 (first published in 1904).   ○

Matthiessen, Peter
AT PLAY IN THE FIELDS OF THE LORD

Four fundamentalist missionaries try to convert the primitive Indians in Oriente province—"the author shines as a naturalist and a storyteller." (BRD) Random, 1965.   ○

Piñeda, Cecile
FACE

Poignant novel of a barber in a coastal city whose face is mutilated in an accident, and who moves to an interior city where he is able to remake his face. Viking, 1985.   ○

Piñon, Nelida
THE REPUBLIC OF DREAMS

Family saga of Brazil, beginning in a Spanish village from whence the patriarch emigrates—"a pointed chronicle of Brazilian history." (FC) Knopf, 1989.   ○

Pryce-Jones, Alan
HOT PLACES

Three novelettes set in Brazil, Chile and Ecuador—"packed with local color." (BRD) Knopf, 1933.   ○

Saint-Exupéry, A. de
NIGHT FLIGHT

The early days of aviation when Buenos Aires was a key airport for night flights of airmail in South America, and the challenge of crossing the Andes. A classic movie, with Helen Hayes, was made from this novel. Century, 1932.   ○

Uys, Errol Lincoln
BRAZIL

Saga, over five centuries, of two remarkable families, and the history of Brazil. S&S, 1986.   ○

Vargas Llosa, Mario
THE WAR OF THE END OF THE WORLD

Based on a bizarre, but true, uprising in northern Brazil at the turn of the century—"brilliant panorama of the forces great and small which fuel a revolution." (FC) FS&G, 1984. Also *The Green House* (1968) set partially in the Amazonian wilderness.   ○

CHILE

Series Guidebooks
(See Appendix 1)

Michael's Guide: Argentina, Chile, Paraguay & Uruguay
Lonely Planet: Chile & Easter Island

Background Reading

García Marquéz, Gabriel
CLANDESTINE IN CHILE
The adventures of Miguel Littin—a first-person account of a movie director's clandestine filming of a documentary on life under Pinochet. HR&W, 1987.   ○

Neruda, Pablo
WINDOWS THAT OPEN INWARD, IMAGES OF CHILE
Translated from Spanish. White Pine, 1984.   ○

Putigny, Bob
EASTER ISLAND
Discovery by the Dutch of the mysterious statues of Easter Island, and current life there. Two Continents, 1976.   ○

HISTORY

Falcoff, Mark
MODERN CHILE, 1970–1989: A CRITICAL HISTORY
Transaction Pubs, 1989.   ○

Loveman, Brian
CHILE: THE LEGACY OF HISPANIC CAPITALISM
Oxford U Pr, 1988.   ○

Novels

Allende, Isabel
THE HOUSE OF SPIRITS
Family saga of politics and violence—highly political story of a family from the early 1900s to the overthrow of Allende in 1973. Knopf, 1985.   ○

Allende, Isabel
OF LOVE AND SHADOWS
The novel takes place in a country much like post-1973 Chile—"skillfully evokes . . . the terrors of daily life under military rule . . . captures the voices of the regime's apologists." (BRD) Knopf, 1987.   ○

Dobyns, Stephen
AFTER SHOCKS, NEAR ESCAPES
A novel about the effect on one family of the 1960 earthquake in Chile—"extended family that is engaging . . . use of the quake as a metaphor for inevitable change is highly effective." (FC) Viking, 1991.   ○

Donoso, José
CURFEW
An expatriate musician returns to Chile and examines what has happened to Chile, and his own life. Weidenfeld, 1988.   ○

Donoso, José
THE OBSCENE BIRD OF NIGHT
The "fading social order of a once-great Chilean estate." (FC) Knopf, 1973.   ○

Pryce-Jones, Alan
HOT PLACES
Three novelettes set in Brazil, Chile and Ecuador—"packed with local color." (BRD) Knopf, 1933.   ○

Skarmeta, Antonio
BURNING PATIENCE
Set in Chile during Allende's presidency—a romance between a postman and the tavern-keeper's daughter, but also a witness to history "and habits of the nation, [poet Pablo] Neruda's immense popularity . . . his death . . . overthrow and death of Allende." (BRD) Pantheon, 1987.   ○

COLOMBIA

Series Guidebooks (See Appendix 1)

Lonely Planet Guide: Columbia
Michael's Guide: Ecuador, Columbia & Venezuela

Background Reading

NOTE: Books on the Andes are listed under South America/The Amazon and the Andes. See also Peru for books on the Incas.

Nicholl, Charles
THE FRUIT PALACE
A portrait of Colombia told by an author sent there to infiltrate and write about the drug traffic. St. Martin, 1986.   o

Rodman, Selden
THE COLOMBIA TRAVELER
History, people, culture, emphasis on the arts, in addition to the usual travel guide information. Devin, 1971.   o

Von Hagen, Victor
THE GOLDEN MAN: QUEST FOR EL DORADO
The legend that the treasure was in Colombia—saga of adventure. Book Club, 1974.   o

GUIDEBOOKS

Meisch, Lynn
A TRAVELER'S GUIDE TO EL DORADO AND THE INCA EMPIRE
See under "Peru/Guidebooks."   o

HISTORY

Galbraith, W.O.
COLOMBIA
Gordon Pr, 1985 (first published 1966).   o

Novels

Clancy, Tom
CLEAR AND PRESENT DANGER
"Clancy's best thriller since . . . *Hunt for Red October*." The national security advisor gets presidential approval for a covert operation against the Columbian drug cartel. Putnam, 1989.   o

Daley, Robert
A FAINT COLD FEAR
A recently widowed star of the New York Police Department is sent to Bogota to "liase" with the Drug Enforcement Agency, and meets a woman journalist from a New York paper. They become allies, friends and lovers—"penetrating inside looks at the N.Y.P.D., 'the paper' [ostensibly *The New York Times*], the D.E.A., South American life and the Medallin cartel." (PW) Little, 1990.   o

García Marquéz, Gabriel
CHRONICLE OF A DEATH FORETOLD
A novella set in a Colombian town reconstructing an actual episode in which the entire town stood by and did nothing while two drunks planned, announced and carried out a murder. Knopf, 1983. Also *The Autumn of the Patriarch* (1976).   o

García Marquéz, Gabriel
THE GENERAL AND HIS LABYRINTH
The last days of Simon Bolivar on his way to exile after being ousted as president. Knopf, 1990.   o

García Marquéz, Gabriel
ONE HUNDRED YEARS OF SOLITUDE
Saga of an "exotic" clan over seven generations that "suggests the mythical development of civilization from Creation to the 20th

century." This novel is one of several set in the mythical town of Macondo (Aracataca, in the Magdalena state of Colombia). HarRow, 1970. Also *In Evil Hour* (1979), and short story collections, *No One Writes to the*

Colonel (1968), *Leaf Storm* (1972), *Collected Stories* (1984). For Marquez fans, Bradt Enterprises in Cambridge, Massachusetts, offers a map in color "with Aracataca precisely located."   ○

E C U A D O R

Series Guidebooks
(See Appendix 1)

Lonely Planet Guide: Ecuador & Galapagos Islands
Michael's Guide: Ecuador, Colombia & Venezuela.

Background Reading

NOTE: Books on the Andes are listed under South America/The Amazon and the Andes.

Angermeyer, Johanna
GALAPAGOS QUEST

"Remarkable story of adventure, romance and the fulfillment of a dream"—the author goes to the Galapagos at age 13, where her family had lived just before she was born, and relates the idyllic Robinson Crusoe-like life she led there with her extended family. Viking, 1990.   ○

De Roy Moore, Tui
GALAPAGOS: ISLANDS LOST IN TIME

"Evokes one of the most haunting landscapes on earth"—reminiscences of the author's childhood on the islands. (TL) Penguin, 1987.   ○

Jackson, M.H.
GALAPAGOS: A NATURAL HISTORY GUIDE

U of Calgary, 1985.   ○

Miller, Tom
THE PANAMA HAT TRAIL: A JOURNEY FROM SOUTH AMERICA

The "Panama" hat is pretext for a book on Ecuador—making and selling these hats

shapes the culture and economy of the country. Morrow, 1986.   ○

Thomsen, Moritz
THE FARM ON THE RIVER OF EMERALDS

Account of farming in the Ecuadoran jungle. See also *The Saddest Pleasure*, under Brazil, above. Random, 1989.   ○

Urrutia, Virginia
TWO WHEELS & TAXI

"A slightly daft adventure in the Andes," is the subtitle. A 70-year-old widow explores the Ecuadoran Andes with a Quito cab driver as guide and bodyguard—Inca ruins, villages, folkways, mountains. Mountaineers, 1987.   ○

GUIDEBOOKS

Boyce, Barry
A TRAVELER'S GUIDE TO THE GALAPAGOS ISLANDS

At-home preparation, choosing a tour, what to do, what to see, wildlife specifics, photo opportunities, reading lists and an introduction to mainland Ecuador. Galapagos Travels, 1990.   ○

Meisch, Lynn
A TRAVELER'S GUIDE TO EL DORADO AND THE INCA EMPIRE

See under Peru/Guidebooks.   ○

Stephenson, Marylee
GALAPAGOS ISLANDS

The essential handbook for exploring, enjoying and understanding Darwin's enchanted islands, claims the subtitle. Full descriptions of the government cruises (the only way to see the islands). Mountaineers, 1989.   ○

HISTORY

Morner, Magnus
The Andean Past (Peru, Bolivia, Ecuador)
Columbia U Pr, 1984.   ○

Novels

Icazu, J.
THE VILLAGERS: HUASIPUNGO
Peasant life in Ecuador. Arcturus, 1973.   ○

Pryce-Jones, Alan
HOT PLACES
Three novelettes set in Chile, Brazil and Ecuador—"packed with excellent local color." (BRD) Knopf, 1933.   ○

THE GUIANAS
(French Guiana, Guyana, Surinam)

Series Guidebooks
(See Appendix 1)

See series guides listed under South America.

Background Reading

Naipaul, Shiva
JOURNEY TO NOWHERE: A NEW WORLD TRAGEDY
"Most thoughtfully wrought" of the Jim Jones/Jamestown books—the "profile of Guyana is a disturbing study of a fraudulent republic . . . the picture of the charismatic Jones [is] bone-chilling." (BL) S&S, 1981.   ○

Naipaul, V.S.
THE MIDDLE PASSAGE
See under "Latin America."   ○

Waugh, Evelyn
NINETY-TWO DAYS
Travelogue of a journey from Georgetown, British Guiana (now Surinam), to Brazil at a time when the area was little known to travelers—"lucid and fascinating picture of places and people." (BRD) FS&G, 1934.   ○

HISTORY

Spinner, Thomas J., Jr.
POLITICAL & SOCIAL HISTORY OF GUYANA, 1945–1983
Westview, 1984.   ○

Novels

Naipaul, Shiva
LOVE AND DEATH IN A HOT COUNTRY
Place and mood of a country modeled on Guyana. Viking, 1984.   ○

Voorhoeve, Jan and Lichtveld, Ursy M., eds.
CREOLE DRUM
An anthology of Creole literature in Surinam. Yale U Pr, 1975.   ○

PARAGUAY

Series Guidebooks
(See Appendix 1)

Michael's Guide: Argentina, Chile, Paraguay & Uruguay

Background Reading

Graham, R.B.
A VANISHED ARCADIA
"Being some account of the Jesuits in Para-

guay, 1607–1767." Reprint of the 1901 edition. Century, 1988.   ○

Warren, Harris G.
PARAGUAY
An informal history and introduction to Paraguay that tells much "about a tragically unimportant country . . . memorable pages on wandering Spaniards, Portuguese, Americans [and] the curious diplomats from Washington." (BRD) Greenwood Pr, 1982 (first published 1949).   ○

HISTORY

Pendle, George
PARAGUAY: A RIVERSIDE NATION
Gordon Pr, 1976 (first published 1954).   ○

Novels

Lieberman, Herbert
THE CLIMATE OF HELL
Suspense story with a chase through the "hell" of the Paraguayan jungle. The plot involves former Nazis who are being protected by the Paraguayan government. S&S, 1978.   ○

PERU

*Series Guidebooks
(See Appendix 1)*

Insight Guide: Peru
Lonely Planet Guide: Peru
Michael's Guide: Bolivia & Peru
Nagel's Encyclopedia Guide: Peru
Real Guide: Peru
Visitor's Guide: Peru

Background Reading

NOTE: Books on the Andes are listed under South America/The Amazon and the Andes.

Bingham, Hiram
LOST CITY OF THE INCAS: THE STORY OF MACHU PICCHU AND ITS BUILDERS
A summing up of archaeological labors of expeditions to Machu Picchu. Greenwood, 1981 (first published 1948). Also *Machu Picchu, A Citadel of the Incas* (1930), which gives an overall picture of archaeological procedures, historical significance, and the excitement of the search.   ○

Engel, Frederic Andre
AN ANCIENT WORLD PRESERVED
"Highly readable, informative, archaeologically current" account of Andean prehistory; places the Incan achievements in perspec-

tive in comparison to other ancient cultures. (BRD) Crown, 1977.   ○

Meyerson, Julia
TAMBO: LIFE IN AN ANDEAN VILLAGE
Observations of daily life in a Quechua community in Peru. U of Texas Pr, 1990.   ○

Morrison, Tony
THE MYSTERY OF THE NASCA LINES
Antique Collect, 1987. Also *Pathways to the Gods* (1979).   ○

Nouwen, Henri J.M.
GRACIAS! A LATIN AMERICAN JOURNAL
See under "Bolivia."   ○

Ridgeway, John
ROAD TO OSAMBIE
Story of the author's return, after 15 years, to an idyllic Peruvian plantation—"extraordinary story of endurance and adventure." The plantation is described in *Amazon Journey*, and the author returns to find the Norwegian-Indian family whose idyllic lifestyle calls him back, only to have his romantic memories dispelled. (PW) Viking, 1987.   ○

Schneebaum, Tobias
KEEP THE RIVER ON YOUR RIGHT
An encounter by an American artist in Peru studying painting with the Indians he wanted to paint—"introspective, wholly engaging adventure." (BRD) Grove-Weidenfeld, 1988.   ○

Wright, Ronald
CUT STONES AND CROSSROADS
"Enticing melange of archaeological fieldwork and exotic travel experiences . . . in search of ancient Inca ruins . . . fascinating personal chronicle of research and travel." (BL) Viking, 1984.   ○

GUIDEBOOKS

Frost, Peter
EXPLORING CUZCO
Includes surrounding area, Machu Picchu, Chinchero, Moray, Vilcabamba Mountains—description and practical tourist information on accommodations, food, shopping, etc. Bradt, 1984.   ○

Meisch, Lynn
A TRAVELER'S GUIDE TO EL DORADO AND THE INCA EMPIRE
"A superbly practical guide to the four Incan countries [Bolivia, Colombia, Ecuador, Peru] . . . stupendously detailed and culturally informed." Chapters on native handicrafts, fiestas, marketplaces, museums, food, etc. (NYTBR) Penguin, 1984.   ○

HISTORY

Morner, Magnus
THE ANDEAN PAST (Bolivia, Ecuador, Peru)
Columbia U Pr, 1984.   ○

Werlich, David P.
PERU: A SHORT HISTORY
For both general reader and scholar. Southern Illinois U, 1978.   ○

Novels

Alegriá, Ciro
THE GOLDEN SERPENT
Incidents of Indian life on the Maranon River, and a classic novel. FS&G, 1943. Also *Broad and Alien Is the World* (1941) about life in an Indian mountain village.   ○

Vargas Llosa, Mario
AUNT JULIA AND THE SCRIPTWRITER
A student who is a newswriter for a radio station in Lima falls in love with his older aunt (by marriage), which develops into a scandalous affair and marriage. FS&G, 1982.   ○

Vargas Llosa, Mario
CAPTAIN PANTOJA AND THE SPECIAL SERVICE
A satire on the Peruvian army and its official prostitution corps. Har-Row, 1978. Also *The Time of the Hero* (1966).   ○

Vargas Llosa, Mario
THE STORYTELLER
"Less a novel than an illustrated meditation, with an anecdotal frame"—the narrator and a storyteller recount the history of the Machiguengas with parallels made between the wandering tribe and the Jewish people. (BRD) FS&G, 1989. Also *The Green House* (1968) set partially in Peru.   ○

Vargas Llosa, Mario
WHO KILLED PALOMINO MOLERO?
The horrific death of a young Air Force recruit, and the web of racism and class hatred untangled by the detectives who handle the investigation. FS&G, 1987. Also *Conversation in the Cathedral* (1975).   ○

Wilder, Thornton
THE BRIDGE OF SAN LUIS REY
The classic novel by a leading American novelist that won a Pulitzer Prize in 1928. It's set in Peru, 200 years ago; five travelers are killed when a bridge built by the Incas collapses. A Franciscan brother then retells their five individual life stories to prove that

the accident "was the culmination of a finite pattern . . . according to God's plan" rather than an accident. (FC) Har-Row, 1967 (first published 1927). ○

URUGUAY

Series Guidebooks
(See Appendix 1)

Michael's Guide: Argentina, Chile, Paraguay & Uruguay

Background Reading

Alisky, Marvin
URUGUAY
"A pleasant survey of Uruguayan society [in] light and readable style"—social structure, physical setting, culture, government of Latin America's "Switzerland." (BRD) Praeger, 1969. ○

HISTORY

Pendle, George
URUGUAY
Reprint of 1965 edition. Greenwood, 1986. ○

Novels

Hudson, W.H.
THE PURPLE LAND
Pseudo-gothic mystery romance—"portrayal of the beauty of nature and the romance of native customs in a strange land." (FC) AMS, 1968 (first published 1885). ○

Onetti, Juan Carlos
A BRIEF LIFE
A major serious novel by one of Uruguay's leading writers and set in the imaginary town of Santa Maria. A man "begins retreating from reality . . . until he is living simultaneously in two fantasy worlds." (BRD) Grossman, 1976. ○

VENEZUELA

Series Guidebooks
(See Appendix 1)

Alive Guide: Venezuela Alive
Michael's Guide: Ecuador, Colombia & Venezuela

Background Reading

Donner, Florinda
SHABONO
"Lush, florid" report on an anthropologist's study of Indian healers and shamans. (PW) Delacorte Pr, 1982. ○

Good, Kenneth and Chanoff, David
INTO THE HEART
"One man's pursuit of love and knowledge among the Yanomama," is the long subtitle. "Spellbinding" both as anthropology and as a moving love story. The author, an anthropologist, went to Venezuela to live among the stone age tribes of the rain forest and came to adopt their life and language and married Yarima. When it seemed that the Venezuelan officials might be a problem, he left with his wife, and now lives and teaches in New Jersey. (PW) S&S, 1991. ○

Lieuwen, Edwin
VENEZUELA
"Brief, skilfull overview." (BRD) Reprint of 1965 edition. Greenwood, 1986. ○

GUIDEBOOKS

Bauman, Janice and Young, Leni
GUIDE TO VENEZUELA
Passport Pr, 1988. ○

HISTORY

Ewell, Judith
VENEZUELA: A CENTURY OF CHANGE
Stanford U, 1984.   ○

Hellinger, Daniel C.
VENEZUELA
Westview Pr, 1990.   ○

Novels

Guernsey, Paul
ANGEL FALLS
A wire service reporter's encounters with people and "his journey of self-knowledge" that turns deadly. (PW) S&S, 1990.   ○

Hudson W.H.
GREEN MANSIONS
Tale of the tropical forests of southern Venezuela where a political outcast, seeking sol-itude and the primitive life of the forest, falls in love with Rima, the Indian bird girl. First published 1893; reprint of 1923 ed., Dover Pub, 1989.   ○

L'Engle, Madeleine
DRAGONS IN THE WATERS
A mystery with a complicated plot involving the return of a portrait of Simon Bolivar (the national hero) to Venezuela. FS&G, 1976.   ○

St. Aubin de Teran, Lisa
THE TIGER
Combination of "legend, fantasy, allegory, and naturalism . . . recounting the myste-rious life of Lucien Schmutter" who is heir apparent to an estate in central Venezuela. (BRD) Watts, 1985.   ○

VII.

NORTH AMERICA

━━━━━━━━━━━━━━━━━━━━━━━━━━━━━━━○

THE ARCTIC AND GREENLAND

Series Guidebooks (See Appendix 1)

Nagel's Encyclopedia Guide: Denmark & Greenland

Background Reading

Note: See also books listed under "Yukon & the Northwest Territory."

Berton, Pierre
THE ARCTIC GRAIL: THE QUEST FOR THE NORTH WEST PASSAGE & THE NORTH POLE
Penguin, 1989. ○

Bruemmer, Fred
THE ARCTIC WORLD
Comprehensive book about the circumpolar world—history, people, animal and plant life of seven Arctic countries, Lapps, Eskimos. Crown, 1989. ○

Freuchen, Peter
ARCTIC ADVENTURE: MY LIFE IN THE FROZEN NORTH
Reproduction of the 1935 edition by the polar explorer. AMS (first published 1935). Also *The Peter Freuchen Reader* (1965), an anthology of his writings, edited by his wife. Also *Ivalu, the Eskimo Wife* (n.d.) and *Book of the Eskimos* (1981). ○

Hall, Sam
THE FOURTH WORLD: THE HERITAGE OF THE ARCTIC AND ITS DESTRUCTION
"A powerful and moving story of the Far North, its people and ominous future" by a British journalist who says that the Arctic has been exploited from the very first contact by Europeans. (PW) Vintage, 1988. ○

Kpomassie, Tété-Michel
AN AFRICAN IN GREENLAND
The author, born in Togoland, was fascinated as a boy with the idea of Greenland.

Eventually, after travel in Europe, he reached his fantasy place and the book relates his adventures in Greenland, and about the people who found him equally astounding. HarBraceJ, 1983.   ○

Lopez, Barry
ARCTIC DREAMS: IMAGINATION AND DESIRE IN A NORTHERN LANDSCAPE
"Captures both the beauty and peril of this frozen land"—the northernmost region of North America. (BL) Scribner, 1986.   ○

Millman, Lawrence
LAST PLACES: A JOURNEY IN THE NORTH
Follows the Viking route from Bergen, Norway, to Newfoundland (via the Shetlands, Faeroes, Iceland, Greenland, Labrador). "Describes the beauty . . . relates the history . . . tells tales of local mythology . . . encounters with the native residents . . . acerbic wit makes the book extremely entertaining." (LJ) HM, 1990.   ○

Mowat, Farley, ed.
THE POLAR PASSION: THE QUEST FOR THE NORTH POLE
With selections from the Arctic journals of various explorers. Also *The Great Betrayal* (1977), about the environmental threat to Northern Canada and the Arctic by gas and oil interests. Gibbs Smith, 1989.   ○

Oxenhorn, Harvey
TUNING THE RIG: A JOURNEY TO THE ARCTIC
"A captivating travel-adventure story"—the author, who is a poet, signed on the training ship *Regina Maris* as an apprentice for oceanographic studies of the humpback whale. The voyage took him to Greenland by way of Newfoundland and Labrador, and his journal reflects the happenings and the effect on his own views. (PW) Har-Row, 1990.   ○

GUIDEBOOKS

Young, Steven B.
EXPLORING THE FAR NORTH: A GUIDE TO ARCTIC REGIONS FOR THE TRAVELER AND NATURALIST
See also Young's background book above on Arctic ecology. P-H, 1987.   ○

HISTORY

Mirsky, Jeanette
TO THE ARCTIC: THE STORY OF NORTHERN EXPLORATION FROM EARLIEST TIMES TO THE PRESENT
With an introduction by Vilhjalmur Stefansson, this history relates with simplicity, the complex, overlapping stories of explorers from the fourth century on, to flights over the pole by Amundsen and others. Originally published in 1948. U of Chicago Pr, 1970.   ○

Rasky, Frank
THE POLAR VOYAGERS: EXPLORERS OF THE NORTH
A two-volume story of polar explorations: the first covers the period from the Vikings to the 18th century; subtitle of the second volume is "North Pole Or Bust." "Entertainment for readers unacquainted with the North and its history" is the author's purpose, with an emphasis on characterization of the many individual explorers. (BRD) McGraw, 1976.   ○

Novels

Davids, Richard C.
LORDS OF THE ARCTIC
See entry under Manitoba.   ○

Freuchen, Peter
WHITE MAN (Greenland)
Historical novel of the early eighteenth century that tells of Norwegian-Danish attempts to colonize Greenland; convicts were sent there to establish settlements. Rinehart, 1946. Also *Eskimo* (1931).   ○

Michener, James A.
JOURNEY

Four British aristocrats and an Irish servant set out to find Klondike gold in 1897. Random, 1989.   ○

Millman, Lawrence, ed.
A KAYAK FULL OF GHOSTS

Folk tales of a civilization at one with nature—"shockingly violent . . . comical . . . magical . . . the best rival Aesop's fables." (PW) Capra Pr, 1987.   ○

Mowat, Farley
THE SNOW WALKER

Short stories about life in the Arctic interwoven with myths, legends and mysteries. Little, 1975.   ○

Mowat, Farley
THE WORLD OF FARLEY MOWAT

Collection of writings by the writer/adventurer—"fine Canadian nature writer, storyteller, humorist, prose poet." Taken from his serious and humorous writings in his many books, including pieces on life in Arctic Canada and Newfoundland. (BRD) Little, 1980.   ○

Smiley, Jane
THE GREENLANDERS

Historical novel of 10th-century Greenland—story of a Scandinavian settlement that lasted 500 years. "Vast, intricately patterned novel . . . meticulous attention to detail" with vivid descriptions of the land and customs. (PW) Knopf, 1988.   ○

CANADA

Series Guidebooks

Birnbaum's: Canada
Berlitz: Canada
Fisher's World: Canada
Fodor: Canada
Insight Guide: Canada
Langenscheidt: Self-Guided Canada
Let's Go: Western Canada & Alaska
Lonely Planet: Canada
Michelin: Canada
Nagel's Encyclopedia Guide: Canada

Background Reading

NOTE: Additional Series Guidebooks, background books and articles that include Canada are listed under the United States and its regions (East, Midwest, West, Pacific Northwest) with an asterisk (*).

Broadfoot, Barry
MY OWN YEARS

By "a kind of Canadian Studs Terkel"— reflects the author's peripatetic life in Canada's west and the characters he's run across, from fishermen and frontiersmen to a dazzling call girl. (BL) Doubleday, 1984. Also

his other chronicles of Canadian life: *10 Lost Years* (1974), *Pioneer Years* (1976), and *Years of Sorrow* (1978).   ○

Brooks, Stephen
MAPLE LEAF RAG

Searching for the Canadian national character from Atlantic Canada to Alaska. Random, 1988.   ○

Fraser, Marian Botsford
WALKING THE LINE: TRAVELS ALONG THE CANADIAN/ AMERICAN BORDER

"Historical perspectives . . . personal reflections and a degree of poetic license"— based on a Canadian Broadcasting Company series of radio documentaries. (LJ) Sierra, 1990.   ○

Leggett, Robert F.
RAILWAYS OF CANADA

How the railways conquered Canada—the story of the Canadian railways from the 1830s, including the smaller companies, capturing much of the romance of Canadian railroading, as well as the facts. Salem Hse, 1983.   ○

Lipset, Seymour M.
CONTINENTAL DIVIDE
The subtitle is "values and institutions of the United States and Canada," and the author's premise is that the difference be-tween the two countries is that America has a sense of destiny and Canada does not. "In its quiet, carefully documented way it chips away at self-flattering illusions on both sides of the border." (NYT) Routledge, 1990.   ○

MacDonald, Ervin J.
THE RAINBOW CHASERS
Spans the period of mid-nineteenth to early twentieth century—"a vivid tale of a family's struggles and triumphs in the Canadian wil-derness . . . [their] elusive dream . . . breathes life into the people and pioneering efforts of the western frontier." (BL) Salem Hse, 1984.   ○

Malcolm, Andrew H.
THE CANADIANS
"Wide-ranging, perceptive view . . . ex-ploring the awesome geography . . . inter-views and personal recollections to describe its people, economy and close ties to the U.S." (PW) Times Bks, 1985.   ○

Moodie, Susanna
ROUGHING IT IN THE BUSH
Reprint of a classic by a Canadian woman writer, of pioneering in the Canadian wil-derness. Also *Life in the Clearing vs the Bush.* Beacon Pr, 1987.   ○

Moritz, Albert and Theresa
**THE OXFORD ILLUSTRATED
   LITERARY GUIDE TO CANADA**
One of a series of country reference books that are extremely useful for those interested in the literary heritage of a country, where authors live, settings for books and stories, etc. Oxford U Pr, 1988.   ○

Morris, Jan
**O CANADA: TRAVELS IN AN
   UNKNOWN COUNTRY**
Ten essays about Canadian cities "capturing their spirit, attitude and personality." (BL) HarperCollins, 1992.   ○

Pindell, Terry
**LAST TRAIN TO TORONTO: A
   CANADIAN RAIL ODYSSEY**
Insights and the variety of life in Canada, based on a year-long, 18,000-mile rail jour-ney—"spellbinding mixture of history, travel, sociology and nostalgia." (PW) Holt, 1992.   ○

Richler, Mordecai
**HOME SWEET HOME: MY
   CANADIAN ALBUM**
"Assorted essays on Canadian themes . . . light but tasty," by a Canadian novelist who returned to the country after twenty years in England. (PW) Knopf, 1984.   ○

Staines, David, ed.
**THE FORTY-NINTH AND OTHER
   PARALLELS**
Contemporary Canadian perspectives. U of Mass Pr, 1986.   ○

GUIDEBOOKS FOR CANADA

NOTE: See also books with asterisk (*) under the United States and subheads for the East, Midwest and West.

Alaska Northwest
THE MILEPOST
"A reliable guide to the entire highway net-work of northwestern Canada, the Yukon and Alaska." Also, *Northwest Mileposts*, cov-ering key highways in Washington, Oregon, Idaho, western Montana and southwestern Canada. (NYT) Alaska Northwest, updated every year.   ○

Erickson, Jack
**BREWERY ADVENTURES IN THE
   WILD WEST**
Redbrick Pr, 1991.   ○

Pratson, Frederick
**GUIDE TO EASTERN CANADA/
   GUIDE TO WESTERN CANADA**
Comprehensive guides to year-round travel. All the information needed by Americans and Canadians alike to discover popular and hidden attractions: history, fairs and festi-vals, outdoor recreation, climate, customs,

practical tourist information on currency, hotels and restaurants. *Eastern Canada* includes: Ontario, Quebec, New Brunswick, Nova Scotia, Prince Edward Island, Newfoundland and Labrador. *Western Canada* includes the provinces of Alberta, British Columbia, Manitoba, Northwest Territories, Saskatchewan and the Yukon. Globe Pequot, 1991.   o

Stanley, David
ALASKA-YUKON HANDBOOK: A GYPSY GUIDE TO THE INSIDE PASSAGE AND BEYOND
See under "Yukon and the Northwest territory."   o

Stephenson, Marylee
CANADA'S NATIONAL PARKS: A VISITOR'S GUIDE
Covers the 29 national parks thoroughly from campsites and visitor facilities to hiking trails, plants, animals. P-H, 1984.   o

Stradiotto, John and Martha
ROAD TO CANADA'S WILD: PARKS ALONG THE TRANS-CANADA HIGHWAY
Hippocrene, 1989.   o

HISTORY

Bothwell, Robert and others
CANADA SINCE NINETEEN FORTY-FIVE: POWER, POLITICS AND PROVINCIALISM
An overview of the period since World War II; a partisan approach popularly written with good cultural sections—"breezy and cheery." (BRD) U of Toronto, 1989. Also *Canada Nineteen Hundred to Nineteen Forty-five* (1987).   o

McNaught, Kenneth W.K.
THE PELICAN HISTORY OF CANADA
Penguin, 1988.   o

Novels

Costain, Thomas B.
HIGH TOWERS
Historical novel of early Canada. Two brothers who explored the Mississippi, one of

whom founded New Orleans, and the Le Moyne family's efforts to establish a French empire in America. Doubleday, 1949.   o

Davies, Robertson
FIFTH BUSINESS
First of a trilogy that includes also *The Manticore* (1972) and *World of Wonders* (1976). Taken together they range over some sixty years, three continents and two wars. It begins with four friends in the Canadian midwest whose lives are profoundly affected by a single badly aimed snowball—"a work of theological fiction that approaches Graham Greene . . . deceptively simple style that is also treacherously entertaining." (FC) Viking, 1970.   o

Ellis, Peter B.
THE RISING OF THE MOON
Fictional treatment of a real, but not well-known, historical event in the mid-19th century when the Irish Republican brotherhood planned to invade Canada and set up a republic in exile. St. Martin, 1987.   o

Francis, Dick
THE EDGE
An undercover investigator, Tor Kelsey, is assigned to protect passengers and horses on the great Transcontinental Mystery Race, a train junket of the Jockey Club. Putnam, 1989.   o

Innes, Hammond
HIGH STAND
A Sussex solicitor on a dangerous search in the Canadian wilds for a missing millionaire. Atheneum, 1986. Also *Campbell's Kingdom* (1952).   o

Munro, Alice
THE MOONS OF JUPITER
Short stories set in rural and urban Canada. Knopf, 1983.   o

Richler, Mordecai
SOLOMON GURSKY WAS HERE
Chronicles several generations of the Gursky family through Canadian history—"unique blend of humor, history and myth

. . . from rawhide to velvet" that begins with the patriarch arriving in Canada as part of an expedition and moves to his bootlegger grandsons. In the course of the novel the Gurskys participate in history's events, from Arctic explorations to Entebbe to Watergate. (BRD) Knopf, 1990.　○

Williams, David
EYE OF THE FATHER
A young Norwegian takes his parents' money and heads for North America to avoid marrying a pregnant girl, and travels to New York, North Dakota and the Canadian prairies. Anansi, 1985.　○

ALBERTA

Background Reading

Abley, Mark
**BEYOND FORGET:
REDISCOVERING THE PRAIRIES**
A journey through the prairie provinces of Manitoba, Saskatchewan and Alberta in 1985, and touching on immigrant colonies and religious sects who live there. "Excellently written and intriguing to read." (PW) Sierra, 1987.　○

Bondar, Barry
**EDMONTON, THE STORY AND
THE SIGHTS**
Whitecap, 1986.　○

Gibson, Morris
A VIEW OF THE MOUNTAINS
Account of the emigration of a British doctor and his physician wife from Yorkshire to a village in southwestern Alberta and their gradual adjustment to the people there and the landscape. Beaufort, 1984.　○

Kowinski, William S.
THE MALLING OF AMERICA
Includes material on the fabulous Edmonton mall. Morrow, 1985.　○

Marty, Sid
MEN FOR THE MOUNTAINS
By a warden at Canada's Banff National Park, evoking "sights, sounds, smells of mountain life guaranteed to arouse nostalgia or anticipation." (BRD) Mountaineers, 1981.　○

Russell, Andy, ed.
ALBERTA ON MY MIND
Falcon Pr, 1990.　○

Russell, Andy
**TRAILS OF A WILDERNESS
WANDERER**
The Canadian Rockies in the early days of this century and now, as seen through the eyes of a man born there and who runs a working ranch in Alberta. Lyons & Burford, 1988.　○

Thomas, Lewis G.
**THE RANCHERS LEGACY:
ALBERTA ESSAYS**
U of Nebraska Pr, 1986.　○

Novels

Adam, Ian
GLASS CANYONS
Poetry and short fiction anthology, with short stories on the theme of change in the city of Calgary. A collage to convince the reader that there is more to Calgary than glass canyons—from gamblers and housewives to tourists and forlorn lovers. N West Pr, 1985.　○

Chalmers, John W. and others
DIAMOND JUBILEE
A set of three anthologies of writing by Alberta-born writers, or those who have lived there for a period of time—fiction, poetry and prose. The anthologies also attempt to include as many works of the fifty identifiable ethnic groups in Alberta as possible. Hurtig, 1979.　○

Freedman, Benedict
MRS. MIKE
Based on true experiences, told secondhand. A Boston girl moves to Canada, marries a Canadian Mountie, and this is the story of their happiness, hardships and courage, with Indian and nature lore interwoven into the novel. Coward, 1947. ⟳

Govier, Katherine
BETWEEN MEN
The focus is on a history professor in Calgary torn between her husband, whom she's divorcing, and a politician, with a second story line about a historical paper she's working on. Viking, 1987. ⟳

Haley, Susan C.
GETTING MARRIED IN BUFFALO
A kindergarten teacher in a small town in Alberta is "just lonely enough" to marry her farmhand, Alexander, a second generation Ukrainian; concerns "the obsession of those around her with a shadowy . . . figure from Alexander's past." (BRD) Dutton, 1987. ⟳

Kinsella, W.P.
THE FENCEPOST CHRONICLES
"Thirteen chronicles narrated by Silas Ermineskin . . . each of these delightful stories has a special glow." Also *The Mocassin Telegraph and Other Tales* and *Dance Me Outside: More Tales from the Ermineskin Reserve,* "alternately poignant, dramatic, frightening, depressing, comic incidents." (BRD) Houghton, 1987. ⟳

ATLANTIC CANADA AND LABRADOR
(New Brunswick, Newfoundland, Nova Scotia, Prince Edward Island)

Series Guidebooks
(See Appendix 1)

Fodor: Maritime Provinces

Background Reading

Armstrong, Bruce
SABLE ISLAND
Highly readable account of the lore and lure of wild horses, seals, flora and fauna, and history of this island southeast of Halifax. Doubleday, 1981. ⟳

Bolger, Francis W., and others
SPIRIT OF PLACE: LUCY MAUD MONTGOMERY AND PRINCE EDWARD ISLAND
Oxford U Pr, 1983. ⟳

Chantraine, Pol
THE LIVING ICE
The story of the seals and the men who hunt them in the Gulf of St. Lawrence and the way of life in the Magdalen community of Acadians where seal hunting is not viewed as frivolous or wasteful but as "a fact of life, a way of life that provides much of the folklore . . . and is still dangerous." (BRD) McClelland & Stewart, 1981. ⟳

Davidson, James W. and Rugge, John
GREAT HEART: THE HISTORY OF A LABRADOR ADVENTURE
"Recounts the intertwined fates of three expeditions to Labrador at the turn of the century," using journals and diaries along with some fictional devices. (LJ) Viking, 1988. ⟳

Harwood, Michael and Durant, Mary
ON THE ROAD WITH JOHN JAMES AUDUBON
Retracing of Audubon's travels in Labrador, Texas and the Dry Tortugas. Dodd, 1980.   ○

*Hay, John and Farb, Peter
THE ATLANTIC SHORE
A history of the human and natural resources of the coast from Long Island to Labrador. It begins with an account of early observers such as Captain John Smith and Cartier, and moves on to the interdependence of animals, birds and habitat—"informative and beautifully written." (NYT) Parnassus, 1982.   ○

Hiller, James and Neary, Peter, eds.
NEWFOUNDLAND IN THE NINETEENTH AND TWENTIETH CENTURIES
Ten essays about the history of Newfoundland and an overview of its literature. U of Toronto, 1980.   ○

Jones, Sonia
IT ALL BEGAN WITH DAISY (Nova Scotia)
Rural life in Nova Scotia and a cow named Daisy who leads a New York couple into the yogurt business. Dutton, 1987.   ○

MacLeish, William H.
OIL AND WATER: THE STRUGGLE FOR GEORGES BANK
"A lively account of people and their work" and the struggle for control involving oil companies, fishermen, and state and federal governments of the U.S. and Canada. (PW) Atl Monthly Pr, 1985.   ○

Merrick, Elliott
TRUE NORTH (Labrador)
Reprint of a journal originally published in 1935, of a couple who moved to Labrador in the 1920s—"fascinating . . . magical chronicle." (PW) U of Nebr Pr, 1989.   ○

Millman, Lawrence
LAST PLACES: A JOURNEY IN THE NORTH (Newfoundland)
See entry under the Arctic & Greenland.   ○

Mowat, Farley
THE ROCK WITHIN THE SEA: A HERITAGE LOST (Newfoundland)
The effects of change on Newfoundland's traditions and its people. Atlantic/Little, 1968. See also *The World of Farley Mowat* under Canada.   ○

Oxenhorn, Harvey
TUNING THE RIG
See entry under the Arctic & Greenland.   ○

O'Connor, D'Arcy
MONEY PIT: THE STORY OF OAK ISLAND AND THE WORLD'S GREATEST TREASURE (Nova Scotia)
Rumors of Captain Kidd's treasure and the searches for it from 1795 to the present. Coward, 1978.   ○

Perkins, Robert F.
AGAINST STRAIGHT LINES: ALONE IN LABRADOR
Journal—and a journey into himself—of a Boston librarian who elects to spend a month on the Palmer River in Labrador: "A couple of leisure hours and this book are all you'll need to follow Robert Perkins to Labrador." (BRD) Atl Monthly Pr, 1983.   ○

Wallace, Dillon
LURE OF THE LABRADOR WILD
Part of Torngat Adventure Classic Series, reproduction of the 1905 edition. Chelsea Green, 1990.   ○

Novels

Currie, Sheldon
THE GLACE BAY MINER'S MUSEUM (Cape Breton)
Short stories with a Cape Breton setting. Deluge Pr, 1979.   ○

Gundy, Elizabeth
LOVE, INFIDELITY AND DRINKING TO FORGET
An artist who paints covers for romances and the owner of a New York antiques store decide to move to an abandoned farm in

New Jerusalem in Atlantic Canada—the story of what they dreamed, the reality they find. The author "describe[s] a community so well that you . . . remember it as if you'd once stayed there." (FC) Dial, 1984.   o

Maillet, Antonine
THE DEVIL IS LOOSE! (New
    Brunswick)
"Rollicking adventures of rum-running days" in the Acadian villages of southeastern New Brunswick during the 1930s. Walker, 1987.   o

Mason, F. Van Wyck
THE YOUNG TITAN
Historical novel of the French and Indian Wars and the battle of Louisbourg. Double-day, 1959.   o

Montgomery, Lucy Maud
ANNE OF GREEN GABLES (Prince
    Edward Island)
The classic story for children, but appreciated by many adults as well, of a young orphan's life on Prince Edward Island. Her home, the setting for the novel, is one of Atlantic Canada's chief attractions for travelers these days. Bantam, 1976.   o

Ogilvie, Elisabeth
THE DEVIL IN TARTAN (Nova
    Scotia)
"What starts out as a glorified babysitting job with a little genealogical research thrown in becomes an adventure in ESP, Scottish history and Nova Scotia living." (FC) Mc-Graw, 1980.   o

Richards, David A.
ROAD TO THE STILT HOUSE (New
    Brunswick)
Poverty-stricken and boring lives of an extended family in semi-rural New Brunswick. Oberon Pr, 1985.   o

Robinson, Spider
TIME PRESSURE (Nova Scotia)
An alien drops in on a commune of hippies on Nova Scotia. Ace Books, 1987.   o

Wright, Eric
**A BODY SURROUNDED BY
    WATER** (Prince Edward Island)
An Inspector Charlie Salter mystery—while on a holiday in a rented cottage on Prince Edward Island, several break-ins occur, and the local historian is murdered. Scribner, 1987.   o

BRITISH COLUMBIA

*Series Guidebooks
(See Appendix 1)*

Fodor: Pacific North Coast
Frommer: Vancouver & Victoria
Let's Go: Vancouver
Moon Handbook: British Columbia

Background Reading
Hellman, Ernest F.
KOOTENAY COUNTRY
One man's life in the Canadian Rockies. Alaska Northwest, 1990.   o

Hoagland, Edward
**NOTES FROM THE CENTURY
    BEFORE**
Experiences on a trip in 1966 when the author followed the trails and talked to the old-timers . . . "about their heydays as trappers, prospectors, traders and explorers." (BRD) North Pt Pr, 1982 (first published 1969).   o

Johnston, Moira
**RANCH: PORTRAIT OF A
    SURVIVING DREAM**
Text and photos in a recreation of the past, the land and its people today—an absorbing

evocation of ranch life and the author's journey, which includes the American high plains, California and British Columbia. Doubleday, 1983.   ○

GUIDEBOOKS

Brook, Paula
VANCOUVER RAINY DAY GUIDE
Chronicle, 1984.   ○

Bryson, Sandy
VANCOUVER ISLAND TRAVELER
Great adventures on Canada's western rim. Windham Bay Pr, 1988.   ○

Carey, Neil G.
A GUIDE TO THE QUEEN CHARLOTTE ISLANDS
Tenth edition of an insider's guide to the island world of British Columbia, by an author who is a longtime resident. Alaska Northwest, 1991.   ○

Patton, Brian
PARKWAYS OF THE CANADIAN ROCKIES
An interpretive guide to Banff, Jasper, Kootenay and Yoho Parks. International Spec Bk, 1988.   ○

Wershler, Terri
THE VANCOUVER GUIDE
"Cover a wide range of topics without . . . extraneous detail"—usual tourist information and a section on things to do with children. (BL) Chronicle, 1991.   ○

Novels

Gerson, Carole
VANCOUVER SHORT STORIES
A collection of 21 short stories published for Vancouver's Centennial, and designed to give a sense of its social and literary history and identity. U of British Columbia Pr, 1985.   ○

St. Pierre, Paul
SMITH AND OTHER EVENTS; STORIES OF THE CHILCOTIN
Short story collection set in Chilcotin country in the 1940s and '50s—"features small-town farmer Smith . . . and characters from the author's CBC television series 'Cariboo Country.' " (FC) Beaufort, 1984.   ○

Watmough, David, ed.
VANCOUVER FICTION
An anthology of short stories published to celebrate Vancouver's Centennial—"an honest witness to place." (BRD) Polestar Pr, 1985.   ○

Whitney, Phillis A.
FEATHER ON THE MOON
Four years after her daughter has been kidnapped from a Connecticut supermarket, Deborah is led to a home in Victoria where the daughter may be living. Doubleday, 1988.   ○

Wright, Laurali
THE SUSPECT
A mystery, winner of an Edgar Allan Poe award, with a focus on psychology rather than plot, involving two octogenarians and set in a town on the coast of British Columbia. Also another mystery, *Sleep While I Sing* (1986). Viking, 1985.   ○

Wright, L.R.
LOVE IN THE TEMPERATE ZONE
Laurali and L.R. are the same person; this is not a mystery, but a story of love in Vancouver. Viking Penguin, 1988.   ○

MANITOBA

Background Reading
Abley, Mark

BEYOND FORGET: REDISCOVERING THE PRAIRIES
See entry under Alberta.   ○

Davids, Richard C.
LORDS OF THE ARCTIC: A JOURNEY AMONG POLAR BEARS

"An enticing collection of legendary facts and eyewitness accounts" of the Arctic bears and interaction with Eskimos and population of Churchill, Manitoba. (BL) Macmillan, 1982. ○

HISTORY

Morton, William L.
MANITOBA: A HISTORY
U of Toronto, 1979. ○

Wells, Eric
WINNIPEG: WHERE THE NEW WEST BEGINS
An illustrated history of the city. Windsor, 1982. ○

Novels

Birdsell, Sandra
AGASSIZ: A NOVEL IN SHORT STORIES

"Mingles genres and voices to re-create the overlapping worlds of a single family," and spanning several generations in the fictional town of Agassiz. Milkweed Editions, 1992. ○

Duncan, Helen
KATE RICE, PROSPECTOR
Novelized account of a woman in the early 1900s who went from school teacher to prospector. The book is based on diaries, letters, tapes—"a well-written portrayal of a strong woman in a harsh, raw land." (BRD) Simon & Pierre, 1984. ○

Laurence, Margaret
A JEST OF GOD
The self-liberation of a spinster school-teacher from her trapped life in provincial Manitoba. Knopf, 1966. Also *A Bird in the House* (1970), short stories set in the 1930s and '40s. ○

Shields, Carol
THE REPUBLIC OF LOVE
"Unabashed love at first sight, with a high I.Q." in Winnipeg, between a 35-year-old folklorist and a three-time divorced radio disc jockey. Viking, 1992. ○

ONTARIO

Series Guidebooks
(See Appendix 1)

American Express Pocket Guide: Toronto, Montreal, Quebec
Berlitz: Toronto
Fodor: Toronto
Frommer: Toronto
Let's Go: Toronto

Background Reading

Galbraith, John K.
THE SCOTCH
A leading economist's boyhood impressions of the small Scottish community where he grew up, on the north shore of Lake Erie. HM, 1985. ○

Stewart, Darryl
POINT PELEE: CANADA'S DEEP SOUTH
A history and guide. Burns & MacEachern, 1977. ○

GUIDEBOOKS

Cantor, George
HISTORIC BLACK LANDMARKS: A TRAVELER'S GUIDE
Significant sites in the U.S. and in Ontario, Canada. Gale, 1991. ○

Kalman, Harold and Roaf, John
EXPLORING OTTAWA
An architectural guide to the nation's capital. U of Toronto Pr, 1983. ○

McKenzie, Rod and Marge
TORONTO GUIDE

"Cover a wide range of topics without . . . extraneous detail"—usual tourist information and a section on things to do with children. (BL) Chronicle, 1991.   o

McKenzie, Rod, Marge and Gregory
TORONTO'S BACKYARD

A guide to nature walks. Salem Hse, 1986.   o

Scharfenberg, Doris
THE LONG BLUE EDGE OF ONTARIO

A vacation guide to Ontario's Great Lakes coast. Eerdmans Pub, 1984.   o

Novels

Atwood, Margaret
CAT'S EYE (Toronto)

The novel is narrated by a Canadian artist who returns to Toronto for a retrospective and a "decoding of childhood's secrets." (FC) Doubleday, 1989. Also *Life Before Man* (1980).   o

Beresford-Howe, Constance
THE MARRIAGE BED (Toronto)

A young pregnant housewife, abandoned by her husband, confronts her friends, parents, mother-in-law and spouse and finds that "they all have personal prisons as confining as hers." (FC) St. Martin, 1982.   o

Cobb, Jocelyn
BELMULLET

"An old-fashioned novel in concept and style" of a ten-year-old girl sent to the family farm in rural Ontario in 1933, ostensibly for a brief visit, but it becomes a permanent change for her. (FC) St. Martin, 1983.   o

Davies, Robertson
MIXTURE OF FRAILTIES (Kingston)

This plus *Leaven of Malice* (1955) and *Tempest Tossed* (1952) are a trilogy (the Salterton trilogy) of "original, wry and amusing social comedy" set in a small Ontario city. Pen-guin, 1980 (first published 1958). See also Davies under Canada/Novels.   o

Davies, Robertson
THE REBEL ANGELS (Toronto)

Involves a stolen Rabelaisian manuscript—"love and scholarship, and secret Gypsy lore" in a small college. (FC) Viking, 1982.   o

De La Roche, Mazo
THE JALNA SAGA

A sixteen-volume family saga of the Whiteoak family and Jalna, their family home on the shores of Lake Ontario. It begins in 1850, and goes on through to the mid-1950s and their centennial celebration. The books were not published chronologically, but are listed here in order of place in the story, to read in proper sequence: *Jalna* (1927), *The Building of Jalna* (1944), *Morning at Jalna* (1960), *Mary Wakefield* (1949), *Young Renny* (1935), *Whiteoak Heritage* (1940), *The Whiteoak Brothers: Jalna 1923* (1953), *Centenary at Jalna* (1958), *Whiteoaks of Jalna* (1929), *Finch's Fortune* (1931), *The Master of Jalna* (1933), *Whiteoak Harvest* (1936), *Wakefield's Course* (1941), *Return to Jalna* (1946), *Renny's Daughter* (1951), *Variable Winds at Jalna* (1954). Little, 1927–1960.   o

Engel, Howard
A CITY CALLED JULY

A Benny Cooperman mystery—Cooperman is asked to look into the disappearance of a synagogue's treasurer. Viking, 1986. Also *The Suicide Murders* (1987), *A Victim Must Be Found* (1989) and *Murder on Location* (1985).   o

Laurence, Margaret
DIVINERS

About a middle-aged writer living on a backwoods farm with her daughter. Knopf, 1974.   o

Munro, Alice
THE PROGRESS OF LOVE

Short stories set in rural Canada. Also *Lives of Girls and Women* (1989), Dance of the Happy Shades (1990), and *The Beggar Maid* (1991), Knopf, 1986.   o

Ondaatje, Michael
IN THE SKIN OF A LION
"Maps high society and the subculture of the under-privileged in Toronto in the 1920s and 30s . . . does for Toronto what Joyce did for Dublin (or Döblin for Berlin)." (BRD) Knopf, 1989. ○

Quarrington, Paul
THE LIFE OF HOPE
The narrative alternates between life in Hope, 1983, and life of the man, J.B. Hope, for whom the town was named, and his cult following in the 1800s. Doubleday, 1985. ○

Ritchie, Simon
THE HOLLOW WOMAN
A Canadian private detective, in Toronto, is hired to find the kidnapped wife and son of a wealthy businessman. Scribner, 1987. ○

Shields, Carol
SWANN
A Canadian farm woman and poet is murdered by her husband, with the culmination at a symposium in Toronto—"a splendid deadpan parody of academic jargon" as each participant distorts aspects of Mary Swann's life and work. Stoddart, 1989. ○

Škvorecký, Josef
THE ENGINEER OF HUMAN SOULS (Toronto)
"First of all the book is an entertainment . . . in humor ranging from slapstick to high wit and people from the utterly wicked to the virtually saintlike." An emigré from Czechoslovakia and his observations of fellow emigrés in Toronto—"provides a bible of exile." (FC) Knopf, 1984. ○

Wood, Ted
DEAD IN THE WATER
Story set in Murphy's Harbor and Reid Bennett (ex-Toronto cop) is its one-man police force—"action-filled story . . . backdrop so real you can almost feel the mosquitoes biting . . . satisfyingly tangled plot." (FC) Scribner, 1983. Also *Murder on Ice* (1984), *Fool's Gold* (1986) and *On the Inside* (1990). ○

Wright, Eric
A QUESTION OF MURDER
Charlie Salter series of police procedurals set in Toronto, about a bombing incident near a visiting princess. Scribner, 1988. Also *The Man Who Changed His Name* (1987). ○

QUEBEC

Series Guidebooks (See Appendix 1)

American Express Pocket Guide: Toronto, Montreal & Quebec
Berlitz: Montreal; Canada
Fodor: Montreal & Quebec City
Frommer: Montreal & Quebec City
Insight Guide: Montreal
Michelin: Quebec

Background Reading

Arnopoulos, Sheila M. and Clift, Dominique
THE ENGLISH FACT IN QUEBEC
English, and other ethnic influences, in Quebec. U of Toronto Pr, 1984. ○

Fitzmaurice, John
QUEBEC AND CANADA: PAST, PRESENT, AND FUTURE
Serious analytic study of Quebec society and politics, focusing on events since 1960—*Choice*, the book review magazine, calls it probably the best synoptic study of the province written in English. St. Martin, 1985. ○

Jacobs, Jane
THE QUESTION OF SEPARATISM: QUEBEC AND THE STRUGGLE OVER SOVEREIGNTY
Random, 1980. ○

GUIDEBOOKS

Lowry, William and Joy
**MONTREAL, QUEBEC AND
    CANADA EAST**
World of Travel, 1989.   ○

Freed, Josh and Kalina, Jon, eds.
**THE ANGLO GUIDE TO SURVIVAL
    IN QUEBEC**
Eden Pr, 1983.   ○

Novels

Atwood, Margaret
SURFACING
Two couples vacation together in a remote
cabin and it puts a strain on their relationship. S&S, 1973.   ○

Beauchemin, Yves
THE ALLEY CAT
Set in Montreal in the 1970s, about a man's
struggle against an Anglo and an Eastern
European who steal his restaurant—"his
Quebecois are mostly splendid souls . . .
evokes Montreal extremely well," but read-
ers may be taken aback by the Anglos and
obsession with things American. (BRD)
McClelland & Stewart, 1986.   ○

Blais, Marie Claire
ST. LAWRENCE BLUES (Quebec
    City)
"Picaresque journey through . . . contemporary Quebec society." (BRD) FS&G, 1974.
Also *The Manuscripts of Pauline Archange* (1970),
about a young girl's life and Catholic
upbringing.   ○

Carrier, Rock
HEARTBREAK ALONG THE ROAD
Deals with "Le Chef," an allusion to a re-
pressive period in the history of the province
and Premier Duplessis. Anansi, 1987. Also
The Hockey Sweater (1979).   ○

Cather, Willa
SHADOWS ON THE ROCK
Evocation of the French Quebec colony in
the early eighteenth century through anecdotes and prose pictures of the homes, marketplace, missionary priests, the Ursuline
convent—"characters historic and imagined . . . a charming idyll." (FC) Knopf,
1931.   ○

Daymond, Douglas, ed.
STORIES OF QUEBEC
Ten short stories by English-Canadian au-
thors set in Quebec. Oberon, 1980.   ○

Hebert, Anne
IN THE SHADOW OF THE WIND
A limbless torso, washed up on the shore,
is the center of the plot—"the story is told
by six narrators [in a] claustrophobic village
where anything and everyone are looked
upon with . . . paranoia." (FC) Stoddart,
1983. Also *Children of the Black Sabbath* (1977)
about exorcism and witchcraft as a nun is
about to take final vows.   ○

Moore, Brian
BLACK ROBE
"An extraordinary novel" of Indians and
priests of the 17th century, with a crisis of
faith as its theme. (FC) Dutton, 1985.   ○

Moore, Brian
THE LUCK OF GINGER COFFEY
    (Montreal)
An Irish family in Montreal survives near-
disintegration. Little, 1960.   ○

Poulin, Jacques
SPRING TIDES
"Allegorical novel . . . a literary caveat to
Quebec concerning the perils of isolationism
. . . preservation of individual values." An-
ansi, 1986.   ○

Richler, Mordecai
JOSHUA THEN AND NOW
A survey of Joshua's life from Montreal slum
childhood to current fame. Knopf, 1980. Also
St. Urban's Horseman (1971).   ○

S A S K A T C H E W A N

Background Reading

Abley, Mark
**BEYOND FORGET:
   REDISCOVERING THE PRAIRIES**
See entry under Alberta.   o

Binnie-Clark, G.
WHEAT AND WOMAN
An early book about Saskatchewan and farming, reissued because of revived interest in its woman author. U of Toronto, 1979 (first published 1914).   o

Stegner, Wallace
WOLF WILLOW
Reminiscences and personalized history of the Saskatchewan southern plains where the author spent his boyhood, with a "wedge of fiction" in the middle recreating the win-

ter of 1906. (BRD) U of Nebraska, 1980 (first published 1962).   o

Novels

Stegner, Wallace
**THE BIG ROCK CANDY
   MOUNTAIN**
Story of a footloose family constantly on the move in the west and Saskatchewan—"cruelty and often crushing poverty, alternating with occasional scenes of a simple family happiness which stand out beautifully and unforgettably." (FC) Duell, 1943.   o

Story, Gertrude
**IT NEVER PAYS TO LAUGH TOO
   MUCH**
Second volume of a trilogy of short story collections about life in a German farming community. Thistledown Pr, 1984.   o

T H E   Y U K O N   A N D   T H E
N O R T H W E S T   T E R R I T O R I E S

Series Guidebooks
(See Appendix 1)

Moon Handbook: Alaska-Yukon

Background Reading

See also books under "The Arctic & Greenland," above.

Berton, Philip
**KLONDIKE FEVER: THE LIFE AND
   DEATH OF THE LAST GREAT
   STAMPEDE**
Carroll & Graf, 1985.   o

Gordon-Cooper, Harry
**YUKONERS: TRUE TALES OF THE
   YUKON**
Hancock Hse, 1990.   o

Hine, Harold
YUKON ANTICS
Hancock Hse, 1987.   o

Iglauer, Edith
DENISON'S ICE ROAD
Suspense-filled, expert reporting of road-building in the Territory, written by a woman who drove the trucks that opened an Arctic truck route. Portions of the book appeared in the *New Yorker*—"excitement, humor, the struggle of man against the elements." (BRD) U of Washington Pr, 1982 (first published 1975).   o

Ives, Rich, ed.
**THE TRUTH ABOUT THE
   TERRITORY**
Anthology of contemporary non-fiction from the Northwest—"offers a rich and panoramic view of the Northwest, its geography,

climate, history, jargon and customs." There are also in this series anthologies of poetry and fiction from the Territory. Owl Creek, 1988.   ○

Moore, Joanne R.
NAHANNI TRAILHEAD: A YEAR IN THE NORTHERN WILDERNESS
"An idyllic year spent in the fabled Nahanni River Valley" along with the author's practical advice, stories, and photographs of wildlife encountered. (BRD) Mountaineers, 1984.   ○

Mowat, Farley
TUNDRA
One of a series of books by "literary naturalists" and a reprint of the 1963 edition. Smith, Gibbs, 1990.   ○

Murray, John A., ed.
A REPUBLIC OF RIVERS: THREE CENTURIES OF NATURE WRITING FROM ALASKA AND THE YUKON
Forty-eight selections in chronological order, from 1741 to 1989; geographical descriptions, animals, man's encounters with the area and themselves. Oxford U Pr, 1990.   ○

Olson, Sigurd
RUNES OF THE NORTH
The "face and facts" of nature as the author describes his experiences on a trip to Hudson Bay, the Northwest Territory, the Yukon and into Alaska. (BRD) Knopf, 1963.   ○

Perkins, Robert F.
INTO THE GREAT SOLITUDE: AN ARCTIC JOURNEY
Holt, 1991.   ○

Thomas, Lowell and others
ALASKA AND THE YUKON
"Splendid evocation of the continent's last frontier"—eight contributors write on history, recreation, sport, people past and pre-

sent, animals, cities, and isolated settlements. Facts On File, 1983.   ○

Novels

Innes, Hammond
HIGH STAND
A solicitor allows himself to be drawn into the Canadian Rockies and the Yukon in his search for a missing millionaire. Atheneum, 1986.   ○

London, Jack
THE CALL OF THE WILD AND OTHER STORIES
Dodd, 1960 (first published 1903). Also *White Fang and Other Stories* (1906).   ○

Michener, James
JOURNEY
See entry under the Arctic & Greenland.   ○

Pronzini, Bill
STARVATION CAMP
A corporal in the Mounted Police finds murder at Molly Malone's roadhouse and sets out on a hunt for vengeance. Doubleday, 1984.   ○

Service, Robert
THE BEST OF ROBERT SERVICE
The "frustrations and splendors" of the Canadian gold rush as seen by the poet of that event. Running Pr, 1990. Also *The Spell of the Yukon and Other Stories* (1987).   ○

Van Herk, Aritha
THE TENT PEG
Reactions of a nine-man uranium prospecting team to a woman in their midst when her disguise as a boy cook is found out. Seaview, 1982.   ○

Whitaker, Muriel, ed.
STORIES FROM THE CANADIAN NORTH
Fourteen tales of Canada's last frontier that explore the land, nature and the people. Hurtig, 1980.   ○

THE UNITED STATES
(Including North America)

Series Guidebooks
(See Appendix 1)

American Guide Series: WPA Guide Reprints: there's a reprint of the original series of WPA guides for every state; as well as **Route 1: Here's New England; The Oregon Trail; The Intracoastal Waterway.**
Berlitz: U.S.A.
Birnbaum's: U.S.
Fisher's World: U.S.A. (also see separate guides on U.S. regions)
Fodor: United States
Frommer: U.S.
Insight Guide: Crossing America
Let's Go: U.S.A.
2–22 Days Itinerary Planning Guides: New England; Around the Great Lakes; Rockies; American Southwest; Pacific Northwest

Background Reading

NOTE: Asterisk (*) indicates that the item applies to North America (Canada and the U.S.) as well.

Baker, Russell
THERE'S A COUNTRY IN MY CELLAR: THE BEST OF RUSSELL BAKER

Essays by a renowned columnist and commentator on American fads, politics, social upheavals—subjects light and serious, including family-style travel around the U.S. "Baker's columns reveal the times in all their richness and idiosyncracy." (BL) Morrow, 1990. ○

Baudrillard, Jean
AMERICA

Translated from the French, a travelogue of a French social thinker—"awestruck . . . aghast." Contains commentary on the differences between European and American lifestyles. (PW) Verso, 1989. ○

Blair, Walter and Hill, Hamlin
AMERICA'S HUMOR: FROM POOR RICHARD TO DOONESBURY
Oxford U Pr, 1980. ○

Conover, Ted
ROLLING NOWHERE
Chronicle of hobo life based on the author's travels, meeting up with classic hobo companions on several freight trains in many states; covering some 12,000 miles. Penguin, 1985. ○

Cooke, Alistair
AMERICA OBSERVED: FROM THE 1940S TO THE 1980S
Compilation of 58 articles by Cooke on the American scene, for the *Manchester Guardian*—"infused with Cook's considerable charm, wit and insight." (BL) Knopf, 1988. ○

*De Voto, Bernard A.
COURSE OF EMPIRE
The exploration of the North American continent for the 300 years prior to 1805—considered one of the best books about the West, "consciously designed to engage the reader's imagination as well as his desire to be informed." (BRD) U of Nebraska, 1983 (first published 1952). ○

Douglas, Patrick
EAST COAST—WEST COAST
Incisive, provocative, witty look at the cultural war between New York and California and who's winning. Donald I. Fine, 1989. ○

Fitzgerald, Frances
CITIES ON A HILL
"A Journey Through Contemporary American Cultures" from Jerry Falwell's church in Lynchburg, Virginia, and a gay neighborhood in San Francisco to a Florida retirement village and the now defunct commune of Rajneesh in Oregon—"triumph of detailed

research and brilliant reportage." (Publisher) S&S, 1986.   ○

Garreau, Joel
EDGE CITY: LIFE ON THE NEW FRONTIER

A book on demographics, on American lifestyles, and the population shift from cities to "edge cities" on the outskirts of 10 American cities. Doubleday, 1991. Also *The Nine Nations of North America* (1981).   ○

Heat Moon, William
BLUE HIGHWAYS: A JOURNEY INTO AMERICA

Traveling the back roads of America—those that rate a blue line on maps—vignettes of people and places with history and philosophy unobtrusively woven into the text. Little, 1983.   ○

Hobson, Archie, ed.
REMEMBERING AMERICA: A SAMPLER OF THE WPA AMERICAN GUIDE SERIES

The editor has culled 500 entries from the auto tour guides written as part of the WPA writer's project from 1935–43, and organized them by theme rather than geographically. Columbia U Pr, 1985.   ○

Hokanson, Drake
THE LINCOLN HIGHWAY: MAIN STREET ACROSS AMERICA

A photo essay on the first transcontinental highway, a "showcase for various writing styles . . . beginning with Emily Post's account of a transcontinental drive in 'By Motor to the Golden Gate.'" (See also books on Route 66 under the Midwest.)   ○

Horwitz, Richard P.
THE STRIP: AN AMERICAN PLACE

A "fun to read" yet academic treatment of a unique aspect of America—the pop culture commercial strips of fast food places and neon on American highways. Focuses on one such strip in Iowa City, and the author conveys the humanness behind the strips and why they are useful. (BL) U of Nebraska, 1985.   ○

Jacobson, Timothy
AN AMERICAN JOURNEY BY RAIL

"Everything to please an armchair traveler"—photos and text, scenery, history, trivia, nostalgia—"eminently browsable and attractive book." (PW) Norton, 1988.   ○

Jenkins, Peter
A WALK ACROSS AMERICA

Literally a walk across America from Connecticut to New Orleans. The walk, and memoirs, were motivated by the author's desire to put his life back together—"vivid and thoughtful." (BRD) Fawcett, 1983. A sequel is *The Walk West* (1982), from New Orleans to the Pacific.   ○

Kuralt, Charles
ON THE ROAD WITH CHARLES KURALT

A continuation of the TV commentator's earlier book, *Dateline America* (1979). More interviews of Americans with a special story to tell that emphasize themes of individuality and altruism—"different drummers." (BL) Putnam Pub Group, 1985. Also *A Life on the Road* (1991), an autobiographical memoir; how he found his niche of covering the pulse of America from a recreational vehicle.   ○

L'Amour, Louis
FRONTIER

The popular author of many novels revisits the settings for them. A blend of history, personal experiences, travelogue—Maine Islands, the Outer Banks of North Carolina, to bayou country and canyons of the Southwest. Bantam, 1984.   ○

Malcolm, Andrew H.
U.S. 1: AMERICA'S ORIGINAL MAIN STREET

U.S. 1 is 2,467 miles long, from northern Maine to the Florida Keys—"strewn with history . . . a delightful and revelatory journey through lost America." (PW) St. Martin, 1991.   ○

McFarland, Gerald
A SCATTERED PEOPLE: AN AMERICAN FAMILY MOVES WEST

History told through an extended family autobiography, atypical in its diversity of experiences . . . its participation in the events of the day as it drifts farther west as did the American people. Full of fascinating historical detail. Pantheon, 1985.   o

*Nicolson, Nigel and Adam
TWO ROADS TO DODGE CITY

A father and son, upper-class Britons, start, respectively, at Miami and Los Angeles, drive some 30,000 miles each through 40 states and three Canadian provinces and write letters to each other daily about the experience, with their ultimate rendezvous in Dodge City, Kansas. Diverse impressions of everything from the Kentucky Derby and Las Vegas to a Wyoming ranch and an anti-apartheid rally. A great book! Har-Row, 1987.   o

O'Gara, Geoffrey
A JOURNEY THROUGH TODAY'S AMERICA IN SEARCH OF AMERICA'S PAST

A Wyoming journalist travels to see how America has changed in the 50 years since the WPA state guides were published in the 1930s—"beguiling . . . will remain in readers' memories long after they put this book down." (PW) Norton, 1989. (Note under Series Guides, above, that reprints of the original WPA American Guide Series are available for those who'd like to traverse those routes again.)   o

Orlean, Susan
SATURDAY NIGHT IN AMERICA

What do people do on Saturday night? The author's premise is that Saturday night is an American icon, and she set out to find the answer to that question. In the process she attended everything from a Hispanic coming-of-age celebration to a New York socialite's dinner party. "Nearly as fun to read" said one reviewer, as the events described— "fascinating, incisive tract [on] unexplored sociological terrain." (LJ) Knopf, 1990.   o

Peirce, Neil R. and Hagstrom, Jerry
THE BOOK OF AMERICA: INSIDE FIFTY STATES TODAY

"Cogent, insightful" survey of the American states, region by region. There's an historical overview of each plus demography, state politics, local personalities, and much more. (BL) Norton, 1984. Also *The Megastates of America* (1972).   o

Pindell, Terry
MAKING TRACKS: AN AMERICAN RAIL ODYSSEY

30,000 miles on Amtrak's 31 lines—"captivating account . . . both travelogue and history lesson." (PW) Grove-Weidenfeld, 1990.   o

Raban, Jonathan
HUNTING MISTER HEARTBREAK

Mr. Raban traveled about the U.S. gathering impressions about the American character, looking at everything from department stores to small-town restaurants. "In holding up a mirror . . . makes us only occasionally wince, more often chuckle . . . at once limpid and rousing." (BL) HarperCollins, 1991.   o

Rawls, Thomas H.
SMALL PLACES: IN SEARCH OF A VANISHING AMERICA

Small towns and their people—"a pleasure to read." (LJ) Little, 1990.   o

Root, Waverly and De Rochemont, Richard
EATING IN AMERICA

A chronicle of American food that is also a history of the United States itself—erudite, sumptuous, witty, marvelously readable study. Ecco Pr, 1981.   o

Rosenblum, Mort
BACK HOME: A FOREIGN CORRESPONDENT REDISCOVERS AMERICA

After 20 years abroad, the author returns and dislikes much of what he sees but is smitten with life along the backroads from the bayous to Kansas City. A very readable perspective from someone distanced from the scene for many years, as to where this country may be headed. Morrow, 1989. ○

Roueche, Berton
SEA TO SHINING SEA

Most of the stories of life in America in this book first appeared in *New Yorker* magazine—"if you really want to know what life is like in Kansas wheat country, aboard a Mississippi River towboat," the author tells you. Avon, 1987. Also *River World* (n.d.) and more miniportraits. ○

Scheer, George F.
BOOKED ON THE MORNING TRAIN: A JOURNEY THROUGH AMERICA

Six weeks of travel on Amtrak, talking to everyone, taking side trips—"takes the pulse of America from the still-romantic vantage point of a window seat on a fast-moving train." (BL) Algonquin, 1991. ○

Silk, Leonard S. and Mark
THE AMERICAN ESTABLISHMENT

What the Establishment is—Harvard, the *New York Times,* the Ford Foundation, Brookings Institute, and the Council on Foreign Relations are the most influential—how it operates and the role it plays in the U.S. today. Avon, 1984. ○

Simmons, James C.
AMERICANS: THE VIEW FROM ABROAD

"Easy-to-read and earnestly middlebrow" collection of reflections on the U.S.A. by non-Americans. (LJ) Crown, 1990. ○

Terkel, Studs
THE GREAT DIVIDE: SECOND THOUGHTS ON THE AMERICAN DREAM

Terkel has established a niche as a perceptive and skilled interviewer of ordinary people. This book recounts the results, along with *Division Street: America* (1967) and *American Dreams: Lost and Found* (1980), which also are collections of statements of Americans, their disappointments, hopes, dreams. *Hard Times* (1986) is an oral history of the Great Depression. Pantheon, 1988. ○

Winegardner, Mark
ELVIS PRESLEY BOULEVARD: FROM SEA TO SHINING SEA, ALMOST

Two graduate students seeing the U.S.A. in a '67 Chevy—"loaded with goofy charm" as they discover that Elvis was wherever they went. (BL) Little, 1988. ○

TRAVELERS AND TRAVEL WRITING OF THE PAST

Allen, Martha M.
TRAVELING WEST: NINETEENTH-CENTURY WOMEN ON THE OVERLAND ROUTES
Tex Western, 1987. ○

*Bird, Isabella
THE ENGLISHWOMAN IN AMERICA

A young English woman's impressions of Canada and America in the 1850s. U of Wisconsin Pr, 1966. Also *A Lady's Life in the Rocky Mountains,* about her journey through those mountains by horseback, some 20 years later. ○

Dickens, Charles
AMERICAN NOTES

Observations on America's manners and morals in 1842. Penguin, 1974. ○

Downs, Robert B.
IMAGE OF AMERICA: TRAVELERS FROM ABROAD IN THE NEW WORLD
U of Illinois Pr, 1987. ○

Janssen, Dale H. and Beaty, Janice J.
TRAVELING WEST MARK TWAIN STYLE
Janssen Ed Enterp, 1989. ○

Lawrence, Bill
THE EARLY AMERICAN WILDERNESS AS THE EXPLORERS SAW IT

Recreation of North America as seen by first explorers—its grandeur, breathtaking beauty, exotic animals—from Norse sagas to excerpts of writings by Lewis and Clark expedition members. Paragon Hse, 1991. ○

Marcy, Randolph B.
THE PRAIRIE TRAVELER
Reproduction of an 1859 guide for those who planned to travel west safely; will give you some idea of what those travelers had to go through. Corner Hse, 1968. ○

*Newcombe, Jack, ed.
TRAVELS IN THE AMERICAS
An anthology of excerpts from fifty larger works that spans North, South and Central America and the Caribbean and five centuries with contributions ranging from Columbus and Twain to Bruce Chatwin and Evelyn Waugh—"armchair traveling at its very best." (PW) Grove-Weidenfeld, 1989. ○

*Trollope, Anthony
NORTH AMERICA
Two-volume set of comments by the prominent English writer. Hippocrene, 1987. ○

ETHNIC AND BLACK AMERICA

Allen, James P. and Turner, Eugene P.
WE, THE PEOPLE: AN ATLAS OF AMERICA'S ETHNIC DIVERSITY
Dividing the population into nine basic origins (Early North America, Asian and Pacific Islands, etc.), this book tells where to find concentrations of ethnic groups, from Basques to Tobagonians. Macmillan, 1988. ○

*Cantor, George
HISTORIC BLACK LANDMARKS: A TRAVELER'S GUIDE
Significant sites in every state except Idaho, Nevada, North Dakota and Wyoming plus the District of Columbia and Ontario, Canada. Gale, 1991. ○

*Frazier, Nancy
JEWISH MUSEUMS OF NORTH AMERICA
A guide to collections, artifacts and memorabilia in collections in the U.S. and Canada. Wiley, 1992. ○

Sowell, Thomas
ETHNIC AMERICA
Traces the historic experience of nine American ethnic groups, combining scholarship and readability in a compact form. Basic, 1983. ○

Thum, Marcella
GUIDE TO BLACK AMERICA
Restores many valuable pages long missing from the literature of travel since it documents the black presence in America's past and present. Organized by state, the book describes historic homes, battlefields, forts, monuments and landmarks of the civil rights movement, as well as art and history museums, colleges and churches—all open to the public. Hippocrene, 1991. ○

Wattenberg, Ben
THE FIRST UNIVERSAL NATION
"Leading indicators and ideas about the surge of America in the 1990s"—Wattenberg's premise is that America's manifest destiny is social, not territorial, that of melding the world's people into a new universal nation both prosperous at home and imitated abroad. (BL) Free Pr, 1990. ○

THE NATIVE AMERICANS

Eagle Walking-Turtle
INDIAN AMERICA: A TRAVELER'S COMPANION
Information on Indian reservations—location, dates of powwows and ceremonies, arts and crafts—for over 300 Indian tribes. The Irish-Choctaw author provides moving descriptions of historic, spiritual and cultural traditions. Muir, 1989. ○

Olson, James S.
NATIVE AMERICANS IN THE TWENTIETH CENTURY
U of Ill Pr, 1986. ○

*Shanka, Ralph
THE NORTH AMERICAN INDIAN TRAVEL GUIDE
Information on observable past and present places of Indian culture. Costano Bks, 1986. ○

RESTORATIONS & HISTORY TOURS, ARCHITECTURE, ARCHAEOLOGY

Eastman, John
WHO LIVED WHERE: A BIOGRAPHICAL GUIDE TO HOMES AND MUSEUMS

"A charming book" of travel/biography, giving some 600 homes and museums of persons (all deceased) whose careers affected U.S. cultural and political history, and ranging "from Abraham Lincoln to Gypsy Rose Lee." (BL) Facts On File, 1983)　ᴑ

Folsom, Franklin and Mary E.
AMERICA'S ANCIENT TREASURES: GUIDE TO ARCHEOLOGICAL SITES AND MUSEUMS

U of N M Pr, 1983.　ᴑ

Gutek, Gerald and Patricia
EXPERIENCING AMERICA'S PAST: A TRAVEL GUIDE TO MUSEUM VILLAGES

Forty-three restored, recreated or reconstructed villages, arranged geographically by region. Includes histories of the villages and practical information on where to eat and stay. Wiley, 1986.　ᴑ

Haas, Irvin
AMERICA'S HISTORIC BATTLEFIELDS

Overview of the famous battlefields from the American Revolution to the Civil War and the Indian wars—battle accounts, visitor information, travel information. Hippocrene, 1987.　ᴑ

Rifkind, Carole
A FIELD GUIDE TO AMERICAN ARCHITECTURE

A "compendious guide to American architectural styles . . . traces the development of residential, church, civic, commercial and utilitarian structures in separate sections . . . includes examples of high style . . . vernacular style . . . provincial adaptations." Crown, 1985.　ᴑ

Stevens, Joseph E.
AMERICA'S NATIONAL BATTLEFIELD PARKS: A GUIDE

"A good blend of history and sightseeing information" for 38 parks—"will captivate history and military literature buffs." (BL) U of Okla Pr, 1990.　ᴑ

Thomas, Bill
TRAVEL AMERICA'S PAST AND FUTURE

The travel guide to America's living restorations and futuristic attractions. Scarborough Hse, 1991.　ᴑ

NATURAL WONDERS & OUTDOOR AMERICA

Abbey, Edward
SLUMGULLION STEW: AN EDWARD ABBEY READER

An anthology of essays and novel excerpts covering "thirty years and thousands of miles of desert, canyon and river rapids" by one of America's "most articulate and engaging environmentalists . . . will delight his fans [while bedeviling his foes]." (PW) Dutton, 1984. See also *Beyond the Wall,* under "West/Background Reading."　ᴑ

*Corrigan, Patricia
WHERE THE WHALES ARE

A guide to whale-watching trips in North America that is at once a nature guide, travel planner and adventure book. It tells how to plan a whale watch trip at all levels from a minimal cost one-hour trip to a two-week expedition. Globe Pequot, 1991.　ᴑ

Frome, Michael
PROMISED LAND: ADVENTURES AND ENCOUNTERS IN WILD AMERICA

Based on thirty years of writing on conservation and travel—"an attempt to define wilderness through descriptions of the places and people he has known. . . . a mosaic of how wild places affect people." (LJ) Morrow, 1985. Also *National Park Guide* (1984), and *America's Favorite National Parks* (1989).　ᴑ

*Harwood, Michael and Durant, Mary
ON THE ROAD WITH JOHN JAMES AUDUBON

Combining their talents of novelist, historian, journalist, and amateur ornithologist, the authors retrace Audubon's travels in Texas, Labrador, the Tortugas, using his journals, essays and letters as a guide. Dodd, 1980.   ○

*Huser, Verne
RIVER REFLECTIONS

"An eclectic collection of . . . writings about North American rivers, covering the past 350 years . . . excerpts from and stories about voyageurs, explorers, white water loggers, naturalists and historians, engineers, recreational boaters and many more." From famous authors such as Steinbeck, McPhee and Twain, to diaries of scientists, women pioneers and so on. (Publisher) East Woods, 1984.   ○

*Jacob, Irene and Walter
GARDENS OF NORTH AMERICA AND HAWAII

Includes Canadian gardens and has a rating system so that you have some idea of whether a garden is OK or a "don't miss." Timber Press, 1985.   ○

McMillon, Bill
NATURE NEARBY: AN OUTDOOR GUIDE TO 20 OF AMERICA'S CITIES

Parks, preserves, conservatories, arboretums in 20 cities, a special daytrip for each area, relevant books for each city area, helpful information sources. Wiley, 1990.   ○

*Miller, Everitt L. and Cohen, Jay S.
THE AMERICAN GARDEN GUIDEBOOK WEST/THE AMERICAN GARDEN GUIDEBOOK EAST

The perfect book for garden lovers who travel—two traveler's guides to extraordinary beauty along the way. "West" includes Hawaii; "East" includes four Canadian provinces. The books provide general information, shops, tours, activities, family fun gardens, gardens where weddings can be held. (BL) M Evans, 1989; Holt, 1987.   ○

Mohlenbrock, Robert H.
THE FIELD GUIDE TO U.S. NATIONAL FORESTS

Arranged by region—practical tourist information on accommodations, activities, information sources, plus evaluations as to the appeal of particular forests, favorite trails and special sights—alternatives to the more crowded national park system. Congdon & Weed, 1984.   ○

National Geographic Society
EXPLORING AMERICA'S VALLEYS: FROM THE SHENANDOAH TO THE RIO GRANDE

"Travel essays [and] photographs describe twenty North American Valleys . . . focus is first on the history of the area and then on the present inhabitants' way of life . . . personal stories of contemporary farmers and crafts people." Natl Geog, 1984. Typical of the many books on natural America published by The Society, some other titles include: *New America's Wonderlands: Our National Parks* (1980); *Exploring America's Scenic Highways* (1979); *Exploring America's Backcountry* (1979); *America's Majestic Canyons* (1979); *America's Hidden Corners—Places off the Beaten Path* (1983); *America's Magnificent Mountains* (1980); *Wild and Scenic Rivers* (1983); and *Wilderness USA* (1973).   ○

National Park Foundation Staff
MIRROR OF AMERICA

An unusual anthology of literary encounters with the national parks; writings about parks and parks-to-be, e.g., Dickens on the mills of Lowell, Massachusetts, Kipling on Yellowstone, Sandburg on the Grand Canyon, and so on. Roberts Rinehart, 1989.   ○

*Ray, Mary H. and Nicholls, Robert P.
THE TRAVELER'S GUIDE TO AMERICAN GARDENS

U of NC Pr, 1988.   ○

Reader's Digest eds.
**OUR NATIONAL PARKS:
AMERICA'S SPECTACULAR
WILDERNESS HERITAGE**

Our parks from Acadia, Maine, to Zion, Utah, in alphabetical order, with a final chapter on the new Alaskan parks. Random, 1985. ○

Rubin, Alan A., ed.
**THE COMPLETE GUIDE TO
AMERICA'S NATIONAL PARKS**

National Park Foundation, 1990. ○

Scott, David L. and Kay W.
**GUIDE TO THE NATIONAL PARK
AREAS**

Volume 1: Eastern States; Volume 2: Western States. Globe Pequot, 1987. ○

Sifford, Darrell
A LOVE OF THE LAND

Farming in America—"by turns amusing, enlightening, sobering and touching"—intended for cityfolks as well as those with an interest in farming. (BL) Farm Journal, 1980. ○

*Ulmer, Jefferson G. and Gower, Susan
LIONS & TIGERS & BEARS

A guide to zoological parks, visitor farms, nature centers, marine displays in the U.S. and Canada. Garland, 1984. ○

Wolverton, Ruthe and Walt
**THE NATIONAL SEASHORES: THE
COMPLETE GUIDE TO
AMERICA'S SCENIC COASTAL
PARKS**

The parks described range from Cape Cod in Massachusetts to Padre Island in Texas and Point Reyes in California, and include history, access, what to do and where to stay, where to get more information. Woodbine House, 1988. ○

Wolverton, Ruthe and Walt
**THIRTEEN NATIONAL PARKS
WITH ROOM TO ROAM**

A guide for travelers in search of undisturbed beauty—description and practical information on 13 parks that are relatively unexplored and uncommercialized. Mills & Sanderson, 1990. ○

LITERATURE, ARTS, MUSIC

Ehrlich, Eugene and Carruth, Gorton
**THE OXFORD ILLUSTRATED
LITERARY GUIDE TO THE
UNITED STATES**

Cities and other places associated with particular authors and books, crossindexed—"delightful and informative production—a pleasure to behold and to browse in." (BL) Oxford U Pr, 1982. ○

Freundenheim, Tom L., ed.
**AMERICAN MUSEUM GUIDES:
FINE ARTS**

A handbook for the general public arranged by category (American, ancient, European, etc.)—collection holdings are surveyed. Also provides tourist information on hours, admissions, etc. Macmillan, 1983. ○

Gusikoff, Lynne
GUIDE TO MUSICAL AMERICA

Guide to all kinds of musical activities organized by region and by genre within each region—"specific references to many of the backwater and less publicized festivals, clubs and discos, arts centers, dance halls . . . where one finds live music today." (Choice) Facts On File, 1984. ○

Kazin, Alfred
**A WRITER'S AMERICA:
LANDSCAPE IN LITERATURE**

"An examination of America as a place and as a metaphor" with excerpts from Emerson, Thoreau, James, Frost, Hemingway, plus other authors both obscure and well known. Knopf, 1988. ○

*McLanathan, Richard
**WORLD ART IN AMERICAN
MUSEUMS**

A guide to museums in the United States and Canada, organized by periods and special collections (modern, primitive, Far East, decorative arts, etc.) Doubleday, 1983. ○

Merrill, Hugh
THE BLUES ROUTE
Taking the pulse of America's great indigenous music at four locales: the Mississippi Delta, Chicago, New Orleans, California. Morrow, 1990. ○

Pearson, Michael
IMAGINED PLACES: JOURNEYS INTO LITERARY AMERICA
Visits the sites that authors such as Twain, Hemingway, Frost and Faulkner used "to shape their literary geographies." (LJ) U Pr of Mississippi, 1991. ○

Rabin, Carol Price
MUSIC FESTIVALS IN AMERICA
A unique planning guide—gives the history of each festival, location, performance dates, ambience, accommodations and more, for all kinds of musical festivals from classical and opera to bluegrass and jazz, new revised edition. Berkshire Traveller. ○

Rappaport Susan
1991 TRAVELER'S GUIDE TO MUSEUM EXHIBITIONS
Suppose you have an hour to spare in a strange city or town—this provides information about major museums in cities all across the country. Abrams, 1991. ○

Turner, Frederick
SPIRIT OF PLACE: THE MAKING OF AN AMERICAN LITERARY LANDSCAPE
Lives and writings of American authors and an account of Turner's visits to the places captured by those authors; interviews with residents. Sierra, 1990. ○

GUIDEBOOKS TO INSPIRE AN ITINERARY OR EXPLORE A THEME

Aaron, Jan
WINE ROUTES OF AMERICA: THE COMPLETE TRAVEL GUIDE TO VINEYARDS AND WINERIES
Dutton, 1989. ○

Barth, Jack, and others
ROADSIDE AMERICA
All those weird and wacky roadside attractions, like Fairyland Caverns with Barbie dolls floating above, the Tupperware museum, and so forth. S&S, 1986. ○

*Berger, Terry and Gardner, Roberta
MCCLANE'S GREAT HUNTING AND FISHING LODGES OF NORTH AMERICA
A sampler of twenty of the top-notch lodges in the United States, Canada and Mexico and a cross-section—remote or just off the highway, expensive and inexpensive, family or to go alone, etc. HR&W, 1984. ○

Carmichael, Suzanne
THE TRAVELER'S GUIDE TO AMERICAN CRAFTS
In two volumes: I, East of the Mississippi, and II, West of the Mississippi. Unique guide to craftspersons and crafts outlets arranged by region, state, town and including description of the work, prices, addresses, mail order information, craft festivals and other craft-related events. Dutton, 1990. ○

Davis, Mary Dymond
GOING OFF THE BEATEN PATH: AN UNTRADITIONAL TRAVEL GUIDE TO THE UNITED STATES
A unique travel guide for the environmentally aware traveller. Noble Pr, 1991. ○

Drury, George H.
GUIDE TO TOURIST RAILROADS AND RAILROAD MUSEUMS
"A fine aid to the touring railroad buff"— notes on over 200 railroad museums and tourist railway lines that range from little streetcar lines to a 470-mile stretch in Alaska. Includes practical touring information. Kalmbach, 1987. ○

Eckert, Allan W.
EARTH TREASURES: WHERE TO COLLECT MINERALS, ROCKS & FOSSILS IN THE UNITED STATES
A four-volume series: Volume I, Northern Section (New England, Middle Atlantic

States, the Midwest); Volume II, Southeast-
ern Section (Middle Atlantic States, the
South); III, Northwest; IV, The Southwest.
Har-Row, 1987.   ⊙

*Fensom, Rod
**AMERICA'S GRAND HOTELS:
EIGHTY CLASSIC RESORTS IN
THE UNITED STATES AND
CANADA**

"Working, historic resorts . . . built between 1847 and 1929 . . . a wonderful book
for armchair travelers" or to use as a practical guide. The author provides anecdotes
of famous guests, history, architecture, de-
cor. (Publisher) East Woods, 1985.   ⊙

Fistell, Ira
AMERICA BY TRAIN

A guidebook by a rail buff who also happens
to be among the most literate of the radio
talk-show hosts. Combines rail information
with history and "sights along the way . . .
story of AMTRAK's 23,000-mile national
network [with] highlights of 49 main streets
. . . thumbnail sketches of hundreds of small
towns and waystations." (NYT) B Franklin,
1985.   ⊙

Hoffman, Paul, ed.
**AMERICAN MUSEUM GUIDE:
SCIENCE**

A handbook of science museums for the
general public arranged by category (air and
space, natural history, science, etc.). Macmillan, 1983.   ⊙

*Howe, Hartley
**NORTH AMERICA'S MARITIME
MUSEUMS: AN ANNOTATED
GUIDE**

Facts On File, 1987.   ⊙

Kenny, Maurice
GREYHOUNDING THIS AMERICA

H Graphics, 1987.   ⊙

Kilgore, Eugene
**RANCH VACATIONS: THE
COMPLETE GUIDE TO GUEST
AND RESORT, FLY FISHING,
AND CROSS-COUNTRY SKIING**

"An extensive, well-organized guide to an
all-American vacation—the dude ranch." (BL)
Muir, 1989.   ⊙

McLendon, Natalie
**GO PUBLIC! THE TRAVELER'S
GUIDE TO NON-COMMERCIAL
RADIO**

Very useful when traveling; 1,100 public radio stations. Wakerobin, 1986.   ⊙

MacNeice, Jill
**A GUIDE TO NATIONAL
MONUMENTS AND HISTORIC
SITES**

Homes of famous Americans, battlefields,
forts, memorials, Mount Rushmore, the
Statue of Liberty, natural wonders—arranged alphabetically by state, with a brief
history and practical information for visiting
the site. P-H, 1990.   ⊙

Model, Eric
**BEYOND THE INTERSTATE:
DISCOVERING THE HIDDEN
AMERICA**

"Unique . . . useful travel guide"—local
celebrations and events arranged by season
and region, includes nearby points of interest, accommodations with a personal touch,
roadside food recommendations, special
bibliographies. Wiley, 1989.   ⊙

*Murphy, Michael and Laura
**FERRYLINE VACATIONS IN
NORTH AMERICA: OCEAN
TRAVEL AND INLAND
CRUISING**

Dutton, 1988.   ⊙

Myers, Arthur
**THE GHOSTLY REGISTER—
HAUNTED DWELLINGS, ACTIVE
SPIRITS**

A journey to America's strangest landmarks,
a guide through 64 haunted dwellings from

Maine to California. Includes the history and profile of the resident ghosts, corroborative reports by witnesses. Contemporary Bks, 1986. ○

*O'Brien Tim
THE AMUSEMENT PARK GUIDE
Fun for the whole family at over 250 amusement parks from coast to coast—a comprehensive guide to both amusement and theme parks in the U.S. and Canada. Globe Pequot, 1991. ○

*Pacheco, Anthony L. and Smith,
   Susan E.
MARINE PARKS AND AQUARIA
Lyons & Burford, 1989. ○

Peterson, Natasha
SACRED SITES: A GUIDEBOOK
   FOR THE NEW AGE TRAVELER
American Stonehenge-type sites, organized by geographical region, with their spiritual significance, tips on meditation (to get the most out of a visit), history and archaeological importance of each, practical tourist information. Contemporary Bks, 1989. ○

*Spivack, Carol and Weinstock,
   Richard A.
BEST FESTIVALS OF NORTH
   AMERICA
"A practical guide to festival/vacations"— arranged by topic (dance, opera, jazz, etc.). "The authors have been very selective . . . criteria such as duration of at least one week, a variety of events or performers, availability of other vacation attractions in the area . . . caliber of talent." Much additional useful information such as nearby festivals and things to do, nearby activities and attractions for children, and so on. (BL) Printwheel Pr, 1989. ○

*Spivack, Carol and Weinstock,
   Richard A.
GOURMET FOOD AND WINE
   FESTIVALS OF NORTH
   AMERICA
Written for those who like to eat well, drink fine wine, when on vacation; provides in-

formation about major annual food and wine festivals in the U.S. and Canada, covering everything from lobster to chocolate and strawberries. Also gives addresses, lodgings available, and other practical information. Printwheel Pr, 1986. ○

Staten, Vince
UNAUTHORIZED AMERICA
"A travel guide to the places the Chamber of Commerce won't tell you about"—like where Frank Sinatra engaged in fist fights, murder sites, Elvis Presley's doctor, *that* kind of low-brow travel trivia. Har-Row, 1990. ○

Tinling, Marion
WOMEN REMEMBERED: A GUIDE
   TO THE LANDMARKS OF
   WOMEN'S HISTORY IN THE
   UNITED STATES
Biographical information and accomplishments of historic women in America that led to their landmark status—arranged geographically. Greenwood, 1986. ○

Wright, Sarah Bird
FERRIES OF AMERICA: A GUIDE
   TO ADVENTUROUS TRAVEL
"The author has done a tremendous job . . . excellent, thorough, detailed"—encourages travelers to incorporate ferries in their travel planning. See also guides to islands of the various regions, just below. Peachtree, 1987. ○

*Wright, Sara Bird
ISLANDS
A natural follow-up to Ms. Wright's ferry guide, just above, are these guides to the islands she encountered while researching the ferry guide. Titles are: *Islands of the Northeastern States & Eastern Canada, Islands of the South & Southeastern United States* (coastal and inland islands from Louisiana to Virginia) and *Islands of the Central United States & the Canadian Great Lakes*. The books include historical background, practical travel information on everything from where to eat to where to camp and dock a boat. (BL) Peachtree, 1989. Continuation of the series into the rest of the country may be in print by the time you read this. ○

Young, Judith
CELEBRATIONS: AMERICA'S BEST FESTIVALS, CARNIVALS, JAMBOREES AND PARADES
Borgo Pr, 1988.   ○

HISTORY

Burns, James MacGregor
THE AMERICAN EXPERIMENT
The overall title of a three-volume series: I, *Vineyard of Liberty*; II, *The Workshop of Democracy: The American Experiment from the Emancipation Proclamation to the Eve of the New Deal*; III, *Crosswinds of Freedom*. Knopf, 1983, 1985, 1989.   ○

Commager, Henry Steele, ed.
THE AMERICAN DESTINY
An illustrated bicentennial history of the United States from discovery and settlement by Europeans to the 1970s. Danbury Pr, 1975.   ○

Garrison, Webb
A TREASURY OF CIVIL WAR TALES
"An unusual but surprisingly accessible approach to Civil War history"—57 tales from history and legend, arranged chronologically, from the publication of *Uncle Tom's*

Cabin to Reconstruction. Rutledge Hill Pr, 1988.   ○

Morison, Samuel Eliot
A CONCISE HISTORY OF THE AMERICAN REPUBLIC
In two volumes. Oxford U Pr, 1983. Also *The Great Explorers: the European Discovery of America*. Oxford U Pr, 1986.   ○

Nevins, Allan and Commager, Henry S.
A POCKET HISTORY OF THE UNITED STATES
Pocket Books, 1986.   ○

Tindall, George B.
AMERICA: A NARRATIVE HISTORY
Two volumes, history from pre-Columbian times to the Reagan administration—"the author's engrossing style makes it possible for readers to dip comfortably here and there . . . and be absorbed in any section that might be of interest." (BL) Norton, 1984. ○

Zinn, Howard
THE TWENTIETH CENTURY, A PEOPLE'S HISTORY
An antidote to establishment history of "those whose plight has been largely omitted from most histories." (LJ) Har-Row, 1990.   ○

THE EAST

Series Guidebooks (See Appendix 1)

Fisher's World: Mid-Atlantic; New England
Fodor: New England; Jersey Shore
Frommer: Atlantic City & Cape May; New England; Mid-Atlantic; Delaware, Maryland, Pennsylvania & the Jersey Shore
Gault-Milau: New England
Insight Guide: New England
Michelin: New England
Sierra: Guide to the National Parks—East & Middle West; Guide to the Natural Areas of New England

Smithsonian: Guide to Historic America—Mid-Atlantic States (N.Y., N.J., Pa.); Northern New England (Me., N.H., Vt.); *Southern New England (Mass., Conn., R.I.)*
2–22 Days Itinerary Planning Guide: New England

Background Reading

*NOTE: Entries with an asterisk (*) pertain also to Canada.

Bell, C. Ritchie and Lindsey, Anne H.
**FALL COLOR AND WOODLAND
HARVESTS**

A guide to the colorful fall leaves, fruits and seeds of the Eastern forests—"designed to be as interesting and informative as possible" for people who enjoy fall foliage, the phenomenon that begins in mid-September in New England, and continues through the Adirondacks, Catskills, Poconos, Cumberlands, Monongahelas and the Blue Ridge, until it ends in the southern Piedmont some six weeks later. (Publisher) Laurel Hill Pr, 1990.   ○

Brill, David
**AS FAR AS THE EYE CAN SEE:
REFLECTIONS OF AN
APPALACHIAN TRAIL HIKER**

"This lyrical book speaks to . . . confirmed hiking enthusiasts [and] to city dwellers wondering what the fuss is about . . . well worth reading for its insight into hiker society on the Appalachian trail." The author tells of his 2,100-mile walk in the summer of 1979 in an attempt to get back in touch with nature, as he had been as a young child. It could be listed under several categories in this book, but since the trail traverses the entire East Coast it is listed here, with a cross-reference under the South. (BL) Rutledge Hill Pr, 1990.   ○

Cantor, George
**WHERE THE OLD ROADS GO:
DRIVING THE FIRST FEDERAL
HIGHWAYS OF THE
NORTHEAST**

"The eccentric charms of small town life . . . all done in such a pleasant, unpretentious way that it makes fine reading for any visitor." (LJ) Har-Row, 1990.   ○

Cronkite, Walter and Ellis, Ray
NORTH BY NORTHEAST

Watercolors and Cronkite's sensitively written text about his sailing trip up the coast from Cape May to Maine; companion volume to *South by Southeast*. Oxmoor, 1986. ○

Frazier, Nancy
**SPECIAL MUSEUMS OF THE
NORTHEAST: A GUIDE TO
UNCOMMON COLLECTIONS
FROM MAINE TO
WASHINGTON, D.C.**

"Fascinating worlds . . . in 144 small but outstanding museums. Discover everything from aircraft to holography, hummingbirds to witches." Factual information on hours, directions, plus evaluative information on whether children will like it, length of a typical visit, atmosphere and scope of each museum. (Publisher) Globe Pequot, 1985.
                                                           ○

*Hay, John and Farb, Peter
THE ATLANTIC SHORE

See entry under Canada/Atlantic Canada & Labrador.   ○

Hill, Kathleen
FESTIVALS USA

Volume II of this series covers festivals in the Eastern States. Hilltop, 1984.   ○

Humphrey, J.R.
TIMELESS TOWNS

A leisurely tour from Maine to Florida for devotees of places as they used to be, to find untouched structures, neighborhoods, entire towns, with sidetrips for each town visited. St. Martin, 1989.   ○

*Kopper, Philip
THE WILD EDGE

Revised edition of this book about life and lore of the great Atlantic beaches, a combination of field guide and handbook for beachcombers—"hard to beat . . . as useful as it is entertaining." It covers beaches all the way from the Bay of Fundy in Canada, to the Carolinas' Outer Banks, from three perspectives. The zoological beach, how the beach evolved and changes, and the art of beaching—clambakes, walks, musings. (PW) Globe Pequot, 1991.   ○

Laskin, David
**ISLANDS OF THE ATLANTIC EAST
COAST**

A guide to unbridged islands from Maine to the Florida Keys—"clear evocative prose . . .

captures and conveys a true sense of place." (LJ) Facts On File, 1990.   ○

Morse, Flo
THE STORY OF THE SHAKERS
This is a book commemorating the 250th anniversary of the birth of Mother Ann Lee who founded the Shakers, a unique religious sect that flourished in utopian communities in New England, New York and Kentucky. The book describes surviving sisters and brothers in Maine and New Hampshire. Their arts, crafts, simple lifestyle and foods are having a renaissance, and the museums and remaining villages are a focus for travelers who admire the Shakers and their way of life. Countryman, 1986.   ○

*Roberts, Bruce
NORTHERN LIGHTHOUSES
Lighthouses from New Brunswick to the Jersey Shore. This is one of a series of books on lighthouses that provide history, geography of the area, anecdotes and stories of past "keepers" and emergencies and dangers endured. They also give directions to reach the lighthouse and visiting hours if they are open to the public. Globe Pequot, 1990.   ○

*Wittemann, Betsy and Webster, Nancy
WATER ESCAPES IN THE NORTHEAST
Information and guidance for planning a water escape on the East Coast, from the Canadian Maritime provinces to Chesapeake Bay. Wood Pond, 1987.   ○

NEW ENGLAND

Bachman, Ben
UPSTREAM: A VOYAGE ON THE CONNECTICUT RIVER
"Leisurely exploration of the river [by tugboat and canoe] with a finely tuned sense of the region's history and ecology . . . mountains and valleys, old mill towns and dams, dairy farms." Plus there are encounters with animals—beaver, otter and moose. The Connecticut River has its source near the Canadian border and flows through the

heart of New England to the Long Island Sound. (PW) Globe Pequot, 1988.   ○

Bailey, Anthony
SPRING JAUNTS
Five jaunts, originally appearing as a series of articles in *The New Yorker*, one of which is along the Maine to Massachusetts coast— "a book to savour . . . wise, funny." (LJ) FS&G, 1986.   ○

Brooks, Paul
THE PEOPLE OF CONCORD—ONE YEAR IN THE FLOWERING OF NEW ENGLAND
A look at the lives and ideas of Emerson, Thoreau, Hawthorne and others who shaped the cultural heritage of the country in 1846— "a watershed year in American cultural history." (Publisher) Globe Pequot, 1990.   ○

Brooks, Van Wyck
THE FLOWERING OF NEW ENGLAND, 1815–65
Classic literary history interpreted as a reflection of the social, political and religious life of the period. Reprint of 1936 edition, AMS Pr, n.d. *New England: Indian Summer 1865–1915* (1940) brings this literary history to 1915.   ○

Faison, S. Lane, Jr.
THE ART MUSEUMS OF NEW ENGLAND
In three volumes: Volume 1: Connecticut and Rhode Island; Volume 2: Massachusetts; Volume 3: New Hampshire, Vermont, Maine. "Critical and art-historical exposition on more than five-hundred works of art [over one hundred museums] . . . a sense of the museums' character . . . like taking a personal tour with this noted art historian." Also includes practical information on hours, admissions, etc. (LJ) Godine, 1982.   ○

Harris, John
SAGA OF THE PILGRIMS
The story from origins in England and exodus to Holland, to the days at sea and life in the New World. Globe Pequot, 1990.   ○

Hubka, Thomas C.
BIG HOUSE, LITTLE HOUSE, BACK HOUSE, BARN
The title is a nineteenth-century children's sing-song describing the connected farm buildings of New England—the book addresses the question of why this unusual style of farmstead was adopted. "A humanistic architectural history . . . an engaging tribute to our nineteenth-century forbears." (LJ) U Pr of New England, 1984.   ○

Levine, Miriam
A GUIDE TO WRITERS' HOMES IN NEW ENGLAND
Relates the authors' lives to the homes—"chatty, even gossipy biographical piece" for each, plus practical information of schedules, addresses, phone numbers. (BL) Apple-Wood Bks, 1984.   ○

Matthews, Diane L.
NEW ENGLAND VISITOR'S GUIDE TO BOTANICAL GARDENS AND NATURE CENTERS
D.L. Matthews, 1984.   ○

Moorhouse, Geoffrey
THE BOAT AND THE TOWN
Through the seasons of a coastal New England town, by a British journalist—trawling, weather, ethnic mix, foreign competition, and summer tourists. Ulverscroft, 1983.   ○

Mutrux, Robert
GREAT NEW ENGLAND CHURCHES: 65 HOUSES OF WORSHIP THAT CHANGED OUR LIVES
A guide to New England's architecturally distinguished churches by a designer of churches. Anecdotes on history and construction of both traditional and modern buildings. Globe Pequot, 1982.   ○

Orleans, Susan
RED SOX AND BLUEFISH: MEDITATIONS ON WHAT MAKES NEW ENGLAND NEW ENGLAND
Essays that originally appeared in the *Boston Globe*—"many curious facets of New England are investigated in a hilarious fashion." (PW) Faber, 1986.   ○

Peirce, Neal R.
NEW ENGLAND STATES: PEOPLE, POLITICS AND POWER IN THE SIX NEW ENGLAND STATES
Patterned after the late John Gunther's series of "inside" books—"part history, part politics, part travel guide" describing the essential character and power structure of each state and the region in which it is located. See also Peirce's books under "U.S.A." Norton, 1976.   ○

Robinson, William F.
COASTAL NEW ENGLAND: ITS LIFE AND PAST
Also *Mountain New England.* The focus is on places at critical periods in their history, taking the reader in time from that period to the present day. Bullfinch Pr, 1989.   ○

Thoreau, Henry D.
THOREAU COUNTRY
Text selections from the words of Thoreau, with photographs. Sierra, 1975.   ○

Tree, Christina
HOW NEW ENGLAND HAPPENED
The modern traveler's guide to New England's historical past. Little, 1976.   ○

Wikoff, Jerold
THE UPPER VALLEY
An illustrated tour along the Connecticut River—local history and evolution of the area enhanced by a collection of rare prints and photographs. Chelsea Green, 1985.   ○

Wood, William
NEW ENGLAND'S PROSPECT
Reprint of the first book that provided reliable first-hand information on British America for prospective colonists. U of Massachusetts Pr, 1977 (first published 1634).   ○

NEW ENGLAND/GUIDEBOOKS

Foulke, Patricia and Robert
DAYTRIPS, GETAWAY WEEKENDS, AND VACATIONS IN NEW ENGLAND

Suggested itineraries that include major attractions and personally discovered, lesser-known favorites of the authors. Globe Pequot, 1988. ○

Landau, Carl and Katie
FESTIVALS OF NEW ENGLAND

All kinds of festivals where you can participate in a local event along with the locals. Landau Comns, 1989. ○

Maynard, Mary
ISLAND HOPPING IN NEW ENGLAND

Guide to 40 islands, or island groups, 11 of which can be reached by bridge; some well-known and popular, some obscure and unheard of. History, folklore for armchair travelers. Yankee Bks, 1986. ○

Riegert, Ray
HIDDEN NEW ENGLAND

Comprehensive guide—history, what to see, where to stay, fall foliage. Ulysses Pr, 1990. ○

Schuman, Michael
NEW ENGLAND'S SPECIAL PLACES

Outings to year-round attractions such as historic villages, working museums, presidential homes, and other cultural and historic places. Countryman, 1990. ○

MID-ATLANTIC STATES

NOTE: See also guides to Civil War battlefields under the South. ○

Cooney, Patrick
DISCOVERING THE MID-ATLANTIC

Historical tours, places to see within 100 miles of Philadelphia. Provides historical background and directions, and other nearby things to do in a given area. Rutgers U Pr, 1991. ○

Foulke, Patricia and Robert
DAY TRIPS AND BUDGET VACATIONS IN THE MID-ATLANTIC STATES

Eight suggested itineraries covering major tourist attractions and lesser-known spots in New York, New Jersey, Pennsylvania, Delaware, Maryland and Washington, D.C. Globe-Pequot, 1989. ○

Peirce, Neal R.
MID-ATLANTIC STATES OF AMERICA: PEOPLE, POLITICS AND POWER IN THE FIVE MID-ATLANTIC STATES

Patterned after the late John Gunther's series of "inside" books—"part history, part politics, part travel guide" describing the essential character and power structure of each state and the region in which it is located. The five mid-Atlantic states are New York, New Jersey, Pennsylvania, Maryland, Delaware and the District of Columbia. Norton, 1977. See also Peirce's books under "U.S.A." ○

THE SOUTH

Series Guidebooks
(See Appendix 1)

Fisher's World: Southeast
Fodor: Carolina & the Georgia Coast; The South; Virginia & Maryland

Frommer: Georgia & the Carolinas; Southern Atlantic States
Smithsonian: Guide to Historic America—Virginia & the Capital Region (Washington, D.C., Va., Md., Del.); The Carolinas & the Appalachian States (N.C., S.C.,

Tenn., Ky., W.V.); The Deep South (La., Miss., Ala., Ga., Fla.); Texas & the Arkansas River Valley

Background Reading

NOTE: Books & articles for the Mississippi are listed under the Midwest.

Binding, Paul
SEPARATE COUNTRY: A LITERARY JOURNEY THROUGH THE AMERICAN SOUTH
The South and its writers, a literary travelogue. U Pr of Miss, 1988. ○

Blount, Roy
CRACKERS
About Southern "crackers" (like himself)—specifically Jimmy Carter and his relatives are the springboard for observations about the South. Portions of the book appeared as articles in *Esquire, New Yorker, Sports Illustrated*, and *Playboy*. Ballantine, 1988. ○

Boney, F.N.
SOUTHERNERS ALL
A new edition of a book originally published in 1984—the author offers the thesis that Southerners were predominantly middle-class without a rigid sense of class identity. The book deals with all sorts of topics—the Civil War, family, land, politics, race, Christianity. "Highly interpretive . . . entertaining and well written . . . subtle distinctions about the south, explodes some myths, enforces others." (LJ) Mercer U Pr, 1990. ○

Brill, David
AS FAR AS THE EYE CAN SEE: REFLECTIONS OF AN APPALACHIAN TRAIL HIKER
See entry under The East. ○

Cash, W.J.
THE MIND OF THE SOUTH
Observations of a loyal son and discerning critic; first published in 1941, it is considered a key book on Southern history and in the influence it has had amongst the reading public and historians. This is a new edition with a new introduction that analyzes the author and the crucial role he played in Southern letters. Random, 1991. ○

Catton, Bruce
THE CENTENNIAL HISTORY OF THE CIVIL WAR
In three volumes. Doubleday, 1961–65. Also *Mr. Lincoln's Army, Glory Road, Stillness at Appomattox, Terrible Swift Sword.* Outlet, 1985. ○

Cooper, William J. and Terrill, Thomas E.
THE AMERICAN SOUTH: A HISTORY
"The sweep of southern history from . . . Jamestown through the rise and fall of the 'Solid South' to . . . transformation of the Sunbelt in the 1970s and 1980s." History for the non-academic reader. Knopf, 1990. ○

Cronkite, Walter
SOUTH BY SOUTHEAST
Companion volume to *North by Northeast* under the East, above. This is about the Intracoastal Waterway from Norfolk to Key West, and adjacent bays, rivers, areas. Oxmoor, 1983. ○

Davis, Burke
SHERMAN'S MARCH
'With as much dramatic flair as *Gone with the Wind* and with . . . factual accuracy [it] reconstructs Sherman's infamous, but vastly consequential, march." (BL) Random, 1988. ○

Escott, Paul D. and Goldfield, David R., eds.
THE SOUTH FOR NEW SOUTHERNERS
A collection of essays for new residents, by authors originally non-Southern—"a primer on ways southern . . . frankness is the book's hallmark, yet a fondness permeates every page, and a refreshing sense of understanding awaits the reader at book's end." (BL) U of North Carolina Pr, 1991. ○

*Hay, John and Farb, Peter
THE ATLANTIC SHORE
See entry under Canada/Atlantic Canada & Labrador. ○

Humphrey, J.R.
TIMELESS TOWNS
A leisurely tour from Maine to Florida for devotees of places as they used to be, to find untouched structures, neighborhoods, entire towns. Includes information on side-trips for each place visited. St. Martin, 1989. ○

*Kopper, Philip
THE WILD EDGE
See entry under the East. ○

Kuralt, Charles
SOUTHERNERS: PORTRAIT OF A PEOPLE
Oxmoor Hse, 1986. ○

Laskin, David
ISLANDS OF THE ATLANTIC EAST COAST
See entry under the East. ○

Lockwood, C.C.
THE GULF COAST: WHERE LAND MEETS SEA
Exploration of this coast from the Florida Keys to southwest Texas—"a splendid excursion for nature lovers. . . . Wildlife refuges, island rookeries, fishing grounds" and the teeming animal life. (PW) Louisiana State U Pr, 1984. ○

Merrill, Hugh
THE BLUES ROUTE
"Setting out to take the pulse of America's great indigenous music" at four locales: the Mississippi Delta, New Orleans, Chicago, California. (BL) Morrow, 1990. ○

Murray, Albert
SOUTH TO A VERY OLD PLACE
Memoir by a black man of letters on growing up in the Deep South during the 1920s and 1930s. In a *New York Times* book review, Toni Morrison commented: "Destroys some fashionable socio-political interpretations of growing up black." Random, 1991. ○

Naipaul, V.S.
A TURN IN THE SOUTH
By an Indian author who grew up in Trinidad, and one who has written many insightful books and novels about other cultures—a unique perspective on the American South based on his travels from farms and plantations to inner cities and Elvis' home in Memphis and speaking to blacks, whites, politicians, country music singers and more. "Part travelogue, part oral history . . . ruminative ramble . . . as only an 'outsider' and novelist could write it." (PW) Knopf, 1989. ○

Peirce, Neal R.
THE BORDER SOUTH STATES OF AMERICA: PEOPLE, POLITICS, AND POWER IN THE FIVE STATES OF THE BORDER SOUTH
Patterned after the late John Gunther's series of "inside" books—"part history, part politics, part travel guide," describing the essential character and power structure of each state and the region in which it is located. The five border states are Virginia, West Virginia, North Carolina, Kentucky and Tennessee. Norton, 1975. In the same series, *The Deep South States of America* (1974), the states covered are Arkansas, Alabama, Florida, Georgia, Louisiana, Mississippi and South Carolina. See also Peirce's books under "U.S.A." ○

Percy, Walker
SIGNPOSTS IN A STRANGE LAND
"Sparkling, fluent essays on the South"—subjects range widely into literature, morality, religion and science. FS&G, 1991. ○

Reed, John Shelton
WHISTLING DIXIE: DISPATCHES FROM THE SOUTH
"Humorous, perceptive" collection of writings that first appeared in Southern publications, written by a professor of sociology at the University of North Carolina. Topics range from religion and politics to "pop" culture. U of Mo Pr, 1990. ○

Roberts, Bruce and Jones, Ray
SOUTHERN LIGHTHOUSES
From Chesapeake Bay to the Gulf of Mexico. This is one of a series of books on lighthouses that provide history, geography of the area, anecdotes and stories of past "keepers" and emergencies and dangers endured. They also give directions to reach the lighthouse and visiting hours if they are open to the public. Globe Pequot, 1989.   o

Summer, Bob
EUGENIA PRICE'S SOUTH
"A guide to the people and places of her beloved region" is the subtitle. Historical places and people that flavor Price's Southern novels. Longstreet Pr, 1991.   o

APPALACHIA, THE BLUE RIDGE, THE GREAT SMOKIES

Blake, William A.
THE BLUE RIDGE
A history of the Blue Ridge region, spanning Georgia to the reaches of the Potomac, and a sympathetic account of the people of that area. Oxmoor, 1984.   o

Bradley, Jeff
A TRAVELER'S GUIDE TO THE SMOKY MOUNTAINS REGION
Embraces the hill country of eastern Tennessee, western North Carolina, southwestern Virginia and northern Georgia—"an idiosyncratic collection of historical facts, anecdotes and descriptive details that will add to the delight of any journey in the area and any encounter with its people." Also has practical tourist information on getting there, sightseeing, seasonal events, facilities for eating and sleeping. (NYT) Harvard Common Pr, 1985.   o

Moore, Warren
MOUNTAIN VOICES: A LEGACY OF THE BLUE RIDGE AND GREAT SMOKIES
Collection of folklore, remembrances, opinions. Globe Pequot, 1989.   o

Wenberg, Donald C.
BLUE RIDGE MOUNTAIN PLEASURES
"An A–Z guide to North Georgia, Western North Carolina and the upcountry of South Carolina"—arts, crafts, festivals, factory outlets, country inns, outdoor recreation, and sports. (Publisher) Globe Pequot, 1988.   o

Wigginton, Eliot and Bennett, Margie
FOXFIRE
A multivolume series of books begun by a teacher in Georgia (see under "Georgia"). Volume 7 of the series is an examination of Appalachian Christianity. Doubleday, 1975–1986.   o

GUIDEBOOKS

Facaros, Dana and Pauls, Michael
DEEP SOUTH: A TRAVELER'S GUIDE TO ALABAMA, MISSISSIPPI & LOUISIANA
With companion volumes for *Mountain South* and *Old South*. "Nicely detailed history; a logical progression for the tourist to follow . . . with emphasis on historically and culturally important spots." Includes practical tourist information. (BL) Hippocrene, 1987.   o

Kennedy, Frances H.
THE CIVIL WAR BATTLEFIELD GUIDE
HM, 1990.   o

Lawliss, Chuck
THE CIVIL WAR: A TRAVELER'S GUIDE AND SOURCEBOOK
Harmony, 1991.   o

McDonald, Jerry N., and others
THE BLUE RIDGE PARKWAY
A guide to the land and culture of the region. M&W Pub Co.   o

Weil, Tom
AMERICA'S SOUTH
Comprehensive and "only single-volume guide" that covers Virginia, the Carolinas,

Georgia, Alabama, Mississippi, Louisiana, Kentucky, Tennessee, Arkansas and Flor-ida. Includes B&Bs, quaint hotels, off-beat festivals. (Publisher) Hippocrene, 1990. ○

THE MIDWEST

Series Guidebooks
(See Appendix 1)

Fisher's World: The Midwest
Fodor: Upper Great Lakes Region
Sierra: Sierra Club Guide to National Parks—East & Middle West; Rocky Mountains & the Great Plains
Smithsonian: Guide to Historic America—Great Lakes States (Ohio, Ind., Ill., Mich., Wis., Minn.); The Plains States; (Mo., Kan., Neb., Iowa, S.D., N.D.); Texas & the Arkansas River Valley (Tex., Okla., Ark.)

Background Reading

*NOTE: Entries with an asterisk (*) pertain also to Canada.

Andrews, Clarence, ed.
GROWING UP IN THE MIDWEST
The "spirit and reality of the Midwest are captured" in selections from poetry, prose and fiction—"a rich patchwork of midwest-ern memories." (BL) Iowa State U, 1981. ○

Beatty, Michael and Nolte, James
GUIDE TO ART MUSEUMS: MIDWEST EDITION
And Bks, 1984. ○

Boyer, Dwight
GREAT STORIES OF THE GREAT LAKES
Also *Ghost Ships of the Great Lakes*. Dodd, 1985. ○

Caplow, Theodore and others
MIDDLETOWN FAMILIES
Muncie, Indiana fifty years after the Lynd sociological study of "Middletown" families. U of Minnesota, 1982. ○

Childs, Marquis
MIGHTY MISSISSIPPI: BIOGRAPHY OF A RIVER
Reminiscences and "a superb history" by a Pulitzer Prize-winning journalist. (BRD) Ticknor & Fields, 1982. ○

Curry, Jane, ed.
THE RIVER'S IN MY BLOOD: RIVERBOAT PILOTS TELL THEIR STORY
"A wonderfully evocative book about the river pilots on the Mississippi and Ohio Riv-ers"; reminiscences, history, technology. (BRD) U of Nebraska, 1983. ○

Cushman, Ruth C. and Jones, Stephen
THE SHORTGRASS PRAIRIE
"Barren beauty and subtle grandeur . . . vast expanses and small, secret delights . . ." often passed over by travelers for areas that are more spectacular. History and ecology, animals and plants, lovely photographs and a selected list of places to see. (BL) Pruett, 1988. ○

Davis, Peter
HOMETOWN: A CONTEMPORARY AMERICAN CHRONICLE
Unforgettable portrait of middle America—the Middletown series on public TV came out of the research. S&S, 1983. ○

Duncan, Dayton
OUT WEST: AN AMERICAN JOURNEY
Traces the route of Lewis & Clark in a camper—"an off-beat story that successfully combines history, travel and personal ad-venture"; and the route takes him from Mis-souri to Washington state via Nebraska, the Dakotas, Montana and Idaho. A reader wrote to ask that this book be included in a new edition of *Traveler's Reading Guide* with the

comment that it has a lot of history, humor and small-town adventures and is one of her all-time favorites, right up there with *Blue Highways.* (PW) Viking, 1987. ○

Flanagan, John T., ed.
AMERICA IS WEST: AN ANTHOLOGY OF MIDDLE-WESTERN LIFE AND LITERATURE
Reproduction of the 1945 edition. Greenwood, 1971. ○

Frazier, Ian
GREAT PLAINS
"Blend of travelogue, local color, geography and folklore" of the area that covers eastern Colorado to western Nebraska, and the Canadian border to Texas. FS&G, 1989. ○

Gjerde, Jon
FROM PEASANTS TO FARMERS
Basically for students of cultural migration, but also a book the reviewer says would be interesting for general readers with a special interest in Scandinavian settlements in the Midwest. It is a study of emigration from Balestrand, Norway, to the upper Midwest, and the effects on each. Cambridge, 1985.
○

Gusewelle, C.W.
FAR FROM ANY COAST: PIECES OF AMERICA'S HEARTLAND
"Essays on America's heartland . . . sketches of small cities, homes, landscapes, people, and institutions." U of Missouri Pr, 1989. ○

Harris, Eddy L.
MISSISSIPPI SOLO: A RIVER QUEST
The black author "seems a combination of Mark Twain's Huck and Jim" in a travelogue of his canoe trip from Minnesota to New Orleans. "Poignant impressions, philosophical reflections, and personal recollections . . . brim with local color, humor and realism." HarperCollins, 1988. ○

Hoy, Jim and Isern, Tom
PLAINS FOLK/PLAINS FOLK II
"Gentle pieces of delightful Americana"—collections of essays from the authors' syndicated column, and touching on topics that range from folklore and landscape monuments to ethnic diversity and tales of the dust bowl era. U of Oklahoma Pr, 1987 and 1990. ○

Kozma, Lu Anne G., ed.
LIVING AT A LIGHTHOUSE
Oral history from the Great Lakes. Great Lakes Lighthouse Keepers Assn, 1987. ○

Lavender, David W.
THE WAY TO THE WESTERN SEA: LEWIS & CLARK ACROSS THE CONTINENT
Using the skills of a master storyteller, Lavender has provided a "lively history of an epochal human exploit," drawing upon the primary source of the Lewis and Clark journals, as well as on earlier books on the subject by DeVoto, Bakeless and others. Doubleday, 1990. ○

Madson, John
UP ON THE RIVER: AN UPPER MISSISSIPPI CHRONICLE
The author views the Upper Mississippi (St. Louis north) as "reflecting the soul of America. . . . Lovingly shares a lifetime's interest, experiences and pleasure [and] moves easily from literary, historical, and bureaucratic accounts to those of his river acquaintances." (LJ) Lyons & Burford, 1985. ○

Madson, John
WHERE THE SKY BEGAN: LAND OF THE TALL GRASS PRAIRIE
Profile of a unique geographical area, the eastern portion of the great grasslands of the United States. Describes the incredulous reactions of those discoverers who first came upon the vast area, pioneer life, geography, weather, natural history, flora and fauna. Sierra, 1985. ○

Martone, Michael, ed.
A PLACE OF SENSE; ESSAYS IN SEARCH OF THE MIDWEST
"Eight prettily composed essays that explore the relationships of Midwesterners to Midwestern landscapes." (PW) U of Iowa Pr, 1988. ○

Merrill, Hugh
THE BLUES ROUTE
See entry under the South, above.   ○

Peirce, Neal R.
**THE GREAT PLAINS STATES OF
    AMERICA: PEOPLE, POLITICS
    AND POWER**
Norton, 1974. This and *The Great Lakes States*
(1980), in the same series, together cover the
Midwest. Patterned after the late John
Gunther's series of "inside" books—"part
history, part politics, part travel guide" describing the essential character and power
structure of each state and the region in
which it is located. See also Peirce's books
under "U.S.A."   ○

Penner, Mil and Schmidt, Carol
PRAIRIE
"Exploration of the history, ecology, evolution and essence of prairie lands," with many
photos. "A paean to both place and life-
style." Sounds of Ks, 1990.   ○

Raban, Jonathan
**OLD GLORY: AN AMERICAN
    VOYAGE**
A British journalist's odyssey down the Mississippi River in a sixteen-foot boat inspired
by longtime dreams of emulating Huck Finn.
One reviewer describes the author's style as
"a sort of English Capote: vivid, funny, accurate [combined with] the ability to make
an instant connection with virtually any human being whomsoever." (NYTBR) S&S,
1981.   ○

Reid, Robert L., ed.
**ALWAYS A RIVER: THE OHIO
    RIVER AND THE AMERICAN
    EXPERIENCE**
Indiana U Pr, 1991.   ○

Rhodes, Richard
**THE INLAND GROUND: AN
    EVOCATION OF THE
    AMERICAN MIDDLE WEST**
Best twelve essays from the original 1970
edition, plus four new ones about life in the
Middle West—"celebrates the essential spirit

and virtues" of the prairies. (PW) U Pr of
Kansas, 1991.   ○

Samuel, Ray, and others
TALES OF THE MISSISSIPPI
A panorama of Mississippi River life—the
many kinds of boats and floating palaces,
fabulous characters who lived, brawled and
died along the river. First published in 1955,
and something of a classic, this is a reprint
with scores of drawings and photographs.
Pelican, 1981.   ○

Scott, Quinta
**ROUTE 66: THE HIGHWAY AND
    ITS PEOPLE**
Route 66 was the major artery between Chicago and Los Angeles from 1926 until the
late 1950s. The book traces the impact of the
route—and the automobiles that drove it—
on the looks of America (tourist cabins, outrageous architecture, billboards, etc.). "Fascinating study of individual entrepreneurs
. . . a paean to a vanished way of life."
(BRD) U of Okla Pr, 1988.   ○

Simmons, Marc
**FOLLOWING THE SANTA FE
    TRAIL: A GUIDE FOR MODERN
    TRAVELERS**
History and text follow the original settlers'
path from Missouri to New Mexico—"any
portion would enrich a vacation . . . through
Kansas, Missouri, Oklahoma, Colorado or
New Mexico." (BL) Ancient City Pr, 1987.
    ○

Snyder, Tom
**ROUTE 66: TRAVELER'S GUIDE
    AND ROADSIDE COMPANION**
Fun to read as armchair travel, as well as
just the thing if you plan to drive, leisurely,
through the Midwest and Southwest. It includes how to follow the old road—it's disappeared in some places and has been
absorbed as an interstate in others—as well
as information on local history, museums,
eating and motels. St. Martin, 1990.   ○

Tassin, Myron, ed.
**THE DELTA QUEEN, LAST OF THE
    PADDLEWHEEL PALACES**
History of how and where she was built,
the facets of her character and the cities to

which she travels, with vintage photographs. Pelican, 1981.   ○

Wallis, Michael
ROUTE 66: THE MOTHER ROAD
A nostalgic book about Route 66, the road that kindled America's wanderlust after World War II; history, entrepreneurs, hustlers, contemporary and period photographs. St. Martin, 1990.   ○

GUIDEBOOKS

Baker, Carol, ed.
THE BOOK OF FESTIVALS IN THE MIDWEST
B L Pub, 1986.   ○

Bogue, Margaret B.
AROUND THE SHORES OF LAKE MICHIGAN
A guide to historic sites, as well as cultural, religious, ethnic, architectural points of interest in a journey around the lake's perimeter, with an overview of areas of Michigan, Wisconsin and Illinois that comprise the lake's shore. U of Wisconsin Pr, 1985. Also *Around the Shores of Lake Superior* (1979).   ○

Cantor, George
THE GREAT LAKES GUIDEBOOK
"Terrific guidebooks by a Detroit journalist" with commentary on the lakeside and island towns, historical information, evocative scenic description, sidetrips. In three volumes: *Lake Huron and Eastern Lake Michigan; Lake Superior and Western Lake Michigan; Lake Ontario and Erie.* (BL) U of Michigan Pr, 1980–84.   ○

*Daniel, Glenda
SIERRA CLUB NATURALIST'S GUIDE
A guide to the northwoods of Michigan, Wisconsin, Minnesota and Southern Ontario. Sierra, 1987.   ○

Edsall, Marian S.
ROADSIDE PLANTS AND FLOWERS
A travel guide to the Midwest and Great Lakes area. U of Wisconsin Pr, 1985.   ○

Grannis, Marjory, and others
VISITING THE MIDWEST'S HISTORIC PRESERVATION SITES
Forty-two sites within a 250-mile radius of Chicago, including where to stay, restaurants, other places of interest in each area. Jameson Bks, 1990.   ○

Gutek, Gerald and Patricia
EXPLORING MID-AMERICA: A GUIDE TO MUSEUM VILLAGES
Hippocrene, 1990.   ○

Middleton, Pat
DISCOVER AMERICA'S GREAT RIVER ROAD
The river road runs through Wisconsin, Iowa, Minnesota, Illinois. A journey from Galena, Illinois, to St. Paul, Minnesota, pointing out sites worth a stop, festivals, towns, shops, lodgings, access to marinas, parks, campgrounds and so on. Heritage Pr, 1989.   ○

Scharfenberg, Doris
THE LONG BLUE EDGE OF SUMMER
A vacation guide to the shoreline of Michigan. Eerdmans, 1982.   ○

Weil, Tom
AMERICA'S HEARTLAND
A travel guide to backroads of Illinois, Indiana, Iowa and Missouri—local history and off-the-beaten path approach. Hippocrene, 1989.   ○

THE WEST

Series Guidebooks
(See Appendix 1)

Fisher's World: West; North West; South West; Rocky Mountains South; Rocky Mountains North

Fodor: Far West; Pacific North Coast; The Rockies

Frommer: Northwest; Southwest

Insight Guide: American Southwest; Pacific Northwest; Rockies

Let's Go: Pacific Northwest

Sierra: Guide to the National Parks—Pacific Northwest & Alaska; Pacific Southwest & Hawaii; Desert Southwest, Rocky Mountains & the Great Plains

Smithsonian: Guide to Historic America—Rocky Mountain States (Colo., Wyo., Id., Mont.); Desert States (N.M., Ariz., Nev., Utah); Pacific States (Cal., Oreg., Wash., Alas., Ha.)

2–22 Days Itinerary Planning Guide: American South West; Pacific North West

Background Reading

NOTE: Entries with an asterisk (*) pertain also to Canada.

Abbey, Edward
BEYOND THE WALL

A collection of previously published essays by a conservationist, transporting readers into "western deserts and exploration of diverse wilderness areas. . . . For aficionados of nature, backpacking, and good writing." (BL) HR&W, 1989. Also *Down the River* (1982), reflections while on river trips, campouts, mountain climbs in the West—"lively, filled with irony, with wonder, and a vivid sense of place."   ○

Backes, Clarus, ed.
GROWING UP WESTERN

An anthology of writings by "the first literary generation that the settled West pro-

duced," with an introduction by Larry McMurtry. (BL) Knopf, 1990.   ○

Berger, Bruce
THE TELLING DISTANCE: CONVERSATIONS WITH THE AMERICAN DESERT

Experiences as a hiker, camper, rafter, bird-watcher and "meditations on the deep psychic link between wilderness and dreams, music, literature." (BL) Breitenbush, 1990.   ○

Conaway, James
THE KINGDOM IN THE COUNTRY

The author spent six months traveling through the West's public lands and visiting a variety of inhabitants from Native Americans and miners to lumberjacks and marijuana growers—"vivid, colorful portraits . . . convey well the complexities of regulation, use, and misuse of these lands." (LJ) HM, 1987.   ○

Cronkite, Walter
WESTWIND

Companion book to *South by Southeast* and *North by Northeast* listed above; like them, combines text, vignettes and watercolors and paintings. Oxmoor Hse, 1990.   ○

DeVoto, Bernard
ACROSS THE WIDE MISSOURI

Story of the mountain men and fur trade of the 1830s described vividly and with "splendid reproductions of sketches made on the trail in 1837–38." (BRD) Crown, 1985 (first published 1947). Also DeVoto's one-volume edition of *Journals of Lewis & Clark* (1953)—"the quintessential American journey"—and *The Course of Empire* (1983).   ○

Duncan, Dayton
OUT WEST: AN AMERICAN JOURNEY

See entry under the Midwest, above.   ○

Eppele, David
ON THE DESERT

"Humorous, poignant, informative essays . . . about people, plants and places" by a botanist, originally published as a column appearing in many Western newspapers. (Publisher) Tortilla Pr, 1990.   ○

Fradkin, Philip L.
A RIVER NO MORE

Historical and political account of the Colorado River and the seven states through which it flows to Mexico. U of Arizona, 1984. Also *Sagebrush Country: Land of the American West* (1989).   ○

Gibbs, Jim
SENTINELS OF SOLITUDE: WEST COAST LIGHTHOUSES

E Z Nature, 1989.   ○

Lavender, David W.
THE WAY TO THE WESTERN SEA: LEWIS & CLARK ACROSS THE CONTINENT

See entry under the Midwest, above. Other books by this writer include *The Great West* (1985), *The Rockies* (1981).   ○

May, Robin
HISTORY OF THE AMERICAN WEST

By a British author—"well researched yet entertaining record of the U.S. frontier era . . . a comprehensive and insightful view of the entire epic." (BL) Exeter, 1984.   ○

Patterson, Richard
HISTORICAL ATLAS OF THE OUTLAW WEST

Vintage (1880) maps plus directions for landmarks—"an indispensable aid to anyone interested in the 'good guys-bad guys' aspect of the American West." (BL) Johnson Bks, 1984.   ○

Peirce, Neal R.
THE PACIFIC STATES OF AMERICA: PEOPLE, POLITICS AND POWER IN THE FIVE PACIFIC STATES

Patterned after the late John Gunther's series of "inside" books—"part history, part politics, part travel guide," describing the essential character and power structure of each state and the region in which it is located. The five Pacific states are California, Oregon, Washington, Alaska and Hawaii. Norton, 1972. In the same series *The Mountain States of America* (1972) covers Arizona, Colorado, Idaho, Montana, Nevada, New Mexico, Utah and Wyoming. See also Peirce's books on America as a whole under "U.S.A."   ○

Pern, Stephen
THE GREAT DIVIDE: A WALK THROUGH AMERICA ALONG THE CONTINENTAL DIVIDE

A native Englishman began this walk at Antelope Wells, N.M., where the Continental Divide enters the United States; the walk lasted over five months, until he arrived at the Canadian border. Ranges between "frivolous observation and ingenuous insight," with many stories and anecdotes along the way. Viking, 1988.   ○

Rochlin, Harriet and Fred
PIONEER JEWS: A NEW LIFE IN THE FAR WEST

An account of Jewish migration to the West beginning with their movement from Spain to the Mexican territory in the sixteenth century and on through the Gold Rush to the 1920s—"a dramatic story and a mind-broadening journey into the past." (PW) Houghton, 1984.   ○

Ross, Nancy W.
WESTWARD THE WOMEN

Account of the roles of various women in the taming of the American West, through diaries and other contemporary writings. N Point Pr, 1985.   ○

Schultheis, Rob
THE HIDDEN WEST: JOURNEYS IN THE AMERICAN OUTBACK

"Profound, haunting travelogue that evokes the magic" of the Western landscape and its ecological precariousness. (BL) N Point Pr, 1983.   ○

Scott, Quinta
ROUTE 66: THE HIGHWAY AND ITS PEOPLE
See entry under the Midwest.   ○

Simmons, Marc
FOLLOWING THE SANTA FE TRAIL: A GUIDE FOR MODERN TRAVELERS
See entry under the Midwest.   ○

Snyder, Tom
ROUTE 66: TRAVELER'S GUIDE AND ROADSIDE COMPANION
See entry under the Midwest.   ○

*Stegner, Page
ISLANDS OF THE WEST: FROM BAJA TO VANCOUVER
Sierra Club, 1986.   ○

Stegner, Page
OUTPOSTS OF EDEN: A CURMUDGEON AT LARGE IN THE AMERICAN WEST
"Part polemical travelogue, part erudite natural history, and all beautifully written . . . a wonderful mix of literary notions concerning the value of a sense of place and the importance of wilderness to the human soul." (BL) Sierra, 1989.   ○

Stone, Irving
MEN TO MATCH MY MOUNTAINS: THE STORY OF THE OPENING OF THE FAR WEST
The story of the West told with the special talents of a novelist dedicated to imparting information with enjoyment and zest. Berkley Pub, 1987 (first published 1956).   ○

Vale, Thomas R. and Geraldine R.
WESTERN IMAGES, WESTERN LANDSCAPES ALONG U.S. 89
Follows U.S. Route 89 along a 1,500-mile route from Mexico to Canada, including the Grand Canyon, Yellowstone, the Tetons, Glacier National Park along the way—what the road means to the people who live there. U of Arizona Pr, 1989.   ○

Wallis, Michael
ROUTE 66: THE MOTHER ROAD
See entry under the Midwest.   ○

Wiley, Peter and Gottlieb, Robert
EMPIRES IN THE SUN: THE RISE OF THE NEW AMERICAN WEST
"From Brigham Young . . . to Ronald Reagan"—with a thesis that government subsidies and military bases provided "the impetus to the phenomenal growth" now reaching a breaking point. (BRD) Putnam Pub Group, 1982.   ○

Woodbury, Chuck
THE BEST FROM OUT WEST
A compilation of the author's best pieces from *Roadside Journal*—"memorable vignettes . . . insightful observations and impressions of the land, towns, the roads, the people—transporting the reader along on . . . his adventures." *Roadside Journal* was the self-published newsletter that this modern-day nomad produced to record his travels in the West. Morrow, 1990.   ○

COWBOYS AND COWGIRLS

Dary, David
COWBOY CULTURE: A SAGA OF FIVE CENTURIES
A scholarly look at the cowboy. Knopf, 1981.   ○

*Davis, Tom
BE TOUGH OR BE GONE! THE ADVENTURES OF A MODERN DAY COWBOY
"Uplifting, true-adventure tale in which Tom Davis set a world record by taking a pack train of horses and mules from El Paso, Texas to Fairbanks, Alaska in less than six months." (BL) Northern Trails Pr, 1984.   ○

Durham, Philip and Jones, Everett L.
THE NEGRO COWBOYS
U of Nebraska, 1983 (first published 1965).   ○

*Johnston, Moira
RANCH: PORTRAIT OF A SURVIVING DREAM

Text and photos in a recreation of the past, the land and its people today. An absorbing evocation of ranch life and the author's journey which includes the American high plains, California and British Columbia. Doubleday, 1983. ○

Jordan, Teresa
COWGIRLS: WOMEN OF THE AMERICAN WEST

Stories of the counterparts to the cowboy based on interviews and excerpts from nineteenth- and early twentieth-century newspaper articles, songs, poetry and diaries. Doubleday, 1982. ○

Roach, Joyce G.
THE COWGIRL

Revised edition, originally published in 1977. History of women of the West who broke with convention to participate in ranching, trail driving, rodeos. U of North Texas Pr, 1990. ○

Steiner, Stan
THE RANCHERS: A BOOK OF GENERATIONS

Vignettes of twenty ranching families from Montana, New Mexico and Oregon and why they hold on to "a way of life and a way of thinking that the rest of the country long ago abandoned and forgot." (BRD) U of Okla Pr, 1985. ○

Youngquist, Erick H.
AMERICA FEVER: A SWEDE IN THE WEST, 1914–1923

The author came to the West without a trade or ability to speak English, and became an expert cowboy and horseman, reveling in the freedom and challenge of wide open spaces—"first hand glimpse of life on the range as seen by an optimistic, romantic youth." A reviewer suggests that this book be read in conjunction with the earlier *Log of a Cowboy: A Narrative of the Old Trail Days* by Andy Adams, first published in 1903 but now available in several reprint editions. ○

GUIDEBOOKS

Black, Naomi and Faller, Will
DUDE RANCHES OF THE AMERICAN WEST

Twenty-nine ranches in Arizona, Colorado, Montana, Wyoming, described with photographs, addresses and rates—"a terrific travel guide." (BL) Stephen Greene, 1988. ○

Brown, Joseph E.
OFF-SEASON: A GUIDE TO VISITING THE WESTERN NATIONAL PARKS WITHOUT THE CROWDS

Parks from the Pacific to the Plains, California and New Mexico. HarBraceJ, 1988. ○

Cromie, Alice H.
TOUR GUIDE TO THE OLD WEST

A guide to settlements, forts, museums, battlegrounds, landmarks, relics, cowboys and characters. Rutledge Hill Pr, 1990. ○

Erickson, Jack
A GUIDE TO WEST COAST MICROBREWERIES AND BREWPUBS

A growing phenomenon—the production of local beers. Redbrick Pr, 1990. ○

Gutek, Gerald and Patricia
EXPLORING AMERICA'S WEST

A guide to museum villages in California, Arizona, New Mexico, Colorado, Wyoming, Oregon and Washington. "A wonderful source of historical information . . . a gold mine for travelers." (LJ) Globe Pequot, 1989. ○

Kaysing, Bill
GREAT HOT SPRINGS OF THE WEST

Hot tubs, primitive hot springs and bubbling mud spas. Capra Pr, 1990. ○

*Olmsted, Gerald W.
THE BEST OF THE PACIFIC COAST: SAN FRANCISCO TO BRITISH COLUMBIA

A guide for the curious traveler is the subtitle—"interesting and delightful places . . .

tiny hamlets off the beaten path . . . history and the present flavor of places." Ideal for the traveler touring the West by car. Practical tourist information is included on places to stay, campgrounds and restaurants. (LJ) Crown, 1989.   ○

Valencia, Kris, ed.
NORTHWEST MILEPOSTS, 1990
Guide to the key highways in Washington, Oregon, Idaho, western Montana and southwestern Canada, with detailed information on major cities, islands and parks in the area; with a new edition each year. Alaska Northwest, 1990.   ○

*Vokac, David
GREAT TOWNS GUIDES
Out-of-the-way vacation spots with a "great town" as focus—selected for being unspoiled and rich in human-scale charms, as well as for scenic splendor. There are guides for the West, the Pacific Northwest and for California. The guides provide history, weather, general employment, lodging of all kinds, including camping, and shopping and so on. West Pr, 1985–87.   ○

PACIFIC NORTHWEST

Bancroft, Hunt N.
PEOPLE OF THE TOTEM
The Indians of the Pacific Northwest, whose art and culture have fascinated Europeans since the eighteenth and nineteenth centuries, before their civilization was changed by the white man—from Alaska to Upper Washington and through British Columbia. Putnam Pub Group, 1979.   ○

Brown, Bruce
MOUNTAIN IN THE CLOUDS: A
    SEARCH FOR THE WILD
    SALMON
"Part lyrical nature writing, part sportsman's adventure story, part . . . political exposé with history and ecology information. (LJ) S&S, 1982.   ○

Franzwa, Gregory M.
THE OREGON TRAIL REVISITED
For those who would like to retrace this historic trail from Missouri to Oregon. Patrice Pr, 1988.   ○

Olmsted, Gerald
LEWIS & CLARK TRAIL
With this book (part of the Fielding series) you can follow in the footsteps of the explorers, from your armchair or for real; excerpts from their journals, practical travel tips, a wealth of historical detail. Morrow, 1987.   ○

Stafford, Kim R.
HAVING EVERYTHING RIGHT:
    ESSAYS OF PLACE
"Having Everything Right" is an Indian place name, and these are personal reminiscences and essays—"vivid, succinct prose . . . a dazzling style . . . summation of a way of living on earth in a spirit of harmony, gratitude and adventure." (BRD) Penguin, 1987.   ○

GUIDEBOOKS/PACIFIC NORTHWEST

*Brewster, D. & Robinson, K.
NORTHWEST BEST PLACES
The *Oregonian* is quoted in a bookstore catalog as having said, "it is so far ahead of its competition in the field that nothing else even comes close." Some 1,500 places are rated: sights, lodgings, restaurants. Covers Washington, Oregon and British Columbia. Sasquatch, 1989.   ○

Hicks-Herman, Julie & Darrin C.
FESTIVAL HOPPER'S GUIDE TO
    THE GREAT NORTHWEST
Arranged geographically, indexed by town and festival name. Creative Chaos, 1990. ○

Landau, Carl and Katie
FESTIVALS OF THE PACIFIC
    NORTHWEST
All kinds of festivals where you can participate in a local event along with the locals. Landau Comns, 1989.   ○

Loam, Jayson
HOT SPRINGS AND HOT POOLS
    OF THE NORTHWEST
The definitive guidebook to places where you can legally put your body in hot water—from natural geothermal pools to where to

rent a hot tub. Aqua Thermal Access, 1991. ○

*McFarlane, Marilyn
QUICK ESCAPES IN THE PACIFIC NORTHWEST

First of a new series of short-trip guides from major U.S. cities. Forty itineraries for trips out of Portland, Seattle or Vancouver that suggest sights to see each morning and afternoon, additional sights, where to take each meal and to stay overnight, and short-cuts home. Globe Pequot, 1991. ○

*Oakley, Myrna
PUBLIC AND PRIVATE GARDENS OF THE NORTHWEST

A guide to gardens and natural areas of the Pacific Northwest and British Columbia. Beautiful America Pub, 1990. ○

THE SOUTHWEST

Abbey, Edward
CACTUS COUNTRY

Part of the American Wilderness series. Time-Life, 1973. ○

Casey, Robert L.
JOURNEY TO THE HIGH SOUTHWEST: A TRAVELER'S GUIDE

"Very personal and engaging guide to the region where Arizona, New Mexico, Colorado, and Utah meet. . . . Natural wonders, archaeological ruins, Indian reservations, parks . . . historic sites" with practical information on housing, restaurants, shopping, and tourist tips. (BL) Globe Pequot, 1988. ○

Dobie, James Frank
CORONADO'S CHILDREN: TALES OF LOST MINES AND BURIED TREASURE IN THE SOUTHWEST

"Packed full of treasure tales"—the myths and legends of buried gold in the old Southwest beginning with the seven cities of Cibola sought by Coronado, with map and charts. (BRD) U of Texas Pr, 1978. *Apache Gold and Yaqui Silver* (1939) is its sequel. Also

Guide to Life and Literature of the Southwest (1981). ○

Horgan, Paul
GREAT RIVER: THE RIO GRANDE IN NORTH AMERICAN HISTORY

Reprint of a book that won a Pulitzer Prize. Pacesetter, 1984 (first published 1954). ○

Keneally, Thomas
THE PLACE WHERE SOULS ARE BORN: JOURNEY TO THE SOUTHWEST

"Observations and impressions" by an Australian novelist fascinated by America's southwest, interweaving history, popular culture, geology, mythology. For Americans, the author feels, do not appreciate "that the native American past still casts a spell over the soul of the land." (BL) S&S, 1992. ○

Lavender, David
THE SOUTHWEST

Exploration of the land, the history and the peoples of the Southwest, with emphasis on Arizona and New Mexico, from Spanish and Indian days to the present. U of New Mexico, 1984. ○

McGaw, William C.
SOUTHWEST SAGA: THE WAY IT REALLY WAS!

Vignettes of characters and episodes to set the record straight—"history presented in its most enjoyable form." (BL) Golden West, 1988. ○

Mays, Buddy
ANCIENT CITIES OF THE SOUTHWEST

Prehistoric ruins and native cultures in Arizona, New Mexico, Utah and Colorado. Chronicle, 1990. ○

Miller, Tom
ON THE BORDER: PORTRAITS OF AMERICA'S SOUTHWESTERN FRONTIER

Documents the lifestyles, competition, cooperation, tensions and conflicts on the "friendship" frontier. U of Ariz Pr, 1985. ○

Querry, Ronald B., ed.
GROWING OLD AT WILLIE NELSON'S PICNIC

Aspects of the Indian, Spanish, Anglo Southwest in a collection of writings—fiction and non-fiction—by 21 writers from D.H. Lawrence to Larry McMurtry. Texas A&M U Pr, 1983.   ○

Sierra Club Guides eds.
NATIONAL PARKS OF THE DESERT SOUTHWEST; NATIONAL PARKS OF THE PACIFIC SOUTHWEST AND HAWAII

Random, 1984.   ○

Simmons, Marc
FOLLOWING THE SANTA FE TRAIL

A guide for modern travelers. Ancient City Pr, 1984.   ○

Turner, Frederick
OF CHILES, CACTI AND FIGHTING COCKS: NOTES ON THE AMERICAN WEST

Essays that explore "the paradoxes of life in the west, the dream versus the reality." (BL) N Point Pr, 1990.   ○

Zwinger, Ann
WIND IN THE ROCK

A naturalist explores the canyon country in the four corners area where Arizona, New Mexico, Utah and Colorado meet—"lively, readable nature writing," with sketches. (BRD) U of Ariz Pr, 1984.   ○

GUIDEBOOKS/SOUTHWEST

Cahill, Rick
BORDER TOWNS OF THE SOUTHWEST

Shopping, dining, fun and adventure from Tijuana to Juarez. How to get a brief glimpse of another culture. Pruett, 1987.   ○

Landau, Carl and Katie
FESTIVALS OF THE SOUTHWEST

All kinds of festivals where you can participate in a local event along with the locals. Landau Comns, 1989.   ○

Lange, Frederick W.
CORTEZ CROSSROADS

A guide to the Anasazi heritage and the four corners (of Utah, Arizona, New Mexico, Colorado) region. Johnson Bks, 1989.   ○

Loam, Jayson
HOT SPRINGS AND HOT POOLS OF THE SOUTHWEST

The definitive guidebook to places where you can legally put your body in hot water—from natural geothermal pools to where to rent a hot-tub. Aqua Thermal Access, 1991.   ○

ALABAMA

*Series Guidebooks
(See Appendix 1)*

See series guides (and non-series guides) listed under United States and the South.

Background Reading

Agee, James
LET US NOW PRAISE FAMOUS MEN

A study in words and pictures of a share-cropper's family in 1936. HM, 1989 (first published 1941).   ○

Carmer, Carl
STARS FELL ON ALABAMA

Tales, sketches and impressions of life in Alabama, first published in 1934, now a classic and published in a new edition as part of the Library of Alabama Classics Series. U of Alabama Pr, 1985.   ○

Greenhouse, Wayne
ALABAMA ON MY MIND
People, politics, history and ghost stories.
Sycamore Pr, 1987.   o

Higgins, Sara W., ed.
**FROM CIVIL WAR TO CIVIL
  RIGHTS**
Alabama from 1860 to 1960, an anthology
from the *Alabama Review*. U of Alabama Pr,
1987.   o

Sangster, Tom
ALABAMA'S COVERED BRIDGES
For anyone who thinks New England has a
monopoly on covered bridges. Coffeetable
1980.   o

GUIDEBOOKS

Kaylor, Mike
**WHERE TO FIND THE BEST OF
  HUNTSVILLE**
Kaylor Co, 1984.   o

McCaig & Boyce
ALABAMA STATE PARKS
Affordable Adventures, 1989.   o

McMinn, Russell
**ANTIQUES: GUIDE TO ALABAMA
  ANTIQUE SHOPS**
Jockey Hollow, 1989.   o

National League of American Pen
  Women, Eds. of
**HISTORIC HOMES OF ALABAMA
  AND THEIR TRADITIONS**
Southern U Pr, 1969.   o

Van der Veer Hamilton, Virginia
SEEING HISTORIC ALABAMA
Fifteen guided tours of historic sights and
museums. U of Alabama Pr, 1982.   o

Wade, Gerald
**FACTS, FOLKS, RESIDENTS AND
  RASCALS**
A slightly irreverent visitors' handbook for
the Shoals (northwest) area. Cypress Creek
Pubns, 1990.   o

HISTORY

Van der Veer Hamilton, Virginia
ALABAMA
One of a series of popular histories for each
state, published as part of the bicentennial
in 1976. Norton, 1984.   o

Novels

Brown, Rita Mae
SOUTHERN DISCOMFORT
Novel of the "rigid class and racial lines of
Montgomery society during the early de-
cades of this century." (FC) Har-Row,
1982.   o

Capote, Truman
A CHRISTMAS MEMORY
Autobiographical story of a boy's Christmas
with elderly relatives. Random, 1966. Also
The Thanksgiving Visitor (1968).   o

Cook, Thomas H.
STREETS OF FIRE (Birmingham)
A crime novel set in Birmingham, 1963, at
the time of Martin Luther King's freedom
marches—"evokes all of the emotionalism
that prevailed at the time." (FC) Putnam,
1989.   o

Flagg, Fannie
**FRIED GREEN TOMATOES AT THE
  WHISTLE-STOP CAFE**
A rural hamlet near Birmingham is the setting—"carefully plotted . . . moods and
people of pre- and post-World War II Alabama is splendidly evoked." (FC) Random,
1987.   o

Groom, Winston
GONE THE SUN
An Alabama newspaper editor covers a story
that precipitates a clash of journalistic ethics
and personal relationships. Doubleday,
1988.   o

Lee, Harper
TO KILL A MOCKINGBIRD
Adult injustice and violence are brought into
the lives of two children when their father
courageously defends a black accused of

rape—set in a small southern town. Lippincott, 1960.   ○

McCammon, R.R.
BOY'S LIFE

Innocence is lost when a 12-year-old, living in a sleepy town in Alabama in 1964, is with his father when a car plunges into the lake and a body is discovered handcuffed to the steering wheel—"haunting yarn of adult demons being faced and fathomed by the young." (FC) Pocket Bks, 1991.   ○

McCammon, Robert
MYSTERY WALK

Two young brothers (one a tent revival faith healer, the other with the gift to help spirits of those who die violently to "pass over")

in a novel of horror and the supernatural—"delivers a good scare with style." (FC) Holt, 1983.   ○

Morris, Phillip Q.
THIRSTY CITY

A dry county is the setting for a novel about a bootlegger and his family—"a celebration of moonshine, fast cars and beautiful women . . . a witty yet loving look at . . . local customs." (PW) Random, 1990.   ○

Norman, Geoffrey
ALABAMA SHOWDOWN

The Alabama-Auburn football game—the big event as a metaphor that transcends college football, revealing much about the region. (FC) Zebra, 1987.   ○

ALASKA

Series Guidebooks

NOTE: See also Series Guides (and nonseries guides) listed under United States and the West and the West/Pacific Northwest, above. You may also find some crossover in guides and books listed under British Columbia and the Yukon and Northwest Territory under Canada.

Fodor: Alaska
Frommer: Alaska
Insight Guide: Alaska
Langenscheidt: Self-Guided Alaska
Let's Go: Western Canada & Alaska
Lonely Planet: Alaska
Moon Handbook: Alaska-Yukon
2–22 Days Itinerary Planning Guide- Alaska

Background Reading

Alaska Geo Staff, eds.
ADVENTURE ROADS NORTH

The story of the Alaska Highway and other roads in the Milepost. Alaska Geo Svc, 1983.   ○

Alaska Geo Staff, eds.
ISLAND OF THE SEALS: THE PRIBILOFFS

History, description, travel and sealing—this is the area of confrontation between conservationists and those who hunt seals for a livelihood each year. Alaska Northwest, 1982.   ○

Bockstoce, John
ARCTIC PASSAGES

"A unique small-boat voyage through the Great Northern waterway" is the subtitle. Using the Umiak, an Eskimo boat, the author sailed for 20 summers in the Bering Strait with crews ranging from Eskimo families to Oxford dons—"uplifting reading . . . a good sense of humor." (LJ) Hearst Bks, 1991.   ○

Connor, Cathy and O'Haire, Daniel
ROADSIDE GEOLOGY OF ALASKA

One of a series of books that is wonderful to take along in the car. To paraphrase the preface, being able to look at the landscape as you travel and (with this book) envision the forces and changes—the dynamics of the landscape you are seeing—is a real achievement of understanding for travelers. Mountain Pr, 1988. ○

Crump, Donald J., ed.
ALASKA'S MAGNIFICENT PARKLANDS
Natl Geog, 1984. ○

Eide, Harold
NORWEGIAN
A rollicking tale of wild trails and the lure of gold—the amazing story of a young man who set out to make his fortune in Alaska, and succeeded. He then spent it on a three-month-long party in San Francisco—"heartwarming, sometimes funny, often exciting." First published in 1975. (Publisher) Alaska Northwest, 1987. ○

Hedin, Robert and Holthaus, Gary, eds.
ALASKA: REFLECTIONS ON LAND AND SPIRIT
An anthology of selections by Muir, John McPhee, Barry Lopez and others—"excellent sampler of some of the best writing on Alaska," with photographs. (LJ) U of Arizona Pr, 1989. ○

Hildebrand, John
READING THE RIVER: A VOYAGE DOWN THE YUKON
A canoe trip searching for life as it used to be on the Yukon—"vivid . . . lyrical picture of people who live off the land in a way the author could not." (LJ) HM, 1988. ○

Johnson, Beth
YUKON WILD
The adventures of four Texas women who paddled through America's last frontier. Their journal includes preparations for and the canoe trip itself—people they met along the way, cafes along the river, weather, bugs, "all add up to a saga that will entertain prospective river travelers and armchair adventurers alike." (PW) Berkshire Traveller Pr, 1984. ○

Lamb, May Wynne
LIFE IN ALASKA: THE REMINISCENCES OF A KANSAS WOMAN
Memoir of a young widow who teaches in the Alaskan bush, 1916–19, with editing, footnotes and introduction added by her niece—"a riveting document of everyday life . . . in a world that can never be reclaimed." (BL) U of Nebraska Pr, 1988. ○

McPhee, John
COMING INTO THE COUNTRY
Story of America's last frontier and of its colorful people, wild animals and magnificent land through all its moods—the next thing to being there. FS&G, 1977. Also, with Galen Rowell, *Alaska: Images of the Country* (1981), color photographs to complement excerpts from the text of *Coming Into the Country*, published by the Sierra Club. ○

Miller, Debbie
MIDNIGHT WILDERNESS: JOURNEYS IN THE ARCTIC
The author and her husband make their living as writers, teachers and wildlife survey pilots. They have explored many remote areas, learning how to survive in the wilderness—"transmits her continual wonder and appreciation of Alaska's magnificence . . . vivid descriptions of immense vistas and fragile wildlife." (BL) Sierra, 1990. ○

Muir, John
TRAVELS IN ALASKA
Reprint of the naturalist's book describing several trips to Alaska, ending with a description of the aurora phenomena. Sierra, 1988. ○

*Murray, John A., ed.
A REPUBLIC OF RIVERS: THREE CENTURIES OF NATURE WRITING FROM ALASKA AND THE YUKON
Forty-eight selections, in chronological order, from 1741 to 1989: geographical descriptions, animals, men's encounters with the area and with themselves. Oxford U Pr, 1990. ○

Nelson, Richard K.
SHADOW OF THE HUNTER: STORIES OF ESKIMO LIFE
Stories of the Inuit Indian by an anthropologist—a descriptive account of a living culture. U of Chicago, 1983. ○

Olson, Sigurd
RUNES OF THE NORTH
The "face and facts" of nature as reflected in the author's experiences on a trip to Saskatchewan, Hudson Bay, the Yukon and into Alaska. (BRD) Knopf, 1963.   ○

Pohl, William L.
DOWN NORTH: PROFILES FROM ALASKA AND THE YUKON
"Colorful comments and recollections" of Alaskans and Yukoners encountered on a trip during the summer of 1979. (LJ) Thorndike, 1986.   ○

Rice, Larry
GATHERING PARADISE
The reviewer was not enchanted with Mr. Rice's writing style but nevertheless found the book absorbing. The author is a wildlife biologist who tells of a dozen of his journeys into the wilderness—parks, white water rivers, refuges, with nuggets of history and some startling experiences. (LJ) Fulcrum, 1990.   ○

Scott, Alastair
TRACKS ACROSS ALASKA
A veteran traveler, but a novice to Alaska and dogsledding, sets out to follow a dream of mushing his way from Manley to Nome, which includes some of the Iditarod Trail route—"awed by the landscape and people . . . does full justice to both in this engaging travel adventure." (PW) Atl Monthly Pr, 1990.   ○

Spencer, Page
WHITE SILK AND BLACK TAR: A JOURNAL OF THE ALASKA OIL SPILL
"Personal, often emotional, account of the *Exxon Valdez* tragedy." (LJ) Bergamot Bks, 1990.   ○

Thomas, Lowell Jr. and others
ALASKA AND THE YUKON
Splendid evocation of the continent's last frontier—eight contributors write on people past and present, animals, recreation, sports,

history, cities and isolated settlements. Facts On File, 1983.   ○

Vick, Ann
THE CAMA-I BOOK
A Foxfire-like project (see "Georgia") of students in the most isolated southwestern region of the state—"kayaks, dogsleds, salmonberry jelly, ivory carving, smoked fish, mukluks" and other crafts, customs and lore. (BL) Doubleday, 1983.   ○

Wulbert, Roland and Laraby, Larry, eds.
A GOOD CREW: AN ALASKAN MEN'S ANTHOLOGY
"First-rate collection of regional writing . . . 25 Alaskan men report male Alaskan experiences . . . their own and those of men . . . known or imagined." (BL) Fireweed Pr, 1986.   ○

GUIDEBOOKS

Eppenbach, Sarah
ALASKA'S SOUTHEAST: TOURING THE INSIDE PASSAGE
A book for traveling in the area of Alaska from Ketchikan to Skagway, whether by ferry, cruise ship or private boat. The first part includes history, geography, flora and fauna and the art and mythology of the peoples; the second part describes individual towns and villages with detailed maps. Globe Pequot, 1988.   ○

Levi, Steven C.
THE ALASKA TRAVELER: YEAR 'ROUND VACATION ADVENTURES FOR EVERYONE
"A practical and engaging guide" organized into four regions, with advice and information to plan an Alaskan vacation around particular interests, from fishing to gold panning. Mills & Sanderson, 1989.   ○

Milepost, Eds. of
THE MILEPOST
"A reliable guide to the entire highway network of northwestern Canada, the Yukon and Alaska." (NYT) Alaska Northwest, up-

dated every year. Also *The Alaska Wilderness Milepost,* if you want to leave the road behind.   ○

Searby, Ellen
THE INSIDE PASSAGE TRAVELER
The author has worked for many years on the ferries—complete information needed to plan a trip as comfortable or adventurous as you choose. Includes minor ports and native villages served by smaller ferries. Windham Bay Pr, 1985.   ○

Simmerman, Nancy L.
ALASKA'S PARKLANDS: THE COMPLETE GUIDE
Comprehensive guide to travel by all means—air, car, foot and boat—in Alaska's parks, refuges and forests; to wild rivers, historic sites. Mountaineers, 1983.   ○

HISTORY

Alaska Magazine, Staff of
BITS AND PIECES OF ALASKAN HISTORY
Volume I covers 1935–1959; Volume II, 1960–1974. "Outstanding overview . . . both humorous and serious stories" and hundreds of nostalgic photographs. (Publisher) Alaska Northwest, 1981.   ○

Hunt, William R.
ALASKA
One of a series of popular histories for each state, published as part of the 1976 bicentennial. Norton, 1976.   ○

Novels

Boyer, G.G.
MORGETTE IN THE YUKON
"Old-fashioned, action-packed tale" of gunfighters, claim-jumpers and a longlost gold mine. (FC) Walker, 1983.   ○

Dailey, Janet
THE GREAT ALONE
Historic, epic novel of Alaska, beginning with arrival of Russian fur traders in the

Aleutians in the 17th century. Poseidon Pr, 1986.   ○

Doig, Ivan
THE SEA RUNNERS
Adventure novel of Alaska's Russian period when Scandinavians worked as indentured servants in the tsar's service. A story of the escape of four of them from Sitka to Astoria, Oregon. Atheneum, 1982.   ○

Elkins, Aaron J.
ICY CLUTCHES
A skeleton detective (one who figures out how people died from their bones), who believes he's on vacation in Alaska, must get back to his profession when human bones are discovered at an old avalanche site. Mysterious Pr, 1990.   ○

Ferber, Edna
ICE PALACE
A public and private tug-of-war over the years between two onetime partners over the issues of statehood for Alaska and affection and loyalty of their granddaughter—"eye-opening glimpses of . . . Alaska." (FC) Doubleday, 1958.   ○

Hawkes, John
ADVENTURES IN THE ALASKAN SKIN TRADE
Her father's story, narrated by Sunny who runs a brothel. S&S, 1985.   ○

Henry, Sue
MURDER ON THE IDITAROD TRAIL
"A stunning portrait of the Alaskan landscape . . . a riveting account" of this annual dog-sled race, combined with an unusual, gripping murder mystery. (Publisher) Atl Monthly Pr, 1991.   ○

London, Jack
CALL OF THE WILD
Classic adventure story of a man and his dog in the Klondike. Dodd, 1960 (first published 1903).   ○

Michener, James A.
ALASKA

The story of Alaska from prehistoric times to the Alcan Highway—blends "fact, fiction and myth . . . in an imagined human and national history." (BRD) Random, 1988.   ○

Roesch, E.P.
ASHANA

An Alaskan woman is taken hostage in 1790 by Russian traders. Random, 1990.   ○

A R I Z O N A

Series Guidebooks
(See Appendix 1)

NOTE: See also Series Guides (and non-series guides) listed under United States and the West and the West/the Southwest.

Compass American Guide: Arizona
Fodor: Arizona
Moon Handbook: Arizona
Sierra Guide: Natural Areas of New Mexico, Arizona & Nevada

Background Reading

Beer, Bill
WE SWAM THE GRAND CANYON

"The true story of a cheap vacation that got a little out of hand" is the lengthy subtitle. An account of an illegal trip through the Grand Canyon that became an exercise in endurance. Also provides information on legal trips. Mountaineers, 1988.   ○

Chapin, Frederick H.
THE LAND OF THE CLIFF DWELLERS

Reprint of an 1892 account of what is now Mesa National Park. U of Arizona Pr, 1988.   ○

Chronic, Halka
ROADSIDE GEOLOGY OF ARIZONA

One of a series of books that is wonderful to take along in the car. To paraphrase the preface, being able to look at the landscape as you travel and (with this book) envision the forces and changes—the dynamics of the landscape you are seeing—is a real achievement of understanding for travelers. Mountain Pr, 1983.   ○

Eikenberry, Alice
PUEBLO: PLAYS, PLAYERS, PLAYHOUSES IN THE GILDED AGE, 1865–1900.

Pueblo Co Hist Soc, 1985.   ○

Fletcher, Colin
THE MAN WHO WALKED THROUGH TIME

New edition of a classic first published in 1968. The author spent two months on a solitary walk through the Grand Canyon from end to end, and the book reflects his perceptions and "the message of the wilderness." (BRD) Random, 1989.   ○

Kant, Candace C.
ZANE GREY'S ARIZONA

"Describes Grey's life in Arizona . . . how his firsthand observations inspired some of his most memorable tales" in their Arizona setting. (BL) Northland, 1984.   ○

Krutch, Joseph W.
GRAND CANYON

Unhurried view of "one of nature's most impressive phenomena . . . nature writing at its best." (BRD) U of Arizona Pr, 1989. Also *Desert Year* (1952), a literary work on the natural setting of the Southwest, desert life, and the author's personal philosophy.   ○

Kurtchner, Kenner C.
FRONTIER FIDDLER: THE LIFE OF A NORTHERN ARIZONA PIONEER

Born on the Arizona frontier to a Mormon family in 1886, he lived a life of adventure, was knowledgeable about the range and wildlife, and was a fine dance hall fiddler from 1902 to the 1920s. The book provides a first-hand account of what life was like during this period bridging pioneer Arizona to modern times. U of Arizona Pr, 1990. o

Lavender, David
RIVER RUNNERS OF THE GRAND CANYON

Early-day river runners and their "breath-taking experiences"—explorers, surveyors, miners, thrill-seekers. (PW) U of Arizona, 1985.
o

Lesure, Thomas B.
ALL ABOUT ARIZONA

"The healthful state where it's great to live and vacation" is the book's subtitle. Allsport Pub, 1983.
o

Morgan, Anne H. and Strickland, Rennard, eds.
ARIZONA MEMORIES

A collection of reminiscences of diverse people, in their own words—an Apache scout, a frontier doctor, a soldier's wife, a cowboy—and about ranching, mining, Christmas, July 4th and more. U of Arizona, 1984.
o

Schullery, Paul, ed.
THE GRAND CANYON: EARLY IMPRESSIONS

Reactions of writers from 1869 to 1941 (Zane Grey, John Muir, etc.), pioneers, scholars, on first seeing the Canyon, and ranging from "scholarly or pioneering reports to enthusiastic travelogues or satiric jabs." (BL) Pruett, 1989.
o

Sikorsky, Robert
FOOLS' GOLD

"The facts, myths and legends of the Lost Dutchman Mine and the Superstition Mountains." The author's experiences as a geologist provide history of this fabled treasure "separating fact from fantasy." (BL) Golden West, 1983.
o

Spangler, Sharon
ON FOOT IN THE GRAND CANYON

For all kinds of hikers (including those who never leave their armchair), the author describes experiences on seven trails, mostly on the South Rim, in every season. "Enriched with natural and human history . . . anecdotes . . . a great appreciation for the beauty"—includes a reading list. (LJ Pruett, 1986.
o

Trimble, Marshall
ROADSIDE HISTORY OF ARIZONA

A history to take along with you, and perhaps read aloud to companions as you drive the state's highways. One of a unique series, written in lively narrative style by authors who know how to bring the past alive. It's like having a knowledgeable friend along who has lived in the state for years, and knows how to illuminate what you are seeing with authentic information about bygone days and the whys and hows of history as it deserves to be told. Mountain Pr, 1987. o

Waters, Frank
BOOK OF THE HOPI
Penguin, 1977.
o

GUIDEBOOKS

Cook, James E. and others
TRAVEL ARIZONA: THE BACKROADS
Arizona Hwy, 1989.
o

DeMente, Boye
GUIDE TO ARIZONA'S INDIAN RESERVATIONS
Phoenix Bks, 1988.
o

Everhart, Ronald E.
GLEN CANYON/LAKE POWELL: THE STORY BEHIND THE SCENERY
Guide to these recreation areas in Arizona and Utah. KC Pbns, 1983.
o

Garrity, John
THE TRAVELER'S GUIDE TO BASEBALL SPRING TRAINING
Spring training sites in Arizona and Florida for all major league teams—all of the practical information along with lists of the author's favorite restaurants and places to stay. Read also for what the reviewer terms the ambience and sheer enjoyment of the author's skewed sense of humor. Andrews & McMeel, 1989.   ○

Hait, Pam
SHIFRA STEIN'S DAY TRIPS FROM PHOENIX, TUCSON, AND FLAGSTAFF
Historic and purely recreational places within a day's drive of the three cities. Includes recommended restaurants and places to stay, festivals, national parks, detailed driving instructions. Globe Pequot, 1990.   ○

Landau, Carl and Katie
FESTIVALS OF THE SOUTHWEST
Your guided tour to festivals in Arizona and New Mexico. Landau Comns, 1989.   ○

Martin, Don W. and Betty W.
COMING TO ARIZONA
The complete guide for future Arizonans—for snowbirds, retirees, jobseekers. Pine Cone Pr, 1991.   ○

Meyer, Michael and Muir, Sarah
DESTINATION SOUTHWEST
This is a guide to wintering and/or retiring in Arizona, New Mexico and Nevada. Oryx, 1990.   ○

Valenti, Dan
CACTUS LEAGUE ROAD TRIP: A GUIDE TO SPRING TRAINING IN ARIZONA
Stephen Greene, 1990   ○

HISTORY

Faulk, Odie B.
ARIZONA: A SHORT HISTORY
U of Oklahoma Pr, 1970.   ○

Powell, Lawrence C.
ARIZONA: A HISTORY
One of a series of popular histories for each state published as part of the bicentennial in 1976; reprint of 1976 edition, with a new preface and bibliography. U of New Mexico Pr, 1989.   ○

Trimble, Marshall
ARIZONA: A CAVALCADE OF HISTORY
Treasure Chest, 1989. Also *A Panoramic History of a Frontier State* (1977), *Arizona Adventure: Action Packed True Tales of Early Arizona* (1982) and *Diamond in the Rough: An Illustrated History of Arizona* (1988).   ○

Novels

Abbey, Edward
THE MONKEY WRENCH GANG
A group of improbable conservationists sabotage bulldozers, power lines and bridges, in their private war against those who would destroy the landscape—"terrific chase sequences . . . eloquent landscapes." (FC) Lippincott, 1975.   ○

Bonham, Frank
THE EYE OF THE HUNTER
Vivid descriptions of Arizona in a novel set in the territory of 1900. Evans & Co, 1989.   ○

Bryant, Will
A TIME OF HEROES
Nostalgia and "great period flavor" of the early 1920s, as a barnstorming pilot gets involved with an orphan and a trip across Arizona to locate a secret mine. (FC) St. Martin, 1987.   ○

Dunlap, Susan
PIOUS DECEPTION
When a young priest is found hanged, a medical examiner turned private eye is hired to investigate—"the desert backdrop proves especially evocative." (FC) Villard Bks, 1989.   ○

Grey, Zane
THE ARIZONA CLAN
Feuding clans in the Tonto Basin. Har-Row, 1958. Also *To the Last Man* (1922).   o

Kingsolver, Barbara
THE BEAN TREES
"Vivid, engaging novel of love and friendship"—a poor young Kentucky woman flees her home, heads west, picks up a two-year-old Cherokee girl and continues on to a Tucson safe house for Central American refugees. (BRD) Harper, 1988. Also *Animal Dreams* (1990).   o

LaFarge, Oliver
LAUGHING BOY
An idyll of the Navajo country—it won a Pulitzer Prize. Buccaneer Bks, 1981 (first published 1929).   o

Lawrence, D.H.
ST. MAWR, AND OTHER STORIES
St. Mawr is a "psychological novella" set in Arizona. (FC) Cambridge U Pr, 1983 (first published 1925).   o

Nye, Nelson C.
DEADLY COMPANIONS
An action novel set in the 1900s—a woman, about to lose her ranch, trades shares in an undiscovered gold mine for the mortgage. Walker, 1987.   o

Seton, Anya
FOXFIRE
Story of the problems and conflicts to be resolved when a cultured Eastern girl marries a mining engineer who is one-quarter Apache. Houghton, 1950.   o

West, Paul
THE PLACE IN FLOWERS WHERE POLLEN RESTS
"A Hopi creation myth" with sub-themes—"a truly striking and ambitious study of contemporary life." (FC) Doubleday, 1988.   o

Whitney, Phyllis A.
VERMILION
A mystery romance of a New York designer who returns to Arizona when she receives a letter that offers to explain her father's mysterious death—"evocation of . . . the Southwest is superb and integral to the plot." (FC) Doubleday, 1981.   o

ARKANSAS

Series Guidebooks
(See Appendix 1)

NOTE: See Series Guides (and non-series guides) listed under United States and the South.

Background Reading

Abbott, Shirley
WOMENFOLKS: GROWING UP DOWN SOUTH
Autobiographical memoir of life in country Arkansas—"the pursuit of one woman's life story becomes an inquiry into the distortions . . . of standard history . . . the way in which myths . . . color the lives of South-

erners." (LJ). First published in 1983. Ticknor & Fields, 1991.   o

Brown, Dee
THE AMERICAN SPA: HOT SPRINGS, ARKANSAS
Anecdotal history of what has been a "hot spot" from DeSoto's discovery in 1541 to the present. Rose, 1982.   o

Fletcher, John G.
ARKANSAS
Combines factual material with the fascination of folk tales, comic interludes, personalities—written by a native son who is a Pulitzer Prize-winning poet. U of Arkansas Pr, 1989.   o

Gerstacker, Friedrich
IN THE ARKANSAS BACKWOODS
The author was a German who gathered material about a trip through Arkansas's frontier, 1837–1843, which he then used as the basis for these tales. A blend of journalism and fiction, they portray backwoods life of the period—"entertaining stories [that] rise far above the regionalism suggested in the title." (PW) U of Missouri Pr, 1990.   ○

Harington, Donald
LET US BUILD A CITY: ELEVEN LOST TOWNS
"Blend of travelogue . . . history, folklore and Indian legend" as the author visits 11 towns that time forgot. HarBraceJ, 1986.   ○

Randolph, Vance
WE ALWAYS LIE TO STRANGERS: TALL TALES FROM THE OZARKS
Americana, both scholarly and entertaining—wild and absurd anecdotes and jokes ". . . a hearty skimming of regional humor." (BRD) Greenwood, 1974 (first published 1951). Also *Pissing in the Snow and Other Ozark Folk Tales*, U of Illinois Pr, 1976.   ○

Reed, Roy
LOOKING FOR HOGEYE
Essays by a professor of journalism at the University of Arkansas—"engaging prose" about the people of the Ozarks, families, cities, back roads, weather, making do. (NYTBR) U of Arkansas Pr, 1986.   ○

Williams, Miller, ed.
OZARK, OZARK: A HILLSIDE READER
"A rich anthology of works by writers from the Ozark Mountain region of Missouri and Arkansas . . . all from the twentieth century . . . imbued with a marvelous combination of naivete and sophistication." (BL) U of Missouri, 1981.   ○

GUIDEBOOKS

Earngey, Bill
ARKANSAS ROADSIDES: A GUIDEBOOK FOR THE STATE
East Mntn Pr, 1988.   ○

Hampel, Bet
THE PELICAN GUIDE TO THE OZARKS
Eleven area tours—what to see, getting there, fairs and events, where to find authentic Ozark food and culture, historic sites. Pelican, 1982.   ○

Leake, Henderson and Dorothy
WILDFLOWERS OF THE OZARKS
Ozark Soc Found, 1981.   ○

McAlister, Wayne H. and Martha K.
GUIDEBOOK TO THE ARANSAS NATIONAL WILDLIFE REFUGE
Mince Country Pr, 1987.   ○

Rafferty, Milton D.
THE OZARKS OUTDOORS
A guide for fishermen, hunters and tourists, with comprehensive background on history, folkways and tourism. U of Oklahoma Pr, 1985.   ○

HISTORY

Ashmore, Harry S.
ARKANSAS
One of a series of popular histories for each state published as part of the bicentennial in 1976; revised edition. Norton, 1984.   ○

Berry, Fred and Novak, John
THE HISTORY OF ARKANSAS
Rose Pub, 1987.   ○

Novels

Baker, William M. and Simpson, Ethel C., eds.
ARKANSAS IN SHORT FICTION
Stories from 1841 to 1984. August Hse, 1986.   ○

Burchardt, Bill
BLACK MARSHALL
A tale of the Oklahoma Territory and a black marshal with an "uncanny knowledge of people and nature." (FC) Doubleday, 1981.   ○

Farris, Jack
**THE ABIDING GOSPEL OF
  CLAUDE DEE MORAN**
Antic novel of an ex-con who becomes a
revivalist preacher and a sheriff in rural
America. St. Luke's Pr, 1987.   ○

Hess, Jean
MISCHIEF IN MAGGODY
Maggody's first female police chief returns
from vacation to find that the local prostitute, and moonshiner, has disappeared—
"an engaging tale, although the raunchy
characters impart a certain vulgarity to the
text." (FC) Also *Malice in Maggody* (1986) and
Madness in Maggody (1991). St. Martin,
1988.   ○

Jones, Douglas C.
ELKHORN TAVERN
The Civil War as experienced by a farming
family in Arkansas. HR&W, 1980.   ○

Jones, Douglas C.
HICKORY CURED
Linked short stories "evoke the full flavor
of life in the imaginary Arkansas town of
Weedy Rough back in the 30s." (FC) HR&W,
1987.   ○

Jones, Douglas C.
**THE SEARCH FOR TEMPERANCE
  MOON**
A bordello madam asks U.S. Marshal Schil-
ler to solve her mother's murder. Holt,
1991.   ○

Jones, Douglas C.
WEEDY ROUGH
"Coming of age of a boy in the small Arkansas town Weedy Rough" during the period
of World War I to the 1930s—"amusing and
tender narrative . . . is actually background
to the novel's climactic event: a bank robbery
in Weedy Rough." (FC) HR&W, 1981.   ○

Leaton, Anne
PEARL
The life and times of a brothel madam on
the American frontier of Fort Smith at the
turn of the century—"original . . . provocative . . . feminist Western." (BRD) Knopf,
1985.   ○

Mickle, Shelley F.
THE QUEEN OF OCTOBER
A first novel about a 13-year-old girl who
has been "dumped in Coldwater" with her
grandparents while her parents sort out the
details of a divorce. She observes her grandfather and his illegal homemade medicines,
her grandmother's feud with the local newspaper editor, befriends a rich neighbor, falls
in love—"descriptions of people and places
are wonderfully on target." (BRD) Algonquin Bks, 1989.   ○

CALIFORNIA

*Series Guidebooks
(See Appendix 1)*

NOTE: See also Series Guides (and non-
series guides) listed under United States and
the West.

Access Guide: Los Angeles; San Francisco
American Express Pocket Guide: San
  Francisco & Los Angeles
Baedeker: San Francisco; California
Berlitz: California
Compass American Guide: San Francisco
  & the Bay Area

Crown Insider's Guide: California
Fisher's World: California; Los Angeles; San
  Francisco
Fodor: Baja & Pacific Coast Resorts; Los
  Angeles, Orange County & Palm Springs;
  San Diego; San Francisco; Pocket Guide
  to San Francisco
Frommer: California & Las Vegas; Los An-
  geles; San Diego; San Francisco
Gault/Milau: The Best of Los Angeles; The
  Best of San Francisco
Insider's Guide: California
Insight Guide: Northern California;

Southern California; Los Angeles; San
Francisco

Let's Go: California & Hawaii (includes
Tahoe, Reno, Las Vegas, Baja); Los Angeles; San Francisco

Michael's Guide: California; Northern
California; Southern California

Moon Handbook: California; Northern
California; Catalina

Nelles Guide: California

Off the Beaten Path: Northern California;
Southern California

Real Guide: California & The West Coast;
San Francisco

Sierra Guide: Natural Areas of California

Background Reading

Femling, Jean
GREAT PIERS OF CALIFORNIA

History, description of life on and near California's piers—for ocean watchers, fishermen, anyone who enjoys the coast. Mostly
Southern California, but also piers from Santa
Cruz heading north. Borgo Pr, 1988.   ○

Georges, Rip and Heimann, Jim
CALIFORNIA CRAZY

Roadside vernacular architecture, which
California is famous for. Chronicle, 1980. ○

Gregory, James N.
AMERICAN EXODUS: THE DUST
BOWL MIGRATION &
CALIFORNIA'S OKIE
SUBCULTURE

Oklahomans, Arkansans, Texans and Mis-
sourians who fled to California in the
Depression years, and their impact on California and the San Joaquin Valley. Oxford
U Pr, 1989.   ○

Hayes, Harold, ed.
THE BEST OF CALIFORNIA, 1976–
86

"Some people, places and institutions of the
most exciting state in the nation, as featured
in *California* magazine . . . comical, critical,
and insightful pieces" on subjects from Napa
Valley wineries and small-town life to crime
and drag racing. Borgo Pr, 1988.   ○

Holliday, J.S.
THE WORLD RUSHED IN: THE
CALIFORNIA GOLD RUSH
EXPERIENCE

Eyewitness account of a nation heading west,
based on the diary of William Swain, who
left his family and farm in New York in 1849
to find gold in California—"an authentic
vicarious experience." (BRD) S&S, 1981. ○

Jackson, Donald D.
GOLD DUST

"A ripe, utterly engrossing version of the
California gold rush of 1848 . . . suspenseful delivery of masses of contemporary information" taken from diaries, journals,
letters, travelogues. (BL) Knopf, 1980.   ○

Lee, Hector
HEROES, VILLAINS AND
GHOSTS: FOLKLORE OF OLD
CALIFORNIA

An anthology of tales based on California
history or pure folklore. Borgo Pr, 1988. ○

Moore, Judith
THE LEFT COAST OF PARADISE:
CALIFORNIA AND THE
AMERICAN HEART

"Eclectic collection of loose essay-type segments on wildly varying people encountered . . . run the gamut from a feminist
lesbian to . . . the author's grandmother
[and] Herbert Marcuse." (LJ) FS&G, 1987.

○

Nadeau, Remi
GHOST TOWNS AND MINING
CAMPS OF CALIFORNIA

Originally published in 1965; should be read
for the dramatic history of each town, or it
can be used as a guide to 170 old gold rush
towns and mining camps. Crest Pubs,
1990.   ○

Pejovich, Ted
THE STATE OF CALIFORNIA:
GROWING UP FOREIGN IN
THE BACK YARDS OF EDEN

The author, now an actor, and his family
emigrated from Montenegro (a Yugoslavian

province) to the Santa Clara Valley. A memoir that is "intriguing . . . excesses in style [but] succeeds in evoking his family's exuberant loyalty to two worlds." (PW) Knopf, 1989.   o

Schad, Jerry
CALIFORNIA DESERTS
Text and photographs that allow you a vicarious visit to the deserts from Death Valley to Mojave. Falcon Pr, 1987.   o

CALIFORNIA IN LITERATURE

Dunaway, David K.
HUXLEY IN HOLLYWOOD
Both a "gossipy socio-cultural-literary compendium" and a serious discussion of Huxley's ideas and writings. He lived for 26 years in California, lecturing and writing and befriending Hollywood greats. (PW) Doubleday, 1991.   o

Eisen, Jonathan and Fine, David
UNKNOWN CALIFORNIA
A diverse collection of essays, letters and stories, spanning California's history from the gold rush on. Authors include Mark Twain, Henry Miller, John Steinbeck, Norman Mailer, a woman's letter from a mining outpost in 1852, Wallace Stegner and more. Macmillan, 1991.   o

Herron, Don
THE LITERARY WORLD OF SAN FRANCISCO & ITS ENVIRONS
"Part traveler's guidebook and part encyclopedic literary history"—both a tour of neighborhoods and of the authors and their writings, including outlying places in the Bay area. "They are all here—Twain and London to Kerouac and Ginsberg." The author, who conducts literary tours of the San Francisco area, "has a way with detail and remarkable anecdote" that makes it worth reading purely as armchair travel. (Choice) City Lights, 1985.   o

Knox, Maxine and Rodriguez, Mary
STEINBECK'S STREET: CANNERY ROW
Guide to Cannery Row's shops, restaurants and historical sites, tales of Steinbeck and

his friends and the local characters who ended up in his books and stories. Presidio Pr, 1984.   o

Lennon, Nigey
THE SAGEBRUSH BOHEMIAN: MARK TWAIN IN CALIFORNIA
"The turbulent California years of Samuel Clemens . . . humorous and well-researched." (Publisher) Paragon Hse, 1991.   o

Mangelsdorf, Tom
A HISTORY OF STEINBECK'S CANNERY ROW
History of the street Steinbeck made famous—traces the models for places and characters. Interesting for the general reader, informative and detailed enough for the student of Steinbeck. Western Tanager, 1986.   o

Michaels, Leonard and others
WEST OF THE WEST: IMAGINING CALIFORNIA
"A distinctive collection of writings—fiction, poetry, essays, travelers' tales, reportage, journals—to analyze the California mystique" on topics ranging from scenery and the desert to Hollywood and cults. Includes writers such as de Beauvoir, Amy Tan, Gore Vidal, M.F.K. Fisher and so on, and is organized around themes—atmosphere, Hollywood, the Sixties, etc. (PW) N Point Pr, 1989.   o

Miller, John, ed.
SAN FRANCISCO STORIES: GREAT WRITERS ON THE CITY
A collection of "splendid reading" that includes all sorts of writing about the city, excerpts from novels set there, poetry, commentary about aspects of the city. (BL) Chronicle, 1990.   o

Reid, Robert L., ed.
A TREASURY OF THE SIERRA NEVADA
A collection of writings by noted authors that celebrate this great mountain range. Wilderness Pr, 1983.   o

Robertson, David
WEST OF EDEN: A HISTORY OF ART AND LITERATURE OF YOSEMITE
Significant authors who have told about Yosemite in their writings, with reproductions of photographs and paintings by artists. Yosemite Assn, 1984. ○

Taper, Bernard, ed.
MARK TWAIN'S SAN FRANCISCO
Compilation of 83 pieces that the author wrote for newspapers and magazines during his years in California and Nevada. Greenwood, 1978. ○

Teale, Edwin Way, ed.
THE WILDERNESS WORLD OF JOHN MUIR
An anthology of Muir's writings arranged chronologically to provide a cohesive portrait of the naturalist's view of life—"reading that is often magnificent and awe-inspiring." (BRD) HM, 1975. ○

Thorpe, Edward
CHANDLERTOWN: THE LOS ANGELES OF PHILIP MARLOWE
Both a biography and a photo-essay of the Los Angeles neighborhoods where Chandler's classic stories were set (1939–58), with Philip Marlowe as the hard-boiled, but sensitive, private eye. "Surviving sites appear in the text . . . graced by liberal quotations from *The Big Sleep* and other tales." (PW) St. Martin, 1984. ○

Wallace, David R.
THE WILDER SHORE
"A stunning book"—an examination of literature about California from Dana and London to Joan Didion. "We see the land as an earthly paradise . . . to be exploited . . . a threat to life." (PW) Sierra, 1984. ○

GUIDEBOOKS

Adams, Rick and Louise
THE CALIFORNIA HIGHWAY ONE BOOK
Ballantine, 1985. ○

Bloch, Louis M., Jr.
OVERLAND TO CALIFORNIA IN 1859
A guide for wagon train travelérs. Bloch & Co, 1990. ○

California Coastal Commission Staff, ed.
COASTAL ACCESS GUIDE; COASTAL RESOURCE GUIDE
Two extremely information-rich books. The first is a guide to piers, beaches, parks along the coast; the second is its companion, with information on plants, wildlife and the geography of the coast, along with information on parks, villages, museums, etc. U of California Pr, 1991. ○

California Travel Assn Staff, ed.
CALIFORNIA WEEKENDER
In two volumes—Volume 1, *Southern California;* Volume 2, *Northern California*. Camaro Pub, 1987. ○

Gleason, Bill
BACKROAD WINERIES OF CALIFORNIA
Small wineries throughout the state. Chronicle Bks, 1985. ○

Landau, Carl and Katie
FESTIVALS OF CALIFORNIA
All kinds of festivals where you can participate in a local event along with the locals. Landau Comns, 1989. ○

Oberrecht, Kenn
DRIVING THE PACIFIC COAST: CALIFORNIA
Wonderful year-round guide for a coastal trip from south to north, from the Hotel del Coronado off the coast of San Diego through Big Sur and Jessica Fletcher's stage set (in Mendocino), in a format that accommodates a two-day side trip or a two-month odyssey along the entire coast. History, where to stay, camp, eat, shop, use the parks and beaches, seasonal events, museums. Globe Pequot, 1991. ○

Olmsted, Gerald W.
**THE BEST OF THE SIERRA
   NEVADA**
Crown, 1991.   o

Riegert, Robert
**CALIFORNIA: THE ULTIMATE
   GUIDEBOOK**
A guide to the best in the state. Ulysses Pr,
1991.   o

Riegert, Robert
**HIDDEN COAST OF CALIFORNIA:
   THE ADVENTURER'S GUIDE**
"A thousand-mile adventure along the edge"
of California—its "culture and history, life
along the shore, vignettes on whales, seals,
seabirds and sharks." Starting with the Mexican border it journeys north, emphasizing
"hidden" aspects of major areas, and intro-
ducing untracked beaches and campgrounds. Ulysses Pr, 1991.   o

Vokac, David
**THE GREAT TOWNS OF
   CALIFORNIA**
A book to entice visitors to look for towns
that don't fit the usual California image—
like Mendocino and St. Helena. West Pr,
1986.   o

Young, Stanley and Levick, Melba
THE MISSIONS OF CALIFORNIA
Chronicle Bks, 1988.   o

*LOS ANGELES & SOUTHERN
CALIFORNIA*

Alleman, Richard
**THE MOVIE LOVER'S GUIDE TO
   HOLLYWOOD**
A guide to over 300 attractions from the
glory days of motion pictures. Har-Row,
1988.   o

Fink, Augusta
**PALOS VERDES PENINSULA: TIME
   AND THE TERRACED LAND**
Western Tanager Pr, 1987.   o

Grimm, Michele and Tom
AWAY FOR THE WEEKEND
Great getaways less than 250 miles from Los
Angeles, is the explanatory subtitle. Gives
driving instructions, sights, lodgings, restaurants from San Simeon to San Diego and
the Baja Peninsula, as well as east to the
mountains. Crown, 1989.   o

LeBien, Sara
**MUSEUMS OF SOUTHERN
   CALIFORNIA**
From Santa Barbara south to San Diego—
170 museums, galleries, ranches, historic
homes, nature centers with necessary tourist
information. Organized by area and indexed
by both name and subject. Peregrine Smith,
1988.   o

Moore, Charles and others
**THE CITY OBSERVED: LOS
   ANGELES, A GUIDE TO ITS
   ARCHITECTURE AND
   LANDSCAPES**
The authors are the "perfect guides to a city
whose chief vernacular icon is Disneyland
. . . travels from Spanish missions to arts-
and-crafts bungalow to art deco to international style [and] post-modern homes." Also
includes theme parks, museums. "A surprising and fascinating handbook." (BL)
Random, 1984.   o

Morley, Sheridan
**TALES FROM THE HOLLYWOOD
   RAJ: THE BRITISH, THE MOVIES
   AND TINSELTOWN**
The cultural invasion of Hollywood, over
several decades, by the British, which the
author terms "India all over again." An "an-
ecdotally rich but perfectly serious account
[of] who these individuals were . . . what
they came for, what they accomplished personally . . . their combined influence." (BL)
Viking, 1984.   o

Riegert, Robert
**HIDDEN LOS ANGELES &
   SOUTHERN CALIFORNIA**
Emphasizes travel experiences beyond the
standard travel guides, to challenge jaded
visitors. Ulysses Pr, 1988.   o

Sehlinger, Bob
**THE UNOFFICIAL GUIDE TO
DISNEYLAND**
An alternative to the Disney promotional
material—"critical evaluations of all rides and
exhibits" and helpful hints on coping with
lines, crowds, planning a one-day stay, and
so on. (BL) Prentice Hall Pr, 1987.   o

Thomas, Bill
NATURAL LOS ANGELES
"A practical source of natural sights . . . for
tourists who want memories of the California countryside as well as the Hollywood
underside." Includes natural areas, parks,
zoos, gardens, tips on picnicking and
camping. (BL) Har-Row, 1989.   o

Varney, Philip
**SOUTHERN CALIFORNIA'S BEST
GHOST TOWNS: A PRACTICAL
GUIDE**
From Inyo to San Diego—"readers will want
to jump in their cars . . . and go. Extremely
readable and informative." (LJ) U of Okla-
homa Pr, 1990.   o

Wolf, Marvin and Mader, Katherine
**FALLEN ANGELS: CHRONICLES
OF LOS ANGELES CRIME AND
MYSTERY**
About the sensational and bizarre crimes
and mysteries, with directions to the scene
of the crime if you care to go. Ballantine,
1988.   o

*SAN FRANCISCO & NORTHERN
CALIFORNIA*

Alt, David and Hyndman, Donald
**ROADSIDE GEOLOGY OF
NORTHERN CALIFORNIA**
One of a series of books that is wonderful
to take along in the car. To paraphrase the
preface, being able to look at the landscape
as you travel and (with this book) envision
the forces and changes—the dynamics of the
landscape you are seeing—is a real achievement of understanding for travelers. Mountain Pr, 1975.   o

Bakalinsky, Adah
**STAIRWAY WALKS IN SAN
FRANCISCO**
The author has connected dozens of stairways into 26 guided walks, each graded for
difficulty and access, and mapped. There's
an appendix listing the stairways by neighborhood and rating them for beauty, safety,
difficulty. Lexikos, 1984.   o

Beebe, Morton
SAN FRANCISCO
Essays by Herb Caen, Herbert Gold, Barnaby Conrad, and others, that reflect the
history of the town, its nightlife and ambiance. Abrams, 1985.   o

Browning, Peter and Holleuffer, Carol
ROAMING THE BACK ROADS
Twenty-eight delightful drives through the
most beautiful countryside in Northern California. Chronicle Bks, 1981.   o

Conaway, James
NAPA
The wine valley—colorful individuals, wine-
drinking in America, history, development
and pollution of its beauty. HM, 1990.   o

Delehanty, Randolph
THE SAN FRANCISCO GUIDE
Six regional day trips by car, 13 walking
tours, history, biographies of founders,
maps—"myriad of details for the traveler
. . . essential reading for any first-time tourist and fun reading for residents and frequent visitors." (LJ) Chronicle, 1989.   o

Dillon, Richard
**NORTH BEACH: THE ITALIAN
HEART OF SAN FRANCISCO**
History and historic photos of North Beach,
the way it was. Presidio Pr, 1985.   o

Emmery, Lena and Taylor, Sally
**GRAPE EXPEDITIONS IN
CALIFORNIA**
Fifteen tours across the California wine
country, intended for cyclists but car will
work also—pass through spectacular scenery and famous wineries. Includes places to

eat, drink, sleep, small motels, B&Bs, camping. Sally Taylor & Friends, 1987.   ○

Gentry, Curt
THE MADAMS OF SAN FRANCISCO: AN IRREVERENT HISTORY OF THE CITY BY THE GOLDEN GATE.
Comstock Edns, 1977 (first published 1964).   ○

Gold, Herbert
TRAVELS IN SAN FRANCISCO
Sketches that originally appeared in local newspapers—"observations are keen and his details amusing." (LJ) Arcade Pub, 1991.   ○

Kingston, Maxine H.
THE WOMAN WARRIOR: MEMOIRS OF A CHILDHOOD AMONG GHOSTS
A Chinese-American girl growing up in San Francisco of the 1940s; originally published in 1976. Random, 1989.   ○

Meyers, Carole T.
WEEKEND ADVENTURES FOR CITY-WEARY PEOPLE
Overnight trips within a 300-mile radius of San Francisco—theme destinations (antique hunting, wildlife, etc.) and practical travel information. Carousel, 1989.   ○

Pierce, Nona
GARDEN GETAWAYS: PUBLIC GARDENS AND SPECIAL NURSERIES IN NORTHERN CALIFORNIA
Tioga, 1989.   ○

Pomada, Elizabeth and Larsen, Michael
PAINTED LADIES: THE ART OF SAN FRANCISCO'S VICTORIAN HOUSES
Celebration of resurrected and restored Victorian houses. Dutton, 1978. Also *Daughters of Painted Ladies: America's Resplendent Victorians* (1987) and *The Painted Ladies Revisited* (1989).   ○

Riegert, Ray
HIDDEN SAN FRANCISCO & NORTHERN CALIFORNIA: THE ADVENTURER'S GUIDE
Emphasizes travel experiences beyond the standard travel guides to challenge jaded visitors. Ulysses Pr, 1988.   ○

Sangwan, B.J.
INDIAN CHIEF TRAVEL GUIDES
A mini-series of guides to Northern California. Titles include: *Complete Santa Barbara, Wine Country, Gold Country, Monterey Peninsula, San Francisco, Vacation Towns, Lake Tahoe.* Indian Chief, 1987–1990.   ○

Shelton, Jack
HOW TO ENJOY 1 TO 10 PERFECT DAYS IN SAN FRANCISCO
Shelton, 1990.   ○

Thomas, Gordon and Morgan-Witts, Max
EARTHQUAKE: THE DESTRUCTION OF SAN FRANCISCO
Graphic history of the 1906 quake. Ulverscroft, 1987.   ○

Van der Zee, John
THE GATE: THE TRUE STORY OF THE DESIGN & CONSTRUCTION OF GOLDEN GATE BRIDGE
A whodunit that sets the record straight—Professor Charles Ellis was the true genius behind the construction, *not* Joseph Strauss. What's more, Ellis was fired after it was designed! S&S, 1988.   ○

Wayburn, Peggy
ADVENTURING IN THE SAN FRANCISCO BAY AREA
The Sierra travel guide to San Francisco, Marin, Sonoma, Napa, Solano, Contra Costa, Alameda, Santa Clara, San Mateo counties and the Bay Islands. Random, 1987.   ○

Whitnah, Dorothy L.
POINT REYES
A guide to trails, roads, beaches, lakes, trees, flowers and rocks of Point Reyes National

Seashore. Wilderness Pr, 1985. Also *An Outdoor Guide to the San Francisco Bay Area* (1985). o

Wollenberg, Charles
GOLDEN GATE METROPOLIS: PERSPECTIVES ON BAY AREA HISTORY
"Short, readable essays" by a social historian, mostly about San Francisco, but also about the Oakland area and Silicon (Santa Clara) Valley—"Geography, history, and political and social influence." (LJ) UCBIGS, 1985. o

Woodbridge, Sally
ARCHITECTURE—SAN FRANCISCO: THE GUIDE
By the Architectural Institute of America, San Francisco chapter. Chronicle Bks, 1988. Also *Bay Area Houses* (1988)—6 essays cover periods from the turn of the century to the present day of a distinctive local tradition in housing. o

CALIFORNIA CENTRAL COAST

Aidala, Thomas
HEARST CASTLE: SAN SIMEON
The building and history of William Randolph Hearst's dream castle—illustrated. S&S, 1981. o

Akeman, Thom
MOVING TO MONTEREY
A newcomer's guide to the peninsula paradise. Kaskaskia Pr, 1990. o

Foster, Lee
MAKING THE MOST OF THE PENINSULA: A CALIFORNIA GUIDE TO SAN MATEO, SANTA CLARA & SANTA CRUZ COUNTIES
A comprehensive guide to a diverse and exciting region, a mix of history, natural history and practical tourist information. Tioga, 1989. o

Knox, Maxine and Rodriguez, Mary
STEINBECK'S STREET: CANNERY ROW
Guide to Cannery Row's shops, restaurants and historical sites, including "tales of Steinbeck, his friends, and local characters who made their way into his books and stories." (Publisher) Presidio Pr, 1984. o

MacDonald, Laclan P.
UNCOMMON GUIDE TO CARMEL, MONTEREY & BIG SUR
Bear Flag Bks, 1990. o

Magary, Alan and Kerstin F.
SOUTH OF SAN FRANCISCO
"California's central coast—San Mateo, Santa Cruz, Monterey, Carmel, Big Sur, Hearst Castle. . . . Interesting, accurate historical information, special events, references to other sources . . . Steinbeck country." (LJ) Har-Row, 1983. o

SAN DIEGO

Bruns, Bill
A WORLD OF ANIMALS: THE SAN DIEGO ZOO AND THE WILD ANIMAL PARK
History of the zoo and an introduction to some of its animal inhabitants—"both narrative and pictures do justice to this great zoo." (PW) Abrams, 1983. o

LeMenager, Charles R.
RAMONA & ROUND ABOUT
A history of San Diego County's little-known back country. Eagle Peak, 1989. o

McKeever, Michael
A SHORT HISTORY OF SAN DIEGO
"Describes the city's growth from the first California mission to one of the world's most refreshing cities"—one of a series of "sprightly, authoritative" city histories. (Publisher) Lexikos, 1985. o

Mills, James R.
SAN DIEGO: WHERE CALIFORNIA BEGAN
San Diego Historical Soc, 1985. o

Peik, Leander and Rosalie
DISCOVER SAN DIEGO
The 15th edition of this guide. Peik's Enterprises, 1988.   ○

Schad, Jerry
AFOOT AND AFIELD IN SAN DIEGO COUNTY
Exploring San Diego's outdoor attractions. Also *Back Country Roads and Trails*. Wilderness Pr, 1986.   ○

Wambaugh, Joseph
LINES AND SHADOWS
True story of Lt. Snider of San Diego who organized the Border Crime Task Force, using Mexican-Americans on the Los Angeles police force to stop the banditry against illegal aliens at the border—"no one writes better about cops than Mr. Wambaugh. . . . An off-trail, action-packed true account of police work and the intimate lives of policemen." (NYTBR) Morrow, 1985.   ○

Wendt, Mary
DESTINATIONS: SAN DIEGO
Hundreds of things to do in America's playground. Fiesta Bks, 1991.   ○

DEATH VALLEY

Clark, William D.
DEATH VALLEY: THE STORY BEHIND THE SCENERY
KC, 1989.   ○

Decker, Barbara and Robert
ROAD GUIDE TO DEATH VALLEY
Double Decker Pr, 1989.   ○

Kirk, Ruth
EXPLORING DEATH VALLEY
A guide to the Death Valley National Monument area—natural and social history, weather and desert survival, sights on the main roads and in the back country, trips by truck and jeep. Stanford U Pr, 1981.   ○

Lingenfelter, Richard E.
DEATH VALLEY & THE AMARGOSA: A LAND OF ILLUSION
"Anecdotal, entertaining, and educational study" of a unique land—49-ers, hermits, Death Valley Scotty, Indians and more. U of California Pr, 1986. Also, *Death Valley Lore* (1988).   ○

Manley, William L.
DEATH VALLEY IN '49
The first edition was published in 1894. Borden Pub, 1990.   ○

HISTORY

Harlow, Neal
CALIFORNIA CONQUERED: WAR AND PEACE IN THE PACIFIC, 1846–50
"Good reading and good history" about the end of the Mexican era in California. (BRD) U of California, 1982.   ○

Lavender, David
CALIFORNIA
One of a series of popular histories for each state, published as part of the bicentennial in 1976. Norton, 1976. Also *California: Land of New Beginnings* (1987).   ○

Starr, Kevin
MATERIAL DREAMS: SOUTHERN CALIFORNIA THROUGH THE 1920s
Part of a multi-volume history of California beginning with *Americans and the California Dream* (1973), which covers the period 1850–1915, and followed by *Inventing the Dream* (1985)—"employs social history and biography as a means of painting the greater picture." (LJ) Oxford U Pr, 1990.   ○

Novels

Boyle, T. Coraghessan
BUDDING PROSPECTS; A PASTORAL
A "quitter" takes on a nine-month stint in northern California, growing marijuana and

resolved not to quit this time. Viking, 1984.   ○

Bristow, Gwen
THE JUBILEE TRAIL
Historical novel of the Spanish trail that led in the 1840s from Santa Fe to Los Angeles, and one family's trek. Crowell, 1950.   ○

DeBlassis, Celeste
THIS PROUD BREED
Three-generation family saga of nineteenth-century California. Coward, 1978.   ○

Dick, Philip K.
MARY AND THE GIANT
"Slice-of-life novel . . . of 50s frustration." Arbor Hse, 1987.   ○

Galloway, David
TAMSEN
A novel about the Donner party's tragic journey. HarBraceJ, 1983.   ○

Gavin, Catherine
THE SUNSET DREAM
A family saga (1846–1941) of California's "rapid, often violent, transition from a pastoral paradise to a thriving, open-ended society. Tumultuous historical events [gold rush, earthquake, war with Mexico] provide a colorful backdrop." (FC) St. Martin, 1984.   ○

Harris, MacDonald
TENTH
A music teacher is asked to do a radio program on the unfinished "tenth" of an obscure composer and is "beset by romantic intentions" of the composer's daughter. (FC) Atheneum, 1984.   ○

Harte, Bret
OUTCASTS OF POKER FLAT AND THE LUCK OF ROARING CAMP
Classic stories set in California gold rush country. Regents, 1973.   ○

Jakes, John
CALIFORNIA GOLD
Saga of a man's rise from rags (in Pennsylvania) to riches (in California)—"conveys the raw, irrepressible vitality of California but the historical backdrop . . . outshines the plot . . . impressive research plus lively depictions of Hearst, Ambrose Bierce, Leland Stanford, Teddy Roosevelt" to enrich the story. (PW) Random, 1989.   ○

Kittredge, Mary
MURDER IN MENDOCINO
"Satisfying complex mystery" with a female detective figure. She is also a freelance writer, hired to write a history of Pelican Road and encounters mystery and murder, with a missing son of local hippies, and a doctor who vanished 60 years earlier. Walker, 1987.   ○

L'Amour, Louis
THE LONESOME GODS
The early years of California—"filled with splendid descriptions of the desert country, historical facts, and nature lore." (FC) Bantam, 1982. Also, *The Californios* (1987).   ○

Longstreet, Stephen
SONS AND DAUGHTERS
Third of a trilogy about a California banking family, preceded by *All or Nothing* (1983) and *Our Father's House* (1985). Putnam, 1987.   ○

MacDonald, John D.
THE GREEN RIPPER
Travis McGee mystery—in this he poses as a cult convert in a remote part of California to spy on the cult's activities and solve the murder of his fiancée. Lippincott, 1979.   ○

O'Hehir, Diana
THE BRIDE WHO RAN AWAY
"Rich sense of the time and place" in a small town in Northern California of the 1950s. The plot concerns a heroine forced to examine her various relationships. (FC) Atheneum, 1988.   ○

Pearson, Ridley
PROBABLE CAUSE (Carmel)
Forensic Investigator James Dewitt takes a job in Carmel to put his troubled past behind him, but again finds that his life, and the lives of his daughters, are in jeopardy—

"fiction for true crime buffs . . . fancy forensic footwork, and intriguing snares." (FC) St. Martin, 1990.   ○

Saroyan, William
THE HUMAN COMEDY
"Thoroughly good characters" in a series of episodes as observed by a fourteen-year-old boy during World War II. (FC) HarBraceJ, 1944.   ○

Searls, Hank
BLOOD SONG
A retired admiral and his 12-year-old granddaughter set out from Manhattan for Nevada City using his ancestor's diaries and letters to duplicate their emigrant trip in 1849. Dangers jeopardize the trip at the same location as the earlier trip was endangered 130 years earlier. "The respective travelogues appear . . . in alternating chapters, eerily paralleling one another." (FC) Villard Bks, 1984.   ○

Silva, Julian
THE GUNNYSACK CASTLE (San Joaquin Valley)
A family saga of the rise of an Americanized Portuguese immigrant in the Valley's fruit-growing region. Ohio U, 1983.   ○

Skimin, Robert
CHIKARA!
"A sweeping novel of Japan and America from 1907 to 1983" is the subtitle of this sage of three generations of a Japanese immigrant family. St. Martin, 1984.   ○

Soto, Gary
A SUMMER LIFE (San Joaquin Valley)
"Lyrically rendered sketches from a gifted poet and story teller" of childhood and adolescence as a Chicano in the San Joaquin Valley. (BL) U Pr of New England, 1990.   ○

Steinbeck, John
CANNERY ROW (Monterey)
Viking, 1945. This and its sequel, *Sweet Thursday* (1954) revolve around a bunch of diverse characters and "Doc" and his labo-

ratory. *Tortilla Flat* (1935) is another funny, bawdy Steinbeck novel set in Monterey.   ○

Steinbeck, John
EAST OF EDEN (Salinas)
Saga of a half-century in the lives of two families. Viking, 1952. *Of Mice and Men* (1937), is also set in Salinas.   ○

Steinbeck, John
THE GRAPES OF WRATH
The Pulitzer Prize-winning novel about Okies during the depression who fled the Oklahoma dust bowl for a new future in California as migrant workers. Viking, 1939. *In Dubious Battle* (1936) is about a strike of migrant workers.   ○

Steinbeck, John
THE WAYWARD BUS
A group of bus passengers and the people who run a gas station and lunchroom where the bus is stranded and the effects of each of them on the others. Viking, 1947.   ○

Whitney, Phyllis A.
EMERALD (Palm Springs)
The heroine, seeking refuge with her great aunt (a former movie star), finds a mystery that leads to murder—"solving the mystery [she] solves her own personal problems." (FC) Doubleday, 1983.   ○

Whitney, Phyllis A.
FLAMING TREE (Carmel, Monterey Peninsula)
A therapist for the brain-damaged comes to Carmel to forget her son's death, becomes involved with the Hammond family and unravels a shocking mystery. Doubleday, 1986.   ○

HOLLYWOOD, LOS ANGELES & ENVIRONS

Allen, Charlotte V.
TIME/STEPS
A dancer is brutally attacked and must make the transition to an acting career instead. Atheneum, 1986.   ○

Atlas, Jacoba
PALACE OF LIGHT
Beginnings of the film industry reflected through the Mishkin family. Dutton, 1989.
○

Barnes, Joanna
SILVERWOOD
Family saga beginning in the early part of this century about the lives of rich, privileged people and of those of the movie colony who infiltrate their set. S&S, 1985.   ○

Bogarde, Dirk
WEST OF SUNSET (Hollywood)
A "strikingly well-observed portrait" of Hollywood as seen through the eyes of a British novelist who is "repelled by the fakery . . . smog, showbiz . . . displaced people." He visits an ex-mistress and becomes involved in the mysterious circumstances of her husband's death. (FC) Viking, 1984.   ○

Bradbury, Ray
DEATH IS A LONELY BUSINESS
  (Venice)
A series of bizarre homicides amongst eccentric inhabitants of the pier district in Venice—"highly gratifying blend of the mysterious and the macabre from a master craftsman." (FC) Knopf, 1985.   ○

Briskin, Jacqueline
EVERYTHING AND MORE (Beverly
  Hills, Los Angeles)
"Love, hate, murder, suicide, rape, incest" in a tri-generational novel based in Beverly Hills. (FC) Putnam Pub Group, 1983. Also *Paloverde* (1978), a family saga set in Los Angeles, beginning in the nineteenth century, and *Dreams Are Not Enough*, the story of a powerful Hollywood family and movie star Alyssia Del Mar (1987).   ○

Bukowski, Charles
HOLLYWOOD
Satirizes a host of well-known movie personalities in a novel of the genre wherein writers are "seduced into screenwriting . . . and live to tell all shamelessly." (BRD) Black Sparrow, 1989.   ○

Cameron, Carey
DADDY BOY
Growing up rich and spoiled in Hollywood in the early 1960s. Algonquin, 1989.   ○

Campbell, R. Wright
JUICE
"Thrilling, atmospheric, gutsy portrayal" of loan sharking in Los Angeles. Poseidon Pr, 1988. Also *In La-La Land We Trust* (1987) and *Alice in La-La Land*, (1990), set in Hollywood.   ○

Chandler, Raymond
THE RAYMOND CHANDLER
  OMNIBUS
Includes *The Big Sleep* (1939), *Farewell My Lovely* (1940), *The High Window* (1942), *The Lady in the Lake* (1944)—mystery classics set in "the big, sordid, dirty city" (as Chandler characterized it) of Los Angeles. Modern Library, 1975. Also *The Little Sister* (1949) and *Playback* (1958).

Note also the book *Chandlertown* under "Background Reading/Los Angeles & Southern California." Also, Aaron Blake Publishers offers the "Raymond Chandler Mystery Map of Los Angeles" which covers Downtown L.A., Hollywood, Santa Monica, Lake Arrowhead and Mexico.   ○

Didion, Joan
PLAY IT AS IT LAYS (Hollywood)
"Using a frenetic milieu of drugs, pills, sexual aberrancy, Didion elliptically etches the self-destruct life of Maria Wyeth." (FC) FS&G, 1970.   ○

Egan, Lesley
CRIME FOR CHRISTMAS (Glendale-
  Hollywood)
One of several mysteries by Egan set in the Glendale-Hollywood area. Doubleday, 1983. Other titles include: *Random Death* (1982), *A Choice of Crimes* (1980), *The Blind Search* (1977) and *Malicious Mischief* (1971).   ○

Ellroy, James
THE BLACK DAHLIA
"A gripping recreation of Los Angeles street life in the 1940s," using the facts of the

unsolved Black Dahlia murder case. Mysterious Pr, 1987. Also *The Big Nowhere* (1988), also set in Los Angeles just after World War II, and involving a converging plot of homosexual murders and a cadre of Hollywood leftists. ○

Fast, Howard
MAX
An engrossing novel that is also a history of the motion-picture industry from nickelodeons to talkies as Max moves from bagel-peddler on the Lower East Side in New York to movie mogul. Houghton, 1982. ○

Fisher, Carrie
POSTCARDS FROM THE EDGE
A starlet's journey from drug addiction to happiness, and basis for the movie of the same name. S&S, 1987. ○

Fitzgerald, F. Scott
THE LAST TYCOON
Unfinished novel about a Hollywood producer, with an outline by Edmund Wilson of how Fitzgerald intended to develop the plot. Scribner, 1969 (first published) 1941. ○

Gage, Elizabeth
A GLIMPSE OF STOCKING
An evil mother, a brutal producer, two half-sisters are protagonists—"guilty pleasure for readers who should know better." (FC) S&S, 1988. ○

Greenleaf, Stephen
THE DITTO LIST
Three unusual women clients come into a lawyer's office. The "ditto list" is a roster he maintains of mostly routine, non-paying divorce cases. Villard Bks, 1985. ○

Jaffe, Rona
AN AMERICAN LOVE STORY
"Hollywood scenes, exploiting the farce and foibles of La-La Land are particularly sharp . . . a book begging to be read while sitting around the pool." (BL) Delacorte, 1990. ○

Kaminsky, Howard
TALENT
"Tale of tinseltown backstabbing . . . southern California life in the fast lane. Irresistibly tacky entertainment." (FC) Bantam, 1989. ○

Karbo, Karen
TRESPASSERS WELCOME HERE
Soviet emigres in the Los Angeles area revealed in a series of satiric monologues "from near slapstick to wry wit . . . Soviet-American relations at their most intimate and basic." (FC) Putnam, 1989. ○

Kellerman, Jonathan
OVER THE EDGE
A complex plot with a "rip-roaring windup" as a Los Angeles child psychologist tries to find out if a former patient is involved in a series of shocking murders. Atheneum, 1987. ○

Leonard, Elmore
GET SHORTY
A loan shark—and one of Leonard's good talkers—pitches a movie idea to a Hollywood producer. Delacorte, 1990. ○

Linington, Elizabeth
SKELETONS IN THE CLOSET (Los Angeles-Hollywood)
One of several police procedurals. Doubleday, 1982. Other titles include: *Crime by Chance* (1973), *Greenmask* (1967), *No Villain Need Be* (1979), *Perchance of Death* (1977), *Policeman's Lot* (1968), and *Practice to Deceive* (1971). ○

Lovesey, Peter
KEYSTONE (Hollywood)
"Takes us back to the era of silent films . . . the hysterical staccato comedy world of Mack Sennett and the Keystone Cops." The plot combines real people from that era with a fictional British vaudevillian who gets mixed up in burglary and homicide. (FC) Pantheon, 1983. ○

Macdonald, Ross
THE UNDERGROUND MAN
One of many mysteries that have been described as "the finest series of detective nov-

els ever written by an American . . . nobody writes Southern California like Macdonald." (FC) Knopf, 1971. Other titles include: *Archer at Large* (1970), *Archer in Hollywood* (1967), and *Archer in Jeopardy* (1979) (all of which are omnibus books containing several mysteries each); also *The Blue Hammer* (1976), *The Goodbye Look* (1969), and *Sleeping Beauty* (1973). ○

Mosley, Walter
DEVIL IN A BLUE DRESS
Easy Rawlins is the black protagonist of this novel of Los Angeles in 1948, and in *A Red Death* (1991), of Los Angeles in 1950. "Portrait of time and place, to the indelible reality of . . a black man in a world not yet ready to accept him . . . may well be in the process of creating a genre classic." (FC) Norton, 1990. ○

Noguchi, Thomas T.
UNNATURAL CAUSES
The drowning death of a sitcom star arouses the suspicions of L.A. medical examiner Dr. Eric Parker (the author is a forensic pathologist)—"accounts of autopsies prove utterly fascinating, although best avoided by the squeamish." (FC) Putnam Pub Group, 1988. Also *Physical Evidence* (1990). ○

Parker, T. Jefferson
LITTLE SAIGON
A surf bum wants to end his family estrangement by assisting in the search for his war-hero brother's Vietnamese wife. (FC) St. Martin, 1988. Also *Laguna Heat* (1986), and *Pacific Beat* (1991). ○

Perry, Thomas
METZGER'S DOG (Los Angeles)
"Smoothly-styled and humorous" novel with an incredible plot—four friends steal a million dollars worth of cocaine. (FC) Scribner, 1983. ○

Rayner, Richard
LOS ANGELES WITHOUT A MAP
A British journalist pursuing a Playboy bunny reports on encounters with people and life in California—"studded with bitingly nasty anecdotes about celebrities . . . as a collec-

tion of observations, it's lethally accurate." (PW) NAL, 1990. ○

Sangster, Jimmy
HARDBALL (Malibu)
A former London cop rents his Malibu home to rich folks until murder and abduction make him decide to put his long-dormant investigative skills to work. Holt, 1988. Also set in Malibu, *Blackball* (1987). ○

Santiago, Danny
FAMOUS ALL OVER TOWN
Coming of age in a Mexican-American barrio in Los Angeles. S&S, 1983. ○

Saroyan, William
PAPA, YOU'RE CRAZY
A 10-year-old boy and his father at Malibu and a Saroyanesque plot—the two talk at the beach of writing and other things, ride bicycles, take a trip up the coast in an old car. Little, 1957. ○

Schulberg, Budd
THE DISENCHANTED (Hollywood)
Based on the life of F. Scott Fitzgerald—a has-been writer gets one more chance in Hollywood. Random 1950. Also *What Makes Sammy Run?* (1941). ○

Shannon, Dell
DESTINY OF DEATH
One of the several police procedurals in which Lt. Luis Mendoza of the Los Angeles Police Department is the key character. Other titles include: *The Motive on Record* (1982), *Exploit of Death* (1983), *Felony File* (1980), *Murder Most Strange* (1981), *Appearance of Death* (1977), *Cold Trail* (1978), *Crime File* (1974), *Felony at Random* (1979), *Kill With Kindness* (1968), and *Streets of Death* (1976). Morrow. New titles include *Chaos of Crime* (1986), *Blood Count* (1987) and *Murder by the Tale*, (short stories, 1988). ○

Simpson, Mona
ANYWHERE BUT HERE
A mother and daughter move from Wisconsin to Los Angeles for a fresh beginning, and flashbacks to stories of Wisconsin point

up the disparities—"any single episode could stand on its own . . . a dynamic and challenging first novel." (FC) Knopf, 1987. ○

Steel, Danielle
FAMILY ALBUM
Traces the fortunes of an actress and director, and her family, from World War II—"characteristic milieu of the beautiful, talented and privileged . . ." (FC) Delacorte Pr, 1985. ○

Tryon, Thomas
ALL THAT GLITTERS
Portrayal of five film star prototypes, from earthy sex symbol to grande dame of the silent era, who share the same lover, agent and friend—"like a great B movie—irresistible." (FC) Knopf, 1986. Also *Crowned Heads* (1976), about the interlocking destinies of four movie stars' lives. ○

Vidal, Gore
HOLLYWOOD: A NOVEL OF AMERICA IN THE 1920S
Part of the author's series of novels on American politics (see under District of Columbia); the main characters first appeared in *Washington, D.C.* (1967). Caroline goes to Hollywood and "begins to understand that cinema has the power to reshape the world." (BRD) Random, 1990. ○

Wambaugh, Joseph
THE GOLDEN ORANGE
The golden orange is Orange County, California—about a drunken ex-cop who meets up with an Orange County grass widow and gets involved in her efforts to investigate why she did not receive the inheritance she feels was due her. Morrow, 1990. ○

Wambaugh, Joseph
THE NEW CENTURIONS (Los
  Angeles)
Little, 1971. This and *The Blue Knight* (1972), *The Delta Star* (1983), *The Black Marble* (1978), are highly regarded novels about policemen in general, and the Los Angeles Police Department in particular. "No one writes better about cops than Mr. Wambaugh" seems

to reflect the opinion of both reviewers and cops. ○

Wambaugh, Joseph
THE SECRETS OF HARRY BRIGHT
A Los Angeles detective takes on a freelance job to find out how the son of a wealthy Californian ended up murdered in a desert canyon. Morrow, 1985. Also *The Glitter Dome* (1981)—"dope, sex and crime ridden" Hollywood. ○

West, Nathanael
THE DAY OF THE LOCUST
"A bitter tale of Hollywood and its hangers-on" in *The Complete Works of Nathanael West*. (FC) Farrar, Straus, 1957 (first published 1939). ○

Westbrook, Robert
THE LEFT-HANDED POLICEMAN
Nicky Rachmaninoff is assigned to solve a series of murders by a lonely man who has decided to target prominent Beverly Hills people. Crown, 1986. ○

Westlake, Donald E.
SACRED MONSTER
Life of a "drug-hazed" movie star in flashback—"pungent . . . satirical asides on today's Hollywood." (FC) Mysterious Pr, 1989. ○

SAN FRANCISCO & THE BAY AREA

Adams, Alice
SECOND CHANCES
This book explores the relationships of several elderly people living near San Francisco. Knopf, 1988. Also *Listening to Billie* (1978). ○

Beagle, Peter S.
THE FOLK OF THE AIR
Science, the supernatural and a League for Archaic Pleasures (they put on medieval plays) are elements of a plot set in the Bay area in a town similar to Berkeley. Ballantine Bks, 1986. ○

Berriault, Gina
THE LIGHTS OF EARTH
"An evocation of her time of despair" at the end of the heroine's love affair—"permeated by a sense of the hills, mists and nearby beaches" of San Francisco. (NYTBR) North Pr, 1985. ○

Bowman, Robert J.
THE HOUSE OF BLUE LIGHTS
Cassandra Thorpe, about to quit being a private eye, gets involved in murder and danger when a street bum hands her an envelope—"long, sensitive look at the underbelly of San Francisco . . . bums and winos, its wheeling and dealing, its missions and flophouses." (FC) St. Martin, 1987. ○

Dick, Philip K.
THE BROKEN BUBBLE
A rock 'n' roll disc jockey of the 1950s is suspended from his job and attempts reconciliation with his former wife—"strong sense of place and time." (FC) Arbor Hse, 1988. ○

Dunlap, Susan
TOO CLOSE TO THE EDGE
"A clever psychological thriller featuring a hair-raising climax"—plot turns on the drowning in San Francisco Bay of a prominent, wheelchair-bound activist. (FC) St. Martin, 1987. ○

Fast, Howard
THE IMMIGRANT'S DAUGHTER
Fifth volume of the California family saga. HM, 1985. Earlier titles, in chronological order, are: *The Immigrants* (1977), *Second Generation* (1978), *The Establishment* (1979), *The Legacy* (1981). ○

Gold, Herbert
DREAMING
The hero is the apotheosis of the California lifestyle and in trouble with the Mob—"moves at a headlong clip . . . beautifully satirical eye and ear for the customs, speech and settings of the hip bourgeoisie of San Francisco." (FC) D.I. Fine, 1988. Also *True Love* (1982), *The Girl of Forty* (1986). ○

Hammett, Dashiell
THE MALTESE FALCON
The classic Sam Spade mystery (see guides by Herron listed under Guidebooks for San Francisco above). North Pr, 1984 (first published 1930). See also Don Herron's *Dashiell Hammett Tour: A Guidebook* under "California in Literature," above. ○

Kingston, Maxine H.
TRIPMASTER MONKEY
About a Chinese-American caught up in the Bay area of the 1960s. Knopf, 1989. ○

Maupin, Armistead
SIGNIFICANT OTHERS
"Trials and adventures of San Francisco lovers, gay and straight," originally published as a newspaper serial. Har-Row, 1987. Also *Sure of You* (1990), another novel about life in San Francisco—"short, delectable, addictive chapters." (NYT) ○

Michael, Judith
POSSESSIONS
A believable modern odyssey of a woman creating a new life for herself in San Francisco when her husband deserts her. (FC) Poseidon, 1984. ○

Michaels, Leonard
THE MEN'S CLUB
Expanded from a prize-winning story of the same name—"men trying to make sense of their lives with women." FS&G, 1984. ○

Morgan, Seth
HOMEBOY
"Autobiographical first novel—the story of street and prison life in and around San Francisco." (BL) Random, 1990. ○

Muller, Marcia
TROPHIES AND DEAD THINGS
About "murderous passions still simmering from the Vietnam anti-war movement." (FC) Mysterious Pr, 1990. Also *Where Echoes Live* (1991). ○

Murphy, Pat
THE CITY, NOT LONG AFTER
After a world plague, surviving artists in San Francisco wage a struggle against those who want to bring about law and order—"vivifying specifics of character and place." (FC) Doubleday, 1989. ⟳

Norris, Frank
McTEAGUE
A "naturalistic novel" first published in 1899 of life in San Francisco of that time—"heredity and environment unleash a series of disasters." Penguin, 1982 (first published 1899). ⟳

O'Marie, C.A.
THE MISSING MADONNA
A gregarious man enlists the San Francisco OWLS (Older Women's League) to help locate a missing college chum—"original and entertaining with a humorist's wit." (FC) Delacorte, 1988. ⟳

Pronzini, Bill
BREAKDOWN
One of a series of "nameless detective" novels. The San Franciscan sleuth is investigating a hit-and-run death that takes him to a beach tavern near San Francisco. Delacorte, 1991. Also *Jackpot* (1990). ⟳

Steel, Danielle
STAR
Cinderella fable set in the California wine country. Delacorte, 1989. Also *Fine Things,*

the story of a rising star in a Bloomingdale-like store chain in New York and San Francisco (1987). ⟳

Tan, Amy
THE JOY LUCK CLUB
The lives of four pre-1949 Chinese women and their American-born daughters, told in alternate chapters—"full of complicated, endearingly human characters and first-rate storytelling." Putnam, 1989. ⟳

Walser, Martin
BREAKERS
A German professor gets a one-semester professorship at a San Francisco college—"an amusing view of America from the German perspective . . . the California setting will have American readers laughing in recognition of the ordinary rendered fresh with a tinge of absurdity." (LJ) Holt, 1987. ⟳

Wilcox, Colin
HIRE A HANGMAN
Frank Hastings, a San Francisco cop, is the protagonist. When a prominent surgeon is shot in the face, and there's a long list of suspects to consider, Hastings has the case. Wilcox has been compared to Dashiell Hammett—"he mines the noir angles of the city with the same restless eye." Also *Doctor, Lawyer . . .* (1977), *Aftershock* (1975), *Stalking Horse* (1982), *A Death Before Dying* (1989). (FC) Holt, 1991. ⟳

COLORADO

Series Guidebooks (See Appendix 1)

NOTE: See also Series Guides (and non-series guides) listed under United States and the West.

Compass American Guide: Colorado
Fodor: Colorado
Frommer: Denver, Boulder & Colorado Springs
Off the Beaten Path: Colorado

Sierra Guide: Natural Areas of Colorado & Utah

Background Reading

Borland, Hal
HIGH, WIDE AND LONESOME
New edition of a classic first published in 1956. The naturalist's boyhood on the eastern Colorado plains where his family homesteaded in 1909—"a narrative of rare charm

and a living document in the history of the last days of the open range." (BRD) U of Arizona Pr, 1990.   ❍

Chronic, Halka
ROADSIDE GEOLOGY
One of a series of books that is wonderful to take along in the car. To paraphrase the preface, being able to look at the landscape as you travel and (with this book) envision the forces and changes—the dynamics of the landscape you are seeing—is a real achievement of understanding for travelers. Mountain Pr, 1980.   ❍

Conover, Ted
WHITEOUT: LOST IN ASPEN
Entertaining assessment of the resort town, beginning with Conover's stint as a driver for the Mellow Yellow Cab Company, and on to his work as a reporter for the *Aspen Times*—"low-key, objective and unpretentious . . . Aspen's events and individuals speak for themselves." (PW) Random, 1991.   ❍

Fradkin, Philip L.
**SAGEBRUSH COUNTRY: LAND
     AND THE AMERICAN WEST**
The Uinta Mountains, bordered by Utah, Wyoming and Colorado, is setting for this account of a lone backpacking trip—"evokes past history from Indians and trappers to emigrants and railroaders, settlers and scientists to regulators and preservers." A companion volume to *A River No More* (see under the West), focusing on land use and public lands of the Uinta Mountains. (PW) Knopf, 1989.   ❍

McTighe, James
ROADSIDE HISTORY
Johnson Bks, 1989.   ❍

May, Stephen
**PILGRIMAGE: A JOURNEY
     THROUGH COLORADO'S
     HISTORY & CULTURE**
Ohio U Pr, 1986.   ❍

Sprague, Marshall
NEWPORT IN THE ROCKIES
The life and good times of Colorado Springs. Ohio U Pr, 1987. Also *Greetings from Colorado* (1988).   ❍

Zamonski, Stanley, W. and Keller,
     Teddy
THE FIFTY-NINERS
Roaring Denver in the gold rush days. Reprint of the 1961 edition. R H Pub, 1983. ❍

GUIDEBOOKS

Ayer, Eleanor B.
COLORADO TRAVELER
A series of individual subject guides for Colorado under this overall title. Subtitles include: *Discover Colorado—The Centennial State; Hall of Fame—a Gallery of the Rich and Famous; Parks & Monuments—A Scenic Guide to Colorado; Wildflowers—A Guide to Colorado's Unique Varieties; Natural Sites—A Guide to Colorado's Natural Wonders; Colorado Day Trips; Railroads of Colorado—A Guide to Narrow Gauge and Modern Trains; Gems & Minerals—A Guide to Colorado's Native Gemstones.* R H Pub, 1987–1988.   ❍

Caughey, Bruce and Winstanley, Dean
THE COLORADO GUIDE
A comprehensive guide by a pair of insiders, with places rated—"the most complete guide to Colorado in existence . . . breezy style and snippets of colorful historical anecdotes . . . not dominated by Denver." (LJ) Fulcrum, 1991.   ❍

Dallas, Sandra
**COLORADO GHOST TOWNS &
     MINING CAMPS**
U of Oklahoma Pr, 1988.   ❍

Gregory, Lee
COLORADO SCENIC GUIDE
Two volumes: *Southern Region, Northern Region.* Johnson Bks, 1990.   ❍

McMinn, Russel
**ANTIQUES: GUIDE TO
     COLORADO ANTIQUE SHOPS**
Jockey Hollow, 1989.   ❍

Wilson, D. Roy
COLORADO HISTORICAL TOUR GUIDE
Itineraries with historical offerings, every museum in the state is listed, and there's an overview of Colorado's history from the cliff dwellers on, with biographies of colorful figures. Crossroads Comns, 1990.   ○

HISTORY

Abbott, Carl, and others
COLORADO: A HISTORY OF THE CENTENNIAL STATE
U Pr of Colorado, 1982.   ○

Sprague, Marshall
COLORADO
One of a series of popular histories for each state, published as part of the bicentennial in 1976. Norton, 1984.   ○

Novels

Blume, Judy
SMART WOMEN(Boulder)
About three families from the east, re-settled into suburban Boulder after broken marriages—"moving, often witty story." (FC) Putnam Pub Group, 1984.   ○

Burns, Rex
PARTS UNKNOWN
A Devlin Kirk mystery. Denver private eye Kirk and his companion own an industrial security business, and the plot in this mystery concerns missing aliens and body-snatching for organ transplants. Viking, 1990. Other mysteries by this author with a Denver and environs setting (not necessarily with Kirk as detective) are: *The Alvarez Journal* (1975), *Speak for the Dead* (1978), *The Avenging Angel* (1983), *Ground Money* (1987), *Suicide Season* (1987), *The Killing Zone* (1988).   ○

Cather, Willa
THE SONG OF THE LARK
A young woman from Moonstone, Colorado, becomes a great singer. Houghton, 1915.   ○

Dailey, Janet
ASPEN BOLD
A soap star gets her first movie break with sex symbol John Travis, but trouble comes, and her return to her hometown, Aspen, brings back sad memories. Little, 1991.   ○

Greenberg, Joanne
THE FAR SIDE OF VICTORY
A "frivolous bachelor" is responsible for the death of a man and his three children, then succeeds in marrying the widow. "His attempt to understand her turns the novel . . . into a thoughtful character study." (FC) HR&W, 1983. Also *Founder's Praise* (1976).   ○

Greenberg, Joanne
SIMPLE GIFTS
An impoverished family participates in a government experiment to live like homesteaders of the 1880s under the aegis of the Social, Cultural and Ethnic Life Placement Program. "A sprightly, thoughtful novel about an age obsessed with the urge to look back and the need to prettify the past." (FC) Holt, 1986.   ○

Grey, Zane
THE VANISHING AMERICAN
An Indian boy is sent to an Eastern university and returns, with an Eastern girl, to help his people—"tragedy of the Indian people, despoiled by government agent and missionary." (FC) Har-Row, 1925.   ○

Haruf, Kent
THE TIE THAT BINDS
Northeastern Colorado is the setting, with a time span from 1896 (when homesteaders arrive) to 1977 and the chief character's 80th birthday. It depicts a way of life—"vividly described . . . the never-ending farmchores . . . Main Street on a Saturday afternoon . . . a fair" and always the land. HR&W, 1984.   ○

King, Stephen
THE SHINING
One of King's scary novels, set in the Overlook Hotel in the Colorado mountains and

involving spirits of the dead who have stayed at the hotel and a precognitive, telepathic caretaker's son—"relentless heightening of horror." (FC) Doubleday, 1977. ○

McCaffrey, Anne
STITCH IN SNOW
An expatriate author of children's books has an affair with a fellow passenger when their airline leaves them stranded in Denver, only to find herself his alibi in a murder later on. Tor Bks, 1986. ○

Michener, James A.
CENTENNIAL
One of Michener's panoramic novels that combine comprehensive history and background with an engrossing plot. This one covers Colorado's history from prehistoric times to the present day. Random, 1974. ○

CONNECTICUT

Series Guidebooks
(See Appendix 1)

NOTE: See Series Guides (and non-series guides) listed under United States and the East and the East/New England.

Background Reading

Bell, Michael
THE FACE OF CONNECTICUT
People, geology and the land. Ct Dep CGNHS, 1985. ○

Jones, Stephen
BACKWATERS
A charming book about the Long Island Sound and its backwaters in Connecticut and Long Island. Norton, 1979. ○

Powers, Ron
FAR FROM HOME
See entry under Illinois. ○

Taber, Gladys
STILLMEADOW SAMPLER
Philosophy and descriptions of life on a Connecticut farm—her writings have become a classic in this genre. Also *Best of Stillmeadow* (1976) and *Illustrated Book of Stillmeadow* (1984). Parnassus Imprints, 1981. ○

Tarrant, John J.
END OF EXURBIA
"Who are all those people and why do they want to ruin our town?" is the outraged question of those who were already there in response to the invasion by outsiders of affluent enclaves in Connecticut. Scarborough Hse, 1976. ○

GUIDEBOOKS

Howard, Andrew R.
**COVERED BRIDGES OF
CONNECTICUT**
Village Pr, 1985. ○

Hochstetter, Nancy, ed.
**TRAVEL HISTORIC
CONNECTICUT: A GUIDE TO
HISTORIC SITES AND MARKERS**
Guide Pr WI, 1987. ○

HISTORY

Roth, David M.
CONNECTICUT
One of a series of popular histories for each state published as part of the bicentennial in 1976. Norton, 1979. ○

Novels

DeVries, Peter
THE PRICK OF NOON
The plot is unexplainable in a brief citation—"an original comic talent . . . you either love or hate." Little, 1985. ○

DeVries, Peter
MADDER MUSIC
"Copiously funny book about a man unfitted either for marriage or adultery." (FC)

Little, 1977. Other funny, satirical novels by DeVries, set in Connecticut, include: *The Tunnel of Love* (1954), *The Mackerel Plaza* (1958), *The Tents of Wickedness* (1959), and *Reuben, Reuben* (1964). ○

Fast, Howard
THE HESSIAN

The trial of a Hessian drummer boy for a war crime during the Revolutionary War. Morrow, 1972. ○

Fast, Howard
THE OUTSIDER

A New Yorker becomes a rabbi in a small Connecticut town. The novel chronicles the growth of "this rural Jewish society [and] historical events [Rosenberg trial, civil rights marches, etc.] in which minor characters embody major conflicts." (FC) Houghton, 1984. ○

Forrest, Richard
DEATH UNDER THE LILACS

A novel of mystery and suspense—a state senator whose husband writes children's books is abducted from a shopping center. Her husband must find her from cryptic hints she gives in the single allowed telephone call. (FC) St. Martin, 1985. ○

Hodgins, Eric
MR. BLANDING BUILDS HIS DREAM HOUSE

Comedy of the trials and tribulations of building a new house just after World War II. S&S, 1946. ○

Kittredge, Mary
POISON PEN

The editor of *Pen and Pencil* finds a prominent novelist dead in her desk chair; her snooping in literary circles "turns up a plethora of suspects." (FC) Walker, 1990. Also *Rigor Mortis* (1991). ○

Kluger, Phyllis
GOOD GOODS

Vicissitudes of a Connecticut woman juggling home, children, and a career, an affair that leads to her divorce—a heroine with "freshness, wit, and intelligence." (FC) Macmillan, 1982. ○

McCarry, Charles
THE BRIDE OF THE WILDERNESS

"Funny, inventive . . . unforgettable caper" in which an 18th-century woman from London, after many vicissitudes, accompanies her godfather to Connecticut and there meets up with more vicissitudes including abduction by Indians. (FC) NAL, 1988. ○

Rice, Luanne
STONE HEART

An archaeologist returns to her hometown, and seeing her family with new eyes realizes that it is a troubled family; understated account of domestic violence with a "sensational climax." (FC) Viking, 1990. ○

Simenon, Georges
THE RULES OF THE GAME

The "rules" are the secret code used by a country club to blackball potential members who don't fit in. HarBraceJ, 1988. ○

Straub, Peter
FLOATING DRAGON

"Examines the consequences of an industrial accident coupled with supernatural evil." (FC) Putnam Pub Group, 1983. ○

Tryon, Thomas
THE WINGS OF MORNING

Set in the early 19th century; a feud between two of Pequot Landing's first families is the theme—"unalloyed pleasure for fans of this genre . . . steeped in the rhythms of Trollope and Scott." (FC) Knopf, 1990. Also *The Other* (1971) and *Lady* (1974). ○

Updike, John
MARRY ME

Affairs of four people in two unsatisfactory marriages—"the world of well-to-do [Connecticut] adultery in the 1960s." (FC) Knopf, 1976. ○

DELAWARE

Series Guidebooks
(See Appendix 1)

NOTE: See Series Guides (and non-series guides) listed under United States and the East and the East/the Middle Atlantic States. Also in some instances you may find Delaware covered in guides under the South or in guides for the District of Columbia, Maryland, Pennsylvania.

Background Reading

Canby, Henry Seidel
THE BRANDYWINE
"Intimately charming"—part history, part reminiscences, part taken from private journals—story of the river area where the author's family settled in the 1700s. Illustrations by Andrew Wyeth. (BRD) Schiffler, 1977 (first published 1941).   ○

Mosley, Leonard
BLOOD RELATIONS
The rise and fall of the Du Ponts of Delaware—a family biography, family intrigue, jealousy, infidelities, etc. Atheneum, 1980.   ○

Vessels, Jane and Fleming, Kevin
DELAWARE: A SMALL WONDER
Text and photographs describe "a uniquely serene yet diverse strip of land on the East coast . . . explicates the nuances of Delaware's high-tech, agricultural, and seaside-resort characteristics, offering tidbits of history and latter-day facts and lore." (BL) Abrams, 1984.   ○

GUIDEBOOKS

See weekend and day-trip guides under District of Columbia, Maryland, New Jersey and Pennsylvania, which often include Delaware destinations.

HISTORY

Albensi, Bill
THE COLONY OF NEW SWEDEN
Napoli Pr, 1987.   ○

Hoffecker, Carol E.
DELAWARE
One of a series of popular histories for each state, published as part of the bicentennial in 1976. Norton, 1977.   ○

Hoffecker, Carol E.
DELAWARE, THE FIRST STATE
Mid Atlantic, 1987.   ○

THE DISTRICT
OF COLUMBIA

Series Guidebooks
(See Appendix 1)

NOTE: See also Series Guides (and non-series guides) listed under United States and the East and the East/the Middle Atlantic States. In some instances you may find District of Columbia covered in guides under the South.

Access Guide: Washington, D.C.
American Express Pocket Guide: Washington, D.C.
Berlitz: Washington, D.C.
Fisher's World: District of Columbia
Fodor: Washington, D.C.
Frommer: Washington D.C. ($-A-Day)
Gault/Milau: Best of Washington, D.C.
Let's Go: Washington D.C.
Michelin: Washington, D.C.

Background Reading

Aikman, Lonnelle
WE, THE PEOPLE
Reprint of the 1963 edition—the story of the United States Capitol. U.S. Capitol Historical Soc, 1991.   o

Becker, Ralph E.
MIRACLE ON THE POTOMAC
About the Kennedy Center from its beginnings—construction, performances and ceremonies. Bartleby Pr, 1989.   o

Bowling, Kenneth
THE CREATION OF WASHINGTON, D.C.: THE IDEA AND LOCATION OF THE AMERICAN CAPITAL
The politics of how our capital came to be located where it is. The author's thesis is that it was a compromise between southern and northern interests to stave off disunion. George Mason U, 1991.   o

Menendez, Albert J.
CHRISTMAS IN THE WHITE HOUSE
Westminster, 1983.   o

Price, Robert L., ed.
THE WASHINGTON POST GUIDE TO WASHINGTON
Both a background book and a guide—essays by *Washington Post* writers on atypical tourist topics such as the presidency, suburban sprawl, along with information tidbits on museums, hotels, restaurants, etc. McRaw, 1989.   o

Rash, Bryson B.
FOOTNOTE WASHINGTON
"Tracking the engaging, humorous and surprising bypaths of Capital history." (Publisher) EPM Pubns, 1983.   o

Ryan, William and Guinness, Desmond
THE WHITE HOUSE: AN ARCHITECTURAL HISTORY
The evolution of the White House from early plans through restorations—"peppered with fascinating accounts of the sometimes make-shift living conditions and grandiose schemes" of several presidents. (LJ) McGraw, 1980.   o

Seale, William
THE PRESIDENT'S HOUSE
"First-rate social history of the White House" in two volumes. Natl Geo Svc, 1986.   o

GUIDEBOOKS

Dilworth, Donald C.
EMBASSIES OF THE WORLD
Walking tours to see the embassies. Broadcasting Pubns, 1986.   o

Douglas, Evelyn and Dickson, Paul
ON THIS SPOT
Pinpointing Washington's historical past. Farragut Pub, 1991.   o

Duffield, Judy and others
WASHINGTON, D.C.
History, description, basic information, as well as information on metro stops, bus lines, parking, special treats for children, etc. Organized to systematically move through each neighborhood. Random, 1989.   o

Fitzpatrick, Sandra and Goodwin, Maria
GUIDE TO BLACK WASHINGTON
A guide to the places and events of historical and cultural significance in the nation's capital that have shaped black history and traditions in Washington and the country. Washington is divided into 15 sections for purposes of organizing the information on "the homes and haunts of African-Americans"; also material on slavery, segregation, gentrification, etc., with off-beat bits of information and an excellent bibliography. Sandra Fitzpatrick has conducted walking tours for the Smithsonian; Maria Goodwin is Historian at the U.S. Mint. (LJ) Hippocrene, 1989.   o

Gilbert, Elizabeth R.
FAIRS AND FESTIVALS: THE SMITHSONIAN GUIDE TO CELEBRATIONS IN MARYLAND, VIRGINIA AND THE DISTRICT OF COLUMBIA

Everything from national holidays and flower festivals to ethnic and religious events. Smithsonian, 1982.   ○

Lee, Richard M.
MR. LINCOLN'S CITY

Illustrated guide to Civil War sites of Washington. EPM, 1981.   ○

Pratson, Frederick
GUIDE TO WASHINGTON, D.C. AND BEYOND

A comprehensive guide, carefully researched and easy to use. Includes those areas that lie just beyond the District (Mt. Vernon, Williamsburg, etc.) and provides background on history, culture, the White House and Congress, as well as visitor sites such as the FBI museum. Practical information for tourists on recreation and amenities will help visitors make the most of their time and money. Globe Pequot, 1991.   ○

Ross, Betty
MUSEUM GUIDE TO WASHINGTON, D.C.

Includes historic houses, galleries, libraries, familiar and unfamiliar museums, practical information (hours, metro stops, etc.), and a selection of highlights for people in a hurry—"a polished work" by a Washingtonian and a travel writer. (LJ) Globe Pequot, 1990.   ○

Smith, Jane O.
ONE-DAY TRIPS THROUGH HISTORY

Two hundred excursions within 150 miles of Washington, D.C. EPM, 1987. Also *Washington One-Day Trip Book: 101 Offbeat Excursions in and Around the Nation's Capital* (1984).   ○

Thomas, Jane O.
BEAUTY & BOUNTY: ONE-DAY NATURE TRIPS AROUND WASHINGTON, D.C.

EPM Pubns, 1987.   ○

HISTORY

Junior League of Washington Staff, eds.
THE CITY OF WASHINGTON

An illustrated history of the city. Knopf, 1985.   ○

Lewis, David L.
DISTRICT OF COLUMBIA

One of a series of popular histories for each state, published as part of the bicentennial in 1976. Norton, 1976.   ○

Smith, Kathryn S., ed.
WASHINGTON AT HOME

An illustrated history of neighborhoods in the nation's capital. Windsor Pubns, 1988.   ○

Novels

Adams, Henry
DEMOCRACY

By the nineteenth-century American novelist and published anonymously in 1879—portrays the political society of Washington during President Ulysses S. Grant's second administration (1873–77). HR&W, 1980.   ○

Benchley, Peter
Q CLEARANCE

Witty story of a former journalist working as a White House speechwriter who accidentally becomes a trusted presidential advisor. Random, 1986.   ○

Breslin, Catherine
FIRST LADIES

"Gossipy Washington novel" about candidates' wives, with an intriguing scenario—the 1980 election is forced into the House of Representatives when neither the Democrat or Republican candidate receives enough electoral votes, and the vice president is sworn in as acting president. McGraw, 1987.   ○

Buckley, C.T.
THE WHITE HOUSE MESS

Satire in the form of a memoir of a personal assistant to a Democrat president, who succeeds Reagan and is, in turn, succeeded by Bush. Knopf, 1986.   o

Carroll, James
FIREBIRD
Tensions and conflicts between the FBI and the State Department in 1949, with a plot about the Soviet-American cold war. Dutton, 1989. Also *Madonna Red* (1976).   o

Cashdan, Linda
SPECIAL INTERESTS
"Realistic, complex and interesting account of politics and journalism in the capital circa 1986." (PW) St. Martin, 1990.   o

Clark, Mary Higgins
STILLWATCH
A young woman moves into a house in D.C. in which she lived as a child, despite being warned not to. She's in town to produce a TV documentary on a senator, and his background is part of the plot of this chiller. S&S, 1984.   o

Dos Passos, John
DISTRICT OF COLUMBIA
Three political novels, from the Spanish Civil War to the New Deal. Houghton, 1952. Also *The Grand Design* (1949), about the New Deal's "merry-go-round."   o

Drury, Allen
DECISION
Two Supreme Court justices are faced with a moral dilemma when they must judge a case involving the deaths of their two daughters. [The reviewer added that in the real world they'd just disqualify themselves.] Doubleday, 1983. Other novels by Drury about the inner workings of Washington are: *Advise and Consent* (1959), *A Shade of Difference* (1962), *Capable of Honor* (1966), *Preserve and Protect* (1968), *Come Ninevah Come Tyre* (1973), *Anna Hastings* (1977).   o

Drury, Allen
PENTAGON
A Soviet invasion of a South Pacific island becomes the scenario to explore how the Pentagon works—"authentic credibility for

events and their consequences." (FC) Doubleday, 1986.   o

Goodrum, C.A.
THE BEST CELLAR
A librarian/detective is the center of this mystery "sure to delight librarians, researchers, and discriminating readers," as he and cohorts try to locate a University of Virginia student on the trail of the 3,000 books that comprised the original Library of Congress. (FC) St. Martin, 1987. Also *Dewey Decimated* (1977).   o

Just, Ward
IN THE CITY OF FEAR
A political novel focused around a Georgetown dinner party during the Vietnam War—"captures the movement of the Washington scene . . . a high comedy of manners and of acid-etched vignettes." (FC) Viking, 1982. Another novel of the Washington political scene is *Nicholson at Large* (1975), about a journalist who joins the federal government to work as spokesman for the Secretary of State. Also *The Congressman Who Loved Flaubert* (1973) (short stories).   o

Just, Ward
JACK GANCE
"The Washington novelists' Washington novelist"—a political chronicle of Jack Gance's year as a White House staffer, his return to Illinois and election to the Senate. (FC) HM, 1989.   o

Kosinski, Jerzy
BEING THERE
A former gardener is propelled into national politics when his simplistic solutions to world problems attract attention. HarBraceJ, 1980.   o

McMurtry, Larry
CADILLAC JACK
A former rodeo man who now scouts for antiques in his Cadillac undergoes a mid-life crisis "in the amiable venality and lechery of Washington, D.C." (FC) S&S, 1982.   o

Michaels, Barbara
SHATTERED SILK

Romantic suspense story set in Georgetown where the heroine attempts to set up a new life for herself after her marriage ends. Atheneum, 1986.   ○

Ravin, Neil
EVIDENCE

Two doctors gather evidence against their hospital's chief of surgery—explores the reluctance of doctors to expose medical ineptitude. Scribner, 1987.   ○

Roosevelt, Elliott
MURDER IN THE BLUE ROOM

The son of President Roosevelt (like President Truman's daughter Margaret) writes a series of mysteries, mostly set in Washington, D.C., and featuring his mother, Eleanor Roosevelt, as mystery solver—"old-fashioned . . . utterly endearing." St. Martin, 1990. Also *Murder and the First Lady* (1984), *The White House Pantry Murder* (1986), *Murder in the Oval Office* (1988), *Murder in the Rose Garden* (1989).   ○

Sheed, Wilfrid
PEOPLE WILL ALWAYS BE KIND

Story of a 1960s president who overcame childhood polio to become a brilliant, cynical politician. FS&G, 1973.   ○

Truman, Margaret
MURDER AT THE NATIONAL CATHEDRAL

One of a series of mysteries by President Truman's daughter that give readers a view of the inside workings of various segments of the government in Washington, along with a pleasant mystery story. Random, 1990. Other titles include: *Murder in the White House* (1980), *Murder on Capitol Hill* (1981), *Murder in the Supreme Court* (1982), *Murder in the Smithsonian* (1983), *Murder on Embassy Row* (1984), *Murder at the FBI* (1985), *Murder in Georgetown* (1986), *Murder in the CIA* (1987), *Murder at the Kennedy Center* (1989).   ○

Vidal, Gore
EMPIRE

Fifth in a series of historical novels about life in the 19th century. Random, 1987. Preceding this are *Washington, D.C.* (below), *Burr, Lincoln, 1876*. Also *Hollywood*, which despite its name is as much about Washington, D.C., as Hollywood.   ○

Vidal, Gore
WASHINGTON, D.C.

Third in a series depicting Washington political life since the Revolutionary War. Random, 1976. Preceding this are *Burr* (1973) and *1876* (1976).   ○

FLORIDA

Series Guidebooks (See Appendix 1)

NOTE: See also Series Guides (and non-series guides) listed under United States and the South. Occasionally a guide listed under the East, especially those pertaining to the coast, will include the southern coast.

Berlitz: Florida; Miami & the Beaches
Fisher's World: Florida
Fodor: Disney World & the Orlando Area; Florida; Miami & the Keys
Frommer: Miami; Orlando, Disney World & Epcot; Tampa & St. Petersburg; Florida

Insight Guide: Florida
Insider's Guide: Florida
Nelles Guide: Florida
Off the Beaten Path: Florida
2–22 Days Itinerary Planning Guide: Florida

Background Reading

Allman, T.D.
MIAMI: CITY OF THE FUTURE

Multifaceted treatment of Miami's growth, a city teeming with money, exotic cargoes, illegal aliens, cocaine and immigrants from everywhere—"colorful anecdotes abound . . . revealing sidelights and personal profiles." The book tells why Miami grew so breathtakingly fast, and the author's insights take us below the surface grit and glitter. (PW/Publisher) Atl Monthly Pr, 1987.   ○

Buchanan, Edna
THE CORPSE HAD A FAMILIAR FACE: COVERING MIAMI, AMERICA'S HOTTEST BEAT
"Tough-as-nails autobiography" of a Pulitzer Prize-winning police reporter for the *Miami Herald* for 16 years, covering some 5,000 murders. (PW) Random, 1987. See also a novel by Buchanan, below.   ○

Carr, Patrick
SUNSHINE STATES
Witty and entertaining account of Florida through the eyes of a British journalist; subtitled *Wild Times and Extraordinary Lives in the Land of Gators, Guns and Grapefruit.* "As a chronicler of American travels, Carr falls somewhere between Charles Dickens and Crocodile Dundee." He thinks of Florida as a frontier and visits with all sorts of people and even goes under cover as a street narc. (NYT) Doubleday, 1990.   ○

Cortes, Carlos E., ed.
THE CUBAN EXPERIENCE IN THE U.S.: AN ORIGINAL ANTHOLOGY
Ayer Co, 1981.   ○

Didion, Joan
MIAMI
Focuses on Miami, since the refugees from Castro's Cuba swarmed there—"brings the novelist's ear and journalist's eye to her work . . . a masterful polemic [that] portrays today's Miami as a hotbed of conspiracy" to overthrow Castro. (PW) S&S, 1987.   ○

Douglas, Marjory S.
THE EVERGLADES: RIVER OF GRASS
Revised edition of a classic, with a new chapter updating its Everglades National Park status since 1947. Mockingbird, 1989.   ○

Green, Ben
FINEST KIND: A CELEBRATION OF A FLORIDA FISHING VILLAGE
Intelligent, down-home treatment of one of the few remaining fishing villages in Florida. Oral history of Cortez, and its people, and a plea to save it from real estate development and drug smuggling. Mercer U, 1985.   ○

Howard, Robert
THE BEST SMALL TOWNS UNDER THE SUN
Florida's most attractive—and inviting—little communities. EPM Pubns, 1989.   ○

Jahoda, Gloria
THE OTHER FLORIDA
About the west Florida panhandle, beyond Pensacola, and first published in 1967 when this area was relatively untouched—travel, history, folklore, sociology. Florida Classics, 1984.   ○

Kaufelt, Lynn
KEY WEST WRITERS AND THEIR HOUSES
Writers who make up the legend of the Keys—Hemingway, Wallace Stevens, Tennessee Williams, others. Pineapple Pr, 1986.   ○

Lane, Jack, ed.
THE FLORIDA READER: VISIONS OF PARADISE
Pineapple Pr, 1990.   ○

Rawlings, Marjorie K.
CROSS CREEK
Recreates vividly the memorable people the author knew from thirteen years of living at Cross Creek—a classic. Scribner, 1984 (first published 1942).   ○

Rothchild, John
UP FOR GRABS: A TRIP THROUGH TIME AND SPACE IN THE SUNSHINE STATE
"Personal memoir [and] history of Florida . . . grand reading. . . . deliciously under-

scores the bizarre quality of Florida life."
(PW) Viking, 1985.   ○

Rudloe, Jack
THE LIVING DOCK AT PANACEA
The author started a business for providing
marine life specimens to colleges—writes
beautifully of the teeming life of his dock.
Fulcrum, 1988.   ○

Shoumatoff, Alex
FLORIDA RAMBLE
An offbeat travelogue of a sixty-two day
sojourn—subjects range from "indigenous
birds and mushrooms to the proliferating
retiree communities." (BRD) Random,
1990.   ○

Toops, Connie
EVERGLADES
Photos and text about places tourists rarely
see—derived from six seasons as a park
ranger. Voyageur Pr, 1989.   ○

Wilkinson, Alec
**BIG SUGAR: SEASONS IN THE
CANE FIELDS OF FLORIDA**
An antidote to the experiences of most tourists—story of the sugar cane industry and
the towns like Clewiston and Belle Glade
where poor, uneducated West Indians work
the fields. Knopf, 1989.   ○

Williams, Joy
THE FLORIDA KEYS
A history and also a guide—"prose encourages the reader to head for the Keys before
things change too much." Written by a novelist from Maine who's made Florida home.
Random, 1987.   ○

Wolfe, Tom
THE RIGHT STUFF
History of the space program and the lives
of the first group of astronauts, their flights,
their training—"technically accurate, learned,
cheeky, touching . . . nostalgic . . . superb." (NYT) Made into a film. Originally
published in 1979. FS&G, 1983.   ○

Zinsser, William
SPRING TRAINING
The Pittsburgh Pirates in 1988, and the spring
training phenomenon in Bradenton. Har-
Row, 1989.   ○

FLORIDA GUIDEBOOKS

Coleman, Ken and Valenti, Dan
GRAPEFRUIT LEAGUE ROAD TRIP
History and guide to baseball for the 18
teams that train in Florida—training lore,
maps of each town, hotels, even some pages
on which to gather autographs. Stephen
Greene Pr, 1987.   ○

DeWire, Elinor
**GUIDE TO FLORIDA
LIGHTHOUSES**
Pineapple Pr, 1989.   ○

Garrity, John
**THE TRAVELER'S GUIDE TO
BASEBALL SPRING TRAINING**
For Florida and Arizona—see entry under
Arizona.   ○

La Freniere, Barbara B. and Ed
**COMPLETE GUIDE TO LIFE IN
FLORIDA**
Pineapple Pr, 1991.   ○

Laurie, Murray and Bardon, Doris
MUSEUMS AND MORE!
Florida's cultural and heritage attractions.
Maupin Hse, 1991.   ○

Leslie, Candace
**HIDDEN FLORIDA KEYS &
EVERGLADES: THE
ADVENTURER'S GUIDE**
Ulysses Pr, 1990.   ○

McCarthy, Kevin
FLORIDA LIGHTHOUSES
U Presses of Florida, 1990.   ○

McMinn, Russell
**ANTIQUES: GUIDE TO FLORIDA
ANTIQUES SHOPS**
Jockey Hollow, 1989.   ○

Pratson, Frederick
ORLANDO & BEYOND
A comprehensive guide to Walt Disney World, Sea World, the Space Center, Busch Gardens, Tampa, beaches. Globe Pequot, 1988.　　　○

Rankin, Anne
EXPLORING FLORIDA
A guide "addressed to those who want to taste more of Florida than florid cocktails and Disney World"—explores the lesser-known historic sites, natural attractions and beaches. Includes a brief history. Hippocrene, 1991.　　　○

Riegert, Ray
HIDDEN FLORIDA: THE ADVENTURER'S GUIDE
Emphasizes travel experiences beyond the standard travel guides to challenge jaded visitors. Ulysses Pr, 1988.　　　○

Ritz, Stacy and Olmstead, Marty
FLORIDA'S GOLD COAST: THE ULTIMATE GUIDEBOOK
Ulysses Pr, 1991.　　　○

Sehlinger, Bob and Finley, John
THE UNOFFICIAL GUIDE TO WALT DISNEY WORLD & EPCOT
"An alternative to the Disney promotional material . . . critical evaluations of all the rides and exhibits"—helpful hints on coping with lines, crowds, planning a one-day stay, etc. P-H, 1987.　　　○

Stone, Lynn M.
SANIBEL ISLAND
Part of the Wilderness Series. Voyageur Pr, 1991.　　　○

Tolf, Robert
FLORIDA WEEKENDS
Fifty-two great getaways throughout Florida and the Keys. Crown, 1990.　　　○

U Presses of Florida, eds.
FLORIDA'S SANDY BEACHES: AN ACCESS GUIDE
County by county guide to beaches on both coasts—facilities for each, how to get there, history, flora and fauna. (BL) U Presses of Florida, 1985.　　　○

Wright, Sarah Bird
ISLANDS OF THE SOUTH AND SOUTHEASTERN UNITED STATES
Entered under United States/Guidebooks. Most of the islands are around Florida.　　○

HISTORY

Derr, Mark
SOME KIND OF PARADISE
"A unique, thorough state history" of everything from ecology and geology to real estate and politics. The "panoramic narrative is animated by anecdotes, novel details and flavorful images." (PW) Morrow, 1989.　　○

Jahoda, Gloria
FLORIDA
One of a series of popular histories for each state, published as part of the bicentennial in 1976. Norton, 1984. Also, *The Other Florida* (1984).　　　○

Muir, Helen
MIAMI, U.S.A.
Revised edition of a history originally published in 1953—"chatty, factual, and personal . . . not-to-be-missed slice of southern living." (BL) Pickering Pr, 1990.　　　○

Novels

Anthony, Piers
SHADE OF THE TREE
A fantasy set in rural Florida where a widower and his two children have come to live in a house left them by an eccentric uncle. Tor Bks, 1985.　　　○

Banks, Russell
CONTINENTAL DRIFT
The intersecting paths of two people told in alternating chapters: one is a New Hampshire native who takes off for Florida with his family, seeking a better life; the other a poverty-stricken Haitian who leaves Haiti for "the bright promise of America." (FC) Har-Row, 1985.　　　○

Barthelme, Frederick
TRACER (Fort Meyers)
A man in the process of being divorced from his wife becomes involved with her younger sister. S&S, 1985.   ⊙

Bell, Christine
PEREZ FAMILY
After 20 years in a Cuban prison, Juan Perez is suddenly released and shipped to Miami, but through bureaucratic errors he ends up in a homeless center. He meets up with sexy Dottie instead of being reunited with his family, and Dottie convinces him to stay—"black comedy . . . feverish plot with wit and humor." (PW) Norton, 1990.   ⊙

Buchanan, Edna
NOBODY LIVES FOREVER
"Relies on the unflinching terror of realistic description" to convey the suspense—"crime-drenched streets become a personal affront" to a detective when his teen-aged neighbor is murdered. (BL) Random, 1990.   ⊙

Dintenfass, Mark
A LOVING PLACE
Three reflective days in the life of a former bookie, now in a Florida retirement community. Morrow, 1985.   ⊙

Elkin, Stanley
STANLEY ELKIN'S THE MAGIC KINGDOM
Seven terminally ill English children go to Disney World in the charge of five adults—"highly comic, and deeply tragic, things happen . . . challenges a resilient and imaginative reader." (FC) Dutton, 1985.   ⊙

Green, Judith H.
SOMETIMES PARADISE
The sordidness, hypocrisy and anti-Semitism beneath Palm Beach's genteel front—"an engrossing read." (FC) Knopf, 1987. ⊙

Hall, James W.
BONES OF CORAL (The Keys)
A fireman's attempt to find out more about his father's suspicious death causes him to fall into the clutches of a garbage dump operator and his son, a loathsome pair. Hall is considered one of the best of the mystery writers today who use Florida for a setting; if you're a fan of the genre and don't mind a few nightmares, take your chances. (BL) Knopf, 1991. Also *Tropical Freeze* (1989) and *Under Cover of Daylight* (1987).   ⊙

Hamill, Pete
LOVING WOMEN; A NOVEL OF THE FIFTIES (Pensacola)
"Tough . . . funny . . . a fierce sense of time, place"—an Irish Catholic from Brooklyn (narrating from middle age and about to get his third divorce) tells how he learned the lessons of life. Random, 1989.   ⊙

Hemingway, Ernest
TO HAVE AND HAVE NOT (Key West; Cuba)
The locale is Key West (and Cuba)—an American gets involved in smuggling when he loses his charter boat in a swindle. Scribner, 1937.   ⊙

Hiaasen, Carl
TOURIST SEASON
A Miami Beach reporter, turned sleuth, "intuits that someone is out to kill Florida's tourist trade" when the president of the Chamber of Commerce meets a horrific death and a Shriner and a Canadian tourist disappear. Like Hall, above, Hiaasen is considered one of the best writers of crime novels set in Florida. (PW) Putnam, 1986. Also, *Skin Tight* (1989).   ⊙

Hunter, Evan
FAR FROM THE SEA
A five-day vigil at the bedside of his dying father results in spiritual rebirth for a New York lawyer. Atheneum, 1983.   ⊙

Hurston, Zora Neale
SERAPH ON THE SUWANEE
By a leading black writer and a best-seller when published—about poor white "crackers" in west Florida at the beginning of the century. AMS (first published 1948). Also the recent reprint *Zora Neale Hurston Reader* (1979).   ⊙

Kaufelt, David A.
AMERICAN TROPIC
A historic saga of two families, from 1512 to Castro's takeover of Cuba. Poseidon, 1986.   ○

Leonard, Elmore
LA BRAVA
A former movie star now living in the South Beach area of Florida, who played a predatory spider woman, is now herself the victim of extortion. Arbor Hse, 1983. Also *Stick* (1983), *Cat Chaser* (1982), *Maximum Bob* (1991).   ○

Levine, Paul
TO SPEAK FOR THE DEAD
"Tense courtroom and medical scenes with expert panache, fluid prose, and sly humor" in a first novel—a physician is accused of malpractice. (LJ) Bantam, 1990.   ○

Littlefield, Bill
PROSPECT
An employee at a rest home befriends former baseball scout Pete Estey, who waits for his death. The employee brings Pete and her grandnephew (a born ballplayer) together for both their sakes—"strong, heartfelt" novel. (FC) HM, 1989.   ○

Lutz, John
TROPICAL HEAT
An ex-cop turned private eye is stalked by a group of Cuban Marielitos when he investigates a suspected suicide. Holt, 1986. Also *Kiss* (1988), and *Scorcher* (1987)—"superb Florida ambience."   ○

McBain, Ed
CINDERELLA
Lawyer Matthew Hope has a penchant for getting involved with women in difficulties; this, and *Snow White and Rose Red*, are two mysteries set in Miami Beach/Fort Lauderdale and a Florida town, respectively. "Hot, hazy and humid Florida serves as an atmospheric backdrop." (FC) HR&W, 1986. Also *Goldilocks* (1977), and *Three Blind Mice* (1990).   ○

MacDonald, John D.
THE EMPTY COPPER SEA
Set on the Florida Gulf coast and one of many Travis McGee mysteries set in Florida. Lippincott, 1978. Other titles include: *A Deadly Shade of Gold* (1974), *The Deep Blue Good-by* (1975), *The Dreadful Lemon Sky* (1975), and *The Turquoise Lament* (1973). Also *The Condominium* (1977), about life in a badly-built condo as Hurricane Ella arrives.   ○

McGuane, Thomas
92 IN THE SHADE (Key West)
A fishing guide is the victim of an extravagant practical joke to drive him out of business—"feeling for the rambunctious oddities, forlorn vulgarity and green beauty of Key West." Also *Panama* (1978), about a rock star trying to get back his lost girlfriend.   ○

Matthiessen, Peter
KILLING MR WATSON
The story behind the legend of Edgar J. Watson, a famous outlaw in the Florida Everglades of a hundred years ago. Random, 1990.   ○

Mayerson, Evelyn W.
NO ENEMY BUT TIME
A hotel in Miami Beach during World War II is the backdrop. Doubleday, 1983.   ○

Palmer, Thomas
THE TRANSFER
"A first-rate thriller" about a man blackmailed by his brother into drug smuggling. Ultimately he is forced to make a decision that will allow him to go back to his former peaceful existence. (FC) Ticknor & Fields, 1983.   ○

Peck, Robert N.
HALLAPOOSA
Set in a south Florida town during the Depression, as the justice of the peace takes in the two children of his murdered younger brother. Walker, 1988.   ○

Rawlings, Marjorie K.
THE MARJORIE RAWLINGS READER
Includes *South Moon Under* and selections from novels and short stories by a leading

Florida writer whose home has become a state historic site. Scribner, 1956.   ○

Sanchez, Thomas
MILE ZERO (Key West)
A "vortex of metaphysical mystery . . . dense, complex . . . murky in its finale . . . uniquely rendered, almost unearthly evocation of Key West." (FC) Knopf, 1989.   ○

Smith, Patrick
A LAND REMEMBERED
Saga of the MacIvey family beginning in 1858. Pineapple Pr, 1985.   ○

Whitney, Phyllis A.
POINCIANA
Atmospherically authentic Palm Beach background and a mildly suspenseful plot. Doubleday, 1980. Also *Dream of Orchids*, "played

against a colorful backdrop of libertines and literati, gold-seekers and sun-worshipers" in Key West. (FC) (1985).   ○

Willeford, C.R.
THE WAY WE DIE NOW
"Trusty . . . comfortable Detective Hoke Mosely lumbers through another case of murder in sunny Florida . . . makes excellent use of the Florida landscape . . . from the big city to the bayou backwaters." (FC) Random, 1988. Also *Miami Blues* (1984).   ○

Yglesias, Jose
HOME AGAIN
A Tampa Latino, and left-wing novelist, returns to Florida after his wife's death, and a cousin involves him in a dangerous scheme to rescue the cousin's daughter. *Tristan and the Hispanics* is a sequel (1989). Arbor Hse, 1987. Also *The Truth About Them* (1971).   ○

GEORGIA

*Series Guidebooks
(See Appendix 1)*

NOTE: See also Series Guides (and non-series guides) listed under United States and the South.

Off the Beaten Path: Georgia

Background Reading

Buck, Polly S.
THE BLESSED TOWN
One of a series of memoirs called "American Places"—this is of Oxford, the town where Emory University began, before Coca Cola endowments moved it to Atlanta. The author's mother boarded Emory students in the early 1900s— "Southern ambiance . . . of the Civil War aftermath . . . a simple time in small-town America evoked with humor, simplicity." (PW) Algonquin, 1986.   ○

Harper, Francis and Presley, Delma
OKEFENOKEE ALBUM
Folklore, language, customs, songs, wildlife of the swamp in southeastern Georgia and northern Florida. U of Georgia, 1981.   ○

McCash, William B. and June H.
THE JEKYLL ISLAND CLUB
This formerly exclusive club is now open for tourists to see, but for 62 years it was "the richest, the most exclusive, the most inaccessible" social organization in the world, as a winter retreat for northeastern financiers. The book is an account of those days using historical records, club records, newspaper accounts, diaries and letters. (BL) U of Georgia Pr, 1989.   ○

Olympic Committee
**WELCOME TO A BRAVE &
    BEAUTIFUL CITY**
How Atlanta beat out Athens, Melbourne and Toronto for the summer Olympics— Volume 1 of the authorized commemorative edition of Atlanta's official Olympic bid books. Volume 2 is entitled *Atlanta: City of Dreams*. Peachtree Pbns, 1991.   ○

Price, Eugenia
AT HOME ON ST. SIMONS
The story of finding the island and writing the St. Simons trilogy of novels (see under

"Novels," below). Peachtree Pbns, 1981. Also *St. Simons Memoir* (1987). ○

Van Story, Burnette L.
GEORGIA'S LAND OF THE GOLDEN ISLES
Georgia's offshore islands, with an introduction by novelist Eugenia Price (see "Novels," below). U of Georgia Pr, (1981). ○

Wigginton, Eliot
FOXFIRE
A landmark series of books that has since been emulated by other high schools in other states. It was begun by a schoolteacher in north Georgia as a classroom writing project that would help to preserve local culture while providing students with an educational experience in research and writing. The series (there are eight books at this time) covers all aspects of "plain living" from log-cabin building to midwifery to musical instruments and gardening, toys and games—every imaginable subject. Doubleday, 1986. ○

GUIDEBOOKS

Harman, Jeanne P. and Harry E., III
GEORGIA AT ITS BEST
Rutledge Hill Pr, 1989. ○

Hoffland, Rusty
MOUNTAIN GETAWAYS IN GEORGIA, NORTH CAROLINA AND TENNESSEE
On the Road Pub, 1990. ○

McCarley, J. Britt, and others
THE ATLANTA CAMPAIGN
A Civil War driving tour of Atlanta-area battlefields, with a reader's guide to the Atlanta campaign. Cherokee, 1989. ○

Miles, James
TO THE SEA: A HISTORY AND TOUR GUIDE OF SHERMAN'S MARCH
Highly anecdotal account of Sherman's march—"offers sympathetic understanding of all sides involved in the epic trek" with narrative skills equaling those of Bruce Catton or Shelby Foote. Each section ends with

a road guide to the route and local historical attractions. (LJ) Rutledge Hill Pr, 1989. Also *Field of Glory: A History and Tour Guide of the Atlanta Campaign* (1989). ○

Wenberg, Donald C.
BLUE RIDGE MOUNTAIN PLEASURES
An A-Z guide to northern Georgia, western North Carolina and the up country of South Carolina. Globe Pequot, 1988. ○

HISTORY

Martin, Harold H.
GEORGIA
One of a series of popular histories for each state, published as part of the bicentennial in 1976. Norton, 1977. ○

Novels

Andrews, Raymond
BABY SWEET'S
One of several novels about black life in a small southern town in Muskhogean County. Baby Sweet's is an eatery turned sporting house. Dial, 1983. In *Appalachee Red* (1978) a mulatto son of an influential white man and a black maid returns to the south to face his father. *Rosiebelle Lee Wildcat* (1980) is a novel of a half-Indian, half-black woman in 1906 who becomes the mistress of the richest man in town. ○

Ansa, Tina McElroy
BABY OF THE FAMILY
"This genial first novel renders the life of a black Georgia family of the 1950s in rich detail." (NYT) HarBraceJ, 1989. ○

Battle, Lois
SOUTHERN WOMEN
Saga of a prominent Savannah family. St. Martin, 1984. ○

Boyd, William
STARS AND BARS
A farce about a "panicky Brit in brash America"—a British art expert is sent to Georgia to evaluate a collection of paintings in an eccentric southern household. Made into a movie. (BRD) Morrow, 1984. ○

Burns, Olive Ann
COLD SASSY TREE

"Humorously poignant coming-of-age story set in turn-of-the-century Georgia. . . . Authentic period piece brimming with charm, sentiment and local color." Made into TV movie. (BL) Ticknor & Fields, 1984.   ○

Burroway, Janet
OPENING NIGHTS

The heroine is on the faculty of a small college in Georgia and raising her son, when her ex-husband arrives, by way of Yale and New York, to direct the summer stage program at the college. Atheneum, 1985.   ○

Caldwell, Erskine
TOBACCO ROAD

Degeneration of a poor-white Georgia family, living on the once-prosperous farm of Jeeter Lester's grandfather—told with humor and irreverence "that verges upon the . . . ribaldry of a burlesque show." (FC) Bentley, 1978 (first published 1932). Also *God's Little Acre* (1932)—"one of the finest studies of the Southern poor white."   ○

Coleman, Lonnie
BEULAH LAND

This, followed by *Look Away Beulah Land* (1977) and *The Legacy of Beulah Land* (1980), begins a trilogy about nineteenth-century, antebellum plantation life. Doubleday, 1973.   ○

Cook, Thomas H.
SACRIFICIAL GROUND

A 16-year-old girl, leading a dual life, is found murdered, and Lt. Frank Clemons because his own daughter committed suicide at 16 is determined to find the killer. Putnam, 1988.   ○

Leamon, Warren
UNHEARD MELODIES

A coming-of-age novel and memoir of a boy's experiences from fourth grade to graduation from high school, in a postwar, white, middle-class neighborhood in Atlanta. The story parallels the growth of Atlanta "from provincial innocence to metropolitan sophis-

tication . . . [evokes] a vivid sense of place . . . introspective even during the most suspenseful and comic episodes." (BRD) Longstreet Pr, 1990.   ○

McCammon, Robert
MYSTERY WALK

Two young brothers (one a tent revival faith healer, the other with the gift to help spirits of those who die violently to "pass over") in a novel of horror and the supernatural—"delivers a good scare with style." (FC) Holt, 1983.   ○

McCullers, Carson
MEMBER OF THE WEDDING

A fictional study in child psychology—the wedding of her older brother seen through the eyes of a twelve-year-old girl "with her six-year-old cousin, and the black cook as chorus." (FC) Houghton, 1946.   ○

Mitchell, Margaret
GONE WITH THE WIND

Winston Churchill called it America's *War and Peace.* The Civil War, and Atlanta and plantation life, just before, during and following the war. Macmillan, 1936. See also *Scarlett* by Alexandra Ripley, below.   ○

O'Connor, Flannery
FLANNERY O'CONNOR'S GEORGIA

Stories by a leading American writer. FS&G, 1980. Also *The Complete Stories of Flannery O'Connor* (1971).   ○

Price, Eugenia
THE BELOVED INVADER (St. Simons Island)

It is the first published of a trilogy that includes *Lighthouse* (1971) and *New Moon Rising* (1969), but chronologically takes place last. Lippincott, 1965.   ○

Price, Eugenia
BRIGHT CAPTIVITY

First of a trilogy of historical Georgia. This one is about St. Simons Island, with some of the action taking place in Scotland. Doubleday, 1991.   ○

Price, Eugenia
SAVANNAH
A leisurely "excursion through 13 years of the city's history" told through the story of an orphan who immigrates to Savannah and is befriended by both imagined and actual historical characters. The story begins in 1812. (Publisher) Doubleday, 1983. *To See Your Face Again* (1984) is a sequel, *Before the Darkness Falls* (1987) is the third volume of the series and *Stranger in Savannah* (1989) the fourth. ○

Ripley, Alexandra
SCARLETT
The sequel to *Gone With the Wind*, Warner, 1991. ○

Siddons, Anne R.
KING'S OAK
"Jumps on the environmental bandwagon" with a story of Andy Calhoun, who moves to the Georgia hunt country with her daughter, is attracted to a man passionately committed to preserving the woods and joins his cause. (LJ) HarperCollins, 1990. Also *Homeplace* (1987) and *Fox's Earth* (1981). ○

Siddons, Anne R.
PEACHTREE ROAD
Forty years of life on Peachtree Road, in Atlanta's Buckhead section, narrated by the reclusive son of an aristocratic family. Har-Row, 1988. ○

Woods, Stuart
UNDER THE LAKE
"Gripping, plausible mystery/ghost story" centered around a man-made lake in a quiet southern town. (FC) S&S, 1987. Also *Grass Roots*, about murder and contemporary politics (1989), *Chiefs* (1981), and *Palindrome* (1991). ○

HAWAII

Series Guidebooks (See Appendix 1)

Access Guide: Hawaii
At Its Best: Hawaii
Berlitz: Hawaii
Birnbaum: Hawaii
Fielding: Hawaii
Fisher's World: Hawaii
Fodor: Hawaii; Maui; Waikiki
Frommer: Hawaii ($-A-Day)
Gault/Milau: The Best of Hawaii
Insider's Guide: Hawaii
Insight Guide: Hawaii
Let's Go: California & Hawaii
Moon Handbook: Hawaii; Oahu; Maui; Kauai; Big Island
Nelles Guide: Hawaii
Off the Beaten Path: Hawaii
2–22 Days Itinerary Planning Guide: Hawaii

Background Reading

Brennan, Joseph
THE PARKER RANCH OF HAWAII
"Saga of a ranch and a dynasty" chronicling the varying fortunes and history of an influential family whose founder jumped ship in 1809 and married the king's granddaughter. (BRD) B&N Bks, 1986. ○

Day, A. Grove, ed.
MAD ABOUT THE ISLANDS: NOVELISTS OF THE SOUTH SEAS
Mutual Pub, 1987. Also *A Hawaiian Reader* (1959), which includes writings by Michener, Jack London, Mark Twain and others, arranged chronologically; and *Mark Twain's Letters from Hawaii* (1979), edited by Mr. Day. ○

Loomis, Albertine
FOR WHOM ARE THE STARS?
Three years starting from 1893, when the last queen of Hawaii surrendered the throne,

the beginning of Hawaii as a republic, and the attempt of the queen's supporters to restore the monarchy. U of Hawaii Pr, 1976.   ○

Nelson, Victoria
MY TIME IN HAWAII
"Probing, witty chronicle of culturally and topographically diverse Hawaii . . . strikingly original . . . a story hard to put down." The author, as a professor at the University of Hawaii in the early 1970s, and an amateur archaeologist, immersed herself in a study of the land and history of Hawaii and the experience of living there as a mainland American. (PW) St. Martin, 1990.   ○

Stephan, John
HAWAII UNDER THE RISING SUN
Japan's plans for conquest of Hawaii after Pearl Harbor and the role that Japanese-Americans in Hawaii were expected to play. U of Hawaii Pr, 1984.   ○

Stevenson, Robert L.
TRAVELS IN HAWAII
The author's experiences and reactions to Hawaii in the nineteenth century. U of Hawaii Pr, 1973.   ○

GUIDEBOOKS

Bone, Robert W.
THE MAVERICK GUIDE TO HAWAII
The Washington Times is quoted as saying: "One of the most complete guides to these paradisiacal islands in the Pacific . . . An invaluable handbook." Pelican, 1991.   ○

Clark, John R.
BEACHES OF HAWAII SERIES
Separate volumes for Maui County, the Big Island, O'ahu, Kaua'i and Ni'ihau—history, anecdotes, shoreline, facilities, access. U of Hawaii Pr, 1985–1990.   ○

Donohugh, Don and Bea
KAUA'I: A PARADISE GUIDE
Historical overview and detailed tourist information—"never hesitant to pick favorites . . . by authors who are permanent residents." (BL) Paradise Pubns, 1989.   ○

Harden, M.J.
MAGIC MAUI: THE BEST OF THE ISLAND
Hawaiian newspapers call this the best, most thorough guide for Maui—"a book to curl up with and enjoy." Equal emphasis is given to the island's magical aspects, and the book includes drawings and paintings by Maui artists. AA Pr, 1987.   ○

Riegert, Ray
HIDDEN HAWAII: THE ADVENTURER'S GUIDE
"For those who like to get away from the tourist lanes and follow a fresh track . . . inexpensive lodgings and restaurants, groceries and gift shops . . . beaches and parks . . . how to live off the land." (LJ) Ulysses Pr, 1989.   ○

Runge, Jonathan
HOT ON HAWAII: THE DEFINITIVE GUIDE TO THE ALOHA STATE
Aimed at travelers who want to pursue a non-typical tourist agenda, with a focus on special interests (nature, sports, "the cerebral option" and so on)—"instructive bits of the author's first hand experiences abound." (BL) St. Martin, 1989.   ○

Zurick, David
HAWAII, NATURALLY
"An environmentally oriented guide to the wonders and the pleasures of the islands." Natural beauty, botanical parks and gardens, nature programs, alternative places to stay, outdoor activities and more. (LJ) Wilderness, 1990.   ○

HISTORY

Daws, Gavan
SHOALS OF TIME
A history of the islands "told with style and, at times, a nice wit." (PW) U of Hawaii Pr, 1974.   ○

Joesting, Edward
HAWAII: AN UNCOMMMON HISTORY
"A very readable work . . . snippets of Hawaiian history" emphasizing personalities

and colorful events of the past. (BRD) Norton, 1988. Also *Kauai: the Separate Kingdom* (1988).   ○

Tabrah, Ruth
HAWAII
One of a series of popular histories for each state, published as part of the bicentennial in 1976. Norton, 1980.   ○

Novels

Bushnell, Oswald A.
THE WATER OF KANE
The Japanese in Hawaii. U of Hawaii Pr, 1980.   ○

Jones, James
FROM HERE TO ETERNITY
The best-seller, in its day, of army life in pre-Pearl Harbor Hawaii and a love affair between an enlisted man and an officer's wife. Delacorte Pr, 1980.   ○

Katkov, Norman
BLOOD AND ORCHIDS
Set in Hawaii in the 1930s and based on an actual case of a group of Hawaiian beach boys accused of raping an American officer's wife; vigilante justice. The ultimate truth revealed is "even more sordid and scandalous than originally supposed." (FC) St. Martin, 1983.   ○

London, Jack
STORIES OF HAWAII
Stories written while London was living in Hawaii, with a wide range of themes—"cap-

tures the flavor of life there at the turn of the century." (FC) Appleton, 1965.   ○

Michener, James A.
HAWAII
A "monumental account of the islands from geologic birth to emergence as a state," explored through its racial origins and several narrative strands. (FC) Random, 1959.   ○

Mo, Timothy
THE MONKEY KING
"A tale both elegant and charming" of a clerk who is "had" when he marries the daughter of a Hong Kong businessman but resourcefully rises to head of the house. Morrow, 1987.   ○

Moore, Susanna
MY OLD SWEETHEART
The narrator, Lily, is the daughter of an "elegant, erratic mother" who becomes dependent on her when on drugs or suffering from delusions. "The lush atmosphere of Hawaii hangs over the reader's armchair." (FC) Houghton, 1982.   ○

Saiki, Jessica
ONCE, A LOTUS GARDEN
Stories of the Japanese in Hawaii and the clash between tradition and contemporary life. New Rivers Pr, 1987.   ○

Whitney, Phyllis A.
SILVERSWORD
A woman decides to return to Maui and find out what really happened the day, 25 years earlier, her parents were killed. Doubleday, 1987.   ○

IDAHO

Series Guidebooks (See Appendix 1)

NOTE: See also Series Guides (and non-series guides) listed under United States and the West.

Sierra: Guide to the Natural Areas of Idaho, Montana & Wyoming

Background Reading

Alt, David and Hyndman, Donald
ROADSIDE GEOLOGY OF IDAHO
One of a series of books that is wonderful to take along in the car. To paraphrase the preface, being able to look at the landscape as you travel and (with this book) envision

the forces and changes—the dynamics of the landscape you are seeing—is a real achievement of understanding for travelers. Mountain Pr, 1989.   ○

Bellavance-Johnson, Marsha and Lee
ERNEST HEMINGWAY IN IDAHO
Part of the Famous Footsteps Series—and also a guidebook. Computer Lab, 1989.   ○

GUIDEBOOKS

Conley, Cort
IDAHO FOR THE CURIOUS; A GUIDE
Backeddy Bks, 1982.   ○

Hendrickson, Borg and Laughy, Linwood
CLEARWATER COUNTRY
The traveler's historical and recreational guide for the area from Lewiston to Missoula. Mountain Meadow Pr, 1989.   ○

Meloy, Betty T.
IDAHO MUSEUM GUIDE
Meloy, 1989.   ○

Moore, Rae Ellen
JUST WEST OF YELLOWSTONE
A comprehensive guidebook and travel sketchbook for the area on the sunset side of Yellowstone National Park—for the traveler and armchair traveler. Great Blue Graphics, 1988.   ○

Sparling, Wayne
SOUTHERN IDAHO GHOST TOWNS
Caxton, 1974.

HISTORY

Peterson, F. Ross
IDAHO
One of a series of popular histories for each state, published as part of the bicentennial in 1976. Norton, 1876.   ○

Novels

Brink, Carol
STRANGERS IN THE RIVER
Story about the efforts of a group of U.S. foresters in the panhandle section of Idaho to conserve the forests there in the early years of the century, and the secret mission of one of them to try to figure out which homesteaders would actually farm the land and which would sell out to the lumber industry. Macmillan, 1960. Other novels with an Idaho background by this author are: *Buffalo Coat* (1944) and *Snow in the River* (1964).   ○

Fisher, Vardis
IN TRAGIC LIFE
One of Fisher's highly realistic novels—"crudities and hardships of life on a western farm a generation ago." (BRD) Caxton, 1932. Other novels by Fisher with an Idaho setting are: *Dark Bridwell* (1931) and *Toilers of the Hill* (1928).   ○

ILLINOIS

Series Guidebooks (See Appendix 1)

NOTE: See also Series Guides (and non-series guides) listed under United States and the Midwest.

Access Guide: Chicago
Fodor: Chicago
Frommer: Chicago
Gault/Milau: The Best of Chicago

Insight Guide: Chicago
Off the Beaten Path: Illinois

Background Reading

Algren, Nelson
CITY ON THE MAKE
New edition of the novelist's hymn to Chicago, with an introduction by Studs Terkel,

first published 1951. U of Chicago Pr, 1987.   ○

Andrews, Clarence
CHICAGO IN STORY; A LITERARY HISTORY
Midwest Heritage, 1983.   ○

Berger, Philip
HIGHLAND PARK: AMERICAN SUBURB AT ITS BEST
Chicago Review Pr, 1983.   ○

Calkins, Earnest Elmo
THEY BROKE THE PRAIRIE
Reprint of 1937 edition—an account of settling the upper Mississippi Valley by pioneers as reflected in the establishment and growth of Galesburg, Illinois and Knox College. U of Ill Pr, 1989.   ○

Cromie, Robert
CHICAGO
"A tribute to a city" by a noted Chicago journalist and broadcaster. "Text and photographs emphasize the geographical features and architectural treasures that set Chicago apart." (BL) Rand McNally, 1990.
○

Guillory, Dan
LIVING WITH LINCOLN: LIFE AND ART IN THE HEARTLAND
Twenty-six essays on aspects of Illinois from barns and restorations, to the Amish—"in search of the soul of the heartland . . . exuberant . . . these essays radiate a feeling for what endures in Midwestern life." (LJ) Stormline Pr, 1989.   ○

Powers, Ron
FAR FROM HOME
The author involved himself in the lives of people in Cairo, Illinois, and Kent, Connecticut. "Ponders the sad levels" to which these two towns have been reduced—Cairo because of its unfulfilled expectations, Kent because of the invasion of summer people that turned it into "bland suburbia." (BL) Random, 1991.   ○

Royko, Mike
LIKE I WAS SAYIN'
Columns from Chicago newspapers over two decades—"observes the passing parade with inimitable wit and intelligence." (PW) Jove Pubns, 1985.   ○

Terkel, Studs
CHICAGO
"Entertaining, nostalgic, a paean" to his hometown—relates his boyhood experiences of Chicago. Pantheon, 1986.   ○

Terkel, Studs
DIVISION STREET: AMERICA
Interviews by a master interviewer with seventy people living in or near Chicago and of diverse ages, ethnic backgrounds and general circumstances—"a remarkable book" evoking city life through the eyes of these people. (BRD) Pantheon, 1982 (first published 1966).   ○

GUIDEBOOKS

Bach, Ira J.
A GUIDE TO CHICAGO'S PUBLIC SCULPTURE
U of Chicago Pr, 1983. Also *Walking Tours of Chicago's Architecture* (1986).   ○

Black, Harry G.
TRAILS TO ILLINOIS HERITAGE
A guidebook for the historic sites of Illinois. HMB Pbns, 1982.   ○

Gutek, Gerald and Patricia
CHICAGOLAND AND BEYOND
Nature and history within 200 miles—the answer to what to do on a weekend. Historical background and specific descriptions and practical information for museums, state parks, historic houses, botanical gardens, museum villages, wildlife preserves. Hippocrene, 1991.   ○

Hochstetter, Nancy, ed.
TRAVEL HISTORIC ILLINOIS
A guide to historic sites and markers. Guide Pr, 1986.   ○

Kelson, Carla, and others
CHICAGO MAGAZINE'S GUIDE TO CHICAGO
"Potpourri of notable sights and activities throughout Chicago's neighborhoods," with lists of shops, phone numbers, chapters on museums, libraries, sport, restaurants—and a foreword by Studs Terkel. (TL) Chicago Magazine, 1988.   ○

McMinn, Russel
ANTIQUES
Guide to Illinois' antique shops. Jockey Hollow, 1989.   ○

Michaelson, Mike
CHICAGO'S BEST-KEPT SECRETS
Museums, sports, children's activities and places to stay and to eat. Passport, 1991. ○

Weil, Tom
AMERICA'S HEARTLAND
Travel guide to the backroads of Illinois, Indiana, Iowa, Missouri. Hippocrene, 1989.   ○

HISTORY

Bridges, Roger D. and Davis, Rodney O.
ILLINOIS: ITS HISTORY & LEGACY
River City Pubs, 1984.   ○

Cromie, Robert
A SHORT HISTORY OF CHICAGO
"Anecdotal . . . entertaining history of Chicago from Marquette's icebound explorations in 1674 to Harold Washington." (BL) Lexikos, 1984.   ○

Cutler, Irving
CHICAGO: METROPOLIS OF THE MID-CONTINENT
Third edition of a history. Kendall-Hunt, 1982.   ○

Jensen, Richard J.
ILLINOIS
One of a series of popular histories for each state, published as part of the bicentennial in 1976. Norton, 1978.   ○

Novels

Bradbury, Ray
DANDELION WINE
Reissue of a book first published in 1957, about the summer of 1928 in a 12-year-old boy's life in a small Illinois town ". . . just having a wonderful time . . . the writing is beautiful and the characters are wonderful living people." (FC) Knopf, 1975.   ○

Ferber, Edna
SO BIG
A young woman's never-ending drudgery as wife of a farmer and her "gay, indomitable spirit" and disappointment in being unable to transmit her view of life to her son. (FC) Doubleday, 1951 (first published 1924).   ○

Greenberg, Marilyn
THE RABBI'S LIFE
Set in a Chicago suburb—a rabbi returns from his sabbatical in Israel only to be asked for his resignation. "A depiction of the tangled motives of a diverse community . . . a saintly man trying to cope with his rejection." (FC) Doubleday, 1983.   ○

Just, Ward
JACK GANCE
See entry under District of Columbia.   ○

Wakefield, Dan
UNDER THE APPLE TREE
A pleasant stroll down Memory Lane of the homefront in Illinois during World War II. Delacorte Pr, 1982.   ○

Wilder, Thornton
THE EIGHTH DAY
Saga of two Coaltown, Illinois, families whose lives intertwine over the period of three generations. Har-Row, 1967.   ○

Woiwode, Larry
BEYOND THE BEDROOM WALL
A family chronicle beginning in Illinois in the 1930s, ending in contemporary North Dakota. FS&G, 1975. The sequel is *Born Brothers* (1988).   ○

CHICAGO

Bellow, Saul
THE ADVENTURES OF AUGIE MARCH
Life of the son of Russian-Jewish immigrants; Bellow won a Nobel Prize in 1976. Viking, 1953. Also set in Chicago, *Humboldt's Gift* (1975) and *Dangling Man* (1944). *The Dean's December* (1982) is set in both Chicago and Bucharest.   o

Brashler, William
TRADERS
"Fast-paced melodrama" about the Chicago stock exchange and the cutthroat futures market, as its sexy heroine tries to succeed there and encounters harassment from a vindictive ex-lover. Atheneum, 1989.   o

Campbell, R. Wright
CAT'S MEOW
When a priest reports that a cat is haunting old St. Pat's Church, it's Chicago sewer inspector Flanner who comes to the rescue "like an urban white knight . . . a captivating read." (FC) NAL, 1988. Also *The Gift Horse's Mouth* (1990) and *Sweet La-La Land* (1990).   o

Collins, Max A.
NEON MIRAGE
One of a series of Private Eye Nate Heller mysteries set in Chicago of the 1940s—tells of a "crime-infested" Chicago and newly developed Las Vegas. St. Martin, 1988.   o

Dreiser, Theodore
SISTER CARRIE
Realistic novel of lower middle class life in Chicago (later New York) and the particular life of a woman's career in vice and a man's moral disintegration. Penguin, 1981 (first published 1900). *Jennie Gerhardt* (1911) is another turn-of-the-century novel of the "realism" genre, set in Chicago.   o

Dybek, Stuart
THE COAST OF CHICAGO
Long and short sketches about growing up in Chicago in the 1960s and '70s—ethnic neighborhoods, early romances. Knopf, 1990.   o

Elward, James
ASK FOR NOTHING MORE
The plot involves a realtor, his ill wife, and the nurse brought in to care for her, who becomes the husband's "back street" mistress. Har-Row, 1984.   o

Farrell, James T.
STUDS LONIGAN
A trilogy that includes the titles *Young Lonigan, The Young Manhood of Studs Lonigan* and *Judgment Day*, about Irish-Americans in Chicago. Vanguard, 1978 (first published 1932–35). Also *The Dunne Family* (1976) and its sequel *The Death of Nora Ryan* (1978), and *A World I Never Made* (1936) set in Chicago and about Irish-Americans.   o

Gash, Jonathan
NEWSPAPER MURDERS: A CHICAGO POLICE MYSTERY
"The grimy underbelly of big city newspapers, politics and police . . . strong, gritty, and compelling work." (FC) HR&W, 1985. Also *Priestly Murders* (1984), another police procedural.   o

Greeley, Andrew M.
LORD OF THE DANCE
Third in a trilogy about the misdeeds of a powerful Irish Catholic family, called "The Passover Trilogy." Warner Bks, 1984. *Thy Brother's Wife* (1982) is first, followed by *Ascent Into Hell* (1983). Also, by Greeley, is *The Cardinal Sins* (1981).   o

Greeley, Andrew M.
PATIENCE OF A SAINT
"Part theological tract, part comedy of manners and part potboiler" about a cynical Chicago newspaperman who has an ecstatic religious experience. (FC) Warner Bks, 1987. Also *Love Song* (1989), about a Chicago D.A. who falls in love with a man whose family destroyed her father.   o

Izzi, Eugene
PROWLERS
Organized crime in Chicago, as Catfeet Millard must outwit the mob or die. Bantam, 1991.   ○

Kaminsky, Stuart M.
LIEBERMAN'S FOLLY
The partnership of two cops—"Rabbi" Lieberman and "Father" Hanrahan—investigates the death of a prostitute, over the objections of their captain. St. Martin, 1991.   ○

McInerny, Ralph M.
ABRACADAVER
This and *The Basket Case* (1987) are two Father Dowling mysteries for fans of "deductive reasoning and clerical detectives" rather than violence. (FC) St. Martin, 1989.   ○

McInerny, Ralph M.
SISTER HOOD
Sister Mary Teresa Dempsey spearheads the investigation when a Carmelite nun takes

shelter with their Chicago Order, and is later found dead. St. Martin, 1991.   ○

Miller, Sue
FAMILY PICTURES
Forty years in the lives of a Chicago family with an autistic child. Har-Row, 1990.   ○

Paretsky, Sara
BLOOD SHOT
One of a series of Chicago-based mysteries with a woman lawyer turned private eye as heroine, by name of V.I. Warshawski. Paretsky's "action-packed style, laced with bitter humor" make Warshawski a welcome addition to the genre. Delacorte, 1988. Also *Killing Orders* (1985), *Bitter Medicine* (1987) and *Burn Marks* (1990).   ○

Spencer, Scott
WAKING THE DEAD
"Absorbing, sharply focused tale of ambition, love and moral confusion"—a novel of south side politics. (FC) Knopf, 1986.   ○

INDIANA

*Series Guidebooks
(See Appendix 1)*

NOTE: See also Series Guides (and non-series guides) listed under United States and the Midwest.

Off the Beaten Path: Indiana

Background Reading

Daniel, Glenda
DUNE COUNTRY
Background reading for a unique natural feature of the state—the dunes near Gary—both for hikers and for those interested as naturalists. Ohio U Pr, 1984.   ○

Hoppe, David
WHERE WE LIVE: ESSAYS ABOUT INDIANA
A variety of viewpoints by Hoosier writers on sports, racism, landscape, history and so

on—what it means to live in Indiana. (BL) Indiana U Pr, 1989.   ○

Lane, James B.
CITY OF THE CENTURY
The story of Gary, which was founded by U.S. Steel as an experiment in industrial planning. Indiana U, 1978.   ○

Lyon, Edward E. and Dillown, Lowell
**INDIANA: THE AMERICAN
    HEARTLAND**
Tichenor, 1986.   ○

Schaeffer, Norma and Franklin, Kay
'ROUND AND ABOUT THE DUNES
Geology and history of a midwestern natural wonder, but also explores the surrounding area "to uncover the most interesting shops, dining spots, recreational facilities and natural sights for visitors." (BL) Dunes Enterprises, 1984.   ○

Schlereth, Thomas J.
U.S. 40: A ROADSCAPE OF THE AMERICAN EXPERIENCE
The author calls his approach "above-ground archaeology"—how to "read" highways as outdoor museums. (LJ) Indiana U Pr, 1985.   ○

GUIDEBOOKS

Black, Harry G.
HISTORIC TRAILS AND TALES OF NORTHWEST INDIANA
Also *Highways and Byways of Indiana* and *Trails to Hoosier Heritage*—guidebooks for historical sites in Indiana. HMB Pubns, 1988.   ○

Hunter, David
SHIFRA STEIN'S DAY TRIPS FROM CINCINNATI
Includes Kentucky and Indiana—see entry under Ohio/Guidebooks.   ○

Jones, Jennifer
EXPLORING INDIANAPOLIS
Lexicon, 1990.   ○

Taylor, Robert M. and others
INDIANA: A NEW HISTORICAL GUIDE
Nineteen circular tours that pass through almost all of the counties and are thoroughly detailed, but no restaurant or accommodations listings. Indiana U Pr, 1989.   ○

Weil, Tom
AMERICA'S HEARTLAND
A travel guide to the backroads of Illinois, Indiana, Iowa and Missouri. Hippocrene, 1989.   ○

HISTORY

Madison, James H.
THE INDIANA WAY: A STATE HISTORY
"An admirable introduction to Indiana history for the student or the scholar." (Choice) Indiana U Pr, 1990.   ○

Peckham, Howard H.
INDIANA
One of a series of popular histories for each state, published as part of the bicentennial in 1976. Norton, 1978.   ○

Novels

Appleman, Philip
APES AND ANGELS
Three families in a small Indiana town and how they are affected by Pearl Harbor and World War II. Putnam, 1989.   ○

Lewin, Michael Z.
AND BABY WILL FALL
A social worker/detective and the Indiana Police Department unearth a ring of baby brokers engaged in illegal adoptions. Morrow, 1988. Also by Lewin and set in Indiana are *Late Payments* and *Hard Line*.   ○

Lockridge, Ross
RAINTREE COUNTY
An epic novel of the period from the Civil War to 1892, in Raintree County, and the lives of the local schoolteacher and his friends. Houghton, 1948.   ○

McInerney, Ralph M.
BODY AND SOIL
A mystery featuring Indiana attorney Broom who represents some unpopular clients, including one who's confessed to murdering a local boy and the divorce of the town's wealthiest couple, whose trial is interrupted by murder—"offers readers front-row seats to observe the villain's activities." Atheneum, 1989.   ○

Stone, Irving
ADVERSARY IN THE HOUSE
A biographical novel—"moving, sympathetic portrait" of Eugene Debs, the socialist labor leader who sacrificed all for the cause of the working man. (FC) Doubleday, 1947.   ○

Tarkington, Booth
ALICE ADAMS
Classic story of small-town life in the 1920s as a young girl must overcome her lack of

money and background—it won the Pulitzer Prize in 1922. Doubleday, 1921. Also *The Gentleman from Indiana* (1899), about the editor of a country newspaper, and *The Magnificent Ambersons* (1918), a saga of a wealthy family in the 1870s.   ○

Tesich, Steve
SUMMER CROSSING
An introspective novel of a young man going through a series of traumatic events, just out of high school, "in the industrial hellhole of East Chicago, Indiana [from which] he emerges a better person and a budding writer." (FC) Random, 1982.   ○

Wakefield, Dan
GOING ALL THE WAY
"Amiable . . . often wonderfully funny" novel of two young men who return to

Indianapolis in 1954 following their army service; their questioning of society and chasing after booze and sex. (FC) Delacorte Pr, 1970.   ○

West, Jessamyn
THE FRIENDLY PERSUASION
Quakers in Indiana during the period following the Civil War. HarBraceJ, 1945. *Except for Me and Thee* (1969) is a companion novel that rounds out the story of the Birdwell family. Also *The Massacre at Fall Creek* (1975), fictional treatment of the Indian slaughter at Fall Creek in 1824, and *The Witch Diggers* (1951).   ○

IOWA

Series Guidebooks
(See Appendix 1)

NOTE: See also Series Guides (and non-series guides) listed under United States and the Midwest.

Off the Beaten Path: Iowa

Background Reading

Andrews, Clarence A., ed.
GROWING UP IN IOWA
Iowa State U Pr, 1988.   ○

Andrews, Clarence A., ed.
A LITERARY HISTORY OF IOWA
U of Iowa Pr, 1972.   ○

Bauer, Douglas
PRAIRIE CITY, IOWA: THREE CITIES AT HOME
Iowa State U Pr, 1982.   ○

Childs, Marquis and Engel, Paul
THIS IS IOWA
Midwest Heritage, 1982.   ○

Harnack, Curtis
GENTLEMEN ON THE PRAIRIE
Story of an unusual British colony and prairie community near Le Mars, of upper-class Britons, begun in the 1880s. Iowa State U Pr, 1985.   ○

Klinkenborg, Verlyn
MAKING HAY
A Fordham professor visits his farming relatives in Iowa, the Rock River Valley of Minnesota and the Big Hole country of Montana—"a marvelous picture of rural life and of families at work . . . a fascinating excursion." (PW) Nick Lyons Bks, 1986.   ○

Pelton, Beulah
WE BELONG TO THE LAND
Memories of a midwesterner. Iowa State U Pr, 1984.   ○

Puckett, Susan
A COOK'S TOUR OF IOWA
Colorful local history with recipes—"the sources . . . and the stories accompanying them are fascinating," and it includes the

recipe for Grant Wood's potato salad! U of
Iowa Pr, 1988.   o

Sayre, Robert F., ed.
TAKE THIS EXIT: REDISCOVERING THE IOWA LANDSCAPE
Sixteen essays on specific sites, what to look
for and how to enjoy them, with historical
perspective and maps and photos. Iowa State
U Pr, 1989.   o

Taylor, Henry C.
TARPLEYWICK
A century of Iowa farming. Iowa State U Pr,
1990.   o

Toth, Susan
BLOOMING: A SMALL-TOWN GIRLHOOD
"A gracefully nostalgic return to a midwestern childhood in Ames, Iowa"—growing up
in the '50s. (BRD) Ballantine, 1985.   o

GUIDEBOOKS

Weil, Tom
AMERICA'S HEARTLAND
A traveler's guide to the backroads of Illinois, Indiana, Iowa and Missouri. Hippocrene, 1989.   o

HISTORY

Hochstetter, Nancy, ed.
TRAVEL HISTORIC IOWA
A guide to historic sites and markers. Guide
Pr, 1987.   o

Wall, Joseph F.
IOWA
One of a series of popular histories for each
state, published as part of the bicentennial
in 1976. Norton, 1978.   o

Novels

Aldrich, Bess
MISS BISHOP
Fifty years in a country teacher's life in
the late nineteenth and early twentieth
centuries. Aeonian, 1975 (first published
1933).   o

Chehak, Susan T.
HARMONY
In the murder story genre but a candidate
for what *The New York Times* called "crossover status" as a novel, and one that seeks
to do more than entertain. "The novel's
fictional small-town Iowa setting, is evoked
with the fine hand of a Grant Wood or a
Thomas Hart Benton." (NYT) HM, 1990. o

Collins, Max A.
SHROUD FOR AQUARIUS
"Well-paced . . . sensitive" mystery, in
which an Iowa mystery writer/detective is
found shot and an apparent suicide. (FC)
Walker, 1985.   o

DeVries, Peter
I HEAR AMERICA SWINGING
"Sly boots commentary on present-day
mores" narrated by an Iowa marriage counselor. (FC) Little, 1976.   o

Harnack, Curtis
LIMITS OF THE LAND
Life on a small Iowa farm in the 1940s and
the "love-hate relationship between men and
the soil." (BRD) Doubleday, 1979.   o

Kinsella, W.P.
SHOELESS JOE
Fantasy of an Iowa farmer who hears a voice
telling him that, if he builds a baseball field,
Shoeless Joe Jackson—legendary Chicago
Black Sox player banned from the game—
will come and play. The movie *Field of Dreams*
was made from the story—"corny and nostalgic . . . a rare talent for conveying pure
joy." HM, 1982. Also *The Iowa Baseball Con-
federacy* (1986).   o

McCoy, Maureen
SUMMERTIME
Set in Des Moines—the story of three generations of women during one summer when
events force them to examine themselves
and each other. Poseidon, 1987.   o

Shields, David
HEROES
The story of a sportswriter for whom basketball is magic, in a quintessential small

town in Iowa. Frustrated with his life and yearning for the big time, his life is changed by a talented young basketball star. Kinsella, author of *Shoeless Joe* (see just above): "Heroes is the only literate fiction ever written about basketball"—a strong sense of the history and geography and texture of Iowa. S&S, 1984. ○

KANSAS

Series Guidebooks (See Appendix 1)

NOTE: See also Series Guides (and non-series guides) listed under United States and the Midwest.

Off the Beaten Path: Kansas

Background Reading

Athearn, Robert G.
IN SEARCH OF CANAAN: BLACK MIGRATION TO KANSAS, 1879–80

The story of the movement to Kansas of Southern blacks—"writes movingly and intelligently about the many disappointments of the settlers . . . excellent historical picture of the 19th-century west." (BRD) U Pr of Kansas, 1978. ○

Bader, Robert
PROHIBITION IN KANSAS

"Sparkling example of how state and local history should be written . . . with clarity and humor on every page"—the story of prohibition in America's most famous "dry state," from the 1850s to the present. (Choice) U Pr of Kansas, 1986. Also *Hayseeds, Moralizers and Methodists: the Twentieth Century Image of Kansas* (1988). ○

Buchanan, Rex and McCauley, James R.
ROADSIDE KANSAS

A guide to the geology and landmarks along the roadsides. U Pr of Kansas, 1987. ○

Dary, David
TRUE TALES OF OLD-TIME KANSAS

Not fiction, but they read like short stories. Also *More True Tales of Old Time Kansas*. U Pr of Kansas, 1987. ○

Dykstra, Robert R.
THE CATTLE TOWNS

"A social history of the Kansas cattle trading centers—Abilene, Ellsworth, Wichita, Dodge City, and Caldwell, 1867–1885," with a conclusion that their "romantic past was no more romantic than Lima, Ohio." (BRD) U of Nebraska Pr, 1983. ○

Haywood, C. Robert
TRAILS SOUTH

There were four "wagon roads" that bound the Oklahoma and Texas Panhandles to Dodge City, and this is a description of the roads as the activities changed from buffalo-hunting to Indian troubles, to ranching and farming. "Exhaustively researched and well documented." (Choice) U of Oklahoma Pr, 1986. Also *Victorian West: Class and Culture in Kansas Cattle Towns* (1991). ○

Heat Moon, William
PRARYERTH

A journey on foot through Case County's tallgrass prairies and grasslands—"a great cornucopia of a book, a majestic, healing hymn to America's potential." (PW) HM, 1991. ○

Parker, Tony
BIRD, KANSAS

The author is a noted British journalist, and this book is about his three months in a small Kansas town ("Bird" is a pseudonym). "Charming, broadly penetrating survey" of a mid-American community. (PW) Knopf, 1989. ○

Stratton, Joanna L.
PIONEER WOMEN: VOICES FROM THE KANSAS FRONTIER

A remarkable book that evolved from memoirs of hundreds of pioneer women, the memoirs collected by the author's grandmother with the intention of editing into book form. They tell of shoot-outs, Indians, grasshopper plagues, and fear. S&S, 1981. ○

GUIDEBOOKS

Fitzgerald, Daniel C.
GHOST TOWNS OF KANSAS: A TRAVEL GUIDE
U Pr of Kansas, 1988. ○

Hochstetter, Nancy, ed.
TRAVEL HISTORIC KANSAS
A guide to historic sites and markers. Guide Pr, 1986. ○

McMinn, Russel
ANTIQUES
A guide to Kansas' antique shops. Jockey Hollow, 1989. ○

Penner, Mil
KANSAS WEEKEND GUIDE
Sounds of Kansas, 1990. ○

Wilson, D. Ray
KANSAS HISTORICAL TOUR GUIDE
Crossroads Comns, 1990. ○

HISTORY

Davis, Kenneth S.
KANSAS
One of a series of popular histories for each state, published as part of the bicentennial in 1976. Norton, 1978. ○

Novels

Day, Robert
THE LAST CATTLE DRIVE
A "new-to-the-saddle schoolteacher" narrates a modern-day cattle drive along the highways to Kansas City—adventures with the law, in bars, and romance along the

way. (FC) U. Pr of Kansas, 1983 (first published 1977). ○

Ehrlich, Leonard
GOD'S ANGRY MAN
The story of John Brown and his fight against slavery in the nineteenth century. S&S, 1932. ○

Hughes, Langston
NOT WITHOUT LAUGHTER
Novel about growing up in a small Kansas town by the noted black poet. Knopf, 1930. ○

Hunter, R. Lanny
LIVING DOGS AND DEAD LIONS
A Vietnam War veteran, in trying to cope with paralyzing flashbacks, travels to Plains, Kansas, to meet the family of his deceased commanding officer. Viking, 1986. ○

Jones, Douglas C.
ROMAN
Sequel to *Elkhorn Tavern* (see under Arkansas). This is set primarily in Leavenworth, Kansas, and depicts the "coming of age of a young man and a nation" through the eyes of Roman Hasford—"dense with accurate historical detail." (FC) Holt, 1986. ○

Matthews, Greg
HEART OF THE COUNTRY
A Kansan village in the last half of the 1800s—"heavily symbolic tale effectively punctures the glorified textbook view of the Wild West." (FC) Norton, 1986. ○

Mead, Robert D.
HEARTLAND
The hero helps found Wichita in 1859—"vignettes of the [buffalo] hunt and of civic and industrial expansion . . . all kinds of anecdotes." (FC) Doubleday, 1986. ○

Parks, Gordon
THE LEARNING TREE
Story of a black boy growing up in the 1920s in Kansas, by the noted photographer. Har-Row, 1963. ○

Pickard, Nancy
BUM STEER
A Jenny Cain mystery. Jenny is director of the Port Frederick Civic Foundation and goes to Kansas City to find out why the foundation has been willed a cattle ranch. Pocket Bks, 1990.   ○

Roderus, Frank
LEAVING KANSAS
A "young misfit" at the turn of the century makes a series of blunders that lead to his leaving his Kansas town and heading west. (FC) Doubleday, 1983.   ○

KENTUCKY

Series Guidebooks (See Appendix 1)

NOTE: See Series Guides (and non-series guides) listed under United States and the South.

Background Reading

Egerton, John
GENERATIONS: AN AMERICAN FAMILY
Social history of a middle-class family viewed as a paradigm of the changes in the American family. U of Kentucky, 1983.   ○

Hirsch, Joe and Bolus, Jim
KENTUCKY DERBY: THE CHANCE OF A LIFETIME
A celebration that captures "the excitement and spirit of the run for the roses through fact, anecdote, and a stunning array of photographs . . . ideally suited for browsing . . . lively text, lush scenes." (BL) McGraw, 1988.   ○

Slone, Verna Mae
WHAT MY HEART WANTS TO TELL
The author is the tenth generation of a family to live in Pippa Passes, within two miles of the place they settled in 1790. Reminiscences that are "beyond the cliches of mountain life" as the author seeks to preserve the culture and traditions of a soon to be forgotten way of life. U Pr of Kentucky (1987).   ○

GUIDEBOOKS

Hunter, David
SHIFRA STEIN'S DAY TRIPS FROM CINCINNATI
Includes Kentucky and Indiana—see entry under Ohio/Guidebooks.   ○

McMinn, Russel
ANTIQUES
A guide to Kentucky's antique shops. Jockey Hollow, 1989.   ○

Strode, William
THE COMPLETE GUIDE TO KENTUCKY HORSE COUNTRY
Where to go, what to see, how to enjoy it. Classic Pub, 1980.   ○

HISTORY

Channing, Steven A.
KENTUCKY
One of a series of popular histories for each state, published as part of the bicentennial in 1976. Norton, 1977.   ○

Novels

Anderson, V.S.
KING OF THE ROSES
Suspense story of bribery at the Kentucky Derby—an intricate plot with "vivid descriptions of . . . Derby Week buffoonery . . . magnificently exciting description of the race itself." (FC) St. Martin, 1983.   ○

Arnow, Harriette
HUNTER'S HORN
"Unforgettable many-sided picture of family life and community life in the Kentucky

hills." (FC) Macmillan, 1949. Also *The Doll-maker* (see under Michigan).   ○

Arnow, Harriette
THE KENTUCKY TRACE: A NOVEL OF THE AMERICAN REVOLUTION
Frontier life in the Cumberland region, descriptive of daily life and customs. Knopf, 1974.   ○

Giles, Janice H.
THE ENDURING HILLS
Twentieth-century rural life in Kentucky. Houghton, 1971 (first published 1950). Also *The Believers* (1957), about the Shaker colony in Kentucky.   ○

Giles, Janice H.
THE KENTUCKIANS
Historical novel of the period 1769–77 when Kentucky was still part of Virginia. G.K. Hall, 1980 (first published 1953). *Hannah Fowler* (1956) is another novel of frontier life.   ○

Gordon, Caroline
THE COLLECTED STORIES OF CAROLINE GORDON
Four decades of stories of Southern landscapes and inbred counties. FS&G, 1981. Also an early saga of a Kentucky plantation family, *Penhally* (1931).   ○

Leonard, Elmore
THE MOONSHINE WAR
In *Double Dutch Treat*, omnibus book of three stores—"charts the exploits of Son Martin, a hell-raising Kentucky moonshiner." (FC) Arbor Hse, 1986.   ○

Mason, Bobbie Ann
SPENCE AND LILA
The story of a happy couple and their children, as Lila faces cancer surgery—"a love story plus . . . with some sly winks at society's contemporary foibles." (BRD) Har-Row, 1988. Also *In Country* (1986), *Shiloh, and Other Stories* (1983) and *Love Life: Stories* (1989).   ○

Stuart, Jesse
TAPS FOR PRIVATE TUSSIE
Comical, regional tale of what sudden wealth does to an improvident family happily living on welfare. Dutton, 1943. Also *The Best-Loved Short Stories of Jesse Stuart* (1982) and *A Jesse Stuart Harvest* (1965) (anthology).   ○

Warren, Robert Penn
BAND OF ANGELS
A girl discovers she's part black, and is sold as a slave. Random, 1955. Also *World Enough and Time* (1950), based on a true 1820 murder trial, and *Night Rider* (1939).   ○

Yount, John
HARDCASTLE
Strikes and labor organizers in the Kentucky coal mines in 1931. Marek, 1980.   ○

LOUISIANA

Series Guidebooks (See Appendix 1)

NOTE: See also Series Guides (and nonseries guides) listed under United States and the South.

Fodor: New Orleans
Frommer: New Orleans
Gault/Milau: The Best of New Orleans
Off the Beaten Path: Louisiana

Background Reading

Ancelet, Barry
CAJUN COUNTRY
History and culture of Louisiana Cajuns for nonspecialists—family structure, courtship, folk medicine, food, dancing, jokes, traditional stories, etc. (PW) U Pr of Mississippi, 1991.   ○

Broven, John
RHYTHM AND BLUES IN NEW ORLEANS

History of a unique music form—"overview of the remarkable music scene inside the borders of this one town." (Publisher) Pelican, 1983. ○

Dundy, Elaine
FERRIDAY, LOUISIANA

The story of a little town in Louisiana that produced Jimmy Swaggart, Jerry Lee Lewis, Mickey Gilley, newscaster Howard K. Smith, trombone player Peewee Whitaker, and General Claire Chennault of World War II fame—"social history, biography, and psychobabble." (BL) Donald I. Fine, 1991. ○

Faulkner, William
NEW ORLEANS SKETCHES

Stories and articles written early in his writing career when working for the *New Orleans Times-Picayune* and *Double Dealer*, with an introduction about the prominent author's years in New Orleans. Random, 1968. ○

Hennick, Louis C. and Charlton, E. Harper
THE STREETCARS OF NEW ORLEANS

Reprint of a book first published in 1965—"the most complete work on . . . traction and urban railways." Provides general history of New Orleans and comprehensive information on all aspect of the streetcars. (Publisher) Pelican, 1975. ○

Kane, Harnett
LOUISIANA HAYRIDE

"Records accurately the wild political hayride [Huey] Long engineered and the scandals that followed his death." (Publisher) Pelican, 1986 (first published 1941). ○

Leavitt, Mel
GREAT CHARACTERS OF NEW ORLEANS

An assemblage of forty-three fascinating characters—"geniuses, madams, and charlatans from every era of the city's tumul-

tuous history." (Publisher) Lexikos, 1984. ○

Rose, Al and Souchon, Edmond
NEW ORLEANS JAZZ: A FAMILY ALBUM

Louisiana State U Pr, 1984. Also, *I Remember Jazz* (1987). ○

Tallant, Robert
MARDI GRAS

"The best general introduction—a sane contemplation of a hopelessly insane subject"—parades, floats, the balls, the crowds. (Publisher) Pelican, 1989. ○

Tassin, Myron
THE LAST LINE: A STREETCAR NAMED ST. CHARLES

Reprint of the 1972 edition; the St. Charles Streetcar is now classified as an historical monument, the last of a system that was once city-wide. A chronicle of public transportation in New Orleans that was recorded, in words and pictures, as a ride on the Last Line. Pelican, 1980. ○

Turner, Frederick
REMEMBERING SONG: ENCOUNTERS WITH THE NEW ORLEANS JAZZ TRADITION

The New Orleans musical story with emphasis on the author's encounters with people and the city and the life histories of several of its musicians. Viking, 1982. ○

GUIDEBOOKS

Calhoun, Nancy H. and James
THE PELICAN GUIDE TO PLANTATION HOMES OF LOUISIANA

Handbook of over 200 homes of architectural and historic significance, both those that are open to the public and some that are not, with suggested tours for the traveler. Pelican, 1988. ○

Cowan, Walter G., and others
NEW ORLEANS YESTERDAY AND TODAY

History, culture, inhabitants, background and atmospheric detail. Louisiana State U Pr, 1983. ○

DeHart, Jess
PLANTATIONS OF LOUISIANA
A basic introduction to the architectural styles of Louisiana plantation homes, with lists of hundreds of them that can be seen, along with history, location, information about the construction and occupants. Pelican, 1988. ○

Griffin, Thomas K.
THE PELICAN GUIDE TO NEW ORLEANS
"Because it provides an excellent overview . . . should be read . . . by anyone planning to visit . . . chatty and entertaining . . . by a man who is a native of New Orleans." Also includes recent information so that it can be used as a guidebook for the frequent visitor. (Publisher) Pelican, 1988. ○

LeBlanc, Joyce Y.
THE PELICAN GUIDE TO GARDENS OF LOUISIANA
A guide to some of America's most enchanting garden spots—complete information for travelers. Pelican, 1989. ○

Lockwood, C.C.
DISCOVERING LOUISIANA
Forty-nine scenic drives explore the natural history of Louisiana—"treasures galore . . . colorful vegetation and diverse wild life," with accounts of journeys by canoe and on foot, and photographs. "Gives the reader a grand tour of Louisiana's wild places." (PW) Louisiana State U Pr, 1986. ○

McMinn, Russel
ANTIQUES
A guide to Louisiana's antique shops. Jockey Hollow, 1989. ○

Taylor, James and Graham, Alan
NEW ORLEANS ON THE HALF SHELL
A native's guide to the city; "informal—and often witty—guide to New Orleans . . . and how to experience the somewhat unconventional sights and sounds . . . see the city as the locals do." (Publisher) Pelican, 1991. ○

Wells, Mary A.
A HISTORY LOVER'S GUIDE TO LOUISIANA
Quail Ridge Pr, 1990. ○

HISTORY

Hall, Bennett H., ed.
LOUISIANA: A HISTORY
Second edition. Forum Pr, 1990. ○

Leavitt, Mel
A SHORT HISTORY OF NEW ORLEANS
Reads like a first-rate historical novel. Lexikos, 1982. ○

Taylor, Joe G.
LOUISIANA
One of a series of popular histories for each state, published as part of the bicentennial in 1976. Norton, 1984. ○

Novels

Basso, Hamilton
SUN IN CAPRICORN
One of several novels based on the life of Huey Long. He's Gilgo Slade in this one—a power-mad politician who wrecks the lives of two lovers who stand in his way. Scribner, 1942. ○

Bradley, John E.
TUPELO NIGHTS
An "archetypal southern gothic" about an ex-football star who gave up his career to return to a small Louisiana town to look after his mother. Atl Monthly Pr, 1988. ○

Bristow, Gwen
DEEP SUMMER
First in a trilogy of plantation life from the eighteenth to the twentieth centuries. Crowell, 1964. *The Handsome Road* (1968) and *This Side of Glory* (1940) complete the trilogy. ○

Burke, James Lee
A MORNING FOR FLAMINGOS
Cajun Detective Dave Robicheaux battles "personal demons" as he stalks an escaped

killer. "Delivers action on churning Gulf waters, in city streets, in deserted fields and within the souls of his memorable characters." (FC) Little, 1990.   ○

Corrington, John W.
SO SMALL A CARNIVAL
Thriller, set in New Orleans. Viking, 1986.   ○

Dos Passos, John
NUMBER ONE
"Fictional portrait of an American demagogue, obviously based on the life and career of Huey Long." (BRD) Houghton, 1943.   ○

Dubus, Elizabeth N.
TO LOVE AND TO DREAM
Third novel of a series about Cajun life, this covers the years 1941–50. Preceding are *Cajun* (1983) and *Where Love Rules.* (1985). Putnam, 1986.   ○

Gaines, Ernest J.
A GATHERING OF OLD MEN
When a white man is found dead on a black man's farm, the aging black population defies the traditional outcome of white revenge. (FC) Knopf, 1983. Also *In My Father's House* (1978), and *The Autobiography of Miss Jane Pittman* (1971).   ○

Grau, Shirley Ann
THE HARD BLUE SKY
Cajun life on Isle aux Chiens and the "nature and character . . . of the island itself." (FC) Knopf, 1958. Also *Keepers of the House* (1964), saga of a Delta family that won a Pulitzer Prize,and *The Black Prince, and Other Stories* (1955), short stories of black life in Louisiana.   ○

Kellerman, Faye
MILK AND HONEY
Police Sergeant Peter Decker tries to learn the identity of a two-year-old girl found playing on a swing set near a housing development. Morrow, 1990.   ○

L'Enfant, Julie
THE DANCERS OF SYCAMORE STREET
A New York choreographer arrives in a small town in Louisiana to direct a gala for its local ballet school. The story is told through the eyes of "a precocious, likeable girl . . . reminiscent of Carson McCullers . . . nothing less than enchanting." (FC) St. Martin, 1983.   ○

Warren, Robert Penn
ALL THE KING'S MEN
Huey Long is embodied in Willie Stark in this fictionalization of the rise of a political leader, with a lust for power, from farm to law and politics. HarBraceJ, 1946.   ○

Wilcox, James
SORT OF RICH
Instant chemistry in a souvenir shop leads to marriage between a fortyish woman of old New York money and a widower from Tula Springs—"insightful, hilarious story of a classic marriage mismatch." (BRD) HarRow, 1989. Also set in Tula Springs are: *Modern Baptists* (1983), *North Gladiola* (1985), *Miss Undine's Living Room* (1987).   ○

NEW ORLEANS

Arnold, Margot
DEATH OF A VOODOO DOLL
New Orleans at Mardi Gras time is the setting. Countryman, 1987.   ○

Burke, James L.
HEAVEN'S PRISONERS
An ex-policeman in New Orleans and his family get involved with Nicaraguan immigrants. Holt, 1988.   ○

Carrington, J.W.
SO SMALL A CARNIVAL
A cynical, ambitious reporter gets an anonymous phone call that brings him to a scene of mass execution, and then he too gets on the hit list—"a screaming climax" and local color. Viking, 1986.   ○

Chopin, Kate
THE AWAKENING
Novel of an early feminist whose books were considered too racy for her time, in the early 1900s, but now as a result of the women's movement are enjoying a revival of interest. Avon, 1972.   ○

Costain, Thomas B.
HIGH TOWERS
See under "Canada/Novels."   ○

Fairbairn, Ann
FIVE SMOOTH STONES
Chronicles a black man's life from poverty in New Orleans through a distinguished career and the civil rights movement. Crown, 1966.   ○

Ferber, Edna
SARATOGA TRUNK
An adventuress in New Orleans of the 1880s who returns to blackmail her father's aristocratic family. Doubleday, 1951 (first published 1941).   ○

Hewat, Alan V.
LADY'S TIME
The life of Lady, a turn-of-the-century lady ragtime pianist, also depicts the birth of jazz and ragtime, and a tragedy that leads to Lady playing in a Vermont resort, passing as white. Har-Row, 1985.   ○

Keyes, Frances Parkinson
DINNER AT ANTOINE'S
A murder mystery and study of the interplay of emotions and desires beginning with a dinner at the famous New Orleans restaurant. S&S, 1948. Also *The Chess Players*, about a New Orleans man who became a world chess champion; based on Paul C. Morphy's life (1837–1884).   ○

Lemann, Nancy
LIVES OF THE SAINTS
Louise Brown, under the sway of the scion of an aristocratic New Orleans family, tells her story—"the luxuriant city is the other object of Louise's affection and . . . more worthy." (BRD) Knopf, 1985.   ○

Leonard, Elmore
BANDITS
"New Orleans is done up with meticulous accuracy"—the plot is about an unlikely trio who decide to intercept money intended for the Nicaraguan Contras. (BRD) Arbor Hse, 1987.   ○

Percy, Walker
THE THANATOS SYNDROME
The psychiatrist from an earlier novel, *Love Among the Ruins*, now out of prison, returns to practicing his profession and finds strange behaviors caused by tampering with the water supply. (FC) FS&G, 1987.   ○

Plain, Belva
CRESCENT CITY
A European Jewish heroine and her brother in New Orleans during the Civil War adjusting to "a bright, promising new land . . . as well as its grimmer aspects." (FC) Delacorte Pr, 1984.   ○

Rice, Anne
THE FEAST OF ALL SAINTS
Historical novel of the Free People of Color in antebellum New Orleans—"a fascinating glimpse into a little known and intriguing segment of American history." (FC) S&S, 1979.   ○

Ripley, Alexandra
NEW ORLEANS LEGACY
Historical romance in pre-Civil War New Orleans and a heroine who survives many vicissitudes as she seeks her mother's family. (FC) Macmillan, 1987.   ○

Warren, Robert Penn
BAND OF ANGELS
See under "Kentucky/Novels."   ○

Williams, Ben Ames, Jr.
THE UNCONQUERED
The Currain family saga,—New Orleans and Louisiana politics during Reconstruction (1865–74), with many historical characters and "unforgettable scenes . . . portrayed as though by eye witness." (FC) HM, 1953. ○

Yerby, Frank
THE FOXES OF HARROW

Historical saga that begins in 1825 and chronicles its hero's rise to wealth, ending with the Civil War and the mansion at Harrow in ruins. Dial, 1946.   ○

MAINE

*Series Guidebooks
(See Appendix 1)*

NOTE: See Series Guides (and non-series guides) listed under United States and the East and the East/New England.

Background Reading

Bailey, Anthony
SPRING JAUNTS

Five jaunts, originally appearing as a series of articles in *The New Yorker,* one of which is the Massachusetts/Maine coast—"a book to savour . . . wise, funny." (LJ) FS&G, 1986.   ○

Barrette, Roy
**A COUNTRYMAN'S JOURNAL;
VIEWS OF LIFE AND NATURE
FROM A MAINE COASTAL
FARM**

"Short sketches [that give] the rich flavor of Maine." (BRD) Godine, 1986. Also *A Countryman's Farewell: Or, Ninety and Counting* (1989). Godine, 1986.   ○

Beston, Henry
**NORTHERN FARM: A CHRONICLE
OF MAINE**

The seasons from dead of winter through the year—"the elusive magic of a year on a Kennebec farm is captured here in truly beautiful prose." Originally published in 1948. (BRD) Down East, 1988.   ○

Brown, Allen D.
THE GREAT LOBSTER CHASE

The real story of Maine lobsters and the men who catch them. Intl Marine, 1987.   ○

Coffin, Robert P. Tristram
YANKEE COAST

Essays on coastal Maine by a native poet. Macmillan, 1947. Also *Lost Paradise* (1934), an autobiographical account of boyhood in Maine, and *Kennebec* (1975), an impressionistic biography of the river.   ○

Dibner, Martin
**SEACOAST MAINE: THE PEOPLE
AND PLACES**

The mystique and beauty of an individualistic region and the natives and outsiders who make it their home—including some surprising celebrities. Harpswell Pr, 1987.   ○

Gould, John
STITCH IN TIME

"Observations of the Maine difference . . . both nostalgia-rich and scholarly-inquisitive." (PW) Norton, 1985. Also *This Trifling Distinction: Reminiscences from Down East* (1978)—"some of the fun it has been to live and write . . . in the Pine Tree State." Also *Funny About That* (1992).   ○

Gould, John
**THERE GOES MAINE! A SORT OF
HISTORY**

Entertaining melange—bits of history orthodox historians skip, local lore, characters, tales of early explorers, colonists and Indians—"just the thing for summer reading." (BL) Norton, 1990.   ○

Nearing, Helen
**CONTINUING THE GOOD LIFE:
HALF A CENTURY OF
HOMESTEADING**

Sequel to *Living the Good Life* (Vermont); this covers the period since 1952. An account of living a Thoreau-like life by the author and her husband who were pioneers in this twentieth-century movement of living simply and resourcefully. Schocken Bks, 1987.   ○

Pike, Robert E.
SPIKED BOOTS
Reprint of a 1959 self-published collection of tales about the north country of Maine and New Hampshire. Logging drives and lumber camps, winters, hunting, fishing, Indian legends—"splendid example of local color." (PW) Yankee, 1987.   ○

Pohl, William L.
THE VOICE OF MAINE
Oral history approach—the 'voices' range from the grandson of L.L. Bean and bush pilots to crafts people and an ex-sea captain. Thorndike Pr, 1983.   ○

Rich, Louise Dickinson
MY NECK OF THE WOODS
Just one of several of this author's books on Maine. Down East, 1976 (first published 1950). Other titles include: *Coast of Maine* (1956), *State o'Maine* (1964), *The Forest Years* (1963), and *Peninsula* (1958).   ○

Roberts, Kenneth
TRENDING INTO MAINE
A lovely mishmash of history, memorable "little" people in Maine's history, his grandmother's recipes, lobstering and so on. Down East, 1975 (first published 1938).   ○

Silber, Terry
A SMALL FARM IN MAINE
"Beautifully written" story of a couple's move to Maine and starting a mail-order business near Buckfield. (PW) HM, 1988.   ○

Smith, Robert
MY LIFE IN THE MAINE WOODS
Autobiographical reminiscences of an 18-year-old clerk in a Maine lumber camp during the Depression—"poignant, highly readable" account of the hard times, character portraits. (LJ) Atl Monthly Pr, 1986.   ○

Stinnett, Caskie
ONE MAN'S ISLAND
Reflections on Maine life from slightly offshore. Down East, 1984.   ○

Ulrich, Laurel T.
A MIDWIFE'S TALE
The life of Martha Ballard along the Kennebec River, based on her diary, 1785–1812. "Belies the image of New England as a haven of quietude," with jottings that tell of back-country violence, suicide, rape, murder. There are interpretive essays by the author illuminating women's status, medicine and the daily life. This book was awarded the Pulitzer Prize for History in 1991. Knopf, 1990.   ○

Wood, Pamela
THE SALT BOOK
This is a book inspired by the Foxfire series (see under "Georgia"); in this case the books are the work of English classes of Kennebunk High School. "Lobstering, sea moss pudding, stone walls, rum running, maple syrup, snow shoes, and other Yankee doings" recorded in this and its sequel *Salt Book 2* (Swan's Island). (BRD) Doubleday, 1977 and 1980.   ○

GUIDEBOOKS

D'Amato, Albert C. and Miriam F.
MAINE ITINERARIES
Two guides under this general title, *Discovering Acadia National Park and Mount Desert Island—12 Places to Begin* and *Discovering the Down East Region*. Pro Edit Serv, 1988.   ○

Howard, Andrew R.
COVERED BRIDGES OF MAINE
Village Pr, 1982.   ○

Huber, J. Parker
THE WILDEST COUNTRY
A guide to Thoreau's Maine. A M C Bks, 1981.   ○

McCaig & Boyce
MAINE STATE PARKS
Affordable Adventures, 1989.   ○

Tree, Christina and Steadman, Mimi
MAINE: AN EXPLORER'S GUIDE
A revised edition of what is considered the most comprehensive guide to Maine, in all its aspects—overviews of each region from beaches to remote parts of the Maine Woods; practical information on where to eat and stay, from posh to family lodgings; and much more. Personal observations and evaluations by two experts on Maine. Countryman, 1991.   o

HISTORY

Clark, Charles E.
MAINE
One of a series of popular histories for each state, published as part of the bicentennial in 1976. Norton, 1977.   o

Novels

Bonnie, Fred
TOO HOT AND OTHER MAINE STORIES
"Superb regional anthology." (BL) Dog Ear Pr, 1987.   o

Chase, Mary Ellen
THE LOVELY AMBITION
About a Methodist minister and his family who emigrate from England to Maine around 1900. Norton, 1960. Other books set in Maine by Chase include: *Mary Peters* (1934), *Silas Crockett* (1935), and *Windswept* (1941).   o

Chute, Carolyn
THE BEANS OF EGYPT, MAINE
A poverty-stricken Maine family—the Beans "are on the very bottom" of the social scale, "devoid of the desire or will to rise above their sordid legacy."(PW) Ticknor & Fields, 1984.   o

Chute, Carolyn
LETOURNEAU'S USED AUTO PARTS
Set in Egypt, Maine, the plot involves a junkyard owner with a heart of gold, and the beneficiaries of his largesse—"poor, ignorant, unwashed . . . and the town fathers

are shaking their heads." (FC) Ticknor & Fields, 1988.   o

Dennison, George
LUISA DOMINIC
An October weekend in 1971 and three houseguests "seek to confront the terrors . . . in the world under the same sun that warms this fortunate Maine family." (BRD) Har-Row, 1985.   o

Findley, Timothy
THE TELLING OF LIES
"A novel of charm and manners . . . also a full-fledged thriller" set in an old hotel on the coast of Maine and narrated by an elderly resident who becomes the detective in solving the murder of a pharmaceutical magnate. (BRD) Viking, 1986.   o

Jewett, Sarah Orne
THE COUNTRY OF THE POINTED FIRS & OTHER STORIES
"Closely knit local-color sketches," first published in 1896, of a seaport town during the era of its decay after the days of the West Indian trade. Norton, 1968.   o

King, Stephen
PET SEMATARY
Their new home in Maine is perfection for the Creed family, except for an old pet burial ground with a terrifying secret. Doubleday, 1983. Other horror stories by Stephen King with a Maine setting include: *Carrie* (1974), *Salem's Lot* (1975), *Cujo* (1981), *It* (1986), *The Tommyknockers* (1987).   o

King, Tabitha
CARETAKERS
"A curious relationship between a member of the Maine gentry and a handyman ten years her senior . . . moving tale, sensitively written." (LJ) Macmillan, 1983.   o

Knowles, Ardeana H.
PINK CHIMNEYS
Set mostly around Bangor, in the first half of the 19th century; the lives of three women become enmeshed at an imposing house in Bangor. Harpswell Pr, 1989.   o

MacLeod, Charlotte
THE GLADSTONE BAG
When "strange events, attempted theft, and a sodden body" enliven Emma Kelling's stay in Maine, she calls for help, starting with her niece-detective Sarah Bittersohn—"eccentricities . . . and a certain luxuriousness of language." (FC) Mysterious Pr, 1990.   o

Mojtabai, A.G.
AUTUMN
A widower's first winter in the retirement home he had planned to live in with his wife—"humorous, achingly real without mawkish sentimentality." (FC) Houghton, 1982.   o

Ogilvie, Elizabeth
THE SUMMER OF THE OSPREY
One of several novels involving lobstering and Maine island life; other titles include *An Answer in the Tide* (1978), *Strawberries in the Sea* (1973), *Waters on a Starry Night* (1968). McGraw, 1987.   o

Ogilvie, Elizabeth
WHEN THE MUSIC STOPPED
Two aging sisters return to a small town on the coast of Maine only to be murdered, and an author finds herself in the midst of local scandal and "terrifying deaths . . . suspects abound." (FC) McGraw, 1989. Also with a plot involving two sisters and set in Maine is *The Road to Nowhere* (1983).   o

Paretti, Sandra
THE MAGIC SHIP
Originally published in Germany in 1977. The captain and crew of a German luxury liner are stranded off Bar Harbor at the outbreak of World War I—"romances blossom and endearing memories are forged among the crew and the people of Bar Harbor." (FC) St. Martin, 1979.   o

Pelletier, Cathie
THE FUNERAL MAKERS
"The main character is Mattagash [Maine] itself . . . hilariously irreverent, comic, tragic and lyrical." (BRD) Macmillan, 1986. Also *Once Upon a Time on the Banks* (1989).   o

Phippen, Sanford, ed.
THE BEST MAINE STORIES: THE MARVELOUS MYSTERY
"A strong, flavorful offering" of 17 stories, spanning 106 years, arranged in seasonal groups, ranging from *A Bunch of Letters* by Henry James to *Berrying*, about Finnish Mainers, by Rebecca Cummings. (BL) Lance Tapley, 1986.   o

Roberts, Kenneth
ARUNDEL
The beginning of a series of historical novels—*Arundel* is about a secret expedition led by Benedict Arnold against Quebec. Doubleday, 1930. Following, in order, to form a complete chronicle from the Revolutionary War to the War of 1812, are *Rabble in Arms* (1933), *The Lively Lady* (1931), and *Captain Caution* (1934).   o

Tapply, William G.
DEAD MEAT
A Brady Coyne mystery—one of his "eccentric, well-to-do clients" summons him to a lodge in the wilds of Maine where a guest has disappeared. "Distinguished by descriptive prose that makes one pine for the Maine woods." (FC) Scribner, 1987.   o

Waugh, Charles G., and others
MURDER AND MYSTERY IN MAINE
"An atmospheric" anthology of 14 stories set in Maine, by authors like Charlotte MacLeod and Janwillem van de Wetering, as well as some lesser-known authors. (BL) Dembner Bks, 1989.   o

MARYLAND

Series Guidebooks
(See Appendix 1)

NOTE: See also Series Guides (and non-series guides) listed under United States and the East/the Middle Atlantic States. You may also find some crossover in guides and books listed under the South.

Off the Beaten Bath: Maryland

Background Reading

Ashe, Dora J., ed.
A MARYLAND ANTHOLOGY, 1608–1986.
U Pr of America, 1987.   ○

Baden, Jacqueline H.
MARYLAND'S EASTERN SHORE, A PLACE APART
"Entertaining, informative, sometimes humorous tale that lets the reader savor the flavor, sniff the smells, hear the sounds and feel the pace of this place apart." (Publisher) Travel on Tape Book Div, 1990.   ○

Beirne, Francis F.
THE AMIABLE BALTIMOREANS
Part of the same series that includes *The Proper Bostonians* (see "Massachusetts")—intended to "portray individual characteristics, underscore the idiosyncrasies . . . local traditions." (PW) Johns Hopkins U, 1984.
○

Hardie, Dee
HOLLYHOCKS, LAMBS AND OTHER PASSIONS: A MEMOIR OF THORNHILL FARM
Reminiscences and anecdotes about a family and a Maryland farm. Atheneum, 1985.   ○

Jopp, Harold D. and Ingersoll, R.H., eds.
SHOREMEN
An anthology of Eastern shore prose and verse. Covers some 300 years of writings. Tidewater, 1974.   ○

Meyer, Eugene L.
MARYLAND LOST AND FOUND
People and places from Chesapeake to Appalachia—"obviously the State makes no sense" is the author's conclusion and provides an easy mix of "history with contemporary accounts of Chesapeake watermen, gambling, tobacco farms, military bases . . . race relations, etc." (LJ) Johns Hopkins, 1986.   ○

Peffer, Randall S.
WATERMEN
The author moved to Tilghman Island and worked as a waterman, crabbing and oystering—"it is a better evocation of life today on the Eastern Shore than Michener" (reference is to *Chesapeake,* listed under "Novels," below). (BRD) Johns Hopkins U, 1985.   ○

Shivers, Frank R., Jr.
MARYLAND WITS AND BALTIMORE BARDS
A literary history. Maclay, 1985.   ○

Warner, William W.
BEAUTIFUL SWIMMERS: WATERMEN, CRABS, AND THE CHESAPEAKE BAY
Lore of the blue crab, history and cycle of the Chesapeake Bay and the watermen who work it, written with "love and flair." Suggestions for additional reading, and places and events in the area for travelers to visit. (BRD) Originally published in 1976. Viking Penguin, 1987.   ○

GUIDEBOOKS

Anderson, Elizabeth B.
ANNAPOLIS, A WALK THROUGH HISTORY
A guide to its historic buildings and architecture. Tidewater, 1984.   ○

Block, Victor and Thomas
THE PELICAN GUIDE TO MARYLAND
Pelican, 1986.   ○

Gilbert, Elizabeth R.
FAIRS & FESTIVALS
The Smithsonian guide to celebrations in Maryland, Virginia and the District of Columbia—everything from national holidays and flower festivals to ethnic and religious events. Smithsonian, 1982.   ○

McCaig & Boyce
MARYLAND STATE PARKS
Affordable Adventures, 1989.   ○

Willis, Gwyn
SHIFRA STEIN'S DAY TRIPS FROM GREATER BALTIMORE
Daytrips that reach into Pennsylvania, Delaware, Virginia and West Virginia, with suggestions for combining these into a longer journey. Globe Pequot, 1991.   ○

HISTORY

Bode, Carl
MARYLAND
One of a series of popular histories for each state, published as part of the bicentennial in 1976. Norton, 1978.   ○

Brugger, Robert J., and others
MARYLAND: A MIDDLE TEMPERAMENT, 1634–1980
"Highly readable" history of the third original colony—the authors find a theme of moderation and balance in this "not-quite Southern but not-quite Northern" state. (LJ) Johns Hopkins, 1988.   ○

Novels

Barth, John
THE SOT-WEED FACTOR
Historical novel of the seventeenth century and a satire of historical novels as well. Doubleday, 1967.   ○

Barth, John
THE TIDEWATER TALES
A minimalist novelist and his maximalist oral historian wife spend a couple of weeks sailing Chesapeake Bay and telling stories. Also *Sabbatical* (1982), about a sailboat trip from the Chesapeake Bay to the Caribbean—

"uses the mock-epic voyage to explore the difficulties of both midlife and artistic passages." Putnam, 1987.   ○

DeBlasis, Celeste
A SEASON FOR SWANS
Last of a trilogy about the Swan family. It begins with *Wild Swan* (1984), in which members of the family emigrate from England to Maryland during the period of pre-Civil War slavery, and is followed by *Swan's Chance* (1986), about a horsebreeding farm and its family. *A Season for Swans* concerns murder and tragedy that threaten the farm in the final years of the 19th century. Bantam, 1989.   ○

Greene, Annie
BRIGHT RIVER TRILOGY
Stories of three women in a Maryland town whose lives intersect in one man—as son, friend, lover, respectively. S&S, 1984.   ○

Hornig, Doug
WATERMEN
Illegal activities in a Virginia town and an ex-CIA agent who settles there, are the bases for the plot. Mysterious Pr, 1987.   ○

Michaels, Barbara
PRINCE OF DARKNESS
In *Dark Duet*, the story of an "orphan turned governess, who marries her charge's guardian"—a gothic with an unexpected ending. Congdon & Weed, 1982.   ○

Michener, James A.
CHESAPEAKE
Four centuries of life on Maryland's eastern shore. Random, 1978.   ○

Robertson, Don
BY ANTIETAM CREEK
Historical novel of the Civil War battles where thousands of lives were lost, weaving together personal stories of soldiers. P-H, 1960.   ○

Tyler, Anne
BREATHING LESSONS
A day in the life of a couple, married 28 years and preparing to attend a funeral in

Pennsylvania. Knopf, 1988. Other novels by Anne Tyler set in Maryland include: *Celestial Navigation* (1974), *Searching for Caleb* (1976), *Earthly Possessions* (1977), *Morgan's Passing* (1980), *Dinner at the Homesick Restaurant* (1982) and *Accidental Tourist* (1985).   o

MASSACHUSETTS

Series Guidebooks
(See Appendix 1)

NOTE: See also Series Guides (and non-series guides) listed under United States and the East and the East/New England.

Access Guide: Boston
Blue Guide: Boston & Cambridge
Fodor: Boston; Cape Cod
Frommer: Boston
Let's Go: Boston
Off the Beaten Path: Massachusetts

Background Reading

Amory, Cleveland
THE PROPER BOSTONIANS
Social history of Boston's first families based on family writings, conversations, anecdotes and Boston stories—by an author who is himself a proper Bostonian. First published in 1947. Parnassus Imprints, 1984.   o

Bailey, Anthony
SPRING JAUNTS
Five jaunts, originally appearing as a series of articles in *The New Yorker*, one of which is the Massachusetts/Maine coast—"a book to savour . . . wise, funny." (LJ) FS&G, 1986.   o

Brooks, Paul
THE PEOPLE OF CONCORD
See entry under the East/New England.   o

Green, Martin
THE MOUNT VERNON STREET WARRENS: A BOSTON STORY, 1860–1910
"Intriguing observations on Boston Society and its antithesis, the Aesthetic movement," through the story of the many-sided, wealthy Warren family, with two key figures—one a homosexual art collector, the other an aristocratic businessman. (LJ) Macmillan, 1990.   o

Horgan, Edward R.
THE SHAKER HOLY LAND
The story of the Shakers' struggle to create a community in Harvard and in Shirley, Massachusetts—how they grew, thrived and died out. Accompanied by rare photographs and an appendix that includes a comprehensive guide to Shaker museums, restorations and libraries. Harvard Common Pr, 1987. o

Lukas, J. Anthony
COMMON GROUND
Account of the decade in Boston when court-ordered busing to integrate the schools took place and tore the city apart. The author provides a history of three stereotypical families—working class Irish Catholic, black Roxbury and an upper-middle-class liberal family. The book is a fascinating social history not only of these families, and of Boston, but also of key figures in the controversy—such as Judge Gerrity, a Catholic cardinal, the editor of the Boston Globe, the mayor. Knopf, 1985.   o

O'Connell, Shaun
IMAGINING BOSTON: A LITERARY LANDSCAPE
"Survey of Boston-oriented writers from Hawthorne to Updike . . . examines how each writer . . . responds to Puritan John Winthrop's 17th-century vision of Boston as a moral beacon." Organized chronologically and thematically, and including some authors not usually associated with Boston. (LJ) Beacon, 1990.   o

Owens, Carole
THE BERKSHIRE COTTAGES: A VANISHING ERA
"A social history of America's Inland Newport . . . the fabulous mansions built in the

Berkshire hills and the fairy tale lives of the families who built them." (Publisher) Cottage Pr, 1984. o

Randall, Peter
SALEM AND MARBLEHEAD
Dwellings and architecture of two historic towns. Down East, 1983. o

Starkey, Marion L.
THE DEVIL IN MASSACHUSETTS
A modern inquiry into the Salem witch trials, first published in 1949. Doubleday, 1969. o

Warner, Sam Bass, Jr.
PROVINCE OF REASON
Incisive sketches of various Bostonians based on the premise that the past can be better understood through the lives of individuals than through statistics and stock phrases. Individuals range from old-time radio comedian Fred Allen and former president of Harvard James Conant to housewives and businessmen. Harvard U Pr, 1984. o

CAPE COD

Beston, Henry
THE OUTERMOST HOUSE
"A year of life on the great beach of Cape Cod"—a classic first published in 1928. (BRD) Penguin, 1988. o

Finch, Robert
COMMON GROUND: A NATURALIST'S CAPE COD
Thirty-two essays from Cape Cod newspaper columns. Godine, 1981. Also *The Primal Place* (1983), about the area around Brewster, and *Outlands: Journey to the Outer Edges of Cape Cod* (1988). o

Hersey, John
BLUES
A young man and an old fisherman meet by chance and go fishing together; they have conversations about fishing and recall poets from Homer to Ciardi who have written about fish. Random, 1988. o

Kane, Tom
MY PAMET: CAPE COD CHRONICLE
A collection of columns from Cape Cod's weekly newspaper and written by the author over 40 years—"captured and communicated the seasonal tenor of life on the Cape . . . delightful chronicle." (BL) Moyer Bell Ltd, 1989. o

O'Brien, Gregory
AN INSIDER'S GUIDE TO CAPE COD AND THE ISLANDS
A guide to Cape Cod, Martha's Vineyard, Nantucket and the Elizabeth Island—a guidebook for natives and newcomers, with comprehensive listings of all sorts of lodgings, restaurants, galleries, antique shops, festivals. Viking Penguin, 1988. o

Pratson, Frederick
GUIDE TO CAPE COD
A four-season guide to the area by a year-round resident. Globe Pequot, 1988. o

Robinson, William F.
CAPE COD
Henry David Thoreau's complete text, with the journey recreated in pictures. Includes watercolors, botanical illustrations, period maps, early photos and contemporary photographs "of a Cape Cod Thoreau would recognize today." Bullfinch Pr, 1985. o

Taber, Gladys
STILL COVE JOURNAL
A journal completed shortly before the author's death of "random thoughts, recipes, neighborhood news and nature reports" written for a local Cape Cod newspaper. (See also this writer's books under "Connecticut.") Har-Row, 1981. Also *My Own Cape Cod* (1971), about her love for the Cape and its seasons, written in 1970. Parnassus Imprints, 1981. o

MARTHA'S VINEYARD & NANTUCKET

Allen, Everett S.
MARTHA'S VINEYARD: AN ELEGY
"Leisurely essays explore the mystique of island existence . . . memorable anecdotes . . . felicitous reading" about a place irrev-

ocably changed by the influx of new residents and tourists. (PW) Little, 1982.   o

Burroughs, Polly
GUIDE TO MARTHA'S VINEYARD; GUIDE TO NANTUCKET
"A sensitive introduction to the history, traditions, and geography of Martha's Vineyard . . . an amazingly thorough and accurate guide to the special places and events found on the Island." (Publisher) Globe Pequot, 1991.   o

Hough, Henry Beatle
REMEMBRANCE AND LIGHT: IMAGES OF MARTHA'S VINEYARD
Impressions of each season on the island by the editor of *Vineyard Gazette*—some of the pieces appeared there first—and photographs. Harvard Common Pr, 1984.   o

O'Brien, Gregory
AN INSIDER'S GUIDE TO CAPE COD AND THE ISLANDS
See entry under Cape Cod, above.   o

Whipple, A.B.
VINTAGE NANTUCKET
Uses walks along the island streets to begin each chapter, tying past to present, and imparting much about Indians, Quakers, whaling wives, eccentrics, old families, etc. Globe Pequot, 1989.   o

GUIDEBOOKS *(Other than Cape Cod/Martha's Vineyard/Nantucket)*

Carlock, Marty
A GUIDE TO PUBLIC ART IN GREATER BOSTON
From Newburyport to Plymouth—a guide to the works of art in public spaces, including murals, statues, abstract works. For both the tourist and the student of art. Harvard Common Pr, 1988.   o

Howard, Andrew R.
COVERED BRIDGES OF MASSACHUSETTS
Village Pr, 1983.   o

McCaig & Boyce
MASSACHUSETTS STATE PARKS
Affordable Adventures, 1989.   o

Maynard, Mary and Dow, Mary-Lou
HASSLE-FREE BOSTON: A MANUAL FOR WOMEN
Geared toward the woman visitor and relocator, with biographical tidbits about the women who lived in and influenced the history of Boston. Greene, 1985.   o

Morris, Jerry
THE BOSTON GLOBE GUIDE TO BOSTON
Comprehensive, easy-to-use guide to Boston and its neighborhoods by a writer for the *Globe*'s travel column. Globe Pequot, 1989.   o

Southworth, Susan and Michael
A.I.A. GUIDE TO BOSTON
A readable and entertaining look at buildings and styles that span three centuries. Globe Pequot, 1984.   o

Tree, Christina M.
THE OTHER MASSACHUSETTS: AN EXPLORER'S GUIDE
A guidebook for the Bay state, other than Boston and Cape Cod, and intended for both residents and visitors, with a focus on areas that often escape notice—upcountry Massachusetts, the southern Berkshires, the Five College Area, Greater Springfield, central Massachusetts, the Merrimack Valley, the north and south shores and Bristol County. Countryman, 1987.   o

HISTORY

Brown, Richard D.
MASSACHUSETTS
One of a series of popular histories for each state, published as part of the bicentennial in 1976. Norton, 1978.   o

NOVELS

Bernlef, J.
OUT OF MIND (Gloucester)
Story of the descent of a Dutch-born man into the tragedy of Alzheimers. Godine, 1989.   o

Boyer, Rick
MOSCOW METAL (Concord)
Doc Adams is a dentist-cum-detective in this story of the KGB and double agents—"the story's cozy, middle-class Concord, Massachusetts ambience is well evoked." Also *Whale's Footprints* (1988), in which Doc Adams' son, studying whales off Cape Cod, is a murder suspect. HM, 1987. ○

Cooney, Ellen
ALL THE WAY HOME
A former athlete's attempt to rebuild her life through establishing Curry Crossing's first female softball team. Putnam Pub Group, 1984. ○

Fast, Howard
APRIL MORNING
Fictionalized version of the shot heard round the world. Crown, 1961. ○

Ford, Elaine
MISSED CONNECTIONS
The "frayed circuits of domestic life" are the missed connections in this novel of family life in a blue-collar suburb of Boston. (FC) Random, 1983. ○

Hodges, Hollis
NORMAN ROCKWELL'S GREATEST PAINTING
Six people who modeled for artist Rockwell plan a reunion party. Eriksson, 1988. ○

Hospital, Janette T.
THE TIGER IN THE TIGER PIT
Reunion of a New England family gathered for their parents' fiftieth wedding celebration. Dutton, 1984. ○

Hunter, Evan
LIZZIE
The author uses actual trial and inquest records along with fictional invention for a fascinating portrait of Lizzie Borden. Arbor Hse, 1984. ○

Langton, Jane
GOOD AND DEAD
Twelve funerals in a town in Massachusetts arouse the suspicion of a former detective,

now on the church's parish committee—"a deep love of New England and its history" and a fictional village peopled with "sunny, sensible parishoners." St. Martin, 1986. ○

Leimbach, Marti
DYING YOUNG
A first novel—"simply told tragic love story . . . creating along the way a Massachusetts landscape that intensifies the cold desolation of the narrator and her two lovers." The plot concerns a young man dying of leukemia who advertises in the *Globe* for a companion and hires her; they fall in love and move to the Massachusetts coast. Doubleday, 1990. ○

Lott, Brett
THE MAN WHO OWNED VERMONT
See under Vermont/Novels. ○

Lovecraft, H. P.
THE DUNWICH HORROR, AND OTHER COLLECTED LOVECRAFT STORIES
First of three volumes of collected Gothic horror stories many of which are set in both a real and an imaginary Massachusetts (Salem, the area around the Quabbin Reservoir, Pioneer Valley). (Dunwich is supposedly based on the villages of Wilbraham, Hampden and Monson.) See also guidebooks on the area under "Background Reading" above, and *Abandoned New England* under "U.S.A., The East/New England." Arkham, 1985. Also Volume 2, *At the Mountains of Madness* (1985) and Volume 3, *Dagon and Other Macabre Tales* (1986). ○

MacLeod, Charlotte
THE CORPSE IN OOZAK'S POND
A death on the campus of an agricultural college that reenacts a crime in 1905 and results in a cooperative effort to solve the mystery by an agronomy professor, the sheriff and a local reporter. Mysterious Pr, 1987.
○

Marquand, John P.
WICKFORD POINT
The "vagaries of [an] ingrown New England family" set in the family home at Wickford Point (Newburyport). (FC) Little, 1939. ○

Pickard, Nancy
NO BODY
Fictitious Port Frederic is the setting for this Jennie Cain mystery involving bodies taken from a cemetery. Scribner (1986). Also *Dead Crazy* (1988).   ○

Seton, Anya
THE HEARTH AND EAGLE
  (Marblehead)
History of Marblehead interwoven with a family's history. Houghton, 1948.   ○

Updike, John
ROGER'S VERSION
A student seeks a grant from a divinity professor to prove the existence of God by use of a computer. Knopf, 1986.   ○

Walker, Walter
**THE IMMEDIATE PROSPECT OF
  BEING HANGED**
A blue-blooded beauty is found strangled, and her husband is charged with the crime. Viking, 1989.   ○

Zaroulis, Nancy
MASSACHUSETTS
Blockbuster novel of the Revell family—"a sweeping saga with just the right blend of history and drama" of the family from its arrival with the Mayflower to the twilight of the 20th century. (BL) Fawcett,1991. Also *Call the Darkness Light* (1979) an account of early nineteenth century immigration and Lowell.   ○

BOSTON & CAMBRIDGE

Banks, Oliver
THE REMBRANDT PANEL
A murder mystery that takes us behind the scenes in the world of art dealers, museum directors and art fakery. Little, 1980.   ○

Barnes, Linda
THE TROUBLE OF FOOLS
Private eye Carlotta Carlyle is an ex-cabbie, ex-policewoman in Boston, and the plot begins with a missing cab driver and some strange activities at a cab company. St. Mar-

tin, 1987. Also *The Snake Tatoo* (1989), about a suburban teenager in the Combat Zone, and *Coyote* (1990), about the world of illegal immigrants.   ○

Bernays, Anne
THE ADDRESS BOOK
A Boston woman is "catapulted into a crisis" when offered a New York job that will make her a commuting wife and mother. She finds five strange names in an old address book, phones each of them, and finds they were part of her life and have definite ideas about the choice she should make. (FC) Little, 1983. Also *The School Book* (1980), a feminist novel set in a private school in Cambridge.   ○

Bernays, Anne
PROFESSOR ROMEO
About a philandering Harvard professor who is done in by contemporary sexual harassment regulations. Weidenfeld, 1989.   ○

Cook, Robin
GODPLAYER
The latest of Cook's medical mysteries set in a Boston hospital. In this, the subject is SSDs—sudden surgical deaths. Putnam, 1983. Also *Fever* (1982) about leukemia and *Coma* (1977) concerns a rash of post-surgery comas.   ○

Fielding, Joy
SEE JANE RUN
Suspense novel of a woman amnesia victim who discovers she's the wife of a prominent surgeon. Morrow, 1991.   ○

Frede, Richard
THE NURSES
Set in a fictional Back Bay hospital—the association of residents and interns stages a walkout, leaving the nurses in charge. HM, 1985.   ○

Healy, J.F.
SO LIKE SLEEP
Boston's wealthy white suburbs and a Roxbury ghetto are settings for a mystery that involves hypnotism and psychiatry. Har-

Row, 1986. Also *Yesterday's News* (1988), about police corruption in Boston.   o

Higgins, George V.
A CHOICE OF ENEMIES

"Mordantly witty and dismayingly believable" novel of Boston-style politics. (PW) Knopf, 1984. Other novels by Higgins on various aspects of the Boston scene include: *The Digger's Game* (1973), *Kennedy for the Defense* (1980), *The Patriot Game* (1982), *The Friends of Eddie Coyle* (1972), and *The Rat on Fire* (1980). *Penance for Jerry Kennedy* (1985) is a sequel to *Kennedy for the Defense*.   o

Higgins, George V.
WONDERFUL YEARS, WONDERFUL YEARS

Troubles with the Feds for a contractor who "did not get rich playing on a level field." (FC) Holt, 1988. Also *Outlaws* (1987)—"brilliant tales of Boston low-life." And *Imposters* (1986), about the D.A. and a publisher trying to learn what a TV anchorman knows about an impending murder trial.   o

James, Henry
THE BOSTONIANS

Satirical novel set in Boston of the late 19th century. A Southern lawyer comes to seek his fortune in Boston and falls in love with a beautiful young woman, who is under the sway of a radical feminist of the day. Also *The Europeans*, about two expatriates who visit Boston—contrasts the sophistication of the expatriates with the straight and strict New Englanders. First published in 1886 and 1878, respectively. Random, 1991.   o

Langton, Jane
MURDER AT THE GARDNER

Boston's Gardner Museum is the focus of this mystery when strange things happen and a benefactor meets an untimely end. St. Martin, 1988. Also, *Memorial Hall Murder* (1981).   o

Lathen, Emma
SOMETHING IN THE AIR

"An observant tale of financial and criminal intrigue" and a Boston commuter airline,

with Wall Street executive John Thatcher as detective. (FC) S&S, 1988.   o

Marquand, John P.
THE LATE GEORGE APLEY

Story of a Boston Brahmin, which won a Pulitzer Prize in 1938. Little, 1937. Also about the socially elite in Boston is *H.M. Pulham, Esquire* (1941).   o

Martin, William
RISING OF THE MOON

Boston's Irish South End is the setting, and the time is 1916, with a complicated plot involving Ireland's Easter Rebellion and two cousins—"sprawling novel . . . also a brawling one." (NYT) Crown, 1987. Also *Back Bay*, another Boston novel.   o

Mason, F. Van Wyck
GUNS FOR REBELLION

The Battle of Bunker Hill from the point of view of a Boston resident who is forced to fight on the side of the British. Doubleday, 1953.   o

Matheson, Don
STRAY CAT

A former computer salesman, doing odd jobs and living on a sailboat in Boston Harbor, gets involved in the rescue of a "larcenous young woman" from death by a hired killer. (FC) Summit Bks, 1987.   o

Myrer, Anton
A GREEN DESIRE

A love triangle "serves as the focal point [for] practically all the major historical events of the present century" through World War II. (FC) Putnam Pub Group, 1982. Also *The Last Convertible* (1978), which takes a group of Harvard students from 1938 through World War II and the years that follow.   o

O'Connor, Edwin
ALL IN THE FAMILY

Story of a rich Irish family's entry into politics. Little, 1966. Also *The Edge of Sadness* (1961), the saga of another Irish-Catholic family in Boston.   o

Parker, Robert B.
PLAYMATES
Parker's Boston private eye Spenser is well-known both through his series of mystery novels and a TV series. In this, the plot focus is on a Boston-area basketball team suspected of point-shaving. Putnam, 1989. Other mysteries set in the Boston area include: *God Save the Child* (1974), *Mortal Stakes* (1975), *Pale Kings and Princes* (1987), *Crimson Joy* (1988).   ○

Reed, Barry
THE VERDICT
"Superb courtroom drama" of medical malpractice in which the two lawyers are "Boston's most upright lawyer [and] a hard-drinking . . . ambulance chasing lawyer who will cheat anyone." Paul Newman starred in the movie. (FC) S&S, 1980.   ○

Sarton, May
THE EDUCATION OF HARRIET HATFIELD
When her lover dies, an aging lesbian fulfills an ambition to open a bookstore for women in a Boston neighborhood. Norton, 1989. Also *Anger* (1982).   ○

Segal, Erich
THE CLASS
Harvardiana, its architecture, the ambiance. The plot follows five stereotypical members of the Harvard '58 class to their 25th reunion. Bantam, 1985.   ○

Smith, Richard
A SECRET SINGING
Death by poison of a Boston Brahmin. NAL/Dutton, 1989. Also *Wild Justice* (1990).   ○

Waugh, Carol-Lynn R. and others, eds.
MURDER AND MYSTERY IN BOSTON
An anthology. Dembner Bks, 1988.   ○

Wolfe, Thomas
OF TIME AND THE RIVER
A young man's three years at Harvard. (See also the author's autobiographical novels under "North Carolina.") Scribner, 1935. ○

Zaroulis, Nancy
THE LAST WALTZ
Boston at the end of the 19th century is the setting—a young woman of culture but little money narrates her story as companion to two wealthy and pampered daughters of a shipping magnate. Doubleday, 1984.   ○

CAPE COD

Clark, Mary Higgins
WHERE ARE THE CHILDREN?
Suspenseful, scary story of an unsolved murder years earlier, which seems about to be repeated in the heroine's new life on the Cape. S&S, 1975.   ○

Kiker, Douglas
MURDER ON CLAM POND
One of TV newsman Kiker's mysteries set on Cape Cod in which the richest woman in town is murdered, out of season—"fills his pages with humor and outstanding characterization." Another, *Death at the Cut* (1987), involves the drowning of a young woman, which creates a politically delicate situation when it is found she worked for a prominent Republican senator who was a potential presidential candidate. (FC) Random, 1986.   ○

Mailer, Norman
TOUGH GUYS DON'T DANCE
Set in Provincetown—a writer wakes up after a night of drinking to find a strange tattoo on his arm, blood in his car and two heads buried with his marijuana supply—obviously he's a prime suspect for the murders. Random, 1984.   ○

Martin, William
CAPE COD
A three-century saga combining romance and suspense to tell Cape Cod's story—"embraces the entire sweep of American history with unflagging relish for authentic detail and private moments." (BL) Warner Bks, 1991.   ○

Piercy, Marge
SUMMER PEOPLE
A *ménage à trois* is ruptured when one of the three becomes discontented. Summit, 1989.   ○

MARTHA'S VINEYARD & NANTUCKET

Benchley, Nathaniel
THE OFF-ISLANDERS (Nantucket)
The book on which the movie *The Russians Are Coming* was based. McGraw, 1961.   o

Carlisle, Henry
THE JONAH MAN (Nantucket)
Grim tale of a 19th-century whaling ship master whose past "taints all his dealings with his neighbors." (FC) Knopf, 1984.   o

Chute, Patricia
EVA'S MUSIC (Martha's Vineyard)
The heroine finds herself pregnant and with a dying mother—she decides to move to Martha's Vineyard with the baby after her mother's death. Doubleday, 1983.   o

Dean, S.F.X.
NANTUCKET SOAP OPERA
A professor, trying to finish a new book, becomes involved in sensational murders in the Nantucket Island community. Atheneum, 1987.   o

Hoffman, Alice
ILLUMINATION NIGHT (Martha's Vineyard)
A couple's marriage, after surviving vicissitudes of "a countercultural transplant to the off-season isolation of Martha's Vineyard," faces an even more threatening situation when a teenage girl develops a fixation on the husband. (FC) Putnam, 1987.   o

Rich, Virginia
THE NANTUCKET DIET MURDERS
Nantucket in winter is the setting—a group of well-to-do widows are seemingly starving themselves to death under the influence of a charismatic diet doctor. Delacorte, 1985.   o

Robertson, Mary E.
FAMILY LIFE (Nantucket)
"Credible and disturbing story" of a man who leaves his family for a woman who reminds him of his first love, and moves with her to another part of Nantucket. Atheneum, 1987.   o

Thayer, Nancy
SPIRIT LOST (Nantucket)
A couple leaves Boston to live in an old house on Nantucket, and the husband becomes obsessed by the ghost of the former owner. Scribner, 1988.   o

MICHIGAN

*Series Guidebooks
(See Appendix 1)*

NOTE: See also Series Guides (and non-series guides) listed under United States and the Midwest.

Off the Beaten Path: Michigan

Background Reading

Conot, Robert E.
AMERICAN ODYSSEY
Life story of America from the perspective of the history and growth of Detroit. Wayne State U Pr, 1986.   o

Lacey, Robert
FORD—THE MEN AND THE MACHINE
"Two books in one"—first the Horatio Alger story of Henry Ford; second, a *Dynasty*-like story of Grosse Pointe—"rich in incident and character as the prime-time soaps and requires no suspension of disbelief, being true." (NYTBR) Little, 1986.   o

Lankton, Larry D.
A MANLY CIVILIZATION: LIFE, WORK AND DEATH IN THE LAKE SUPERIOR COPPER MINES
Oxford U Pr, 1991.   o

Love, Edmund G.
THE SITUATION IN FLUSHING
First published in 1965. "Joyful account of being a small boy in a lovely town" and his love for the coal-burning freight trains that came through—"sharp and funny calendar of the townsfolk . . . social history . . . portrait of a place and a time that has vanished." (BRD) Wayne State U Pr, 1987. ○

Piljac, Pamela A. and Thomas M.
MACKINAC ISLAND
History, background, as well as a guide to the island as historic frontier, vacation resort and a timeless wonderland where no cars are permitted, with a section on its permanent residents. Bryce-Waterton, 1988. ○

Stocking, Kathleen
LETTERS FROM THE LEELANAU: ESSAYS OF PEOPLE AND PLACE
"Zestful glimpse of the citizens and environment" of the Leelanau Peninsula by an essayist "unafraid to plunge into deeper water." (NYT) U of Michigan Pr, 1990. ○

Wamsley, James S.
AMERICAN INGENUITY: HENRY FORD MUSEUM AND GREENFIELD VILLAGE
Story of the Ford indoor-outdoor museum of American industry and cultural history and its contents—everything from the chair on which Lincoln was sitting when shot to a replica of the Menlo Park lab where Edison worked to an entire nineteenth-century jewelry store transplanted to the museum. (PW) Abrams, 1985. ○

GUIDEBOOKS

Dodge, R.L.
MICHIGAN GHOST TOWNS: LOWER PENINSULA/UPPER PENINSULA
Reproduction of the 1970 two-volume edition—history and guide to the old logging and mining towns, some surviving as a building or two, some completely gone. Glendon, 1990. ○

Hunt, Don and Mary
DETROIT & SOUTHEASTERN MICHIGAN
Midwestern Guides, 1989. ○

McMinn, Russell
ANTIQUES
A guide to Michigan's antique shops. Jockey Hollow, 1989. ○

Powers, Tom
MICHIGAN STATE AND NATIONAL PARKS: A COMPLETE GUIDE
Also *Natural Michigan* (1987). Friede Pubns, 1989. ○

HISTORY

Catton, Bruce
MICHIGAN
One of a series of popular histories for each state, published as part of the bicentennial in 1976. Norton, 1984. ○

Novels

Arnow, Harriette
THE DOLLMAKER
A country woman with a passion for whittling objects out of wood is forced in World War II to leave her home for Detroit's mean streets so that her husband can work in a factory. Macmillan, 1954. Also, *The Weedkiller's Daughter* (1970). ○

Briskin, Jacqueline
THE ONYX
A chronicle of the early days of the automobile industry, with a lead character who bears a striking resemblance to Henry Ford. Delacorte, Pr, 1982. ○

Caputo, Philip
INDIAN COUNTRY
A Vietnam veteran's return to Upper Peninsula offers hope for salvation from psychological trauma—"a strong sense of place . . . a boondocks with its own special flavor." (BRD) Bantam, 1987. ○

Dickinson, Charles
WALTZ IN MARATHON
Life in Marathon, Michigan, a small town, as seen through the life of a gentlemanly loan shark. His life is greatly changed when he meets a fortyish woman lawyer. Knopf, 1983. ○

Estleman, Loren D.
SWEET WOMEN LIE
One of a series of crime novels set in Detroit, "classic hard-boiled style . . . evocation of the seamy, forlorn ambience of Detroit." (FC) HM, 1990. Also in the series are: *Motor City Blue* (1980), *The Midnight Man* (1982), *The Glass Highway* (1983), *Killzone* (1984), *Sugartown* (1985), *Every Brilliant Eye* (1985), *Lady Yesterday* (1986), *General Murders* (1988), *Downriver* (1988), *Silent Thunder* (1989), *Whiskey River* (1990). ○

Harrison, Jim
SUNDOG (Upper Peninsula)
A writer tape-records a dying man's life story as foreman on dam construction projects. Dutton, 1984. Also *Farmer* (1976), about a Swedish-American teacher and farmer and midwest Americana of a generation ago. ○

Hemingway, Ernest
THE TORRENTS OF SPRING
(Petosky)
A working-class comedy by the noted writer. Scribner, 1972 (first published 1926). ○

Kakonis, Tom
MICHIGAN ROLL
A professor imprisoned for a crime of passion returns to Traverse City and is drawn into nightmarish adventures—"conducted in a state of high suspense and in a lofty literary style." (FC) St. Martin, 1988. ○

Kienzle, William X.
EMINENCE
One of a series of Father Robert Koesler mysteries that combine theology and logic to assist the Detroit police in solving crimes. Other titles in the series include: *The Rosary Murders* (1979), *Death Wears a Red Hat* (1980), *Mind Over Murder* (1981), *Assault With Intent* (1982), *Shadow of Death* (1983), *Kill and Tell* (1984), *Sudden Death* (1985), *Deathbed* (1986), *Deadline for a Critic* (1987), *Marked for Murder* (1988), *Masquerade* (1990) and *Chameleon* (1991). Andrews & McMeel, 1989. ○

Leonard, Elmore
FREAKY DEAKY
Ghosts from their activist past return to seek vengeance on two wealthy brothers. Arbor Hse, 1988. Also *Killshot* (1989). ○

Matheson, Richard
BID TIME RETURN (Mackinac Island)
This is the story that was the basis for a movie that has become a cult film—about a love between an actress and a playwright that crosses time barriers. I understand that its devotees have formed a club that meets annually on Mackinac Island. Buccaneer Bks, 1986. Another edition under the title *Somewhere in Time* (the name of the movie) is published by Scream Press. ○

Oates, Joyce Carol
DO WITH ME WHAT YOU WILL
(Detroit)
Examination of personalities and motives, back to their childhoods, of two people involved in an extramarital affair. (FC) Vanguard, 1973. Also *Them* (1969), "violence and poverty in the lives of . . . a blue-collar white family" from 1930–67; and a book of short stories, *The Wheel of Love* (1970). ○

Traver, Robert
PEOPLE VS. KIRK
A murder mystery that uses hypnotism to probe the chief suspect's guilt. St. Martin, 1981. Also *Anatomy of a Murder* (1958), the story of an Army officer who murders his wife's rapist. Made into a popular movie. ○

Woiwode, Larry
WHAT I'M GOING TO DO, I
  THINK
A honeymoon in northern Michigan— "touching . . . deeply moving novel" about loss and "the puzzle of love." (FC) FS&G, 1969. ○

MINNESOTA

Series Guidebooks
(See Appendix 1)

NOTE: See also Series Guides (and non-series guides) listed under United States and the Midwest.

Frommer:　City Guide—Minneapolis/St. Paul
Off the Beaten Path:　Minnesota

Background Reading

Bly, Carol
LETTERS FROM THE COUNTRY
Essays "to raise rural consciousness" by a fiction writer about the "essence of small town life." (BRD) Har-Row, 1988.　◦

Hampl, Patricia
A ROMANTIC EDUCATION
"Begins as an extended essay on sensitivity to one's family and ends as a sort of travelogue describing the author's visits to Prague." The author was born into a St. Paul, Minnesota, family that "cultivated nostalgia for the past." (BRD) Houghton, 1983.　◦

Holm, Bill
PRAIRIE DAYS
The author writes of his heritage, the land and people and a vanishing way of life, with whimsical echoes of Lake Wobegone. Saybrook, 1987.　◦

Klinkenborg, Verlyn
MAKING HAY
See entry under Iowa.　◦

Leschak, Peter M.
LETTERS FROM SIDE LAKE
The author is "part philosopher, part nature writer, part hell raiser, so each entry in this delightful book is a treat." It begins in the city, and then the author moves with his new wife back to northern Minnesota—from whence he'd always wanted to escape—builds a cabin, and takes the reader along on the adventure. (LJ) Har-Row, 1987.　◦

Mohr, Howard
A MINNESOTA BOOK OF DAYS (AND A FEW NIGHTS)
Adventures of an eccentric farmer and his wife in western Minnesota, Minneapolis and St. Paul, by a man who used to do the tongue-in-cheek commercials for "A Prairie Home Companion" radio show. Penguin, 1989. Also *How to Talk Minnesotan* (1987).　◦

GUIDEBOOKS

Deblinger, Paul
CULPEPPER'S MINNEAPOLIS-ST. PAUL
"The essential guide to the twin cities," is the book's subtitle. Culpepper Pr, 1990.　◦

Hereid, Nancy and Gennaro, Eugene D.
A FAMILY GUIDE TO MINNESOTA'S NORTH SHORE
U of Minnesota Pr, 1986.　◦

McCaig & Boyce
MINNESOTA STATE PARKS
Affordable Adventures, 1989.　◦

Olsenius, Richard
MINNESOTA TRAVEL COMPANION
A unique guide to the history along the highways. Bluestem, 1981.　◦

HISTORY

Lass, William E.
MINNESOTA
One of a series of popular histories for each state, published as part of the bicentennial in 1976. Norton, 1977.　◦

Novels

Clark, Mary Higgins
A CRY IN THE NIGHT
One of Clark's page-turning mysteries, a neo-gothic thriller. The plot concerns a young woman with two daughters, working in a

Manhattan art gallery, who meets the artist whose paintings are being exhibited, marries him and moves to rural Minnesota. S&S, 1982.   o

Hassler, Jon
NORTH OF HOPE
A young man responds to his mother's dying request to become a priest after the girl he loves marries someone else; they meet again 25 years later. Ballantine Bks, 1990. Also set in Minnesota is *Staggerford* (1977), about a week in the life of a high school teacher, *Four Miles to Pinecone* (1977) and *Grand Opening* (1987).   o

Keillor, Garrison
LAKE WOBEGONE DAYS
"History and season-by-season chronicle of his imaginary hometown . . . exposes the foibles and faults of Lake Wobegonians with affection and sympathy." (BRD) Viking, 1985. Also *Leaving Home* (1987), a collection of radio monologues from PBS's weekly radio show, "Prairie Home Companion."   o

Larsen, Eric
AN AMERICAN MEMORY
The narrator grows up on a remote Minnesota farm and tells the stories of his parents, grandparents and siblings—"as much a prose poem as a novel." (NYT) Algonquin, 1988.
      o

Lewis, Sinclair
MAIN STREET
The classic novel of Sauk Center and middle America in the 1920s. S&S, 1950 (first published 1920). Also *Cass Timberlane* (1945), the story of a second marriage.   o

Moberg, Vilhelm
UNTO A GOOD LAND
S&S, 1954. Originally written in Swedish, it follows *The Emigrants* (see "Sweden"). This tells of the emigration experience of a farmer and his group of peasants from a parish in Smaland, who left in 1850 for America. They arrive in New York and reach Minnesota by riverboat, steam wagon, foot, ox-drawn cart, to create a new home. S&S, 1954. Also *The Last Letter Home* (1961), final volume in the epic story.   o

Powers, J.F.
WHEAT THAT SPRINGETH GREEN
A mid-western Catholic priest is pastor of a suburban parish—saved from "spiritual drought" by the arrival of a priest of the '60s. Also *Morte d'Urban* (1962). Knopf, 1988.   o

Sandford, John
RULES OF PREY
"Tense action, chilling excitement, and thrilling suspense . . . and romantic sidelines"—a mad dog killer of Minneapolis women, and Policeman Lucas Davenport, are the protagonists. (FC) Putnam, 1989. o

Weaver, Will
RED EARTH, WHITE EARTH
The owner of an electronics company in the Silicon Valley gets a call for help from his grandfather and returns to Minnesota—"carefully cultivated indifference to his past dissolves as he grapples" with family problems. (FC) S&S, 1986.   o

MISSISSIPPI

*Series Guidebooks
(See Appendix 1)*

NOTE: See Series Guides (and non-series guides) listed under United States and the South.

Background Reading

Dunbar, Tony
DELTA TIME: A JOURNEY THROUGH MISSISSIPPI
"Semi-travelog with a heavy dose of nostal-

gia'' by the author of *Our Land Too,* which was a report on social conditions written some 20 years ago. The author finds that black participation in political and economic life has increased, but the unique Delta life is being destroyed. (LJ) Pantheon, 1990.   ○

Taylor, Herman E.
FAULKNER'S OXFORD
The author's family, like Faulkner's, has been in Oxford for generations. The author shares reminiscences of ''Mr. Billy'' and identifies landmarks in ''Yoknapatawpha'' and Jefferson counties in detail. Rutledge Hill Pr, 1990.   ○

Yates, Gayle G.
MISSISSIPPI MIND: A PERSONAL CULTURAL HISTORY OF AN AMERICAN STATE
A blend of personal narrative and scholarly inquiry into the state's culture since the 1960s and the civil rights movement—how changes there illuminate changes in the South and the nation as a whole. U of Tennessee, 1990.   ○

GUIDEBOOKS

Cornwell, Ilene J.
TRAVEL GUIDE TO THE NATCHEZ TRACE PARKWAY
A guide to the parkway between Natchez and Nashville. Southern Resources, 1984.   ○

Kempe, Helen K.
THE PELICAN GUIDE TO OLD HOMES OF MISSISSIPPI
Maps, photographs and information to help sightseers discover the famous, architecturally and historically significant homes and landmarks. In two volumes: Volume I covers Natchez and the South; Volume II, Columbus and the North. Pelican, 1989.   ○

Wells, Mary A.
HISTORY LOVER'S GUIDE TO MISSISSIPPI
Quail Ridge Pr, 1988.   ○

HISTORY

Skates, John R.
MISSISSIPPI
One of a series of popular histories for each state, published as part of the bicentennial in 1976. Norton, 1979.   ○

Novels

Brown, Rosella
CIVIL WARS (Jackson)
A couple brought together by the civil rights movement two decades earlier find a growing distance between them that is further complicated when, as the result of an auto accident, they are bequeathed two additional children who have been raised in a racist atmosphere. Knopf, 1984.   ○

Childress, Mark
TENDER
A novel that sounds like the novelized life of Elvis Presley—''poor . . . singer who in the 1950s rises to extraordinary fame . . . eccentric Southern manager . . . drafted . . . lives out his later years overweight . . . in a drugged stupor'' and so on. (FC) Harmony Bks, 1990.   ○

Douglas, Ellen
CAN'T QUIT YOU, BABY
A white woman and her black servant, making preserves together, reveal their life stories—''powerful, poignant and wise.'' (FC) Atheneum, 1988.   ○

Faulkner, William
THE HAMLET
First in the trilogy of the Snopes saga. Following is *The Town* (1957) and *The Mansion* (1959). Random, 1964 (first published 1940).   ○

Faulkner, William
SANCTUARY
Random, 1962 (first published 1931). This, and its sequel, *Requiem for a Nun* (1951), tell the story of Temple Drake from college coed to eight years later.   ○

Faulkner, William
SARTORIS
Family saga of the Sartoris family. *Flags in the Dust* (1929) is the uncut version, extending from the Sartoris clan "to the full range of Faulkner's Yoknapatawpha social structure." *The Unvanquished* (1938) is a series of stories of the Sartoris family during the Civil War. NAL, 1983 (first published 1929).   ○

Faulkner, William
THE SOUND AND THE FURY
The disintegration of "a southern family of gentle blood." Random, 1966 (first published 1929). Other tales set in Mississippi by Faulkner, in order of publication, are: *Light in August* (1932), *Absalom, Absalom!* (1936), *Go Down Moses* (1942) (short stories), *Intruder in the Dust* (1948) and *The Portable Faulkner* (1948) (short stories).   ○

Hill, Rebecca
BLUE RISE
"A delightful story of small-town life in the South with its long-established rituals and codes of behavior." (FC) Morrow, 1983.   ○

MacDonald, John D.
BARRIER ISLAND
Bribery and chicanery involved in turning a barrier island into a national park. Knopf, 1986.   ○

Spencer, Elizabeth
THE SALT LINE
Set in a Mississippi Gulf Coast town—"one man's efforts to halt rampant commercialization" following a hurricane that levels the town, and rivalry with a former colleague over both his cause and the colleague's wife. (FC) Doubleday, 1984. Also *The Face at the Back Door* (1956), about a new county sheriff and the changing pattern of race relations, *Fire in the Morning* (1948) and *The Stories of Elizabeth Spencer* (1981), with foreword by Eudora Welty.   ○

Street, James
TAP ROOTS
Family saga of the Civil War era (1858–65). Dial, 1942. Also *Oh, Promised Land* (1940), historical novel of Natchez during the period 1794–1817, and *Good-Bye My Lady* (1954) a contemporary story of a boy and his dog.   ○

Welty, Eudora
DELTA WEDDING
Story of a large southern family—"presents the essence of the deep south." HarBraceJ, 1946. Also by this distinguished writer, with a Mississippi background, are: *The Ponder Heart* (1954), *Losing Battles* (1970), *The Optimist's Daughter* (1972), *The Golden Apples* (1949).   ○

MISSOURI

*Series Guidebooks
(See Appendix 1)*

NOTE: See also Series Guides (and non-series guides) listed under United States and the Midwest. You may also find some crossover in guides and books listed under Arkansas and about the Ozarks.

Off the Beaten Path: Missouri

Background Reading

Kinney-Hanson, Sharon, ed.
ART MUSEUMS AND GALLERIES IN MISSOURI
An annotated directory. Sheba Rev, 1983. ○

Knittel, Robert
WALKING IN TOWER GROVE PARK: A VICTORIAN STROLLING PARK
Grass-Hooper, 1985.   ○

Pearson, Nathan W., Jr.
GOING TO KANSAS CITY
Reminiscences of the jazz musicians that made Kansas City a jazz center in the 1920s and '30s. U of Illinois Pr, 1987.   ○

Powers, Ron
WHITE TOWN DROWSING
This is about Mark Twain's Hannibal from the viewpoint of its TV news anchor author who grew up there, left at 17 and returned for the sesquicentennial year—"beautifully written account . . . of the author and the town coming to grips with the past and moving on." (LJ) Atl Monthly Pr, 1986.   ○

Rafferty, Milton D.
THE OZARKS OUTDOORS
See under "Arkansas."   ○

Rhodes, Richard
FARM: A YEAR IN THE LIFE OF AN AMERICAN FARMER
The monumental achievement of the independent farmer is chronicled, the result of a year spent on a central Missouri farm. S&S, 1989. Mr. Rhodes has also written an stunning book called *A Hole in the World: An American Boyhood* (1990), which recounts the shocking story of his boyhood in Missouri and the abuse he and his brother endured before being rescued.   ○

Williams, Miller, ed.
OZARK, OZARK: A HILLSIDE READER
"A rich anthology of works by writers from the Ozark Mountain region of Missouri and Arkansas . . . all from the twentieth century . . . imbued with a marvelous combination of naivete and sophistication." (BL) U of Missouri, 1981.   ○

GUIDEBOOKS

Boyer, Chris
MISSOURI PARKS GUIDE
Affordable Adventures, 1988.   ○

McMinn, Russell
ANTIQUES
A guide to Missouri's antique shops. Jockey Hollow, 1989.   ○

Stein, Shifra
DAYTRIPS FROM KANSAS CITY
Spills over into Illinois. Two Lane Pr, 1990.   ○

Weil, Tom
AMERICA'S HEARTLAND
A travel guide to the backroads of Illinois, Indiana, Iowa and Missouri. Hippocrene, 1989.   ○

Wilson, D. Ray
MISSOURI HISTORICAL TOUR GUIDE
Crossroads Comns, 1988.   ○

HISTORY

Foley, William E.
THE GENESIS OF MISSOURI
From wilderness outpost to statehood. U of Missouri Pr, 1989.   ○

Nagel, Paul C.
MISSOURI
One of a series of popular histories for each state, published as part of the bicentennial in 1976. Norton, 1977. Also U Pr of Kansas, 1988.   ○

Novels

Bellamann, Henry
KING'S ROW
The underside of small-town life in a midwestern town in the 1890s (said to be based on Fulton, Missouri). S&S, 1940.   ○

Connell, Evan S.
MRS. BRIDGE; MR. BRIDGE (Kansas City)
Set in Kansas City. Companion volumes of the marriage of a suburban couple, its everyday incidents, loneliness, and boredom of middle age—"the cumulative effect of these episodic snapshots is a discerning full-length portrait." Viking, 1959, 1969.   ○

Dew, Robb F.
THE TIME OF HER LIFE
Set in a provincial university town in Missouri—story of an unhappy marriage and

the struggle for psychological survival visited upon the children when parents split up. Morrow, 1984.   ○

Franzen, Jonathan
THE TWENTY-SEVENTH CITY
A female Bombayan is the new police chief of St. Louis, and she sets out to take control of the city. FS&G, 1988.   ○

Hearon, Shelby
A SMALL TOWN
"Wry account" of the heroine's life in Venice, Missouri, as an abused child, high school Lolita, principal's wife and trailer park adulteress. (FC) Atheneum, 1985.   ○

Kantor, MacKinlay
THE VOICE OF BUGLE ANN
Bugle Ann is a very special fox hunting dog; the plot is set in rural Missouri—"a story of primitive passions." (FC) Coward, 1935. Also *The Romance of Rosy Ridge* (1937).   ○

Lutz, John
RIDE THE LIGHTNING
Alo Nudger is a St. Louis private investigator in this mystery; the fiancée of a man condemned to death hires investigator Nudger in a desperate attempt to save him from wrongful execution. St. Martin, 1987. Also *Time Exposure* (1989), in which Nudger takes on City Hall.   ○

Shange, Ntozake
BETSEY BROWN
Three generations of black women and the life of this prosperous family in St. Louis during 1957 school desegregation. St. Martin, 1985.   ○

Twain, Mark
THE ADVENTURES OF TOM SAWYER
Classic story of boyhood adventures. U of California, 1982 (first published 1876). Also *The Adventures of Huckleberry Finn* (1883) and *Pudd'nhead Wilson* (1894).   ○

MONTANA

*Series Guidebooks
(See Appendix 1)*

NOTE: See also Series Guides (and non-series guides) listed under United States and the West.

Compass American Guide: Montana
Sierra Guide: Natural Areas of Idaho, Montana & Wyoming

Background Reading

Alt, David and Hyndman, Donald
ROADSIDE GEOLOGY OF MONTANA
One of a series of books that is wonderful to take along whether you travel by car, train or plane—to paraphrase the preface, being able to look at the landscape as you travel and (with this book) envision the forces and changes, the dynamics of the landscape you are seeing, is a real achievement of

understanding for travelers. Mountain Pr, 1986.   ○

Ambrose, Stephen E.
CRAZY HORSE AND CUSTER
"The parallel lives of two American warriors . . . curious and suggestive social history." (BRD) NAL, 1986.   ○

Bass, Rick
WINTER: A JOURNEY TO MONTANA
"Juxtaposes realistic accounts of ordinary chores . . . with stunning insights into nature and self." (NYT) HM, 1990.   ○

Beirs, William H.
TEN TOUGH TRIPS: MONTANA WRITERS AND THE WEST
Essays of literary journeys by 10 writers linked by the Montana landscape. U of Washington Pr, 1990.   ○

Doig, Ivan
**THIS HOUSE OF SKY:
LANDSCAPES OF A WESTERN
MIND**
"Extraordinary, eloquent memoir" that recreates the hardscrabble lives of the last generation of aging cowboys and ranch hands in rural Montana. (BRD) HarBraceJ, 1980. o

Howard, Joseph K.
**MONTANA HIGH WIDE AND
HANDSOME**
"Colorful, amusing, and quick-moving. . . . A history and a description of that great and beautiful and various state." First published in 1943. (BRD) U of Nebraska Pr, 1983. Also *Montana Margins* (1987), reprint of a state anthology first published in 1946.   o

Johnson, Dorothy M.
**THE BLOODY BOZEMAN: THE
PERILOUS TRAIL TO
MONTANA'S GOLD**
Mountain Pr, 1987 (first published 1971). o

Johnson, Dorothy M.
**WHEN YOU AND I WERE YOUNG
WHITEFISH**
Collection of stories of the author's childhood at the turn of the century—"delightful . . . social and personal history" of Whitefish, a western Montana town. (BL) Mountain Pr, 1982.   o

Klinkenborg, Verlyn
MAKING HAY
See entry under Iowa.   o

Lang, William L. and Myers, Rex C.
**MONTANA, OUR LAND AND
PEOPLE**
Pruett, 1989.   o

Murray, Robert A.
THE BOZEMAN TRAIL
The trail today for travelers and a history of military and pioneer days along this historic route—"outstanding work . . . exceptional photos and maps." (BL) Pruett, 1988.   o

Rudner, Ruth
**GREETINGS FROM WISDOM,
MONTANA**
An account of working and living in Montana, and the author's transformation from "superior Easterner to relaxed, if not gregarious, Westerner." (PW) Fulcrum, 1989.   o

Simpson, Ross W.
**THE FIRES OF '88: YELLOWSTONE
PARK AND MONTANA IN
FLAMES**
See under Wyoming. American Geo, 1989.
        o

Toole, K. Ross
**MONTANA: AN UNCOMMON
LAND**
Reprint of a book first published in 1957— "fascinating tale" of Montana's history, "one which the native author has told with insight and understanding." (BRD) U of Oklahoma Pr, 1984.   o

GUIDEBOOKS

Miller, Donald C.
GHOST TOWNS OF MONTANA
Pruett, 1982.   o

Newby, Rick
**GREAT ESCAPES: MONTANA
STATE PARKS**
Falcon Pr Mt, 1988.   o

Van West, Carroll
**A TRAVELER'S COMPANION TO
MONTANA HISTORY**
Mt Hist Soc, 1986.   o

Yuill, Clifford D., Sr., and Ellen R.
MONTANA'S HISTORIC HOMES
Vis Yuill Ent, 1986.   o

HISTORY

Malone, Michael P. and Roeder,
    Richard B.
**MONTANA: A HISTORY OF TWO
CENTURIES**
U of Washington Pr, 1976.   o

Spence, Clark C.
MONTANA
One of a series of popular histories for each state, published as part of the bicentennial in 1976. Norton, 1978. ○

Novels

Blew, Mary C.
ALL BUT THE WALTZ: ESSAYS ON A MONTANA FAMILY
"Haunting memoir of life on the high Montana plains . . . sadness, fierce pride and an unforgettable clarity of their struggle to survive drought, disaster and economic depression." It is a hundred-year history of the author's family. (NYT) Viking, 1992. ○

Dallas, Sandra
BUSTER MIDNIGHT'S CAFE
The narrator has shared childhood and adolescence in Butte with movie star Marion and decides to set the record straight in a novelized version of the events. "Every detail of 1930s and '40s Butte, Montana, rings true." (LJ) Random, 1990. ○

Doig, Ivan
RIDE WITH ME, MARIAH MONTANA
The "crown volume" of the McCaskill family trilogy in which "Montana . . . is virtually another character." Began with *English Creek* (1984), which takes place in the summer of 1939 and introduces the family; *Dancing at the Rascal Fair* (1987) brings to life the ancestors of the people in *English Creek*, when they arrive in Montana, and covers the period up to 1919. In this last book, it is the centennial of Montana's statehood, 1989, a blend of "travelogue, family drama, history and newspaper lore." (PW) Macmillan, 1990. ○

Dorris, Michael
A YELLOW RAFT IN BLUE WATER
"Three generations of Indian women offer varying perspectives of their lives on a Montana reservation," in successive narratives. (BRD) Holt, 1987. ○

Farris, Jack
ME AND GALLAGHER
Setting is Virginia City, Montana, in 1863. The story of a frontier man with "golden-rule righteousness" who helps form a vigilance committee to deal with a county sheriff who is victimizing Montana territory citizens. (FC) S&S, 1982. ○

Ford, Richard
WILDLIFE
A 16-year-old boy confronts human frailties in his parents—the author's landscape, his characters . . . the elegance of his declarative prose . . . brings the early Hemingway to mind." (FC) Atl Monthly Pr, 1990. ○

Guthrie, A.B.
ARFIVE
Set in a small Montana town at the beginning of the twentieth century. Houghton, 1971. A sequel with some of the same characters is *The Last Valley* (1975) which covers the period 1920–40, when the town is becoming beset with some of the common contemporary problems. ○

Guthrie, A.B.
PLAYING CATCH-UP
"Sensitive and well-written"—a novel about rape and murder in Montana. (FC) HM, 1985. Also *These Thousand Hills* (1956), and *No Second Wind* (1980). ○

McGuane, Thomas
KEEP THE CHANGE
"A lost soul" trying to find himself in Key West, New York City and finally back in Montana—"the dialogue is often uproariously funny . . . supporting cast is thoroughly engaging." (BL) HM, 1989. Also *Nobody's Angel* (1981). ○

MacLean, Norman
A RIVER RUNS THROUGH IT
A novella, first published in *A River Runs Through It, and Other Stories* in 1976. The author and his brother ("one of the West's greatest fly fishermen") go fishing on the Big Blackfoot River—"unique and marvelous" (FC) U of Chicago Pr, 1983. ○

Savage, Thomas
**THE CORNER OF RIFE AND
PACIFIC**
A family saga covering the period 1890–
1920. Morrow, 1988.   ○

Svee, Gary D.
INCIDENT AT PISHKIN CREEK
A Montana rancher must convince his mail-
order bride to stay—"wonderful characters
and strikingly beautiful descriptions of the
Montana prairie." (FC) Walker, 1989.   ○

Taylor, Robert L.
A ROARING IN THE WIND
"Being a history of Alder Gulch, Montana,
in its great and its shameful days." (FC)
Putnam Pub Group, 1978.   ○

Welch, James
FOOLS CROW
Traditions crumble amongst the Pikunis
branch of the Blackfoot Indians in post-Civil
War Montana, as the invasion of the whites
(Napikwans) inevitably exerts its influence.
Viking, 1986. Also *The Indian Lawyer* (1990),
about an Indian who has fought his way to
the top and is now being wooed to run for
Congress. Two earlier novels are *Winter in
the Blood* (1974) and *The Death of Jim Loney*
(1979).   ○

NEBRASKA

*Series Guidebooks
(See Appendix 1)*

NOTE: See also Series Guides (and non-
series guides) listed under United States and
the Midwest.

Background Reading

Faulkner, Virginia, ed.
ROUNDUP: A NEBRASKA READER
U of Nebraska, 1975.   ○

Janovy, John R.
KEITH COUNTRY JOURNAL
"A very different look at the wonders of
nature, fascinating, well written, and enlightening"—west central Nebraska, including the sand hills, the Platte rivers, lakes,
bluffs, canyons, marshes and creeks. St.
Martin, 1980. Also *Back in Keith County*
(1983).   ○

Luebke, Frederick C., ed.
**A HARMONY OF THE ARTS: THE
NEBRASKA STATE CAPITOL**
Nebraska's capitol building, built in 1932,
can be seen for miles on the Plains—this
book tells, in words and illustrations, about

the architectural achievement, and the artists involved in its creation. U of Nebraska
Pr, 1990.   ○

Welsch, Roger
**IT'S NOT THE END OF THE EARTH
BUT YOU CAN SEE IT FROM
HERE**
Tales of the Great Plains—a collection of
essays, stories, monologues by the CBS cor-
respondent who contributes regularly to CBS
Sunday morning program of news and life
in the United States. "Celebrates small-town
America's leisurely pace, human scale" and
ordinary people. (BL) Random, 1990.   ○

GUIDEBOOKS

Boye, Alan
**THE COMPLETE ROADSIDE GUIDE
TO NEBRASKA**
Saltillo Pr, 1989.   ○

Wilson, D. Ray
**NEBRASKA HISTORICAL TOUR
GUIDE**
Crossroads Commns, 1988.   ○

HISTORY

Creigh, Dorothy W.
NEBRASKA
One of a series of popular histories for each state, published as part of the bicentennial in 1976. Norton, 1977. Also *Where Dreams Grow* (1990), reprint of the 1980 edition. ○

Olson, James C.
HISTORY OF NEBRASKA
U of Nebraska Pr, 1966.   ○

Novels

Cather, Willa
O PIONEERS!
A classic novel of Swedish immigrants in Nebraska in the 1880s, by one of America's leading writers, and winner of a Pulitzer Prize. Houghton, 1929 (first published 1913). Other novels by Cather with a Nebraska setting are: *My Antonia* (1918), *One of Ours* (1922), and *A Lost Lady* (1923).   ○

Chehak, Susan T.
THE STORY OF ANNIE D.
Wiser River, Nebraska—its past, Annie's friends, her love affair, the town's unsolved murders. HM, 1989.   ○

Hansen, Ron
NEBRASKA: STORIES
"Belongs in the best tradition of truly American literature." (FC) Atl Monthly Pr, 1989.   ○

Harrison, Jim
DALVA
"Lyrical and atmospheric book" about Dalva's reconciliation with the things that have happened to her, an eccentric family, wasted years and return to her Midwestern roots. (FC) Dutton, 1988.   ○

Morris, Wright
PLAINS SONG
Saga of farm life from 1900 to the 1970s— "the textures of farm life on the plains are beautifully rendered. Animals . . . contribute to the novel's quiet humor." (FC) Har-Row, 1980. Also *Ceremony in Lone Tree* (1960), about the Scanlon family's reunion in a Nebraska ghost town where a 90-year-old Scanlon is the only resident.   ○

Sandoz, Mari
MISS MORISSA, DOCTOR OF THE GOLD TRAIL
Story of a woman doctor on the Nebraska frontier in the 1870s. Hastings, 1975 (first published 1955).   ○

Wiltse, David
HOME AGAIN
"Sensitive and interesting . . . with, incidentally, a good deal of action"—an FBI agent, tired of the violence he encounters in his work, returns to his Nebraska hometown with his wife and adolescent son. Ultimately the father must involve himself in finding the murderer of two young women and a boyhood friend. (FC) Macmillan, 1986.   ○

NEVADA

Series Guidebooks

NOTE: See also Series Guides (and non-series guides) listed under United States and the West.

Compass American Guide: Las Vegas
Fodor: Las Vegas
Frommer: Nevada
Let's Go: California & Hawaii (includes Reno, Las Vegas, Tahoe, and Baja)

Moon Handbook: Nevada
Sierra Guide: Natural Areas of New Mexico, Arizona & Nevada

Background Reading

Alvarez, A.
THE BIGGEST GAME IN TOWN
Sketches of professional poker players at the World Series of Poker held annually at the

Horseshoe Casino in Las Vegas; some sketches originally appeared in the *New Yorker*—"this field guide is the equivalent of an inside straight." (BRD) Houghton, 1985.   ○

Lewis, Oscar
SILVER KINGS

The lives and times of Mackay, Fair, Flood and O'Brien, lords of the Comstock Lode. U of Nevada Pr, 1986.   ○

Marshall, Howard W. and Ahlborn, Richard E.
BUCKAROOS IN PARADISE

The workings of a modern ranch in Paradise, Nevada—people, tools and artifacts. U of Nebraska, 1981.   ○

Shepperson, Wilbur S., ed.
EAST OF EDEN, WEST OF ZION

Essays on Nevada. U of Nevada Pr, 1989.   ○

Toll, David W.
THE COMPLEAT NEVADA TRAVELER

Historical background, perceptive observations beyond the purely practical travel guide. Practical information on points of interest for the entire state with emphasis on the countryside rather than on Las Vegas. Gold Hill, 1985.   ○

GUIDEBOOKS

Castleman, Deke
NEVADA HANDBOOK

A guide to casinos and desert oases. U of Nevada Pr, 1991.   ○

Edwards, Mary Jane and Greg
BET ON IT!: THE ULTIMATE GUIDE TO NEVADA

Mustang, 1991.   ○

Lambert, Florin
NEVADA GHOST TOWNS

Nevada Pubns, 1986.   ○

Meyer, Michael and Muir, Sarah
DESTINATION SOUTHWEST

A guide to retiring and wintering in Arizona, New Mexico, Nevada. Oryx Pr, 1990.   ○

HISTORY

Elliott, Russell R. and Rowley, William D.
HISTORY OF NEVADA

U of Nebraska Pr, 1987.   ○

Laxalt, Robert
NEVADA

One of a series of popular histories for each state, published as part of the bicentennial in 1976. Norton, 1977.   ○

Novels

Clark, Walter Van Tilburg
THE OXBOW INCIDENT

Nevada in 1885 is the setting and this is a story, based on a true incident, of a group of citizens who form an illegal posse that lynches some cattle rustlers for the murder of one of their members. Random, 1940. Also *The Track of the Cat* (1949).   ○

Cummings, Jack
THE ROUGH RIDER

A struggle over the governorship between a ranch owner and the top "hand" who saved his life at San Juan Hill—"a bang-up surprise finish." (FC) Walker, 1988.   ○

Demaris, Ovid
THE VEGAS LEGACY

Plot traces the life of a potential vice-presidential nominee with Las Vegas background and atmosphere, and a Nevada-style Republican convention. Delacorte Pr, 1983.   ○

Erdman, Paul E.
THE PALACE

The economist author gives readers an education in the machinations of investment banking, casinos and money laundering through the novel's antihero, Danny Lehman. Doubleday, 1988.   ○

Goldman, William
HEAT
Violence and explicit sex in an action novel of an ex-Marine freelance bodyguard who looks like tennis player Pancho Gonzales. Warner Bks, 1985.   ○

Laxalt, Robert
THE BASQUE HOTEL
"Short, beautifully written, semi-autobiographical novel" of growing up in Carson City where his father, formerly a Basque sheep rancher, runs a small hotel during Prohibition and the Depression—"a small gem . . . of a childhood tranquilly recollected." (BRD) U of Nevada Pr, 1989.   ○

McMurtry, Larry
THE DESERT ROSE
The decline of a topless dancer approaching thirty-nine as her teenage daughter becomes her contender for the title of 'the best legs in Las Vegas'—"touching, low-key, convincing novel." (FC) S&S, 1983.   ○

Murray, William
WHEN THE FAT MAN SINGS
The casinos of Las Vegas, opera houses of New York, and racetracks are the settings for a mystery featuring Shifty Anderson, who is hired to act as a lucky charm for a world-famous tenor who is also a compulsive gambler. Bantam, 1987.   ○

Petievich, Gerald
SHAKEDOWN
The plot pits an F.B.I. agent against organized crime and a Las Vegas mobster; by an author who "knows how to milk every character and plot point for maximum suspense." (FC) S&S, 1988.   ○

Roderus, Frank
FINDING NEVADA
The plot revolves around an inherited, unprofitable mine, which turns up other hostile claimants. Doubleday, 1985.   ○

NEW HAMPSHIRE

Series Guidebooks
(See Appendix 1)

NOTE: See Series Guides (and non-series guides) listed under United States and the East and the East/New England.

Background Reading

Duncan, Dayton
GRASS ROOTS: ONE YEAR IN THE LIFE OF THE NEW HAMPSHIRE PRIMARY
The author follows a group of campaign workers in Cheshire County as they work to have their respective candidates win the New Hampshire primary in 1988—"a rare, warmhearted look at the electoral process" in the state that seems to be requisite to winning the White House. (PW) Viking, 1991.   ○

Gilmore, Robert C.
NEW HAMPSHIRE LITERATURE: A SAMPLER
U Pr of New England, 1981.   ○

Hall, Donald
HERE AT EAGLE POND
Essays by New Hampshire's poet laureate, Donald Hall, of his childhood and family in Wilmot—"captures the essence of New England, past and present," touching on aspects of New Hampshire life with a few jabs at Vermont. (PW) Ticknor & Fields, 1990. Also *Seasons at Eagle Pond* (1987), and *String Too Short to Be Saved* (1979), first published in 1962, recalls summers on the farm.   ○

Hill, Ralph Nading
YANKEE KINGDOM: VERMONT & NEW HAMPSHIRE
Lively, informal, entertaining social history beginning with coastal settlements in the

17th century—tells of the rivalry between the two states over the years and their differences and similarities rooted in a common heritage. Countryman, 1984.   ○

Keyes, Donald
THE WHITE MOUNTAINS: PLACE AND PERCEPTIONS
U Pr of New England, 1980.   ○

Kumin, Maxine
IN DEEP: COUNTRY ESSAYS
Living on a New Hampshire hill farm, the author has won a Pulitzer Prize for her poetry—"her country essays are captivating." (PW) Viking, 1987.   ○

Pike, Robert E.
SPIKED BOOTS
See entry under Maine.   ○

Tolman, Newton F.
NORTH OF MONADNOCK
A single year in Nelson, New Hampshire—pieces that originally appeared in *Atlantic Monthly* and local journals—"written in sophisticated crackerbarrel style." (BRD) Bauhan, 1978. Also *Our Loons Are Always Laughing* (1963).   ○

Van Diver, Bradford B.
ROADSIDE GEOLOGY OF VERMONT & NEW HAMPSHIRE
One of a series of books that is wonderful to take along in the car—to paraphrase the preface, being able to look at the landscape as you travel and (with this book) envision the forces and changes, the dynamics of the landscape you are seeing, is a real achievement of understanding for travelers. Mountain Pr, 1987.   ○

GUIDEBOOKS

Bolnick, Bruce R. and Doreen
WATERFALLS OF THE WHITE MOUNTAINS
Alerts travelers to waterfalls they can add to their itinerary as they drive through the state; how to reach them, difficulty, etc. Countryman, 1990.   ○

Frost, Ed and Roon
COAST GUIDE
Seabrook, New Hampshire, to Freeport, Maine. Glove Compart Bks, 1987.   ○

McMinn, Russell
ANTIQUES
A guide to New Hampshire antique shops. Jockey Hollow, 1989.   ○

Sloan, Bruce
NEW HAMPSHIRE PARKLANDS
A guide to public parklands in the Granite State. P E Randall Pub, 1985.   ○

Tree, Christina
NEW HAMPSHIRE: AN EXPLORER'S GUIDE
One of a series of first-rate guides. See also under Maine and Massachusetts.   ○

HISTORY

Jager, Ronald and Grace
NEW HAMPSHIRE
A history (illustrated) of the Granite State. Windsor, 1983.   ○

Morison, E.F.
NEW HAMPSHIRE
One of a series of popular histories for each state, published as part of the bicentennial in 1976. Norton, 1976.   ○

Novels

Banks, Russell
AFFLICTION
Tragic saga of an older brother's self-destruction, narrated by a bookish history teacher. Har-Row, 1989. Also, *Trailerpark* (1981).   ○

Benet, Stephen Vincent
THE DEVIL AND DANIEL WEBSTER
A twentieth-century version of the Faust legend—"a poor New Hampshire farmer, the devil in a new guise, and New Hampshire's famous native son, Daniel Webster." (FC) Rinehart, 1937.   ○

Cannon, Le Grand
LOOK TO THE MOUNTAIN
Novel of a young bride and groom who left the settlements to pioneer in the New

Hampshire Grants, 1769–77—"simple, vivid and beautiful . . . partly idyl . . . partly realistic adventure story." (BRD) Holt, 1942.   ◌

Hebert, Ernest
LIVE FREE OR DIE
The fifth and final volume of a series of novels set in the fictional town of Derby ("no postcard-perfect town"), in the fictional county of Tuckerman, that has been compared to Faulkner's Yoknapatawpha County in Mississippi. *The New York Times* says of *Live Free or Die:* "Creates a satisfyingly complete environment between hard covers . . . imbued with a palpable spirit of place." The plot of this final volume centers on a tragic Romeo and Juliet-like love affair between a member of the upper crust and the son of the main character in *Dogs of March* (1979), which began the series. Titles in between are: *Little More Than Kin* (1982), *Whisper My Name* (1985) and *The Passion of Estelle Jordan* (1987).   ◌

Houston, James
GHOST FOX
"Stunning frontier novel" of the French and Indian Wars in the eighteenth century. (FC) HarBraceJ, 1977.   ◌

Irving, John
A PRAYER FOR OWEN MEANY
Set in a fictional town in New Hampshire (Exeter is the guess)—"a fable of political predestination" in which the narrator accidentally kills his mother and because of Owen Meany becomes a Christian. (FC) Morrow, 1989.   ◌

Knowles, John
PEACE BREAKS OUT
Set in a boys' school in New Hampshire in 1945. A group of boys viciously turn on a classmate. HR&W, 1981. Also *A Separate Peace* (1960).   ◌

MacDougall, Ruth D.
THE FLOWERS OF THE FOREST
Stark rural life in turn-of-the-century New Hampshire. Atheneum, 1981. Also *Aunt Pleasantine* (1978).   ◌

Sherman, Steve
THE MAPLE SUGAR MURDERS
    (Lyme)
Romance and mystery—a Lyme real estate agent's body is found while an ex-policeman from Boston collects maple sugar. Walker, 1987.   ◌

Tolman, F.B.
MORE SPIT THAN POLISH AT
    TOLMAN POND (Nelson)
The setting is a boarding house at Tolman Pond near Nelson—the plot concerns "the bevy of curious and eccentric characters who populate this weedy household." (PW) Yankee Bks, 1987.   ◌

Weesner, Theodore
THE TRUE DETECTIVE (Portsmouth)
The sex-related murder of a 12-year-old as seen through the eyes of the policeman in charge of the case, the boy's mother, his brother and the pathetic and lonely murderer—"sometimes so real it makes the heart pound." (FC) Summit, 1987.   ◌

Williams, Thomas
THE FOLLOWED MAN
Penetrating study of life in a small town in northern New Hampshire—the plot is about a writer, living in Paris after World War II, called back home because of his brother's illness. Marek, 1978. Also *Whipple's Castle* (1969), chronicle of a Dartmouth student, crippled in an auto accident, from the 1930s to the Korean War.   ◌

Williams, Thomas
MOON PINNACE
A coming-of-age novel of a young veteran, just after World War II, who returns to the home in New Hampshire provided by his mother and stepfather. He falls in love with a neighbor girl, parts and sets off to find his absent father on a cross-country motorcycle trip—"superb on unsettled postwar America." (BRD) Doubleday, 1986. Also *Town Burning* (1987).   ◌

NEW JERSEY

Series Guidebooks

NOTE: See also Series Guides (and non-series guides) listed under United States and the East and the Middle Atlantic States.

Off the Beaten Path: New Jersey
Frommer:

Background Reading

Beck, Henry C.
THE ROADS OF HOME: LANES & LEGENDS OF NEW JERSEY

Rutgers U Pr, 1983. Also *Tales and Towns of Northern New Jersey* (1983), *The Jersey Midlands* (1984), *Forgotten Towns of Southern New Jersey* and *More Forgotten Towns of Southern New Jersey* (1984). o

Bernard, April and Sante, Luc
NEW JERSEY: AN AMERICAN PORTRAIT

Taylor Pub, 1986. o

Cunningham, John T.
THIS IS NEW JERSEY

County by county guide, including the shore area—history, description, and travel. Rutgers U Pr, 1983. o

Funnell, Charles E.
BY THE BEAUTIFUL SEA

"The rise and high times of that great American resort, Atlantic City. . . . Atlantic City in its prime [1890s] . . . depicted in all of its variety and vitality." (BRD) Rutgers U Pr, 1983 (first published 1975). o

Gillespie, Angus K. and Rockland, Michael A.
LOOKING FOR AMERICA ON THE NEW JERSEY TURNPIKE

"Funny, engagingly anecdotal, yet well researched and organized"—traces people's changing attitudes toward the turnpike, including that of artists such as Ginsberg and Springsteen who have romanticized the road. Despite the scorn and humor with which it has been sometimes viewed, it may be, the authors say, America's "most apt symbol . . . functionalism gone awry." (LJ) Rutgers U Pr, 1989. o

McPhee, John
THE PINE BARRENS

"The special atmosphere of the Barrens," a unique wilderness area in the center of New Jersey; a new edition with photographs. (BRD) FS&G, 1981 (first published 1968). o

Moonsammy, Rita Z., and others
PINELANDS FOLKLIFE

"Informal survey of a thriving folk culture"—in the area of pine forests along the coast, which has given rise to regional crafts and occupations and has given the people a separate identity. (BL) Rutgers U Pr, 1987. o

Sternlieb, George and Hughes, James
THE ATLANTIC CITY GAMBLE

Two Rutgers professors examine the results and consequences of legalized casino gambling in Atlantic City. Harvard U Pr, 1983. o

GUIDEBOOKS

Cudworth, Marsha
SELF-GUIDED ARCHITECTURAL TOURS, CAPE MAY

Lady Raspberry, 1985. o

Santelli, Robert
THE JERSEY SHORE: A TRAVEL & PLEASURE GUIDE

"The ultimate guide . . . everything from beaches and boardwalks to blueberry farms and bed and breakfasts." It is organized into nine regions from north (Sandy Hook) to south (Cape May). (Publisher) Globe Pequot, 1986. o

Zatz, Arline
NEW JERSEY'S SPECIAL PLACES
Scenic, historic and cultural treasures in the Garden State, organized into 52 outings—one for each week of the year—working farms, gardens, woods, museums, unusual villages, etc. Countryman, 1990.   o

HISTORY

Fleming, Thomas J.
NEW JERSEY
One of a series of popular histories for each state, published as part of the bicentennial in 1976. Norton, 1984.   o

Kross, Peter
NEW JERSEY HISTORY
Mid Atlantic, 1987.   o

Novels

Algren, Nelson
THE DEVIL'S STOCKING
"The story is built up around a black boxer from New Jersey . . . convicted of murder . . . released and convicted again." (FC) Arbor Hse, 1983.   o

Calisher, Hortense
THE BOBBY-SOXER
"Labyrinthine" novel of the complicated past and twisted secrets of a family living in a New Jersey town. (FC) Doubleday, 1986.   o

Clark, Mary Higgins
THE CRADLE WILL FALL
A can't-put-it-down spine tingler involving a young woman assistant prosecutor who believes she's seen a body loaded into a car, while she was in the hospital recovering from a car accident. S&S, 1980.   o

Kaminsky, Stuart M.
SMART MOVES
It is 1942 at Princeton, as Albert Einstein enlists the aid of investigator Toby Peters to find out who is trying to brand him a traitor, and to protect him from a Nazi group; with a climax that includes both Einstein and Paul Robeson. St. Martin, 1986.   o

Krist, Gary
THE GARDEN STATE
Collection of eight stories with a suburban setting of northern New Jersey "near Route 4 . . . knows his territory . . . a cultural ambiance that nourishes smiles of recognition." (PW) Random, 1989.   o

Leonard, Elmore
GLITZ
Alternates between Atlantic City and Puerto Rico—the world of casino gambling with a "steady flow of intrigue and action." (FC) Arbor Hse, 1985.   o

Updike, John
THE POORHOUSE FAIR
A "handful of marvelously eccentric people" in a New Jersey poorhouse. (FC) Knopf, 1977 (first published 1959).   o

Wolff, Geoffrey
THE FINAL CLUB
About the initiation of Nathaniel Clay, a half-Jewish public high school graduate, in the Princeton class of '60, and his next 20 years as a Princeton alumnus. Does for Princeton "what Waugh did for Oxbridge . . . impart a sense of real drama to the social rites of young men and young women too fortunate to know all clubs are fragile." (FC) Knopf, 1990.   o

NEW MEXICO

Series Guidebooks (See Appendix 1)

NOTE: See also Series Guides (and non-

series guides) listed under United States and the West and the West/the Southwest.

Compass American Guide: New Mexico

Fodor: New Mexico
Frommer: Santa Fe, Taos and Albuquerque
Sierra Guide: Natural Areas of New Mexico, Arizona & Nevada

Background Reading

Chronic, Halka
ROADSIDE GEOLOGY

One of a series of books that is wonderful to take along in the car—to paraphrase the preface, being able to look at the landscape as you travel and (with this book) envision the forces and changes, the dynamics of the landscape you are seeing, is a real achievement of understanding for travelers. Mountain Pr, 1987.   ○

Fugate, Francis
ROADSIDE HISTORY OF NEW MEXICO

A history to take along with you and perhaps read aloud to companions as you drive the state's highways. One of a unique series, written in lively narrative style by authors who know how to bring the past alive. It's like having a knowledgeable friend along who has lived in the state for years. Mountain Pr, 1989.   ○

Gibson, Arrel
THE SANTA FE AND TAOS COLONIES

History of the cultural renaissance of these two interesting places before and after the "artistic invasion," which included (among many others) D.H. Lawrence and Georgia O'Keeffe. (BL) U of Oklahoma Pr, 1983. ○

Hillerman, Tony
THE GREAT TAOS BANK ROBBERY—AND OTHER INDIAN COUNTRY AFFAIRS

Essays, first published in 1973, by a leading novelist who has written many highly regarded mysteries set in New Mexico (see below). U of New Mexico Pr, 1980.   ○

Hillerman, Tony, ed.
SPELL OF NEW MEXICO

Essays by writers of the 20th century, first published in 1976. U of New Mexico, 1984.

Also *Hillerman Country* (1991) a photographic journey.   ○

Maurer, Stephen G.
SOLITUDE AND SUNSHINE

Images of a Grand Canyon childhood. Pruett, 1983.   ○

Nichols, John
THE LAST BEAUTIFUL DAYS OF AUTUMN

A "paean to Taos and the surrounding country" by a novelist. "An extraordinary personal essay about one of the most stunning sections of the country." (LJ) HR&W, 1982. Also *If Mountains Die: A New Mexico Memoir* (1979).   ○

Nichols, John
ON THE MESA

"Beautifully written appreciation" of the sagebrush plain in northwestern New Mexico, through both its tranquil season and season of explosive growth. (PW) Peregrine Smith, 1986.   ○

Simmons, Marc
RANCHERS, RAMBLERS AND RENEGADES

True tales of territorial New Mexico. Ancient City Pr, 1984.   ○

Sinclair, John
COWBOY RIDING COUNTRY

Reminiscences of years as a young cowpoke in the early 1900s in the El Capitan Mountains. U of New Mexico, 1982. Also *New Mexico: The Shining Land* (1983).   ○

GUIDEBOOKS

Chilton, Lance and others
NEW MEXICO: A NEW GUIDE TO THE COLORFUL STATE

A rewritten version of the classic WPA guidebooks written in the 1930s and '40s. (See Appendix 1.)   ○

Hilleson, K.
ROUTE SIXTY-SIX REVISITED

A wanderer's guide to New Mexico, from Albuquerque to the Arizona border. Nakii Ent, 1988.   ○

Jamison, Bill
THE INSIDER'S GUIDE TO SANTA FE
Delves into local history and heritage, historic streets, mountain trails, to ancient Taos and old Spanish villages. Fiestas, festivals, art galleries, exhibits, shops, nightlife, where to eat, hotels and motels—all are covered. Harvard Common Pr, 1987. ◦

Landau, Carl and Katie
FESTIVALS OF THE SOUTHWEST
Your guided tour to festivals in Arizona and New Mexico. Landau Comns, 1989. ◦

McCaig & Boyce
NEW MEXICO STATE PARKS
Affordable Adventures, 1989. ◦

Mays, Buddy
INDIAN VILLAGES OF THE SOUTHWEST
Chronicle, 1985. ◦

Meyer, Michael and Muir, Sarah
DESTINATION SOUTHWEST
A guide to retiring and wintering in Arizona, New Mexico and Nevada. Oryx Pr, 1990. ◦

Sheck, Ree, ed.
EXPLORE NEW MEXICO: INSIDER'S GUIDE
Tours to favorite spots for locals and out-of-staters; arranged by region, with major cities in each region and their nearby attractions. New Mexico Magazine, 1989. ◦

Simmons, Marc
FOLLOWING THE SANTA FE TRAIL: A GUIDE FOR MODERN TRAVELERS
Ancient City Pr, 1986. ◦

Varney, Philip
NEW MEXICO'S BEST GHOST TOWNS: A PRACTICAL GUIDE
U of New Mexico Pr, 1987. ◦

Young, John V.
THE STATE PARKS OF NEW MEXICO
U of New Mexico Pr, 1984. ◦

HISTORY

Ellis, Richard N., ed.
NEW MEXICO PAST AND PRESENT
A historical reader. U of New Mexico Pr, 1971. ◦

Simmons, Marc
NEW MEXICO
One of a series of popular histories for each state, published as part of the bicentennial in 1976. Norton, 1977. Also *New Mexico: An Interpretive History* (1988). ◦

Sonnichsen, C.L.
TULAROSA: LAST OF THE FRONTIER WEST
Definitive and lively history of the area. U of New Mexico Pr, 1980. ◦

Novels

Bradford, Richard
SO FAR FROM HEAVEN
A group of Mexicans in the United States attempt to claim federal land. Lippincott, 1973. Also *Red Sky at Morning* (1968), about life in the Southwest during World War II. ◦

Butler, Robert O.
COUNTRYMEN OF BONES
Set in 1945, a time-is-running-out story involving an archaeologist and a member of Oppenheimer's team working on the atomic bomb. Horizon, 1983. ◦

Cather, Willa
DEATH COMES FOR THE ARCHBISHOP
A classic by one of America's leading writers—based on the lives of two French clerics who won the Southwest for the Catholic Church in the period of the mid-1800s. Modern Lib, 1984 (first published 1927). ◦

Clarke, Richard
THE COPPER DUST HILLS
"Vivid depiction of animal life and the beauty of the west enhance this engrossing tale" of a cowhand's determination to avenge his brother's hanging. (FC) Walker, 1983.   ○

Hillerman, Tony
A THIEF OF TIME
Hillerman is the author of a series of mysteries in which Lt. Joe Leaphorn and Officer Jim Chee of the Navaho Tribal Police do the detective work. "The complex relationship between Leaphorn and Chee . . . the rich view of Navaho culture . . . landscape that shimmers with realism . . . combines P.D. James' taut, precise narrative style with a consistently sensitive portrayal of the native American experience." (BL) Har-Row, 1990. Other titles in the series include *Blessing Way* (1970), *Dance Hall of the Dead* (1973), *Listening Woman* (1978), *People of Darkness* (1980), *Dark Wind* (1982), *The Ghostway* (1985), *Skinwalkers* (1987), *Talking God* (1989), *Coyote Waits* (1990).   ○

Horgan, Paul
THE THIN MOUNTAIN AIR
Setting is the early 1920s as a young man leaves college to accompany his father to Albuquerque to a tuberculosis ranch—"sense of place is palpable and magical." (BRD) FS&G, 1977. Also *Far from Cibola* (1938) and *The Common Heart* in *Mountain Standard Time* (1942).   ○

Johnston, Velda
SHADOW BEHIND THE CURTAIN
A wealthy New Yorker discovers her real parenthood and goes to New Mexico to explore the mystery of her roots. Dodd, 1985.   ○

Kunetka, James
SHADOW MAN
A high-tech thriller; a scientist working on Star Wars at the Los Alamos Laboratory is murdered. It looks like a ritual Indian murder, but the truth proves to be far more complex—"distinguished by easy familiarity with scientific and military matters . . . colorful southwestern setting." (BL) Warner Bks, 1988.   ○

Nichols, John
THE MILAGRO BEANFIELD WAR
"A bawdy, slangy, modern proletarian novel" of Chicanos vs. land developers. (FC) HR&W, 1974. Also *The Magic Journey* (1978), and *American Blood* (1987).   ○

Parker, F.M.
THE SHADOW MAN
"Superbly written and detailed" novel of the New Mexico territory in the 1840s and of Tamarron who marries the daughter of a landholding family and, with a Comanche brave, sets out to take revenge after the family is destroyed by the American plans to take the territory by force. (PW) NAL, 1988.   ○

Smith, Martin Cruz
STALLION GATE
"A monumental thriller in which . . . Oppenheimer, Edward Teller, General Leslie Groves and other historic figures live again." (FC) Random, 1986.   ○

Van Gieson, Judith
THE OTHER SIDE OF DEATH
Death in an Indian cove near Santa Fe—"the rich atmosphere of north New Mexico and some offbeat and intriguing characters . . . give a sharp and appealing edge." (PW) HarperCollins, 1991.   ○

NEW YORK

Series Guidebooks
(See Appendix 1)

NOTE: See also Series Guides (and non-series guides) listed under United States and

the East and the East/the Middle Atlantic
States.

Access: New York
American Express Pocket Guide: New York
  City
Baedeker: New York City
Berlitz: New York
Blue Guide: New York City
Cadogan Guide: New York
Crown Insider's Guide: New York City and
  State
Fodor: New York City; Pocket Guide to
  New York City; Sunday in New York;
  New York State
Frommer: New York City; New York
Gault/Milau: Best of New York
Insight: New York State
Let's Go: New York City
Michael's Guide: New York City
Michelin: New York City
Off the Beaten Path: New York
Real Guide: New York

Background Reading

NOTE: For New York State, background
books and guides are included under Background Reading. See also New York City/
Guidebooks for guides that use the city as a
base for trips into surrounding areas of New
York State and Long Island.

Adams, Arthur Gray
**THE HUDSON RIVER IN
  LITERATURE: AN ANTHOLOGY**
Fordham, 1988.   ○

Boyce, Chris and McCaig, Barbara
NEW YORK PARKS GUIDE
Affordable Adventures, 1988.   ○

Carmer, Carl
**THE TAVERN LAMPS ARE
  BURNING**
A literary journey through six regions and
four centuries of New York State. McKay,
1964. Also *Listen For a Lonesome Drum* (1936)—
historical sketches, folklore and tall stories—
and *The Hudson* (1939).   ○

Champlin, Charles
**BACK THERE WHERE THE PAST
  WAS: A SMALL TOWN
  BOYHOOD**
"Touchingly poignant recollection of grow-
ing up in Hammondsport, a small town in
Western New York . . . his evocation of
place and time resonates far beyond a little
town . . . have a universal quality." (BL)
Syracuse U Pr, 1989.   ○

Chilberg, Joe and Baber, Bob
NEW YORK WINE COUNTRY
Fifty-five wineries arranged by district (Long
Island, Finger Lakes, etc.), with descriptions
of the wineries, what they produce, names
and addresses. North Country Bks, 1986.
                                             ○

Dumbleton, Susanne and Older, Anne
IN AND AROUND ALBANY
Guidebook for the capital of the state and
its environs. Washington Park Pr, 1985.   ○

Epstein, Jane and Barlow, Elizabeth
THE HUDSON RIVER VALLEY
A history and guide. Random, 1985.   ○

Evers, Alf
**THE CATSKILLS FROM
  WILDERNESS TO WOODSTOCK**
Lore, legend, flora and fauna, natural and
unnatural wonders, history and present of
the region. Overlook Pr, 1984 (first published 1972).   ○

Frommer, Harvey and Katz-Frommer,
  Myrna
IT HAPPENED IN THE CATSKILLS
"Exuberant oral history" of the Borscht Belt,
the 500 resorts of the Catskills area that
served in their heyday as birthplace and
proving ground for comedians and show
business people. Reminiscences of Grossin-
ger's, the Concord, the Nevele, bungalo colonies, ethnic jokes, photos. (PW) HBJ,
1991.   ○

Jamieson, Paul
THE ADIRONDACKS READER
Anthology. Adirondack Mountain Club,
1983.   ○

Kennedy, William
O ALBANY! AN URBAN TAPESTRY

"Improbable city of political wizards, fearless ethnics, spectacular aristocrats, splendid nobodies, and underrated scoundrels. . . . fascinating view of the American experience." (Publisher) Viking, 1983. See also Albany/Novels below.   ○

Klinkenborg, Verlyn
THE LAST FINE TIME

The story of a bar in Buffalo and two generations of the Polish-American family who run it. This is a biography of a family and the tavern, working class life, Polish immigration, social and cultural aspects of Buffalo—"incredibly moving . . . ability to capture a watershed period in the transition of American cities." (LJ) Knopf, 1991.   ○

Kohlhagen, Gale and Heinbach, Ellen
WEST POINT AND THE HUDSON VALLEY

Brings to life the history and traditions of the U.S. Military Academy and includes trips to the estates, towns and wineries in the Hudson Valley region. Directions are given from either West Point or New York City. Hippocrene, 1990.   ○

Linhorst, Sue C.
DAYTRIPS AND WEEKEND JAUNTS THROUGH CENTRAL NEW YORK

Stephanus Pub, 1988.   ○

McMinn, Russell
ANTIQUES

A guide to New York antique shops. Jockey Hollow, 1989.   ○

Michaels, Joanne and Barile, Mary
THE HUDSON VALLEY AND CATSKILL MOUNTAINS

By two local women, this is a guide to an area known for its antiques, fairs, skiing and hiking. Harmony, 1988.   ○

Mulligan, Tim
THE HUDSON RIVER VALLEY: A HISTORY GUIDE

First of a new travel series to be enjoyed before, during, and after a trip. Random, 1985.   ○

Roseberry, C.R.
FROM NIAGARA TO MONTAUK: THE SCENIC PLEASURES OF NEW YORK STATE

"Extensive, delightful view" of the natural wonders and why they are of interest to scientists and tourists; directions for finding and exploring them. (BL) State U of NY, 1981.   ○

Schuman, Michael A.
NEW YORK STATE'S SPECIAL PLACES

All kinds of daytrips and weekend outings in the state that are chosen to offer insights into an aspect of the state's character; touches as many of its corners as possible. The author attempts to recommend only those places he would recommend to a friend. Globe Pequot, 1988.   ○

Smiley, Jane
CATSKILL CRAFTS: ARTISANS OF THE CATSKILL MOUNTAINS

"Eloquent tribute" to crafts people in the region—15 are profiled in revealing interviews as to their daily life and how they work. (BL) Crown, 1987.   ○

Van Diver, Bradford B.
ROADSIDE GEOLOGY OF NEW YORK

One of a series of books that is wonderful to take along in the car—to paraphrase the preface, being able to look at the landscape as you travel and (with this book) envision the forces and changes, the dynamics of the landscape you are seeing, is a real achievement of understanding for travelers. Mountain Pr, 1985.   ○

Webster, Harriet
FAVORITE SHORT TRIPS IN NEW YORK STATE

Weekend jaunts to historic sites, museums, beaches, craft classes and so on. Yankee Bks, 1986.   ○

Wilson, Edmund
**UPSTATE: RECORDS AND
RECOLLECTIONS**
"Anecdotal combination of family reminiscences, explorations . . . visits with literary
figures . . . sketches of local characters"—
much of the material appeared originally in
the *New Yorker*. (BRD) Syracuse U Pr,
1990.   o

Wright, Leonard M., Jr.
**NEVERSINK: ONE ANGLER'S
INTENSE EXPLORATION OF A
RIVER**
The "intense exploration" of a Catskill fish-
ing stream "yields a scientific and literary
angling book . . . firmly in the tradition of
the 19th century . . . offers up odd angling
epiphanies in an urbane writing style." (PW)
Atl Monthly Pr, 1991.   o

*LONG ISLAND/FIRE ISLAND/SHELTER
ISLAND*

Bookbinder, Bernie
LONG ISLAND
People and places, past and present. Abrams,
1983.   o

Capon, Robert F.
THE YOUNGEST DAY
"Shelter Island's seasons in the light of
grace." (subtitle) Har-Row, 1983.   o

Hamilton, Harlan
LIGHTS AND LEGENDS
A historical guide to lighthouses of Long
Island Sound, Fishers Island Sound and Block
Island Sound. Wescott Cove, 1987.   o

Jones, Stephen
BACKWATERS
All about the Long Island Sound, both its
Connecticut and Long Island backwaters—
"a charming book." (BRD) Norton, 1979.   o

Masters, James I.
**THE HAMPTONS GUIDEBOOK
AND NORTH FORK & SHELTER
ISLAND GUIDEBOOK**
Blue Claw Pr, 1981.   o

Matthiessen, Peter
**MEN'S LIVES: THE SURFMEN AND
BAYMEN OF THE SOUTH FORK**
Affectionate account of the commercial fishermen of the east end of Long Island, their
way of life and losing battle with the resort
economy. Random, 1987.   o

Randall, Monica
**MANSIONS OF LONG ISLAND'S
GOLD COAST**
Rizzoli Intl, 1987.   o

Rattray, Everett T.
THE SOUTH FORK
The land and the people of Eastern Long
Island—natural and social history by the
publisher of the local newspaper and a lifelong resident of the Hamptons. Pushcart Pr,
1989.   o

Spinzia, Raymond, and others
**LONG ISLAND: A GUIDE TO NEW
YORK'S SUFFOLK AND
NASSAU COUNTIES**
Hippocrene, 1990.   o

NEW YORK CITY

Allen, Oliver E.
NEW YORK, NEW YORK
"A history of the world's most exhilarating
and challenging city" is the subtitle for this
book. New York's harbor shaped the city
from the beginning; using this as a motif,
the author provides an entertaining biography from the 1700s to the present. Atheneum, 1991.   o

Auchincloss, Louis
**THE VANDERBILT ERA: PROFILES
OF A GILDED AGE**
"Lively, anecdotal histories . . . in the felicitous style of his many novels"—examines
the lives of New York's privileged families
from 1880 to 1920. (PW) Collier, 1990.   o

Bailey, A. Peter
**HARLEM TODAY: A CULTURAL
AND VISITOR'S GUIDE**
"Captures the essence of Harlem's colorful
history"—churches, cultural institutions,

restaurants, events, landmarks, maps and a bibliography. Gumbs & Thomas, 1986. ○

Barnes, Djuna
NEW YORK

The author was one of the "Lost Generation" and a personality of the day who wrote for newspapers and magazines between 1911 and 1931; "will interest the general reader" as well as literary and history buffs. (LJ) Sun & Moon Pr, 1989. ○

Blanchet, Christian and Dard, Bertrand
STATUE OF LIBERTY: THE FIRST HUNDRED YEARS

Illustrated history of the Statue, translated from the French for American readers—from idea for the Statue to its unveiling in 1886, and its subsequent history as an international symbol and American shrine. American Heritage, 1985. ○

Bontemps, Arna, ed.
THE HARLEM RENAISSANCE REMEMBERED

First published in 1972; note also the book by Nathan Huggins listed below. Dodd, 1984. ○

Bookbinder, Bernie
CITY OF THE WORLD: NEW YORK AND ITS PEOPLE

"A bonanza for the Gothamophile"—a history with 200 photos of New York that emphasizes the city's ethnic diversity "not as a . . . melting pot but as a cauldron" in which waves of newcomers fail to blend. It tells of their struggles "with natives (and one another) . . . politics . . . Tammany Hall . . . the school system . . . pop culture." (PW) NY Newsday/Abrams, 1989. ○

Brown, Claude
CHILDREN OF HAM

Twelve young Harlemites in an urban commune in an abandoned apartment and their survival over drugs and inhumanity. Scarborough Hse, 1987. ○

Charyn, Jerome
METROPOLIS: NEW YORK AS MYTH, MARKETPLACE, AND MAGICAL LAND

A "love song" by a novelist to his hometown, with personal memories, history, profiles of people—"a scintillating portrait." (BL) Putnam, 1986. ○

Cohen, Barbara, ed., and others
NEW YORK OBSERVED: ARTISTS & WRITERS LOOK AT THE CITY, 1650 TO THE PRESENT

Excerpts from novels, plays and poems, ranging from Truman Capote to Charles Dickens—a book for browsing "serving both to ease the souls of city-weary natives and to introduce the amazing show to first-timers." (Esquire) Abrams, 1987. ○

Conrad, Peter
WHERE I FELL TO EARTH: A LIFE IN FOUR CITIES

The four cities—Oxford, London, Lisbon, and Greenwich Village in New York City—provide a map for a memoir evoking the settings "with particular distinction . . . a number of marvelous and disturbing images of the human condition." (BL) Poseidon, 1990. ○

Ellerin, Bunny
NEW YORK CITY: IT'S A GREAT COLLEGE TOWN!

This was compiled by the Association for a Better New York and has contributions by students of the 87 colleges in the city; they touch on everything from academic and internship offerings to housing and pubhopping in all five boroughs. Globe Pequot, 1987. ○

Fox, Ted
SHOWTIME AT THE APOLLO

Chronicle of the Apollo Theatre in Harlem which was a showcase for black performers from 1934 to the 1980s—famous personalities from Bessie Smith to Aretha Franklin. HR&W, 1983. ○

Hanff, Helen
APPLE OF MY EYE
Humorous anecdotes and little-known facts about some of the author's favorite places. Moyer Bell Ltd, 1989.   o

Karp, Walter
THE CENTER: A HISTORY AND GUIDE TO ROCKEFELLER CENTER
History, planning, construction, expansion, the Music Hall, photos and maps of the complex. Van Nostrand, 1983.   o

Kisseloff, Jeff
YOU MUST REMEMBER THIS
Oral history: "a torrent of verbatim recollections" from the period 1890 to World War II; anecdotes, reminiscences of ethnic neighborhoods and of privileged citizens. "Lusty, sad, startling, funny, bawdy—even cruel—stories . . . one becomes convinced anew that New York is . . . a wonderful town." (PW) HarBraceJ, 1989.   o

Klein, Alexander, ed.
THE EMPIRE CITY
"All the best ever written about New York" is the subtitle to this anthology, first published in 1955. Essays and articles by people such as Mumford, Tallulah Bankhead, Walter Winchell, Mark Twain. See also two other anthologies listed herein, more recently published. Ayer Co, 1975.   o

Leisner, Marcia
LITERARY NEIGHBORHOODS OF NEW YORK
By a native New Yorker who "describes with empathy and insight the rich literary life" of New York, "skillfully evoking the diverse worlds of Edith Wharton, I.B. Singer, Zora Neale Hurston, Auden, Millay and many more." (Publisher) Starrhill Pr, 1989.   o

Lewis, David L.
WHEN HARLEM WAS IN VOGUE
The Harlem renaissance of the 1920s when "almost everything seemed possible"—achievements in writing, music, and art. (PW) Oxford U Pr, 1989.   o

McCullough, David W.
BROOKLYN AND HOW IT GOT THAT WAY
Extensively illustrated history of the borough by a Brooklyn aficionado—"the varied, colorful stream of residents who have passed through . . . its indomitable though sorely tried spirit." (BL) Doubleday, 1983.   o

McDarrah, Fred W.
MUSEUMS IN NEW YORK
Newly revised descriptive reference guide to fine arts, local history, and specialized museums such as museums of science, natural history, botanical parks, etc. Prentice Hall Pr, 1983.   o

Marqusee, Mike and Harris, Bill, eds.
NEW YORK: AN ANTHOLOGY
"The complexity and wonder, the naughtiness and niceties, the silliness and splendor, or life in the world's first city." Includes writings of Dorothy Parker, Henry James, E.B. White, Gorky, Chesterton, others. Salem Hse, 1988.   o

Moorhouse, Geoffrey
IMPERIAL CITY: NEW YORK
A look at the city's dynamism and extremes of wealth and poverty—by an English journalist. HR&W, 1988.   o

Morris, Jan
MANHATTAN '45
"Wonderfully readable word picture of New York City in the year 1945," as the troops come home after World War II on the *Queen Mary*—"a nostalgia nosh for many, and a come-on book for a younger generation." (PW) Oxford U Pr, 1987.   o

Reynolds, Donald M.
THE ARCHITECTURE OF NEW YORK CITY
"Weaves little-known stories of eighty buildings and landmarks into a colorful tapestry of New York's whirlwind history. . . . can be read from beginning to end with great pleasure." (PW) Macmillan, 1988.   o

Schoener, Allon, ed.
CULTURAL CAPITAL OF BLACK AMERICA, 1900–1968
Conceived as a supplement to a Metropolitan Museum of Art exhibition—text and photos on events and personalities associated with Harlem's literature, theater, politics, music, art and business. First published in 1968. Dell, 1979.   ○

Shapiro, Mary J.
GATEWAY TO LIBERTY: THE STORY OF THE STATUE OF LIBERTY AND ELLIS ISLAND
"The pick of the pack" of books on the statue and Ellis Island, with a lively narrative "brimming with human interest and political fascination." (BL) Random, 1986.   ○

Shaw, Arnold
FIFTY-SECOND STREET: THE STREET OF JAZZ
"New York's fabled 52nd Street—and the bootleggers, comics, characters, strippers, club owners and jazzmen that made it swing." (Publisher) DaCapo, 1977.   ○

Trager, James
PARK AVENUE: STREET OF DREAMS
Chronicle of New York City's fashionable street. Atheneum, 1990.   ○

Ultan, Lloyd and Hermalyn, Gary
THE BRONX IN THE INNOCENT YEARS
The Bronx from 1920–50, with assistance from the Bronx County Historical Society. Har-Row, 1985.   ○

White, E.B.
HERE IS NEW YORK
Reprint of a magazine article and an essay that have the status of classics; about the author's love affair with New York—"one man's private vision of the city." (BRD) Warner Bks, 1988.   ○

GUIDEBOOKS FOR NEW YORK CITY

Alleman, Richard
THE MOVIE-LOVER'S GUIDE TO NEW YORK
The ultimate guide to movie New York—an inside look at over 25 attractions from motion pictures past and present. Har-Row, 1988.   ○

Berman, Eleanor
AWAY FOR THE WEEKEND: NEW YORK
Fifty-two ideas for getaways within 200 miles of New York City, arranged by season "to take advantage of special events and seasonal activities . . . historic restorations and museums, seaports, gardens, beaches, summer theater," etc. (LJ) Crown, 1991.   ○

Dunhill, Priscilla and Freedman, Sue
GLORIOUS GARDENS TO VISIT
Sixty-one gardens within a three-hour drive of New York City. Crown, 1989.   ○

Frontero, Vince
WHAT'S FREE AND CHEAP IN NEW YORK
"Highly recommended . . . a guidebook that lives up to its title . . . based on an article in *New York* magazine in 1989." The arrangement is by subject and all five boroughs are included. (LJ) Viking Penguin, 1991.   ○

Garrett, Robert
NEW YORK'S GREAT ART MUSEUMS
Tours of 18 permanent collections in seven museums (including the Cloisters, Brooklyn Museum and the Frick Collection), with the Metropolitan Museum covered most extensively. "Free of pretension, academic clutter and overburdening facts . . . a warm intelligent book that will make cultural pleasures more accessible." (PW) Chelsea Green, 1988.   ○

Lawliss, Chuck
THE NEW YORK THEATRE SOURCEBOOK
"The ultimate guide to theatre in New York and its environs" is the lengthy subtitle.

Organized around eight New York areas, plus companies without a permanent location. Includes a list of restaurants and nightclubs that cater to theatergoers. Finally, there is a collection of essays on theater-related topics, from how to enjoy it more to backstage tours. (BL) Fireside, 1990.   ○

McDarrah, Fred W.
MUSEUMS IN NEW YORK
A guide to all kinds of museums, from fine and folk art to natural history, museums for children, libraries with collections. St. Martin, 1990.   ○

Newberry, Lida
DAYTRIPS FROM NEW YORK
One hundred one-day adventures by car, in any kind of weather, any time of the year. Hastings, 1991.   ○

Penguin, Editors of
PENGUIN GUIDE TO NEW YORK CITY
A guide for travelers "who already know that the Bronx is up and the Battery's down . . . neatly balanced between practical and more-specialized information." Eighteen New Yorkers contribute sections on neighborhoods, attractions, restaurants and hotels. And for armchair travelers who prefer to stay home and read about New York, there's a reading list on New York history and literature. (BL) Penguin, 1989.   ○

Plumb, Stephen W.
A WALKING GUIDE TO THE RESIDENCES OF FAMOUS NEW YORKERS
Thirty-six tours ranging from 15 to 60 minutes in length, exploring haunts of 400 notables. MarLor Pr, 1989.   ○

Stern, Zelda
THE COMPLETE GUIDE TO ETHNIC NEW YORK
St. Martin, 1980.   ○

Wilensky, Elliott and White, Norval
AIA GUIDE TO NEW YORK CITY
For architecture buffs. HarBraceJ, 1988.   ○

HISTORY

Bliven, Bruce
NEW YORK
One of a series of popular histories for each state, published as part of the bicentennial in 1976. Norton, 1981.   ○

Ellis, David M.
NEW YORK STATE AND CITY
Explores the growth, literature, regional conflicts and politics of the state. Cornell U Pr, 1979.   ○

Novels
UPSTATE NEW YORK

Adams, Samuel H.
CANAL TOWN
The building of the Erie Canal in the 1820s and attendant social and economic conflicts. Random, 1944.   ○

Barth, Richard
FURNISHED FOR MURDER
A furniture salesman in Westchester believes his daughter's music teacher took his cuff links; he did, but in reporting that to the police, the salesman find himself a murder suspect. A former Soviet policeman (now a chess coach) comes to his aid. St. Martin, 1990.   ○

Blakeslee, Mermer
SAME BLOOD (Catskills)
"Remarkable first novel . . . reminiscent of *The Color Purple*"—Margaret is a semi-literate young woman who begins as a cleaning lady and blossoms into a woman "holding together an odd household of friends and family." (BL) HM, 1989.   ○

Boyle, T. Coraghessan
WORLD'S END (Westchester)
Contemporary re-creation in the Hudson River Valley of a historical tale, with the sins of the fathers visited upon the children, and involving 17th-century Dutch settlers, modern-day hippies and Indians who want to reclaim their territory. Viking, 1987.   ○

Busch, Frederick
HARRY AND CATHERINE
A divorcee is "living in pleasant upstate surroundings" with children, gardening, cooking, curating, and a relationship with a local contractor, when a former lover shows up. (BL) Knopf, 1990. Also *Sometimes I Live in the Country* (1986), and *Closing Arguments* (1991). ○

Carmer, Carl
GENESEE FEVER
The story of English settlers in the Genesee region "written with high ardor" for this section of the state, which the author knows well. (FC) McKay, 1980 (first published 1941). ○

Cheever, John
BULLET PARK
Contemporary issues and problems reflected in interplay between suburbanites. Knopf, 1969. ○

Dobyns, Stephen
SARATOGA BESTIARY (Saratoga)
One of a series of mysteries with a Saratoga setting "vividly described" and Detective Charlie Bradshaw as main protagonist—"interesting, frightening, suspenseful and often unbearably gory." (FC) Viking, 1988. Also *Saratoga Headhunter* (1986) and *Saratoga Snapper* (1987). ○

Doctorow, E.L.
RAGTIME
An anti-nostalgic novel of the fictions and realities of the era of ragtime as lives of an upper-middle-class New Rochelle family, a Jewish immigrant family, and a black musician are intertwined. Random, 1975. ○

Dreiser, Theodore
AN AMERICAN TRAGEDY
The classic of an impoverished young man, corrupted by promise of wealth and social position, leading to the murder of the young woman who stands in his way. Bentley, 1978 (first published 1925). ○

Edmonds, Walter D.
DRUMS ALONG THE MOHAWK
The Revolutionary War and frontier life in the Mohawk Valley. Little, 1936. Also three novels of Erie Canal life in the early 1800s: *Erie Water* (1933), *Rome Haul* (1929), and *The Wedding Journey* (1947). ○

Elfman, Blossom
THE STRAWBERRY FIELDS OF HEAVEN
Story of a family's sojourn in the Oneida Community of the 1870s—"how a cult develops and maintains its hold on its members." (FC) Crown, 1983. ○

Feist, Raymond E.
FAERIE TALE; A DARK FANTASY
Three children and their parents, who move to an old farm house in upstate New York, are caught in a love-hate relationship with mythical creatures who live in the forest nearby. Doubleday, 1987. ○

Ferber, Edna
SARATOGA TRUNK
An adventuress from New Orleans takes on society and big business in Saratoga, when it was a prominent resort for the very wealthy. Doubleday, 1951 (first published 1941). ○

Furman, Laura
TUXEDO PARK
The heroine lives in the past and future, refusing to believe her estranged husband will not return, until near-tragedy forces her to commit to the present. Summit, 1986. ○

Gardner, John
NICKEL MOUNTAIN (Catskills)
A plain, good-hearted man marries a pregnant girl. Knopf, 1973. Also *The Sunlight Dialogues* (1972), a mystery set in Batavia. ○

Godwin, Gail
THE FINISHING SCHOOL
Ursula De Vane, descendant of Hudson Valley aristocracy, enthralls 14-year-old Justin who has moved north to live with an aunt—

told from the perspective of Justin, 30 years later. Viking, 1985.   ○

Holland, Isabelle
FLIGHT OF THE ARCHANGEL
Romantic suspense novel set in an Episcopal Church retreat center. Doubleday, 1985. Also *Counterpoint* (1980). (See also mysteries listed under New York City.)   ○

Kennedy, William
IRONWEED
Third volume in "the Albany cycle," about the Albany underworld from the 1920s and on. (FC) Viking, 1983. The first two are *Legs* (1975) and *Billy Phelan's Greatest Game* (1978)— "rich in plot and dramatic tension." Also *Quinn's Book* (1988).   ○

Oates, Joyce Carol
MYSTERIES OF WINTERTHURN
Set in upstate New York—three cases of a detective that are failures, not successes— "takes a satirical look at 19th-century society as well as the beginnings of criminology." (FC) Dutton, 1984. *Unholy Loves* (1979), also set in upstate New York, is a contemporary novel about faculty life, focusing on a novelist "struggling with fears of failure as an artist," and *You Must Remember This.* (1988).   ○

Quindlen, Anna
OBJECT LESSONS
"A summer in the life of an Irish American family in suburban New York in the 1960s" and conflicts of family and ethnic pride. (FC). Ivy Books, 1992.   ○

Roosevelt, Elliott
HYDE PARK MURDER
One of Roosevelt's pleasant mysteries in which his mother, Eleanor Roosevelt, is the sleuth. Most of them are set in Washington, D.C., but this is in Hyde Park, the Roosevelt family home—"fascinating glimpses into history, into the Roosevelts at home." (FC) St. Martin, 1986.   ○

Russo, Richard
THE RISK POOL
Set in a decaying town in New York—"maliciously funny . . . haunting power and

insidious charm" despite the characters "most of us would back away from." (FC) Random, 1988.   ○

Shaw, Irwin
RICH MAN, POOR MAN
Success-to-failure, poor-to-rich spectrum is experienced in this saga of the Jordache family from 1940s to 1970s. Delacorte Pr, 1970. *Beggarman, Thief* (1977) continues the chronicle of the second generation of the family.   ○

Shreve, Anita
EDEN CLOSE
A recently divorced man returns to his hometown for his mother's funeral, and it recalls a tragedy that happened when he was 17. The man next door was murdered, while his daughter Eden was raped and blinded by a gunshot in the melee. He reconnects with Eden, still living next door with her mother—"evocative prose and elegiac voice." (PW) HarBraceJ, 1989.   ○

Taylor, E.A.
MURDER AT VASSAR
Two murders rock the campus when Private Eye Maggie Elliot comes East from San Francisco to attend her college reunion. St. Martin, 1986.   ○

Taylor, Robert L.
NIAGARA
Niagara Falls when it was a fashionable resort in the early 1800s. "Rich in historical details . . . rife with comic wit . . . the story is outrageous and delicious." (FC) Putnam Pub Group, 1980.   ○

Westlake, Donald E.
DROWNED HOPES
One of Westlake's series in which John Dortmunder is the hero (see under New York City). In this the story takes place in upstate New York—"dizzying plot twists . . . bewilderment of Runyonesque New Yorkers at life up state." (PW) Mysterious Pr, 1990.   ○

Wilhelm, Kate
SWEET, SWEET POISON
A couple from the Bronx invest their lottery winnings in a rural estate. When both their dog and young friend David die, the conclusions of accident or suicide come into doubt. "Studied prose . . . local color . . . tightly knit plotting in a novel that isn't like most mysteries." (FC) St. Martin, 1990.   o

LONG ISLAND & FIRE ISLAND

Benchley, Peter
JAWS
A shark terrorizes a summer resort on Long Island's east end. Doubleday, 1974.   o

Berger, Thomas
THE HOUSEGUEST
The ideal house guest gradually becomes target of a plot to kill him—"quintessential weekend/houseguest horror story." (FC) Little, 1988.   o

DeMille, Nelson
THE GOLD COAST
Established members of the Gold Coast set become involved with a Mafia don who moves into the estate next door. (BL) Warner, 1990.   o

Fitzgerald, F. Scott
THE GREAT GATSBY
Long Island society in the 1920s—"its false glamor and cultural barrenness." (FC) Scribner, 1953 (first published 1925).   o

Hirschfield, Burt
RETURN TO FIRE ISLAND
A sequel to *Fire Island* (1970), which introduced readers to "the sizzling summer scene" on the island. In this are the same characters, years later, with most of them bitter and cynical, their earlier bright futures unfulfilled. (PW) Avon, 1984.   o

Isaacs, Susan
MAGIC HOUR (Hamptons)
Mystery in which a movie producer is shot near his swimming pool in Southampton—"tension between the hardworking locals

. . . snooty summer people, phony Manhattan culture hounds and social climbers." (PW) HarperCollins, 1991. Also *Compromising Positions* (1978) and *Close Relations* (1980).   o

Leonard, George
THE ICE CATHEDRAL
A thriller about a Long Island Bay man turned mass murderer. The setting is the Great South Bay, Whole Neck (Merrick) and Crab Meadow (Freeport), with an aging south shore detective as the main protagonist. S&S, 1983.   o

McDermott, Alice
THAT NIGHT
Doomed love affair of two teenagers in the early 1960s. FS&G, 1987.   o

Nagy, Gloria
A HOUSE IN THE HAMPTONS
"Satisfying soaper bubbling with plots and personalities . . . mocks the artifice of the Hampton life-style." (BL) Delacorte, 1990.   o

Sheed, Wilfrid
THE BOYS OF WINTER
(Southampton)
Literary politicking and the world of publishing are satirized. An editor, living year-round in the Hamptons, is secretly planning to incorporate all the characters and expatriates he meets at Jimmy's Bar into a novel—only to find that another regular at the Bar is doing the same. Knopf, 1987.   o

Vonnegut, Kurt
BLUEBEARD
An Armenian-American (a minor character in *Breakfast of Champions*) tells his life story as son, husband, father, World War II soldier, artist. Delacorte, 1987.   o

Weinman, Irving
HAMPTON HEAT
A New York City detective, on vacation in the Hamptons, ends up helping the local police solve a complex murder case. Fawcett, 1989.   o

Whitney, Phyllis A.
RAINSONG (Cold Spring Harbor)
An estate, on the north shore of Long Island, and the pop music field are the background for this mystery/romance of a heroine trying to put her life back in order following the suicide of her husband. Doubleday, 1984. Also *The Golden Unicorn* set in East Hampton (1976).   ○

Wolitzer, Hilma
SILVER
A couple's upcoming silver wedding anniversary, and son Jason's relationship with his girl friend, bring back old memories and exacerbate unresolved problems—"Wolitzer is unbeatable at explaining why New Yorkers love New York . . . suspenseful, wildly funny and deeply moving." (FC) FS&G, 1988.   ○

Yates, Richard
COLD SPRING HARBOR
Set in a small Long Island town "on the eve of World War II . . . a strain of soap opera plotting" about two marriages—that of Charles Shepard, and his son Evan. (FC) Delacorte, 1986.   ○

NEW YORK CITY (Manhattan)

Adams, Jane
TRADEOFFS
The tradeoffs women make in choosing between career and home—authentic background in journalism, advertising and government. Morrow, 1983.   ○

Armstrong, Campbell
JIG
A British officer is sent to America to find an IRA folk hero and recover IRA money. Morrow, 1987.   ○

Auchincloss, Louis
THE BOOK CLASS
Seemingly a Manhattan upper-crust version of . . . *and Ladies of the Club* (see "Ohio/ Novels")—the son of one of the members of the Book Class narrates the story of a collection of Park Avenue debutantes who meet for book discussions beginning in 1908 and

lasting 64 years. "No one excels his finely etched portraits of sophisticates of good breeding and inherited wealth." Houghton, 1984. Other novels set in this milieu are (in order of publication date): *The House of Five Talents* (1960), *Portrait in Brownstone* (1962), *The Embezzler* (1966), *A World of Profit* (1968), *The Dark Lady* (1977), *The Country Cousin* (1978), *Watchfires* (1982). Also two collections of short stories with a Manhattan setting: *Tales of Manhattan* (1967) and *Second Chance* (1970).   ○

Auchincloss, Louis
DIARY OF A YUPPIE
Novel of ethics and corporate takeovers. HM, 1986. Also *Skinny Island; More Tales of Manhattan* (1987); *The Golden Calves* (1988), about a Manhattan museum and diverse motives of its staff; *Fellow Passengers* (1989), about an attorney, his relatives, clients and friends. See also entry above for earlier novels by Auchincloss, and *The Lady of Situations* (1990).   ○

Baker, Dorothy
YOUNG MAN WITH A HORN
The book about a young American jazz artist inspired by Bix Beiderbecke's music; first published in 1938. Amereon, 1977.   ○

Baldwin, James
IF BEALE STREET COULD TALK
New York City and Puerto Rico are the settings for a novel of a love between two young people that helps them to deal with racial oppression. Dial, 1974. Other books by this author about black life and New York are *Go Tell It on The Mountain* (1963), *Another Country* (1962), and *Tell Me How Long the Train's Been Gone* (1968).   ○

Barnhardt, Wilton
EMMA WHO SAVED MY LIFE
Appealing first novel of looking back from Evanston, Illinois, on the decade he spent trying to make it on Broadway and the "dauntingly literate . . . neurotic Emma for whom he carried a torch." (BL) St. Martin, 1989.   ○

Barth, Richard
THE CONDO KILL
A mystery in which the last tenants of an upper West Side apartment, slated to go condo, organize to fight off the real estate developer—"humor and authentic New York City street scenes." (FC) Scribner, 1985.   ○

Bayer, William
SWITCH
An introspective police officer with a psychological approach to crime is assigned to a gruesome double murder. S&S, 1984.   ○

Bell, Madison S.
THE WASHINGTON SQUARE ENSEMBLE
Drug dealers in Washington Square on a summer weekend narrate their individual pasts—"brilliantly evokes a world of violence, depravity and despair without inducing lowering of the spirits." (FC) Viking, 1983.   ○

Benedict, Elizabeth
THE BEGINNER'S BOOK OF DREAMS
"Engaging story of personal triumph" and the coming-of-age of a young girl living in a posh area of New York City with her divorced mother, as she gradually comes to terms with herself and life. (FC) Knopf, 1988.   ○

Block, Lawrence
OUT ON THE CUTTING EDGE
A Matt Scudder mystery distinguished by "humanity . . . understated style." (FC) Morrow, 1989. Also *Eight Million Ways to Die* (1982), *When the Sacred Gin Mill Closes* (1986), set in Hell's Kitchen, and *A Ticket to the Boneyard* (1990). Block also writes an interesting series, set in New York City, in which bookseller/burglar Bernie Rhodenbarr is the protagonist; titles in this series include *The Burglar in the Closet* (1978), *The Burglar Who Liked to Quote Kipling* (1979), *The Burglar Who Studied Spinoza* (1980), *The Burglar Who Painted Like Mondrian* (1983), all of which were reissued in paperback in 1986.   ○

Bram, Christopher
IN MEMORY OF ANGEL CLARE
Michael is gay, 23, estranged from his family, mourning the death of his older lover, Clarence, and his only friends are Clarence's friends—the author has "the ability to ferret out the humor within emotional conflicts, to make the reader see and touch his characters." (BL) Fine, 1989.   ○

Breslin, Jimmy
HE GOT HUNGRY AND FORGOT HIS MANNERS
Satiric novel about a priest sent by the Vatican to stamp out sin in New York who, instead, gets involved with the homeless and victims of the welfare system. Ticknor & Fields, 1988.   ○

Bringle, Mary
MURDER MOST GENTRIFIED
Murder and other events in a Manhattan condominium lead to former tenants. Doubleday, 1988.   ○

Brownmiller, Susan
WAVERLY PLACE (Greenwich Village)
The Greenwich Village milieu in a novel based on the brutal story of Joel Steinberg and his abuse of an adopted child—"investigative journalism disguised as fiction." (FC) Grove Pr, 1989.   ○

Bush, Lawrence
BESSIE
Bessie, the American-Jewish radical heroine, is part of major events in the various movements of the century—the Triangle fire, the Sacco-Vanzetti trial, and so on. The novel is based on experiences of the author's grandmother. Putnam Pub Group, 1983.   ○

Caunitz, William J.
BLACK SAND
Begins with murder in Greece, when ancient scrolls and Alexander the Great's copy of *The Iliad* are stolen; this mystery becomes a New York police procedural when the stolen property ends up in New York. Crown,

1989. Also *One Police Plaza* (1984) and *Suspects* (1986).   ○

Chute, B.J.
THE GOOD WOMAN
Symbolic novel of a Manhattan woman, reflecting on the hollowness of her life, who dons the clothes of a bag lady and begins wandering. Vanguard, 1986.   ○

Clark, Mary Higgins
A STRANGER IS WATCHING
Murder-horror story with "precise and evocative sense of place . . . particularly Grand Central Station." (FC) S&S, 1978.   ○

Collins, Michael
RED ROSA
"Tight, gritty, uncompromising" mystery of the attempted murder of a bag lady who turns out to have been a member of the Communist Party, with a tangled family background that includes three former husbands, a son, two rich brothers, a granddaughter who is linked to a militant black organization. (FC) Fine, 1988.   ○

Condon, Richard
PRIZZI'S HONOR
Novel of an enforcer for the Prizzi mob who falls in love with a woman who is a freelance killer for the Mafia—"full of action and surprises" and basis for movie of the same name. (FC) Coward, McCann, 1982. Also *Prizzi's Family* (1986) and *Prizzi's Glory* (1988).   ○

Cook, Robin
BRAIN
One of the author's medical mystery novels—this one involves the stealing of a dead patient's brain, and is set at Hobson University Medical Center in New York. Putnam, 1981.   ○

Cook, Thomas H.
FLESH AND BLOOD
"Many-layered and shimmering tale" of the Seventh Avenue garment industry in which a New York private eye is asked to find the next of kin of a couturier's elderly assis-

tant—"history, locale and personality build to an unsuspected, satisfying end." (FC) Putnam, 1989. Also *The City When It Rains* (1991).   ○

Corbin, Steven
NO EASY PLACE TO BE (Harlem)
"Immensely readable novel"—the saga of three sisters and Harlem's renaissance period of the 1920s. One is a follower of Marcus Garvey, one a Cotton Club dancer, one a Barnard student. (FC) S&S, 1989.   ○

Cunningham, E.V.
THE WABASH FACTOR
"Endlessly fascinating police procedural" involving the death of an Israeli leader and a kidnapped Vermeer. (FC) Delacorte, 1986.   ○

Daley, Robert
A FAINT COLD FEAR
See entry under Columbia.   ○

Daley, Robert
MAN WITH A GUN
The right-hand man to the New York City police commissioner has to deal with the complications of police politics and the results of his "bravery, idealism and naivete" that get him in trouble with police chief buddies. (BL) S&S, 1988. Also *Prince of the City* (1979) and *Year of the Dragon* (1981), about Chinatown.   ○

Davies, Valentine
MIRACLE ON 34TH STREET
The classic movie about Santa Clause coming true in Macy's department store is based on this happy novel. HarBraceJ, 1947.   ○

DeLynn, Jane
REAL ESTATE
About the housing crunch and how it dictates some relationships—"a scathing commentary on the New York upwardly mobile life-style." (FC) Poseidon Pr, 1988.   ○

Dennis, Patrick
AUNTIE MAME
A nephew reminisces about his unconventional aunt who played each of the roles life

handed her—shopgirl, showgirl, authoress, etc.—to the hilt. Vanguard, 1955.   ○

DiDonato, Pietro
CHRIST IN CONCRETE
Italian-American bricklayers in New York, and the specific story of a young boy who takes over financial responsibility for his family when his father is killed working on a construction job. Bobbs, 1980 (first published 1939).   ○

Dunne, Dominick
PEOPLE LIKE US
Story of social distinctions in Manhattan, with several story strands. Crown, 1988.   ○

Ellin, Stanley
THE DARK FANTASTIC
"Expertly horrifying tale" of stolen art and a racist landlord's plan to blow up his building, with an "incredibly ingenious" finale. (FC) Mysterious Press, 1983. Also *Very Old Money* (1985), about two school teachers who decide to become live-in servants for a wealthy woman.   ○

Ellison, Ralph
INVISIBLE MAN
A black's loss of identity—final invisibility—in a world of rejection that has been compared to Dostoevski's *Notes from the Underground.* Modern Lib (first published 1952).   ○

Feinberg, David B.
EIGHTY-SIXED
Contrasts pre-AIDS 1980s with post-AIDS 1986—"the scorched voice of New York City gay culture, of its repertory, its codes, its excesses and its curse." (FC) Viking, 1989.   ○

Fitzgerald, F. Scott
THE BEAUTIFUL AND DAMNED
A story of the roaring twenties set in Manhattan. Scribner, 1950 (first published 1922).   ○

Flynn, Don
ORDINARY MURDER
The owner of a bar asks a newspaper reporter to look into the murder of his son—

"very New Yorkish, very amusing, very nice." (FC) Walker, 1987.   ○

Garfield, Brian
DEATH WISH
A man avenges the brutal death of his wife and destruction of his daughter's sanity by becoming a one-man vigilante against criminals in New York. McKay, 1972.   ○

Greenfield, Robert
TEMPLE
Each member of a Jewish family experiences a major trauma during the period between the Jewish and secular New Years and each "emerges changed and with a new understanding of friends and family." (FC) Summit Bks, 1983.   ○

Guy, Rosa
A MEASURE OF TIME (Harlem)
Picaresque novel of a woman from Montgomery, Alabama, who seeks her fortune in Harlem in 1926—"an evocative tour of 20th-century black America from the rural South to streets of New York City." (BRD) HR&W, 1983. Also *Ruby* (1976) about a young woman from the West Indies adjusting to a lonely and frustrating life in Harlem in the 1970s.   ○

Hailey, J.P.
THE BAXTER TRUST
A starving New York lawyer is contacted through the yellow pages by an orphaned heiress when she finds a corpse in her apartment—with complications from a married boyfriend and a Scrooge-like trustee who makes her live on a small allowance. Fine, 1988.   ○

Harris, Ruth
MODERN WOMAN
The lives of three women who "dabble in the sexual, cultural and political freedoms . . . thrust upon the new generation" at the time of the Kennedy assassination, who all end up in Greenwich Village, in publishing, while aspiring to writing careers. (FC) St. Martin, 1989.   ○

Herlihy, James Leo
MIDNIGHT COWBOY
"An appalling story, told with great skill"
of three misfits living in an abandoned
building. (FC) S&S, 1965.   o

Highsmith, Patricia
FOUND IN THE STREET (Greenwich
   Village)
Two men are drawn together by their inter-
est in a young girl—"powerfully disturbing"
creation. (FC) Mysterious Pr, 1987.   o

Hijuelos, Oscar
**THE MAMBO KINGS PLAY
   SONGS OF LOVE**
The lives and loves of two Cuban musicians
aiming for stardom in the U.S.—"traced in
exuberant and colorful detail . . . Latin music's invasion of American popular taste in
the 1940s and 1950s." (FC) FS&G, 1989. o

Hobson, Laura Z.
UNTOLD MILLIONS
Manhattan in 1923. A talented newcomer
falls in love with an agency copywriter and
supports him in his ambition to write a
novel. Har-Row, 1982. Also *Gentleman's
Agreement* (1947), about a journalist who pre-
tends to be a Jew to research anti-
Semitism.   o

Holland, Isabelle
A FATAL ADVENT
A series of mysteries in a unique setting, St.
Anselm's Episcopal Church, with a woman
minister—"Holland uses the church setting
deftly . . . Told with reverent wit . . . ter-
rific." (FC) Doubleday, 1989. Also *A Death
At Anselm's* (1984), *A Lover Scorned* (1987).
Also *Flight of the Archangel* (1985), set in an
Episcopal Church retreat center in upstate
New York.   o

Holland, Isabelle
THE LONG SEARCH
In this, Episcopal minister Aldington (see *A
Fatal Advent,* above) is just a link to the main
characters—an editor for a New York City
publishing company and her newly-ac-
quired author. Doubleday, 1990.   o

Hughes, Langston
SIMPLE SPEAKS HIS MIND
   (Harlem)
First of three novels in which a Harlem black
speaks his mind in a sardonic spoof of race
relations, followed by *Simple Takes a Wife*
(1953) and *Simple Stakes a Claim* (1957). Also,
a collection of short stories, *Simple's Uncle
Sam* (1965). S&S, 1950.   o

Janowitz, Tama
A CANNIBAL IN MANHATTAN
The "savage-meets-society gambit . . . ironic
and knowledgeable vision of New York"—
an heiress working as a Peace Corps volunteer brings a South Sea island native to
New York. (FC) Crown, 1987.   o

Jhabvala, Ruth Prawer
**IN SEARCH OF LOVE AND
   BEAUTY**
An emigre from Austria in the 1930s is the
focus around which the story of three generations of an emigre family is told. Morrow,
1983.   o

Johnston, Jane
PAINT HER FACE DEAD
A free-lance writer infiltrates an est-like encounter group to uncover charlatanism, only
to be accused of poisoning the woman sitting next to her—"enhanced by depictions
of the Big Apple." (PW) St. Martin, 1987.
                                            o

Jong, Erica
**ANY WOMAN'S BLUES; A NOVEL
   OF OBSESSION**
Attempts to free herself from addiction to a
younger man leads to a "sensual and spiri-
tual odyssey." (FC) Har-Row, 1990.   o

Kazan, Elia
THE ANATOLIAN
A sequel to *America, America* (see "Turkey/
Novels"), it begins in 1909 when the hero's
family arrives in New York and he is expected to "take up the patriarchal mantle
[and of the] struggle for wealth, influence
and an illusive Americanization." (FC) Knopf,
1982.   o

Kluger, Phyllis and Richard
GOOD GOODS
See "Connecticut/Novels."   ○

Korda, Michael
THE FORTUNE
A fictional family—sort of a hybrid of the Rockefellers and the newspaper Binghams of Louisville—and what happens when one of them dies under scandalous circumstances. Summit Bks, 1989.   ○

Kotzwinkle, William
THE MIDNIGHT EXAMINER
Life at a magazine conglomerate in Manhattan, as editors try to survive—"relentlessly funny . . . a delight to read." (FC) HM, 1989.   ○

Krantz, Judith
I'LL TAKE MANHATTAN
Saga of a beautiful heroine's career in the New York publishing world. Crown, 1986.   ○

Lawrence, Kathleen R.
THE LAST ROOM IN MANHATTAN
"Witty, gritty depiction of down-and-out life in contemporary Manhattan." (FC) Atheneum, 1988.   ○

L'Engle, Madeleine
A SEVERED WASP
"A New York novel, filled with big-city tensions." (FC) FS&G, 1982. The plot includes a character from one of her other novels, *The Small Rain* (1984), a retired concert pianist, who becomes involved in the lives of Episcopal clergy, their wives and children. FS&G, 1982.   ○

Leuci, Bob
DOYLE'S DISCIPLES
A newly promoted detective has to deal with conflicts between friendship and personal integrity when a murder investigation points to police corruption. Freundlich, 1984.   ○

Levin, Ira
SLIVER
"A gleaming 'sliver' of an apartment house" is the setting for this suspense story. When

a book editor moves into the building, where there have been several murders, the owner begins electronic surveillance of her activities—the author "constructs an edifice of terror." (FC) Bantam, 1991. Also *Rosemary's Baby* (1967).   ○

Lutz, John
SWF SEEKS SAME
Psychological thriller—"Allison Jones takes in a seemingly innocuous room mate." (FC) St. Martin, 1990.   ○

McBain, Ed
WIDOWS: A NOVEL OF THE 87TH PRECINCT
One of many, many police procedurals based on the fictional 87th Precinct, with continuing characters. In more recent volumes the author knows his audience and is so familiar with the characters that he no longer has to even "introduce" them. (FC) Morrow, 1991. Here's a partial list of forerunners, in chronological order beginning in 1968 and ending in 1991: *Fuzz, Jigsaw, Sadie When She Died, Blood Relatives, Ghosts, Heat, Ice, Lightning, Eight Black Horses, Poison, Lullaby, Tricks, Vespers, Widows.*   ○

McInerney, Jay
BRIGHT LIGHTS, BIG CITY
"Very funny, oddly touching" novel of a would-be writer—"elements of a *roman a clef* about life at *The New Yorker*," the protagonist's employer. (BRD) Vintage, 1984.   ○

McInerney, Jay
STORY OF MY LIFE
"Chronicle of zonked-out, affluent, young urban life . . . vivid and heartbreaking." (FC) Atl Monthly Pr, 1988.   ○

Murdoch, Anna
FAMILY BUSINESS
Chronicles the beginning and growth of a newspaper and telecommunications conglomerate from the 1920s on. Morrow, 1988.   ○

O'Donnell, Lillian
A PRIVATE CRIME
One of a series of Lt. Norah Mulcahaney mysteries—"a strong, determined woman

holding her own in a male-dominated police force" and lately involved romantically with a TV newsman. (PW) Putnam, 1991. Also *Dial 577 R-A-P-E* (1974), *No Business Being a Cop* (1979), *The Children's Zoo* (1981), *Cop Without a Shield* (1983), *The Other Side of the Door* (1987), *A Good Night to Kill* (1988), *Wreath for the Bride* (1990). ○

Oster, Jerry
CLUB DEAD
Two detectives, assigned by computer to investigate the fall of a newspaper reporter from a Park Avenue highrise, find that despite their antipathy their techniques complement each other in solving the mystery. Har-Row, 1988. ○

Parent, Gail
A SIGN OF THE EIGHTIES
"Freewheeling romp" of a feminist ready to chuck it all for a husband—the TV comedy writer she wants to marry. (FC) Putnam, 1987. ○

Patrick, Vincent
FAMILY BUSINESS
The American family as "an ethnic smorgasbord" with criminal genes. (FC) Poseidon Pr, 1985. ○

Paul, Barbara
GOOD KING SAUERKRAUT
One of several "sophisticated, original mysteries"—this one is the saga of King Sarcowicz. "The descriptions of New York are wonderful." (PW) Scribner, 1989. Also *Kill Fee* (1985), *The Renewable Virgin* (1982), *Chorus of Detectives* (1987), *In-Laws and Outlaws* (1990). ○

Plimpton, George
THE CURIOUS CASE OF SIDD FINCH
A baseball pitcher, whose fast ball is unhittable, signs on with the New York Mets and turns out to be far more complicated a personality than expected—he's studying to be a Buddhist monk. Macmillan, 1987. ○

Puzo, Mario
THE GODFATHER
The blockbuster novel of an Italian-American crime family. Putnam Pub Group, 1969. Also *The Fortunate Pilgrim* (1965) about a close-knit Italian family and community life in 1928. ○

Renek, Morris
BREAD AND CIRCUS
Historical novel of Boss Tweed in the 1860s—"stunningly graphic" in portraying events and people such as Cornelius Vanderbilt and Jay Gould. (FC) Weidenfeld, 1987. ○

Runyon, Damon
GUYS AND DOLLS
Short stories, some of which were the basis for the musical. Lippincott, 1950. Also *Best of Runyon* (1938). ○

Salinger, J.D.
THE CATCHER IN THE RYE
Classic of a young boy on his own for three days in New York, first published in 1951.○

Sanders, Lawrence
THE SEVENTH COMMANDMENT
A series of "Deadly Sins and Commandments" mysteries whose trademarks are "murder, greed, lust, corruption and an extraordinary preoccupation with food and drink." (PW) Putnam, 1991. Other titles include: *First Deadly Sin* (1973), *The Second Deadly Sin* (1977), *The Sixth Commandment* (1979), *The Tenth Commandment* (1980), *The Third Deadly Sin* (1981), *The Eighth Commandment* (1986), *The Fourth Deadly Sin* (1989). ○

Schulberg, Budd
WATERFRONT
An indictment of racketeering and labor unions on the waterfront. Bentley, 1979 (first published 1955). ○

Schwartz, Lynne S.
DISTURBANCES IN THE FIELD
"Journey from resignation to a grudging reaffirmation of living" as a Manhattan chamber musician and her artist husband

face profound tragedy and marital problems. (FC) Har-Row, 1983.   ⟳

Solomita, Stephen
A TWIST OF THE KNIFE
A detective tracks his girlfriend's killers
throughout Manhattan, and members of a
political terrorist group make random at-
tacks—"captures perfectly the resignation
. . . that true New Yorkers use" to describe
the city. (FC) Putnam, 1988.   ⟳

Stewart, Edward
PRIVILEGED LIVES
Police Lieutenant Vince Cardozo links a
young man's ritual murder and a woman
awakening from an insulin-induced coma
after seven years—"high sleaze factor . . .
it's difficult to put down." (FC) Delacorte,
1988.   ⟳

Swift, Edward
**THE CHRISTOPHER PARK
   REGULARS**
About an odd assortment of cultural misfits
who congregate at a Greenwich Village park.
British Am Pub, 1989.   ⟳

Tanenbaum, Robert
NO LESSER PLEA
A story of the failing judicial system and a
dedicated assistant district attorney striving
to work within it. Watts, 1987. Also *Immoral
Uncertainty* (1991).   ⟳

Tax, Meredith
RIVINGTON STREET
Family chronicle of a woman-dominated
Lower East Side family as well as the garment industry and suffragist movement of
the early 1900s. Morrow, 1982. Its sequel is
Union Square (1988), which takes the Rus-
sian-born family through the Depression and
a family split over socialist politics.   ⟳

Thomas, Michael M.
HANOVER PLACE
"Charts the triumphs, losses and peccadil-
loes" of the Warrington family, owner of
Hanover Place, a brokerage firm. A portrait
of high finance from 1924 and on through
the Depression to modern-day junk bonds
and unfriendly takeovers, with a secondary
theme of anti-Semitism and the WASPS who
dominate New York society. (BL) Warner
Bks, 1989. Also *Someone Else's Money*
(1982).   ⟳

Uhnak, Dorothy
FALSE WITNESS
"The investigative process prevails" in the
story of an ambitious female in the D.A.'s
office involved in a political bombshell case
that presents conflicts both for her career
ambitions and her personal life. (FC) S&S,
1981. Other novels by Uhnak with a New
York City setting are *Law and Order* (1973),
saga of an Irish family, and two police mysteries, *The Ledger* (1970) and *The Witness* (1969),
and *Victims* (1986).   ⟳

Vachss, Andrew H.
SACRIFICE
Private investigator Burke "works both sides
of the law" to save an eight-year-old sus-
pected of murder. (FC) Knopf, 1991. Also
Blossom (1990).   ⟳

Verlaine, M.J.
A BAD MAN IS EASY TO FIND
Short stories that catch "the flash and dash"
of New York City and its inhabitants' will
for survival and love. (FC) St. Martin,
1989.   ⟳

Villars, Elizabeth
LIPSTICK ON HIS COLLAR
"Glitzy New York publishing setting," with
a heroine who has just made the cover of
Time when she discovers that her husband
is having an affair with a colleague. (FC)
Warner, 1990.   ⟳

Wallach, Anne T.
WOMEN'S WORK
"Fast-paced . . . plenty of dazzle" novel
about the advertising industry from a feminist woman's viewpoint ("sexist, cynical and
degrading"). (FC) NAL, 1986. Also *Private
Scores.* (1987).   ⟳

Wallant, Edward L.
THE PAWNBROKER (Harlem)
A bitter Harlem pawnbroker, haunted by memories of the concentration camp, and self-hating, rejoins the "emotionally living." HarBraceJ, 1961. Also *The Tenants of Moonbloom* (1963), about a humanistic hero working as rental agent for his slumlord brother. ○

Westlake, Donald E.
GOOD BEHAVIOR
One of a series of comic crime capers with John A. Dortmunder, a professional thief, as hero. In this one Dortmunder falls through the roof of a convent while fleeing an attempted robbery and ends up with a deal to rescue a nun from her father's deprogramming. Mysterious Pr, 1985. Also *The Fugitive Pigeon* (1965), *The Hot Rock* (1970), *Cops and Robbers* (1972), *Brother's Keeper* (1975), *Dancing Aztecs* (1976) and *Why Me* (1983). ○

White, Edmund
THE BEAUTIFUL ROOM IS EMPTY
Continues the story of a nameless hero begun in *A Boy's Own Story* (1982); from prep school through college to the turning point in his life in 1969, when patrons of a New York gay bar turned on the police trying to close it down—the narrator's struggle to come to terms with himself "is universal . . . clearly transcends its 'gay' theme." (FC) Knopf, 1988. ○

Williams, John A.
CLICK SONG
Set in and around New York since World War II with a plot about a black novelist's experience in establishing himself as a "novelist of distinction." (FC) Houghton, 1982. ○

Wolfe, Tom
THE BONFIRE OF THE VANITIES
"Immensely entertaining . . . brilliant evocation of New York's class, racial and political structure in the 1980s." When Sherman McCoy mistakenly drives off the expressway into the South Bronx, after picking up his mistress at the airport, it precipitates a series of disastrous consequences that end his charmed and privileged life. (FC) FS&G, 1987. ○

Wouk, Herman
MARJORIE MORNINGSTAR
Story of a Jewish girl growing into womanhood. Doubleday, 1955. Also *Youngblood Hawke* (1962), an aspiring novelist from Kentucky who makes it big in the city. ○

Yglesias, Rafael
ONLY CHILDREN
The first five years of life of two boys and their upper-middle-class parents. Morrow, 1988. Also *The Murderer Next Door* (1990). ○

BROOKLYN, THE BRONX AND QUEENS

Bonanno, Margaret W.
EMBER DAYS (Brooklyn)
Saga of the women in an Irish-Catholic family in a close, rigid culture in the first generation, that culture virtually gone by the fourth. Seaview, 1980. Also *A Certain Slant of Light* (1979), in which one of the earlier novel's main characters is a secondary character. ○

Boyle, Thomas
POST-MORTEM EFFECTS
Racial trouble, anti-Semitism, the drug scene in Brooklyn. Viking, 1987. ○

Breslin, Jimmy
FORSAKING ALL OTHERS (Bronx)
"A tough, unflinching look at the lower depths"—the plot involves a Harvard-educated Puerto Rican lawyer, the daughter of a Mafia don, and the murder of a dope seller. (FC) S&S, 1982. ○

Breslin, Jimmy
THE GANG THAT COULDN'T SHOOT STRAIGHT (Brooklyn and Queens)
Story of a disorganized crime family, and Kid Sally Palumbo's attempt to take over from the big boss. Viking, 1969. Also *Table Money* (1985). ○

Dintenfass, Mark
OLD WORLD, NEW WORLD
(Brooklyn)
Family chronicle of Jewish immigrants—
"spins the multi-colored, multi-faceted
threads of the family into a huge . . . tapestry." (FC) Morrow, 1982. Also with a
Brooklyn setting, *Montgomery Street* (1978),
about a filmmaker producing a movie about
the Brooklyn neighborhood where he grew
up.   o

Doctorow, E.L.
BILLY BATHGATE
The education of Billy, brought up in poverty on Bathgate Avenue in the Bronx, who
becomes a gangster-in-training for Dutch
Schultz and falls for Dutch's girlfriend. Random, 1989.   o

Doctorow, E.L.
WORLD'S FAIR
A memoir of the Bronx and New York in
the 1930s. Random, 1985.   o

Eisenstadt, Jill
FROM ROCKAWAY
"Coming-of-age" novel of Irish working-class
teenagers during the early 1980s, "going
nowhere" and working at the beach in Rockaway as lifeguards. (BRD) Knopf, 1987.   o

Flaherty, Joe
TIN WIFE (Brooklyn)
A "tin wife" [cop's wife] reviews her life on
the day she's due to receive her husband's
posthumous award from the mayor. S&S,
1984.   o

Green, Gerald
THE CHAINS (Brooklyn)
Family chronicle of a "brawling, semi-crim-
inal" Jewish family—"passionate, violent
story, streetwise and rich in authentic detail." (FC) Also set in Brooklyn are *The Last
Angry Man* (1957), about a doctor's life in
the Brooklyn slums, and *To Brooklyn With
Love* (1967), Brooklyn youth during the
depression. Seaview, 1980.   o

Kellerman, Faye
DAY OF ATONEMENT
Los Angeles detective Pete Decker, with his
new wife, visits her Jewish kin in Brooklyn
and gets involved in events that include his
natural mother and her missing grandson—
"entrancing page turner." (FC) Morrow,
1991.   o

Malamud, Bernard
THE ASSISTANT (Brooklyn)
A Jewish grocer and his family—"simple
people struggling to make their lives better
in a world of bad luck." (FC) FS&G, 1957.
                                           o

Potok, Chaim
THE CHOSEN (Brooklyn, Bronx)
Friendship between two boys in the Williamsburg section of Brooklyn. S&S, 1967.
The Promise (1969) continues the story as the
boys grow up. Also *In the Beginning* (1975),
about growing up in the Bronx in the early
1900s, *My Name is Asher Lev* (1972), about a
boy who wants a career as an artist in a
family of intense religious beliefs, and its
sequel *The Gift of Asher Lev* (1990).   o

Smith, Betty
A TREE GROWS IN BROOKLYN
Life in an impoverished family for an excep-
tional young girl in the early 1900s. Har-
Row, 1947. Also *Maggie-Now* (1958), a girl
grows into responsible womanhood.   o

Styron, William
SOPHIE'S CHOICE
A Southern writer, a Polish Catholic survivor of the Holocaust, and her Jewish lover,
living in a Brooklyn boardinghouse—the
novel traces the writer's "intense involvement with the lovers . . . and his growing
fascination with the horror of Sophie's past."
(FC) Random, 1979.   o

Uhnak, Dorothy
THE INVESTIGATION (Queens)
A Queens mother is suspected of murdering
her two children. S&S, 1977.   o

Wouk, Herman
INSIDE, OUTSIDE (Bronx)
The story of the life and times of David Goodkind, moving between present and past, as he recalls his immigrant background, the Bronx, Columbia University, political events from World War II to Watergate. Little, 1985. Also *Cityboy* (1948).   o

NORTH CAROLINA

Series Guidebooks
(See Appendix 1)

NOTE: See also Series Guides (and non-series guides) listed under United States and the South. You may also find some cross-over in guides and books listed under the East that have to do with the eastern coast.

Michael's Guide: North Carolina
Off the Beaten Path: North Carolina

Background Reading

Bailey, Anthony
THE OUTER BANKS
"Irresistible combination of personal experience, natural and local history and people." (PW) FS&G, 1989.   o

Ballance, Alton
OCRACOKERS
About the Ocracoke, accessible only by ferry, and its residents. U of North Carolina Pr, 1989.   o

Bishir, Catherine W.
UNPAINTED ARISTOCRACY
The beach cottages of old Nags Head, North Carolina. Archives, 1987.   o

Bledsoe, Jerry
CAROLINA CURIOSITIES
"Jerry Bledsoe's outlandish guide to the dadblamedest things to see and do in North Carolina." A combination of tour guide and "believe it or not" book of North Carolina oddities. (BL) Globe Pequot, 1989. Also *Just Folks: Visitin's with Carolina People* (1990) and *You Can't Live on Radishes: Some Funny Things Happened on the Way Back to the Land* (1990), both published by Down Home.   o

Bledsoe, Jerry
FROM WHALEBONE TO HOT HOUSE
A journey along North Carolina's longest highway. Globe Pequot, 1986.   o

Claiborne, Jack and Price, William, eds.
DISCOVERING NORTH CAROLINA
A Tar Heel Reader. U of North Carolina Pr, 1991.   o

Kupperman, Karen O.
ROANOKE: THE ABANDONED COLONY
"Cogent and vivacious account of the twice-failed settlement. . . . also interprets Roanoke's significance in both British imperial history and the development of the U.S." (BL) Rowman, 1984.   o

Kuralt, Charles
NORTH CAROLINA IS MY HOME
Reminiscences in prose and poetry of customs, folklore and cultural history; stories by a master storyteller. East Woods, 1986.
     o

Powell, Lew
LEW POWELL'S CAROLINA FOLLIES
"A nose-tweaking look at life in our two great and goofy states" is the subtitle. Down Home Pr, 1990.   o

Ready, Milton
ASHEVILLE: LAND OF THE SKY
Cultural and architectural history. Windsor, 1986.   o

Redford, Dorothy
SOMERSET HOMECOMING
A *Roots* story—the author researched her background, identified 2,000 descendants and brought them together in a homecoming at the place where their ancestors had been slaves. Fascinating social history. Doubleday, 1988.   ○

Schoenbaum, Thomas J.
ISLANDS, CAPES AND SOUNDS:
  THE NORTH CAROLINA COAST
John F. Blair, 1982.   ○

Shears, David
OCRACOKE: ITS HISTORY AND
  PEOPLE
By a British author who is a frequent visitor to this unique area—uses interviews with residents to tell the story of Ocracoke. Starfish Pr, 1989.   ○

Simpson, Bland
THE GREAT DISMAL: A
  CAROLINIAN'S SWAMP
  MEMOIR
Interviews, visits, history—"an endlessly fascinating subject of literature, music, and legend." (LJ) U of North Carolina Pr, 1990.   ○

Stick, David
NORTH CAROLINA
  LIGHTHOUSES
NC Dept of Cultural Resources, 1984.   ○

Wilkinson, Alec
MOONSHINE: A LIFE IN PURSUIT
  OF WHITE LIQUOR
About moonshine and a likable "revenooer" working under cover—"captures a small bit of Americana that is both esoteric and entertaining." (BRD) Knopf, 1985.   ○

GUIDEBOOKS

Hill, Michael, ed.
GUIDE TO NORTH CAROLINA
  HIGHWAY HISTORICAL
  MARKERS
NC Div of Archives & History, 1990.   ○

McCaig & Boyce
NORTH CAROLINA STATE PARKS
Affordable Adventures, 1989.   ○

McMinn, Russell
ANTIQUES
A guide to North Carolina antique shops. Jockey Hollow, 1989.   ○

Ockershausen, Jane
THE NORTH CAROLINA ONE-DAY
  TRIP BOOK
"150 excursions in the land of dramatic diversity" is its lengthy subtitle. EPM Pubns, 1990.   ○

Wenberg, Donald C.
BLUE RIDGE MOUNTAIN
  PLEASURES
An A-to-Z guide to northern Georgia, western North Carolina and the up country of South Carolina. Globe Pequot, 1988.   ○

HISTORY

Powell, William S.
NORTH CAROLINA
One of a series of popular histories for each state, published as part of the bicentennial in 1976. Norton, 1988.   ○

Novels

Anderson, Ferrell
WHERE SHE WAS
The setting is the tobacco country of North Carolina, and the plot revolves about the farm wife's attempts to find answers in Old Time religion. Knopf, 1985.   ○

Athas, Daphne
ENTERING EPHESUS
In this novel, first published in 1971, a family is forced to move "from relative grandeur in the north to frank squalor" in Ephesus (bearing strong resemblance to Chapel Hill)—the mother clings to her origins, the three daughters "take on the world . . . an unforgettable story." (PW) Permanent Pr, 1990.   ○

Edgerton, Clyde
THE FLOATPLANE NOTEBOOKS
Story of the blue-collar Copeland family, from 1956 to the Vietnam War years—"demonstrates the ability to reveal character through sharply etched dialogue and wildly hilarious circumstance." (FC) Algonquin, 1988. ○

Edgerton, Clyde
WALKING ACROSS EGYPT
Novel of a 78-year-old widow whose life is revived when a reform school graduate touches her heart and she can provide the grandmotherly love he needs—"warm, innocent . . . a charming central character." (FC) Algonquin, 1987. Its sequel is *Killer Diller* (1990). ○

Ehle, John
LAST ONE HOME
A family leaves the farm to try the insurance business in the growing little city of Asheville at the turn of the century—"strong place description [of city and country] . . . regional writing at its best." (FC) Har-Row, 1984. ○

Ehle, John
THE WINTER PEOPLE
Set during the depression, and part of a series of novels about two North Carolina mountain families over several generations. Har-Row, 1982. Preceding it are: *The Land Breakers* (1964), *The Journey of August King* (1971), and *The Road* (1967). ○

Fletcher, Inglis
RALEIGH'S EDEN
Fletcher's first historical novel (1940) set in Albemarle County. Other titles in the series include: *Men of Albemarle* (1942), *Lusty Wind for Carolina* (1944), *Toil of the Brave* (1946), *Roanoke Hundred* (1948), *The Scotswoman* (1954), and *The Wind in the Forest* (1957). Queens Hse, 1976–78. ○

Gingher, Marianne
BOBBY REX'S GREATEST HIT
The "greatest hit" is a song about a high school love affair that shakes up its heroine and the North Carolina town where she lives. Atheneum, 1986. ○

Godwin, Gail
A SOUTHERN FAMILY
Focuses on each member of a Mountain City family when one member, a New York City novelist, comes for a visit. Morrow, 1987. Also *A Mother and Two Daughters* (1982). ○

Johnston, Velda
A GIRL ON THE BEACH
A novel of suspense; a New York commercial artist on a North Carolina island needs to recover from an auto accident and sort out her life. She discovers the house she's renting has been the scene of a murder. Dodd, 1987. ○

McCammon, Robert R.
USHER'S PASSING
"Spine-tingling, atmospheric" suspense story of the descendants of Poe's Usher family as they gather to see who will inherit the ill-gotten Usher fortune. One of the descendants is a horror novelist intent on discovering the family's secrets. (FC) HR&W, 1984. ○

McCloy, Kristin
VELOCITY
After her mother is killed in a car accident, a grief-stricken daughter spends the summer in North Carolina with her father—"feverish behavior inevitable and credible . . . atmosphere of a small Southern town and the people who live there." (FC) Random, 1988. ○

McCorkle, Jill
FERRIS BEACH
Ferris Beach is a fictional place that exists in the mind of Katie Burns as she grows up in a small town in central North Carolina—"a nexus of illusions and fantasies." (NYT) Algonquin, 1990. Also *Tending to Virginia* (1987), about a young, married, pregnant woman dealing with personal insecurities, and *July 7th* (1984). ○

Malone, Michael
TIME'S WITNESS
A "page-turning" suspense novel of sleeze and corruption in Hillston—"the southern literary tradition at its finest." (FC) Little, 1989. Also *Uncivil Seasons* (1983).   ∘

Marshall, Edison
THE LOST COLONY
Fictional version of the vanished Raleigh Colony. Doubleday, 1964.   ∘

Pearson, T.R.
A SHORT HISTORY OF A SMALL PLACE
This, along with *Off for the Sweet Hereafter* (1985) and *The Last of How It Was* (1987), form a trilogy of novels about a mythical town called Neely, N.C.—"the language, earthy and elaborate, creates a world the reader will long to return to . . . the complete entering into the writer's dream." (NYT) S&S, 1985.   ∘

Price, Reynolds
KATE VAIDEN
Kate narrates her own story "to justify herself to a son she abandoned as a baby"— her life and the events that led up to his birth. (FC) Atheneum, 1986. Also *The Tongues of Angels* (1990), in which a famous painter looks back to 1954 and works as a counselor at a camp in North Carolina, and *Good Hearts* (1987).   ∘

Shivers, Louise
HERE TO GET MY BABY OUT OF JAIL
"Two men in love with one woman, and the consequences of such a triangle. . . . Sights, sounds, smells, textures" of the North Carolina tobacco country in 1937. (FC) Random, 1983.   ∘

Wolfe, Thomas
LOOK HOMEWARD ANGEL
Autobiographical novel of a native son of Asheville (Altamont in the book). Scribner, 1957 (first published 1929). Also *The Web and the Rock* (1939). A Thomas Wolfe memorial has been established in Asheville.   ∘

NORTH DAKOTA

*Series Guidebooks
(See Appendix 1)*

NOTE: See Series Guides (and non-series guides) listed under United States and the Midwest.

Background Reading

Berg, Francie M.
LAND OF CHANGING SEASONS
Flying Diamond Bks, 1983. Also *Ethnic Heritage in North Dakota* (1983).   ∘

Martin, Christopher
PRAIRIE PATTERNS: FOLK ARTS IN NORTH DAKOTA
ND Council on the Arts, 1989.   ∘

Schneider, Mary J.
NORTH DAKOTA INDIANS: AN INTRODUCTION
Kendall-Hunt, 1986.   ∘

GUIDEBOOKS

Hanson, Nancy E.
GETTING TO KNOW DAKOTA
An insider's guide to North Dakota. Prairie Hse, 1988.   ∘

McCaig, Barbara
DAKOTA'S PARKS GUIDE
Affordable Adventures, 1988.   ∘

Roehrick, Kaye L., ed.
BREVET'S NORTH DAKOTA HISTORICAL MARKERS & SITES
Brevet Pr, 1975.   ∘

HISTORY

Rezatto, Helen
THE MAKING OF THE TWO DAKOTAS
Media Publishing, 1989.   o

Wilkins, Robert P. and Wynona H.
NORTH DAKOTA
One of a series of popular histories for each state, published as part of the bicentennial in 1976. Norton, 1977.   o

Novels

Bojer, Johan
THE EMIGRANTS
Story of a group of land-hungry, impoverished Norwegian immigrants who settled in the Red River Valley area of North Dakota, and their battle against the elements. Greenwood, 1974 (first published in Norway in 1924).   o

Deloria, Ella C.
WATERLILY
The life of a Plains Sioux—a cultural narrative of the role of Native American women before the white settlers arrived. U of Nebraska Pr, 1988.   o

Erdrich, Louise
THE BEET QUEEN
With *Love Medicine* (1984) and *Tracks* (1988), a cycle of novels about the Chippewas in North Dakota. *Tracks* is earliest in time (1912–24) and uses characters from *Love Medicine* to depict "the escalating conflict between two Chippewa families . . . a riveting novel . . . as readable as [it] is complex." *Beet Queen* concerns the adventures of Mary Adare, abandoned in 1932 by her mother—"bizarre comedy, ordinary Midwestern facts and vigorous tragedy." (LJ) Holt, 1986.   o

Jones, Douglas C.
ARREST SITTING BULL
The story of what happened when the order "arrest Sitting Bull" went out—"of the Indians, trapped between a fight to the death and a willingness to try to assimilate." (FC) Scribner, 1977.   o

Rolvaag, O.E.
PEDER VICTORIOUS
Realistic portrayal of pioneer life on the plains—"penetrating study of pioneer psychology." Published in 1929. (FC) U of Nebraska Pr, 1982.   o

Unger, Douglas
LEAVING THE LAND
"Set in the west Dakotas dramatizes the destruction of the American family farm . . . a whole way of life"—compared to Willa Cather's *O Pioneers!* (Publisher) Har-Row, 1984.   o

Wolwode, Larry
BEYOND THE BEDROOM WALL
Family chronicle beginning in the 1930s (in Illinois), to present-day North Dakota—the "real theme [is] about the love between parents and children." (FC) FS&G, 1975. *Born Brothers* (1988) is the sequel.   o

OHIO

Series Guidebooks (See Appendix 1)

NOTE: See also Series Guides (and non-series guides) listed under United States and the Midwest.

Off the Beaten Path: Ohio

Background Reading

Davis, Peter
HOMETOWN
The author selected Hamilton, Ohio, with the assistance of the Bureau of Census, as a typical town of 50,000 to 100,000 population. His chapters focus on various events—a basketball game, a wedding, a policeman's rou-

tine day, a day in court, a fundamentalist church, and so on. Several of the chapters were produced as a PBS TV series. S&S, 1982.   ○

Joyce, Rosemary O.
A WOMAN'S PLACE
The life history of a rural Ohio grandmother. Ohio State U Pr, 1983.   ○

Kline, David
GREAT POSSESSIONS: AN AMISH FARMER'S JOURNAL
Amish farmer Kline describes life on his farm in southern Ohio—"keenly observed, personal, reverent, and wondrous natural history . . . may well become a quiet classic." (BL) N Point Pr, 1990.   ○

GUIDEBOOKS

Hochstetter, Nancy, ed.
TRAVEL HISTORIC OHIO
A guide to historic sites and markers. Guide Pr, 1986.   ○

Hunter, David and Nickell, Julie
SHIFRA STEIN'S DAY TRIPS FROM CINCINNATI
Getaways less than two hours away—16 itineraries that include the highlights of Ohio, Kentucky, Indiana, including museums, parks, special restaurants, Fort Knox, a riverboat trip, unique towns, architecturally fascinating Columbus, Indiana, and so on. Globe Pequot, 1991.   ○

McMinn, Russell
ANTIQUES
A guide to Ohio antique shops. Jockey Hollow, 1989.   ○

Soli, Lynn and McCaig, Barb
OHIO PARKS & FOREST GUIDE
Affordable Adventures, 1986.   ○

Traylor, Jeff and Nadean D.
LIFE IN THE SLOW LANE
A series of guides for Sunday drivers, bicyclists, and other explorers for Central Ohio, Northwest Ohio, Southwest Ohio and Beau-

tiful Ohio. Backroad Chronicles, 1987–88.   ○

Traylor, Jeff and Nadean D.
OHIO PRIDE
A guide to Ohio roadside history. Backroad Chronicles, 1990.   ○

HISTORY

Havighurst, Walter
OHIO
One of a series of popular histories for each state, published as part of the bicentennial in 1976. Norton, 1976.   ○

Knepper, George W.
OHIO AND ITS PEOPLE
History of "the most 'middle' of the midwestern states . . . sufficient anecdotes to make it interesting popular reading and enough detail and interpretation to satisfy a scholar's need for a historical synthesis." (LJ) Kent State U Pr, 1989.   ○

Novels

Anderson, Sherwood
WINESBURG, OHIO
The classic autobiographical novel of small-town life (Clyde is Winesburg)—"trials of adolescence [and] barren narrowness of small town life." (FC) Viking, 1960 (first published 1919). Also *Tar: A Midwest Childhood* (1926), and *Poor White* (1920).   ○

Chase, Joan
DURING THE REIGN OF THE QUEEN OF PERSIA
Three generations of women on a farm in northern Ohio in the 1950s, whose story is told by two pairs of cousins. The "Queen of Persia" is the matriarch—"language as rich and fertile as the farm land she writes about." (FC) Har-Row, 1983.   ○

Dell, George
THE EARTH ABIDETH
A novel of pioneer life in Fairfield County, written in 1938 and published recently for the first time—"a rich find." (FC) Ohio State U Pr, 1986.   ○

Eckert, Allan W.
JOHNNY LOGAN, SHAWNEE SPY
A novel based on fact of a captured Shawnee Indian youth who spies for the Americans—"the only Indian in Ohio history to be buried with military honors." (FC) Little, 1983.   o

Goldman, James
FULTON COUNTY
Annie, who's "had it" with Beaver County, Pennsylvania, signs on with a traveling strip show headed for Fulton County, Ohio—"proffering the new Peyton Place." (BL) Morrow, 1989.   o

McInerny, Ralph M.
THE SEARCH COMMITTEE
"Wicked insights" into academe at the Fort Elbow campus of University of Ohio when the chancellor has to be replaced after being picked up for drunken driving. (FC) Atheneum, 1991.   o

Nissenson, Hugh
THE TREE OF LIFE
The edge of the American frontier—"vivid account of the elemental cycle of life in the wilderness . . . the indefatigable nature of the pioneer spirit." (FC) Har-Row, 1985.   o

Richter, Conrad
THE AWAKENING LAND
Comprised of three separate novels: *The Trees* (1940), *The Fields* (1946), and *The Town* (1950). "Fictional Americana"—depicting the settlement of Ohio, beginning with primitive pioneering in the American wilderness north of the Ohio River, and on through making a farm out of the cleared land and the establishment of the town. (FC) Knopf, 1966.   o

Santmyer, Helen Hoover
". . . AND LADIES OF THE CLUB"
A small Ohio town from the perspective of a women's literary club, the lives of its members and their descendants. Putnam Pub Group, 1984.   o

Valin, Jonathan
**SECOND CHANCE: A HARRY
   STONER MYSTERY**
One of a series of crime novels set in Cincinnati, with Private Eye Harry Stoner as the "Chandleresque" detective. The daughter of a wealthy psychiatrist has disappeared, and Stoner deduces that she's "on a mission of vengeance." (FC) Delacorte, 1991. Other titles in the series include *Dead Letter* (1981), *Day of Wrath* (1982), *Fire Lake* (1988), *Extenuating Circumstances* (1989).   o

OKLAHOMA

*Series Guidebooks
(See Appendix 1)*

NOTE: See Series Guides (and non-series guides) listed under United States and the Midwest. You may also find some crossover in guides and books listed under Texas.

Background Reading

Debo, Angie
PRAIRIE CITY
"Partly fictionalized history of an Oklahoma town from founding in the 'run' of 1889" to the 1940s—a composite and typical community rather than an actual community, written with warmth and "rich in stories of

people." First published in 1949. (BRD) Council Oak Bks, 1985. Also *Oklahoma, Footloose and Fancy Free* (1987), first published in 1950 and now in a new edition by U of Oklahoma Press.   o

Faulk, Odie B. and others
**OKLAHOMA CITY: A
   CENTENNIAL PORTRAIT**
Windsor Pubns, 1989.   o

Jordan, Tom
**THE ROBBINS: OKLAHOMA HILL
   FOLK**
Oral history of the Robbins clan of southeast Oklahoma, from the days when it was a

territory through World War I, statehood, oil booms and busts, moonshining (with recipes) to contemporary days—"you'll laugh along with them as they share experiences but be prepared to cry." (Publisher) Didymus Pub, 1990.   ○

Morgan, Anne H. and Strickland, Rennard
OKLAHOMA MEMORIES
A collection of reminiscences of diverse people in their own words. U of Oklahoma Pr, 1977.   ○

Newson, D. Earl
DRUMRIGHT
The glory days of a boom town. Evans Pubns, 1985.   ○

Stephens, Donna M.
ONE-ROOM SCHOOL: TEACHING IN NINETEEN THIRTIES WESTERN OKLAHOMA
Written by a daughter about her mother's experiences as a Depression-era teacher in Oklahoma. U of Oklahoma Pr, 1990.   ○

GUIDEBOOKS

Kent, Ruth
OKLAHOMA TRAVEL HANDBOOK
U of Oklahoma Pr, 1987.   ○

McMinn, Russell
ANTIQUES
A guide to Oklahoma antique shops. Jockey Hollow, 1989.   ○

HISTORY

Gibson, Arrell M.
THE HISTORY OF OKLAHOMA
A history of five centuries. U of Oklahoma Pr, 1989. Also *The History of Oklahoma* (1981) and *The Oklahoma Story* (1978).   ○

Morgan, H. Wayne
OKLAHOMA
One of a series of popular histories for each state, published as part of the bicentennial in 1976. Norton, 1984.   ○

Novels

Braun, Matthew
THE KINCAIDS
A western, and a family saga, spanning several generations in which the first Kincaid "parlays a saloon won in a poker game into a business empire." (FC) Putnam Pub Group, 1976.   ○

Capps, Benjamin
THE WHITE MAN'S ROAD
A Comanche son of a white father and an Indian mother, and his quest for manhood in a society where Indian lands have been taken over. Set in the 1890s. Har-Row, 1969.   ○

Ferber, Edna
CIMARRON
Life in the land rush days of the 1880s as seen through the eyes of Sabra, the wife of a pioneering newspaper editor. It continues through the years of the oil boom, her husband's disappearance and her eventual election to Congress. Doubleday, 1930.   ○

Harris, Marilyn
WARRICK
An Oklahoma oil magnate revealed through reminiscences of grandchildren and associates as he lays dying. Doubleday, 1985.   ○

Lehrer, Jim
KICK THE CAN
Yes, this is the same Jim Lehrer who cohosts a news program for PBS-TV. It has been reviewed as a "delightfully engaging coming-of-age odyssey" of a young man who lost an eye in a "kick-the-can" game accident. (BL) Putnam, 1988. There's a series of sequels that continue One-Eyed Mack's odyssey as lieutenant governor of Oklahoma: *Crown Oklahoma* (1989), *Lost and Found* (1990) when Carter is in the White House and about the me generation attitudes and mid-

life crises. A new addition is *The Sooner Spy* (1991), a take-off on the espionage genre; One-Eyed Mack mixes it up with Russian spies. ○

Morgan, Speer
BELLE STARR
Novelization of the notorious woman outlaw's life and death. Little, 1979. ○

OREGON

Series Guidebooks (See Appendix 1)

NOTE: See also Series Guides (and nonseries guides) listed under United States and the West and the West/the Pacific Northwest.

Frommer: Seattle & Portland
Off the Beaten Path: Oregon
Sierra Guide: Natural Areas of Oregon & Washington

Background Reading

Alt, David and Hyndman, Donald
ROADSIDE GEOLOGY OF OREGON
One of a series of books that is wonderful to take along in the car—to paraphrase the preface, being able to look at the landscape as you travel and (with this book) envision the forces and changes, the dynamics of the landscape you are seeing, is a real achievement of understanding for travelers. Mountain Pr, 1978. ○

Applegate, Shannon
SKOOKUM: AN OREGON PIONEER FAMILY'S HISTORY AND LORE
A fifth generation descendant of the Applegate family tells their story from 1843, when three brothers settled in Yoncalla Valley— "reads like a novel." (PW) Beech Tree, 1988. ○

Franzwa, Gregory M.
OREGON TRAIL REVISITED
Excerpts from diaries and writings of early pioneers who traveled the Oregon Trail, along with a mile-by-mile driving guide. Patrice Pr, 1988. ○

Gulick, Bill
ROADSIDE HISTORY OF OREGON
A history to take along with you and perhaps read aloud to companions as you drive the state's highways. One of a unique series, written in lively narrative style. It's like having a knowledgeable friend along who has lived in the state for years. Mountain Pr, 1991. ○

McCarthy, Bridget B.
WHERE TO FIND THE OREGON IN OREGON
Read for background and as a guide to what is uniquely Oregonian—regional crafts, museums, foods, theater, music, celebrations. The state is divided into regions, with suggested tours and excursions. Self-published, 1989. ○

Ronda, James P.
ASTORIA AND EMPIRE
An interesting footnote for history buffs— in 1810, John Jacob Astor tried to create his own empire out of the Pacific Fur Company, at the mouth of the Columbia River. This is the history of that endeavor. U of Nebraska Pr, 1990. ○

Sullivan, William L.
LISTENING FOR COYOTE
A walk across Oregon's wilderness. Morrow, 1988. ○

Thoele, Mike
FOOTPRINTS ACROSS OREGON
Biographical sketches of a varied group of Oregonians, by a Eugene journalist. Graphic Arts Center, 1989. ○

Webber, Bert and Margie
OREGON'S COVERED BRIDGES: AN OREGON DOCUMENTARY
Webb Research Group, 1991.   o

Webber, Bert
RAJNEESHPURAM: WHO WERE ITS PEOPLE?
About the sect and its leader that for a time took over a town in Oregon. Webb Research, 1990.   o

GUIDEBOOKS

Holden, Glendon and Ronald
TOURING THE WINE COUNTRY OF OREGON
Holden Pac, 1984.   o

McCaig, Barbara
OREGON PARKS GUIDE
Affordable Adventures, 1988.   o

Mainwaring, William L.
EXPLORING THE OREGON COAST
Westridge Pr, 1990.   o

Oberrecht, Kenn
DRIVING THE PACIFIC COAST: OREGON AND WASHINGTON
Wonderful year-round guide for a coastal trip through the two states—"comprehensive yet selective" guide to 33 towns along 101, with history and covering museums, recreation, lodgings, restaurants, shopping. (Publisher) Globe Pequot, 1990.   o

Rank, Steve and Kincade, Kathy
FESTIVALS OF THE PACIFIC NORTHWEST
Your guided tour to festivals of Washington and Oregon. Landau Comns, 1989.   o

Smith, Kathy
PORTLAND RAINY DAY GUIDE: THE NATIVE'S HANDBOOK
Chronicle, 1983.   o

HISTORY

Dodds, Gordon
THE AMERICAN NORTHWEST: A HISTORY OF WASHINGTON & OREGON
Forum Pr, 1986.   o

Dodds, Gordon B.
OREGON
One of a series of popular histories for each state, published as part of the bicentennial in 1976. Norton, 1977. Also, *The American Northwest: A History of Washington & Oregon* (1986).   o

Novels

Berry, Don
TRASK
The book is based on the life of an actual person—Eldridge Trask—who pioneered in the Oregon Territory in the 1840s. "One of the few [books] that attempt to deal with the quality, character, and motives of the Indian." (FC) Viking, 1960.   o

Davis, H.L.
HONEY IN THE HORN
A novel about homesteading in the early 1900s that won a Pulitzer Prize in 1936. Larlin, 1975 (first published 1935).   o

Duncan, David J.
THE RIVER WHY
"Relates the reclusive backwoods exploits" of a man in pursuit of his true love—fly fishing." (FC) Sierra Club, 1983.   o

Lesley, Craig
WINTERKILL
A modern-day Nez Percé Indian rodeo performer drives from Oregon to Nebraska to find the son he's not seen for years and to teach him Indian tribal ways. Houghton, 1984.   o

Wilhelm, Kate
THE HAMLET TRAP
A mystery set in Ashland, home of the Oregon Shakespeare festival, with a husband and wife detective team. St. Martin, 1987. o

PENNSYLVANIA

Series Guidebooks

NOTE: See also Series Guides (and non-series guides) listed under United States and the East and the East/the Middle Atlantic States.

Fodor: Philadelphia (with Amish Country, Bucks County & Valley Forge)
Frommer: Philadelphia
Off the Beaten Path: Pennsylvania

Background Reading

Altick, Richard D.
OF A PLACE AND TIME: REMEMBERING LANCASTER
Reminiscences of a city with "paradoxical" communities—citified, Amish, farm-oriented—and how the city changed when tourism discovered the Amish, "nostalgic and infused with regional charm." (PW) Archon, 1991.　　　　　o

Dillard, Annie
AN AMERICAN CHILDHOOD
A memoir of growing up—"luminous prose . . . partly a hymn to Pittsburgh" in the 1950s. (PW) Har-Row, 1987.　　o

Gallery, John A.
PHILADELPHIA ARCHITECTURE
MIT, 1984.　　　　　　　　o

Good, Merle
WHO ARE THE AMISH?
Many of the general questions raised by outsiders about activities of the Amish are answered. Good Bks, 1985.　　o

Lukacs, John
PHILADELPHIA: PATRICIANS AND PHILISTINES, 1900–1950
The unique spirit of Philadelphia life, 1900–1950, with biographical sketches of seven people who flourished. FS&G, 1980.　o

Oplinger, Carl S. and Halma, J. Robert
THE POCONOS
Natural history of the area. Rutgers U Pr, 1988.　　　　　　　　o

Sharpless, Richard and Miller, Donald L.
THE KINGDOM OF COAL
As the northeast's "rust valleys" increase in number, the memory of America's heavy industry fades away. This is about coal and mining in the 19th and 20th centuries, how heavy industry developed nearby, the multiethnic coal towns, the strikes, John L. Lewis, the Molly Maguires. U of Pennsylvania Pr, 1985.　　　　　　　　o

Van Diver, Bradford B.
ROADSIDE GEOLOGY OF PENNSYLVANIA
One of a series of books that is wonderful to take along in the car—to paraphrase the preface, being able to look at the landscape as you travel and (with this book) envision the forces and changes, the dynamics of the landscape you are seeing, is a real achievement of understanding for travelers. Mountain Pr, 1990.　　　　　　o

Walters, Phil
JOHNSTOWN, MY UNCLE AND THE FLOOD
"Folksy, nostalgic . . . peppered with down-home humor"—eyewitness accounts of one of America's greatest natural disasters that happened 100 years ago. It conveys a feel for the era and "the hopelessness that immediately followed the disaster." (Publisher) Cliffwood, 1989.　　　o

Wolf, Edwin
PHILADELPHIA: PORTRAIT OF AN AMERICAN CITY
Updated edition of a book first published in 1975 as part of the Revolution bicentennial—a chronicle of the city, events and people. Camino Bks, 1990.　　　　　o

GUIDEBOOKS

Bonta, Marcia
OUTBOUND JOURNEYS IN PENNSYLVANIA
A guide to natural places for individual and group outings. Pennsylvania State U Pr, 1987.　　　　　　　　o

Boyce, Chris
PENNSYLVANIA PARKS GUIDE
Affordable Adventures, 1988.   ○

Curson, Julie P.
A GUIDE'S GUIDE TO PHILADELPHIA
A guide to history, culture, transportation, museums, sightseeing and sports of Philadelphia. Curson Hse, 1986.   ○

Hoffman, William N.
GOING DUTCH
A visitor's guide to the 14 southeastern counties that make up Pennsylvania Dutch country—"sensitivity to the needs of the quiet people who reside there." Arranged by county, with a historical overview of each and a description of tours, historic sites, museums, markets and shops, and an appendix listing accommodations and restaurants. (BL) Spring Garden, 1989.   ○

Keehn, Sally M. and David C.
HEXCURSIONS
Daytripping in and around Pennsylvania's Dutch country. Hastings, 1982.   ○

Seitz, R.
PENNSYLVANIA'S HISTORIC PLACES
A guide mostly to state-owned historical sites such as the Daniel Boone homestead, plus several parks such as Gettysburg. "Well-written essays" tell about the site and its significance with advice on what to do and see. (LJ) Good Bks, 1989.   ○

HISTORY

Cochran, Thomas C.
PENNSYLVANIA
One of a series of popular histories for each state, published as part of the bicentennial in 1976. Norton, 1978.   ○

Klein, Philip S. and Hoogenboom, Ari
A HISTORY OF PENNSYLVANIA
Pennsylvania State U Pr, 1980.   ○

Swetnam, George and Smith, Helene
THE GOVERNORS OF PENNSYLVANIA, 1790–1990
A bicentennial history. McDonald-Sward, 1990. Also *A Guidebook to Historic Western Pennsylvania* (1976).   ○

Novels

Allen, Hervey
THE CITY IN THE DAWN
An abridgement of the Colonial saga of a backwoodsman's progress from the forest primeval (as a Shawnee captive) to the civilization of a provincial Philadelphia. Rinehart, 1950. Titles in the original series are: *The Forest and the Fort* (1943), *Bedford Village* (1944), and *Toward the Morning* (1948).   ○

Caldwell, Taylor
ANSWER AS A MAN
Saga of an Irish immigrant's rise to wealth and power. Putnam Pub Group, 1981. Another family saga set in Pennsylvania is *Dynasty of Death* (1938), about the armaments industry and three generations of a family involved in it. Also with a Pennsylvania setting are *Testimony of Two Men* (1968) and *Ceremony of the Innocent* (1976).   ○

Carr, Robyn
WOMAN'S OWN
A 19th-century historical romance of three generations of Philadelphia Main Line women, who are unlucky when it comes to men. St. Martin, 1990.   ○

Constantine, K.C.
SUNSHINE ENEMIES
One of a series of mysteries, featuring Mario Balzic as chief of police of a western Pennsylvania town; reviews comment—"one of the most completely realized milieux in mystery fiction." (BRD) Mysterious Pr, 1990. Other titles in the series are: *The Man Who Liked Slow Tomatoes* (1982), *Always a Body to Trade* (1983), *Upon Some Midnight Clear* (1985), *Joey's Case* (1988).   ○

Davenport, Marcia
THE VALLEY OF DECISION
Saga of an Irish family in Pittsburgh, from 1873 to World War II. Bentley, 1979 (first published 1942).　　　　　○

Dexter, Pete
GOD'S POCKET
"A tough, funny articulate book about violent, sad, tragically inarticulate people" in a Philadelphia blue-collar neighborhood. The plot centers around a man who is killed for taunting a fellow worker. (FC) Random, 1983.　　　　　○

Dreiser, Theodore
THE BULWARK
"The shattering effects of twentieth-century materialism on the life of . . . a devout Pennsylvania Quaker." (FC) Doubleday, 1980 (first published 1946).　　　　　○

Fast, Howard
CITIZEN TOM PAINE
Fictionalized biography of the Revolutionary figure. Duell, 1943.　　　　　○

Hartog, Jan de
THE PEACEABLE KINGDOM
Recreation of Quaker life in Pennsylvania beginning in England in the seventeenth century, from which they were forced to flee to America. Atheneum, 1972.　　　　　○

Jakes, John
NORTH AND SOUTH
First in a projected series of three books that will chronicle the parallel lives of the Main and Hazard families from South Carolina and Pennsylvania, respectively, beginning in 1842, who are tied through their sons' attendance at West Point. Their lives also parallel America's struggles. "The characters, both fictional and real, make this era seem almost current." (FC) HarBraceJ, 1982. This is followed by In Love and War (1984), and the third book in the trilogy is Heaven and Hell (1987).　　　　　○

Kantor, MacKinlay
VALLEY FORGE
A recreation of the battle. Coward, 1934. Also Long Remember (1934), which depicts daily life on a day in July 1863.　　　　　○

King, Stephen
CHRISTINE
For horror fans—a car named Christine with "mysterious regenerative powers" is bought by a teenager who becomes both "obsessed by the car and possessed by its previous owner." (FC) Viking, 1983.　　　　　○

Marshall, Catherine
JULIE
Julie's father, a minister, gives up his post as an Alabama minister to purchase a small-town newspaper—"a family's triumph . . . during a critical time in America's history." (FC) McGraw, 1984.　　　　　○

Oates, Joyce Carol
SOLSTICE
The "parasitical relationship" of a recently divorced woman working as a teacher in a boys' school, and a locally famous woman artist. (FC) Dutton, 1985.　　　　　○

O'Hara, John
TEN NORTH FREDERICK
Character study of Joe Chapin, "first citizen of Gibbsville," and the woman he marries. Random, 1955. Also about people in the author's fictional hometown of Gibbsville, Pennsylvania (Pottsville), are: The Cape Cod Lighter (1962), And Other Stories (1968) and Sermons and Soda Water (1960).

　　Other novels by O'Hara with a Pennsylvania setting include: A Rage to Live (1949), From the Terrace (1958), Ourselves to Know (1960), Elizabeth Appleton (1963) and The Lockwood Concern (1965).　　　　　○

Parini, Jay
THE PATCH BOYS
A 15-year-old's summer in an Italian-Polish neighborhood of a Pennsylvania mining town of 1925. Holt, 1986.　　　　　○

Pulver, Mary M.
MURDER AT THE WAR

A medieval murder with a modern setting takes place at the annual event of a "medieval recreationist" organization in eastern Pennsylvania. St. Martin, 1987.   ○

Shaara, Michael
THE KILLER ANGELS

Recreation of the battle of Gettysburg, first published in 1974. PB, 1987.   ○

Shreve, Susan R.
MIRACLE PLAY

An "engaging Quaker family saga" set in Bucks County. (FC) Morrow, 1981.   ○

Updike, John
OF THE FARM

A visit to his mother's farm reveals the complicated interrelationships of four characters. Knopf, 1965. Also *The Centaur*, a modern version of the myth of the wisest centaur who gave up his immortality on behalf of Prometheus (1963).   ○

Updike, John
RABBIT, RUN

"Grotesque allegory of American life with its myth of happiness and success." Knopf, 1960. Also *Rabbit Redux* (1971) (10 years later) and *Rabbit Is Rich* (1981).   ○

Wideman, John E.
REUBEN

Reuben is a humpbacked black man in Homewood (Pittsburgh), serving as advocate and lawyer for the poor—"a series of powerful images that will burn long in the mind and conscience." (FC) Holt, 1987. Also *Philadelphia Fire* about destruction of the MOVE headquarters in 1985 (1990).   ○

Wideman, John E.
SENT FOR YOU YESTERDAY

A young black writer returns to Pittsburgh to assume the roles of son and father. The setting, "Homewood," is an imaginary place, a black ghetto, based on an actual district in Pittsburgh. Schocken, 1984. Also *Hiding Place* (1981) and *Damballah* (1981), a collection of short stories.   ○

Williamson, Chet
ASH WEDNESDAY

A horror story with overtones of Peyton Place—all the folks who ever died in Merridale return as blue ghosts in the same form as when death struck. Tor Bks, 1989.   ○

Zellerbach, Merla
RITTENHOUSE SQUARE

A woman real estate dealer is determined to get revenge on those who snubbed her as a child by reshaping Philadelphia through her real estate dealings. Random, 1989.   ○

RHODE ISLAND

*Series Guidebooks
(See Appendix 1)*

NOTE: See Series Guides (and non-series guides) listed under United States and the East and the East/New England.

Background Reading

Bradner, Lawrence H.
THE PLUM BEACH LIGHT

The birth, life and death of a lighthouse. Self-published, 1989.   ○

Crolius, Peter C., ed.
A WICKFORD ANTHOLOGY

Dutch Island Pr, 1985.   ○

Dow, Richard A. and Mowbray, E. Andrew
NEWPORT

Mowbray, 1976.   ○

Lippincott, Bertram
INDIANS, PRIVATEERS AND HIGH SOCIETY
"A collection of historical sketches about Rhode Island from earliest days through to the 1960s Jazz Festival riots." (BRD) Lippincott, 1961. ○

O'Connor, Richard
THE GOLDEN SUMMERS
"An antic social history" of Newport and anecdotal account of its wealthy. Putnam, 1974. ○

Warburton, Eileen
IN LIVING MEMORY: A CHRONICLE OF NEWPORT, RHODE ISLAND: 1888–1988
RI Publications Soc, 1988. ○

GUIDEBOOKS

Meras, Phyllis
EXPLORING RHODE ISLAND: A VISITOR'S GUIDE TO THE OCEAN STATE
Providence Journal Co, 1984. ○

Weber, Ken
WALKS AND RAMBLES IN RHODE ISLAND
A guide to the natural and historic wonders of the Ocean State. Countryman, 1986. ○

Whitman, Herbert
EXPLORING OLD BLOCK ISLAND
Chatham Pr, 1988. ○

HISTORY

McLoughlin, William G.
RHODE ISLAND
One of a series of popular histories for each state, published as part of the bicentennial in 1976. Norton, 1978. ○

Novels

Auchincloss, Louis
THE HOUSE OF FIVE TALENTS
"The effects of great wealth upon . . . numerous members of the family and those who marry into it"—with a Newport setting. (FC) Houghton, 1960. ○

Casey, John
SPARTINA
Spartina is pond grass and also the name of Dick Pierce's boat and his key to independence. When Dick starts poaching clams to finance the boat, he gets involved with a woman officer of the Department of Natural Resources—"possibly the best American novel about going fishing since The Old Man and the Sea." (FC) Knopf, 1989. ○

Farrelly, Peter
OUTSIDE PROVIDENCE
"Hilarious yet melancholy novel of a man's coming of age in the 1970s." Atl Monthly Pr, 1987. ○

Paul, Raymond
THE TRAGEDY AT TIVERTON: AN HISTORICAL NOVEL OF MURDER
When a 29-year-old unmarried, pregnant woman is found hanged, suicide is presumed, but evidence in her belongings results in the first trial for murder in America in which the accused is a minister. Based on historical fact—"a riveting tale . . . all the more tragic and lurid in its puritanical New England setting. . . . sure to please readers of both historical fiction and mysteries." (FC) Viking, 1984. ○

Plante, David
THE FAMILY
First of a trilogy about a French-Canadian family in Providence, beginning in the 1950s—"takes on the dimensions of O'Neill's Long Day's Journey into Night," in its exploration of relationships between parents and sons. Atheneum, 1978. Following are The Country (1981), The Woods (1982) and The Native (1988), which is a generation away and set in Boston. ○

Ravin, Neil
INFORMED CONSENT
A medical novel set in Newport, in which a young researcher in endocrinology makes a remarkable diagnosis of adrenal cancer—

"good local color of the College Hill section of Providence [and] real insight into medicine and medical ethics." (FC) Putnam Pub Group, 1983.   o

Sapir, Richard B.
SPIES

The co-owner of a hardware store has a World War II past of being leader of a German spy ring; his pleasant life since then is endangered when the FBI reopens investigation of the ring. Doubleday, 1984.   o

Updike, John
WITCHES OF EASTWICK

Three women with failed marriages are the witches, empowered by their new independence and "the very air of Eastwick." (FC) Knopf, 1984.   o

Wilder, Thornton
THEOPHILUS NORTH

A schoolteacher defines nine social classes in Newport—nine "separate cities" within the city—and the novel tells of his encounters with each. The period is the 1920s. (FC) Har-Row, 1973.   o

Wolff, Geoffrey
PROVIDENCE

A "magnetic tale of corruption and redemption," with a patrician criminal lawyer, a hood, an honorable cop and a "coked-up good-time girl"—all living in Providence. The *New York Times Book Review* said, "A splendid novel . . . wonderfully well-written, restrained and exuberant at once." (Publisher) Viking, 1986.   o

SOUTH CAROLINA

Series Guidebooks
(See Appendix 1)

NOTE: See also Series Guides (and non-series guides) listed under United States and the South. You may also find some crossover in guides and books listed under the East about the eastern coast.

Michael's Guide: South Carolina

Background Reading

Bethel, Elizabeth R.
**PROMISELAND, SOUTH
CAROLINA**

A century of life in a Negro community. Temple U, 1982.   o

Bresee, Clyde
**HOW GRAND A FLAME: A
CHRONICLE OF A
PLANTATION FAMILY**

Reconstruction from original documents, diaries and letters, of the life of a South Carolina plantation family—"transcends time and locale. . . . This splendidly evocative visitation neither condemns nor celebrates the certain way of life it captures, simply remembers it." (BL) Algonquin, 1991.   o

Bresee, Clyde
SEA ISLAND YANKEE

Eloquent memoir of the author's early years on James Island—"evokes great times in a lovely locale." (PW) Algonquin, 1986.   o

Carawan, Guy and Candie
**AIN'T YOU GOT A RIGHT TO THE
    TREE OF LIFE?**

The people of Johns Island, South Carolina—their faces, their words, their songs. The author and his wife lived on Johns Island from 1963 to 1965, collecting interviews and recording a way of life that was falling victim to the ravages of time. This is the second edition of their book, originally published in 1967. U of Georgia Pr, 1989.   o

Fields, Mamie G. and Karen
**LEMON SWAMP AND OTHER
    PLACES: A CAROLINA MEMOIR**

Memoir of a black grandmother (born in 1888) written for her granddaughters—"her youth, teaching school on John's Island, of

parties and courtship . . . of the easy relation between the races before Jim Crow rules
. . . a simple life but an engrossing one."
(BL) Free Pr, 1985.   ○

Gragg, Rod
**PIRATES, PLANTERS AND
    PATRIOTS**
Historical tales from the South Carolina Grand
Strand. Book Service Assoc, 1984.   ○

Powell, Lew
**LEW POWELL'S CAROLINA
    FOLLIES**
"A nose-tweaking look at life in our two
great and goofy states" is the subtitle. Down
Home Pr, 1990.   ○

Roberts, Nancy and Bruce
**SOUTH CAROLINA GHOSTS:
    FROM THE MOUNTAINS TO
    THE COAST**
U of South Carolina, 1983.   ○

Wells, Randall A.
ALONG THE WACCAMAW
Culture shock of a couple who settle in a
small town near Myrtle Beach—"engaging
account of adjusting to a different rhythm."
(PW) Algonquin, 1990.   ○

GUIDEBOOKS

McMinn, Russell
ANTIQUES
A guide to South Carolina antique shops.
Jockey Hollow, 1989.   ○

Rhyne, Nancy
**THE GRAND STRAND: AN
    UNCOMMON GUIDE TO
    MYRTLE BEACH AND ITS
    SURROUNDINGS**
"A lively and informative tour of an area
steeped in history and tradition . . . there
is much more to do in Myrtle Beach, S.C.
than lie in the sun." (Publisher) Globe Pequot, 1985.   ○

Wenberg, Donald C.
**BLUE RIDGE MOUNTAIN
    PLEASURES**
An A-to-Z guide to northern Georgia, west-
ern North Carolina and the up country of
South Carolina. Globe Pequot, 1988.   ○

HISTORY

Rosen, Robert N.
**A SHORT HISTORY OF
    CHARLESTON**
"Sprightly and entertaining . . . has cap-
tured the flavor and flair of Charleston."
(Publisher) Lexikos, 1982.   ○

Wright, Louis B.
SOUTH CAROLINA
One of a series of popular histories for each
state, published as part of the bicentennial
in 1976. Norton, 1977.   ○

Novels

Basso, Hamilton
THE LIGHT INFANTRY BALL
A Carolina planter's experiences during the
Civil War is the plot for this romantic his-
torical novel. Doubleday, 1959.   ○

Conroy, Pat
THE LORDS OF DISCIPLINE
A Carolina military school in the 1960s.
Houghton, 1980.   ○

Conroy, Pat
THE PRINCE OF TIDES
About a feminist poet's suicide attempt in
New York City and the need for reconstruc-
tion and analysis of her early life in South
Carolina. HM, 1986.   ○

Fast, Howard
FREEDOM ROAD
Historical novel of Reconstruction and Gid-
eon Jackson, the black leader who rose to
be a member of Congress. Duell, Sloan &
Pearce, 1944.   ○

Heyward, DuBose
PORGY
Classic story, and plot for the opera, of a
crippled black and his love for Bess. Larlin,

1970 (first published 1925). Also *Mamba's Daughters* (1929).   o

Humphreys, Josephine
DREAMS OF SLEEP

A first novel that "provides a fresh, new perspective" of alienation and parent/child, black/white, male/female relationships. (FC) Viking, 1984.   o

Humphreys, Josephine
RICH IN LOVE

Set in a town near Charleston, described "in vivid and loving detail" with a plot about one summer's events in the life of a 17-year-old whose mother leaves abruptly to begin a new life. (BRD) Viking, 1987. Also *The Fireman's Fair* (1991).   o

Jakes, John
NORTH AND SOUTH

First in a projected series of three novels that chronicles the parallel lives of the Main and Hazard families in South Carolina and Pennsylvania, respectively, beginning in 1842, who are tied through their sons' attendance at West Point. Their lives also parallel America's struggles. "The characters both fictional and real, make this era seem almost current." (FC) HarBraceJ, 1982. This is followed by *In Love and War* (1984); the third book in the trilogy is *Heaven and Hell* (1987).   o

L'Engle, Madeleine
THE OTHER SIDE OF THE SUN

A gothic novel about a young English girl who is sent alone to the South, after the

Civil War, and finds "a brace of aging eccentric relatives" and racial strife. (FC) FS&G, 1971.   o

Powell, Padgett
EDISTO

Set in a coastal town—the adolescent education of a "Holden Caulfield for the 1980s." (FC) FS&G, 1984.   o

Ripley, Alexandra N.
ON LEAVING CHARLESTON

Sequel to *Charleston* (1982)—saga of a decadent southern plantation family. Doubleday, 1984.   o

Sayers, Valerie
HOW I GOT HIM BACK, OR UNDER THE COLD MOON'S SHINE

Characters in this book were introduced in its predecessor, *Due East* (1987), and their lives go on—"writes clearly and forcefully, with her own version of the humor that Southern writers . . . use so tellingly." (FC) Doubleday, 1989. Also *Who Do You Love* (1991), which takes place at the time of Kennedy's assassination and parallels the loss of innocence of a young girl.   o

Whitney, Phyllis A.
WOMAN WITHOUT A PAST

A rising star in the suspense novel genre has a chance meeting that leads to the discovery of the truth about her parentage. Doubleday, 1991.   o

SOUTH DAKOTA

Series Guidebooks (See Appendix 1)

NOTE: See Series Guides (and non-series guides) listed under United States and the Midwest.

Background Reading

Berg, Francie M.
SOUTH DAKOTA: LAND OF SHINING GOLD

One of the Old West regional series—"an enticement to tourists . . . a source book for the researcher [includes] business and industry, agriculture, the arts, early ranching, the fur trade, vacation spots." (BL) Flying Diamond, 1982.   o

Froiland, Sven G. and Weedon, Ronald R.
NATURAL HISTORY OF THE BLACK HILLS AND BADLANDS
Center for Western Studies, 1990.   o

Garfinkel, Martin
STURGIS, SD: MOTORCYCLE MECCA
A photoessay on this town and the annual Black Hills Motorcycle Classic, which convenes for a week every August when Sturgis becomes the motorcycle mecca of the world— "the mystique encompasses them, leather-clad and tattoo-ridden . . . symbolizing danger and rebellion." (BL) ZG Pub, 1990.
                                        o

Hasselstrom, Linda
WINDBREAK
The author is a poet, essayist, working ranchwoman, wife—this book and *Going Over East* (1987) are about what it's like to live on and run a ranch in South Dakota. Contains "the essential goodness of ranching life" and her attempts to integrate the seemingly disparate roles she plays. (BL) Bani Owl Bks, 1987.   o

Parker, Watson
DEADWOOD: THE GOLDEN YEARS
"Lively, colorful . . . amusing" account of the gold-mining boom in South Dakota's Black Hills and in Deadwood—"boss city of the Hills." (PW) U of Nebraska, 1981.   o

Smith, Rex A.
THE CARVING OF MOUNT RUSHMORE
Gutzon Borglum, creator of Mount Rushmore, "revealed as a talented but contentious man with a dream . . . the politics and technique surrounding the carving . . . interviews with many of the participants" and many photos. (Choice) Abbeville Pr, 1985.   o

GUIDEBOOKS

Fielder, Mildred
A GUIDE TO BLACK HILLS GHOST MINES
North Plains, 1972.   o

HISTORY

Milton, John R.
SOUTH DAKOTA
One of a series of popular histories for each state, published as part of the bicentennial in 1976. Norton, 1989.   o

Rezatto, Helen
THE MAKING OF THE TWO DAKOTAS
Media Publishing, 1989.   o

Novels

Adams, Harold
THE MAN WHO MISSED THE PARTY
One of several mysteries set in South Dakota towns in the 1930s, in which Carl Wilcox, with an ex-con and ex-cop background, is the detective—"Adams paints vividly realistic settings and creates memorable characters that are involving and enjoyable to read about." (FC) Mysterious Pr, 1989. Other titles include: *The Fourth Widow* (1987), *The Barbed Wire Noose* (1987), *The Man Who Met the Train* (1988).   o

Dexter, Pete
DEADWOOD
"Unpredictable, hyperbolic" novel of Deadwood, Wild Bill Hickok, Calamity Jane and other legendary characters of the late 1800s. (FC) Random, 1986.   o

Jones, Douglas C.
A CREEK CALLED WOUNDED KNEE
Last book in a trilogy about the tragedy of Wounded Knee from three perspectives— Indians, the press, the Federal troops. Scribner, 1978. Previous titles are: *The Court-Martial of George Armstrong Custer* (1976) and *Arrest Sitting Bull* (1977) (listed under "North Dakota").   o

O'Brien, Dan
THE SPIRIT OF THE HILLS
"Exciting, absorbing" novel with several plot threads—some animal is killing the cattle at night, a Vietnam veteran is seeking revenge and there's an Indian sit-in at Mount Rushmore. (LJ) Crown, 1988. ❍

Rolvaag, O.E.
GIANTS IN THE EARTH
Prairie saga of Norwegian immigrants and life on the frontier. Har-Row, 1965 (first published 1927). Also with similar themes, *The Third Life of Per Smevik* (1912) and *Peder Victorious* (1929). ❍

Spenser, LaVyrle
FORGIVING
The setting is Deadwood in 1876, when South Dakota was still part of the Dakota Territory. A woman arrives with her father's printing press and two goals, to open a newspaper and to find her sister. Putnam, 1991. ❍

Unger, Douglas
LEAVING THE LAND
"Set in the west Dakotas. Dramatizes the destruction of the American family farm . . . a whole way of life"—compared to Willa Cather's *O Pioneers!* (Publisher) Har-Row, 1984. ❍

TENNESSEE

Series Guidebooks
(See Appendix 1)

NOTE: See also Series Guides (and non-series guides) listed under United States and the South.

Off the Beaten Path: Tennessee

Background Reading

Acuff, Roy and Neely, William
ROY ACUFF'S NASHVILLE
The life and good times of country music. Putnam Pub Group, 1983. ❍

Callahan, North
TVA: BRIDGE OVER TROUBLED WATERS
History of the TVA by an early participant and a lifetime resident of the area—intended for the general reader. Cornwall Bks, 1980. ❍

Jenkins, Peter, and others
THE TENNESSEE SAMPLER
Definitive guide to the author's adopted state. He tells about the state's music, wit and wisdom, where to eat and sleep, the outdoors, in homespun prose along with local expert commentary. Nelson, 1985. ❍

Lomax, John, III
NASHVILLE: MUSIC CITY USA
Celebration of Nashville offers a fine overview of country music and enjoyable tour of Music City USA. Abrams, 1985. ❍

Lynn, Loretta
COAL MINER'S DAUGHTER
Autobiography of the country singer, first published in 1976. Contemporary Bks, 1990. ❍

Tassin, Myron and Henderson, Jerry
FIFTY YEARS AT THE GRAND OLE OPRY
With a foreword by Minnie Pearl. Pelican, 1975. ❍

GUIDEBOOKS

Cornwell, Ilene J.
TRAVEL GUIDE TO THE NATCHEZ TRACE PARKWAY
The parkway runs between Natchez, Mississippi, and Nashville. Southern Resources, 1984. ❍

Schemmel, William
HOW, WHEN AND WHERE IN TENNESSEE
A guide to Knoxville, Nashville, Memphis, Chattanooga, Gatlinburg and the Smoky

Mountains. Also *Marmac Guide to Nashville.* Marmac, 1982 and 1984. ○

HISTORY

Dykeman, Wilma
TENNESSEE
One of a series of popular histories for each state, published as part of the bicentennial in 1976. Norton, 1977. ○

Novels

Agee, James
A DEATH IN THE FAMILY
A few days in the lives of a Knoxville family at the turn of the century, from just before a man dies until the day of his funeral—poses "a universal human situation most affectingly." (FC) McDowell, 1957. ○

Alther, Lisa
KINFLICKS
Story of a woman's life told in flashback, as she moves from cheerleader, to collegian, anti-war lesbian, organic farmer, and finally to her present predicament. Knopf, 1981. Also *Original Sins* (1981), growing up of a mill owner's daughter, the mill foreman's sons, and the black maid's son. ○

Bell, Madison S.
SOLDIER'S JOY
"A tale of rich religious and political symbolism infused with a compelling, rewarding sense of place." The plot concerns a Vietnam vet's return to his Tennessee home near Nashville. (FC) Ticknor & Fields, 1989. ○

Clouse, Loletta
WILDER
"Vivid imagery" in a first novel by a Knoxville librarian, picturing "a way of life slowly coming to an end." (LJ) Rutledge Hill Pr, 1990. ○

Faulkner, William
THE REIVERS
Reminiscence of a youthful escapade—"smuggling a horse across country, plan-

ning a bizarre race, and ending in jail." (FC) Random, 1962. ○

Ford, Jesse Hill
THE LIBERATION OF LORD BYRON JONES
A black man files a divorce suit charging his wife with having an affair with a white policeman. "The involvements and responses of each major and minor character . . . revealed from his particular personal point of view." (FC) Little, 1980 (first published 1965). Also *Fishes, Birds and Sons of Men* (1967), short stories set in the same town of Summerton. ○

Ford, Jesse Hill
THE RAIDER
Historical novel, based on stories passed down in his own family, of a frontiersman in west Tennessee who carves a plantation out of the wilderness only to lose it, his slaves, his wife and son, in the Civil War. Atlantic Monthly Pr, 1975. ○

Grisham, John
THE FIRM
A Harvard Law School graduate is hired by a Memphis law firm and finds that the front-office clientele is a facade for Mafia activities. He agrees to work as an undercover agent for the FBI—"suspense, wit, and polished writing." (FC) Doubleday, 1991. ○

Harris, Charlaine
A SECRET RAGE
Following a successful career as a New York model, the heroine returns to Tennessee to finish college and finds "mannered dignity . . . distrust . . . overt racism" and becomes victim to violence—"extraordinary novel [that] offers more than a saga of victimization and recovery." (FC) Houghton, 1984. ○

McDonald, Gregory
A WORLD TOO WIDE
A jazz pianist offers his Tennessee farm as the setting for a wedding. Hill, 1987. ○

Mason, F. Van Wyck
WILD HORIZON
Historical novel of frontier life during the Revolutionary War. Little, 1966. ○

O'Connor, Flannery
WISE BLOOD
"An important addition to the grotesque literature of Southern decadence" (FC) and religious fanaticism. FS&G, 1962 (first published 1952). Also *The Violent Bear It Away* (1960). ○

Taylor, Peter H.
A SUMMONS TO MEMPHIS
"Delicious novel about minute social discriminations"—the bachelor son of the family is summoned home because his widowed father is planning to remarry at 81. (BRD) Knopf, 1986. Also *In the Miro District* (1977) and *Collected Stories of Peter Taylor* (1969). ○

Warren, Robert Penn
THE CAVE
A young hillbilly becomes trapped in a cave and the effects of this event on many people in a small town. Random, 1959. *Flood* (1964) is another novel about the reactions of a town in western Tennessee—the building of a dam is the event around which the plot develops. Also *At Heaven's Gate* (1943) and *Circus in the Attic and Other Stories* (1948) have Tennessee settings. ○

TEXAS

*Series Guidebooks
(See Appendix 1)*

NOTE: See also Series Guides (and nonseries guides) listed under United States and the West. You may also find some crossover in guides and books listed under the West/ the Southwest or the South.

Fodor: Texas
Insight Guide: Texas
Moon Handbook: Texas
2–22 Days Itinerary Planning Guide: Texas

Background Reading

Brook, Stephen
HONEYTONK GELATO: TRAVEL THROUGH TEXAS
A British author's "whirlwind romp around Texas. . . . a fresh, informative look at the larger-than-life state." (PW) Paragon Hse, 1988. ○

Burns, Mamie Sypert
THIS I CAN LEAVE YOU: A WOMAN'S DAYS ON THE PITCHFORK RANCH
The author lived on the ranch from 1942 to 1965, while her husband was ranch manager. These are her observations, notes and journals, "kept as a tribute to D (her husband) and a legacy for her grandchildren . . . her book is delightful and humorous, a true picture of ranch people and ranch life in the 20th century." (LJ) Texas A&M Pr, 1987. ○

Corder, Jim W.
LOST IN WEST TEXAS
"Heady brew of folklore, history and philosophy . . . nostalgia and wonderment . . . result is a sense of place that proves as vivid as the depicted western landscape." (BL) Texas A&M U Pr, 1988. ○

Dobie, J. Frank
OUT OF THE OLD ROCK
Profiles and portraits of people of the past—writers, cowmen, gunmen, preachers, wits and others—"pure Dobie . . . leaves the partaker wanting more." (BRD) U of Texas Pr, 1982. ○

Eisen, Jonathan and Straugh, Harold, eds.
UNKNOWN TEXAS
Anthology of lively memoirs, stories, "higher journalism" and excerpts from novels set in Texas; arranged around themes such as the

vast size of Texas or the 19th-century mythos, oil boom days and so on. (BL) Macmillan, 1988. ○

Graham, Don
TEXAS: A LITERARY PORTRAIT
A photo book with selections from writings of Texans and non-Texans, divided into geographical regions with an essay on each region plus additional suggested readings. Corona, 1985. ○

Graves, John
FROM A LIMESTONE LEDGE: SOME ESSAYS AND OTHER RUMINATIONS ABOUT COUNTRY LIFE IN TEXAS
Essays on septic tanks, patching a leaky trough for heifers, vain hunts for legendary riches of Spanish silver, beekeeping, etc.— "delightfully fresh figures of speech and literary allusions." (BRD) Pacesetter Pr, 1984. Also *Hard Scrabble* (1974)—"folklore, people and natural history of north central Texas." ○

Greene, A.C.
DALLAS USA
"Past, present, and future of Big D . . . treasure trove of worthwhile information . . . invaluable [for in-depth visit or relocation]." (BL) Pacesetter Pr, 1984. ○

Greene, A.C.
TEXAS SKETCHES
Essays that cut through the tall tales, by a Texas historian—"succinctly rendered prose . . . fascinating reading." (BL) Taylor Pub, 1985. Also *It's Been Fun: Oil Field Stories from the Texas Boom Days* (1986). ○

Haley, James L.
TEXAS: AN ALBUM OF HISTORY
Key events, quotes from primary sources, provide a vivid history of the state. Doubleday, 1985. ○

Harrigan, Stephen
A NATURAL STATE
A collection of "engaging essays . . . the fresh outlook of a city-bred tourist rejoicing

in the exhilaration of discovery . . . his fascination with land, plants, animals, and history." Topics range from the Gulf Coast and Chihuahuan Desert to the Houston Zoo. Pacesetter Pr, 1988. ○

Hurt, Harry
TEXAS RICH
"A composite biography of the Hunt family from the early oil days through the silver crash." (BRD) Norton, 1982. ○

Kramer, Jane
THE LAST COWBOY
"The plight of the cowboy in the age of computer ranching." (BRD) FS&G, 1988. ○

Lea, Tom
THE KING RANCH
Two-volume story by a Texas writer-artist of the making of a man, a ranch and a way of life. Little, 1957. ○

Lich, Lera Tyler
LARRY MCMURTRY'S TEXAS: EVOLUTION OF A MYTH
Literate study of McMurtry's life, fictional themes and literary influence—"astute analysis of his novels." (BL) Eakin Pr, 1988. ○

McDonald, Archie P.
THE TEXAS EXPERIENCE
Commemorates the sesquicentennial of the founding of the Texas Republic in 70 brief essays by recognized authorities, on events, famous people, ordinary people, the Alamo, oil, Prohibition and so on. (BL) Texas A&M U Pr, 1986. ○

McMurtry, Larry
IN A NARROW GRAVE: ESSAYS ON TEXAS
S&S, 1989. ○

Porterfield, Bill
THE GREATEST HONKY-TONKS IN TEXAS
History and lore of honky-tonks on the outskirts of Texas towns and a guide to the best—"entertaining anecdotes and back-

ground details for each [with a] concluding primer on country-and-western dance steps." (BL) Taylor Pub, 1983. Also *Texas Rhapsody: Memories of a Native Son* (1981).   ☊

Presley, James
A SAGA OF WEALTH: THE RISE OF THE TEXAS OILMEN
Anecdotal and popular history of Texas oil. Texas Monthly Pr, 1983.   ☊

Prindle, David F.
TEXAS MONTHLY'S POLITICAL READER
Pacesetter Pr, 1985.   ☊

Robinson, Charles M.
FRONTIER FORTS OF TEXAS
The key role that the forts played in Texas history—people, events. There is also "guidebook" information about where they are located and the extent of restoration, etc. Lone Star Bks, 1986.   ☊

Spearing, Darwin
ROADSIDE GEOLOGY OF TEXAS
One of a series of books that is wonderful to take along in the car—to paraphrase the preface, being able to look at the landscape as you travel and (with this book) envision the forces and changes, the dynamics of the landscape you are seeing, is a real achievement of understanding for travelers. Mountain Pr, 1991.   ☊

Strickland, Ron
TEXANS: SELF PORTRAITS FROM THE LONE STAR STATE
"A lively and nostalgic collection of oral histories from one of our most flamboyant states"—Pecos rodeo announcer Buck Jackson, the oldest living Texas Ranger, tales of an outlaw train robber, an S&L banker and much more—50 individuals in all. (Publisher) Paragon Hse, 1991.   ☊

GUIDEBOOKS

Albright, Dawn
TEXAS FESTIVALS: THE MOST COMPLETE GUIDE TO CELEBRATIONS IN THE LONE STAR STATE
"A delightful romp through the cultural diversity of the Lone Star State" and a profile of over 300 festivals. Palmetto Pr, 1991.   ☊

Barrington, Carol
SHIFRA STEIN'S DAY TRIPS FROM HOUSTON: GETAWAYS LESS THAN TWO HOURS AWAY
Part of a series that provides maps and detailed information on day-tripping from a particular city. "Twenty-two day trips with information on museums, shops, restaurants, farms, campgrounds, trails, canoe routes, sporting events, celebrations, historic sites, and much more." (BL) Globe Pequot, 1991.   ☊

Germaine, Elizabeth
TEXAS: AN A–Z GUIDE
Outlet Bks, 1989.   ☊

Houk, Rose
HEART'S HOME: L.B.J.'S COUNTRY HOME
Southwest Parks & Monuments Assn, 1986.   ☊

McCaig, Barbara
TEXAS PARKS GUIDE
Affordable Adventures, 1988.   ☊

McMinn, Russell
ANTIQUES
A guide to Texas antique shops. Jockey Hollow, 1989.   ☊

Rafferty, Robert
TEXAS COAST
"Discover delights along the Gulf coast of Texas . . . a complete guide to the Texas Riviera in chatty, informal style." (LJ) Pacesetter Pr, 1986.   ☊

Tall, Delena and Miller, George
A TEXAS MONTHLY FIELD GUIDE TO WILDFLOWERS, TREES, AND SHRUBS OF TEXAS
Gulf Pub, 1991.   ☊

Tyler, Paula E. and Ron
TEXAS MUSEUMS: A GUIDEBOOK
U of Texas, 1983.   ☊

Wiley, Nancy
THE GREAT STATE FAIRS OF TEXAS: AN ILLUSTRATED HISTORY
Taylor Pub Co, 1985. ○

Zelade, Richard
THE HILL COUNTRY: THE TEXAS MONTHLY GUIDEBOOK
"Pleasures and surprises in central Texas" via back road itineraries, restaurants and "water holes." (Publisher) Pacesetter Pr, 1987. ○

HISTORY

Calvert, Richard and DeLeon, Arnoldo
THE HISTORY OF TEXAS
Harlan Davidson, 1990. ○

Frantz, Joe B.
TEXAS
One of a series of popular histories for each state published as part of the bicentennial in 1976. Norton, 1984. ○

McComb, David G.
TEXAS: A MODERN HISTORY
For the general reader, with anecdotes, folklore, historical photos—Texas history from earliest Indian inhabitants to the present, with an emphasis on the 20th century and on ethnic groups, blacks, women and how Texas has managed modern-day problems. U of Texas Pr, 1989. ○

Weems, John E. and Jane
DREAM OF EMPIRE
First published in 1971—"highly readable and interesting human history" of Texas during the time it was a sovereign state (1836–46); derived from diaries, journals and letters of 12 people who lived during the period. (BRD) Texas Christian U Pr, 1986. ○

Novels

Barthelme, Frederick
NATURAL SELECTION
Midlife crisis and marital problems in a Houston suburb. Viking, 1990. ○

Bird, Sarah
THE MOMMY CLUB
Surrogate motherhood in San Antonio. Doubleday, 1991. ○

Brammer, Billy L.
THE GAY PLACE
"Three related novels . . . portraying a southern state which is obviously Texas" with three protagonists: a state legislator, the state's senator, the governor's press secretary. The reviewer for *People Magazine* who complained about the omission of this novel in the previous edition, called this "probably the best novel ever written about Texas" in contrast, he said, to James Michener's *Texas,* which he termed "probably the dumbest book ever written about the state." Random, 1983. ○

Erdman, Loula Grace
THE EDGE OF TIME
Frontier life in the panhandle in 1885— "honest, literate telling of one of the lesser-known chapters" in the American saga. Dodd, 1950. Also *The Far Journey* (1955), about a pioneer woman heading west. ○

Ferber, Edna
GIANT
Epic of Texas and Texans through the eyes of the Virginia-born wife of the owner of the huge Benedict Ranch. Doubleday, 1952. ○

Gent, Peter
NORTH DALLAS AFTER FORTY
North Dallas Forty 20 years later—"a brilliantly written novel, equal parts sports, politics, philosophy, and social commentary." (FC) Villard Bks, 1989. ○

Gipson, Fred
SAVAGE SAM
Frontier life in the 1870s and a very special dog. Har-Row, 1962. Two other novels in which special dogs are important to the plot are *Old Yeller* (1956) and *Hound-Dog Man* (1949). ○

Hailey, Elizabeth Forsythe
A WOMAN OF INDEPENDENT MEANS

A woman's life from 1899 to the 1970s told through letters, cables and newspaper clippings. Viking, 1978.   o

Hearon, Shelby
OWNING JOLENE (San Antonio)

The travails of a 19-year-old—"vivid, quirky characters as outsized as the Lone Star State." (FC) Knopf, 1989. Also *A Prince of a Fellow* (1978) and *Group Therapy* (1984).   o

Hines, Alan
SQUARE DANCE

An eleven-year-old girl is needed by her "isolated, cranky, half-blind" grandfather on their chicken farm outside Twilight, Texas. She runs away briefly to see her mother in Fort Worth, but returns. (FC) Har-Row, 1984.   o

Irving, Clifford
TRIAL

A Houston attorney, trying to make a comeback after having been suspended from practicing law, finds himself with two murder cases to defend: one an illegal immigrant, the other the hostess of a topless bar. Summit, 1990.   o

Islas, Arturo
MIGRANT SOULS

Second novel of a trilogy about the Angel family—the first is *The Raingod* (1984)—set primarily in the border town of Del Sapo and about the migration of a Mexican family into America. (BL) Morrow, 1990.   o

Jenkins, Dan
FAST COPY

Set in 1935—Betsy and her husband take over a newspaper and a radio station, which becomes catalyst for the husband's death. S&S, 1988. Also *Baja Oklahoma* (1981), set mostly in a Fort Worth cafe, about "middle-class Texas low-life."   o

Kelton, Elmer
STAND PROUD: A TEXAS SAGA

A combination mystery novel and western set in West Central Texas at the turn of the century—a Texas pioneer on trial for his life. Doubleday, 1984. Other Texas frontier novels by Kelton include *The Good Old Boys* (1978), *The Day the Cowboys Quit* (1971) and *The Wolf and the Buffalo* (1980).   o

Lea, Tom
THE WONDERFUL COUNTRY

Story of the return to Texas of Matthew Brady, having fled to Mexico after killing his father's murderer—"marvelous action throughout . . . an extraordinarily well written costume-piece of 'Western.' " (FC) Texas A&M U Pr, 1984.   o

Lindsey, David L.
A COLD MIND

Three of Houston's most beautiful call girls die and the detective's investigation takes him from "shadowy wharves and warehouses of the city's back streets to the exotic world of Houston's wealthy Brazilian expatriate community." (FC) Har-Row, 1983. Also *Mercy* (1990) a psychological thriller.   o

Lowry, Beverly
BREAKING GENTLE (Austin)

"Illuminates the difficulties of negotiating family accord"—a contemporary family in which the parents aim for a simple life near Austin. (FC) Viking, 1988.   o

McMurtry, Larry
SOME CAN WHISTLE

"A fat, lonely and rich" recluse begins the slow journey back toward reconnection when his daughter, who he's not seen since the night of her birth, contacts him. (FC) S&S, 1989. Also *Terms of Endearment* (1975).   o

McMurtry, Larry
TEXASVILLE

A return to the town of *Last Picture Show*, with some of the same characters as in the earlier novel, as the town faces hard times after the oil boom. S&S, 1987.   o

Martin, Lee
A CONSPIRACY OF STRANGERS

Deb Ralston, a Fort Worth police detective, stars in a "frightening almost-too-believable thriller centered on abortion, murder and black-market babies." (FC) St. Martin, 1986. ○

Mathis, Edward
DARK STREAKS AND EMPTY PLACES
Investigator Dan Roman lives in a fictional city between Dallas and Fort Worth and is hired to find the missing granddaughter of a lumber tycoon. Scribner, 1986. ○

Michener, James A.
TEXAS
The latest of Michener's fictionalized histories, following several generations of the prototype characters in the novel—Mexicans, Scotch-Irish, German and Spanish. A modern-day governor appoints a task force to come up with an outline of what students should be taught of Texas history—and this provides a framework for the book. Random, 1985. See also *The Eagle and the Raven* under Mexico/Novels. ○

Mojtabai, A.G.
ORDINARY TIME
"Mundane and metaphysical concerns" are intertwined around a group of three lonely people in a Texas town, all believers—a teen-aged boy, a priest, a Pentecostal convert. (BRD) Doubleday, 1989. ○

Pringle, Terry
A FINE TIME TO LEAVE ME
"Tranquil" novel of a marriage of a Navy vet, son of a Texas farmer, and a Baptist-American princess, daughter of a rich oil

man, in a life of "quiet desperation and commitment." (FC) Algonquin, 1989. ○

Smith, C.W.
COUNTRY MUSIC
Highly accurate descriptions of the people, towns and countryside of West Texas. FS&G, 1975. ○

Swarthout, Glendon
THE SHOOTIST
More than a western—story of the last of the gunfighters, in 1901, who is dying of cancer in El Paso. Doubleday, 1975. ○

Swift, Edward
PRINCIPIA MARTINDALE
"About a naively religious young woman who becomes a faith healer. . . . she is taken up by hucksters, with disastrous results." Har-Row, 1983. Also *Splendora* (1978), about a young man who returns to his east Texas town in a rather unusual way. ○

Thompson, Thomas
CELEBRITY
Three friends from high school "whose lives, in complex sort, bear out their roles in a high school play" are haunted by an adolescent crime they committed. (FC) Doubleday, 1982. ○

Wall, Judith H.
LOVE AND DUTY
A family chronicle of three women raised in a straightlaced German town in Texas. Viking, 1988. ○

UTAH

Series Guidebooks
(See Appendix 1)

Note: See also Series Guides (and non-series guides) listed under United States and the West. You may also find some crossover in guides and books listed under the West/the Southwest.

Compass American Guide: Utah
Frommer: Salt Lake City

Moon Handbook: Utah
Sierra Guide: Natural Areas of Colorado & Utah

Background Reading

Abbey, Edward
DESERT SOLITAIRE
The author worked as a park ranger at Arches National Monument in southeastern Utah

and this is his account of "day-to-day desert" with information about the desert—"literature, not just a guidebook." First published 1968. (BRD) S&S, 1990.   ○

Arrington, Leon
BRIGHAM YOUNG: AMERICAN MOSES
"Even-handed" biography of one of the most controversial figures of 19th-century America. (BL) Knopf, 1985. Also *The Mormon Experience* (1979).   ○

Chronic, Halka
ROADSIDE GEOLOGY OF UTAH
One of a series of books that is wonderful to take along in the car—to paraphrase the preface, being able to look at the landscape as you travel and (with this book) envision the forces and changes, the dynamics of the landscape you are seeing, is a real achievement of understanding for travelers. Mountain Pr, 1990.   ○

Gottlieb, Robert and Wiley, Peter
AMERICA'S SAINTS: THE RISE OF MORMON POWER
"The church's role in conservative politics . . . the lives of Mormon women . . . an excellent portrait of a major but often overlooked power in contemporary America." (LJ) Putnam Pub Group, 1984.   ○

Stegner, Wallace E.
THE GATHERING OF ZION: THE STORY OF THE MORMON TRAIL
The epic migration of the Mormons—"interweaving diarists' accounts with historical data . . . with freshness and perspective." (BRD) Howe Bros, 1982 (first published 1964).   ○

GUIDEBOOKS

Akens, Jean
HIGH DESERT TREASURES: THE STATE PARKS OF SOUTHEASTERN UTAH
Four Corners Pubs, 1990.   ○

Reed, Allen C.
GRAND CIRCLE ADVENTURE
Traveling to national parks and reserves in Arizona, Colorado and Utah. KC Pubns, 1983.   ○

Wharton, Tom
UTAH! A FAMILY TRAVEL GUIDE
"Explores the natural and human-made wonders of the State . . . emphasis on the scenery and activities with children . . . all sorts of places that invite enjoyment of the countryside." (Basic facts are suited to visitors of any age.) (BL) Wasatch Pubs, 1987.   ○

Young, John
STATE PARKS OF UTAH
Forty-eight parks—facilities, recreation available, historic facts and folklore, significance of the park in the region. U of Utah Pr, 1989.   ○

HISTORY

May, Dean
UTAH: A PEOPLE'S HISTORY
U of Utah Pr, 1987.   ○

Peterson, Charles S.
UTAH
One of a series of popular histories for each state, published as part of the bicentennial in 1976. Norton, 1977.   ○

Novels

Abbey, Edward
THE MONKEY WRENCH GANG
About a band of conservationists trying to preserve the wilds. Lippincott, 1975.   ○

Cook, Thomas H.
TABERNACLE
A series of Mormons are murdered and by approaching the murders from a new perspective a former New York City cop figures out who the next victim will be. Houghton, 1983.   ○

Fisher, Vardis
CHILDREN OF GOD

Novelization of the Mormon epic by an author of Mormon descent. "Glosses over neither misdeeds of the Mormons nor the brutality of their enemies as he depicts . . . the trek west, or minutely envisages domestic conflicts resulting from plural marriage." (FC) Holmes, 1977 (first published 1939). o

Grey, Zane
RIDERS OF THE PURPLE SAGE

Mormon vengeance in southwestern Utah in 1871. Har-Row, 1980 (first published 1912). o

Henry, Will
ALIAS BUTCH CASSIDY

The saga of Butch Cassidy and Robbers' Roost, a notorious Utah hideout for outlaws. Random, 1968. o

Irvine, Robert
CALLED HOME

Mr. Irvine writes mysteries in which a Salt Lake City private eye, Moroni Traveler, is the chief protagonist, and plot lines involve Mormons. St. Martin, 1991. Also *Angel's Share* (1989) and *Gone to Glory* (1990). o

Mailer, Norman
THE EXECUTIONER'S SONG

A documentary narrative of Gary Gilmore from April 1976, when he was released from prison, until early 1977 when he was executed for the murder of two people. The second half is about the "marketing of Gilmore as he awaits—and demands—death in the Utah state prison." (FC) The novel won a Pulitzer Prize. Little, 1979. o

Stegner, Wallace
RECAPITULATION

A man returns to Salt Lake City fifty years after having left to attend law school and faces what he's spent his whole life trying to live down—by an author with an often praised gift for the recreation of place. Doubleday, 1979. o

Stewart, Gerry
THE ZARAHEMIA VISION

A private eye in Salt Lake City, engaged mostly in routine divorce cases, is plunged into a dangerous investigation that involves the president of the Mormon Church, right-wing crazies and the Indian problem—"superbly witty writing and full scale credible characterization." (FC) St. Martin, 1986. o

VERMONT

*Series Guidebooks
(See Appendix 1)*

NOTE: See Series Guides (and non-series guides) listed under United States and the East and the East/New England.

Background Reading

Conger, Beach
**BAG BALM AND DUCT TAPE:
TALES OF A VERMONT
DOCTOR**

By a Harvard M.D. who moves from California to Vermont—what doctors can learn from patients and nurses. "Alternately scorching and good-natured." (BL) Little, 1988. o

Fago, D'Ann Calhoun
**A DIVERSITY OF GIFTS:
VERMONT WOMEN AT WORK**

A look into the lives of contemporary Vermont women, in traditional and non-traditional roles. Countryman, 1989. o

Gilbert, G.E., ed.
VERMONT ODYSSEYS

Contemporary tales from the Green Mountain State. NAL/Dutton, 1991. o

Hastings, Scott E., Jr.
THE LAST YANKEES: FOLKWAYS IN EASTERN VERMONT AND THE BORDER COUNTRY

History of crafts and crafts people, generously illustrated, synthesis of oral interviews with natives of regions where these arts flourished. U Pr of New England, 1990.   o

Hill, Lewis
FETCHED UP YANKEE: A NEW ENGLAND BOYHOOD REMEMBERED

"Couched in Yankee cadences these vivid recollections preserve the hardships as well as the pleasures of growing up in rural America during the Depression." (PW) Globe Pequot, 1990.   o

Jennison, Peter S.
ROADSIDE HISTORY OF VERMONT

A history to take along with you and perhaps read aloud to companions as you drive the state's highways. One of a unique series, written in lively narrative style by authors who know how to bring the past alive. It's like having a knowledgeable friend along who has lived in the state for years. Mountain Pr, 1989.   o

Keizer, Garret
NO PLACE BUT HERE: A TEACHER'S VOCATION IN A RURAL COMMUNITY

An Episcopal minister's seven-year stint as teacher at Lakes Region Union High School in the Northeast Kingdom. Viking, 1988. Also *A Dresser of Sycamore Trees* (1991), "an arresting and entertaining journal." (PW) o

Lindberg, Reeve
THE VIEW FROM THE KINGDOM

Chronicle of regional life—"essays are graceful evocations of the farmer's year . . . a stunning rendering of life defined by land and climate." Photographs, by the author's husband, of some quintessential Vermonters. (PW) HarBraceJ, 1987.   o

Meeks, Harold A.
TIME AND CHANGE IN VERMONT

The author calls this "human geography"— Vermont over four centuries "from the ar-

rival of Samuel de Champlain to the recent advent of General Electric and IBM. . . . the many changes . . . in the use of the land and the changing population." (Publisher) Globe Pequot, 1985.   o

Mitchell, Don
LIVING UPCOUNTRY

A novelist and his wife move to a farm in Vermont—"anecdotal account of the joys and travails of country living . . . A literate and completely engaging country journal." (BL) Yankee Bks, 1986. Also *Moving Up Country* (1984) and *Growing Upcountry: Raising a Family and Flock in a Rural Place* (1991).   o

Nearing, Helen
LIVING THE GOOD LIFE

Account of self-sufficient homesteading long before its vogue in the 1960s. Published privately in 1954. See also the Nearing book under "Maine" in which Mrs. Nearing and her husband continued their self-sufficient life-style. Schocken, 1989. Also *The Maple Sugar Book* (1970).   o

Perrin, Noel
LAST PERSON RURAL

Continues a series of essays. This is divided thematically into farmer problems, politics of ecology, evocations of rural life and New England. Previous books are *First Person Rural* (1978), *Second Person Rural* (1980), *Third Person Rural* (1983).   o

Pistorius, Alan
CUTTING HILL

An account of four seasons on a Vermont dairy farm, with a couple and their four children—"acquaints us with folk of grit, a family that . . . tenaciously holds fast to its farm." (PW) Knopf, 1990.   o

Sherman, Joe
FAST LANE ON A DIRT ROAD: VERMONT TRANSFERRED, 1945–1990

Changes in Vermont in the author's lifetime, socioeconomic and personal observations. Countryman, 1991.   o

Van Diver, Bradford B.
ROADSIDE GEOLOGY OF VERMONT AND NEW HAMPSHIRE
One of a series of books that is wonderful to take along in the car—to paraphrase the preface, being able to look at the landscape as you travel and (with this book) envision the forces and changes, the dynamics of the landscape you are seeing, is a real achievement of understanding for travelers. Mountain Pr, 1987.   ○

Weber, Susan B., ed.
THE VERMONT EXPERIENCE
Photographs, arranged by season, and accompanied by poetry and prose selections "so lyrical and sagacious . . . they may induce mass migration to the State"—with a reading list. (BL) Vermont Life, 1987.   ○

Wright, Catharine and Nancy M.
VERMONTERS AT THEIR CRAFT
Vermont craftspeople talk about their life and work—24 interview/profiles "offer a glimpse into . . . life styles" of full-time craftspeople who produce everything from quilts and pottery to dulcimers and marionettes. There's an appended directory of craftspeople in Vermont. (BL) New England Pr, 1987.   ○

GUIDEBOOKS

Bucholt, Margaret, ed.
AN INSIDER'S GUIDE TO SOUTHERN VERMONT
The editor of the *Manchester Journal* collaborates with local writers in a personal and vivid guidebook. Includes anything a traveler would need to know and more. NAL, 1991.   ○

McMinn, Russell
ANTIQUES
A guide to Vermont antique shops. Jockey Hollow, 1989.   ○

Tree, Christina and Jennison, Peter S.
VERMONT: AN EXPLORER'S GUIDE
One of a series of first-rate guides. See also under Maine and Massachusetts.   ○

HISTORY

Morrissey, Charles T.
VERMONT
One of a series of popular histories for each state, published as part of the bicentennial in 1976. Norton, 1981.   ○

Novels

Alther, Lisa
BEDROCK
"A novel that is as funny as it is moving in its portrait of life and love . . . in the midst of the tranquil, snow-draped beauty of Roches Ridge, Vermont." (BL) Knopf, 1990.   ○

Beattie, Ann
LOVE ALWAYS
Satire of the "last remaining vestiges of the counter culture . . . the stresses of an overprivileged country life-style." (FC) Random, 1985.   ○

Borgenicht, Miriam
BOOKED FOR DEATH
When her former fiance is found dead and everyone assumes suicide, Celia knows he could not have done anything so tasteless, and takes a job with a literature professor who seemingly has the key to it all. St. Martin, 1988.   ○

Brown, Reeve Lindbergh
MOVING TO THE COUNTRY
Problems of transition when a family moves from suburban Massachusetts to rural Virginia—honest and believable portrait of marriage changes and putting down roots. Doubleday, 1983.   ○

Clark, Eleanor
CAMPING OUT
A camping trip by two women to a remote Vermont Lake—a strange story, "the ironical close [will] leave the reader shaken." (FC) Putnam, 1986. Also, *Gloria Mundi* (1979).   ○

Heffernan, William
BLOOD ROSE
"Gore tempered by a touch of romance" when a young woman and her brother settle

in a Vermont town to escape an abusive husband—only to encounter murder. (FC) Dutton, 1991.   o

Higgins, George V.
VICTORIES
The author leaves his usual Boston setting for a novel set in Vermont. A former baseball player, now a game warden in Vermont, is tapped by Democratic leaders to run for Congress against the incumbent, which sets off a look into his past. Holt, 1990.   o

Koenig, Joseph
SMUGGLER'S NOTCH
A cop who resigns in disgrace gets a second chance to arrest the killer of a young woman—"stunningly set and executed on snowbound roads and ice-packed ridges in the Green Mountains." (FC) Viking, 1989.
    o

Lott, Brett
THE MAN WHO OWNED VERMONT
When his wife miscarries their first baby, Rick Wheeler blames himself and throws himself into his job as a soda pop salesman based in Northampton, Massachusetts. "A gripping novel about ordinary people . . . strong regional pungency . . . bits of country are the parts of Connecticut, Massachusetts and Vermont threaded together by Interstate 91 and the Merritt Parkway." (PW) Viking Penguin, 1987.   o

Metz, Don
CATAMOUNT BRIDGE
A twin, gung-ho to get to Vietnam and the war, suspects his wife is carrying the child of his pacifist twin brother—"captures . . . remote environment with loving care . . . brief Vietnam scenes are harrowing." (NYT) Har-Row, 1987.   o

Schaeffer, Susan F.
THE MADNESS OF A SEDUCED WOMAN
Invention of experiences and emotions to "fill in the outlines" of the life of a young Vermont woman who was tried for murder early in this century and judged insane— "portrays a difficult and complicated woman . . . no easy answers." (FC) Dutton, 1980. Also, *Time in Its Flight* (1978).   o

VIRGINIA

Series Guidebooks
(See Appendix 1)

NOTE: See also Series Guides (and nonseries guides) listed under United States and the South. You may also find some crossover in guides and books listed under the East about the eastern coast. Washington, D.C., guidebooks also may include information on Virginia.

Off the Beaten Path: Virginia

Background Reading

Adams, William H.
JEFFERSON'S MONTICELLO
Text "perfectly suited to . . . 'the quintessential example of the autobiographical house,' " with photographs and illustrations. (Publisher) Abbeville Pr, 1988.   o

Frye, Keith
ROADSIDE GEOLOGY OF VIRGINIA
One of a series of books that is wonderful to take along in the car—to paraphrase the preface, being able to look at the landscape as you travel and (with this book) envision the forces and changes, the dynamics of the landscape you are seeing, is a real achievement of understanding for travelers. Mountain Pr, 1986.   o

Lee, Hilde G. and Allan C.
VIRGINIA WINE COUNTRY
Comprehensive information on wineries engaged in a revival of the wine industry in Virginia. Also data for those who wish to tour the region—even a few recipes from wineries and local inns. Betterway Pubs, 1987.   o

Mulligan, Tim
VIRGINIA
Both history and guidebook—to quote the catalog from Traveller's Bookstore, "Tim Mulligan takes you by the hand and introduces you to all the best to see and do in the Old Dominion," a state that has been at the center of America's history. Random, 1986. ○

Sherry, John
MAGGIE'S FARM
Memoir by an author who decided to buy a dairy farm in southwest Virginia to provide income and the time to write—"an entertaining account [of dairy farming] and getting along with the natives." (PW) Permanent Pr, 1984. ○

Smith, Daniel B.
INSIDE THE GREAT HOUSE: PLANTER FAMILY LIFE IN 18TH-CENTURY CHESAPEAKE SOCIETY
Explores the character of family experience in the pre-industrial South in Maryland and Virginia. Cornell U, 1980. ○

Woodlief, Ann
IN RIVER TIME: THE WAY OF THE JAMES
The James River, a chronology from prehistoric times to the present—"novels, poems, art work, and exploration accounts . . . emphasize a predominantly human river relationship." History, biology, and ecology lessons become part of the reading. (LJ) Algonquin, 1985. ○

GUIDEBOOKS

Gilbert, Elizabeth R.
FAIRS AND FESTIVALS
The Smithsonian guide to celebrations in Maryland, Virginia and the District of Columbia—everything from national holidays and flower festivals to ethnic and religious events. Smithsonian, 1982. ○

McCarg, Margie
VIRGINIA PARKS GUIDE
Affordable Adventures, 1988. ○

McMinn, Russell
ANTIQUES
A guide to Virginia antique shops. Jockey Hollow, 1989. ○

Morris, Shirley
THE PELICAN GUIDE TO VIRGINIA
Organized alphabetically by city, plus a calendar of annual events. Pelican, 1989. ○

Peters, Margaret T., ed.
A GUIDEBOOK TO VIRGINIA'S HISTORICAL MARKERS
U Pr of Virginia, 1985. ○

Robertson, James I.
CIVIL WAR SITES IN VIRGINIA: A TOUR GUIDE
U Pr of Virginia, 1982. ○

Smith, Jane O.
THE VIRGINIA ONE-DAY TRIP BOOK
EPM Pubns, 1986. ○

HISTORY

Rubin, Louis D., Jr.
VIRGINIA
One of a series of popular histories for each state, published as part of the bicentennial in 1976. Norton, 1984. ○

Novels

Adams, Alice
FAMILIES AND SURVIVORS
Spans 30 years (1941–1970), following Louisa Calloway from girlhood in Virginia, on through college, marriages, affairs, motherhood, California—"her search for a usable identity." (FC) Knopf, 1975. ○

Brown, Rita Mae
HIGH HEARTS
A Civil War saga and the effects of the war on women and blacks. Bantam Bks, 1986. ○

Brown, Rita Mae
WISH YOU WERE HERE
The postmistress in Crozet attempts to gather clues after two murders in the community—

"writes with wise, disarming wit about . . . country-bred neighbors and their not-always-neighborly ways." (FC) Bantam, 1990.   ○

Cornwell, Patricia D.
BODY OF EVIDENCE
A romance writer is stabbed to death in Richmond. Also *Postmortem* (1990). The crime-solver is Kay Scarpetta, chief medical examiner of the Commonwealth of Virginia in both of these mysteries—"accomplished novel[s] . . . autopsy gore wisely down-played." (FC) Scribner, 1991.   ○

Glasgow, Ellen
IN THIS OUR LIFE
Story of "decayed aristocrats" in Virginia that won a Pulitzer Prize in 1942. HarBraceJ, 1941. Also set in Virginia are *Vein of Iron* (1935), a family saga set in the Virginia mountains, and *Barren Ground* (1925), about a poor farm family.   ○

Godwin, Gail
FATHER MELANCHOLY'S DAUGHTER
The family of an Episcopal rector in the Shenandoah Valley is the focus of this novel, and the daughter dealing with the loss of her parents—"social comedy and setting [are] richly realized . . . religious conventions of small-town, upper-middle-class life." (BL) Morrow, 1991.   ○

L'Amour, Louis
TO THE FAR BLUE MOUNTAINS
Begins in England and is a sequel to *Sackett's Land* (1974). In this, Sackett decides to leave England for Virginia, assembles a band of "brave settlers and strong women" and they follow the James River to rich farmland to establish a community. Saturday Review Pr, 1976.   ○

McCaig, Donald N.
NOP'S TRIALS
About stock dogs and stock dog trials, set in rural Virginia—"refreshing, heartwarming, well crafted." (FC) Crown, 1984.   ○

Mason, F. Van Wyck
THE SEA VENTURE
The early years of Jamestown (and the Bermuda settlement) are the basis for the plot. Doubleday, 1961.   ○

Mason, F. Van Wyck
TRUMPETS SOUND NO MORE
Picking up the pieces after the Civil War, for a Confederate officer. Little, 1975.   ○

Michaels, Barbara
BE BURIED IN THE RAIN
A medical student and an archaeologist try to solve the mystery of an old house and two graves. Atheneum, 1985. Also *Witch* (1973), a suspenseful gothic.   ○

Settle, Mary Lee
O BEULAH LAND
"Excellently written chronological novel with a fascinating story told in the idiom of the day and place." (FC) The plot centers on a Virginia gentleman and the group of early Americans he takes west with him to "Beulah," beyond the king's proclamation line. Period is 1754–75. See "Novels/West Virginia." Viking, 1956.   ○

Shreve, Susan R.
A COUNTRY OF STRANGERS
A white midwesterner moves his family during World War II to Virginia, where he plans to live and farm "in harmony with . . . a family descended from the slaves who once worked the farm." (PW) S&S, 1989.   ○

Smith, Lee
FAIR AND TENDER LADIES
"A 20th-century history of Virginia's Appalachian region as well as a compelling saga . . . literate . . . and entertaining." (BRD) Putnam, 1988.   ○

Smith, Lee
FAMILY LINEN
The Hess clan gathers at the death of its matriarch and recounts family history—"a companionable, chatty book." (FC) Putnam, 1985.   ○

Styron, William
THE CONFESSIONS OF NAT TURNER

A Pulitzer Prize-winning novel of the 1831 slave rebellion. Random, 1967.   ○

Thane, Elswyth
DAWN'S EARLY LIGHT

First of a whole series of novels, a saga of the Day/Murray/Sprague families of Williamsburg (and also English cousins). The story begins in 1774 and ends just before World War II. The books were written from 1943 through 1957. The titles in chronological order are: *Dawn's Early Light, Yankee Stranger, Ever After, Light Heart, Kissing Kin, This Was Tomorrow, Homing.* Amereon Reprints.   ○

Theroux, Alexander
DARCONVILLE'S CAT

An instructor in a small woman's college in Virginia is spurned by one of his students, moves on to teach at Harvard but plots his revenge. Doubleday, 1981.   ○

Wicker, Tom
UNTO THIS HOUR

Civil War novel by the *New York Times* columnist—defeat of the North at Manassas is the focus of the plot. Major historical figures—Lee, Longstreet, others—combined with many and varied ordinary characters. Viking, 1984.   ○

Williams, Ben Ames
HOUSE DIVIDED

Novel about the Civil War and its effect on an old Virginia family. Houghton, 1947.   ○

WASHINGTON

Series Guidebooks (See Appendix 1)

NOTE: See also Series Guides (and non-series guides) listed under United States and the West and the West/the Pacific Northwest. You may also find some crossover in guides and books listed under British Columbia.

Frommer: Seattle and Portland
Moon Handbook: Washington
Sierra Guide: Natural Areas of Washington

Background Reading

Alt, David and Hyndman, Donald
ROADSIDE GEOLOGY OF WASHINGTON

One of a series of books that is wonderful to take along in the car—to paraphrase the preface, being able to look at the landscape as you travel and (with this book) envision the forces and changes, the dynamics of the landscape you are seeing, is a real achievement of understanding for travelers. Mountain Pr, 1984.   ○

Doig, Ivan
WINTER BROTHERS: A SEASON AT THE EDGE OF AMERICA

A diary within a diary—the discovery of the diaries of James G. Swan, an obscure nineteenth-century artist and observer of Indian life, leads the author to interweave his own contemporary diary of a winter with that of Swan for a unique reading experience. HarBraceJ, 1982.   ○

Espy, Willard R.
OYSTERVILLE: ROADS TO GRANDPA'S VILLAGE

Family chronicle and that of a small coastal village. Crown, 1985.   ○

Gotchy, Joe
BRIDGING THE NARROWS

Story of the Tacoma Narrows Bridge, dedicated July 1, 1940, and nicknamed "Galloping Gertie" because of its undulating movements when the wind blew. It fell into Puget Sound on November 7, 1940, and was replaced in 1950. Peninsula Historical Soc, 1990.   ○

Kirk, Ruth
EXPLORING THE OLYMPIC PENINSULA

Culture, history, people, nature and facts for enjoying all of them. U of Washington Pr, 1990. Also (with Carmela Alexander), *Exploring Washington's Past* (1990), under guidebooks.   ○

Manning, Harvey
WALKING THE BEACH TO BELLINGHAM

An account of a walk from Seattle to Bellingham (150 miles), done in increments over two years—"ample time and space for a variety of historical, scientific, and personal asides." (BL) Madrona, 1987.   ○

Morgan, Murray
PUGET'S SOUND: A NARRATIVE OF EARLY TACOMA AND THE SOUTHERN SOUND

History of the region in terms of selected historical personalities, from the arrival of Vancouver until the establishment of Fort Lewis—lively history and fascinating characters. (BRD) U of Washington Pr, 1981. ○

Nisbet, Jack
SKY PEOPLE

Colville Valley—"collage of impressions . . . a cast of vivid and unforgettable characters, human and otherwise . . . nature, legends and people." (BL) Quartzite Bks, 1984.   ○

Shane, Scott
DISCOVERING MOUNT ST. HELENS: A GUIDE TO THE NATIONAL VOLCANIC MONUMENT

To aid tourists visiting the monument. An account of volcanism in general and the Mt. St. Helens eruption in 1980, in particular; the plant and human culture of the area. U of Washington Pr, 1985.   ○

Ward, Andrew
OUT HERE: A NEWCOMER'S NOTES FROM THE GREAT NORTHWEST

"Beautifully crafted pieces," some of which have been part of National Public Radio's

"All Things Considered," about life on Bainbridge Island. (PW) Viking, 1991.   ○

GUIDEBOOKS

Boyce, Chris
WASHINGTON PARKS GUIDE

Affordable Adventures, 1988.   ○

Gardner, Booth, ed.
DESTINATION WASHINGTON

The official Washington State Traveler's Guide. Alaska Northwest, 1990.   ○

Keith, Gordon
THE FERRYBOAT ISLANDS

A practical guide to Washington's San Juan Islands. Dolphin Bay, 1989.   ○

Kirk, Ruth and Alexander, Carmela
EXPLORING WASHINGTON'S PAST

A road guide to history—"encyclopedic . . . explores the visible history of that lovely state . . . a wealth of carefully coordinated detail." (LJ) U of Washington Pr, 1990.   ○

London, Bill
UMBRELLA GUIDE TO THE INLAND EMPIRE

"Chops up areas around Spokane and the Idaho Panhandle and treats them in small, focused pieces"—can serve either as an auto or biking guide. (LJ) Umbrella Bks, 1990. ○

McMinn, Russell
ANTIQUES

A guide to Washington antique shops. Jockey Hollow, 1989.   ○

Nelson, Sharlene P. and Ted W.
UMBRELLA GUIDE TO WASHINGTON LIGHTHOUSES

Lists all 25, with histories, keepers, visiting hours and more. Umbrella Bks, 1990.   ○

Oberrecht, Kenn
DRIVING THE PACIFIC COAST: OREGON & WASHINGTON

See entry under Oregon.   ○

Rank, Steve and Kincade, Kathy
FESTIVALS OF THE PACIFIC NORTHWEST

Your guided tour to festivals in Washington and Oregon. Landau Comns, 1989. ◦

Satterfield, Archie
THE SEATTLE GUIDEBOOK

The *Seattle Times* says "Everything you need to know about Seattle," from its natural beauty to cultural attractions, wildlife of Puget Sound, a special section on its ethnic cuisines, all kinds of lodgings, including B&Bs, special things for kids, and even how to break into the social scene. Globe Pequot, 1991. Also by Satterfield, *Country Roads of Washington* (1989). ◦

Youra, Dan and Thompson, Pat
TRAVELING AROUND MOUNT ST. HELENS

A guide for a 400-mile scenic loop. Olympic Pub, 1981. ◦

HISTORY

Clark, Norman H.
WASHINGTON

One of a series of popular histories for each state, published as part of the bicentennial in 1976. Norton, 1976. ◦

Duncan, Don
WASHINGTON: THE FIRST ONE HUNDRED YEARS, 1889–1989

An anecdotal history. Seattle Times, 1989. ◦

Ficken, Robert E. and LeWarne, Charles P.
WASHINGTON: A CENTENNIAL HISTORY

"Popular, rigorous history" of 100 years since 1889. U of Washington Pr, 1988. ◦

Novels

Emerson, Earl W.
BLACK HEARTS AND SLOW DANCING

"Crisp, no-nonsense prose . . . superb use of his firefighting background"—a fireman from the East settles in a small town and ends up both running the fire department and acting as temporary police chief, with a murder to handle first day on the job. (FC) Morrow, 1988. ◦

Pearson, Ridley
UNDERCURRENTS

A brutal killer, supposedly dead, is again on the loose—"not for the squeamish." (FC) St. Martin, 1988. ◦

Roberts, Willo Davis
THE SNIPER

Inheritance from a distant relative of a Victorian house leads to murders—the heroine must solve them or be next. Doubleday, 1984. ◦

Robinson, Margaret A.
COURTING EMMA HOWE

A young woman from Virginia agrees to cross the country and marry a young homesteader in Washington State after courtship by correspondence in 1904. Adler & Adler, 1987. ◦

Smith, Janet
SEA OF TROUBLES

A former trial lawyer's business trip to the San Juan Islands involves her in a kidnapping and murder. Perseverence, 1990. ◦

WEST VIRGINIA

*Series Guidebooks
(See Appendix 1)*

NOTE: See Series Guides (and non-series

guides) listed under United States and the South.

Background Reading

McNeill, Louise
THE MILKWEED LADIES
"Graceful, poignant memoir" of the West Virginia land that has been in the author's family for nine generations. Chronicles a rustic childhood with stories of family, chores, that mark the passing of seasons. The author is a published poet. (PW) U of Pittsburgh Pr, 1988.   ○

White, Betty W.
THE PAST IS A KEY TO THE FUTURE
A social history of Terra Alta and its environs, from its geology to nostalgic verse; the book captures the atmosphere in this town in the era of the Baltimore & Ohio Railroad, as business floundered and the Irish and Italian workers came in. Melody Mountain, 1990.   ○

HISTORY

Williams, John A.
WEST VIRGINIA
One of a series of popular histories for each state, published as part of the bicentennial in 1976. Norton, 1976.   ○

Novels

Abbey, Edward
THE FOOL'S PROGRESS; AN HONEST NOVEL
Henry Lightcap tells of his journey from Tucson back to his boyhood home in West Virginia and the family farm—"bitterly humorous commentary . . . hauntingly beautiful novel." (BRD) Holt, 1988.   ○

Currey, Richard
THE WARD OF HEAVEN
Collection of short stories and a novella—"sorrow-filled tales . . . cutting to the heart of West Virginia's working class." (BL) HM, 1990.   ○

Ehrlich, Leonard
GOD'S ANGRY MAN
Fictionalized story of John Brown, the fanatical foe of slavery, and the raid on Harper's Ferry. S&S, 1932.   ○

Giardina, Denise
STORMING HEAVEN
Story of the United Mine Workers' threat to overthrow two West Virginia counties in 1921, crushed by the U.S. Army—"an exciting story in vigorous, elegant prose." (FC) Norton, 1987.   ○

Grubb, Davis
THE NIGHT OF THE HUNTER
Suspense novel of a young boy pitted against an evil man masquerading as "the preacher," who wants the boy to reveal information about hidden money. This was made into a great movie with Robert Mitchum as the menace. Har-Row, 1953.   ○

Pancake, Breece D'J.
THE STORIES OF BREECE D'J. PANCAKE
Short stories—"a dark Faulknerian view of contemporary West Virginia hill life . . . with a naturalist's sensitivity." (FC) Little, 1983.   ○

Phillips, Jayne Anne
MACHINE DREAMS
"The transformations [of] individuals and . . . society as a whole" from years of the depression to the Vietnam War—a "postmodernist" family saga. (FC) Dutton, 1984.   ○

Settle, Mary Lee
CHARLEY BLAND
"Condensed lyric novel"—the heroine fled the small-town environment of West Virginia, re-creating herself as a writer in postwar Paris. She returns, meets Charley Bland who she adored as a child—"the affair they begin . . . demolishes everything" she's accomplished in her years away. (FC) FS&G, 1989.   ○

Settle, Mary Lee
THE KILLING GROUND
FS&G, 1982. Final novel of a five-book saga by a leading contemporary writer. *The Beulah Quintet* traces a family and the land for 300 years. Prior titles are *Prisons* (1973), *O Beulah Land* (1956) (see "Virginia"), *Know Nothing* (1960) and *The Scapegoat* (1980).   ○

WISCONSIN

Series Guidebooks
(See Appendix 1)

NOTE: See also Series Guides (and non-series guides) listed under United States and the Midwest.

Off the Beaten Path: Wisconsin

Background Reading

Derleth, August W.
WALDEN WEST; RETURN TO WALDEN WEST

"Remembered scenes and remembered village people . . . sights and sounds and smells" of the river town Sac Prairie. See also books by Derleth under "Novels," below. (BRD) Stanton & Lee, 1962, 1970.   ○

Engelmann, Ruth
LEAF HOUSE: DAYS OF REMEMBERING

Memoir of a Finnish immigrant family in Rivier during the 1920s and '30s—the author leaves at eighteen for Milwaukee to work as a domestic and later to attend university. Har-Row, 1982.   ○

Leopold, Aldo
SAND COUNTRY ALMANAC

Essays for each month of the year about the author's Wisconsin farm—a classic of nature/ecology writing. First published in 1949. Ballantine, 1986.   ○

Logan, Ben
LAND REMEMBERS: THE STORY OF A FARM AND ITS PEOPLE

Remembrance of growing up on a Wisconsin farm in the 1920s and '30s, and the farm itself as it changes through the seasons. Northwood, 1975.   ○

Murray, Robert D.
THUNDER OVER THE DOOR

The ships, shores and woods of Wisconsin's Door Peninsula. William Caxton, 1991.   ○

Patterson, Elsie E.
A PORTRAIT OF EVERYDAY LIFE IN WISCONSIN

Patterson Comns, 1988.   ○

Ribbens, Dennis, ed.
WISCONSIN LITERARY TRAVEL GUIDE

Cross-referenced by author and arranged alphabetically by city—the homes, cities and landscapes of Wisconsin writers. Wisconsin Library Assn, 1990.   ○

GUIDEBOOKS

McCaig & Boyce
WISCONSIN STATE PARKS

Affordable Adventures, 1989.   ○

Umhoefer, Jim
GUIDE TO WISCONSIN'S OUTDOORS

A guide to Wisconsin's state parks, wildlife refuges and trails—"outdoor attractions to 'satisfy the city-soft as well as the wilderness experience.' " (BL) NorthWord, 1989. Also, *Guide to Wisconsin's Parks, Forests, Recreation Areas and Trails* (1982).   ○

Zimmerman, H. Russell
THE HERITAGE GUIDEBOOK

Landmarks and historical sites in southeastern Wisconsin. Harry W. Schwartz, 1989.   ○

HISTORY

Current, Richard N.
WISCONSIN

One of a series of popular histories for each state, published as part of the bicentennial in 1976. Norton, 1977.   ○

Nesbit, Robert C.
WISCONSIN: A HISTORY

Second edition. U of Wisconsin Pr, 1990.   ○

Novels

Derleth, August W.
THE HILLS STAND WATCH
Marriage of an easterner to a Wisconsin tradesman and life in a mining village in the 1840s. Duell, 1960. Also *Wind Over Wisconsin* (1938) and *Still Is the Summer* (1937). *Sac Prairie People* (1948) and *Wisconsin Earth: Sac Prairie Sampler* (1948) are, respectively, a collection of the author's short stories and an anthology of selections from his novels. ○

Dickinson, Charles
CROWS
An ex-sportswriter searches for a professor/father figure—"authenticity of landscape and of the seasonal and social cycles of a small Wisconsin town" come alive. (BRD) Knopf, 1985. ○

McPherson, William
TESTING THE CURRENT
A story seen through the eyes of a seven-year-old boy at his family's island summer home in 1939, and his gradual awareness that family members and friends are not what they seem to be. S&S, 1984. *To the Sargasso Sea* (1987) is a sequel—the seven-year-old is now 40, happily married, a father, yet "plainly enmeshed in a midlife crisis." He encounters an older woman who enchanted him as a child. (FC). Pocket Books, 1987. ○

Spencer, LaVyrle
BITTER SWEET
The heroine returns to Wisconsin when she is widowed, after 20 years, and decides to open a bed and breakfast—"journey of self-discovery and reawakening." (FC) Putnam, 1990. ○

WYOMING

Series Guidebooks
(See Appendix 1)

NOTE: See also Series Guides (and non-series guides) listed under United States and the West.

Compass American Guide: Wyoming
Sierra Guide: Natural Areas of Idaho, Montana & Wyoming

Background Reading

Anderson, Susan
LIVING IN WYOMING: SETTLING FOR MORE
Compass American, 1990. ○

Blevins, Winfred
ROADSIDE HISTORY OF YELLOWSTONE PARK
A history to take along with you and perhaps read aloud to companions as you drive the state's highways. One of a unique series, written in lively narrative style by authors who know now to bring the past alive. It's

like having a knowledgeable friend along who has lived in the state for years. Mountain Pr, 1989. ○

Budd, Bob
A WIDE SPOT IN THE ROAD
Everyday life in Friendly Creek, Wyoming— "honest and funny picture of small town life . . . and characters" in a ranching community. (Publisher) Portfolio Pub, 1990. ○

Burt, Nathaniel
JACKSON HOLE JOURNAL
Memoir of a poet-novelist-composer of life in Jackson Hole in the 1920s and '30s when his writer parents managed a dude ranch. U of Oklahoma Pr, 1985. ○

Craighead, Frank C.
TRACK OF THE GRIZZLY
A study of the grizzly bear at Yellowstone. Sierra, 1982. ○

Ehrlich, Gretel
THE SOLACE OF OPEN SPACES
"A paean to Wyoming"—begun as a journal, later arranged into 12 chapters, each of which can stand on its own. "Captures the essence of a huge, desolate, yet cozy place." (BRD) Penguin, 1986.   o

Fishbein, Seymour L.
YELLOWSTONE COUNTRY: THE ENDURING WONDER
Profile of Yellowstone Park and the Tetons and wildlife refuges in the area, with a section on the recent fires. Natl Geo Society, 1989.   o

Fritz, William J.
ROADSIDE GEOLOGY OF THE YELLOWSTONE COUNTRY
See entry under Lageson, below—this is a separate volume for Yellowstone. Mountain Pr, 1985.   o

Haines, Aubrey L.
THE YELLOWSTONE STORY
A two-volume history of America's first national park by a retired park historian and touching on major themes in American history as well. U Pr of Colorado, 1977.   o

Lageson, David and Spearing, Darwin
ROADSIDE GEOLOGY OF WYOMING
One of a series of books that is wonderful to take along in the car—to paraphrase the preface, being able to look at the landscape as you travel and (with this book) envision the forces and changes, the dynamics of the landscape you are seeing, is a real achievement of understanding for travelers. Mountain Pr, 1988.   o

Madsen, R. Scott
THE BOMBER MOUNTAIN CRASH: A WYOMING MYSTERY
A B-17 Flying Fortress disappeared one stormy night in 1943 in Wyoming's Big Horn Mountains. The author's long fascination with the event began in 1982, and he has researched Air Force and other records, interviewed local residents and families of four of the 10-man crew (whose average age was 19), to provide a touching tribute to the young men who died. Mountain Man, 1990.   o

Moore, Rae Ellen
JUST WEST OF YELLOWSTONE
See entry under Idaho.   o

Ritthaler, Shelly
THE GINGER JAR
"Unassuming, subtle, perceptive depictions of everyday life" and a ranch in Wyoming, 100 miles from a grocery store. (BL) Raven Creek Pr, 1990.   o

Sagebrush Elementary School Scholars
OUR WYOMING HERITAGE
History as seen through the eyes of the students of Sagebrush Elementary School in a collection of essays, letters and drawings in the tradition of the Foxfire series (see under Georgia). "Vibrates with an authentic sense of history and reverence for the Wyoming countryside." The collection includes unpleasant facts, too, like the Teapot Dome scandal and treatment of the Sioux Indians, and provides a reading list at the end of each chapter. Achievement Pr, 1990.   o

Schullery, Paul
MOUNTAIN TIME
"A splendid private tour of [Yellowstone Park]" by an author who worked there as a ranger-naturalist—reminisces about his experiences as a ranger and casts a "jaded eye at the American tourist." (PW) S&S, 1988.   o

Simpson, Ross W.
THE FIRES OF '88: YELLOWSTONE PARK AND MONTANA IN FLAMES
Simpson was a newsman who covered the great fires, when nearly a million acres burned. "Imparts . . . the action . . . the thoughts and feelings of these brave men and women along with hard facts." (BL) American Geo, 1989.   o

Williamson, Chilton
LIFE IN THE OVERTHRUST
The author of *Saltbound* (see entry under "Rhode Island") ventures to the "overthrust belt" of Wyoming—"colorful and trenchant observations on American types and life-styles . . . ranchers, oil-field roughnecks, law-and-order politicians." (BRD) S&S, 1982.   o

GUIDEBOOKS

Banks, James
WYOMING'S BEST
Pruett, 1991.   o

MacAdams, Cliff
GRAND TETON NATIONAL PARK
Guide and reference book. Caxton, 1983. o

Wilson, D. Ray
WYOMING HISTORICAL TOUR GUIDE
Brief history, stories about historical characters and events, lists of museums and historical sites, with schedules and fees plus photos and maps. Crossroads Comns, 1990.   o

HISTORY

Larson, Taft A.
WYOMING
One of a series of popular histories for each state, published as part of the bicentennial in 1976. Norton, 1984.   o

Novels

Ehrlich, Gretel
HEART MOUNTAIN
A group of Japanese-Americans "interact with each other and with the inhabitants of a tight-knit ranching community" in Wyoming, where they have been relocated during World War II. (BL) Viking, 1988.   o

L'Amour, Louis
BENDIGO SHAFTER
"Marvelous mural of post-Civil War Wyoming and the people who settled it." (FC) Dutton, 1979.   o

Lutz, Giles
THE FEUD
A greedy banker connives to resurrect from Old West days the conflict between cattlemen and sheep ranchers. Doubleday, 1982.   o

Schaefer, Jack
SHANE
Story of the stranger who comes into the life of a homesteading family, affects them all profoundly, and moves on. Houghton, 1954. Also *Collected Short Novels* (1967).   o

Williamson, Chilton
THE HOMESTEAD
Older brother Sam returns to small-town Wyoming to help his younger brother face an attempted murder charge. Grove Weidenfeld, 1990.   o

APPENDIX 1

Key to Source Codes

Travel Guidebook Information Sources

Going Places: A Guide to the Guides by Greg Hayes and Joan Wright (Harvard Common Pr, 1991)

This book is completely devoted to evaluation and review of the kind of guidebooks listed under Series Guides, as well as many other guidebooks such as outdoor and recreation guides, that are beyond the scope of *Traveler's Reading Guide*.

Travel Bookstores

The following are travel bookstores that provide mail order service and wonderful catalogs that include capsule descriptions of travel books:

Book Passage, 51 Tamal Vista, Corte Madera, CA 94925 (800-321-9785)

Complete Traveller Bookstore, 199 Madison Avenue, New York, NY (212-685-9007)

The Literate Traveller, 8306 Wilshire Blvd., Beverly Hills, CA 90211 (213-934-7280)

Travel Books & Language Center, 4931 Cordell Avenue, Bethesda, MD 20814 (301-951-8533)

Traveler's Bookcase, 8375 West Third St., Los Angeles, CA 90048 (213-655-0575 FAX: 213-655-1197)

Series Guides

Series Name	Publisher
Access Guides	Access Pr Ltd (Prentice-Hall Pr)
American Express Pocket Guides	Prentice Hall Press
At Its Best	Passport Bks (Natl Textbook Co)
Baedeker's Guides	Prentice Hall Press
Berlitz Guides	Macmillan Publishing Co., Inc.

Series Guides

Birnbaum's Guides	Houghton Mifflin Co.
Blue Guides	W.W. Norton Co., Inc.
Cadogan Guides	Globe Pequot Press
Crown Insider's Guides	Crown Publications, Inc.
Exploring Rural Europe	Passport Books (Natl Textbook Co)
Fielding's Guides	William Morrow & Co.
Fisher's World	Fisher's World, Inc. (NAL)
Fodor Guides	Fodor (David McKay Co)
Frommer Guides	Prentice Hall Press
Gault Milau	Prentice Hall Press
Hildebrand Guides	Hunter Pub
Independent Traveller	Harper-Row
Insider's Guides	Hunter Pub
Insight Guides	Prentice Hall Press
Langenscheidt Self-Guided Guides	Langenscheidt
Let's Go	St. Martin's
Lonely Planet	Lonely Planet Pubns
Michael's Guides	Hippocrene Books
Michelin Guides	Michelin Travel
Moon Handbook	Moon Publications
Nagel's Encyclopedia Guides	Passport Books (Natl Textbook Co)
Nelles Guides	R McCarta
Off the Beaten Track	Harper-Row
Passport China Guides/Asia Guides	Passport Bks (Natl Textbook Co)
Post Guides	Hunter Pub
Real Guides	Prentice Hall Press
Times Travel Library	Hunter Pub
2–22 Days Itinerary Planning Guides	John Muir
Visitor's Guides	Hunter Pub

APPENDIX 2

A Reading List about Travel Literature

Adams, Percy G. *Travel Literature and the Evolution of the Novel.* University of Kentucky Press, 1983.

Adams, Percy G., ed. *Travel Literature Through the Ages: An Anthology.* Garland, 1988. Selections from ancient times to 1900.

Birkett, Dea, ed. *Spinsters Abroad: Victorian Lady Explorers.* Basil Blackwell, 1989. Social history of the intrepid lady explorers of the 19th century.

Downs, Robert B. *In Search of New Horizons: Epic Tales of Travel and Exploration.* ALA, 1978. First recorded accounts of the explorers' discoveries, and the impact of what was discovered. Also, for impressions of America, *Images of America: Travelers from Abroad in the New World* (1987).

Feifer, Maxine. *Tourism in History: From Imperial Rome to the Present.* Stein & Day, 1986.

Fussell, Paul. *Abroad: British Literary Traveling Between the Wars.* Oxford University Press, 1980. Essays by a scholar about the travel and writings of people such as Evelen Waugh, Graham Greene, many not as well known.

Fussell, Paul, ed. *The Norton Book of Travel.* Norton, 1987. Historical tour through the world of travel writing, from Herodotus to contemporary writers such as Paul Theroux and Jan Morris.

Jones-Griffiths, Philip, ed. *Great Journeys.* Simon & Schuster, 1990. Seven journeys of myth, history, personal challenge, as chronicled by seven travel writers. The book was the basis for a PBS series. Destinations include China on the Silk Road, Polynesia (navigator's route), the Pan American Highway, the Burma Road, the Salt Road (Morocco to Niger and Mali), the Viking invasion route in Russia, and the Ho Chi Minh Trail.

Keay, John. *Eccentric Travellers.* J.P. Tarcher, 1984. Reconstructs for readers the exploits of English travelers of the 18th and 19th centuries.

King, Peter, ed. *Travels with a Superior Person.* Salem House, n.d. Lord Curzon, before he became a viceroy, writes of his voyages around the world, to the Near and Far East. "The quintessence of late-Victorian travel writing . . . humorous anecdotes . . . rich and poetic descriptive writing" along with 90 contemporary photographs. (Publisher)

Leed, Eric J. *The Mind of the Traveler: From Gilgamesh to Global Tourism.* Basic Books,

1991. "A historian's account, wonderfully rich in material, of travel through the ages, exploring the nature of the journey, and the ways in which the mind of the traveler is transformed by what it encounters." Surveys writings on the nature of travel by authors ranging from Plato and Capt. James Cook to Albert Einstein and Joan Didion. (NYT)

Morrison, Helen B. *Golden Age of Travel: Literary Impressions of the Grand Tour.* Reprint of the 1951 edition. AMS Press, n.d..

Newby, Eric, ed. *A Book of Traveler's Tales.* Viking, 1986. An anthology of writings by over 300 writers, from ancient times to modern, arranged geographically and in chronological order—described by the *Wall Street Journal* as "a dazzling kaleidoscope."

Newcombe, Jack, ed. *Travels in the Americas.* Grove-Weidenfeld, 1989. An anthology that spans two continents and five centuries, with contributions ranging from Columbus and Mark Twain to Bruce Chatwin and Evelyn Waugh.

Norwich, John J., ed. *A Taste for Travel.* Knopf, 1987. Contemporary and classic writing, from Robert Louis Stevenson to Jonathan Rabin, arranged around aspects of travel, i.e., departures, first impressions, bad times, homecomings and so on.

Packard, Robert. *Refractions: Writers and Places.* Carroll & Graf, 1990. How writers reinvent locales is the theme for eight essays—"adventurous, engaging . . . full of the pleasures of discovery, literary and geographic." (PW).

Robinson, Jane. *Wayward Women: A Guide to Women Travellers.* Oxford University Press, 1990. About women who traveled and wrote about it and have been published; arranged by travel purpose with a geographic index.

Sprengnether, Madelon and Truesdale, C.W., eds. *The House on Via Gombito: Writing by North American Women Abroad.* New Rivers, 1991.

Thorn, John and Reuther, David, eds. *The Armchair Traveler.* An anthology of travel writing by gifted travel writers, American and otherwise. Prentice-Hall Press, 1989.

Yapp, Peter. *The Traveller's Dictionary of Quotation: Who Said What About Where?* Routledge. 1985.

Zinsser, William, ed. *They Went: The Art and Craft of Travel Writing.* HM, 1991. Essays that grew out of a lecture series at the New York Public Library; by the author of the classic *On Writing Well.*

APPENDIX 3

Collections of Travel Writings

Barich, Bill. *Traveling Light*. Penguin, 1985. Essays resulting from a year of travels, focusing on the ordinary activities of the places visited.

Bowles, Paul. *Their Heads Are Green and Their Hands Are Blue*. Ecco Press, 1984. Morocco and other places.

Cahill, Tim. *Jaguars Ripped My Flesh: Adventure Is a Risky Business*. Bantam, 1987. "Literate adventure writing . . . ranging from parachuting to exploring jungles." (LJ) Also *A Wolverine Is Eating My Leg* (1988), travel pieces about off-the-beaten-path fun and trouble.

Chatwin, Bruce. *What Am I Doing Here?* Viking, 1989. A mosaic of travelogues, semi-fictionalized stories, fragments—"an endless feast" about everything from nomads and art auctioneering to Indira Gandhi and French couturier Vionnet. (PW)

Crichton, Michael. *Travels*. Knopf, 1988. Essays in search of redefining himself in the experience of new places and cultures.

Dillard, Annie. *Teaching a Stone to Talk*. Har-Row, 1988. Impressionistic images of real and metaphoric places.

Eames, Andrew. *Crossing the Shadow Line*. David & Charles, 1988. Travels in Southeast Asia—a two-year odyssey on a shoestring, at times working his way, in Thailand, Philippine Islands, Singapore, Indonesia, Bali, Timor, Australia, and a solo trek from Nepal to England. "Will attract the young and fit, and turn their elders green with envy." (PW)

Fisher, M.F.K. *As They Were*. Random, 1983. Memoir of food, places and people by a leading food and travel writer.

Girling, Richard, ed. *The Best of Sunday Times Travel*. David & Charles, 1989. Travel pieces from *The London Sunday Times*—journeys, perspectives on the U.S.

Granta Travel, eds. *The Best of Granta Travel*. Penguin, 1992. Selections from the first 35 issues; pieces that its editors believe to be the most enduring—"part memoir, part reportage, part old-fashioned story." (Publisher)

Greene, Graham. *Reflections*. Viking, 1991. Previously uncollected travel pieces— "superbly crafted . . . combining politics and sociology seamlessly with history and scenery." (PW)

Hibbert, Christopher. *Cities & Civilizations*. Weidenfeld, 1986. Visits to 21 cities that have been vital and important centers of influence at some point in their history, from ancient days to the present—"imparting the essential atmosphere and visages of these places at the height of their consequence." (BL)

Holmes, John C. *Displaced Person: Travel Essays*. University of Arkansas Press, 1987. Travel essays of a novelist and scholar of the beat generation movement.

Howard, Jean. *Travels with Cole Porter*. Abrams, 1991. Reminiscences in text and photos and excerpts from Porter's diaries—by a former showgirl who joined Porter and friends in luxurious mid-50s travels to the south of France, the Greek islands, Switzerland, Egypt and more, by yacht, private railroad cars and limousines.

James, Clive. *Flying Visits: Post Cards from The Observer*. Norton, 1986. "Literate, brilliantly perceptive and witty"—a collection of travel pieces that originally appeared in *The London Observer*, and including Australia, Moscow, Salzburg, Jerusalem, Japan, the United States. (PW)

Krich, John. *Music in Every Room: Around the World in a Bad Mood*. Atlantic Monthly Press, 1988. Macao, Hong Kong, Thailand, Nepal, Iran, Turkey—"absolutely marvelous . . . a kind of *Divine Comedy* in which everyone has strayed from the straight path, and we are all punished for the sins of the twentieth century." (NYT)

Maugham, W. Somerset. *A Traveller in Romance*. Crown, 1985. Uncollected writings, 1901–1964, by an inveterate traveler.

Morris, Jan. *Among the Cities*. Oxford University Press, 1985. Collection of short pieces on cities, written from 1956 through 1984—"elevates travel writing to the level of fine literature without losing any of the comfortable-walking-shoes tone." (BL) Other collections of Morris's writing you may still find at the library include *Destination Essays from Rolling Stone, Places, Journeys*. A new collection (1992) is *Locations*.

O'Rourke, P.J. *Holidays in Hell*. Atlantic Monthly Press, 1988. The subtitle is: "In which our intrepid reporter travels to the world's worst places and asks, 'what's funny about this?' " By one of the funniest writers in America today.

Pritchett, V.S. *At Home and Abroad*. North Point Press, 1989. Travel essays of the 1950s and 1960s that originally appeared in *Holiday*. "Keen insights into human nature and marvelous portrayals of national character." (LJ)

Pyle, Ernie. *Ernie's America: The Best of Ernie Pyle's 1930s Travel Dispatches*. Random, 1990.

Reid, Alastair. *Whereabouts: Notes on Being a Foreigner*. North Point Press, 1987. Seven stories that first appeared in *The New Yorker*, about the author's experiences in Los Angeles, New York, Scotland and Spain. (LJ)

Spectator, eds. *Views From Abroad: The Spectator Book of Travel Writing*. Random, 1990. Four decades of the best from *Spectator* of Great Britain, with a foreword by Colin Thubron. Includes writings by Evelyn Waugh, Graham Greene, Ludovic Kennedy, Colin Thubron, etc.

Theroux, Paul. *Sunrise with Seamonsters*. Houghton Mifflin, 1986. An anthology of the novelist/travel writer's pieces from 1964 to 1984, beginning with a stint in the Peace Corps in East Africa, and arranged chronologically.

Trillin, Calvin. *Travels with Alice*. Ticknor & Fields, 1989. Italy, France, the Caribbean—travels with wife Alice and two daughters, with food always a key part of the experience.

Twain, Mark. *The Innocents Abroad* and *A Tramp Abroad*. Hippocrene, 1989. Reprints of Twain's two classic travel books.

Waugh, Alec. *Hot Countries*. Paragon House, 1989. The hot countries are Tahiti, Siam, the West Indies—"keen observations . . . one of the best." (NYT)

Waugh, Evelyn. *When the Going Was Good*. Little, 1985. Excerpts from four of the author's travel books written in the 1920s and '30s—"the prose is flawless, the observation razor-sharp, the comedy incomparable." (BRD)

Winchester, Simon. *The Sun Never Sets: Travels to the Remaining Outposts of the British Empire*. Prentice Hall Press, 1991. Three years of crisscrossing the world from Pitcairn Island to Gibraltar and other forgotten bits of the Empire.

APPENDIX 4

List of Authors of Novels with English Settings

Because of the inordinate number of novels (and mysteries) with an English setting, it was necessary to limit those listed herein to books indicated in review materials as being set in a specific place, i.e., London or one of the counties; left unlisted are the many novels and mysteries set in England in general.

Fortunately for Anglophiles, there are several literary guides, and books about authors and books, that armchair travelers can use to locate additional place-set fiction. Books by classic and standard authors (Dickens, Trollope, etc.) can be located through one of these guides, listed under England/Literary and Book-Related Guides.

Also, you can check the *Fiction Catalog* or *Book Review Digest* at your library.

Then, with the following list of authors who have written novels with an English setting, you can scan the bookshelves of the fiction section at your library to help you locate additional novels. An asterisk (*) indicates the author has written mysteries set in England—but has not, necessarily, written only mysteries. Some libraries shelve their mystery collection separately. Names in parentheses are alternate pen names under which the author has written books.

Adams, Richard
Aiken, Joan
*Aird, Catherine
Aldiss, Brian W.
Allbeury, Ted
*Allingham, Margery
*Amis, Kingsley
Amis, Martin
*Anderson, James
*Anderson, John R.L.
Anthony, Evelyn
Archer, Jeffrey
*Ashford, Jeffrey
Attoe, David
*Babson, Marian

Bagnold, Enid
Bainbridge, Beryl
Banks, Lynne Reid
*Bannister, Jo
Barker, Pat
*Barnard, Robert
Barnes, Julian
Bates, H.E.
Bawden, Nina
Beckett, Samuel
*Bell, Josephine
Benson, E.F.
*Bentley, E.C.
Bentley, Ursula
Berckman, Evelyn

Bermant, Chaim
Billington, Rachel
Binchy, Maeve
Blackstock, Charity
Bottome, Phyllis
Bowen, Elizabeth
Braddon, Russell
Bradford, Barbara T.
Braine, John
*Brand, Christianna
Brent, Madeleine
*Brett, Simon
Brookes, Owen
Brookner, Anita
Brown, Christy
Bruce, Leo
Buchan, John
Burgess, Anthony
*Burley, W.J.
Butler, Gwendoline
Butler, W.V.
*Cadell, Elizabeth
Campbell, Ramsey
*Candy, Edward
*Cannell, Dorothy
*Canning, Victor
Carey, Philippa
*Carr, J.D.
Carr, J.L.
Carr, Philippa
Carson, Michael
*Carter, Youngman
*Carvic, Heron
Cary, Joyce
Caudwell, Sarah
*Charteris, Leslie
Cheek, Mavis
Chesney, Marion
*Chesterton, G.K.
*Christie, Agatha
Clarke, Anna
Clarkson, Ewan
*Cleary, Jon
Clifford, Francis
*Cody, Liza
Colegate, Isabel
*Collins, Wilkie
Compton-Burnett, Ivy
Cooke, Judy
Cookson, Catherine (Catherine Marchant)
Cooper, William
Cornwell, Bernard
Crane, Teresa

*Creasey, John (J.J. Marric)
Crichton, Michael
Crisp, N.J.
*Crispin, Edmund
Cronin, A.J.
*Cutter, Leela
Dale, Celia
*Davies, L.P.
*Dean, S.F.X.
Deighton, Len
Delderfield, R.F.
*Delving, Michael
*Derleth, August
Dewhurst, Eileen
*Dexter, Colin
*Dickinson, Peter
Disch, T.M.
Donleavy, J.P.
Drabble, Margaret
DuMaurier, Daphne
Durrell, Gerald
Eden, Dorothy
Edwards, G.B.
*Egleton, Clive
Elliott, Janice
*Ferrars, E.X.
Fitzgerald, Penelope
*Fleming, Joan
Follett, Ken
Forster, E.M.
Forster, Margaret
Fowles, John
*Fox, Peter
*Francis, Dick
Frankau, Pamela
*Fraser, Anthea
*Fraser, Antonia
Freeman, Cynthia
*Fremlin, Celia
Galsworthy, John
Gardner, John
*Garfield, Leon
*Garve, Andrew
*Gash, Jonathan
Gaskin, Catherine
Gee, Maggie
*George, Elizabeth
Gibbons, Stella
Gilbert, Anna
*Gilbert, Michael
*Gill, Bartholomew
Gilliatt, Penelope
*Giroux, E.X.
Glendinning, Victoria

Gloag, Julian
Godden, Jon
Godden, Rumer
Godwin, Gail
Golding, William
Goodwin, Suzanne
*Gosling, Paula
Goudge, Elizabeth
*Graham, Caroline
Graham, Winston
Grant-Adamson, Leslie
Greene, Graham
Greenwood, L.B.
*Grimes, Martha
Grossman, Judith
Haines, Pamela
Hambly, Barbara
Hanley, James
Hardwick, Mollie
Harris, Marilyn
Harrison, Harry
*Harrison, Ray
Harrison, Sarah
Hart, Roy
*Haymon, S.T.
*Heald, Tim
Heath, Catherine
*Heyer, Georgette
Higgins, Jack
Hill, Fiona
*Hill, Reginald
*Hilton, James
*Hilton, John B.
Hoban, Russell
Holland, Isabelle
Hollinghurst, Alan
Holt, Victoria
Horwood, William
Hough, Richard
*Household, Geoffrey
Howard, Elizabeth Jane
Howatch, Susan
*Hunter, Alan
Huxley, Aldous
*Huxley, Elspeth
*Innes, Michael (J.I.M. Stewart)
Ishiguro, Kazuo
Jagger, Brenda
*James, P.D. (Phyllis D. White)
Jeffreys, J.G.
Johnson, Pamela Hansford
Jolley, Elizabeth
Jones, Mervyn
Jordan, Lee

*Keating, H.R.F.
Kells, Susannah
Kennedy, Lena
*Kenney, Susan
Kyle, Duncan
Laker, Rosalind
LeCarre, John
*Lemarchand, Elizabeth
Leslie, Josephine A.C.
Lessing, Doris (Jane Somers)
Lively, Penelope
Llewellyn, Richard
Lodge, David
Lofts, Norah
*Lovesey, Peter
Lyall, Gavin
McCarry, Charles
Macdonald, Malcolm
*MacDonald, Phillip
McGown, Jill
MacInnes, Colin
MacKenzie, Donald
MacKintosh, Elizabeth (Josephine Tey)
McMullen, Mary
*Malcolm, John
Mankowitz, Wolf
*Mann, Jessica
Marchant, Catherine (Catherine Cookson)
*Marric, J.J. (John Creasey)
*Marsh, Dame Ngaio
Masters, John
Maybury, Anne
*Meek, M.R.D.
Melville, Anne
*Meyer, Nicholas
*Michaels, Barbara (Elizabeth Peters)
*Milne, A.A.
*Mitchell, Gladys
Moorcock, Michael
Moore, Brian
*Morice, Anne
Mortimer, John C.
Mortimer, Penelope
*Moyes, Patricia
Murdoch, Iris
Naylor, Charles
*Oliver, Anthony
Orwell, George
*Page, Emma
Parkin, Frank
*Parrish, Frank
Pearce, Mary E.
Pearson, Diane

Pearson, John
Penman, Sharon K.
*Perowne, Barry
*Perry, Anne
*Peters, Elizabeth (Barbara Michaels)
Phillips, Dee
Pilcher, Rosamunde
Plaidy, Jean
Powell, Anthony
Pownall, David
*Priestley, J.B.
Pritchett, V.S.
Pym, Barbara
Pynchon, Thomas
*Quest, Erica
*Radley, Sheila
Raymond, Ernest
Rayner, Claire
Read, Miss
Read, Piers Paul
*Rendell, Ruth (Barbara Vine)
Rhys, Jean
Rock, Phillip
*Ross, Jonathan
Ross, Malcolm
Rubens, Bernice
Sackville-West, Victoria
*Sayers, Dorothy L.
Scholefield, Alan
*Selwyn, Francis
Shannon, Doris
Sharp, Margery
*Shaw, Howard
Shelby, Graham
*Sherwood, John
Sillitoe, Alan
*Simpson, Dorothy
*Snow, C.P.
Somers, Jane (Doris Lessing)
Spark, Muriel
Stevenson, D.E.
Stewart, J.I.M. (Michael Innes)
Stewart, Mary
Stirling, Jessica
Storey, David
Struther, Jan
*Stubbs, Jean

*Symons, Julian
*Taylor, Andrew
Taylor, Elizabeth
*Tey, Josephine (Elizabeth Mac-Kintosh)
Thane, Elswyth
Theroux, Paul
Thirkell, Angela
*Thomas, June
Thomson, June
Thomson, Rupert
*Tine, Robert
*Tourney, Leonard
Townsend, Sue
Trapido, Barbara
Trollope, Joanna
*Underwood, Michael
Uris, Leon
Van Slyke, Helen
Veryan, Patricia
Vine, Barbara (Ruth Rendell)
Wain, John
*Wainwright, John
Walpole, Hugh
*Watson, Colin
Waugh, Evelyn
Waugh, Hilary
Way, Peter
Weldon, Fay
Wells, H.G.
Wesley, Mary
West, Dame Rebecca
West, Pamela E.
White, Patrick
White, Phyllis D. (P.D. James)
Williams, Emlyn
Wilson, Angus
Wilson, A.N.
Winch, Arden
Wodehouse, P.G.
*Woods, Sara
Woolf, Virginia
Worboys, Anne
Wright, Patricia
Wyndham, Francis
*Yorke, Margaret
Zilinsky, Ursula

INDEX OF AUTHORS